BELIEFS IN GOVERNMENT

Volumes of a Research Programme of the European Science Foundation

Series Editors: Max Kaase, Kenneth Newton, and Elinor Scarbrough

THE IMPACT OF VALUES

This set of five volumes is an exhaustive study of beliefs in government in post-war Europe. Based upon an extensive collection of survey evidence, the results challenge widely argued theories of mass opinion, and much scholarly writing about citizen attitudes towards government and politics.

The **European Science Foundation** is an association of its fifty-six member research councils, academies, and institutions devoted to basic scientific research in twenty countries. The ESF assists its Member Organizations in two main ways: by bringing scientists together in its Scientific Programmes, Networks, and European Research Conferences to work on topics of common concern, and through the joint study of issues of strategic importance in European science policy.

The scientific work sponsored by ESF includes basic research in the natural and technical sciences, the medical and biosciences, the humanities, and the social sciences.

The ESF maintains close relations with other scientific institutions within and outside Europe. By its activities, ESF adds value by co-operation and co-ordination across national frontiers, offers expert scientific advice on strategic issues, and provides the European forum for fundamental science.

This volume arises from the work of the ESF Scientific Programme on Beliefs in Government (BiG).

Further information on ESF activities can be obtained from:

European Science Foundation
1, quai Lezay-Marnésia
F-67080 Strasbourg Cedex
France

Tel. (+33) 88 76 71 00
Fax (+33) 88 37 05 32

BELIEFS IN GOVERNMENT VOLUME FOUR

THE IMPACT OF VALUES

Edited by

JAN W. VAN DETH

and

ELINOR SCARBROUGH

OXFORD UNIVERSITY PRESS

1995

Oxford University Press, Walton Street, Oxford OX2 6DP

Oxford New York
Athens Auckland Bangkok Bombay
Calcutta Cape Town Dar es Salaam Delhi
Florence Hong Kong Istanbul Karachi
Kuala Lumpur Madras Madrid Melbourne
Mexico City Nairobi Paris Singapore
Taipei Tokyo Toronto
and associated companies in
Berlin Ibadan

Oxford is a trade mark of Oxford University Press

Published in the United States
by Oxford University Press Inc., New York

British Library Cataloguing in Publication Data
Data available

Library of Congress Cataloging in Publication Data
The impact of values / edited by Jan W. van Deth and Elinor Scarbrough.
—(Beliefs in government ; v. 4)
Includes bibliographical references and index.
1. Social Values—Europe. 2. Social change—Europe. I. Deth, Jan W. van.
II. Scarbrough, Elinor. III. Series.
HM73.I48 1995 303.4'094—dc20 95–20297

ISBN 0–19–827957–4

1 3 5 7 9 10 8 6 4 2

Typeset by J&L Composition Ltd, Filey, North Yorkshire
Printed in Great Britain
on acid-free paper by
Biddles Ltd, Guildford and King's Lynn

FOREWORD

This is one of five volumes in a series produced by the Beliefs in Government research programme of the European Science Foundation. The volumes, all published by Oxford University Press in 1995, are as follows:

The first chapter of *Beliefs in Government* presents a brief history of the research project, its general concerns, approach and methods, and an outline of the relationship of each volume to the project as a whole.

All five books share a debt of gratitude which we would like to acknowledge on their behalf. The European Science Foundation (ESF) supported and funded the research programme throughout its five long and arduous years. Eleven of the research councils and academies that are members of the ESF have made a financial contribution to the overall costs of the project—Belgium, Denmark, Finland, France, the Federal Republic of Germany, Ireland, Italy, the Netherlands, Norway, Sweden, and the United Kingdom. We would like to thank the ESF and these member organizations five times over—once for each book.

All five volumes were copy-edited by Heather Bliss, whose eagle eye and endless patience are unrivalled in the Western world. At Oxford University Press we were lucky indeed to have two understanding editors in Tim Barton and Dominic Byatt.

In particular, John Smith, the Secretary of the ESF's Standing Committee for the Social Sciences, and his staff put in huge efforts and gave us encouragement at every stage of the project. Having gone through the process with other ESF research programmes a few times before, they knew when we started what an immense task lay in wait for us all, but were not daunted. We cannot lay claim to any such bravery, and have only our innocence as an excuse.

Max Kaase
Kenneth Newton
Elinor Scarbrough

December 1994

PREFACE

From the outset, the study of values was part of the research design for Beliefs in Government. As a large-scale, longitudinal, and comparative project on the attitudes and behaviour of citizens in Western Europe, it was clear that we had to examine political values and value change. Our research group was formed to study 'The Impact of Values', and this is reflected in the title of our book.

Studying developments in several countries over a relatively long period of time requires serious commitments from a number of people. A wide variety of experience, research interests, and knowledge of social and political developments in different countries is represented by the contributors to this volume. We worked together closely between 1990 and 1994, discussing our plans, findings, and draft chapters in detail. This volume, then, is the result of a truly collaborative effort and the willingness of each member of the group to stimulate and help other members.

A work of this kind, however, cannot be completed by a group of thirteen social scientists without assistance from other people. When the first drafts of the contributions were completed, Ronald Inglehart and Helmut Klages kindly agreed to discuss our work in detail. Their stimulating comments proved very useful when it came to revising our manuscripts. So did the many suggestions offered to us by the directors of the project.

During the time our research group worked together, a number of people and institutes provided us with much valued support. The Zentralarchiv in Cologne compiled several cross-national and long-itudinal data sets for our use, while the ZUMA institute in Mannheim kindly hosted us for a data confrontation seminar. Secretarial and organizational assistance was provided at the home institutes of several members of our group. In later stages of the project Christine Wilkinson, Helen Sibley, and Sharon Duthie at Essex University, and Carmelita Verbeet at Nijmegen University, succeeded in producing a decent manuscript from a large number of folders with drafts, revisions, revisions of revisions, final drafts and very final drafts. Much patience and forebearance was needed to ensure the accurate presentation of

tables and figures. Heather Bliss proved a very professional and con-
scientious copyeditor who suggested many improvements to the texts.

This book could not have been written without the energetic efforts
of Max Kaase and Kenneth Newton in bringing together in a single
project the major themes in European comparative research. Nor would
it have been possible without the generous financial support of the
European Science Foundation and the organizational skills of Dr John
Smith. Besides greatly extending our understanding of political and
social change, the project has stimulated personal relationships and
appreciation between the members of our group. We are grateful to
all those people who made that possible.

Jan van Deth
Elinor Scarbrough

December 1994

CONTENTS

LIST OF FIGURES

LIST OF TABLES

ABBREVIATIONS

ADP	Average percentage difference
EC	European Commission
ICPSR	Inter-university Consortium for Political and Social Research (University of Michigan)
IPOS	Institut für praxisorientierte Sozialforschung
NATO	North Atlantic Treaty Organization
OECD	Organization for Economic Co-operation and Development
ZUMA	Zentrum für Umfragen, Methoden und Analysen

Standard country abbreviations used in the tables and figures are:

AU	Austria
BE	Belgium
DK	Denmark
FI	Finland
FR	France
GB	Britain
GE	Germany
GR	Greece
IC	Iceland
IR	Ireland
IT	Italy
LU	Luxembourg
NL	Netherlands
NO	Norway
PO	Portugal
SP	Spain
SV	Sweden
SW	Switzerland

LIST OF CONTRIBUTORS

SAMI BORG, Researcher, Research Institute of Social Sciences, University of Tampere

KAREL DOBBELAERE, Professor of Sociology and Sociology of Religion, Catholic University of Leuven; Professor of Sociological Research, University of Antwerp

OSCAR W. GABRIEL, Professor of Political Science, University of Stuttgart

JOHN R. GIBBINS, Senior Lecturer, Department of Politics, Social Policy, and Philosophy, School of Human Studies, University of Teesside

PETER GUNDELACH, Professor of Sociology, University of Copenhagen

WOLFGANG JAGODZINSKI, Professor of Sociology; Director, Institute for Applied Social Research; Director, Central Archive for Empirical Research, University of Cologne

ODDBJØRN KNUTSEN, Professor of Political Science, University of Oslo

CARINA LUNDMARK, Doktorandtjähnst, Department of Political Science, University of Umeå

MASJA NAS, Researcher, Department of Political Science, University of Nijmegen, and Social and Cultural Planning Office for the Netherlands

BO REIMER, Senior Lecturer, Department of Journalism and Mass Communication, University of Gothenburg

ELINOR SCARBROUGH, Lecturer, Department of Government, University of Essex

ETIENNE SCHWEISGUTH, Researcher, Centre d'étude de la vie politique Française, Fondation Nationale des Sciences Politiques, Paris

JAN W. VAN DETH, Professor of Political Science and International Comparative Research, University of Mannheim

1

Introduction: The Impact of Values

JAN W. VAN DETH

The idea of rapid political change in Western Europe is, by now, a platitude. Within just a few decades, political institutions, party systems, and political cultures seem to have lost their traditional roots. The reconstruction era immediately following the Second World War would probably have revealed political conflicts and orientations along the historic lines of industrialization and rising capitalism. These 'frozen' cleavages were apparent in the distinction between proletarian (left-wing), bourgeois (right-wing), and religious (mostly right-wing or centre) parties and political organizations. The following decade, however, was not characterized by a gradual decline of ideological thinking and the rise of a more pragmatic approach to political life. Even without the exaggerations of the 1960s as a 'revolutionary epoch' or a 'fundamental break' with the past, it is clear that major shifts took place in the political systems of the advanced industrial countries of Western Europe and North America.[1] In the late 1960s and early 1970s a wave of political unrest, radicalization, and polarization swept these countries, most visible in an expanding repertoire of political action, such as demonstrations and boycotts, and the rise of new social movements, such as the women's movement and the ecological movement. These changes have been institutionalized in many countries, and the label 'unconventional political behaviour' lost most of its original meaning during the 1980s. The 'élite directed' modes of political participation of the first two decades following the Second World War have been replaced by the 'élite directing' or 'élite challenging' behaviour of the more recent period (cf. Inglehart 1990: ch. 10).

Although these shifts in political behaviour are the most visible aspects of a process of political change, the accompanying changes in political orientations among the populations of advanced industrial societies are equally relevant for our understanding of political life. Researchers with quite different approaches appear to agree that these populations show an increased emphasis on non-material and emancipatory goals; shifting away from tradition, respect for authority, and material well-being towards self-fulfilment, independence, and emancipation. The label 'individualization' is commonly used for these developments, but it would be more appropriate to apply terms such as the rise of 'post-conventional' norms, the 'de-traditionalization' of society, or the growing relevance of 'postmaterialism'. In spite of the strong emphasis on the independent individual in debates about social and political change, it is clear that for most people 'connectedness to others in work, love, and community is essential to happiness, self-esteem, and moral worth' (Bellah *et al.* 1985: 84). Moreover, we do not seem to be witnessing the emergence of completely new values, but the gradual replacement of older, traditional values by less strict or less authoritarian ideas. It is this combination of slowly disappearing traditional values and the growing independence and self-reliance of individuals, as well as the need for belongingness in modern society, which characterizes the broad lines of the process of changing values.

Shifts in value orientations are likely to induce change in the modes and levels of political participation. These shifts have implications for other aspects of political life: in the nature of support, in the basis of legitimacy and the party systems, and in the lines of political conflict. In this way, the concept of changing values is at the core of interpretations of almost every aspect of political change in advanced industrial societies. Although the nature, scope, and impact of political change in advanced industrial societies are much disputed, most researchers underline the central role of some value concept in understanding social and political change in these societies. Thus, the value concept has *analytic* primacy in our work.

Beliefs in Government

The processes of value change have important consequences for many aspects of social life in advanced industrial societies. As one observer (Zinn 1990: 526) noticed about the rapid changes in the 1960s and the 1970s:

There was a general revolt against oppressive, artificial, previously unques-
tioned ways of living. It touched every aspect of personal life: childbirth,
childhood, love, sex, marriage, dress, music, art, sports, language, food,
housing, religion, literature, death, schools.

This picture is somewhat exaggerated but basically correct. There
seems to have been a massive change in many aspects of social and
personal life, and several of the consequences of these changes did not
disappear in the 1980s. However, our interest here is not with some
general phenomenon of rapid cultural change in advanced industrial
societies. What is relevant for us is that these cultural changes are
presumed to be based on a more general feeling of emancipation and
self-fulfilment, as a 'revolt' against 'oppressive' forces. So it is no
surprise that Zinn (1990: 581–2) concludes: 'never before was there
such a general withdrawal of confidence from so many elements of the
political and economic system'. Social and political scientists like
Habermas, Inglehart, Offe, and Rose formulated similar ideas long
before the tides of cultural change seemed to slow down in the 1980s.

We can acknowledge the cultural changes of the last decades,
however, without having to accept the idea of a general revolt against
government, or even a weakening of the legitimacy of the existing
political order. What we do see, however, is a change in the position
of government in society, and increasing pressures on governments to
deal with all manner of problems. The implications of value change for
these developments can be approached from two perspectives. The first
is based on the notion that the *content* of changing values can raise
problems, while the second refers to an ongoing process of *fragmentation* or *pluralization* as new values are added to existing orientations.
Both variants are summarized here from the 'bottom-up' perspective:
that is, we indicate the consequences of changing values for government action, paying less attention to the impact of government activities
on the orientations of citizens. This perspective follows directly from
our search for the impact of changing values.

Immediately after the Second World War the predominant values
were in line with the needs of economic recovery and, in several
countries, the reconstruction of the political system. The traumatic
experiences of large-scale unemployment and poverty during the Great
Depression paved the way for the political goals of economic growth,
reindustrialization, and law-and-order to dominate industrial societies
in the 1950s, while material advantage, security, and tradition were the

major concerns for individual citizens. In the 1960s the picture changes. People took traditional goals and values for granted and started to stress independence and emancipation. Since the political systems of West European countries were, by and large, still addressed to the goals and values of the previous decades, actual government performance increasingly diverged from the demands of citizens. In other words, a shift in values urges governments to reconsider their policies.

Readjustment takes time. During a period of flux in the outlook of citizens, governments will be under constant pressure to adjust to cultural changes—and government policies will always lag behind popular developments. Such disjunctures between government policies and the new demands of citizens may lead to the questioning of beliefs in government and threaten the legitimacy of the political system.[2] This will be especially true if people are becoming less deferential. Moreover, almost by definition, the authority of government is questioned in a culture stressing individual autonomy. In a society where people seek emancipation rather than security, support and legitimacy becomes increasingly instrumental, based on calculations of interest rather than feelings of belonging. Consequently, while government performance is measured against these new values, its actual output is largely based on goals that correspond to yesterday's values. Frustration, dissatisfaction, and protest will be the result.

Existing values are not, however, simply replaced by other values. It is obvious that cherished values disappear gradually in advanced industrial society, thus the process is better described as a continuous development towards a more fragmented culture. In a changing environment, people adjust to new values without giving up every element in their previous orientations. Moreover, if independence and self-fulfilment are stressed, people will be inclined to design their own set of values and choose their orientations *à la carte*. Postmodernist commentators, especially, suggest the breakdown of structurally shaped social identities, along with the value orientations which are historically characteristic of industrial society. In contrast to the moral certainties associated with the class roles typical of 'modernism', the emergent 'postmodern' cultural order is marked by value heterogeneity with an emphasis on 'structures of feeling' and individual identities based on differences in life-styles and tastes. In contrast to the instrumental and materialist concerns of modernist outlooks, 'expressivism' and 'cultural concerns' are the hallmarks of postmodernist outlooks. Moreover, in this environment of radical social and moral diversity, the familiar structures and practices of party politics become inappropriate and irrelevant (Taylor 1989).

Thus the modernist–postmodernist debate suggests not only opportunities for value change but also a progressive disengagement from the public activity of politics. This fragmentation of political life may eventually confront politicians with a burgeoning of dispersed and conflicting demands, while government policies can no longer be based on some dominant ideology or overarching set of goals. This will be especially relevant if individual independence is emphasized, with no broadly accepted set of values available as a criterion for balancing conflicting interests.

These roughly sketched scenarios were at the roots of the debates on the 'crisis of the welfare state' and the revival of neo-conservative thinking in the late 1970s and early 1980s. The empirical validity of these claims, however, is not undisputed. In the midst of cultural changes which seemed to affect many aspects of people's lives, satisfaction with the way democracy works, trust in government, or attachments to the status quo do not appear to have declined any further after a drop in the late 1960s.[3] This leaves us with the paradox that the cultural changes evident in advanced industrial societies appear to have missed a major target: the national state as an instrument of repression. Both perspectives—value change as a major threat to the political system and value change in the non-political aspects of life—require close examination of the available data, over time and across several countries. Thus, the value concept has *substantive* primacy in this volume.

A Simple Analytic Scheme

Values and value research have become a minor branch of industry in political science. Empirically oriented subfields such as electoral behaviour, political participation, party competition, policy preferences are all influenced by the idea that values deserve a place in models of prediction and explanation. And, as noted, values appear to be crucial to interpreting social and political change.

Despite several differences, a simple scheme seems to underlie many of the specific approaches and interpretations in value research. Only two assumptions are needed for this scheme. The first is that individual behaviour is determined by behaviourial intentions, which, in turn, are shaped by values and political orientations. The second assumption is that people's values are highly influenced by the social environment and by their social position in that environment. These two assumptions provide two chains for the connections between three analytic levels: macro-level circumstances, individual orientations, and individual behaviour. Obviously, individual behaviour is not a terminal stage. In the long run, changes in individual behaviour imply changes in macro-level circumstances, so we are dealing with a complex circular process. This process is reduced to a simple three-level model only for analytic purposes. This so-called 'E→P→R model' (Environment→Predisposition→Response) has long been used as a starting point in social research.[4] Its main aspects for our research are depicted in Figure 1.1.

The upper part of this schema consists of the most straightforward interpretation of the position of values in theories of political change. Macro-level developments shape the values of individuals, and these values determine the behaviour of individuals via behavioural intentions. An additional line of reasoning is included by recognizing that macro-level developments have a direct impact on the social position of individuals and that the relationship between macro-level developments and values should be interpreted with respect to these changing social positions. Finally, we include political orientations as co-determinants of behavioural intentions. The values of individuals can be transformed into political orientations which have some impact on their behavioural intentions. These two additional lines of reasoning, however, are side-walks in our analyses. Our emphasis is on the central position of values in the link between macro-level developments and the behaviour of individuals as depicted in the upper part of Figure 1.1.

The most common variant of this approach identifies the twin processes of technological development and economic growth as the

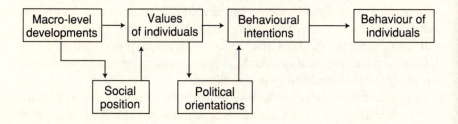

FIGURE 1.1. *A simple analytical scheme for analysing the impact of values*

underlying dynamics of change in macro-level circumstances in general and the rise of industrial capitalism in particular. The several aspects and consequences of this modernization process include the spread of affluence, the ongoing division of labour, decline of the agricultural sector, urbanization, rising levels of education, increasing mobility, growth of mass media, and a stabilization of birth and death rates at historically low levels. These systemic properties of a society are at the first analytic level. Changes at this level will have some impact on individual values and on the social position of individuals. This is the second analytic level. The third level is the behaviour of individuals. So the two quite different chains in the schema are, first, the relationships between systemic properties and individual orientations and positions, and, secondly, the relationships between individual orientations and political behaviour.

Two interpretations of social and political change can be discerned from this analytical scheme. The first takes political orientations, especially values, as the concept mediating between the systemic properties of a society, on the one hand, and individual behaviour, on the other. This line of reasoning is a classic theme in macro-sociological theory. Perhaps the best-known contemporary work in this vein is the theory of the 'Silent Revolution' (Inglehart 1977b; 1990). According to Inglehart, the unprecedented increase in economic prosperity and security has induced a shift in value priorities among the most recent cohorts in advanced industrial societies. This spread of 'postmaterial-ism', in turn, has led to a change in the modes and levels of political participation and to new forms of political conflict.

In the second interpretation of social and political change according to our simple scheme, social position is directly linked to values. From this perspective, social and economic changes have resulted in the rise of new groups consisting of people with high levels of education who are relatively autonomous or authoritative in their work roles. The jobs of these professionals involve information, communication, and the creation of cultural messages—in the mass media, liberal arts, publishing, and the like—or the delivery of welfare and other social programmes. Their outlook, it is argued, is characterized by the rejection of every kind of authority. They spurn conventional modes of thinking and the ideologies associated with traditional political cleavages, developing instead more 'modern' ideas in line with their social position.

Both variants of our simple scheme stress the importance of values for understanding the consequences for individuals of systemic, long-term, social and economic developments. The analytic and substantive primacy of the value concept, then, and the simple scheme representing the two interpretations of social and political change, enable us to present our central research questions in a systematic way. Accordingly, in this volume, we deal with the following questions:

1. What is the meaning, status, and relevance of the value concept in perspectives on social and political change?
2. What are the major characteristics of advanced industrial societies, and to what extent is a process of value change actually taking place in Western Europe?
3. What distinct value orientations can be empirically documented, what traces of newly arising value orientations are evident, and what are the major socio-structural antecedents of specific value orientations?
4. What is the impact of value orientations on political orientations and behavioural intentions among the publics in West European countries?
5. What are the implications of our findings about changing value orientations for the beliefs in government of citizens in Western Europe?

With the obvious exception of the first question, the goal in this volume is to answer these questions by analysing data which cover both the longitudinal and the cross-national components of the presumed processes of changing value orientations and their consequences for beliefs in government.

Central Value Orientations

The ongoing processes of value change and fractionalization seem to have led to an almost endless list of values, value orientations, value dimensions, value patterns, and value clusters in advanced industrial societies. In addition to traditional value orientations such as authoritarianism, deference, conservatism, progressiveness, religiosity, and materialism, the last two decades or so have witnessed the rise (and sometimes already the decline) of new orientations such as postmaterialism, environmentalism, postmodernism, ecologism, and feminism. For both theoretical and practical reasons, we cannot deal with the full range of these broad and divergent 'old' and 'new' orientations. Just one, but important, limitation is the lack of appropriate data. We have searched through national and cross-national surveys to find comparable or functionally equivalent indicators. However, while data on postmaterialism seem to be everywhere and, for instance, surrogate indicators for secular value orientations are easy to find, it is virtually impossible to create a data base for cross-national developments in authoritarian and libertarian values. Moreover, in many instances, crucial dependent variables are missing for a study of the *impact* of values.

These practical limitations, and the need to concentrate on major trends, urge a pragmatic approach to selecting the value orientations examined in this volume. We decided to concentrate, for the most part, on three central value orientations which cover important aspects of advanced industrial society, as well as the legacies of industrial and pre-industrial societies.[5] But we also consider some specific value orientations which are relevant for political developments in advanced industrial societies. When examining the impact of values, however, our analyses focus mainly on the consequences of the three central value orientations.

The most prominent of the debates about changing values in advanced industrial societies centres on the rise of *materialist–postmaterialist value orientations*—sometimes simply referred to as 'postmaterialism'. This is our first central value orientation. According to Inglehart (1990: 68–9), the expectation of value change derives from the economic and physical security experienced during the post-war years in Western Europe, which has made for the declining relevance of values related to those 'material' concerns which were at the centre of class conflicts. Instead, values related to 'such non-material goals as a less impersonal, more participatory society, in which ideas, self-expression, and aesthetic concerns' (1990: 160) have become increasingly relevant to politics. The pace of this value change will be slow and uneven, as the process is borne by cohorts socialized in different economic and social environments; the 'silent revolution' consists in successive post-war cohorts, who are more given to a postmaterialist orientation, gradually replacing earlier cohorts who are more given to a materialist orientation. As this value shift takes hold, the 'old' politics of class conflict—and, to some extent, religious conflict—is being overlain, and will be steadily displaced, by a 'new' politics centred on the conflict between materialist and postmaterialist value orientations.

As the extensive debate about postmaterialism testifies, Inglehart's approach is both innovative and problematic. At this stage, we note only that there seems little reason for the effects of postmaterialist value change to be confined to electoral politics, a point which Inglehart himself makes: 'we would expect the impact of Postmaterialism to be weakest on voting behavior . . . and relatively strong on support for social change' (1990: 306). Even so, Inglehart's claims about the effects of postmaterialist orientations have been generalized to account for several features of the 'new politics' apparent in many West European countries since the late 1960s: the appearance of 'new' political issues such as the environment, nuclear power, gender, abortion, human rights (Flanagan 1982; Dalton 1988); the growth of 'unconventional' political action (Barnes, Kaase, *et al.* 1979; Jennings, Van Deth, *et al.* 1989); the emergence of new social movements and new parties of the left (Müller-Rommel 1985*a*; Poguntke 1987*b*). Inglehart's claims and their implications for mass politics are examined in several chapters in this volume.

The rise of postmaterialism and the focus on 'new politics' might easily give the false impression that industrial and pre-industrial society have left virtually no traces on political life in today's societies of Western Europe. As an indicator of the cultural consequences of industrial society we use the concept of *left–right materialist value orientations* (or left–right materialism). This is our second central value orientation and reflects the class conflicts typical of industrial society. As the simple concepts 'left' and 'right' are too general for analysing change in value orientations as between industrial and advanced industrial society, we follow Lafferty and Knutsen (1984) in distinguishing between 'right' and 'left' materialist orientations. Right materialism is associated with economic liberalism, emphasizing market competition, personal freedom, a relatively weak state, the rights of private property, resistance against government regulation, and opposition to notions of social and economic equality. Left materialism is centred on active government, designed to achieve economic security, solidarity, equality of income and living conditions, and social harmony between classes and strata. Left–right materialist value orientations, then, are mainly economic in nature, referring to the quite different role of markets and governments in economy and society— which have strong political implications. These orientations are not simply exclusive, but are conceptualized as polar opposites which remain highly relevant to the structuring of political conflict.

Pre-industrial sources of political conflict, too, have left their imprint on political life in advanced industrial societies. Thus, for our third central value orientation we take *religious–secular value orientations*. In this instance, value change concerns the erosion of religious beliefs and the spread of rationalism—a process often obscured by the excessive attention to socio-economic cleavages in political research. Religious orientations have a persisting relevance in advanced industrial societies but, in line with Max Weber's view, we see the process of 'occidental rationalization' as undermining the authority of institutionalized churches. In consequence, other agents of the status quo are approached with the same critical attitudes. This development is stimulated not only by the scientific rationality which disenchants the world and undermines institutionalized authority, but also by people's daily life experiences in rationally organized bureaucracies or industrial enterprises. These experiences strengthen the belief that the world can only be controlled by planned and rational human action, not by prayer or any form of magic. In the long run, occidental rationalization may destroy the pre-industrial basis of religiosity.

The rise of secular value orientations can be conceptualized as a process—originating in occidental rationality—of detachment from the beliefs, values, and practices of traditional churches. This process has become evident in many West European countries in the last decades. From one point of view, if churches lose their monopoly to define religious and moral norms, the whole moral system of a society, of generally accepted norms and fundamental values, might break down. A less dramatic scenario points to the gradualness of change, to the diversity and more flexible interpretation of norms, within which individuals arrange their own private set of religious beliefs. Whether one accepts the dramatic or the gradual approach, clearly the dissemination of secular value orientations will have consequences for political orientations and the legitimation of political decision-making processes. For this very same reason, the 'religious cleavage' has been prominent in the seminal treatment of political change in Western Europe by Lipset and Rokkan (1967).

Materialism–postmaterialism, left–right materialism, and religious–secular orientations reflect long-term developments in West European countries. But actual developments in advanced industrial societies require the introduction of more specific value orientations in order to deal with aspects of political change not covered by general concepts like postmaterialism. For these reasons, we pick out three additional value orientations which deserve attention in their own right; that is, the demarcation and description of these orientations are more important than studying the impact of these values on, say, participation or trust in government. The further orientations, which are discussed in subsequent chapters, are feminism, 'green' orientations, and postmodernism. The discussion of these more specific orientations is largely confined to a single chapter, whereas the three central value orientations are examined in some detail in separate chapters and are introduced into every chapter in Part III of this volume, where we examine the impact of values.

Research Design

The search for answers to the second, third, and fourth of our questions makes some specific demands on the organization of our study. For the empirical inquiries we have to select a research method, select the countries to be included, decide on the time span to cover, and identify the data sets to be analysed. As we explain in this section, the limitations of the data record meant making a number of compromises in our research.

In a study focusing on value change, we are necessarily committed to secondary analysis. Unfortunately, this strategy restricts the range and depth of our study. Our method relied on obtaining data from large-scale national and comparative surveys featuring the same questions, or questions sufficiently similar to be regarded as yielding functionally equivalent indicators. Although the use of survey techniques is not undisputed in the field of value research, responses to questionnaire items are the only data we have for the analyses of value orientations, political orientations, and behavioural intentions among mass publics. In-depth interviews may yield data of higher quality, with more detail about individual value orientations, but they are too restricted in sample size for our purpose. The question, however, is not whether we are able to apply excellent or rather poor instruments; more often the question is whether we accept a poor instrument in order to obtain some information. The alternative was not having any empirical evidence at all. The upshot is a compromise between what we wanted to do and what we could do with the available data.

Our research is focused on the advanced industrial countries of Western Europe. Although the 'revolution of 1989' created opportunities for a broader approach to political change in Europe, clearly the countries of Central and Eastern Europe have had political and economic systems very different from the frec-market economies and the representative democracies of the West. The countries which are the objects of our search for value change and its consequences, then, are: Denmark, Finland, Iceland, Norway, Sweden in northern Europe; Austria, Belgium, Germany, Ireland, Luxembourg, the Netherlands, Switzerland, Britain[6] in the central belt of countries; and France, Italy, Greece, Spain, Portugal in southern Europe. We endeavoured to find relevant data for all these eighteen countries. However, there are only sparse data for some of them, hence in most of our analyses the full list is reduced by the limitations of the data record. As we shall see, this means that we often examine a much smaller number of countries.

The time span of our study is also restricted by the available data. Although the roots of advanced industrial societies are to be found in the era of rising industrial capitalism and representative democracy in the late nineteenth and early twentieth centuries, the political systems we look at were shaped after the Second World War with the rise of the welfare state and the expansion of the service sector. Thus, ideally, the time span we want to cover is the post-war period, with an emphasis on developments in the late 1960s and early 1970s. But the data situation imposes strong restrictions on what is possible. Data sets of acceptable quality which include indicators of value orientations are very rare for the 1950s and 1960s; most of the research on the questions we address started only in the 1970s. Thus, we looked for data which cover as much as possible of the time span from the late 1960s through to the 1990s.

In an ideal world we would have comparative data sets covering a large number of countries, and stretching back some thirty years or so. But the world of survey research is not perfect and the available data sets are just a shade of what we would wish. In terms of the instruments applied, the countries and periods covered, and the equivalence of instruments in different settings, our opportunities are indeed far from the ideal. Hence we used pragmatic criteria for selecting our empirical material. First, we specified that surveys should cover at least two countries of Western Europe; nation-specific data sets are only used where comparable data are available from at least one other country. Secondly, we selected data sets which allow for longitudinal comparisons. And thirdly, we required that the data sets should be drawn from either the total population or from the electorate as the sampling base.[7]

These criteria have not been used blindly; any relevant piece of empirical information is included even if it comes from a data set which does not meet our criteria. The most useful data set proved to be the Eurobarometer series of biannual, large-scale surveys in the member states of the European Community. In addition, data from the two Political Action studies (1973–76 and 1979–80) and the two European Values Surveys (1981 and 1990) were used for exploring some aspects of our research questions. We also used data from national election surveys for tackling some questions for which no comparative data are available.

Outline of the Book

The three parts of this volume deal with different aspects of the process of value change and its consequences for the politics of the advanced industrial societies in Western Europe. We cannot deal with all, nor even with most, aspects of these developments. The topics we have selected, however, cover the most salient aspects of the shifts in political orientations among the populations of these countries. The outline of the book broadly follows the five research questions presented above.

The backdrop to our research is set out in Part I which consists of four chapters. In this introductory chapter we have been using phrases such as 'values', 'value change', and 'value orientation' in a rather uncomplicated way. Our first task, then, is to set out the status and the meaning of the value concept in our approach. In Chapter 2, Jan van Deth and Elinor Scarbrough propose a conceptualization of values as notions of the desirable used in moral discourse. These conceptions are not directly observable but are hypothetical constructs. Researchers can establish a claim for the empirical relevance of values by uncovering some pattern, or constraint, among attitudes. When such patterning or constraint is established, we use the term 'value orientation'.

The analytic scheme presented in Figure 1.1 points to the influence of the societal environment in shaping value change. So in Chapter 3, before turning to examine value orientations, Jan van Deth draws out those macro-level developments which constitute the setting for micro politics in advanced industrial societies, with particular attention to economic development and the position of government. The major developments are highlighted by looking at several indicators of economic growth during the last decades, the growth and shifts in government intervention, the spread of mass communications and transport, and some characteristics of electoral systems and political processes.

In Chapter 4, Wolfgang Jagodzinski and Karel Dobbelaere document the decline of church religiosity, a major trend in advanced industrial society. This decline is manifest in a process of alienation from one of the most traditional aspects of pre-modern and modern societies. The spread of secularization and its causes are examined at the individual level by concentrating on the long-term change in church involvement in Western Europe. The pluralization of values entailed in this process may have wide-ranging consequences, as religion may also lose its power to structure beliefs and attitudes in other domains.

The chapters in Part II deal with the value orientations and their social antecedents. We start with a discussion of our central value orientations—materialism–postmaterialism, left–right materialism, and religious–secular orientations—in the first three chapters. In Chapter 5, Elinor Scarbrough examines the development of *materialist–postmaterialist value orientations* in Western Europe. As we noted earlier, this has been a dominant theme in empirical research on values. Her discussion focuses on the theory of postmaterialism, and the growth and stability of these orientations. In Chapter 6, we turn to the traces of industrial society detectable in *left–right materialist value orientations*. After introducing this concept, Oddbjørn Knutsen summarizes the distributions and trends in these value orientations, together with an account of their social-structural antecedents.

Religious and secular orientations are discussed in the next two chapters. Karel Dobbelaere and Wolfgang Jagodzinski focus first on religious cognitions and beliefs, or church religiosity in a narrow sense, in Chapter 7. They examine socio-demographic variables such as age, gender, and education as indicators of particular socialization influences, along with work and life experiences. Within this framework they can readily interpret the impact of national contexts on religiosity, as well as the changing influence of education within Catholic countries. In Chapter 8, they go on to discuss the rise of religious and ethical pluralism. They consider value change, first of all, as a process of re-interpreting old values and moral norms, rather than the emergence of new orientations. They then investigate two potential consequences of the breakdown of the religious fundament: a new, less rigid understanding of norms, and an increasing pluralism of religious beliefs and moral norms.

The remaining chapters in Part II examine the three other value orientations which deserve attention without rising to the status of a central value orientation in our work. Carina Lundmark, in Chapter 9, deals with the spread of *feminist value orientations* in Western Europe. The situation of women changed radically in many respects after the war: women entered the labour force and, in several countries, women's political representation increased remarkably. Her analyses reveal a distribution of feminist value orientations which is clearly correlated with sex, age, and education. This study also shows that the emancipation of women has led to changes in the wider political culture. In the same vein, in Chapter 10, Masja Nas applies the ideas of value change to the rise of *green orientations* in Western Europe. As she shows, the label 'green' covers different shades of 'greenness', running from environmental concern to bio-centrism. Her findings reveal that, although related to postmaterialism, greenness cannot be reduced to simply one expression of postmaterialism.

The most recent approach to changing values in advanced industrial societies is the concept of *postmodernism*. John Gibbins and Bo Reimer explore the concept and its relationship with value change, political attitudes, and beliefs in government in Chapter 11. The core notion of postmodernism is 'expressivism', but expressivists divide between materialist 'instrumentalists' and communal 'humanists'. Their analysis shows that, while expressivism has an impact on political attitudes and behaviour, this does not imply declining support for democratic institutions.

In the final contribution to Part II, Chapter 12, Etienne Schweisguth examines the relationship between value orientations and socio-economic status. He argues that the link between social status and value orientations engages tensions: the highly educated tend to be libertarian in social matters but neo-liberal or conservative on economic matters; the working class tends to be authoritarian on social questions but to hold egalitarian socio-economic values. This contributes to the blurring of ideological conflict, which tends to mute the intensity of traditional class conflicts.

The direct impact of values and value change on political behaviour in the advanced industrial societies of Western Europe is considered in Part III. The first contribution, in Chapter 13, is Oscar Gabriel's analyses of the relationship between value orientations and political efficacy and political trust. After discussing theoretical aspects of the concepts of trust and efficacy, he reports several empirical tests of claims that changing values imply increasing political efficacy and declining political trust. His findings show that the impact of value orientations on trust and efficacy are highly variable and much influenced by national, or situational, circumstances. In Chapter 14, the attitudinal component of political involvement—political interest—is examined by Oscar Gabriel and Jan van Deth. Measuring political interest by subjective political interest and the frequency of political discussion, the chapter assesses the incidence of political interest and its variation according to the impact of value orientations. They conclude that, although value change is engaged in the higher levels of political involvement witnessed in the 1970s, changing value orientations do not directly explain the variations in political interest found across Western Europe.

A rather different aspect of political participation is presented by Peter Gundelach in his treatment of grass roots activities and social movement participation in Chapter 15. After reviewing the measurement problems, he shows that the best indicator of protest potential is grass-roots activity. Multivariate analyses reveal that value orientations are better predictors of grass-roots activities than demographic factors. However, closer analysis of the relationship between value orientation and activity indicates that value orientations may be changed, even created, by grass-roots activity—contrary to the more conventional view that 'new' value orientations stimulate grass-roots activity. Sami Borg takes up another classic theme in his analyses of electoral participation in Chapter 16. He evaluates the impact of postmaterialism and secular values in promoting turnout levels in both national elections and elections for the European Parliament. Perhaps surprisingly, secular orientations emerge as more powerful predictors of electoral participation than postmaterialism.

The relationship between values and party choice is dealt with by Oddbjørn Knutsen in Chapter 17. By combining left–right materialist orientations and materialist–postmaterialist orientations he is able to show that there are clear cross-national differences in the impact of left–right materialism in several countries. He also shows that the libertarian–authoritarian aspect of postmaterialism has more impact on voting than the quality of life–economic security aspect. Then, in Chapter 18, Oddbjørn Knutsen and Elinor Scarbrough assess the contemporary relevance of the classic cleavage model of political conflict.

Posing a confrontation between the traditional cleavage model and 'new politics', they examine the relative impact of social structure and value orientations on party choice. It turns out that while value orientations are generally more significant, neither the impact of social location nor value orientations has changed much over the last two decades.

In Part IV, our concluding chapter draws together the major findings of our research and, more specifically, we assess the relevance of these findings for beliefs in government among West European citizens. We conclude that, although a process of value change seems to be under way, its direction cannot be described by some simple continuous function or trend. Certainly, political processes are increasingly characterized by ongoing value pluralization and differentiation, a development which accounts for the fact that most findings in this volume do not show very clear patterns or very high correlation coefficients. In a world so ambiguous, 'beliefs in government' are fragmented too—a situation which puts even more pressure on the legitimacy of political decision-making processes than would be produced by a crystalline, unidirectional shift in value orientations.

NOTES

1. We use the term 'advanced industrial societies' if the agricultural and industrial sectors of the economy are gradually being replaced by the service sector and the information processing sectors. Thus there are different degrees of being 'advanced'. See Bell (1973: 14 ff.) for a discussion of the major features of these societies. In order to avoid confusion or conceptual complexity, we do not use terms such as 'post-industrial society', 'technetronic society' or 'information society' in this volume.
2. See Vol. i, Chs. 1 and 11 for a more extensive discussion of this claim.
3. See Vol. i, Chs. 9, 10, and 11 for a report on these findings.
4. For a short overview of this model and a summary critique of its assumptions, see Greenstein (1975: 6).
5. Inglehart (1977b, 181–2) introduces the terms 'pre-industrial', 'industrial', and 'post-industrial'. His description of the distinctions is not followed here since he mixes the distinctions with empirical statements about the generational transmission of values which are not relevant for the present discussion.
6. We include data from Northern Ireland if they are available. So the terms 'United Kingdom' and 'Britain' are used here to identify the different data sets. But Northern Ireland is not considered separately.
7. The differences between samples based on the total population, the adult population, and the electorate are very modest in terms of the type of research reported in this volume.

PART I

Value Orientations and Value Change

2

The Concept of Values

JAN W. VAN DETH AND ELINOR SCARBROUGH

The concept of values was used in an uncomplicated, rather naïve way in the introductory chapter. Values were presented there as simply core elements in theories, or interpretations, of social and political change in advanced industrial societies. This reflects the widely held assumption in the social sciences that values are at the root of behaviour. Despite that, in comparison with the attitude–behaviour axis, the influence of values on political behaviour is relatively poorly researched—perhaps due to the behavioural orientations of political science, or even a certain calculated indifference due to worries that explaining behaviour in terms of values may not explain anything very much. But before embarking on an assessment of the impact of values and value change on beliefs in government in Western Europe, we have to face up to the conceptual problems surrounding the notion of 'values'.

In this chapter, we discuss, first, some of the difficulties with conceptualizations of values used in the social sciences and then, secondly, set out the understanding of values which inform this volume. We do not attempt to summarize the vast literature in this field, nor to discuss every aspect of controversies about the value concept. Rather, we begin by reviewing several approaches which, we anticipated, might yield a definition of values that could be adopted, or adapted, for our purposes. Our general conclusion is that

Parts of this chapter are based on earlier discussions and overviews published in J. W. van Deth, *Politieke waarden* (1984: ch. 4) and Elinor Scarbrough, 'The Concept of Values and the Concept of Cleavages' (1991, unpublished).

agreement about the value concept is hard to find, but some common aspects of different definitions prove useful. Building on those notions, we go on to set out our own understanding of values. We shall propose that values are non-empirical—that is, not directly observable—conceptions of the desirable, used in moral discourse, with a particular relevance for behaviour. We argue that such conceptions are to be treated, analytically, as hypothetical constructs, used for heuristic purposes without any presumption about their empirical status. Researchers can establish the empirical relevance of these constructs by uncovering some pattern, or constraint, among attitudes. A set of patterned, or constrained, attitudes we will call a *value orientation.* Finally, we outline some debates that are relevant to our concern with value change.

Our aim is to arrive at a conceptualization of values which is 'neither eclectic nor arbitrary, but strategic' (Middendorp 1991: 55) to our research project. We need an understanding of the value concept which allows us to explore the place of values in social and political change in Western Europe in the last few decades. That appears a limited task, but it is not uncomplicated.

The Many Faces of Values

Our task would be easier if we could draw on some general understanding of the term 'values' commonly used in the social sciences. It would also avoid adding to conceptual proliferation. Our first question, then, is whether there is such a common understanding, or, at least, some grounds for consensus about the meaning of the value concept.

In psychology, the term 'values' is frequently used to refer to a 'modality of selective orientation' (Williams 1968; Pepper 1958) which is linked to individual-level preferences, motives, needs, and attitudes. Sociologists employ the term as a social concept when they talk of norms, customs, manners, ideologies, commitments, and the like. In economics, too, there is a long tradition of using values: the distinction between the Ricardian, Marxist, and marginalist approaches to economic life centres on concurrent definitions of values; basic economic concepts such as utility, exchange, and price are all related to values. The concept of values is applied also in many anthropological and philosophical studies. Wright summarizes these differences: 'The psychological, scientific, philosophical, and sociological school of general ethics have respectively based values on desire, necessity, reason and custom' (1955: 449). Willi (1966: 118) comes to much the same conclusion, but does not restrict himself to even 'general ethics'.

Commenting on early research on values, Folsom noted the tendency to use the term to cover 'any general pattern, situation or aspect of human behaviour, society, culture, or the physical environment, or their interrelationships' (1937: 717). That is, more or less the whole world. And clarity does not seem to have been achieved subsequently. Lautmann's search for the distinct meanings of the term 'value' in some 4,000 publications resulted in no less than 180 different definitions (Kmieciak 1976: 147). There does not, then, seem to be a general or common understanding of the value concept in the social sciences; no dominant or accepted conceptualization that we can take up.

We might do better to look for some common meaning of the value concept in a specific discipline. Psychology, social-psychology and political science seem particularly relevant to the scheme of social and political change outlined in the previous chapter. Is there, then, a generally agreed definition of the value concept in the approaches adopted in psychology, social-psychology, or political science?

Even a brief review of the psychological and social-psychological literature shows a lack of consensus comparable to that found across the social sciences. Many authors settle for listing the cognates of values, so subsuming values within other notions. McLaughlin (1965) discusses values as 'preferences', 'needs', 'motivators', 'concepts' and 'situational relationships'; Scholl-Schaaf (1975) suggests that 'Trieb', 'Bedürfnis', 'Motiv', 'Einstellung', and 'Norm' are closely related to the value concept. Both Williams (1968) and Kmieciak (1976) cite even longer lists of related notions: 'values may refer to interests, pleasures, likes, preferences, duties, moral obligations, desires, wants, needs, aversions, and attractions' (Williams 1968: 283); 'Einstellung, Meinung, Vorurteil, Stereotyp, Ideal, Ideologie, Erwartung, Norm, Rolle, Fähigkeit, Selbstkonzept, Bedürfnis, Motiv, Interesse, Zeit und Zukünftperspektieve, Aspiration, Ziel, etc.' (Kmieciak 1976: 151).

Other researchers have presented an abstract, general conceptualization of values, avoiding enumerations. According to Woodruff and Divesta, for example, a value is 'a generalized condition of living which the individual feels has an important effect on his well-being' (1948: 645). Similarly, Nye proposes that a value is 'a high-level abstraction which encompasses a whole category of objects, feelings and/or experiences' (1967: 241). But this kind of definition is so vague as to be virtually meaningless; by covering almost everything in the world, it does not tell us what is specific about values. Psychology and social-psychology, then, seem to offer no generally accepted conceptualization of values.

In political science, the concept of values is at the core of Easton's famous definition of politics as 'those interactions through which values are authoritatively allocated for a society' (1965: 21). More specifically, it has been used in debates about political issues, participation, deprivation, democracy—usually as a rather general term implying some dynamic associated with opinions or behaviour. According to C. Wright Mills, for example, an issue should be seen as a public matter in which 'some value cherished by publics is felt to be threatened' (1959: 15). Political participation has been defined as 'those types of behaviour which enable the citizen(s) to take part in the creation and allocation of values' (Van Deth 1980: 2). Gurr conceptualizes relative deprivation as 'actors' perception of discrepancy between their value expectations and their value capabilities' (1970: 24). Neubauer's review of democratic practices in several countries concludes that their nature and extent 'appears to be less a function of their state of social and economic development than of certain values embodied in their political culture' (1969: 233). We could easily extend the list, showing how the notion of values has been used to elaborate concepts like legitimacy, representation, power, or policy. Indeed, political science itself might be defined as 'the study of the shaping and sharing of values' (cf. Lasswell and Kaplan 1952). But these uses of the value concept are no less vague, leaving us still to ponder how we might identify values or specify the relationship between values, attitudes, and behaviour.

Clearly, the definitions of values used in the social sciences are not very helpful. We are offered either cognate terms such as needs, preferences, desires, and the like, or only a very general, abstract basis for any kind of consensus. One denudes the value concept of discrete content, the other yields a consensus which is too all-embracing for an empirical study. With a clear sense of understatement, Albert (1968: 288) concludes: 'it is doubtful whether a definition of values can be produced that embraces all the meanings assigned to the term and its cognates or that would be acceptable to all investigators'. Our review leads to the same conclusion. The next step, then, is to arrive at our own conceptualization. First, we search for aspects of the value concept which are common to several definitions. That is, instead of searching for some common definition, it may be more fruitful to look for common elements in divergent definitions. We then go on to elaborate the principle elements in this conceptualization.

Conceptions of the Desirable

McLaughlin (1965: 266) identifies three features of values common to many different conceptualizations: (i) values cannot be observed directly; (ii) values have cognitive, affective, and connotive aspects; (iii) values do not operate independently from biological organisms or social environments. But claiming that values have cognitive, affective, and connotive aspects means that we have no meaningful demarcation between values and other aspects of attitudes. That is, McLaughlin's second point leaves us exposed to equating values with attitudes. Much the same difficulty arises with McLaughlin's third point: it is difficult to conceive of an object of social science research that is independent of biological or social influences. We conclude that the second and third features of McLaughlin's characterization of values refer to aspects of values but do not amount to criteria for distinguishing the value concept from other concepts. That leaves only McLaughlin's first point; a common feature of different characterizations of values is that they cannot be observed directly. This apparently trivial conclusion has important implications for our conceptualization.

That values cannot be observed directly has not gone undisputed. The more sociologically oriented approaches, in particular, have a long tradition of conceptualizing values as inhering in objects. This tradition is much influenced by Thomas and Znaniecki's seminal study of Polish immigrants in the Western world. They defined values as: 'any datum having an empirical content accessible to the members of some social group and a meaning with regard to which it is or may be an object or activity' (1918: 21). Thus coins, poetry, a university, a scientific theory could all be considered as values. Another example of the 'objects' approach comes from Hilliard who defined a value as 'affectivity in the reaction of an organism to a stimulus object'. Thus values are represented as an emotive response to encounters with objects, whether a 'thing, situation, action, occurrence, symbol, even a symbol of a non-existent object, "a figment of the imagination"' (1950: 42).

Although *The Polish Peasant* started a torrent of research on values, the 'values-as-objects' approach has long since been discarded. The major problem arose from the way Thomas and Znaniecki distinguished between attitudes and values; attitude referred to 'a process of individual consciousness', while a value referred to the object stimulating this attitude, or orientation, which, for them, were the rules governing social behaviour. This distinction soon proved to be inadequate for understanding social processes, largely because the actor/object dichotomy confused values as objects of orientation and values as elements of orientation (Kolb 1957: 94–7). Several scholars have identified this problem as an obstruction to applying the value concept in social science (Scholl-Schaaf 1975: 41); others have simply observed that the approach is not efficacious (Kmieciak 1976: 148) or should be dropped now that alternatives are available (Parsons 1968: 136). It was the consensus on this point that led McLaughlin to conclude that values should be conceptualized as not directly observable.

McLaughlin emphasized that all specifications of the value concept not included in the three features discussed above are either arbitrary or depend on the theoretical context of the research project. According to McLaughlin (1965: 266), three questions in particular need to be addressed: (i) Do values refer to desire or desirability? (ii) Are values hierarchically ordered in some personality system? (iii) Are values determinants of behaviour? In the context of our research, the second and third questions are matters for empirical testing, not questions to be answered *a priori*. It makes no sense to include answers to empirical questions in a conceptualization of values. This leaves us to answer McLaughlin's first question: are values desires or desirabilities?

The distinction between desire and desirable is based on the explicitly intentional element suggested by the word 'desirable'. A desire is simply a wish or a preference. The term 'desirable', however, goes beyond the idea of wish or want to bring in considerations with moral content—principles, ideals, virtues, and the like—in which 'want' is modified by 'ought'. The two notions are closely related because desirabilities are a subset of desires; people can desire what they consider desirable, and label desirable things as desires. That is, every wish or demand can be interpreted in several ways, as needs, instincts, customs, motives, and the like; introducing moral considerations to identify certain kinds of desires is just one of the many opportunities available to people to give meaning to their thoughts and behaviour. This emphasis on values as desirabilities is indicated by replacing terms such as 'I want' with 'I ought' (cf. Parsons 1935; Folsom 1937; White 1951; Rose 1956; Scott 1965; Rokeach 1973). Our conceptualization of values, then, incorporates the idea of desirability—that values are wishes or demands engaging moral considerations. This conceptual move means that, in our approach, values are expressed not as descriptive statements—as responses to stimuli—but as prescriptive statements.

Many scholars, however, have taken the view that values should be seen not as something desirable but as a conception of the desirable (Kluckhohn 1951; Albert 1956; R. T. Morris 1956; Catton 1959; McLaughlin 1965; Williams 1968; Bengston and Lovejoy 1973; Glenn 1980). Even contemporary scholars who do not explicitly refer to desirabilities as conceptions of the desirable seem to have something similar in mind. The classic definition of values as conceptions is presented by Kluckhohn (1951: 395): 'a value is a conception, explicit or implicit, distinctive of an individual or characteristic of a group, of the desirable which influences the selection of available modes, means and ends of action'.

Several objections can be put against this definition. In the first place, it is less precise than it appears. Scholl-Schaaf (1975: 58) has pointed out that the pairs 'implicit or explicit' and 'individual or group' do not specify the definition but enumerate all possibilities. So we drop them from our conception. Secondly, Kluckhohn's definition contains functional elements, suggesting that values are to be defined by their purpose. Other authors do much the same, usually referring to the function of values, like Kluckhohn, as selecting between alternatives. Indeed, the selection function is underlined in descriptions of values as preferences; Scholl-Schaaf even identifies values as 'Preferenzmodelle' (1975: 60). These scholars seem unaware of the pitfalls of bringing functions into concepts, particularly when the definitions involve relationships which have to be empirically tested. If we go along with this functional interpretation of the value concept, we risk a tautology; we cannot use values to explain specific choices if values are already defined in those very same terms (cf. Adler 1956; Scholl-Schaaf 1975: 117). And there is, of course, the additional question mark over 'conceptions of the desirable' which do not serve (only) to select from 'available modes, means and ends of action'. Are these not values?

The third difficulty with Kluckhohn's definition is its circularity. The English language masks complications with the words 'value' and 'desirable' but, for instance, the German words 'Wert' and 'wunschenswert', and the Dutch 'waarde' and 'waardering', clearly indicate that parts of the *definiens* are included in the *definiendum*. This touches on whether something is a value because it is desirable, or is desirable because it is a value. But the essential point is that if values cannot exist without desire, then including one of those terms in the *definiens* makes the definition circular. Following this line of reasoning, Scholl-Schaaf (1975: 60) concludes:

the concept of values, indeed, is a basic term which cannot be defined in the strict sense of a nominal definition. However, it is possible to describe what is meant, and to identify the relationships within the framework that provides its meaning.[1]

McCracken's (1949: 460) analogy between the concepts 'cause' and 'values' is illuminating here. He argues that both notions should be conceptualized as *a priori* categories in the Kantian tradition; they are to be understood not as empirical concepts derived from experience, but as concepts introduced by individuals to deal with their environment. These kinds of concepts can be defined only when the meaning of the *definiendum* is clear. Once we accept this conclusion, it becomes clear that searching for a nominal definition of values is senseless. After all, any definition of values will contain circular elements since we have to introduce the term in our arguments and elucidations in order to describe its meaning. We conclude, then, along with Kluckhohn, that values are to be conceived as *conceptions of the desirable*. We come back to the notion of conceptions as *a priori* categories.

To summarize our argument so far. We found no consensus about the meaning of 'values' across the social sciences or within any subdiscipline. Instead, from reviewing common features in divergent definitions, we have arrived at a conceptualization of values based on three propositions:

1. Values cannot be directly observed.
2. Values engage moral considerations.
3. Values are conceptions of the desirable.

The first proposition implies that we have to establish how we can make any empirical claims about values, which means examining the relevance of values for attitudes and behaviour. The second requires that we spell out the nature of moral considerations, which points to the social character of values. The third takes us on to consider values as a heuristic device. We explicate these ideas, in turn, in the next sections.

Values, Action, and Attitudes

That values cannot be directly observed is a major problem if we set out to examine the impact of values, whether on attitudes or behaviour; if they cannot be observed, what kind of evidence do we need before we can claim that values, rather than something else, are at work? This is a particularly tricky problem in our research because few of our data come from surveys directly concerned with values. We observed earlier that political science has tended to use the term as a very broad concept. But there is a long political science tradition of analysing attitudinal data to uncover some pattern, or evidence of constraint, among several attitudes, which is interpreted as revealing, for example, the influence of ideology (Campbell *et al.* 1960: 189–94; Butler and Stokes 1971: 261; Nie *et al.* 1976: 133) or the significance of the left–right dimension (Converse 1964; Inglehart and Klingemann 1976). Something akin to this approach is adopted in the following chapters, but, in contrast to the conceptual pragmatism of this tradition in electoral research (cf. Scarbrough 1984: 8–22), our strategy follows from clarifying the relationship between values, attitudes, and action.

Several scholars have incorporated into their definition of values the notion that values relate to action. As we have seen, Kluckhohn depicted a value as a conception which influences 'the selection of available modes, means and ends of action'; Thomas and Znaniecki pointed to a value as something which 'is or may be an object of activity' (1918: 21). More directly, Rokeach presents values as a species of belief about 'a specific mode of conduct or end-state of existence' (1973: 5), the one governed by 'instrumental values', the other by 'terminal values' (1976: 160). From a rather different perspective, Moscovici depicts the 'consensual universes' (1984: 186–7) of social life as essentially moral communities; ways of thinking, talking, judging, acting among members of social groups are shot through with moral content. As Moscovici puts it: 'Neutrality is forbidden by the very logic of the system' (1984: 30). In a similar vein, Billig, too, conceptualizes values as modes of 'arguing and thinking [that] make possible a communion with regard to particular ways of acting' (1987: 209).

There appears, then, to be a broad consensus that values are significant in their bearing on action. Quite what is the relationship between values and action is not explicated in that literature, but from the consensus we conclude that values are distinctive not only because they are desirabilities but, more importantly for our purpose, they are *desirabilities in matters of action*. This conclusion fits readily with our later discussion about values and attitudes. However, it still leaves unresolved our earlier question about the selection function of values. What place do values have in the process of selecting from the 'available modes, means and ends of action', as posited by Kluckhohn, or in settling upon 'a specific mode of conduct or end-state of existence', as proposed by Rokeach? Before we can be confident in our conceptualization of values as the moral dimension of action, we have to look more closely at the 'selection function' of values.

That 'selection' is a process engaging evaluations, judgements, and decisions is evident enough. We do not need the panoply of Kantian arguments to recognize that evaluations, judgements, and decisions are the work of active, thinking subjects engaged in wrestling with notions of what is good or bad. These notions might be consciously ethical or merely 'elements of common-sense whose truth or desirability is taken for granted' (Billig 1987: 210). Whatever the case, the process of selecting between alternatives engages some form of value-imbued reasoning. Mannheim puts the point well: 'Every real decision (such as one's evaluation of other persons or how a society should be organized) implies a judgement concerning good and evil' (1960: 17).

Values, then, we understand as desirabilities in matters of action—taking action in its wider sense to cover evaluations, judgements, decisions, and the like. However, while values are relevant to questions of action, they do not prescribe any particular type of action. For example, Rokeach talks of 'humility' and 'justice' as values which might guide conduct, 'salvation' and 'freedom' as values which might be life goals (1976: 124); Inglehart classes 'economic and physical security' as materialist values, 'self-expression and aesthetic concerns' as postmaterialist values (1990: 160). But these abstract principles tell us nothing about what actions constitute 'justice' or 'self-expression', or ensure 'freedom' or 'physical security'. In order for these values to see the light of day, as it were, in action, they need to be joined to notions of 'what is to be done'; to notions of what actions are consistent with what values. In this sense, values are not about action as such but, rather, abstract principles with which action is to conform; concepts of purposes or ends to be realized in determining courses of action, rather than determinate principles of action.

We can now see more clearly why values are particularly difficult to research. Not only are values not directly observable because they are manifest in action but not constitutive of action, but they need to be tied in with a much larger array of ideas, beliefs, concepts, understandings before they can have effects for action. As Mannheim points out, before individuals can 'act out' their values, they need some 'definition of the situation' (1960: 19); that is, an understanding of the field of action, its possibilities and constraints, and the status of objects and persons in that field. In other words, values are embedded in other things—in ways of thinking, talking, and acting, in judgements, decisions, attitudes, behaviour, and the like. We can conceptualize values as separate from these other things, but we cannot 'get to them' separately from their place in other things. Values cannot be researched on their own because they do not stand on their own. So we have to decide where, in the forest of activities which engage values, we look for evidence of the empirical relevance of values.

In part, our decision is influenced by the data we have, and most of the available surveys were concerned with political behaviour in some way. However, as we cannot presume a direct relationship between values and behaviour, we cannot use behavioural data to infer values. Yet most of these surveys followed the early 'Michigan model', not only in collecting attitudinal data but using them to provide a 'proximal mode of explanation' (Campbell *et al.* 1960: 34). And while we cannot presume a direct relationship between values and attitudes, attitudes are generally recognized to consist of cognitive, evaluative, and behavioural elements (cf. McGuire 1985: 242), but with the behavioural element understood as a predisposition to act, not the equivalent of action itself (cf. Rokeach 1976: 113–14; Barnes, Kaase, *et al.* 1979: 62). Thus, in view of the greater proximity of attitudes to behaviour, we focus on the relationship between values and attitudes, looking for evidence of values by examining data about attitudes.

In his seminal article, Thurstone uses the concept 'attitude' to 'denote the sum total of a man's inclinations and feelings, prejudice or bias, preconceived notions, ideas, fears, threats, and convictions about any specific topic' (1928: 531). Many other scholars, too, employ the term 'attitude' to identify orientations towards a specific object; and from the way they use the term, it is clear that a general notion of action is incorporated in the phrase 'specific object'. But how are we to disentangle the value elements from the other elements in such orientations? Dukes (1955: 33) summarizes three possible approaches:

1. Values and attitudes in a stimulus–response schema.
2. Values and attitudes as desirability and individual desire.
3. Values as more than general attitudes.

Several scholars have identified the first approach as the distinction between the social and the individual level; individuals observe a value (stimulus) and their attitude (response) reflects their reaction. We commented earlier on the inadequacy of representing values and attitudes as dichotomies. The second approach, distinguishing between values as desirability and attitudes as individual desire, would amount to rephrasing our earlier distinction between desire and desirability in terms of attitudes and values. But we gain nothing from restating earlier arguments in different terms. That leaves the third approach, that values are more general than attitudes. This approach allows us to conceptualize values not as stimuli but, rather, as *underlying orientations*, which are relevant for, or inform the process of, arriving at attitudes.

A similar account of the relationship between values and attitudes is proposed by Woodruff and Divesta: 'One's attitude toward a specific object or condition in a specific situation seems to be a function of the way one conceives that object from the standpoint of its effects on one's most cherished values' (1948: 657). What is noticeable here, however, is that they propose a one-way traffic between values and attitudes. Wright, too, proposes a one-way traffic in his discussion of the transfer of 'meaning' as 'a movement from symbols to opinions, from opinions to attitudes, and from attitudes to values' (1955: 284), but he reverses the direction.

More recently, Klages and Herbert formulated the *grundsätzliche Hypothese* for their research on values in Germany: 'that social attitudes, dispositions and ways of conduct . . . to a large degree are guided by [the fact that] "behind them" stand basic directional forces of an attitudinal nature, that can be understood as "value orientations" in the broadest sense of the word' (1983: 29).[2] This characterization of the way values are used is clearly in line with our conceptualization of values as 'desirabilities in matters of action'. In a different vocabulary Sniderman, Brody, and Tetlock (1991: 269–70) similarly suggest that the relationship between values and attitudes (or 'opinions') should be seen as the most important aspect of values because it allows individuals to deal with an indefinitely large number of specific policies:

It would be hard to explain how the average person keeps a myriad of specific opinions about particular policies well organized, given how little attention he or she tends to pay to political issues; it is considerably easier to give an account of how the average person could keep track of a small number of general values, which in turn give him direction on how to respond to a large number of specific issues.

There seems, then, to be no reason to opt for one-way traffic, in whichever direction. Rather, we conceive the values–attitudes axis as a reciprocal relationship. Values have an impact on attitudes in the way researchers like Klages, Sniderman, and their colleagues suggest. In turn, attitudes influence values by the way individuals learn from their own experience in engaging values, and from the influence of the attitudes of other people. Although he neglects the link in terms of attitudes, MacIntyre suggests the social process at work in this two-way traffic: 'We use moral judgements not only to express our own feelings and attitudes, but also precisely to produce effects in others' (1981: 12). As we shall see in the next section, the mutual influence between values and attitudes provides opportunities for the modification and adaptation of values at the individual level. Indeed, the idea of two-way traffic leads directly to the notion of change: values will change as attitudes are changing, and attitudes are modified if values change. At the aggregate level, these individual-level changes may provide a clue to the understanding of processes of social and political change for which we are looking.

We conclude, then, that attitudes are influenced by values and values by attitudes. Bear in mind, however, that there are elements other than values in attitudes and that values can be used in ways other than as an influence on attitudes. But the conceptual point we draw out from this discussion is the place of values in the formulation of attitudes. Taking attitudes as the most immediate antecedents of behaviour, we conceptualize values as becoming manifest in action—or, more modestly, behaviour—by the contribution they make to the formulation of attitudes. We have yet to consider the empirical complications of this conceptualization of the values–attitudes relationship. Before that, however, we consider the social nature of values.

The Social Nature of Values

In the earlier literature, there was an evident divide between 'individual' and 'social' accounts of values. As we have seen, Thomas and

Znaniecki identified a value as a social concept (1918: 22). But later scholars, such as Allport, who systematically edited out the social and collective elements in *The Polish Peasant* (Jaspers and Fraser 1984), worked with individualized concepts of beliefs, values, and attitudes. This left a persisting legacy construing values as personality traits. For Adorno *et al.* (1950), the authoritarian personality is authoritarian in all things; Wilson suggests that conservative values follow from a 'generalized susceptibility to feeling threat or anxiety in the face of uncertainty' (1979: 65). Here we concur with Rokeach in arguing that traits have an immutability—a 'fixedness'—which forecloses the possibility of change or 'situational variation' (1973: 21). Even more to the point, conceptualizing values as personality traits means adopting an over-individualized model of persons. As Farr comments, in another context, 'the individualization of the social goes hand in hand with the desocialization of the individual' (1990: 55). These considerations lead us to reject a conceptualization of values as 'fixed' entities characterizing individual persona.

From a very different perspective, Moscovici emphasizes values as the stuff of everyday social exchanges; the 'concepts, statements and explanations originating in daily life in the course of inter-individual communications' (1981: 181) are permeated with values because 'words . . . create things and pass their properties to them' (1981: 202). This discursive, 'noisy, public activity' of creating active images of the world takes place 'in the streets, in cafés, offices, hospitals, laboratories etc', characterizing those 'consensual universes' found in the everyday life of 'clubs, associations and cafés' (1984: 16). Other scholars, too, conceptualize values as at the heart of modes of 'arguing and thinking' (Billig 1987: 209) which characterize communities. And this emphasis on the social nature of values is shared by writers from other research traditions. Gibbs talks of values as referring to 'shared' and 'collective evaluations' (1965: 586); Folsom made much the same point somewhat earlier in claiming that 'Anything which people want exclusively for themselves is not a value' (1937: 716). Likewise, the discursive nature of values is asserted by Kluckhohn, for example, who contends that 'verbalizability is a necessary test of a value' (1951: 397), and by Fallding, in his assertion that values 'will scarcely consent to be born unless they are swaddled in verbalizations' (1965: 233). And in declaring that values are 'banners under which one can fight', Rescher (1969: 9) takes us close to our concern with the impact of values on political behaviour.

From these different directions, then, it becomes evident that values are not individual properties but the social properties of persons who share a universe of meaning. Individuals share a universe of meaning by dint of the language they talk in common—which bears the values they hold in common. To turn to Mannheim again: 'We belong to a group . . . primarily because we see the world and certain things in the world the way it does' (1960: 19). This leads us to modify Kluckhohn's claim that values are 'distinctive of an individual or characteristic of a group' to assert, instead, that it is from participation in a group, or membership of a community, that individuals come to their distinctive values. The language of a community constitutes its moral discourse—by which we mean the commonly recognized conversational conventions about what is fit, meet, and right—from which individuals draw, and to which they contribute, in a process of continuous inter-subjective exchange.

But this emphasis on the social, discursive nature of values rather speaks against our earlier conclusion that values constitute underlying orientations. This suggests a certain 'fixity' about values, which accords with a general presumption that values are universal principles, or, at least, relatively immutable entities, which individuals carry about with them and upon which they draw whenever action is called for. Certainly, notions of freedom and justice would seem to be 'banners under which one can fight' in all circumstances. None the less, we argue, conceptualizing values as universal 'desirabilities' neglects the relationship between values and context; that is, the simple proposition that different contexts call upon different values. Claiming the universality of values, however, would mean assuming that individuals live their lives in a single domain, and, moreover, that the domain constitutes a continuum. In that event, a single set of values would serve whenever and wherever action is called for. Rokeach suggests something of this kind in his definition of a value system as 'an enduring organization of beliefs concerning preferable modes of conduct or end-states of existence along a *continuum of relative importance*' (1973: 5; emphases added).

The clear implication here is that individuals adhere to a relatively determinate, 'enduring', body of values, in which the only difference between one value and another is their place in a hierarchy of salience—the 'continuum of relative importance'. This is plainly an implausible rendering of 'lived realities' (Berger and Luckmann 1967). To paraphrase the work of several scholars, the 'modernization' thrust of economic development brings with it an intensification of social and cultural differentiation (Apter 1965; Lash and Urry 1987), creating in its wake a 'disjuncture of realms' (Bell 1976: 14) and a disruption of 'the natural rootedness and automatic structures of belonging' (Martin 1981: 18). Such a severing of continuities is particularly relevant to discussions of social and political change. Thus a more sensitive, and intelligible, account of individual lives would point to the several worlds people take part in; the worlds of family, work, leisure, as parents or children, employers or workers, bureaucrats or clients, as citizens or members of classes. As MacIntyre (1981: 190) puts it:

Modernity partitions each human life into a variety of segments, each with its own norms and modes of behaviour. So work is divided from leisure, private life from public, the corporate from the personal . . . [each is] made over into distinct realms . . . it is the distinctiveness of each and not the unity of the life of the individual who passes through those parts in terms of which we are taught to think and feel.

Once we recognize the 'multi-worldedness' of people's lives, we have to forgo the notion that values are universal desirabilities. Perhaps there are some values that 'transcendentally guide actions and judgements across specific objects and situations' (Rokeach 1976: 160). But that is an empirical matter. On the contrary, if people live in a 'variety of segments', we have to anticipate that they participate in several different universes of meaning, each governed by situationally appropriate values—what is 'seemly in different places' (Billig 1987: 209). Indeed, talk of 'family values', 'spiritual values', 'commercial values' and the like is part of our everyday language. More specifically, Becker (1981) has contrasted the altruistic values embedded in family relations with the competitive values of the business world; we have no difficulty in recognizing winning as an important value among athletes but inappropriate among aesthetes. We argue, then, in accord with our conceptualization of values as elements in moral discourse, that modes of thinking and arguing are features of domains of behaviour, of the social setting of behaviour, rather than universal 'all-purpose' desirabilities in matters of action.

What this means, of course, is that people do not conduct their lives according to a—singular—moral discourse but according to several, and not necessarily compatible, discourses. Which discourse is engaged is a contingent matter, according to 'what is seemly' in the world in question. Moreover, we can anticipate the interpenetration of discourses, and tensions between discourses, as the different worlds of, say, work and family, intersect. This is not to argue against the general assumption that values are relatively stable, but to suggest some of the opportunities for those shifts, slides, and mutations of 'conceptions of the desirable' which may amount, over time, to value change.

Explicating the moral dimension of values in this section has led us to reject a conceptualization of values as either objects or individual properties. Instead, we emphasize the social, intersubjective nature of values, which is evident from their appearance as elements in moral discourse. From these arguments we conclude that values have to be studied in their social context, and that the objects of our analyses are individuals as members of groups. It also means, of course, that, ideally, we would want to examine qualitative data which capture the elements of moral discourse in different domains. However, in the comparative and national surveys used in this research project, quantitative attitudinal data are the best measures available to us. This brings us on directly to consider the value concept as a heuristic device.

Values as a Heuristic Device

Earlier we argued that values are not empirical concepts derived from experience but *a priori* concepts introduced by individuals to deal with their environment. This is consistent with the consensus that values are not directly observable. At the same time, we noted that the social, discursive nature of values presumes verbalization. But these arguments, taken together, raise a number of new questions. What can be the status of a non-observable, *a priori* concept in a scientific theory? How can we depict any verbal expressions as the 'verbalization' of values if values are non-observable? What criteria can we use to distinguish, empirically, between the value elements and other elements in verbalizations identified as attitudes? In this section, we establish the theoretical grounds for a methodological move which allows us, as researchers, to infer values from data about attitudes.

Rescher (1969: 55) suggests that the first problem with identifying values concerns whether we are dealing with aspects of objects, or with the relationship between an object and a subject. We encountered this problem when noting Thomas and Znaniecki's work, and decided against conceptualizing values as objects. An alternative approach is to look at values as aspects of individuals in their social context: individuals use their values as underlying orientations to structure their particular attitudes and behaviour in specific contexts—and, we argued, vice versa. Since values are not observable, the status of these orientations is that of a *disposition* or a *dispositional concept*. In that case, the existence and the relevance of values can be demonstrated by studying the realization of values in defined situations: the meaning of the concept follows from the definition of these conditions (cf. Carnap 1936: 440; Hempel 1965: 457–63).[3] For example, if we want to capture the meaning of the dispositional concept 'dissolvable', we have to describe the process of dropping sugar into water, stirring until it has disappeared, evaporating the water, and recovering a white substance.[4] The concept 'dissolvable' is defined by this simple procedure. A similar argument applies to value orientations as a dispositional concept; by describing a social context in which values are elements in the pattern of behaviour, the meaning and relevance of the concept is defined in the description of the process. However, by embracing values as a strong dispositional concept, we risk falling back to suggesting the 'real' existence of values, so re-opening the door to the notion of values-as-entities. Thus, depicting values as dispositional concepts requires an important limitation.

According to MacCorquodale and Meehl's (1948) classic definition, the behaviour analogue of Carnap's 'dispositional constructs' is an intervening variable, not a hypothetical construct. The distinction between these two concepts is based on their status in our theories and descriptions. Intervening variables, however, are abstractions of empirical relationships. Each term in the description has a clear empirical meaning; no phrases are used which cannot be reduced to empirical statements. Every intervening variable, then, can be measured and has a place in empirical descriptions. But hypothetical constructs are typified by the presumption of processes or phenomena which cannot be observed. In order to delineate these constructs, we have to use terms that cannot be reduced to empirical statements; that is, hypothetical constructs have some non-empirical surplus meaning. This is where the notion of values as *a priori* categories, in the Kantian sense, comes in. As they are constructs delineating some non-observable processes or phenomena, we cannot adduce direct evidence for their existence or relevance. Rather, they are constructs introduced by researchers to make sense of the evidence before them. In other words, we use the concept of value orientations as a *heuristic device* to facilitate our understanding of attitudes. We have good theoretical grounds upon which to predicate the influence of value orientations on attitudes, but we have to use the values concept heuristically, not empirically, in order to capture the value elements in attitudes.

An example of the 'realist' approach to value orientations as heuristic devices is presented by Sniderman, Brody, and Tetlock. They want to explain how people can work out what they favour or oppose in politics, while, at the same time, they know little about politics. Their argument is that ordinary citizens reduce their 'investments' by using values (1991: 269): 'We suppose there is a strong tendency to resolve problems of reasoning and choice in the simplest way possible. Which is the reason, of course, for the appeal of values as an explanatory category. A value is a simple but general consistency generator.' For Sniderman and his colleagues, then, the use of value orientations as a heuristic device is not confined to researchers; individuals apply values in a straightforward way to achieve consistency at a low 'cost'. Much the same point is made by Butler and Stokes when they comment, 'many of the issues of electoral politics owe more to the voters' orientation towards values and goals than to their assessment of policy alternatives' (1971: 230).

The way values are used in these examples illustrates our argument for using the value concept heuristically. However, we do not go along with the suggestion that values are 'real' entities. If we did, we would be back to the values-as-entities conceptualization which we rejected earlier. For our purposes, the Kantian notion of *a priori* categories and the heuristic status of hypothetical constructs are more appropriate to describe the value concept. To be clear on this point: we, *the researchers*, apply the value concept as a way of enhancing our understanding of the evidence before us, but we do not make any empirical claim about the use of values in this way by *individuals themselves* (as Sniderman and others do). This approach is depicted quite clearly by Kluckhohn (1951: 398): 'The observer notes certain kinds of patterned behaviour. He cannot "explain" these regularities unless he subsumes certain aspects of the processes that determine concrete acts under the rubric "value".'

One of the strengths of our approach is that it avoids the pitfalls of identifying values in functional terms. Indeed, looking at the literature, values are expected to perform so many different functions that it is virtually impossible to specify the conditions for values to be expressed.[5] That is, we cannot specify the meaning of the value concept by describing some kind of object or situation which shows the 'real' nature of the concept—simply because there are too many different and divergent objects and situations in which values are used. Moreover, as Billig puts it, 'Contained within the general principles are many different possibilities' (1988: 20); to put it more directly, the outcome of 'values in action' is too variable, uncertain, and situationally specific to allow us to read off values from particular courses of action. Conceptualizing values as a dispositional predicate would require an exact and unique identification of the conditions for discerning the consequences of values. We cannot present such a description of any object or situation. Thus we depict values neither as strong dispositional predicates nor as attributes of an object or subject. Rather, to repeat, in our approach the concept of values is a hypothetical construct used as a heuristic device by us, as researchers, without any presumption that our subjects—respondents in surveys—use the value concept in the same way. Kmieciak (1976: 150–1) and, implicitly, Krippendorff (1970: 510–11) come to a similar conclusion.

What does this discussion mean for understanding the relationship between values and attitudes? We have argued that values are relevant for action but get to see 'the light of day' by their contribution to the formulation of attitudes. However, we rejected the conceptualization of values as an intervening variable, so we cannot presume an empirical link between values and attitudes. Indeed, suggesting an empirical link would run us into all the problems associated with the 'functions' of values noted above. This is where our use of the value concept as a heuristic device becomes important. If values are elements 'behind' attitudes, then uncovering some pattern among several attitudes suggests there is some non-observable phenomenon or process at work. Introducing the value concept as a heuristic device allows us to capture these non-empirical features of the values–attitudes relationship. In other words, we use a non-observable concept in order to understand a non-empirical phenomenon (cf. Hempel 1965). And the proof of the pudding will be, of course, the explanation of empirical phenomena which we cannot understand without introducing a non-observable concept like values.

As our research rests, crucially, on deploying a non-observable concept, we have to be particularly careful about laying out our strategy. Data about one kind of category (attitudes) can be interpreted as evidence of another kind of category (values) only if we have clear rules of assignment (cf. Scarbrough 1984: 10–11). If attitudes engage values, and people can hold many attitudes but there are relatively few values (Rokeach 1976: 162), there cannot be a one-to-one relationship between values and attitudes. So in our approach, we look for evidence of some pattern among several attitudes, and this patterning we interpret as evidence of *constraint*. Such constraint is not directly observable, but it is the assumption of constraint on our part—as researchers—which renders intelligible some patterning between several attitudes. That is, evidence of constraint demonstrates the empirical relevance of the value concept; and the summary measure for patterned attitudes is what we term *value orientation*. Indeed, our approach is in line with Inglehart's comment that values 'can be inferred from a consistent pattern of emphasis on given types of goals' (1990: 74),[6] and with the proposal by Sniderman *et al.* that values are a 'general consistency generator' (1991: 269). The major differences are that we do not subscribe to the notion of values as 'real', and we have gone to some lengths to set out the theoretical grounds for presuming that individuals hold certain abstract, morally and socially imbued conceptions of the desirable which renders individual behaviour 'meaningful', 'comprehensible', even predictable. Attitudes are our data but, in our approach, those data are rendered intelligible, and yield a coherent account of behaviour, by employing the value concept heuristically.

Value Orientations

Conceptions of the desirable can be discerned by uncovering some pattern among attitudes. However, these patterns are likely to show considerable variation, suggesting different degrees of constraint. Some groups of people may be characterized by a well-integrated set of attitudes on some topics—on matters of income and wealth, say—but only weak constraint between attitudes on other topics. Some groups may show very little constraint at all between their attitudes on any topics; yet others, such as politicians and political activists, may show very high levels of constraint between attitudes on a wide range of topics. This route, of course, leads to the Pandora's box of discussions about ideologies and 'mass belief systems'. But this route is barred to us—simply because few of the available data are appropriate to a more elaborate, ideological account of attitudes (cf. Scarbrough 1984;

Middendorp 1991). Instead, our focus is kept firmly on the patterning of attitudes, interpreted as evidence of constraint.

So far, we have been preoccupied with explicating the value concept, saying little about how 'conceptions of the desirable' might stand in relationship to one another. Clearly, our emphasis on the discursive, inter-subjective nature of values suggests that such conceptions are loosely articulated. We made the point that values do not determine attitudes or courses of action; in just the same way, our conceptualization does not propose any *a priori* rules about which values 'go together'. This is something we, the researchers, have to establish on theoretical grounds—which we come to shortly. The point to establish here is that we do not assume evidence of constraint between some number of attitudes as evidence of the effects of some singular 'conception of the desirable'. Rather, the loose articulation of the elements in moral discourse suggests that the substantive interpretation of constraint between attitudes requires several conceptions of the desirable before an entire pattern is intelligible. We capture these multiple conceptions of the desirable as *value orientations*. In order to apply this term to any constellation of attitudes, two requirements have to be met: (i) a set of attitudes which can be shown to be patterned in some empirical way; (ii) a theoretical interpretation of the pattern in terms of desirability. These two requirements are necessary and sufficient conditions for the use of the term value orientations.

Our strategy, then, is to identify the value orientations which, on theoretical grounds, we have reason to believe are relevant for attitudes and behaviour on questions of politics. We discuss those theoretical considerations in the next section; how the value orientations are operationalized is set out in the relevant chapters. These value orientations constitute configurations of conceptions of the desirable which tend to be juxtaposed in politically relevant discourses. Thus we avoid phrases like 'value dimensions' to refer to patterns of constraint; that would suggest we are dealing with some space defined by specific properties in which clusters of values are identified according to their relative position in that space. Although it is not unusual to place attitudes in analytic spaces of some two or three dimensions, this approach would be too schematic and restrictive for our purposes. All we need in order to apply the term 'value orientations' is a theoretically meaningful pattern among attitudes. Our last task in this chapter is to identify the value orientations examined in this volume.

Theories of Value Changes

Our central concern in this volume is the impact of value change on social and political change. At several points in our earlier discussion, we indicated opportunities for modifications and shifts in values which are inherent in the discursive nature of 'conceptions of the desirable': the loose articulation of the elements; the effects of experience and the attitudes of others; the interpenetration of different discourses. But such opportunities neither point to value change in any particular direction nor suggest the possibility of longer-term, relatively irreversible, value change. In identifying the value orientations on which this volume focuses, we turn to theories which anticipate not only long-term change but value change in particular directions.

Much of our understanding of mass politics in Western Europe has been derived from the seminal work of Lipset and Rokkan (1967). Their 'model' of party systems identified four types of historically rooted cleavages which, by the mid-1960s, had structured electoral politics since the advent of adult suffrage: (i) a centre–periphery cleavage, reflecting resistance to the dominant culture; (ii) a religious cleavage, engaging conflicts between church and state or between different confessional groups; (iii) an urban–rural cleavage, stemming from competition between agriculture and industry; and (iv) a class cleavage, centring on conflicts between employers and workers. Subsequent empirical research has revealed the predominance of the class and religious cleavages—except in Ireland (Rose and Urwin 1969; Lijphart 1982; Whyte 1974).[7] The urban–rural cleavage has been largely a distinctive feature of Scandinavian politics, and the cultural cleavage has had major effects only for the politics of Belgium and Spain (Lijphart 1981).[8]

Lipset and Rokkan, however, paid scant attention to the underlying values, as opposed to the issues, which inform class and religious conflicts. More recently, Bartolini and Mair (1990: 212–20) have urged a conceptualization of cleavage which both incorporates the three aspects of cleavage politics—social structure, values and beliefs, organization—and yet allows them to be treated as empirically distinct; each of these aspects of a cleavage, they argue, 'have histories of their own . . . [and] . . . may vary quite autonomously' (1990: 219). This elaboration of the 'cleavage model' enables us to examine class values and religious values as empirical phenomena detached from their place in a cleavage model of electoral politics. We are, of course, interested in developments in 'cleavage politics', but our concern with the impact of these values extends beyond their influence on voting behaviour.

The cleavage model also suggests circumstances conducive to value change. In representing parties as élite responses to the 'givens' of social divisions, Lipset and Rokkan imply that parties and the values they embody are the outgrowths of conflicts between specific social groups. With changes in the environment, the political relevance of such group memberships can be expected to wane, along with their characteristic values. The transformation of economic and social life in West European countries, documented in the next chapter, represents just such changes in the environment. One of our concerns, then, against this background, is to examine trends in the values associated with class and religious conflicts and to assess their relevance for political attitudes.

A rather different approach to the prospects for value change is proposed by Inglehart in his studies charting the progress of the 'Silent Revolution' as agricultural and industrial societies are transformed into advanced industrial societies. Although Inglehart anticipates the demise of the class cleavage and its associated values, he is ambivalent about the future of the religious cleavage, sometimes anticipating its decay (1985: 486), at other times anticipating its enhanced relevance (1990: 305), and at yet other times suggesting that religious values will retain their individual-level significance despite the demise of the religious cleavage (1990: 177). However, whereas Lipset and Rokkan hint only that post-cleavage politics will show 'greater fluctuations than before' (1967: 56), Inglehart predicts the emergence of a new cleavage centring on conflicts between 'materialist' and 'postmaterialist' values. That is, the demise of class and (perhaps) religion as sources of political conflict heralds not only the end of cleavage politics but also, at the same time, the emergence of political conflicts based on values alone. This implies both a disconnection between structure and values, and a transformation in politically relevant values.

From the cleavage model and Inglehart's approach we derive three value orientations which are central to political change, as already noted in the introductory chapter. The first is religious in nature and refers to the process of secularization. The value orientations identified by these values are derived by analysing data on religious belief and church membership. Religious values might be regarded as pre-industrial since their origins go back to the sixteenth and seventeenth centuries. We use the term *religious–secular value orientations* to characterize changes in the religious value orientation (see Chapter 7). The second value orientation is based on one of the principal characteristics of industrial society: the expression of class conflict in terms of left and right. However, as the terms left and right engage no reference to conceptions of the desirable, this value orientation is not operationalized by using data about left–right self-placement. Rather, we derive *left–right materialist value orientations* from attitudes towards the several socio-economic issues at the heart of political conflict in industrial societies (see Chapter 6). The third value orientation refers to the specific values of advanced industrial societies, introduced by using the idea of postmaterialism as developed by Inglehart. This value orientation refers to the priority given to goals such as self-fulfilment and emancipation rather than economic security or law and order. Attitudes towards a number of these goals appear to be patterned and can be summarized as *materialist–postmaterialist value orientations* (see Chapter 5). On account of its widespread use in empirical studies, it is this materialist–postmaterialist measure which receives our first attention in Part II of this volume.

Obviously, the three value orientations identified here do not cover every politically relevant value orientation, nor do the debates we have outlined cover every aspect of value change in Western Europe. Indeed, in analytic terms, quite distinct processes of value change can occur: constraint among certain attitudes can weaken or grow stronger; prevailing attitudes can come to be grouped in new patterns; large patterns of constraint encompassing many attitudes might become fragmented, giving rise to several more specific patterns. Moreover, people with a specific pattern of attitudes may be replaced by people with new ways of articulating constraints among attitudes.

The process of value change, then, can be conceptualized in many different ways. In this volume we restrict ourselves to the most obvious variants of value change. First, we describe the three central value orientations and their major socio-structural antecedents. Secondly, with some specific questions in mind, we derive further value orientations by looking for meaningful constraint among attitudes in other politically relevant domains. Several chapters in this volume show the fruitfulness of our approach by introducing value orientations such as feminism, 'greenness', and postmodernism. By looking at the three central value orientations, we are tracing aspects of major trends in value change; by looking at less widespread value orientations, we are identifying more specific developments.

Conclusion

To sum up what the discussion in this chapter contributes to the research reported in this volume, our task is to examine the impact of values and value change on beliefs in government across Western Europe in both a cross-national and a longitudinal perspective. We are not alone in attending to values; several chapters in the companion volumes suggest explanations for trends in terms of values. But, in contrast to the other volumes, the notion that changing attitudes about government and politics originate in changing values is at the heart of our research. Rather than starting out from behaviour and turning to value-type explanations to account for trends, our starting point is the significance of values in politics.

Our first step was to establish a conceptualization of values suited to our research task. Our strategy sought to describe the value concept in terms which optimizes its usefulness for our purposes. Values are seen here as conceptions of the desirable which are not directly observable but are evident in moral discourse and relevant to the formulation of attitudes. For heuristic purposes, we understand these conceptions as hypothetical constructs which constrain attitudes. The claim for the empirical relevance of values, we argue, is demonstrated by evidence of patterning among attitudes. We call these meaningful patterns *value orientations*. This approach places attitudinal measures at the centre of our empirical work.

A final word: we have laid out our strategy with some care, but it has to be borne in mind that few of the data available to us were collected with any clear, fully explicated, concept of values in mind. As we commented in our opening remarks, attempts to study systematically the impact of values on political behaviour have not been a major feature of the political science agenda. Election surveys, one of our main data sources, are largely wedded to an amalgam of sociological and 'issue' models of electoral behaviour; attitudinal data leave us only the footprints of how people think about politics and government. The strategic approach outlined in this chapter endeavours to give meaning to these footprints, rather as a detective or an archaeologist reconstructs events from inconclusive and indirect evidence. This means that claims based on these data must necessarily be modest. Our purpose is to delineate the main lines of development and change, rather than to tackle larger questions about the role of values in politics.

NOTES

1. Translated from the original: 'bei dem Wertbegriff haber wir tatsächlich mit einem Grundterminus zu tun, der nicht mehr im strengen Sinne einer Nominaldefinition zu definieren ist. Es kann aber umschrieben werden, was gemeint ist; es können die Beziehungen angezeigt werden, innerhalb deren ein solcher Begriff steht und innerhalb er einen Sinn gewinnt.'
2. Translated from the original: 'dass soziale Einstellungen, Verhaltensdispositionen und Verhaltensweisen . . . in einem starken Masse van "hinter ihnen" stehenden elementaren Richtungskräften einstelhungsbestimmender Natur gesteuert werden, die sich als "Wertorientierungen" im weitesten Sinne des Wortes verstehen lassen.'
3. Notice that this suggestion raises, again, the question of the circularity of definitions as, for instance, when values are defined in terms of the selections that could be predicted or explained by introducing this concept. We follow Popper (1963: 118–19, 278–9) in his observations that there are many non-defined concepts in scientific theories and that the dispositional character of a concept is not a valid argument to drop dispositions.
4. Note that, if the remaining substance is sugar, a characteristic of sugar is that it is dissolvable. So, in order to prove that the substance really is sugar, it has to be dropped into water. And so on. This endless procedure is a feature of dispositional concepts.
5. Examples of the many functions of values are: goal (Fallding 1965), criterion (Kluckhohn 1951), order principle (Fallding 1965; Kmieciak 1976), legitimation (Folsom 1937), satisfaction of needs (Katz 1960), the prevention of chaos (Parsons 1935).
6. Inglehart suggests this approach to values and attitudes in several places, but his selection of terms is highly ambiguous. He talks varyingly of 'attitudinal continuities' (1990: 105), 'behavioural predispositions' (1990: 106) and refers to the 'index of Materialist/Postmaterialist values' as providing 'a measure of *something* pervasive and enduring in one's outlook' (1990: 131; emphasis added).
7. Contrary to much of the conventional wisdom, religion has until recently been a significant influence on political attitudes and voting behaviour in Britain (cf. Heath 1991: 85–8, 174–5, 203–5).
8. The cultural cleavage has had some relatively minor effects in Britain, and some—but still disputed—effects on the politics of the so-called 'consociational' democracies (cf. Lijphart 1969; Daalder 1974; Halpern 1986).

3

A Macro Setting for Micro Politics

JAN W. VAN DETH

The countries of Western Europe differ widely in their economic, social, and political life, yet it is generally assumed that there are more or less similar processes going on which may explain the value orientations and political involvement of their citizens. Such a macro setting for micro politics consists in the development of advanced industrial societies in democratic countries. More specifically, the central characteristics of that setting are a combination of highly developed economic systems and representative political regimes. But the bare facts of these twin developments are less relevant than the mutual interdependence and intensive interaction between them. Governments increasingly intervene in the economic process, especially to deal with aspects of macro-economic policy—inflation, unemployment, investment, exchange rates, and the like—while the political process has become dominated by these economic issues. Thus, we see the conversion of social and political conflict into budgetary claims— the 'fiscalization of politics'.

Although the nature of these developments remains controversial, there seems to be a consensus about their consequences: as per capita real income increases, governments spend a higher proportion of the national product (Wagner's Law). This is only one among a number of 'laws' characterizing the relationship between economic growth and government spending (Wilenski's First and Second Law, Schmidt's Law, or Castles' Law; cf. Lane and Ersson 1991: 340–1). But it is not only the amount of money spent by government which grows continuously. When the number of government activities increases, the scope of government regulation, subsidy, and taxation increases as well. The result is that democratic government in advanced industrial societies absorbs a substantial part of the national product, and government becomes party to such divergent aspects of social life as housing, education, transport, social security, and health care.

Besides demand-side theories, there are a number of supply-side 'laws' describing the relationship between economic and political developments (Niskanen's Law, Tullocks's Law, Downs' Law; cf. Lane and Ersson 1991: 340–1). With each expansion of government tasks and increase in spending, the number of interests organizing around government grows. As Webber and Wildavsky (1986: 493) remark: 'Big government breeds big pressures. Each new program creates interests organizing around it.' Thus, both demand-side and supply-side theories of the relationship between economic and political developments predict ever-growing levels of government intervention and regulation in the economies of advanced industrial societies.

The main elements of a macro setting for micro politics in advanced industrial societies, then, are economic development and the growth of government. A brief overview of these twin processes is presented here by looking, first, at several aspects of economic development over the last decades and its correlates in terms of rising levels of education, increasing mobility and communication, and the position of women in society. Secondly, the growth and shifts in government intervention during the same period are noted. In the final part of the chapter we look at the characteristics of the political processes in Western Europe in terms of involvement and protest. But before moving to these themes, we say something about the information selected.

Selecting Information

The macro setting provides the background against which to interpret the data on micro politics in the following chapters. In this way, the atomized individuals found in our survey data are placed in their societal and historical contexts.[1] The traditional approach in political sociology is to consider political phenomena as a function of the socio-economic structure of society. This type of structural determinism is especially related to the work of Rokkan and his followers in analysing political cleavages in Western Europe. This approach has been criticized by advocates of a cultural approach, and by researchers arguing for a more institutional frame of reference. From this perspective, political culture is a major aspect of political systems, and political institutions are seen to have a life and a logic of their own. The macro setting presented here takes into account both perspectives, so avoiding the Scylla of structural determinism and the Charybdis of social indeterminism by referring to socio-economic developments as well as to institutional and cultural changes.

Before describing the macro settings, the period we cover should be made clear. Obviously, the period spanned by the survey data has to be covered. But explanations of developments in recent years have to be consistent with interpretations of similar developments in earlier years, so we have to lengthen our perspective. For example, if growing affluence is identified as significant in predicting the growth of postmaterialism in the early 1970s yet ten or fifteen years later we find postmaterialism is declining amidst continuing high levels of affluence, we need to explain why affluence is now accompanied by opposite effects. Thus, the macro setting cannot neglect developments in years prior to our survey data. The end of the period is determined by the most recent information available to us. At the time of writing, in the early 1990s, reliable time series for many of our indicators are available only until the mid- or late 1980s. So, for both theoretical and pragmatic reasons, the macro settings presented here cover, roughly, the forty-five years since the end of the Second World War.

A more complicated question when analysing social and political change is how to discriminate between basic trends and the impact of particular events. Three types of political events dominated public debate and received wide media coverage throughout Western Europe during the 1960s and 1970s. The first was the war in Vietnam, which generated political protest in the United States and many other Western countries. The second type was the spread of terrorism, ranging from hijacking planes and trains to the assassination of prominent figures. Political violence became a major political issue. The third type was wrongdoing among political élites. Revelations of burglary, bugging, bribery, espionage, and the like, eventually led, for example, to the resignation of the president of the United States, Richard Nixon, the withdrawal from public life of the Dutch prince consort, and the end of the career of Bundeskanzler Willy Brandt.

The impact of these kinds of events on individual citizens cannot be pinpointed, but clearly the political climate changed in the 1970s. Even so, these kinds of events are short term in character. They may colour general developments at particular moments, but they do not provide the broader picture against which to set the longer-term trends discussed in this volume. Hence, we focus on those broader developments which have characterized a period of rapid economic and social change in Western Europe.

Next, there is the question of data sources. Obviously, in view of the vast amount of data available, we have to be selective on two counts. First, we had to decide which aspects of development are relevant, according to our theoretical perspective. This was discussed in Chapter 1. The second decision is technical and involves the sources to be used. The general strategy pursued here is summarized by Zapf and Flora (1971: 63):

The major problem . . . does not arise from a scarcity of sources but concerns the choice among abundant data of unequal quality. Of course, there is no ideal strategy to deal with these problems. In general, we prefer *a*) primary sources to secondary sources, *b*) historical comparative sources to non-comparative sources, *c*) cross-national comparative sources to non-comparative sources, *d*) compendia to monographs.

But neat criteria frequently conflict in real life. Primary sources are usually non-comparative monographs; comparative sources do not always cover the historical or cross-national dimensions of our study. The original intention to use only primary sources was abandoned as unnecessarily time consuming. Instead, we turned to data collections such as the *World Handbook of Political and Social Indicators* (Taylor and Jodice 1983) and its predecessors (Russett *et al.* 1964; Taylor and Hudson 1972). The most recent publication of this type is the *Political Data Handbook: OECD Countries* (Lane, McKay, and Newton 1991), while more specific data on national accounts are included in 'The Penn World Table (Mark 5)' (Summers and Heston 1991). Thus, the data in this chapter are either official statistics available from organizations such as the OECD and the United Nations, or they are drawn from publications such as the handbooks. We used country-specific data only in the last resort.

Economic Development

Although economic conditions in most West European countries look fairly similar today, the picture was very different at the end of the Second World War. In many countries, large parts of the economic infrastructure were destroyed. For instance, the Netherlands had lost about 30 per cent of its productive capacity. Conditions in Germany were even more miserable: many cities lay in ruins, and huge numbers of displaced persons had entered the country. However, the economies of countries which retained their independence during the war—such as Sweden and Switzerland—were largely untouched. Post-war reconstruction in many countries was stimulated by aid under the Marshall Plan, which made available US$13.15 billion for economic recovery in Europe, especially for (re)industrialization, during the four years 1948–52. Thereafter, economic development, on almost every indicator, was rapid. We present data on those developments which were most relevant to the individual citizen.

The most obvious measure of macro-economic development is gross domestic product (GDP) per capita. This shows the total products and services in a country on a yearly basis, and the year-on-year changes are a straightforward indicator of the economic performance of a country. In the period 1950–5, GDP per capita showed an average annual growth of 3.8 per cent in Western Europe. The levels of GDP per capita were also quite remarkable in the first post-war decades. In 1950 this was highest in Switzerland (US$8,019) and lowest in Portugal (US$1,050).[2] Of course, in historical and global terms, these are impressive figures;

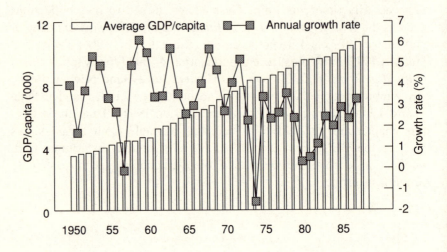

FIGURE 3.1*a*. *Average real GDP per capita, Western Europe, 1950–88*
Notes: 1985 prices; chain index.
Source: Summers and Heston (1991: var. 2).

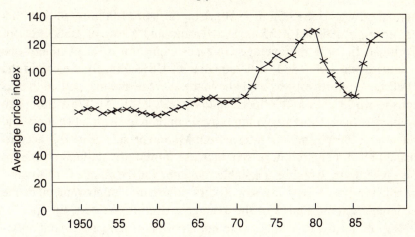

FIGURE 3.1*b*. *Average price level of GDP (controlled for exchange rates),*
Western Europe, 1950–88

Source: Summers and Heston (1991: var. 13).

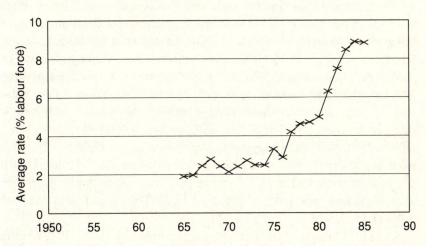

FIGURE 3.1*c*. *Standardized unemployment rates, Western Europe, 1965–85*

Source: Lane, MacKay, and Newton (1991: table 3.12).

even the 'low' figure for Portugal meant that it ranked forty-fifth out of
sixty-one countries, with Switzerland in the third rank. It is not supris-
ing that, with a rise of GDP per capita from US$3,128 in 1950 to
US$6,038 in 1960, Germany proudly referred to its *Wirtschaftswunder*.

In Figure 3.1*a* we show the average real GDP per capita and the
annual growth rate 1950–88 for Western Europe. The average real GDP

per capita was US$3,455 in 1950, rising to US$11,005 in 1988, with a record high of US$16,155 in Switzerland and a low of US$5,321 for Portugal. In 1988 the average GDP per capita for a set of ninety-two countries was US$4,884, with a median of US$3,598. By the end of the 1980s, even Portugal was well above the average and the median figures for the world with a GDP per capita of US$5,321. All West European countries, then, show very impressive economic growth, absolutely and relatively, during the post-war period. Moreover, this growth is accompanied by an equally impressive increase in real private final consumption per capita, which is a reliable indicator for the standard of living.[3] In all, the post-war years saw a very substantial improvement in the economic circumstances of the average citizen in Western Europe.

But the post-war decades were not a period of smooth or continuous growth. There are several indications of the darkening of the economic skies in the early 1970s. Although GDP per capita grew impressively, the year-on-year changes were almost zero or even negative in the late 1960s, the mid-1970s, and the early 1980s. Average annual growth rates fell to 2.25 per cent for 1971–88. The fluctuating but declining line for the average annual growth rate of GDP per capita in Figure 3.1*a* shows this structural weakening of the economic systems, although the explosion of oil prices in the 1970s certainly contributed to this deterioration. The index for the average price level 1950–88, shown in Figure 3.1*b*, rose steeply across Western Europe during the 1970s. Although it dropped in the early 1980s, the average price level increased again after 1985. And unemployment levels, shown in Figure 3.1*c*, rose from about 2 per cent of the labour force during 1965–75 to about 9 per cent in the mid-1980s. A typical case was the Netherlands, where unemployment rose from 1 per cent in 1970 to 6 per cent in 1980 (OECD 1985: 183).

A clear indicator of the darkening economic sky in the 1970s is the unemployment figures. At first, the economic problems of the 1970s were considered a minor cyclical downswing or a recession stimulated by the multiplication of oil prices and the end of the Vietnam war. In the early 1980s, however, it became clear that 'crisis' was a more appropriate term for the economic situation. Most striking was the return to pre-war unemployment levels. In 1984, an average of 8.9 per cent of the labour force was out of a job. Growth rates in the real domestic product were negative in 1982, and other economic indicators underline severe problems. Only the level of inflation dropped in the

1980s. So, the stagflation of the 1970s was replaced by economic depression of a more 'normal' nature in the early 1980s.

Clearly, then, the earliest survey data used in this volume, dating from the early 1970s, were collected at a time when economic growth and prosperity could be taken for granted by the average citizen. The threat to living standards from economic dislocations seemed to belong to the past. Some six to seven years later, economic stagnation had set in. Without exaggerating the differences in absolute figures, the economic outlook for individual citizens changed for the worse during the period between the surveys of the early 1970s and those of the late 1980s.

Industrialization

The figures presented above describe a general process of economic recovery, growth, and stagnation. None the less, differences between the West European countries remained substantial. Rather than presenting separate data on every aspect for each country, we summarize general trends by looking at the development of GDP per capita in relation to the proportion of the workforce employed in the industrial sector of the economy.

Figure 3.2*a* shows the relationship between the proportion of the workforce employed in industry and GDP per capita in 1950. It is clear that low levels of employment in industry are accompanied by low GDP per capita. At one extreme, Greece, Ireland, and Portugal have low scores on both indicators; at the other, Switzerland, Belgium, and Britain show high industrial employment and relatively high GDP per capita. This relationship is reflected in a correlation coefficient of 0.75 (Pearson's *r*). On this basis, the future of industrial society could readily be predicted: increasing industrialization, an ever higher proportion of the workforce employed in industry, and economic growth. However, the relationship between these two indicators thirty-five years later, shown in Figure 3.2*b*, substantially modifies this picture. By 1985, it is hard to find a systematic relationship between employment in the industrial sector and economic growth. For example, industrial employment is relatively low in Norway and Denmark, but their economic performance in terms of GDP per capita is clearly very high. The absence of a linear relationship between these two variables in 1985 is evident in the correlation coefficient of 0.07 (Pearson's *r*).

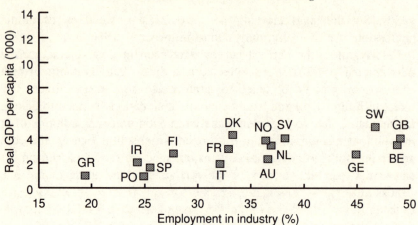

FIGURE 3.2*a*. *Employment in industry and GDP per capita in Western Europe,*
1950

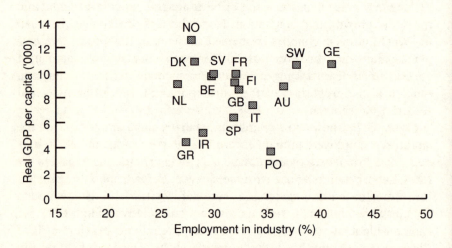

FIGURE 3.2*b*. *Employment in industry and GDP per capita in Western Europe,*
1985

There is, then, no simple function to describe the relationship
between industrialization and economic growth in Western Europe
during the post-war period. In some countries—Greece or Spain, for
instance—employment in industry increased and GDP per capita rose;
in others, GDP per capita rose but the proportion of the workforce
employed in industry declined. The pattern of industrial and economic
development for each country is shown in Figure 3.2*c*, which combines

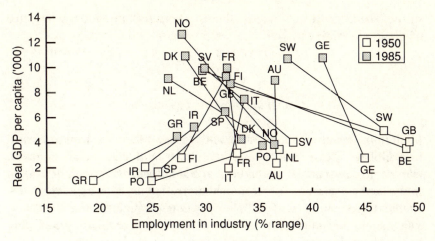

FIGURE 3.2c. *Employment in industry and GDP per capita in Western Europe, 1950 and 1985*

Source: Lane, McKay, and Newton (1991: tables 3.4–4.1).

the data in Figures 3.2*a* and *b*. Each country is represented by two squares (one for 1950 and one for 1985); the straight lines summarize developments in each country. Even a glance at Figure 3.2*c* shows that the relationship between industrialization and economic development has taken two different routes. First, we have countries starting with relatively low levels of both industrial employment and GDP per capita in which both the size of the industrial labour force and the total product increases: Greece, Ireland, Portugal, Spain, and Finland. Their development confirms the traditional notion of industrialization and rising economic performance.

The second group of countries is more heterogeneous in development. Here, increasing GDP per capita is accompanied by a decline in the size of the industrial labour force. However, there is only a modest decline, even a very small increase, in industrial employment in Germany, Austria, Italy, and France, while economic growth is very impressive. In Norway, Denmark, Sweden, the Netherlands, Britain, Belgium, and Switzerland, the relationship between industrialization and economic growth is reversed: a massive decline in industrial employment is accompanied by even more impressive growth in GDP per capita. Industrialization stimulated economic growth up to a certain level, but a further rise in economic performance entailed a gradual shift of the labour force from the industrial sector into the service sector of these economies.

Communication and Transport

Modern means of communication and transport have reduced the world to a global village in less than a century. With the spread of radio, television, newspapers, telephones, and satellites, events can be known in the furthest corners almost immediately. Trains, cars, and aeroplanes enable large numbers of people to bridge unprecedented distances. Television especially seems to reach people in a particularly penetrating way, influencing their attitudes and opinions.

With this shrinking of the world, local customs are no longer the only frame of reference; going abroad for holidays or work is not unusual and those remaining at home get the world delivered to their door. Confrontations with other cultures make familiar environments look less self-evident, perhaps even dampening feelings of hostility or superiority. When peasants did not know very much about the outside world, they were unaware of different values and cultures, or what they might demand from their government.[4] Confronted with diverse cultures, norms, and values, people are under pressure to evaluate or re-evaluate their own ways of life, attitudes, and values. In other words, value change in advanced industrial society follows, among other things, from the exposure of people to different cultures.

Of the many indicators available to identify these processes, we use only the figures for television sets and cars. Other indicators, relating to radios, telephones, air travel and the like show much the same pattern. The spread of television sets, depicted in Figure 3.3, shows that although there are clear differences between countries, there is a more or less similar pattern in most countries. In the first ten years after the arrival of television, there is a sharp rise in the distribution of television sets; except in Greece and Portugal, all West European countries experienced a television 'explosion' in the early 1960s. The rate of growth slowed by the late 1960s but the general growth trend has continued to the present day. There are, of course, country-specific differences: Ireland, Greece, and Portugal have substantially lower figures than the other countries; Italy and especially Spain are closing the gap with the more advanced countries. In the 1990s, there are more

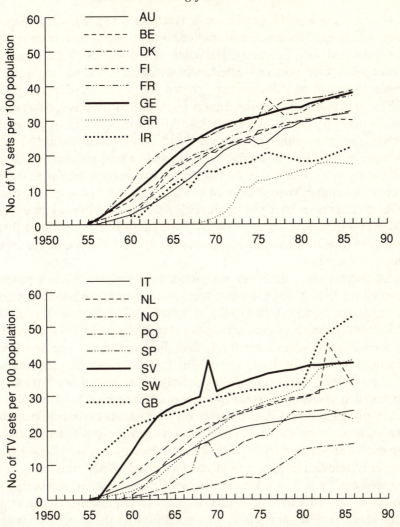

FIGURE 3.3. *Distribution of television sets in Western Europe, 1955–86*
Source: UN Statistical Yearbooks.

than thirty television sets for every hundred people in most West European countries.

More recently, the television 'revolution' is being overtaken by even greater opportunities for communication. Computers, satellites, cable television, video recorders, subscription television, interactive compact disks, teletext, and the like are making information increasingly accessible to ordinary citizens. Electronic mail, video conferencing, teleconferencing, and telepolling allow information to be exchanged without regard for space and time. Although television is probably still the principal source of information and entertainment for most people in Western Europe, its position is increasingly shared with other facilities.[5]

The expansion of communication is paralleled by the expansion of car ownership, shown in Figure 3.4. After slow growth in the early 1950s, car ownership grew rapidly and almost monotonically. The exceptions are Greece, Spain, and Portugal, where ownership started expanding in the late 1960s, and car ownership in these countries is still well below other West European countries. Ireland is a special case, with initial growth taking off in the 1950s but slowing down in the early 1970s and flattening out thereafter. By the end of the 1980s, most West European countries had an average of some thirty to forty cars for every hundred people.

Although these trends are not perfectly correlated with economic development, they suggest that developments in communication and transport are closely linked to the economic performance of a country. The graphs show that the richer countries tend to have the highest levels of communication and transport, and the least developed countries (Portugal, Greece, Ireland, and Spain) the lowest levels. The impact of these developments, however, can only be estimated when we have information about the content of the messages derived from travel and the media. Unfortunately, there is no systematic cross-national and longitudinal evidence about their impact. But there are some strong arguments about fundamental changes in public discourse following the spread of television. A slogan of the 1960s and 1970s, 'the medium is the message', emphasized the triviality of media content. According to Postman, the shift from the printing press to television has meant an emphasis on entertainment and superficiality, with the effect that 'much of our public discourse has become dangerous nonsense'; we are 'amusing ourselves to death' (Postman 1985: 16).

Education

According to Schumpeter, the vigorous expansion of education is 'one of the most important features of the later stages of capitalist civilization' (1942: 152). The greater complexity of production processes and the bureaucratization of daily life require new and more sophisticated

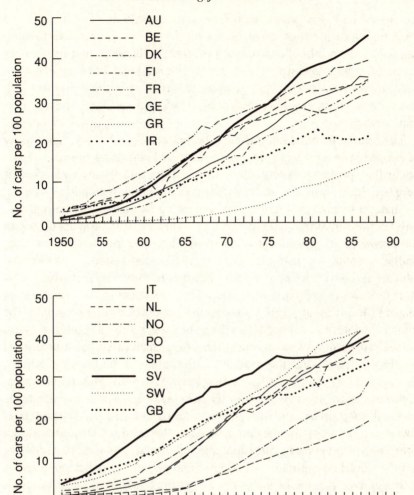

FIGURE 3.4. *Distribution of cars in Western Europe, 1950–87*
Source: UN Statistical Yearbooks.

skills, which have manifold consequences for socialization practices and educational systems. With basic schooling a statutory requirement in most countries during the first phases of industrialization, very high literacy rates have been more or less normal in Western Europe for some time. But the labour market of an advanced industrial society requires a more diverse and specialized workforce; in these terms, teenagers with ten years schooling are 'unskilled'. The result is a lengthening of the time spent in school, the modernization and diversification of curricula, the expansion of higher education and its opening up to all social classes. These developments have been labelled the *educational revolution*, which emphasizes their speed and their impact; more than thirty years ago Young (1958) noted the arrival of a meritocracy.

The spread of education affects the behaviour, attitudes, and values of people in several ways. In cognitive terms, education informs people about the specific nature of their own culture and the culture of other peoples. Moreover, the skills developed in school—gathering and re-ordering information, learning and operating formal rules, dealing with bureaucratic institutions, and the like—are necessary for dealing with the complicated procedures of life in highly developed societies. Secondly, schools are institutions of formal socialization.[6] Historically, education is based on a liberal, bourgeois view of the world, and educational systems still transmit several of these values (politeness, respect for others, abjuring violence, the importance of arguments). The longer people are exposed to education, the more they absorb these values. A third way to interpret the consequences of the educational revolution focuses on the growth of discontent. Schumpeter predicted the spread of discontent as many people fail to find employment appropriate to their education (1942: 152–3). Thus capitalism is doomed to produce its own severest critics. From this perspective, social and political change can be seen as the result of tension between ever higher levels of education and restricted job opportunities for highly qualified people. Although Schumpeter's prediction appears too negative, it is clear that—ceteris paribus—rising education levels imply a growth in the proportion of people with critical attitudes towards society and politics.

Several indicators can be used to identify changes in educational systems and levels of education in Western Europe. Literacy levels reflect the degree to which the population is already educated. Already in the early 1960s literacy was as high as 99 per cent among people aged 15 years and older in countries such as Germany and the Netherlands. The corresponding average among 130 countries is 54 per cent (cf. Taylor and Hudson 1972: 232–4). Another indicator is the school enrolment ratio, but the different systems of primary education in West European countries make it difficult to compare these ratios. Less equivocal are the data for higher education. In Figure 3.5 the gross

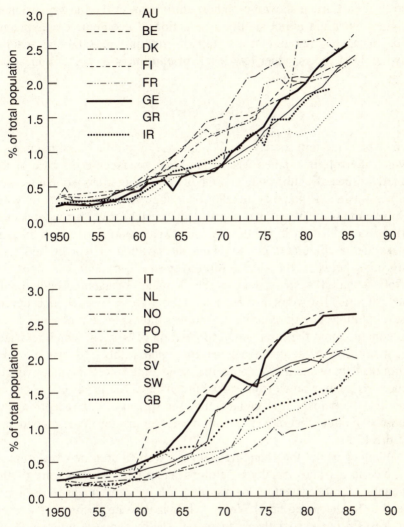

FIGURE 3.5. *Student participation in higher education in Western Europe, 1950–86*

Source: UN Statistical Yearbooks.

enrolment ratios for higher education are presented as a percentage of the total population in these countries. A clear increase in these ratios is evident in every country since the late 1950s. In 1985, with the exception of Portugal, all countries have an enrolment ratio higher than 1.5 per cent. However, although the most advanced countries of north-west Europe show the highest enrolment levels, the expansion of higher education is not simply a reflection of economic development. For instance, although at the top of the list for GDP per capita, Switzerland shows rather low levels of enrolment in higher education.

Position of Women

The rise of modern society entailed the rise of middle-class practices in which the role of women was in the home overseeing the care of the family, especially the young and the old. Working-class women worked either outside the home or, in addition to their family role, took in work. Only a minority of women succeeded in establishing an independent career or a position in public life. The expansion of education and the mass media stimulated debate about the position of women and relationships between the sexes. Moreover, the economic boom of the 1960s entailed a sharp rise in the demand for labour, opening up opportunities for women to enter the labour force. The 'second feminist revolution' emerging around 1970 was the expression of widespread discontent about the disadvantaged position of women, which resulted, in many countries, in an agenda for equal rights and specific programmes for women. At about the same time, the contraceptive pill liberated many women from casual pregnancy. The needs of the labour market, the demands for equal rights, the spread of contraception, and the rise of a feminist movement, all have their origins in the second half of the 1960s.

Whether or not the changing status of women and the revolution in sexual norms and social conventions should be seen as part of the process of modernization or as some of its consequences does not need to be discussed here. What is clear is that the position of women in West European societies is changing. The most direct indicator is the position of women in the labour market. The proportion of women in the labour force of West European countries, shown in Figure 3.6, has increased almost monotonically in every country since the second half of the 1960s, with particularly sharp increases in Portugal, the Netherlands, Sweden, and Denmark.

Figure 3.6 also shows that despite the continuous expansion of women's participation in labour markets, women are still not on a par with men.[7] At the end of the 1980s, female participation is highest in the four Scandinavian countries, but even there the figures do not reach

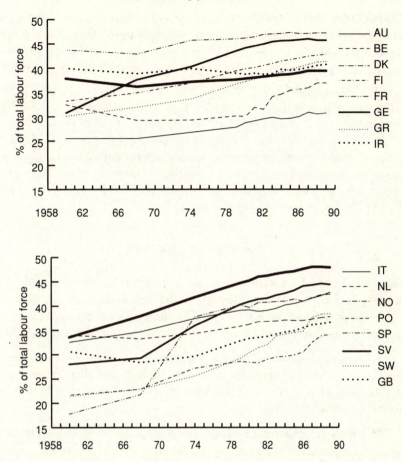

FIGURE 3.6. *Female labour force in Western Europe, 1960–89*
Source: OECD (1991: 39).

50 per cent. Female participation is consistently low in Ireland, Greece, and Spain, countries with less advanced economies. However, the high participation rate in Portugal and the relatively low rates in the Netherlands, Italy, and Switzerland suggest that we cannot ascribe the place of women in labour markets simply to the level of economic development.

If women are approaching equal participation in labour markets, especially in Scandinavia, the same cannot be said for the participation of women in political decision-making. A survey of members of parliament in the twelve EC countries (Commission of the European

Communities 1992) found that, on average, only 11 per cent were women; seven countries are below this average. Denmark had the highest female representation (33 per cent), followed by the Netherlands (24 per cent), Germany (22 per cent), Spain (14 per cent), and Luxembourg (13 per cent). Women had 19 per cent of the seats in the European Parliament. Moreover, with some singular exceptions, women are still hard to find in leadership roles in either parliamentary assemblies or in other political decision-making institutions in Western Europe—trade unions, employers' organizations, public administration, and consultative committees or councils (Commission of the European Communities 1992). Women's emancipation, in other words, is mainly a social and economic phenomenon.

Expansion of Government

The link between social-economic developments and the political process is most clearly expressed in the redefinition of the role of government. Almost without exception there has been a rapid expansion of government activities since 1945. As Rustow put it (1968: 48):

The prodigious expansion of governmental functions, in education, conscription, taxation, economic regulation, social welfare, information, propaganda, and so forth, clearly is one of the most striking and significant aspects of modernization.

The traumatic experience of the Great Depression in the 1930s and post-war economic chaos, led to the abandonment of traditional *laissez-faire* doctrines. Crude income maintenance measures appeared inadequate. Governments and legislatures accepted that there was a duty to ensure full employment even when this threatened stable prices. The Maximum Employment Act (1946) in America was designed to promote employment, production, and purchasing power. Governments in Western Europe, inspired by Keynesian economics and the social programmes proposed by Beveridge and Bevan in Britain, were prepared to go much further. For example, the Germans had in mind a transformation of capitalism into a *Soziale Marktwirtschaft*. The Dutch tried to reorganize their social and economic life along more corporatist lines.

In every country the result was a considerable strengthening of the role of central government in economic, social, and cultural life. However, differences between countries have always been evident.

Broadly speaking, the only common ground is that government should provide some form of minimal care for the young, the old, the sick, and the disabled. How this should be done, and to what extent government intervention and regulation is desirable, have remained matters of dispute, and national governments have answered such questions differently. The research evidence suggests that besides economic development, differences in political traditions account for differences in the size and the growth rates of governments (Heidenheimer *et al.* 1983: ch. 10; Webber and Wildavsky 1986: ch. 10).

The total current receipts of government as a proportion of the GDP is an indicator of the position of government in the economic and social sectors of society.[8] These figures show clear differences between countries and time periods. In the early 1960s, government receipts were around 30–35 per cent of GDP in most West European countries. They were at their highest, above 35 per cent, in Germany, Norway, and Sweden; at their lowest, about 20 per cent, in Greece. In the following decades, government receipts grew in every country in line with Wagner's Law. Within twenty years government receipts rose to about 55 per cent of GDP in Sweden, Norway, and the Netherlands. Governments started trying to cut their spending, and to reduce both their share of the national product and its rate of growth, only after economic recession became evident in the early 1980s. These attempts eventually resulted in a slight reversal of the post-war trend towards ever-expanding government receipts. As the total outlays of government show much the same pattern as government receipts, we do not need to discuss general trends in those data.[9]

For the most part, the rise in government expenditure was a consequence of the growth of social security provision. This process was most evident in countries where total government receipts and outlays rose sharply. For instance, in the Netherlands social security outlays amounted to 8 per cent of GDP in the early 1950s, rising to almost 30 per cent in 1980. In the same period, Germany spent 15 per cent and 25 per cent, respectively, of GDP on social security.[10]

The current receipts of government are clearly related to the social expenditure of government. In 1960, in most countries considered here, the current receipts of government were between 25 and 35 per cent of GDP while social expenditures were in the range of 12 to 20 per cent. Only Greece, Ireland, and Switzerland show lower levels on both indicators. The positive relationship between current receipts and social expenditure is indicated by a correlation coefficient of 0.66

(Pearson's *r*). Twenty years later, current receipts and social expenditure were much higher in every country; most had current receipts between 35 per cent and almost 60 per cent of GDP while social expenditure was between 25 per cent and almost 40 per cent of GDP in 1980. The correlation is 0.74 (Pearson's *r*), indicating a somewhat stronger relationship in 1980 than in 1960. Moreover, the similarities in the strong growth of both receipts and expenditures in different countries is striking. Particularly large increases occurred in countries like Belgium, Sweden, and the Netherlands, but there were impressive growth figures in other countries too. In two decades West European welfare states were shaped by increases in both the current receipts and the social expenditures of governments.

Despite the similarities, West European countries differ considerably on these indicators too. Belgium, the Netherlands, Sweden, Denmark, and Norway are typical welfare state leaders with relatively high levels of current receipts and government expenditures, while Greece and Switzerland show much lower figures on both indicators. In all, then, the development of the welfare state shows many similarities in West European countries between 1960 and 1980, but large cross-national differences persist if we look at the level of social welfare.

With the expansion of government, new tasks were added to old without a substantial reduction of the old tasks. The new social security tasks, however, do not conform to the classic definition of 'public goods'—goods which no one is excluded from consuming. This implies that, broadly speaking, governments have two options in the provision of welfare goods: direct provision or income transfers.[11] Although governments in Western Europe have used both policy instruments, there are evident differences between countries. Some governments, as in the Netherlands, rely heavily on transfer payments, functioning more or less as a clearing-house for funds rather than as a direct provider of services. Other governments, as in Finland, have relatively low levels of transfer payments but high levels of direct provision.

We can distinguish three clusters of countries based on combining social transfer payments and other forms of social security (data not shown here). The first consists of the typical welfare states with high levels of social security expenditure: the Netherlands, Belgium, Sweden, Germany, and Denmark. The second cluster consists of countries with modest levels of total social security spending and transfer payments ranging from high to low levels: France, Austria,

Ireland, Italy, Norway, and Finland. Finally, we have a cluster of countries showing low levels of social security spending: Switzerland, Britain, and Greece. Note, however, that the clustering of countries according to government receipts or the levels and nature of social security payments is not even a rough reflection of the clustering of countries according to their economic development, as presented earlier. This underlines, once more, that non-economic factors have to be taken into account when comparing developments in Western Europe.

The unprecedented levels of economic growth during the post-war period allowed West European governments to develop extensive social security provision for their citizens without forgoing the traditional tasks of government. However, with the halting of economic growth after 1970, the financial position of governments became burdensome. Familiar Keynesian remedies seemed only to make the patient even more sick. By the early 1980s, many West European governments were faced with serious budget deficits. In 1950 the average surplus of government income as a proportion of GDP was 3.9 per cent; this figure increased monotonically to reach 5.1 per cent in 1970. But there was a dramatic decline of government surpluses in the 1970s and the early 1980s, with an average deficit of 0.4 per cent in 1985. However, this average figure again conceals large cross-national differences; for example, Norway had an impressive surplus in 1985 (mainly owing to oil resources), while Greece was confronting severe budgetary problems. The other countries fall into two clusters, with Switzerland, Spain, Germany, Austria, France, and Denmark showing a modest surplus, and the Netherlands, Finland, Britain, and Sweden showing a modest deficit.

In spite of national differences, it is evident that governments play an important role in West European countries and that government intervention and regulation grew rapidly in the 1960s and 1970s. This expansion of government implies the rise of all manner of special interests. The result is the increasing visibility and relevance of the political process for the average citizen. Thus every West European government, perhaps with the exception of Norway, was dealing with complex economic, budgetary, and fiscal problems during the 1980s. However, while the development of welfare states in the 1960s and early 1970s positioned governments as problem solvers for all manner of problems of citizens, the fiscal problems of the 1980s suggested that ever-expanding government intervention was part of the problem.

These developments suggest the conditions for a shift in attitudes towards the role of government in society.

Participation and Stability

In democratic political systems, government activities should be controlled by the electorate, expressing its preferences through regular elections. With the rapid growth of government intervention, the control function of elections becomes even more important. The interdependencies between the economic and political spheres are most directly expressed in national political processes; contrary to the notion that personal economic conditions are major determinants of political preferences, collective economic circumstances seem more influential in shaping political choice.[12] We might expect, then, that extensive and rapid change in government activity might have effects for political involvement and the stability of party systems.

TABLE 3.1. *Total votes as a percentage of the electorate in sixteen West European countries, 1950–4 and 1985–9*

	1950–54	1985–89	Difference	Avg., 1950–89
DK	81.1	86.3	+5.2	85.8
FI	77.3	72.1	−5.1	77.0
NO	79.3	84.0	+4.7	81.3
SV	79.1	88.0	+8.9	86.5
AU	95.8	90.4	−5.4	93.3
BE	92.9	93.5	+0.6	92.9
GE	85.8	84.3	−1.5	78.3
IR	75.9	73.4	−2.5	74.3
NE	95.0	85.8	−9.2	90.0
SW	69.8	46.8	−23.0	58.7
GB	—	75.4	—	75.0
FR	80.2	71.9	−8.3	87.9
IT	93.9	90.5	−3.4	92.2
GR	76.3	83.8	+7.5	80.1
SP	—	70.8	—	74.3
PO	—	72.4	—	80.6
Average	82.7	79.3	−3.4	82.4

Note: The data for Britain include Northern Ireland.

Source: Lane, McKay, and Newton (1991: table 7.2).

In most countries, well above 75 per cent of the electorate vote in national elections. The other side of that coin is that, in any particular election, substantial numbers of electors neglect the opportunity to influence the political process by participating in elections. As we can see in Table 3.1, showing the average level of electoral participation in the early 1950s and the late 1980s, the overall picture is of a very modest but discernible decline in most countries, almost entirely confined to the late 1980s. In all, average levels of non-voting among West European electorates show a modest increase over the last three decades, from 17.3 per cent for 1950–4 to 20.7 per cent for 1985–9.[13]

Thus, the enlarged role of government in Western Europe has not resulted in higher levels of involvement in national elections. Equally, citizens have not turned away from their political systems. If there were widespread alienation or frustration among West European populations, this would be evident in severely declining electoral participation— voting being the most traditional, least radical mode of political participation.

Instead of examining election results more closely, we look at several characteristics of the party systems. Three indicators are particularly interesting: fractionalization (the chance that two randomly selected citizens vote for the same party); polarization (the skewness of the distribution of the electorate on a left–right scale); and volatility (the net changes for all the parties between two elections). Lane and Ersson's (1991: 183–9) analysis of these measures revealed, first, that whereas fractionalization has not varied much between countries, there are clear country variations in the levels of polarization and volatility; and, secondly, there has been an increase in polarization since the 1960s, an increase in volatility since the 1970s, but an increase in fractionalization only in the 1980s. Lane and Ersson conclude that the remarkably high level of stability attributed to West European political systems does not apply to the party systems.[14] Contrary to the famous Lipset and Rokkan assertion about 'frozen' party systems, the party systems of Western Europe have changed in the last decades (cf. Bartolini and Mair 1990).

The modest decline, on average, in electoral participation suggests a rather high degree of political stability in many West European countries over the last few decades. On the other hand, Lane and Ersson's findings do not suggest the high degree of stability which justifies describing developments as 'frozen'. So, before we reach any firm conclusion about the extent of political change, we examine other

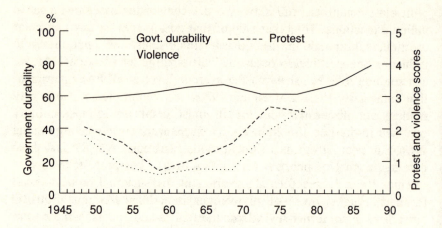

FIGURE 3.7. *Government durability, protest scores, and violence scores in Western Europe, 1948–87*

Source: Lane and Ersson (1991: 304–6).

indicators of political stability. Three measures allow us to make a more subtle evaluation of political stability in Western Europe.

The first is a government durability index, calculated as the length of time a government is in power as a proportion of its legal maximum period. In the early post-war period this indicator shows no clear cross-national differences nor a similar trend across many countries (Lane and Ersson 1991: 304). However, as we can see in Figure 3.7, the index of government durability starts to rise in the 1960s, with more prominent increases in the 1980s. As measured by this indicator, government stability has generally been rising in Western Europe over the post-war period, but with a clear concavity in the 1970s.

Our second measure is a protest index, reflecting the willingness of citizens to engage in protest. Using figures for different types of protest and violence, available for the period 1948–77, the protest index measures the occurrence of strikes, demonstrations, and the like. Our third measure, using the same data, is a violence index, recording the incidence of violent political acts such as armed attacks and assassinations.[15] The average scores on these two indicators are also shown in Figure 3.7. The graph shows the parallel, and then converging, development of the two measures; after a decline in the 1950s, the late 1960s and the early 1970s see an impressive increase in both political protest and violence. These developments are in line with the commonplace claim that protest activity by individual citizens is increasing.

Clearly, then, the political systems of Western Europe show considerable change if we look at activities among citizens since the late 1960s. On the other hand, this growth of protest and political violence does not seem to have affected the overall picture of stability in terms of electoral participation, party systems, or government durability.

Conclusion

The macro settings of politics in the 1960s, the 1970s, and the 1980s clearly differed. By the late 1960s, economic growth along with the expansion of welfare had given rise to the notion that society was manageable, and that all social and economic problems could, and should, be tackled by government intervention. But the harbingers of less prosperous times were already visible. By the mid-1970s, economic stagnation ended the impression that politics would be a positive sum game forever and established some limits to government expansion. Furthermore, the settings of politics changed: the Vietnam war ended, political protest and terrorism became familiar, political scandals seemed rife. By the mid-1980s, governments were grappling with budget deficits, high and rising unemployment, and the need to reorganize parts of the welfare system. The limits of growth along with the relentless expansion of government were the precursors of long-term developments coming to surface in changes in the economic, social, and political constellations within the countries of Western Europe. It turns out, then, that the surveys used in this volume cover a rather critical period in contemporary history.

The macro settings sketched here set the stage for our empirical analyses of the value orientations and political involvements of citizens in Western Europe. However, it would be impossible and foolish to try to determine how the factors outlined in this chapter contribute to the shaping of those orientations and involvements. None the less, there are three general points to make about the relevance of the macro settings for changing value orientations in Western Europe. The simple analytical scheme of the relationships between circumstances, orientations, and behaviour, presented in the introductory chapter, is again our starting point.

First, we have documented several impressive changes in economy and society in Western Europe. Economic growth and the expansion of government are the most striking. At the same time, we identified clear differences between countries and time periods. Thus, we expect to find substantive differences in value orientations among West European citizens. More to the point, however, on account of the similar trajectories of development, we expect to find that the value orientations of citizens in different countries are changing in the same direction.

Secondly, value orientations are to be thought of not only as the consequences of the modernization process but also as co-determinants of many aspects of advanced industrial societies. For instance, although women's participation in the labour market is related to levels of economic development, a number of non-economic factors are required to explain differences between countries. The structural aspects of the modernization process are intertwined with cultural developments, and this dual process results in differences between the value orientations of citizens in different countries.

Finally, our search for a macro setting has uncovered several indicators showing that the substantive and rapid shifts in economy and society have not led to widespread unrest or revolt among the citizens of Western Europe. Figures for electoral turnout and government stability do not indicate alienation among citizens. By analysing the value orientations discussed in the next chapters, we may gain some understanding of the paradox of revolutionary shifts in the macro settings of politics accompanied by more or less persistent representative decision-making procedures.

NOTES

1. Deutsch suggested the basic idea behind this chapter many years ago when he stated that it seems 'vitally important . . . to maintain and restore the unity of the study of politics—to strengthen and revive communication between the bearers of its historical and descriptive scholarship and those practitioners engaged in the more analytic, behavioral and quantitative aspects of political research' (1960: 35).
2. The economic indicators presented here are all standardized in order to neutralize the impact of changes in price levels and to facilitate cross-national and longitudinal comparison. The GDP figures are based on the 1985 international price level and computed per capita (cf. Summers and Heston 1991). All economic figures in this section are derived from the 'Penn World Table' (Summers and Heston 1991).
3. The assumption that 'when the economy grows, the standard of living improves' is not self-evident (cf. Olson 1963).

4. For an early discussion of the impact of the mass media on traditional life and the relationship with the modernization process, see Pye (1963).
5. Data on the spread of new media are hard to find. See, among others, Gabriel (1992: 528–32) for some figures on the traditional media, and Abramson *et al.* (1988) for a discussion of the impact of new media technologies on democratic politics.
6. See Jennings and Niemi (1974; 1981) for a detailed analysis of schools as socialization agents.
7. The position of women in the labour market is worse than these figures suggest. Women are more likely to have part-time jobs, and are over-represented in lower income brackets. These observations, however, do not contradict our general discussion.
8. Current receipts of government consist mainly of direct and indirect taxes, and social security contributions paid by employers and employees. All figures presented in this section are for general government; i.e. all departments, offices, organizations, and other bodies which are agents or instruments of central or local public authorities.
9. See Vol. iii, Ch. 2.
10. See Heidenheimer *et al.* (1983: 202). For a more general discussion of the rise of welfare states, see Flora and Heidenheimer (1981).
11. Social security transfers consist of social security benefits, social assistance grants, unfunded employee pension and welfare benefits, and transfers to private non-profit institutions serving households.
12. For a discussion of pocket-book voting versus socio-tropic voting, see Kinder and Mebane (1983) and Thomassen (1989).
13. A detailed analysis of trends in turnout over the post-war period is presented in Vol. i, Ch. 2.
14. Using a wide variety of indicators, Lane and Ersson conclude that the party systems of Denmark, France, Greece, Portugal, and Spain must be described as unstable (1991: 192).
15. The index scores are per capita and logarithmically transformed. See Lane and Ersson (1991: 302, 305–6, 324).

4

Secularization and Church Religiosity

WOLFGANG JAGODZINSKI AND KAREL DOBBELAERE

Values are rooted in metaphysical beliefs. Philosophers have not only eternalized values, but have established the independent reality of values alongside the physical world and have derived systems of values from metaphysical assumptions. If values are seen as fundamental, unchangeable, sacrosanct or holy, this is largely due to their metaphysical origin. But the relationship between values and metaphysics is almost completely ignored in modern value research. We do not try to make good this lacuna, but pursue a more modest aim: to investigate the relationship between some ethical norms and principles on the one hand, and church religion on the other hand. In this chapter, we analyse change in church religiosity in Western Europe during the last decades.

Approaching value change from this perspective has two advantages. First, by analysing long-term religious change, it becomes apparent that changes in values often cannot be reduced to the emergence of some

This chapter could not have been written without the help of many people throughout Western Europe who provided us with national data sets and additional information. We are greatly indebted to Oddbjørn Knutsen from the University of Oslo and the Norwegian Data Archive, Per Nielsen and the Danish Data Archive, Elinor Scarbrough from the University of Essex, Eric Roughley from the ESRC Data Archive, Loek Halman from the Social Research Institute in Tilburg, Masja Nas from the University of Nijmegen, Paul Dekker and Rene Vinke from the Social and Cultural Planning Office in Rijswijk, and Erwin Rose and Steffen Kühnel from the Central Archive in Cologne. Hermann Dülmer and Klaus Stöppler helped us to produce data files and charts.

new preferences or needs. Rather, value change may be better understood as a complex process of re-interpreting old, highly abstract value
concepts. Secondly, conceptualizing value change as a process of
changing interpretations of value concepts emphasizes the role of
intellectuals and institutions in the process of value change. Since the
translation of values into coherent sets of preferences and norms
requires special skills, the task is frequently assigned to experts or
specialized institutions. As long as they have a monopoly on interpreting norms and values, they may also influence the pace of value change.
However, it is important to analyse not only the influence of institutions
on value change, but also to investigate the consequences of institutional decay: is the loss of institutional power accompanied by increasing value pluralism and value instability, as many conservative authors
suspect?

We are interested in three aspects of church religiosity: changes in
behaviour, changes in beliefs, and whether moral norms are more
heterogeneous among people emancipated from institutionalized
churches. In this chapter, the empirical analyses focus on the behavioural aspect, using the terms *church integration* and *disengagement* to
designate religious behaviour. Specifically, we describe the process of
disengagement from institutionalized churches after the Second World
War. In the first section, we present some explanatory sketches relating
the decline of church religiosity to other macro- and micro-level
changes. They are based on fairly broad and general hypotheses which
cannot be tested with the available data, but they are helpful in
formulating research questions for the empirical analysis in later sections. Comparative research on church disengagement is rare, probably
because comparative measures of church integration are difficult to
obtain. We tackle this difficulty by building simple indices from church
attendance and denomination. The second section is devoted to an
aggregate-level analysis of West European countries, using pooled data.
In the third section, we examine trends over time, using longitudinal
national and comparative data. In the final section we investigate generational differences in the process of disengagement from churches.

Explanatory Sketches

For more than two centuries, philosophers and social scientists have
predicted the death of God and the decline of religiosity. We review

some of the major arguments, most of which come under the heading 'secularization' or 'de-sacralization'. We use a broad concept of church religiosity which relates to belief and practice. We consider church religiosity to be the greater the more a person accepts the core dogmas of one of the institutionalized churches and the more he or she participates in activities related to the church, such as services or Christian associations. Our research concentrates on this traditional form of religiosity and does not deal with religion in a broader sense.[1]

A popular hypothesis postulates a negative relationship between economic wealth and church religiosity. According to the Bible, it is easier for a camel to pass through the eye of a needle than for a rich man to get to heaven. In taking up this old idea, we might expect a close correspondence between long-term economic cycles and religiosity: religiosity increases under deteriorating economic conditions and declines under improving economic conditions. Others have attributed a different meaning to the same principle and derived from it a long-term trend. In particular, Inglehart (1990) argues that traditional religion satisfies the need for shelter and safety, but the unprecedented wealth of post-war Western societies has, for the first time in history, satisfied these basic needs, thereby destroying the basis of church religion. Thus, whereas in the early stages of industrialization materialism and church religiosity co-existed, the traditional forms of church religiosity are expected to wither away gradually in advanced industrial societies. In contrast, Stark and Bainbridge (1985) have argued that religion will persist since it provides general compensators for not directly satisfiable desires.

According to a second approach, the decline of church religiosity is largely due to the development of 'occidental rationality'. Max Weber (1975) outlined the basic features of this process (see also Lepsius 1990: 40–52). In science, occidental rationality implies the mathematical foundation of theories, and the indispensable role of laboratories and experiments; in economic life, it implies the calculability of costs and benefits, and free working contracts. Obviously, underlying the whole process of occidental rationalization is the belief that the world is calculable, predictable, and controllable (cf. Wilson 1976; 1985). These beliefs apply to the psychological world and the social world, as much as to the physical world. Occidental rationality disenchants the world because God is no longer required in explanations of natural and social phenomena; catastrophes, sickness, wars, are seen not as the work of God but as the outcome of this-wordly processes. Moreover, the basic tenets of a rational science may come into conflict with the requirements of religion. In science, it must always be possible to doubt even the most basic axioms of scientific theories, whereas religion rests on belief (see also Schluchter 1981). Those who do not believe in God and Christ are not members of the Christian community.

Other authors stress the effects of functional or structural differentiation (Dobbelaere and Voyé 1990: 4–5) on secularization and individuation. Functional differentiation has produced societal subsystems, which have become increasingly specialized in their functions, and some have developed increasingly rational organizations. Consequently, the churches have lost their influence in many domains, and the traditional functions of churches have become less important, even unimportant. Functionalists doubt whether religion still has a societal function in a rational world, since control is assumed to be no longer based on religious or moral principles. Control has 'become impersonal and amoral, a matter of routine techniques and unknown officials'— legal, technical, mechanized, computerized, and electronicized (Wilson 1976: 20, 202). Religion may even be a menace to modern, rational institutions; by asking questions, it disturbs the smooth functioning of organizations (Fenn 1972). For example, by stressing that a sick person is more than a body but an individual with psychological, social, and spiritual dimensions, religion criticizes both medical specialization, which analyses sickness, and the economic rationality of paying for medical treatment (Dobbelaere 1988*b*: 16, 31–2). Accordingly, functional rationality typical of a societalized environment conflicts with the value rationality of religion, which is communally oriented.

The old principles of Christian education have also become obsolete in a functional world. Education had to be emancipated from ecclesiastical authority, to stress science and technical knowledge. Thus secularization 'is more than a social-structural process. It affects the totality of cultural life and ideation, and may be observed . . . most important of all, in the rise of science as an autonomous, thoroughly secular perspective on the world' (Berger 1967: 107). Science and the technologies dependent on it make up the major part of modern education, desacralizing the content of learning (Wilson 1976: 68, 128).

Following on from functionalist arguments, others claim that the religious subsystem has not only lost its function at the macro level, but that religious beliefs are also transformed at the individual level. Swanson (1960), among others, has argued that individuals develop a concept of personified supernatural beings from the model provided by their society. Thus, where beliefs about the calculability of the world have not completely destroyed belief in God, the growing impersonality of societal relationships could be expected to undermine the conception of God as a 'person'. And, as Durkheim suggested, the more general and vague God becomes, the more removed He is from this world and the more ineffective (1960: 272–6). Belief in God then becomes an abstract notion without any real impact on people's lives—and is thus easily disposed of. The same holds, of course, for traditions associated with belief in God. In a society where role relations have become impersonal and segmented, belief in God as a person declines, so celebration of a personal relationship with Him in a religious service seems an anachronism, hence the decline in church-going (Dobbelaere 1988*b*: 61–6).

The preceding argument links the idea of secularization at the macro level to changes at the micro level. The link between the impersonal society and God as an abstract notion is set within this framework because the impersonal character of rationally organized institutions seems to be a typical experience of modern citizens. Moreover, the depersonalization of God may also be regarded as a component of the disenchantment of the world: modern science has removed anthropomorphism from our thinking. The world is not governed by a perfect individual but by abstract principles. Thus, one does not need to agree with the premiss of an impersonal society in order to accept the hypothesized transformation of the belief in God as a person.

The individuation hypothesis about the transformation of religious beliefs is often elaborated within the framework of functionalism. At heart, the hypothesis is rooted in the assumption that, in contrast to the past, religious matters can be decided by autonomous individuals. Thus, modern religiosity has developed several peculiar features. Due to competition from other, more attractive leisure activities, religious activities are declining. Since religious consumers can satisfy their metaphysical needs from a large basket of competing religious and non-religious offers, their belief system becomes a patchwork of heterogeneous elements.

More sophisticated sociological arguments use complex notions of collective identity and identity construction. In traditional societies, it is argued, a homogeneous lifeworld gave people their identity. In 'modern' times, people lived in a *monde éclaté*: the lifeworld of family, neighbourhood, and community became dissociated from the social system and its subsystems. Typical of this period was the

'Privatisierung des Entscheidens' in the world of the subsystems (Luhmann 1977: 232–42). Collective identities survived only in the lifeworld of family, religion, leisure, and friendships. In advanced modernity, sometimes called postmodernity, individualization is assumed to extend into the lifeworld (Laermans 1992: 63–72), and a de-traditionalization of the lifeworld occurs. This led to a liberation in which people faced the new experience of having to make their own decisions, their own choices, to build their own identity (Beck 1992).[2] Collective identities no longer function and fixed identities may only survive in older generations.[3] In the religious domain, terms like *bricolage, religion à la carte,* and *patchwork* point towards very similar phenomena.

One can accept much of the preceding analysis without adopting the whole conceptual framework. Even though one may be uneasy about the notion of identity construction, hardly anyone disputes that individuals are now confronted with a larger number of alternatives in the lifeworld than in past centuries. And it is at least conceivable that the range of options available to people determines the homogeneity and stability of religious beliefs—a topic we address in Chapter 8.

The last approach we mention emphasizes differences between the Catholic and Protestant religions. According to this view, the seeds of individualism were manifest much earlier in Protestantism. In contrast to Catholics, Protestants are personally responsible before God in religious matters, and the church has a lesser role as mediator between the believer and God. The Catholic Church, with its extensive, dog-matic, collective creed imposes a more collective identity upon its faithful (Kaufmann 1979; Gabriel and Kaufmann 1980). Thus, as a general rule, the decline of church religiosity is thought to have started earlier and to be more advanced in the Protestant world than in the Catholic world—all other things being equal.

Even so, there is great variety in the Protestant world. Calvinism, for example, laid greater stress than Lutheranism on the loneliness of the individual before God and the need for impersonal, objective relations in rational organizations (Weber 1958: 104–9; for a critique, see McKinnon 1989a; 1989b). But even the Calvinist world is far from homogeneous; in the Netherlands, for example, the neo-Calvinist Church (the Gereformeerden) is more integrated than the Netherlands Reformed Church (the Hervormden). Consequently, we may hypothe-size that individualization will be less advanced there. In the Catholic world, since we expect that church disengagement occurred more recently, the pace of disengagement presumably differs according to the way Catholics were incorporated. In some countries, as in Belgium and the Netherlands, Catholics were organized in a Catholic 'pillar', protected from the secularized world. Catholics lived in their own Catholic world, with their own schools, youth and adult organizations, trade unions, hospitals, and with their own mass-media magazines, newspapers, and libraries. In other countries, such 'pillarized' structures were not established. This leads us to hypothesize that the decline of involvement in the Catholic Church occurred earlier in countries where no Catholic pillar existed, as in France for example.

Finally, we anticipate that in the pillarized countries also the decline of involvement in the Catholic Church set in during the mid-1960s and early 1970s. Why? During the 1960s religious controversy was stirred by, among other things, Bishop John Robinson's (1963) *Honest to God*. As a result of Vatican Council II (1962–6), the traditional Catholic creed came into question; people publicly questioned the dogmas, the ethics, and the authority of the church. All this had an effect on the clergy and members of religious orders, who, in the late 1960s and early 1970s, massively left the church—or, at least, asked for laïcization— which had further consequences for the beliefs, attitudes, and behaviour of lay people. This was also a consequence of generally more critical attitudes towards rigid social institutions.

In this matter, 1968 remains a symbolic date. For the first time in social discourse and the media, one could acknowledge that the religious understanding of ethics and church authority was undermined through the rationalization process. Implicit belief—a general, uncritical subjection to the teachings of the church—was no longer possible. Public debate undermined authoritarian church teachings in matters of beliefs and ethics, as with the papal encyclical *Humanae Vitae*. Reflexivity was intensified by the collapse of traditions. A faltering belief system could no longer hold up traditional behaviour. Attendance at Sunday mass, still very high in the early 1960s, adapted to inner convictions. Public behaviour and personal disbelief in the doctrines and values of the church converged. Thus, we anticipate that, since then, social control has increasingly had a quite different impact— keeping people out of the church (Dobbelaere 1988*b*).

Research Questions

We have brought together several different arguments for the decay of church religion. They are not integrated into a more coherent theoretical framework because that might lead us into a secondary theatre. For instance, agreement with the hypothesis of occidental rationality might not quell doubts about functionalist arguments; if we embedded the rationality hypothesis in a functionalistic framework, we might provoke other criticisms. For the same reason, we point occasionally to the possibility of alternative explanations for the same phenomenon.

We cannot distil testable empirical hypotheses from the explanatory sketches. Nevertheless, they are helpful in formulating our research questions. Since longitudinal data for measuring the belief component of church religiosity are not available, we focus on the behavioural component and speak of church integration or affiliation. Precise measurement rules are set out below, but the general rule is that the less individuals participate in church rites and services, the less they are considered to be integrated in the church.

According to the arguments about the effects of economic wealth, occidental rationality, and functional differentiation, we would expect church religiosity to be negatively related to economic wealth. Although macro indicators of economic performance are not direct measures of the degree of rationalization, in the long run, rationality should become manifest in high productivity and economic wealth. Similarly, if functional differentiation is a concomitant of rationality or vice versa, economic performance should also, in general, be influenced by the degree of functional differentiation.[4] However, since we use the gross domestic product (GDP) per capita as a crude indicator in our aggregate analyses, the assumption of a negative relationship between economic performance and church integration has to be qualified.

First, small improvements in economic performance at the aggregate level do not always reflect greater economic or scientific rationality or greater mass affluence. Secondly, even if increasing economic wealth is due to rationalism or reflects increasing mass affluence, this need not cause a similar development in church disengagement. Recent observations suggest that, like a contagious process, religious participation declines sharply within fairly short periods. We cannot, then, expect a strong (linear) relationship between economic wealth and church disengagement in longitudinal national studies which cover only a relatively short period of some ten to twenty years. A much clearer pattern should emerge in a cross-sectional or pooled analysis which includes countries at different levels of economic development.

Bivariate analyses always run the risk of interpreting spurious associations as causal relationships. The effect of GDP per capita on church integration would be spurious if either occidental rationality or functional differentiation—not economic performance—are the causes of declining church religiosity. It might also be that individualism is the decisive cause and that all other associations are spurious. Unfortunately, we cannot test these assumptions because we have no indicator other than economic performance for rationality and functional differentiation, and we have no indicator at all for individualism. Only a crude measure of individualism—denomination—can be included in our macro-level analysis. For technical reasons, set out below, we use the percentage of Catholics for the absence of Protestant individualism.

Then we have two interesting questions. Does the impact of Protestant individualism disappear if the level of economic performance is held constant? And vice versa: does the impact of economic performance persist if we control for Catholicism? In the long run, differences between members of the two churches should vanish. However, at present, one can hardly imagine that disengagement from the Catholic Church has reached the same level as in the major Protestant churches and that, therefore, Catholicism has no impact on church disengagement.

We described some fairly persistent differences between Catholicism and Protestantism, and elaborated some assumptions about the timing and pace of disengagement in both churches. If de-traditionalization of the lifeworld has an immediate impact on church religiosity, then the process of disengagement in both churches should have accelerated during the 1960s. But the process probably started at different levels of church integration. In the Protestant world—apart from some orthodox denominations in Britain and the Netherlands—it may have led to a stampede from the church, whereas in the pillarized Catholic world the process may have started at a much higher level of integration and developed later. Unfortunately, longitudinal data for the 1960s are available only for France, Britain, and West Germany. A further issue concerns the speed of church disengagement: have the pillarized Catholics disengaged later but more rapidly than the Protestants and the non-pillarized Catholics? Finally, we investigate how the smaller Protestant denominations weathered the crises of the 1960s and 1970s.

Clearly, a crucial question is whether the process of church disengagement will continue during the next decades. Any statement about long-term developments amounts to prophecy rather than prediction. However, if we want to obtain at least some evidence of what to expect in the next few years, we can do two things. First, we can use longitudinal national aggregate studies to see if periods of rapid decay are followed by a revival of church religiosity. Is there a continuous or discontinuous, but in any case irreversible, process of alienation from the churches? Secondly, we can use cohort analysis to see if our data display intergenerational change. If so, we can expect a steady decline of church religiosity in future years due to generational replacement.

However, there are good reasons to expect a quite different type of generational change. If church disengagement is a stepwise—or contagious—process, it may affect all generations during periods of rapid change. The decline at each step may be larger than the generational differences during periods of stability or slow change. As a consequence, we should observe a massive decline in church integration in society at large as well as in all cohorts—intra-cohort change—within fairly short time-spans. Since the older generation may adapt less rapidly to the new norms and beliefs, the generational differences may increase during periods of rapid change. Obviously, the contagion model, elaborated below, does not preclude period effects and intra-cohort change. However, it is not compatible with a long-term increase of church integration in any generation, and it is hardly compatible with opposite developments in different generations.

Analytic Strategy

Unfortunately, the data base is too small to permit the construction of a data sequence covering a period of at least twenty to thirty years. Furthermore, the available surveys usually contain items in different format so comparisons are almost impossible. Hence, we do not measure both components of church religiosity. Instead, we constructed an index of church integration from two items which belong to the standard repertory of almost all election studies and social surveys: church attendance and denomination. We also introduce another dimension of church religiosity which is subsequently equated with individual internal states; broadly, we regard individuals as more church religious the more core dogmas of their church they accept and the higher their commitment to these beliefs.

Our central indicator is church integration. We consider people the more church integrated the more frequently they participate in rites and services. To operationalize our definition, we rely predominantly on church attendance. In both the 1981 and 1990 European Values Study, the church attendance variable has eight categories, ranging from more than once a week to never.[5] For constructing our index of church integration, we reversed the original rank order. In general, the higher a person's score on church integration, the more integrated into the church they are and the more frequently they attend services. In our correlation analyses, we assign the lowest score to unchurched respondents—those who do not report any denomination[6]—because there is some evidence that these people are most distant from the churches, even more distant than nominal Christians. In other analyses, it is possible to distinguish only between a church-integrated and an unaffiliated group; the latter consists of nominal Christians and unchurched people.[7]

Concentrating on church integration in this narrow sense may seem very restrictive because individual orientations and beliefs are disregarded. Protestants frequently stress that a person can be deeply religious without regularly attending church. However, whether or not church integration is related to church religiosity is an empirical question—which we try to answer, using four variables which are more directly linked to church religiosity. The first, importance of God, is a ten-point scale which has proved an excellent indicator of the centrality of church religion in other studies. The higher the score on this variable, the more important God is to the respondent. The second indicator, religiosity, is a crude measure of an individual's religiosity: respondents can classify themselves as religious, not religious, or atheist. The third variable, number of religious beliefs, simply counts positive answers to seven questions asking respondents whether they believe in God, the soul, sin, life after death, heaven, the devil, and hell. The last variable, type of God, is intended to measure the gradual transformation of the image of God during the secularization process. This ranges from belief in a personal God, to a more abstract spirit or life force, to a point where the individual has no image of God, and, finally, to disbelief.[8]

We expect a high positive association between church integration and the other four variables because most people need the interaction within the church community to support their religiosity. However, the correlation may be somewhat lower in the Protestant countries except in small but cohesive Protestant denominations. Whereas for Catholics church attendance is an almost indispensable manifestation of their beliefs, Protestants usually attribute less importance to attendance at religious services.[9] We expect the relationship to be fairly stable across time.

We refrain from any attempt to improve the correlations. For instance, we apply the church integration index to all respondents with a valid code on church attendance even though it might be argued that the index is applicable only to Christian and unchurched respondents.[10] Furthermore, we have not corrected for the different operationalizations of church attendance—measured with a filter question in 1990 but not in 1981. Finally, we always assign the lowest value on church integration to respondents reporting no denomination whether or not they attend church more or less regularly.

Church Integration and Church Religiosity

In Table 4.1*a* we present the correlations between church integration and our four measures of religiosity for the relevant sub-populations in ten countries. In Table 4.1*b* separate coefficients are reported for Protestants and Catholics in the religiously mixed countries.[11] Since we want to make use of the full variance of church integration in these subgroup analyses, each of the two groups is supplemented randomly by 50 per cent of the unchurched respondents. Both sub-tables display the correlation coefficients for the 1981 survey, the 1990 survey, and the pooled data set which combines the data for 1981 and 1990.

Bearing in mind that our design is biased against the postulated relationships, the results in Table 4.1 are really beautiful. Probably because of their low measurement quality, religiosity and type of God correlate only moderately with church integration. The coefficients usually range between 0.40 and 0.55. The correlation of 0.32 with type of God in the Irish 1990 survey is an outlier. The correlations with importance of God and number of religious beliefs are extremely high. If we concentrate on the pooled data set, the coefficients range between 0.48 (Denmark) and 0.73 (Netherlands) for importance of God, and between 0.41 (Denmark) and 0.63 (Netherlands) for number of religious beliefs. In non-experimental research, correlations of this

TABLE 4.1. *Church integration and four direct measures of church religiosity in Western Europe, 1981 and 1990*

Countries/ Date source	Importance of God	Religiosity	No. of religious beliefs	Type of God	N (min.)
(a) Correlations for total population					
CATHOLIC					
Belgium					
Pooled sample	0.66	0.57	0.59	0.56	3,434
Survey 1981	0.61	0.50	0.58	0.45	953
Survey 1990	0.67	0.59	0.59	0.59	2,481
France					
Pooled sample	0.65	0.54	0.61	0.44	2,048
Survey 1981	0.64	0.53	0.62	0.45	1,104
Survey 1990	0.65	0.56	0.61	0.42	928
Italy					
Pooled sample	0.65	0.51	0.59	0.49	2,897
Survey 1981	0.60	0.48	0.55	0.43	933
Survey 1990	0.66	0.53	0.62	0.56	1,906
Spain					
Pooled sample	0.59	0.58	0.61	0.44	4,704
Survey 1981	0.58	0.56	0.62	0.42	2,187
Survey 1990	0.60	0.60	0.61	0.46	2,500
Ireland					
Pooled sample	0.54	0.38	0.47	0.39	2,158
Survey 1981	0.59	0.38	0.50	0.44	1,172
Survey 1990	0.48	0.40	0.43	0.32	985
MIXED					
Britain					
Pooled sample	0.55	0.42	0.47	0.42	2,597
Survey 1981	0.52	0.37	0.46	0.39	1,174
Survey 1990	0.57	0.46	0.48	0.45	1,420
West Germany					
Pooled sample	0.63	0.55	0.59	0.55	2,795
Survey 1981	0.61	0.56	0.62	0.53	1,058
Survey 1990	0.64	0.55	0.57	0.56	1,737
Netherlands					
Pooled sample	0.73	0.60	0.63	0.55	2,084
Survey 1981	0.74	0.57	0.62	0.57	1,090
Survey 1990	0.73	0.62	0.64	0.54	994
PROTESTANT					
Denmark					
Pooled sample	048	0.38	0.41	0.41	1,919
Survey 1981	0.52	0.42	0.46	0.43	956
Survey 1990	0.45	0.34	0.35	0.39	995

Table 4.1. *Cont.*

Countries/ Data source	Importance of God	Religiosity	No. of religious beliefs	Type of God	N (min.)
Norway					
Pooled sample	0.56	0.41	0.50	0.45	2,340
Survey 1981	0.55	0.39	0.48	0.43	1,173
Survey 1990	0.56	0.43	0.51	0.47	1,167

(b) Comparisons between Catholics and Protestants in mixed religious cultures

BRITAIN

Protestants and unchurched					
Pooled sample	0.50	0.39	0.40	0.41	1,830
Survey 1981	0.44	0.32	0.35	0.35	902
Survey 1990	0.55	0.45	0.44	0.45	928
Catholics and unchurched					
Pooled sample	0.62	0.46	0.59	0.46	617
Survey 1981	0.66	0.52	0.65	0.47	191
Survey 1990	0.58	0.44	0.55	0.45	423

NETHERLANDS

Protestants and unchurched					
Pooled sample	0.77	0.60	0.75	0.59	897
Survey 1981	0.77	0.57	0.74	0.60	483
Survey 1990	0.77	0.61	0.75	0.59	414
Catholics and unchurched					
Pooled sample	0.70	0.60	0.54	0.52	1,111
Survey 1981	0.71	0.57	0.53	0.56	547
Survey 1990	0.70	0.62	0.55	0.48	557

WEST GERMANY

Protestants and unchurched					
Pooled sample	0.56	0.51	0.53	0.46	1,396
Survey 1981	0.54	0.49	0.56	0.45	560
Survey 1990	0.57	0.52	0.51	0.47	836
Catholics and unchurched					
Pooled sample	0.68	0.59	0.62	0.59	1,380
Survey 1981	0.67	0.60	0.64	0.55	492
Survey 1990	0.69	0.58	0.61	0.61	888

Notes: Entries are correlation coefficients. All correlations are significant at the 0.001 level. The data are unweighted. Pairwise deletion of missing data.

Sources: European Values Survey (1981, 1990).

magnitude are rare. They also indicate that the centrality of God can be quite successfully predicted from church integration. By knowing how often a person attends services, we can estimate the (reported) importance of God fairly accurately. Thus, if correlations among indicators of values are the yardstick, church integration can be classified as an excellent indirect indicator of church religiosity.

Our other expectations are also confirmed. Among the Catholic countries, the most homogeneous—Ireland—displays the lowest correlations between all variables. The Norwegian and Danish correlations are approximately at the same level. However, in general, the Catholic countries display higher correlations than the Protestant Nordic countries. With the exception of the Netherlands, where the high correlations among Protestants may be due to the neo-Calvinists, the same relationship holds within mixed religious countries.[12]

Finally, the correlations of the 1981 and 1990 samples correspond closely. Of the forty pairs of correlations in Table 4.1a only five differ by more than 0.1 in magnitude. Obviously, with large sample sizes, much smaller differences would become significant in single-stage probability samples. However, even if both studies had the quality of probability samples, the question would still arise of whether the differences reflect systematic change or are due solely to period effects. In our view, there are good reasons to reject the assumption of systematic change. For instance, if we examine the relatively large differences between the 1981 and 1990 results in Denmark, it turns out that the direct indicators of church religiosity in 1981 display up to 20 per cent missing values, which is at least three times larger than in 1990. That may be the only reason for obtaining rather different correlation coefficients. Thus, on balance, our crude index of church integration is an excellent indicator of church religiosity. It is not a direct indicator because it measures reported behaviour; but, indirectly, it reflects the degree of individual religiosity.

In Chapter 2 of this volume, Van Deth and Scarbrough propose the term *value orientation* when a patterning of attitudes can be interpreted as an indicator of specific values. Our measure of church religiosity is not based on this approach. However, our measure is clearly an excellent indicator of the religious beliefs and attitudes of our respondents. Hence, this measure of church religiosity is used to operationalize religious—secular orientations in this volume. But for most of the empirical analyses in this volume, the data situation forces the authors to use church attendance as an indirect measure of this value orientation. When dealing with more sophisticated approaches to religiosity in Chapters 7 and 8, we retain the more refined terminology.

Change in Church Integration and Church Religiosity

We cannot conclude from the preceding results that a change in church integration reflects a similar change in church religiosity. There are serious substantive and technical arguments why, in spite of high cross-sectional correlations, church integration may not be suitable for measuring changing religiosity. First, it is often argued that a change in religious beliefs usually precedes a change in behaviour; people call into question the basic tenets of their religion before altering their behaviour. Thus a change in church integration may not be paralleled by a change in church religiosity.[13] Secondly, even if the time-lag between the two processes is negligible, we may get the impression of an unparalleled change simply because the indicators are more or less sensitive to change.

It follows, then, that we have to be much more careful in operationalizing our measure than in the preceding analysis. So we apply the index of church integration only to those respondents who belong either to a Christian denomination or to the unchurched subpopulation; members of other denominations are excluded from the analysis.[14] Moreover, we have to take into account the distorting effect of the filter question in the 1990 survey,[15] which seems to have produced an increase in the no-denomination category in almost all countries. The change is most dramatic in Britain where the proportion of the unchurched increases by more than 30 percentage points between 1981 and 1990; it still amounts to more than 10 percentage points in the Netherlands, France, and in Italy, but is negligible in Ireland and West Germany (less than two points). Obviously, these differences may indicate true change, but their magnitude suggests that the increase is primarily due to different question formats, and only in small part to true change. However, as the two surveys did not take denomination as a filter question for church attendance, we can correct for the distorting effect of the filter question by constructing our index of church integration almost exclusively from the variable church attendance.

Our index does not distinguish between nominal Christians and the unchurched. Respondents are classified as unaffiliated if they never

TABLE 4.2. *Changes in church integration in Western Europe, 1981 and 1990*

(a) Church attendance

Change in church integration	Categories of church attendance				4 categories (d.f. = 3)		8 categories (d.f. = 7)		N	Importance of God	
	Percentage difference between 1981 and 1990				χ^2	p	χ^2	p		Pearson's χ^2	p with 9 d.f.	N
	Nuclear	Moderate	Marginal	Unaffiliated								
More integration												
Italy	+4.6	+2.2	−1.0	−5.9	22.24	0.00	39.38	0.00	3,328	26.05	0.00	3,249
France	−2.2	+4.8	+2.2	−4.8	12.44	0.01	16.77	0.02	2,153	18.75	0.03	2,103
No macro-level change												
Denmark	−0.6	−1.1	+0.1	+1.5	1.29	0.73	11.17	0.13	2,179	54.70	0.00	2,088
Britain	+0.7	+3.2	−1.9	−2.1	4.99	0.17	8.79	0.27	2,553	21.59	0.01	2,514
Less integration												
Belgium	−7.7	+4.7	−5.5	+8.5	58.53	0.00	88.73	0.00	3,859	84.91	0.00	3,622
Spain	−8.1	+2.0	+2.5	+3.6	35.98	0.00	88.26	0.00	4,894	20.20	0.02	4,722
Netherlands	−6.7	+4.7	+1.8	+0.2	17.02	0.00	50.80	0.00	2,151	25.25	0.00	2,079
West Germany	−3.1	+1.0	+4.6	−2.5	11.98	0.01	18.02	0.01	3,370	11.67	0.23	3,246
Ireland	−1.9	+4.0	−1.9	−0.3	13.73	0.00	22.09	0.00	2,194	33.03	0.00	2,180
Norway	−0.6	−7.2	+1.5	+6.2	15.08	0.00	37.36	0.00	2,215	29.53	0.00	2,176

TABLE 4.2. *Cont.*

(b) *Religious beliefs*

Change in church integration	Number of religious beliefs (percentage difference between 1981 and 1990)								Statistics		
	7	6	5	4	3	2	1	0	Pearson's χ^2	p with d.f. $= 7$	N
More integration											
Italy	+5.5	−0.6	+1.1	−0.5	−2.0	−0.2	−3.7	+0.4	22.79	0.00	3,328
France	−0.6	+1.3	−1.6	+2.0	−0.3	+1.4	−1.0	−1.3	8.32	0.31	2,153
No macro-level change											
Denmark	−1.0	−0.2	−0.4	+0.7	+2.5	+0.3	+1.5	−3.5	7.83	0.35	2,179
Britain	+0.5	+1.3	+0.6	+0.4	−4.9	−1.0	+0.1	+3.1	18.53	0.01	2,553
Less integration											
Belgium	−1.5	−0.8	−0.9	−1.0	−0.9	+1.9	−3.5	+6.8	27.99	0.00	3,859
Spain	−7.4	+0.4	+1.1	+2.1	−1.2	−0.4	+0.5	+4.9	63.15	0.00	4,894
Netherlands	−2.3	−1.9	−2.2	+0.9	+1.4	+3.2	+2.0	−1.2	15.76	0.03	2,151
West Germany	−1.7	−1.1	+1.5	−1.4	−2.2	+3.4	+0.1	+1.5	17.62	0.01	3,370
Ireland	−4.9	+0.5	+5.7	—	+1.0	−0.9	−0.6	−0.7	15.92	0.03	2,194
Norway	−1.5	−2.0	−2.3	−3.0	−0.9	−1.3	+1.7	+9.4	35.74	0.00	2,215

Notes: The original weights from the European Values Surveys have been used. The χ^2 tests are based on weighted data. Since normalized weights are used, the weighted N is more or less the same as the unweighted N. Respondents who are not Catholics, Protestants, members of the free churches, or unchurched have been excluded from the analysis with one exception: in order to reduce the distorting effect of the filter question in the 1990 survey, we have included respondents with a missing value on denomination but a valid code on church attendance. Furthermore, since the French survey does not distinguish between 'other' and 'no denomination' in the 1981 survey, both groups had to be treated as unchurched. A negative percentage indicates a decrease from 1981 to 1990; a positive sign an increase.

Sources: European Values Survey (1981, 1990).

attend church (whether or not they have a valid code on denomination), or if they classify themselves as unchurched and if there is no information about their church attendance. Thus, our new index consists of only eight categories. A collapsed version of this index distinguishes only between nuclear Christians (weekly or more), moderate (once a month or on Christian festivals), marginal Christians (once a year or less often), and the disengaged (never or unchurched).

We get a rough impression about the process of change by simply comparing the distributions of church integration in 1981 and 1990.[16] Relying on the χ^2 statistics of the original index (at a 10 per cent level of significance), we first divided the countries into those which have experienced a change in church integration during the 1980s, and those which have not. In the former group, we distinguished further between countries with increasing and countries with declining church integration. If the percentage differences for a particular country are not compatible with a model of unidirectional stepwise change (USC model), we have based the decision exclusively on the influx or outflow of the extreme categories. According to these criteria we obtain two countries with more or less stable church integration (Denmark, Britain), two countries where church integration is increasing (Italy, France), and six where church disengagement has increased. The number of categories has virtually no impact on the χ^2 test statistics since the collapsed and the extended index lead to the same classification.

At a first glance, Table 4.2*a* does not overwhelmingly support the secularization hypothesis. In 40 per cent of the countries church integration has not declined during the last decade. West Germany is a borderline case since the outflow of the unaffiliated is almost equal to the decline of nuclear church members. To be sure, most theoretical arguments do not forbid a short-term recovery of church religion since they are only concerned with long-term developments. Nevertheless, reverse tendencies should remain the exception.

Church integration increased between 1981 and 1990 only in Italy and France. And France remains a dubious case. If we consult the Eurobarometer data, the percentage of nuclear church members appears quite stable throughout the 1980s, while the percentage of unaffiliated individuals increased. Two reasons may account for our deviating result. First, we may not have been able to correct completely for the distorting effect of the filter question in the 1990 survey. Secondly, the widely used church attendance scales may not differentiate adequately at lower levels. Semantically, there is almost no difference between attending church at Christmas and attending church once a year, and there is only a small difference between these two categories and attending church less than once a year. However, these responses constitute three distinct levels of church integration even on the collapsed index. If church integration is not measured reliably at lower levels, fluctuation at these levels can also be produced by measurement error. The influence of measurement error will be more detrimental the smaller the true change in church integration.

On the basis of these results we can now turn to our core question in this section: has church integration changed in parallel with church religiosity? To answer this question, we have added to Table 4.2*a* and Table 4.2*b* the χ^2 test statistics and the *p*-values for our two best direct indicators of church religiosity: the number of religious beliefs and the importance of God. For lack of space, percentage differences are displayed only for number of religious beliefs.

Despite our qualifications, the degree of correspondence between the three indicators is remarkably good. Belgium and Spain have experienced the most dramatic decline of church integration during the last decade, and the direct indicators of church religiosity also display a significant decline. The percentage differences of all three variables are also significant at the 5 per cent level in Ireland and Norway, and church integration and number of religious beliefs display very similar patterns of change. In Ireland, there is not a unidirectional decline of church religiosity but a massive concentration in the moderate category. By contrast, in Norway the percentage differences of the two variables follow the model of unidirectional stepwise decline. In the Netherlands, the change in the number of religious beliefs is not perfectly consistent with the USC model but it is nearly so. West Germany is the only country in the last group where the three χ^2 tests lead to different conclusions: there is a significant change in church integration and the number of religious beliefs but not in the importance of God. However, since the change in the first two variables is fairly small, there is still a close correspondence between the three variables.

Moving from the bottom to the top of the tables, the same holds for France. In Italy, the three indicators again reveal a very similar pattern: church religiosity and church integration seem to have increased during the last decade. Finally, in Denmark and Britain the three indicators display different patterns of change. In Denmark, the change in church integration and the number of religious beliefs is insignificant but the change in importance of God is highly significant. In Britain, the two indicators of church religiosity point to a significant change, but church integration does not. Here, our earlier conclusions apply: the index of church integration may be distorted by the filter question in 1990 and/or by measurement error. Therefore, the direct indicators of church religiosity are probably more reliable than our index.

Our analyses suggest that pronounced changes in church integration are paralleled by similar changes in church religiosity. However, our index of church integration may suffer from reliability problems at low levels of church attendance; small changes in church integration may be drowned out by measurement error. Clearly, this is a tentative conclusion because the measurement problems at low levels of integration may result exclusively from the filter question in 1990.

In the next section, we examine differences in church integration over time and between countries. Here we rely on a number of national surveys which were not designed for comparative purposes.[17] We use the categories at the upper (weekly or more) and lower (never or rarely) ends of the church attendance scales found in a number of studies. The surveys do not always include weekly or more as a category, but where it is included, nuclear church membership can be quite accurately determined. But at low levels of church integration, item wordings as well as filter questions have an impact on the percentage unaffiliated and this impact may also differ from one country to another (see Jagodzinski 1991). Consequently, we cannot reliably identify those who have already severed bonds with the institutionalized churches.

When examining differences between countries, we include only those countries where the same definition of church disengagement can be applied; when examining differences within countries, we use a more liberal criterion.[18]

Differences between Countries

From our theoretical discussion we conclude, tentatively, that the process of church disengagement is more advanced the more rationalized a society and the more influential the Protestant church has been in the past. As we argued earlier, the rationalization hypothesis does not imply a close correspondence between economic performance and church integration within short time intervals. Rather, we have to contrast levels of church integration within a single country at distant time points or compare countries at different levels of economic development. The same holds for the impact of Protestant individualism. The empirical evidence from these comparisons will always remain shaky, because the number of cases necessarily becomes very small. Hence, in order to examine the influence of rationalization and Protestantism, we pool the data from the 1981 and 1990 European Values Study. However, we stress that our results will be determined predominantly by the differences between countries because they are much larger than the differences between time points within countries.

We use regression analysis to examine our first hypothesis. The country at a given point in time is the unit of analysis. We compute four alternative measures of the level of church integration: the percentage unaffiliated; the percentage of nuclear church members or highly integrated; the median integration; the logarithm of the geometric mean (mean integration), which has been calculated from a metric version of the church attendance scale.[19] The four variables are regressed one by one on indicators of rationalization and Protestantism. As an imperfect indicator of rationalization we take the GDP per capita, correcting for different inflation and exchange rates by measuring the GDP per capita in standard purchasing power units. With regard to Protestantism, we construct an additional variable—percentage Catholics—as a measure of Protestant versus Catholic dominance.[20] In general, the higher the proportion of Catholics, the more influential the Catholic Church has been in the past; the lower the proportion of Catholics, the more influential Protestantism has been.

To give an impression of the relationship between economic performance, percentage Catholics, and church integration, the data in Figure 4.1 are arranged in a cube. The two data points for each country, 1981 and 1990, are depicted by the same symbol. The name of the country is written beside the 1990 data point. Thus to identify a country's 1981 data point, one has to look for the same symbol at the back of the cube. For instance, the empty square on the back right side represents Italy in 1981. Usually, one can find the data point for 1981 by moving at approximately the height of the 1990 data point in parallel with the GDP per capita axis to the back of the cube.

In most cases, the percentages of nuclear church members are almost stable over the nine years. A sharp decline can be observed only in Belgium and Spain. By contrast, church integration seems to have increased in Italy.[21] We can also see that change in church integration

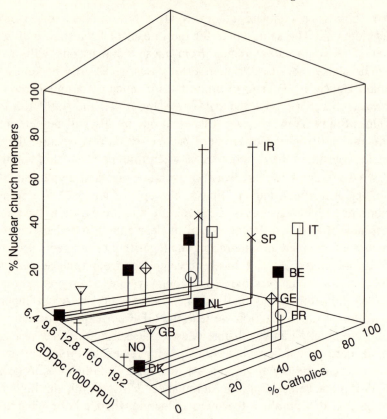

FIGURE 4.1. *Church integration, economic performance, and Catholicism in Western Europe, 1981 and 1990*

Note: See text and Table 4.3 for an explanation of this figure.

is not strongly dependent on the degree of economic development: large differences between GDP per capita in 1981 and 1990 are not accompanied by a large decline in church integration.

According to our first hypothesis, the percentage of Catholics should have a positive impact on the percentage of the highly integrated, medium integration, and mean integration, and a negative impact on the percentage unaffiliated. By contrast, if the rationalization hypothesis is true, the effects of GDP per capita should show the opposite sign. Figure 4.1 already suggests that this hypothesis will be confirmed; a regression plane where the slope increases with the percentage of

Catholics (positive effect) and declines with increasing GDP per capita (negative effect) will fit the observed data fairly well. To obtain more precise results we first estimate the model:

$$C = \beta_i * GDPpc + \beta_2 * Cath + \varepsilon, \tag{1}$$

where C is Church integration/disengagement, β_i is the ith standardized regression coefficient, ε is the residual term, $GDPpc$ is the standardized GDP per capita, and $Cath$ is the standardized percentage Catholics.[22] In addition, we specify the equation

$$C = \beta_i * \ln(GDPpc) + \beta_2 * Cath + \varepsilon, \tag{2}$$

because the logarithms of GDP per capita have performed almost consistently as better predictors than the untransformed variables in quantitative aggregate analyses.

Finally, we also explore a context effect. Individual church practice may not be determined by denomination alone but may be mediated by the homogeneity of the religious context, for instance by the proportion of Catholics within the country. The impact of denomination on church practice may be stronger the more homogeneous is the religious context. In specifying this assumption at the individual level, we multiplied Catholic denomination by percentage of Catholics. In an aggregate analysis this interaction term becomes the square of the percentage of Catholics.[23] If we observe a significant increase in the coefficient of determination, the context effect is empirically established. We proceed accordingly, comparing the R^2 of equation (1) with the R^2 of the regression:

$$C = \beta_i * GDPpc + \beta_2 * Cath + \beta_3 * Cath^2 + \varepsilon. \tag{3}$$

Similarly, we expand equation (2) by the quadratic term $Cath^2$. The results of the four regressions for all four dependent variables are reported in Table 4.3. The first three columns refer to the first step of each regression, and the last column reports the amount of variance explained in the second step. The regressions with the logarithm of GDP per capita ('Transformed') consistently yield higher percentages of explained variances than those with the untransformed GDP per capita. The signs of the regression coefficients are always in the expected direction, and percentage Catholics, without exception, has a stronger impact on church integration than the indicator for rationalization. This result is not very surprising. First, percentage Catholics is also, to some extent, a measure of church integration since a member of the Catholic church cannot be unchurched. Thus, the strong effect of percentage Catholics may only partly reflect the impact of Protestant individualism since the independent variable and the dependent variables are confounded. Secondly, GDP per capita is only a very crude measure of rationalization, and the high degree of measurement error in this variable may reduce its standardized regression coefficient.

We should note that the regression equations suffer from deficiencies due to the small number of cases. For instance, as can be seen in Figure 4.1, the results are largely determined by the outliers—Ireland and Spain on the one hand, Denmark and Norway on the other. We also cannot adequately correct for autocorrelated residuals which almost certainly occur in our pooled design. On balance, the regression analyses should be taken as a parsimonious description of the relationships and not as a statistical test. Thus, it is too early to conclude that the cultural factor—Protestant versus Catholic dominance—is more important than economic rationalization.

As for the percentage of explained variance, the percentage of highly integrated can be predicted best (about 65 per cent of the explained variance in the first step regression) and the percentage of unaffiliated predicted least well (about 38 per cent). Although the two measures of central tendency (median integration and mean integration) yield somewhat lower R^2 than the percentage of highly integrated, we prefer the former for cross-sectional and longitudinal comparisons because they are less affected by outliers. The large gap in terms of explained variances between the percentage unaffiliated and the other three dependent variables can be explained in two different ways. One may argue either that Protestant individualism is manifest, so far, in a dissolution of the core and not in a massive exodus from the church. Accordingly, we would observe much less systematic fluctuation at lower levels of church integration. Or the low R^2 could be due to the unreliable measurement of disengagement. Although both factors may have contributed to the large differences in explained variances, we consider the latter to be more important.

There are also some hints of a context effect for percentage Catholics since the R^2 in the fourth column of Table 4.3 are always considerably higher than the R^2 in the third column. The increase is most remarkable in the case of percentage unaffiliated where, after the inclusion of squared percentage Catholics, the R^2 climb from about 38 per cent to more than 49 per cent. Similar results are obtained in the regressions

TABLE 4.3. *Regression of church integration on GDP per capita and percentage of Catholics: aggregate analysis*

Dependent variable	Standardized regression coefficients (first step)		Coefficient of determination $(100 * R^2)$	
	GDPpc/PPU (1)	% Catholics (2)	First step (%) (3)	Second step (%) (4)
% unaffiliated				
Untransformed	0.20	−0.53	38.09	49.38
Transformed	0.21	−0.51	38.32	49.46
% highly integrated				
Untransformed	−0.14	0.75	64.49	72.92
Transformed	−0.15	0.74	64.78	72.99
Median integration				
Untransformed	−0.16	0.61	45.30	56.18
Transformed	−0.17	0.60	45.45	56.21
Mean integration (Geometric mean)				
Untransformed	−0.11	0.72	57.71	65.66
Transformed	−0.12	0.71	57.94	65.68

Notes: $N = 20$. Entries are standardized regression coefficients and R^2. In order to correct for different inflation rates and exchange rates, the GDPpc is measured in purchasing power standard units (PPU). Data for 1981 are from Eurostat, 1987; data for 1990 are from Eurostat, 1992. Since the new series uses 1990 and the old series uses 1975 as the base year, we have adapted the new series to the old basis. 'Untransformed' refers to regression analyses with untransformed GDPpc/PPU. 'Transformed' refers to regression analyses with the logarithm of GDPpc/PPU as the independent variable. Further details about these computations can be obtained from the authors. To obtain a metric variable, we transformed the response categories of church attendance into a metric scale. By imputing a time frame of two years and using an exponential function e^x, the exponent x comes fairly close to the natural numbers 1, 2, . . ., 5.

of median integration. However, even in the other regressions the coefficient of determination improves by about 5 percentage points. Thus, the aggregate level analysis offers weak evidence that church integration declines with economic rationalization and Protestant dominance, but also that the retardative influence of Catholicism is largest in a homogeneous Catholic culture. Clearly, the latter conclusion is not at all surprising, and the former is open to a variety of critical objections. Nevertheless, in our view, these comparisons between countries offer the most convincing evidence in favour of the Weberian secularization hypothesis.

Church Integration within Countries

Since we cannot construct identical measures of central tendency for our longitudinal study, we rely exclusively on two complementary indices in this and the following section: the percentage of highly integrated or nuclear church members and the percentage unaffiliated. The former index is more reliable (see Jagodzinski 1991), but it is less sensitive to changes in the Protestant world. Since the nucleus of the dominant Protestant churches fell apart immediately after the Second World War or earlier, the process cannot be adequately documented by our time series. Thus, we can expect the percentage of nuclear church members to reflect mainly the effects of the de-traditionalization of the Catholic lifeworld.

We restrict the analysis to those countries where surveys of church attendance are available at least since 1970. Thus, Spain[24] and Ireland have to be dropped from our set of ten West European countries. In Norway, an almost perfect time series since 1954 can be built from election studies. However, Norwegian respondents were asked about church attendance during the last month, so the Norwegian church integration scale is not comparable to the other scales. Therefore, Norway is included only in our cohort analysis.

Since election studies and comparable national surveys usually have the best sample quality, our analysis is based on these surveys wherever possible. Unfortunately, among the seven remaining countries, long-term sequences can be constructed only for Denmark, Britain, the Netherlands, and West Germany. For Belgium, Italy, and France, we have to rely on the 1970 and 1973 European Community Studies, and the Eurobarometer series—but with additional data on weekly church attenders in France.[25]

The data sets, coding rules, and definitions need not be recapitulated in detail.[26] In general, we have calculated the percentage of respondents attending church weekly or more. Non-Christian religions have been excluded from the percentage base. In the Netherlands and Britain, three groups have been distinguished: Catholics, members of the dominant Protestant church, and members of smaller Protestant denominations. In Britain, in particular, the latter group is still quite heterogeneous. In West Germany, only members of the Catholic and Protestant churches are included, and Catholics were excluded in the analysis of the Danish data. As the excluded groups consist of less than 2.5 per cent of the total sample, their exclusion almost certainly has no

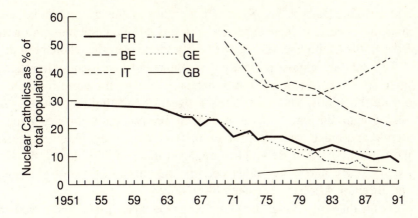

FIGURE 4.2. *Nuclear Catholics in six West European countries, 1951–91*

Sources: For Belgium and Italy, EC studies and Eurobarometer studies; for France, data made available by Yves Lambert, Centre National de Recherche Scientifique, Groupe de Sociologie de Religion, for Paris; for Britain, British election studies and British Social Attitudes Surveys; for Netherlands, national election studies and Cultural Change Survey; for West Germany, social surveys and various other studies.

discernible impact on the results. Since few of these surveys have an upper age limit, we have not defined a general upper limit. The distortion caused by upper age limits is negligible compared to the impact of sampling error and short-term period effects. We have weighted the data if the data set included a reasonable weight. Our results, showing the percentage of nuclear Catholics in the total population, are displayed in Figure 4.2.

The figure represents the erosion of the Catholic core. In Belgium, France, the Netherlands, and West Germany, we observe a dramatic decline of nuclear Catholics during the 1960s and 1970s. As the German data suggest, the decay probably started at the end of the 1960s. Other studies have confirmed this for the Netherlands and Belgium (Dobbelaere 1988*a*: 88, 94). France, a so-called Catholic country, displays figures similar to the mixed countries.[27] The process of disengagement occurred earlier in France than among the pillarized Catholic population of the mixed countries, West Germany, and the Netherlands, confirming our surmise that the process started earlier in non-pillarized countries than in pillarized countries (cf. Dobbelaere and Voyé 1991: 206). The only exceptions from the general trend are Italy and Britain. During the 1970s, Italy followed the general trend, but since then seems to have experienced a revival of church integration. In Britain, the Catholic core remains nearly stable over the whole period.[28]

The data are almost perfectly consistent with our assumption that a large step towards the de-traditionalization of the lifeworld took place during the 1960s. The differences between the Catholic countries also accord with our expectations. In France, the process of disengagement started at a much lower level than in Belgium or Italy. However, since the Catholic core in Belgium disengaged more rapidly during the last twenty years than in any other country, the difference between France and Belgium has been considerably reduced.

As for the large Protestant churches in Denmark, Britain, the Netherlands, and West Germany, the core had almost dissolved by the end of the 1960s. Usually, less than 10 per cent of church members were highly integrated; in Denmark, even by 1964, less than 3 per cent of church members were highly integrated. In Britain, in 1964 less than 10 per cent of Anglicans were nuclear church members. West Germany is almost an exception, since the percentage of nuclear church members at the beginning at the 1960s was above 10 per cent, but there was a continuous decline between 1963 and 1973; by the mid-1970s, the West German Protestants do not differ much from the major Protestant groups in other West European countries.

While integration is low in the dominant Protestant churches, it remains very high in certain Protestant denominations. This can be inferred from data for the Netherlands (Oudhof 1988: 8; cf. Oudhof and Beets 1982: 17). The neo-Calvinists have a much more solid and cohesive collective creed, and their parish communities are much more integrated, than is the case with the Dutch Reformed Church. They also had a solid pillar. All these factors delayed the losses of the neo-Calvinists.

Comparing the total percentage of nuclear church members without distinguishing between denominations, the differences between Catholic and Protestant countries had almost disappeared by the end of the 1980s. The percentage of nuclear church members in France (about 12 per cent) is approximately at the same level as in Britain or the Netherlands, but lower than in Germany (nearly 15 per cent). Belgium is still somewhat behind but in view of the pace of change during the 1980s, we expect the 10 per cent level to be approached fairly soon. From our preceding results, we have to conclude that the process of church disengagement has been accompanied by a major transformation of religious belief systems.

Turning next to the percentages of unaffiliated, we repeat our warning that disengagement cannot be measured with the same precision as nuclear church membership. For some countries we had to use surveys with different item wordings or different church attendance scales. Since the OESI (1989) figures point to a considerable increase of non-attenders in Spain, these percentages have been included in this analysis although we have no control over data definitions and operationalizations. Leaving these problems aside, we can see from Figures 4.3*a* and 4.3*b* that the percentage unaffiliated increased in almost all countries under investigation between 1970 and 1990. The change was most pronounced in France, Belgium, Britain, and the Netherlands.

From comparing the graphs in Figure 4.3, we can infer that church disengagement is most advanced in France, Britain, and the Netherlands where already more than 50 per cent of the population have left the churches. At the end of the 1980s, Belgium and Denmark are fairly close to a fifty–fifty split. In West Germany and, in particular, Italy, church disengagement was less widespread. Nevertheless, the de-traditionalization of the lifeworld during the 1960s and 1970s had also become manifest in an increase of the unaffiliated population. The dominant Protestant churches, in particular, suffered from the exodus. Although the timing and pace differ from one country to the next, the general tendency is quite stable: in the long run, the percentage of unaffiliated is increasing.

Intergenerational Change?

Several different processes might result in a steady decline of church involvement. Three models of change are considered here. Two originate in the standard model of generational change, according to which individual level change is largely restricted to 'formative' years. Once beliefs, norms, and values are internalized and behaviour becomes routinized, change is less likely to occur. On the assumption that the process of rationalization and functional differentiation gradually undermines the basic tenets of traditional religion, each new birth cohort should be less church religious than its predecessors. At the aggregate level, church religiosity should gradually decline because

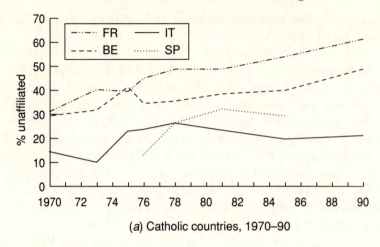

(*a*) Catholic countries, 1970–90

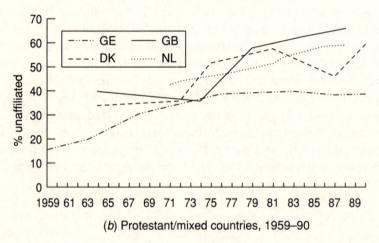

(*b*) Protestant/mixed countries, 1959–90

Figure 4.3. *Church disengagement in eight West European countries,
1959–90*

Sources: Danish Data Archives; Officina de Estadistica y Sociologia de la Iglesia, Spain
(1989: 221); West German election studies. For other countries, see Figure 4.2.

older cohorts are replaced by younger ones (*gradual model*). The
standard model of generational change can also be combined with
Inglehart's (1990) idea of formative affluence. Then we would not
expect a gradual decline of church involvement but a watershed
between post-war and older cohorts (*watershed model*).

Our model of religious change does not make different assumptions about long-term causes. Rationalization and functional differentiation will gradually undermine the basic tenets of traditional religion, but for a long time this erosion of religion will not become manifest in behavioural change. Although religious doubts may increase, people will remain within the churches, participate in rites and services, and consider themselves Christians. Specific events are necessary before these internal doubts turn into overt protest or exit. Criticism of the churches by political élites, the mass media, or theologians can work in this direction. We would then expect an exodus from the churches in all cohorts. The younger cohorts might react more rapidly, simply because they do not have to give up familiar beliefs and habits. Older cohorts might always remain at higher levels of church integration, partly because they are less affected by the process of rationalization and partly because some older people are unwilling to change their religious beliefs. However, in general, we expect a change in all cohorts within fairly short time periods. Since disengagement from religion spreads out rapidly we speak of a *contagion model* of religious change. To be sure, the contagion model also postulates a kind of generational change because all cohorts after the period of rapid decay are much less church religious than earlier cohorts. However, change in our model is not restricted to the formative years nor is it produced by post-war affluence.

Which of the three models fits our data best? Figures 4.4–4.5 help to give an answer. Here we have depicted the percentage of nuclear church members (Figure 4.4) and the percentage unaffiliated (Figure 4.5) within cohorts. Each cohort is represented by a distinct symbol; for instance, members of the oldest cohort in Belgium, France, and Italy were born between 1906 and 1915. In general, ten year cohorts have been chosen in order to reduce sampling error.[29] Wherever possible, we have determined the cohort intervals so that a clear distinction can be made between post-war and older cohorts; in most countries, the first post-war cohort was born between 1946 and 1955.

Change between cohorts in Belgium, Italy, and France is depicted in Figure 4.4*a*. Since the process of secularization was pushed ahead in France by the political élites much earlier than in most other European countries (Martin 1978), the Catholic nucleus was already fairly small in 1970. Church integration was much higher in the other two countries. While we observe a rapid decay of the Catholic core in Belgium, and a smaller decay in France, the curvilinear aggregate-level relationship in

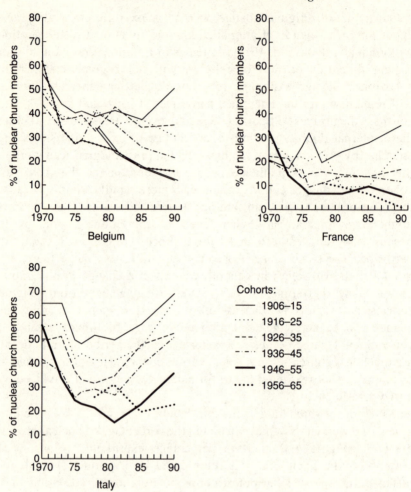

Figure 4.4*a*. *High levels of church integration in Catholic countries, 1970–90*

Sources: EC studies and Eurobarometer surveys.

Italy is replicated in almost all cohorts. Only the youngest cohort seems to be more resistant to the revival of church religion. Despite these differences, the three countries share two important properties: the younger cohorts are almost consistently less church integrated than the older cohorts, and the differences between cohorts are much larger at the end of the 1980s than at the beginning of the 1970s.

With some qualifications, these features can also be observed in the

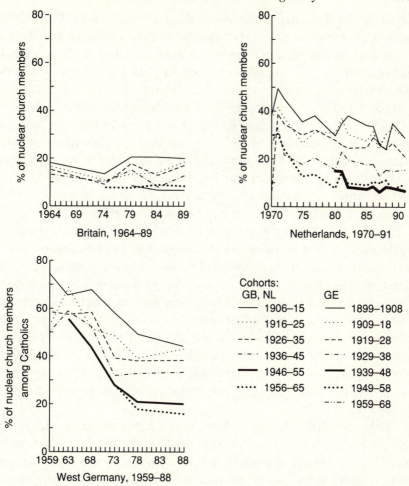

FIGURE 4.4*b*. *High levels of church integration in mixed countries*

Sources: British election studies and British Social Attitudes Surveys; Dutch national election studies and Cultural Change Survey; West German social surveys and various other studies.

three religiously mixed countries depicted in Figure 4.4*b*. In Britain, the differences between the cohorts are very small, but even here the generations seem to have drifted apart since the mid-1970s. In the Netherlands, there were already considerable gaps between the cohorts in 1970 which grew slightly in the following period.

The small numbers of cases do not allow us to run separate cohort analyses for each denomination in the Netherlands and Britain. The graphs for these countries are based on nuclear Catholics and Protestants. But the sample numbers are sufficiently large to allow separate analyses of the denominations in Germany. Developments among the West German Catholic cohorts since 1959 show a general process of decline. However, the percentage of nuclear church members is much higher in this instance than in Figure 4.2 because here we have the percentage of nuclear church members among Catholics. Although there is a small difference in the timing of the process, the dissolution of Catholicism in Belgium and West Germany takes a similar course: the proportion of nuclear church members drops in all cohorts but it drops most sharply in the war and post-war cohorts.

In our view, Figures 4.4*a* and 4.4*b* clearly reject the gradual and the watershed models of generational change. The de-traditionalization of the lifeworld has affected all cohorts, not only the younger ones. At least until the mid-1970s we do not observe a watershed between the pre- and post-war generations. Since then, the gap sometimes increases, but it increases as a result of different developments within cohorts. The differences between cohorts become largest in those countries where the core has fallen apart most recently—in Belgium, Italy, the Netherlands, and (Catholic) West Germany. The youngest cohorts are almost always in the lead, displaying the lowest percentage of nuclear church members.

Differences between the cohorts may be due either to (small) age effects or to the persistence of traditional beliefs and behaviour among the older cohorts. The contagion model, however, is compatible with both assumptions, so we do not need to speculate about the relative size of either effect. On the other hand, one might argue, in support of the first two models, that period effects can be superimposed on cohort effects. Thus, if after a period of public criticism of religion, the older cohorts return to their former levels of church integration, either the gradual model or the watershed model is confirmed. The oldest cohorts in Belgium, France, and Italy did indeed reintegrate to some extent. However, this process is confined to one or two cohorts; it could also result from sampling error, owing to the small sample size and high male mortality. The exception is Italy, where all cohorts but the youngest returned to higher levels of church integration during the 1980s. Accordingly, it could be argued that in Italy period effects were superimposed on stable cohort differences during the 1980s. However, developments in the two post-war cohorts are not completely consistent with this explanation.

On balance, the contagion model is supported best by our cohort analyses. In our view, rationalization, functional differentiation, the de-traditionalization of the lifeworld, and ensuing individualism have gradually undermined traditional religiosity after the Second World War. However, for a long time, the renunciation of traditional religion did not become manifest at the mass level. Only when public criticism of the churches in general, and of the Catholic Church in particular, started in the mid-1960s, did internal doubts turn into overt behaviour and result in a large-scale exodus from the churches. The contagion model does not deny differences between pre-war and post-war cohorts. However, these differences are not attributable to post-war affluence. Rather, the younger cohorts are more affected by a process which affects all cohorts. Younger people are more susceptible to new norms and beliefs; and in post-war Western Europe, are better educated, more mobile, and more often engaged in rationalized sectors of the economy. Moreover, in an environment of declining church religiosity, younger people have internalized religious beliefs and norms to a lesser degree than older people.

The results for church disengagement, shown in Figures 4.5a–4.5c, are less unique. First, our discussion of measurement problems with respect to Figure 4.3 also applies here. In four countries—Italy, Britain, the Netherlands, and Denmark—there seems to be a persistent watershed between post-war and older cohorts. Older cohorts may be slightly more reluctant to detach themselves completely from the institutionalized churches. This might be an argument in favour of a modified watershed model with period effects superimposed. On the other hand, we observe rapid intra-cohort change in most of the countries: over almost the whole period in Belgium, France, and the Netherlands; between 1969 and 1972 in West Germany; and in Britain between 1974 and 1979. In Denmark, distance from the Protestant church may have increased after 1972, but the evidence remains ambiguous.[30]

Thus, these graphs suggest that long-term intra-cohort change is larger than cohort differences. On balance, we consider the contagion model applicable in most of the countries, with modifications in a few exceptional cases. More specific statements can only be made after a statistical cohort analysis which is beyond the scope of this chapter.

To summarize: distance from the institutionalized churches has

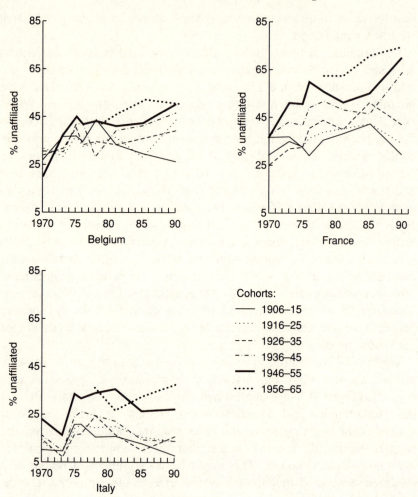

FIGURE 4.5a. *Church disengagement in three Catholic countries, 1970–90*
Sources: EC studies and Eurobarometer surveys.

become fairly large in younger cohorts. In Belgium and West Germany, nearly 40–50 per cent of the youngest cohorts practically never attend church or consider themselves unchurched. In France, Britain, Denmark, and the Netherlands, far more than 50 per cent are already unaffiliated. The figures for Norway are not strictly comparable, but we know (from the European Values Study) that the Norwegian figures are not far below the Danish.

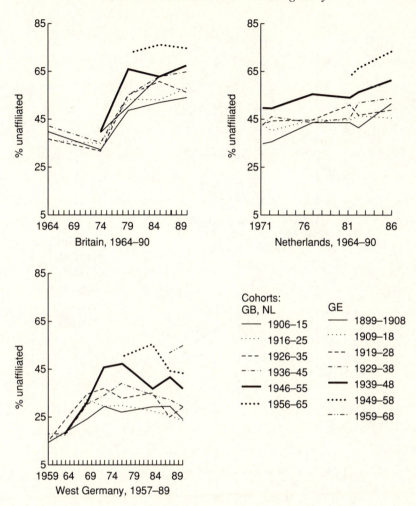

FIGURE 4.5*b. Church disengagement in mixed countries*

Sources: British election studies and British Social Attitudes Surveys; Dutch national election studies; West German election studies and various other studies.

Conclusion

This chapter has concentrated on church religiosity, particularly membership in established churches, and church integration. In Chapters 7 and 8 we go on to consider religious beliefs. However, we have

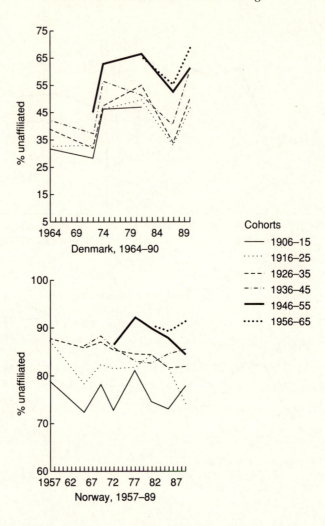

FIGURE 4.5*c*. *Church disengagement in two Protestant Scandinavian countries*

Note: Since the Norwegian church attendance scale is completely different from all other scales, the results for that country cannot be compared with other countries.

Sources: Danish Data Archives; Norwegian election studies.

demonstrated here that church integration is an acceptable indirect indicator of church religiosity. Focusing on church integration allowed us to make comparisons between countries and churches, and to build time series to test the impact of secularization.

All the empirical analyses in this chapter are compatible with the assumption that functional rationalization related to functional differentiation, de-traditionalization, and ensuing individualization have a cumulative influence on the decline of church involvement, especially among the post-war generation. Apart from Italy, among the younger cohorts the percentage of nuclear church members varies between (almost) zero and 10 per cent of the population. In our view, this almost complete dissolution of the religious core has far-reaching consequences for the institutionalized churches and the traditional form of religiosity. Moreover, the decline has occurred not just at higher levels of church involvement.

The consequence of this development for religious belief systems, political involvement, and support for the political system may be important. The churches have lost most of their impact *ad intra*: as a consequence, individuals may reject the 'menu' of church beliefs and practices, instead recomposing a religion *à la carte*—constructing their own religious patchwork. As for the impact *ad extra*, church leaders are allowed to give moral advice, but legitimized on humanitarian—not religious—grounds. Sin is an inadmissible concept but human rights is a legitimate referent. No strict rules are accepted; among people—and political leaders—who refuse to be regimented, only value orientations may provide general guidance or inspiration (Voyé and Dobbelaere 1992: 232–3).

Such developments will presumably also have an impact on people's political behaviour. Politics and religion will become even more differentiated; church guidelines on political questions will no longer be accepted; they may even provoke a negative reaction. The crumbling of church integration may, in the long run, change voting patterns and the appeal of Christian parties. Currently, the declining influence of traditional religiosity may be concealed by the association between church integration and conservatism. This relationship, too, may crumble if political conservatism becomes emancipated from its religious basis. Changes in religiosity may also have their impact on beliefs in government. With religiously inspired deference fading away, political leaders may have much more difficulty mustering political support for the institutions of government. We return to this discussion in Chapter 8.

NOTES

1. Although religion in a broader sense is of considerable interest, the data available on religious belief and practice do not permit an empirical assessment.
2. Obviously, freedom of choice does not necessarily make people free in their decisions. For instance, people are still members of networks or tribes (Maffesoli 1988) which have an impact on their life-style. What we stress in characterizing advanced modernity is that individuals are confronted with many more options or alternatives than in the past.
3. Several authors have stressed this kind of development. Bell (1976) suggested that modernity stimulated 'identity construction'; Schimank (1985) talked about 'reflexiver Subjektivismus'; Gastelaars emphasized that traditional norms and values have become relativized, and that individuals have gained freedom of action in an open, no longer self-evident world (1987: 154).
4. See Dobbelaere (1989) for a discussion of the concept of functional differentiation.
5. In the European Values Study, church attendance is coded: (1) More than once a week; (2) Once a week; (3) Once a month; (4) Christmas; (5) Holy days; (6) Once a year; (7) Less often; (8) Never; (9) No denomination; (99) Missing.
6. We admit there is a good argument to base the church integration index exclusively on church attendance: in most countries it seems to be a matter of attachment and feelings whether respondents assign themselves to a denomination. Withdrawal from the church is an internal, rather than external, formal act. Consequently, respondents' response to the denomination question becomes extremely volatile and dependent on the item format. The question about church attendance is easier to decide and responses are presumably more reliable. Yet many surveys automatically assign a missing value on church attendance to respondents without denomination. To keep our study consistent with these surveys, we almost have no choice but to classify respondents without a denomination as unaffiliated. Furthermore, we are frequently interested not only in church integration in general, but in integration into the Catholic or the Protestant churches. However, more or less regular church attenders without a denomination cannot be assigned to either group. We assigned these respondents to the unchurched group rather than as cases of missing values.
7. For technical reasons, we enlarge the unaffiliated group with respondents who attend church less than once a year.
8. Only 'Number of religious beliefs' is a ratio scale. None of the other variables even approach the level of interval measurement. Nevertheless, we report the product moment correlation in Table 4.1 since most of the variables are better than pure ordinal scales. In the Catholic countries, we have included only Catholics and unchurched people in the calculations; in Norway and Denmark, only Protestants and the unchurched. In the religiously mixed countries, we have included all three groups. In the Netherlands and Britain, the Protestants also include a number of smaller Protestant denominations, for instance neo-Calvinists in the Netherlands, and Presbyterians in Britain.
9. Since the product moment correlation coefficient is fairly sensitive to measurement error and skewness combined, it may assume a somewhat smaller value if the

population is more or less homogeneous with respect to belief or/and church integration. If all citizens believe in a personal God and all attend church weekly, the correlation is not even defined. If a few people behave randomly and the remainder is homogeneous, the correlation will be close to zero. This may be the case in Ireland.

10. In both surveys, the proportion of non-Christian denominations is well below 5%, so that group has a negligible impact on the strength of the association.

11. Separate analyses of Protestants and Catholics in the other countries would not produce meaningful results. The minority religion in these countries is always very small, so we would not obtain stable correlation coefficients for this group and the correlation coefficient for the majority religion would be almost identical to the one depicted in Table 4.1*a*.

12. The lower correlations may also be because our measure of church integration is less sensitive to changes at low levels of church religiosity.

13. Our study may suffer from the same problem. If the change in church religiosity took place either before 1981 or shortly before 1990 and if the decline in church integration followed with a time lag of one year or more, we would observe only a change in church integration in the first case, and only a change in church religiosity in the second.

14. This also applies to small Protestant sects, if they are not separately coded on our measure of denomination. This reduces the sample size by about 2% or less. Thus the impact on the results is probably very small.

15. In 1981, respondents were asked directly for their denomination, but in the 1990 survey a filter question was used asking respondents whether they belonged to a religious denomination. The denomination question was only put to respondents who answered the filter question positively. We know from studies in the Netherlands that similar filter questions produce higher proportions of unchurched respondents and deviate much more from the figures in the official statistics (Oudhof 1988; Oudhof and Beets 1982). Thus, if the category 'No denomination' is intended to measure the volatile, temporary, internal, and emotional withdrawal from the church, the filter performs worse and not better than the direct question. The same distorting effect almost certainly occurs in these two surveys.

16 Since the representative weights in the World Values Survey are not suited for our purposes, the analyses in Table 4.2*a* and 4.2*b* are based on the original European Value Study and were performed in Tilburg. We are greatly indebted to Loek Halman for the computations. The χ^2 tests reported in Table 4.2*a* for the extended (d.f. = 7) and the collapsed (d.f. = 3) index of church integration are only crude criteria, whether or not the two frequency distributions are markedly different from each other. This is not only because of sampling and measurement problems but also because the test is not based on any assumptions about the underlying process of change; it tests only whether or not the two samples can be assumed to come from the same population. So, the χ^2 test statistics may not become significant even if a more restrictive model of change would yield highly significant parameters.

17. It is therefore not surprising that the wording of the church attendance question frequently alters even within national surveys, so producing fairly different frequency distributions. We cannot address these problems here but they are important, since the results of comparisons might be interpreted as substantive

change while they are, in fact, no more than the effect of different question wording (see Jagodzinski 1991).

18. We cannot solve all the comparability problems, but as some studies use crude church attendance scales, we consider that the following rules produce the most comparable results: if a scale distinguishes between once a year, less than once a year, and never, respondents in the two latter categories are classified as unaffiliated; if a cruder scale with fewer categories is used, only respondents in the categories never or practically never are considered unaffiliated.

19. To make the metric scale robust against measurement error, it was constructed as an exponential function. In addition, no distinction has been made between attendance less than once a year and never.

20. Percentage Protestants is not suitable for operationalizing the concept of Protestant *v.* Catholic dominance because in some Protestant countries a large part of the population has already left the churches. There is some ambiguity in the middle range of the measure: if we observe about 50% Catholics in France, this does not imply that the other 50% have been influenced formerly by the Protestant Church. Apart from this exception, the countries are plausibly rank-ordered on the underlying continuum.

21. The directors of the European Values Study suggest that the changes registered in Italy since 1981 might be unreliable.

22. All other variables are assumed as standardized also. We restrict the analysis to standardized regression because our data do not allow any form of statistical inference, and because the relative strength of the effects is best reflected by the standardized coefficients.

23. It has been suggested elsewhere (see Jagodzinski and Weede 1981) that to test the context effect in aggregate level analysis in a stepwise regression the quadratic term has to be entered into the equation as a second step after all the linear terms have been included.

24. Apart from Fig. 4.3, where Spain is included.

25. The European Community studies and the Eurobarometer surveys have advantages in terms of comparability but cannot compete with national studies for sampling quality. For France, we are indebted to Yves Lambert from the Centre National de Recherche Scientifique, Paris, who provided us with the percentages of weekly church attenders from various national surveys. These percentages have been included in Fig. 4.2. We do not have percentages of the unaffiliated in France; therefore, we had to rely on the same data base as for the other Catholic countries in Fig. 4.3.

26. These can be obtained from Wolfgang Jagodzinski.

27. However, as percentages of the total population, Fig. 4.2 does not adequately reflect the disengagement of Catholics in mixed countries. For example, if the percentage of Catholics in the total population is about 40% and if 10% of the nuclear Catholics become unaffiliated, we will observe a decline of only 4%.

28. We have no well-founded explanation for the astonishing increase in church religion in Italy; there might be a connection to the decay of the Communist Party (see also n. 20 above). The stability in Britain is probably due to the large proportion of Catholics who are Irish immigrants still living in close contact with their mother country.

29. Theoretically, smaller cohort intervals may appear advantageous, but they frequently come into conflict with the requirements of statistical estimation theory. We do not report percentages at all if the number of cases in the respective cohort remains below 50.
30. The apparently rapid change in Britain in 1974–9 may be due to measurement error. The high percentage of unaffiliated people in Denmark in 1981 and 1990 may partly result from the different item format of the European Values Study.

PART II

Value Orientations and their Antecedents

5

Materialist–Postmaterialist Value Orientations

Much research on values and value change during the last twenty years or so has focused on the claim that advanced industrial societies are in the throes of a shift from materialist to postmaterialist value orientations. The claim is largely associated with the work of Ronald Inglehart, who has mined this seam since the late 1960s. Aside from Inglehart's own researches, the emergence of postmaterialist orientations has been deployed to explain the waves of political unrest which broke during the late 1960s (Barnes, Kaase, *et al*. 1979); the appearance of new forms of political action in the early 1970s (Marsh 1977; Dalton 1988); and the arrival of new issues on the political agenda during the 1980s (Dalton, Beck, and Flanagan 1984; Dalton 1989). Postmaterialist theory also carries weight in accounting for the appearance of new social movements (Kriesi 1989; Rohrschneider 1990) and the arrival of 'green' and 'new left' parties (Müller-Rommel 1985a; 1990) in several West European countries. Moreover, materialist–postmaterialist conflicts are thought, by several observers, to be displacing the politics of class conflict, with effects for electoral realignments and the reshaping of party systems (Baker, Dalton, and Hildebrandt 1981; Dalton 1991). In all, what Inglehart (1977a; 1990) identifies as a 'silent revolution'

The data for this chapter were kindly and generously supplied by Oscar Gabriel, University of Stuttgart, and Richard Topf, London Guildhall University. Simon Price, University of Essex, gave advice on time series analysis. I am much indebted to them.

heralds widespread change, transformation even, in political life in Western Europe.

The value orientations associated with conflicts centred around class and religion relate to a politics largely unchanged over the entire period of mass mobilization (Lipset and Rokkan 1967; Bartolini and Mair 1990). But the politics of materialist–postmaterialist conflict takes us into new and uncertainly charted territory. Several of the chapters in this volume examine, among other things, the impact of postmaterialist value orientations on political behaviour and beliefs in government. Our purpose in this chapter is to set out the background to those discussions. First, we review postmaterialist theory; secondly, we look at trends in the development of materialist–postmaterialist orientations; and thirdly, we assess the social distinctiveness of postmaterialism.

Postmaterialist Theory

The theory of postmaterialist value change rests on two simple hypotheses: a *scarcity hypothesis*, asserting that 'one places greatest subjective value on those things that are in relatively short supply'; and a *socialization hypothesis*, asserting that, largely, 'one's basic values reflect the conditions that prevailed during one's preadult years' (Inglehart 1990: 56). The scarcity hypothesis is comparable to the principle of marginal utility in economic theory, predicting that people turn to new concerns once prior concerns are settled; the socialization hypothesis is a generalization of the relationship between formative influences and adult personality. People's basic values are defined simply as 'relatively central, deep-rooted, and early-instilled part of one's outlook on life' (Inglehart 1990: 130), and varyingly referred to as 'needs', 'goals', 'behavioural predispositions', or 'attitudinal continuities'.

Neither the scarcity hypothesis nor the socialization hypothesis are startling or original. By combining them, however, Inglehart arrives at a generational theory which yields innovative propositions about value change in advanced industrial societies. Two propositions focus on the process of value change. First, value change follows from the different environments in which successive generations spend their formative years. Inglehart says little about the concept of generation but seems to share something of Mannheim's (1952) view of a generation as an aggregation of individuals who experience a common early environment which has lasting effects on them. In this sense, value change is a social process, effected through generational replacement, by which wider societal developments come to affect individual outlooks. Secondly, the theory implies a lag of some years before shifts in value orientations are expressed in people's attitudes. Hence, the explanation for value change is to be found in the circumstances prevailing some thirty years, even fifty or sixty years, earlier (Inglehart 1990: 57, 424). The 'silent revolution' originates in the different value priorities as between older and younger generations, which, as younger generations replace older generations, result in a slow but steady shift in the cultural character of a society.

Propositions about the content of value change are less straightforward. Initially, postmaterialist theory drew on Maslow's (1954) notion of a needs hierarchy: once first order needs for security are ensured, individuals become more concerned with higher order needs for 'self-actualization'. Explicitly following Maslow, Inglehart proposed that 'individuals pursue various goals in hierarchical order' (1971*b*: 991; cf. 1977*b*: 22)—manifest in the 'bourgeois' values of older generations and 'post-bourgeois' values among younger generations. In later accounts, the scarcity hypothesis replaces the needs hierarchy and changing value orientations are recast in the materialist–postmaterialist distinction. Thereafter, Inglehart refers to Maslow's needs hierarchy as a 'complementary concept' or 'a provocative hypothesis' (1990: 68, 15).[1]

The Maslovian heritage persists in postmaterialist theory, however, in the notion that value orientations follow a particular developmental path. Materialist orientations, emphasizing 'physiological sustenance and safety', are characteristic of people who have experienced insecurity and privation during their formative years, whereas postmaterialist orientations express people's need for 'self-expression, belonging, and intellectual or esthetic satisfaction' (Inglehart 1990: 134). These needs come to the fore among people who have enjoyed 'formative security'. In other words, postmaterialist orientations do not represent 'new' values in the sense that they are *ab initio* notions, or that values of any kind might emerge once people are released from insecurity. Rather, postmaterialist orientations are ever present, but take priority when the experience of 'formative security' allows individuals to be more concerned about the quality of life than the conditions of life. As the 'needs' reflected in materialist and postmaterialist priorities shape the potentialities of people free of want and fear, the 'silent revolution' represents the re-ordering of priorities—not a new vision of possibilities.

The dynamics underlying generational differences in outlook are security and economic development. Here, too, there is a certain shift in postmaterialist theory. In discussing the different pace of value shift in West European countries, Inglehart (1977*b*: 1990) emphasizes the conjunction between economic growth and social development. Postmaterialism is more likely to spread among 'the publics of relatively rich societies' (1990: 57) not as a direct consequence of greater wealth, but from the very different societal environment characteristic of advanced industrial societies—extensive welfare provision, expansion of education, and the growth of 'high tech' employment which 'allows wide scope to individual judgement and creativity' (1990: 10). Differences at the individual level are similarly the outcome of different economic and social experiences. The children of better-off parents enjoy greater 'formative security', are more likely to enter higher education, and more likely to take up higher status occupations. Thus, in the advanced industrial societies of the West, postmaterialism is linked not just to 'one's subjective sense of security' (1990: 122) due to prosperity but also to educational and occupational opportunity (1977*b*: 21–2).

Exploring value change across a range of forty countries, however, Inglehart and Abramson suggest that the process of postmaterialist value shift is not confined to Western advanced industrial societies but is 'potentially a universal process' (1994: 347). The emergence of postmaterialist values in countries such as South Korea, China, Russia, and Poland, is linked directly to the impact of economic growth alone; due to significant economic growth in the last decades, as a direct effect of greater prosperity, younger people have known greater economic security during their formative years than older people. In brief: 'Intergenerational value differences reflect a society's rate of economic growth' (1994: 351). Thus, in contrast to postmaterialist value shift as the outcome of a complex intertwining of economic and social developments in the advanced industrial societies of the West, Inglehart and Abramson conclude that 'the shift from materialist to postmaterialist values is not a uniquely Western phenomenon. Rather, it is found in societies with widely different institutions and cultural traditions' (1994: 351).

Universalizing the concept of postmaterialism, however, does not impinge on the generational nature of value change. In the West

European context, the central empirical claim derived from postmaterialist theory is that, consequent on the 'historically unprecedented prosperity and the absence of war that has prevailed in Western countries since 1945' (Inglehart 1990: 56), generations born after the Second World War place less emphasis on materialist goals and more emphasis on postmaterialist goals than earlier generations. Thus, the 1968 'student events' reflected the political arrival of the first generation raised in circumstances not dominated by the fear of war and economic privation (1971*a*). With successive post-war cohorts being more postmaterialist and steadily replacing older generations, 'there has been a gradual but pervasive shift in the values of [West European] publics' (1990: 56), averaging an increase of about 1 percentage point in postmaterialism per year (Abramson and Inglehart 1992). As this process works its way down the generations, by the year 2000 'Materialists will outnumber Postmaterialists only narrowly (which) may be a sort of tipping point in the balance between the two value types' (Inglehart 1990: 103); by 2010, postmaterialists are clearly likely to outnumber materialists (Abramson and Inglehart 1992: 227).

Despite the definitive effects of socialization and the 'deep-rooted' nature of values, postmaterialist orientations are not invariant. Fluctuations are specifically anticipated by the scarcity hypothesis: 'Periods of prosperity lead to increased Postmaterialism, and periods of scarcity lead to Materialism' (Inglehart 1990: 82). Although generational replacement 'exerts a continuous pressure pushing Postmaterialism upwards' (Abramson and Inglehart 1992: 187), periods of high inflation, in particular, tend to lead to a fall in the proportion of postmaterialists 'not as a result of fundamental value change, but simply because this was currently a serious problem' (Inglehart 1990: 131). The sharp dips in postmaterialism among the European Community countries in 1977, 1980–1, and the early 1990s, reflect rising inflation; upwards movements during 1978–9 and 1982–7 reflect the abatement of inflation, with a lag of about one year (Inglehart 1990: 94–5; Inglehart and Abramson 1994: 341). Such period effects are largely short term, with inflation inhibiting but not stemming the advance of postmaterialism, and spurts of prosperity yielding an exaggerated picture of the inter-generational trend towards postmaterialism (Inglehart 1990: 96–7). But period effects can have a longer-term impact, as for those born during 1966–75 among whom the general trend towards rising levels of postmaterialism with each successively younger cohort is arrested—reflecting the persistently negative impact of two recessions during the cohort's formative years (Inglehart 1990: 87). Thus, the shift towards postmaterialism consists of a long-wave, inter-generational shift in value priorities with short-term boosts or set-backs.

Although postmaterialist theory lays out a horizon beyond the distributional conflicts which characterized the politics of industrial societies, materialist–postmaterialist opposition is not devoid of a class dimension. By the 1980s postmaterialism had 'moved out of the student ghetto' as the first post-war generation entered the 'ranks of young professionals, civil servants, managers and politicians' (Inglehart 1990: 331, 67). The shift to postmaterialism is thus a major force in the rise of a 'new class' in Western society: 'a stratum of highly educated and well-paid young technocrats, who take an adversarial stance toward their society', in sharp contrast with the 'politically conservative' outlook characteristic of earlier highly educated groups (Inglehart 1990: 67, 332). Both the location of this new class near to the centre of policy-making and its involvement in new social movements makes it 'the major vehicle through which social change is attained in advanced industrial society' (1990: 332). Moreover, more generally, as 'Postmaterialists tend to be more highly educated and articulate than Materialists, they are likely to have a substantial impact on many issues, for they can often set the political agenda' (Abramson and Inglehart 1992: 227).

As is the fate—or fortune—of bold excursions, the claims made for postmaterialist theory have been seized upon by proponents and critics alike. Several aspects of these controversies are touched upon in this volume. We note just two points. First, postmaterialist theory often entwines macro-level propositions about the kind of societal environment which is conducive to the rise of postmaterialist orientations with micro-level propositions about what kind of people hold postmaterialist values. We shall need to distinguish between these levels, and be cautious about the notion of 'cause', in reviewing the empirical evidence. Secondly, while the shift to postmaterialist priorities is seen to have effects for democratic politics, postmaterialist theory lacks specifically political content. In the West European context, postmaterialist value shift originates in the different social and economic conditions of everyday life as experienced by older and younger generations; it owes little or nothing to the dynamics of democratic regimes or the potentialities of democratic citizens. According to postmaterialist theory, political transformation in advanced industrial societies originates in a shift in value orientations, which, in turn, stems from the dynamics of economic and social development—not in the character of the political environment.

Instrument and Data Base

Part of the force of the postmaterialist case derives from the massive data base accumulated from the Eurobarometer surveys conducted in the European Community (and subsequently the European Union) member states since 1970. These surveys yield a twenty-year time series for Belgium, France, Italy, the Netherlands, and Germany. For Denmark, Britain, Ireland, and Luxembourg, the data series starts in 1973. The series starts in 1980 for Greece, and in 1985 for Spain and Portugal. Although the full series starts in 1970, our starting point is 1973 when the survey was extended from five countries to nine. We use data from twenty-six Eurobarometer surveys for the period 1973–91.[2] Data from the spring and autumn surveys are pooled to give annual estimates.

The standard instrument for measuring materialist–postmaterialist orientations is a forced-choice question asking respondents to select their first and second priority from among four items. The introduction to the question varies but the items have remained unchanged:

A. Maintain order in the nation
B. Give people more say in the decisions of the government
C. Fight rising prices
D. Protect freedom of speech

Responses combining items (A) and (C) indicate a materialist orientation; items (B) and (D), a postmaterialist orientation. All other combinations constitute a 'mixed' value orientation. Variants of this measure, elaborated as three sets of four items or a combined set of four and eight items, have been used in some surveys. Although the twelve-item measure is considered more reliable (Inglehart 1990: 115; Abramson and Inglehart 1992: 339), we use data based on the four-item instrument as it provides the longest time series.

Underlying this instrument is the assumption that the rank order of people's priorities reveal 'something pervasive and enduring' (Inglehart 1990: 131) in their outlook. People's values are not directly observable but can be 'inferred from a consistent pattern of emphasis on given types of goals' (Inglehart 1990: 74). According to the evidence adduced by Inglehart (1990: 133–44), and others (Van Deth 1983*a*), the items in the instrument constitute a relatively robust structure which is, thus, interpretable as tapping two distinct value orientations. This approach to the interpretation of patterned—or constrained—attitudes is directly in line with the analytic strategy adopted in this volume (see Chapter 2).

General Developments

We start by looking at the two most general claims derived from postmaterialist theory. First, that there is a general shift from materialist to postmaterialist orientations across Western Europe as a whole. Secondly, within that general shift, postmaterialism has progressed further among the more advanced countries. We assess these claims by looking at trends in the materialist–postmaterialist index, calculated as the percentage of materialists minus the percentage of postmaterialists, shown in Figure 5.1.[3] As the data base varies, we look at the mean value of the index for the nine countries (EC-9) for which the data series starts in 1973. Following Van Deth's discussion in Chapter 3, Belgium, Denmark, Germany, France, Britain, Luxembourg, and the Netherlands are in the group of more advanced countries; Ireland, Spain, Greece, Portugal, and Italy in the group of less advanced countries.[4] The trend line for the less developed countries starts in 1973 with data for Italy and Ireland.[5]

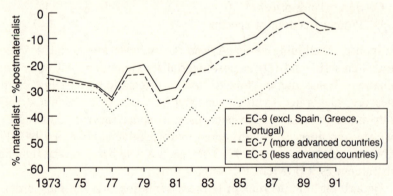

FIGURE 5.1. *Materialist–postmaterialist index in twelve West European countries, 1973–91*

Note: The trend lines are based on annualized percentages.

Source: Eurobarometer cumulated data (1973–91).

Despite some sharp dips, particularly during the 1970s, the percentage difference index indicates an overall rise in postmaterialism across much of Western Europe over the last twenty years or so. Moreover, the level of postmaterialism is consistently higher over the period in the group of more advanced countries. It is also evident that the general shift to postmaterialist orientations is entirely a feature of the 1980s, which is consonant with the effects of generational replacement (Inglehart and Abramson 1994: 341). Developments during the 1970s, however, give rise to a puzzle. With the arrival in the electorate of successive post-war birth years, we would expect the materialist–postmaterialist index to show some steady, if slow, advance. What we see, however, is erratic movements of the index with an overall fall, compared to 1973, until the early 1980s. Both the failure of the index to advance and the erratic movements can be attributed to period effects—which is consonant with the 'darkening of the economic skies' noted by Van Deth (Chapter 3). But if period effects inhibited the shift to postmaterialism during the 1970s, it seems odd that similar effects are not evident during the 1980s when, as Van Deth makes clear, most economic indicators pointed to troubled times. It appears, then, at a general level, that postmaterialism advanced during the 1980s despite a largely unpropitious environment. According to postmaterialist theory these different patterns are due to rising or falling inflation rates. We return to this point shortly.

The percentage difference index conceals interesting details about the raw distributions of the materialist, postmaterialist, and 'mixed' types.[6] Both among the EC-9 countries and in the richer and poorer group of countries, the mixed type predominates: the proportion of respondents with 'mixed' values seldom drops below 50 per cent, and often approaches 60 per cent.[7] Moreover, overall, the retreat from materialism is more evident than the advance of postmaterialism. Among the EC-9 countries, over the period, the proportion of materialists fell by some 12 percentage points whereas the proportion of postmaterialists rose by less than 8 points; among the seven richer countries, there was an 11 point decline in materialism but a 7 point increase in postmaterialism; and among the five poorer countries, an 11 point decline in materialism was accompanied by an increase in postmaterialism of only 3 percentage points. In short, the decline of materialism is not paralleled by an increase in postmaterialism: materialism and postmaterialism are not, it seems, two sides of the same coin. Rather, much of the change in the materialist–postmaterialist index consists of bulges in the 'mixed' value type as materialism declines.

Finally, the trends in Figure 5.1 indicate that electorates in Western Europe became, as predicted, increasingly polarized between materialists and postmaterialists during the 1980s. Among the more advanced countries, the 'tipping point' was virtually achieved by 1989 when the index stood at −0.2, although deteriorating thereafter. But the distributions of the value types reveal that, most of the time, the trend towards polarity is confined to less than half the public in these countries. The other half, and often more, is in the 'mixed' category. In other words, materialist–postmaterialist polarization characterizes only some half of the West European electorate. Discounting the other half sharpens the picture of value change but presents only half the picture.

Developments within Countries

Next, we consider whether these general trends represent typical developments. We noted that much of the apparent trend towards postmaterialism is actually due to declining materialism. So, at the same time as dropping down to a lower level of aggregation, we shift focus to concentrate on the progress of postmaterialism: how has

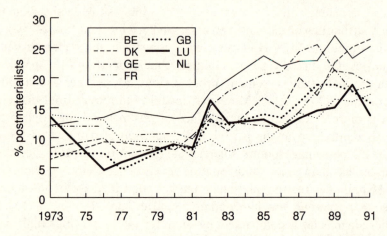

FIGURE 5.2. *Postmaterialism in seven more advanced West European countries, 1973–91*

Note and Source: See Figure 5.1.

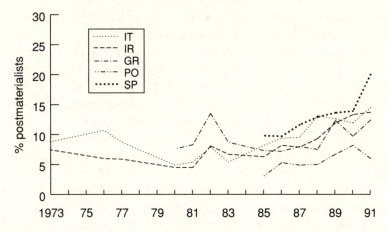

FIGURE 5.3. *Postmaterialism in five less advanced West European countries, 1973–91*

Note and Source: See Figure 5.1.

postmaterialism, rather than the materialist–postmaterialist index, fared over this period? The trends lines, based on the proportion of postmaterialists in each country, are shown in Figures 5.2 and 5.3.

Apart from the stubbornly low levels in Portugal, the trend lines here confirm the general advance of postmaterialism during the 1980s in both groups of countries. However, we now see much more fluctuation in the incidence of postmaterialism. Some part of the fluctuation, of course, can be put down to sampling error; pooling the data and using the summary index, as in Figure 5.1, smooths out some part of these fluctuations. None the less, it is evident that, within the overall advance of postmaterialism, progress is erratic and halting, particularly among the more advanced countries during the 1980s. Moreover, it becomes evident from Figure 5.2 that advance to the 'tipping point' is not a general development among the more advanced countries, but largely a function of the spectacular advance of postmaterialism in Denmark and the Netherlands. Indeed, the raw distributions reveal that, in 1991, postmaterialists outnumbered materialists only in Denmark (16 percentage points) and the Netherlands (10 points). The postmaterialist majorities in Germany during 1985–90, and the narrow majority in Luxembourg in 1990, were reversed by 1991; earlier high points in Britain and France had also fallen back by 1991.

The two figures also reveal that the differences between the more and the less advanced countries are less distinctive than suggested by a simple dichotomy. For example, in 1981 the proportion of postmaterialists in Germany (7 per cent) slipped close to the proportion in Italy (5 per cent); in 1991, postmaterialism was as pervasive in Ireland as in Luxembourg (14 per cent). Again, postmaterialism is at a higher level in Spain (20 per cent) in 1991 than in any advanced country except Denmark (26 per cent) and the Netherlands (25 per cent). Note, moreover, the continuing rise of postmaterialism, overall, in the less advanced countries during 1989–91 (with the partial exception of Portugal) and the turndown in the more advanced countries (with the exception of Denmark). Such a difference is unlikely to be due to differential population replacement rates (see Abramson and Inglehart 1992) but, rather, hints at a 'ceiling' effect—just as the low points of around 5 per cent in Ireland (1980 and 1981) and Portugal (1985), for example, suggest that there is a 'floor' of postmaterialism. However, in view of the fluctuations in these trends, we should not make too much of the particular numbers here.

These data yield two overriding impressions: the rapid progress of postmaterialism during the 1980s compared with the 1970s; and considerable fluctuation within a general trend towards postmaterialism. According to postmaterialist theory, the socialization hypothesis accounts for the general trend, the scarcity hypothesis accounts for the fluctuations. The fluctuations are particularly important as they suggest that the effects of scarcity can overtake the effects of socialization, rendering postmaterialist value orientations labile.[8] We look more closely at these fluctuations in the next section.

Fluctuations and Inflation

According to postmaterialist theory, fluctuations in the level of postmaterialism reflect period effects due to the impact of inflation, lagged by a year or so. High inflation rates following the oil shocks led a retreat towards materialism in the late 1970s and early 1980s; falling inflation rates after 1982 encouraged advances in postmaterialism in the later 1980s. Moreover, based on data for Germany, France, Britain, Italy, and the Netherlands for the 1970–87 period, Inglehart concludes (1990, 96): 'Not only overall, but on a nation by nation basis, there is an extremely close fit between inflation rates and short-term changes in [the materialist–postmaterialist index].'

Our initial tests revealed that, on the face of it, there is some systematic relationship between inflation and the materialist–postmaterialist index. Plotting the mean values for the index and the mean annual inflation rate lagged by one year across the EC-9 countries for 1973–90 (not shown here) displayed the one as almost a mirror image of the other. The results from regression analysis, shown in Table 5.1, indicate that, overall, inflation accounts for about 65 per cent of the variance in the materialist–postmaterialist index. However, both the index and inflation are trended variables, so we have to be wary about interpreting the relationship between them: what appears as a determinate relationship may turn out to be merely the effect of strong trends. One test is to see if the error terms are serially correlated. If so, a regression model may produce coefficients which are largely spurious. The results from applying the regression model to each of the EC-9 countries, along with the Durbin–Watson test for autocorrelation, are shown in Table 5.1.

Looking first at the EC-9, the b coefficient of -2.11 and t value of -5.68 suggest that the impact of inflation on changes in the index is significant if not strong. However, as d values of around 2.0 indicate a non-spurious correlation, the d of 0.96 suggests that this relationship is, indeed, suspect. Moreover, a plot of the residuals from the regression analysis (not shown here) reveals considerable variation in the index over and beyond what might be attributed to the effects of inflation.

TABLE 5.1. *Impact of inflation on postmaterialism: regression analysis*

Country	b coefficient	t ratio	R^2	Durbin–Watson d statistic
EC-9	-2.11	$-5.68**$	0.65	0.96
BE	-0.57	-0.99	-0.001	0.25
DK	-3.10	$-3.63*$	0.42	0.97
FR	-1.63	$-5.02**$	0.59	1.41
GE	-5.75	$-4.71**$	0.55	0.58
GB	-1.43	$-4.66**$	0.55	1.12
IR	-1.15	$-5.01**$	0.59	0.71
IT	-1.43	$-4.45**$	0.53	1.05
LU	-2.34	$-3.39*$	0.38	0.94
NL	-2.99	$-6.15**$	0.68	1.23

* $p< 0.01$ ** $p< 0.000$

Notes: Results based on OLS regression with postmaterialism as the dependent variable. Both postmaterialism and inflation are trended variables.

Sources: Eurobarometer cumulated data (1973–90); OECD (1986, 1992).

Furthermore, the residuals oscillate unpredictably around the mean instead of approaching towards zero, again suggesting that the apparent relationship between inflation and the index is largely spurious.

A very similar picture emerges from applying the same model to the (unweighted) data for each country. All the b coefficients have the correct sign, indicating a negative relationship between inflation and the index. Except for Belgium,[9] all the t values are statistically significant, and, except for Belgium, Luxembourg, and perhaps Denmark, the proportion of variance explained suggests that inflation accounts for a high proportion of the variance in the index. But, with the partial exception of France, all the models have a d value well below 2—indicating that what appears to be a significant relationship is actually the spurious effect of serially correlated variables. Furthermore, again with the partial exception of France, plotting the residuals (not shown here) reveals both considerable variation in the index unrelated to the impact of inflation and rather wild oscillations around the mean.

The poor fit of the model might, of course, be due to misspecification, either because some relevant variable is 'missing' or because the actual relationship between inflation and fluctuations in postmaterialism is complex.[10] Other research[11] indicates that the materialist–postmaterialist index is sensitive to a model of the macro economy which includes, in addition to inflation, the level of unemployment and changes in real gross domestic product per capita; following Inglehart and Abramson (1994), rates of economic growth might also be included.[12] However, to extend the model we used would substantially alter the application of postmaterialist theory in the case of West European societies. Another possibility is that the serial correlation in the model 'drowns' the impact of inflation. Experiments with 'correcting' for autocorrelation did, indeed, improve the fit of the model, but the relationships became difficult to interpret.[13] We conclude that the relationship between inflation and postmaterialism is either spurious in some considerable measure or more complex than the period effects implied by the scarcity hypothesis.

But focusing on fluctuations deflects attention from the main thrust of postmaterialist theory and the evidence of an overall increase in postmaterialist orientations in West European countries since the early 1970s. Postmaterialist theory is essentially a theory of generational change, of different value priorities as between pre-war and post-war generations. In the next section, we drop down to a yet lower level of aggregation, to examine levels of materialism and postmaterialism among different generations.

Inter-Generational Change

The shift to postmaterialist orientations is depicted as a development among the post-war generation which becomes a more widespread phenomenon as younger people replace older, pre-war generations.[14] More specifically, postmaterialist theory anticipates that each successively younger post-war cohort is more postmaterialist than its predecessor, and 'the existence of a significant watershed' (Inglehart 1981: 886) between the pre-war and post-war generations. The only deviation from this general pattern is among the youngest cohort, those born 1966–75, which, having lived through two recessions during their formative years, is less postmaterialist than the second youngest cohort (Inglehart 1990, 87).

The distribution of materialist and postmaterialist value types among eight cohorts in the twelve EC countries (EC-12) is shown in Table 5.2. The data for each country are pooled, allowing us to focus on underlying trends. To accommodate changes in the data base, the mean percentages for both EC-9 and EC-12 are shown. As sample numbers fall off sharply among those born before 1900, the oldest cohort consists of people born 1901–10. Those born 1941–50 spent most of their formative years in the environment of the post-war boom, so they are our first post-war cohort. Sample numbers are again rather lower among the youngest, post-1970 cohort, but it is included so that we can examine postmaterialism among people coming to maturity in the tougher times of the 1980s. As we are primarily interested in the advance of postmaterialism and the retreat of materialism, the distinction between materialists and postmaterialists is retained.

As anticipated, postmaterialism is consistently higher among post-war cohorts than pre-war cohorts, and, in most instances, each successive post-war cohort is more postmaterialist than its predecessor until the youngest cohort appears. Materialism is more widespread among pre-war cohorts than post-war cohorts, and there is a general downwards trend in materialism among successive post-war cohorts—with some exceptions among the two youngest cohorts. These trends are both an EC-wide phenomenon and a common, if not uniform, development in each country. The details may vary but the general pattern is clear:

materialists far outstrip postmaterialists among the oldest cohorts, but among the youngest cohorts the two groups are of roughly equal size.

However, while some of the deviations from these general patterns appear as aberrations, variations in the falling way of postmaterialism among the youngest cohort seem more systematic. Except in Spain, the shift towards postmaterialism with each successive cohort is arrested only in countries where 20 per cent or more of the second youngest cohort are postmaterialists; with the exception of Belgium, the arrest is evident only in the more advanced countries. In Italy, Ireland, Portugal, Spain, and Greece, postmaterialist advance continues through to the youngest cohort. These differences imply that the halting of the inter-generational trend towards postmaterialism among the youngest cohorts is confined to the more advanced countries. This, again, suggests that some 'ceiling' effect is at work: below the 20 per cent level, post-materialism continues to progress; above a level of about 20–25 per cent, further advance seems fragile.

The distributions in Table 5.2 also reveal a steady trend towards postmaterialism among pre-war cohorts. In most instances, the trend starts in the second oldest cohort and then advances at an increasing pace down through (most) post-war cohorts. This suggests that younger cohorts may be caught up in some long-term but accelerating develop-mental process. According to postmaterialist theory, however, post-war cohorts differ in outlook from pre-war cohorts not on account of some general long-term process but because of their socialization during the specific and 'historically unprecedented' conditions of the post-war years. Thus the question is not whether younger generations are more postmaterialist than older generations; the continuation of the trend towards postmaterialism among successive pre-war cohorts would have yielded higher levels of postmaterialism among post-war cohorts. Rather, the question is a matter of different *rates of change* in the shift towards postmaterialism as between pre-war and post-war cohorts.

Similar considerations apply to the shift away from materialism. The process is firmly established among the third oldest cohort, born 1921–30, and proceeds almost monotonically through to the youngest cohort; except in France, and perhaps Denmark and Britain, interruptions among the two youngest cohorts appear to be aberrations. Hence, the continuation of the trend among pre-war generations would have yielded declining levels of materialism among post-war cohorts. So,

TABLE 5.2. *Distribution of postmaterialists and materialists in eight birth cohorts, 1973–91*

Birth cohorts	BE	DK	FR	GE	GB	GR	IR	IT	LU	NL	PO	SP	EC-9 mean	EC-12 mean
(a) Postmaterialists														
1901–10	2	2	2	4	4	3	3	2	4	5	3	3	3.2	3.1
1911–20	5	5	5	7	7	4	3	3	4	8	2	3	5.1	4.7
1921–30	7	8	8	8	8	5	4	4	7	10	3	3	7.2	6.3
1931–40	9	10	10	10	10	6	5	6	7	13	4	5	8.6	7.7
1941–50	12	15	14	14	12	9	7	8	10	19	6	10	12.4	11.4
1951–60	14	21	17	21	14	13	8	13	17	24	6	18	16.6	15.5
1961–70	16	21	20	27	19	16	12	14	22	28	9	23	20.0	19.1
post-1970	17	18	16	24	19	17	20	17	17	27	10	24	19.4	18.8
(b) Materialists														
1901–10	33	33	40	30	31	51	38	43	29	29	51	56	34.1	38.7
1911–20	33	30	37	31	30	51	39	44	33	27	59	53	33.8	38.9
1921–30	31	25	33	30	25	47	38	42	30	24	54	51	30.8	35.7
1931–40	30	23	30	26	23	45	34	39	28	21	52	48	28.0	33.1
1941–50	25	20	23	22	22	41	32	33	24	18	45	38	24.2	28.5
1951–60	23	17	21	16	19	33	26	24	19	16	42	27	20.2	23.4
1961–70	24	15	22	13	15	25	23	25	17	14	36	18	18.6	20.6
post-1970	20	19	24	13	17	23	14	19	14	13	32	13	17.0	18.4

Notes: Entries are annualized and rounded percentages. The mixed types are excluded. The size of the pooled samples ranges between 11,703 (Luxembourg) and 40,464 (Italy).

Source: Eurobarometer cumulated data (1973–91).

again, what matters is the rate of change underlying the shift away from materialism among pre-war and post-war cohorts.

In Figure 5.4, we have plotted two measures of the incidence of postmaterialism across the eight cohorts, calculated as a mean for the EC countries. The level of postmaterialism within successive cohorts is shown in the lower plot; the rate of change towards postmaterialism between successive cohorts is shown in the upper plot. Although the mean levels among the EC-9 and the EC-12 countries are very similar, both are shown.

The trend line for the level of postmaterialism shows an almost smooth continuous development across the pre-war cohorts; indeed, if the progressively higher levels of postmaterialism among successive pre-war cohorts had been maintained, the level of postmaterialism would have been around 15 per cent (16 per cent for EC-9, 14 per

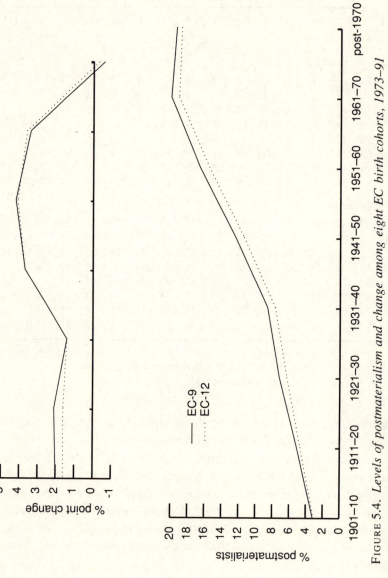

FIGURE 5.4. *Levels of postmaterialism and change among eight EC birth cohorts, 1973–91*

Source: Eurobarometer cumulated data (1973–91).

cent for EC-12) among the youngest cohort. The actual levels are around 19 per cent (see Table 5.2). None the less, the level of post-materialism rises more steeply among the post-war cohorts except the youngest. Turning to the rates of change between successive cohorts, we find two regimes: rates of increase of rather less than 2 percentage points between pre-war cohorts; rates of almost 4 percentage points between post-war cohorts except between the two youngest cohorts. If we exclude the very youngest cohort, the pace of the shift towards postmaterialism is rather more than twice as fast among post-war cohorts as among pre-war cohorts. Moreover, the first large jump in the rate of change does, indeed, occur between the last pre-war cohort (born 1931–40) and the first post-war cohort (born 1941–50). The pace of this shift accelerates between the first (1941–50) and second (1951–60) post-war cohorts, falls to a lower rate with the next cohort, and then goes into reverse. The war years, then, do mark a step shift towards postmaterialism. But the slow down and then reversal of the rate of change suggest that this step shift was a short-term boost—affecting the first and second post-war cohorts—to a long-term trend rather than a turning point. Moreover, and perhaps a chastening thought, postmaterialism is not much more widespread among post-war cohorts than it would have been had there been no post-war years of 'unprecedented' peace and prosperity.

In Figure 5.5, we have similarly plotted the incidence of materialism among the eight cohorts. The differences between the EC-9 and the EC-12 averages are more marked here, but the indicators run broadly parallel.

From the lower plot we see that materialism falls away fairly smoothly after the second oldest cohort but rather flattens out among the two youngest cohorts. Again, however, if we extrapolate the decline of materialism among the second and third pre-war cohorts, the war years are something less than a 'watershed'. The trend line for the EC-9 indicates that materialism might have fallen to a comparably low level among the youngest cohort if the decline among the two immediately pre-war cohorts (born 1911–20 and 1921–30) had been maintained. The actual level is 17 per cent; extending the pre-war trend yields an estimate of about 16.5 per cent. A similar estimate for EC-12 differs rather more—about 21.5 per cent as against an actual level of 18.4 per cent. As for the rate of change, again we have two regimes: one marked by the distinctively faster rate of decline as between the last pre-war cohort and the first post-war cohort, and between the first two post-war

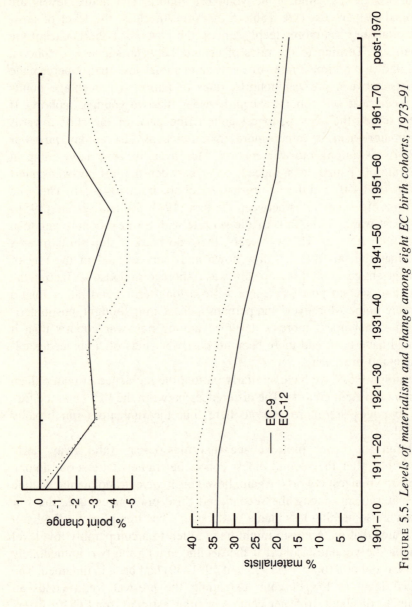

FIGURE 5.5. *Levels of materialism and change among eight EC birth cohorts, 1973–91*

Source: Eurobarometer cumulated data (1973–91).

TABLE 5.3. *Materialists and postmaterialists in eight birth cohorts,*
1973, 1981, and 1990

Birth cohorts	1973		1981		1990	
	Materialists	Post-materialists	Materialists	Post-materialists	Materialists	Post-materialists
1901–10	48	4	53	4	36	5
1911–20	42	6	50	4	36	7
1921–30	39	7	50	7	32	9
1931–40	35	8	44	7	26	15
1941–50	27	14	40	10	22	18
1951–60	23	20	34	13	20	20
1961–70	–	–	31	15	16	23
post-1970	–	–	–	–	15	24
N	4,601	1,291	10,586	2,383	6,096	4,100

Note: Entries are EC-9 means in annualized and rounded percentages.

Sources: European Community Survey; Eurobarometer, Nos. 15, 16, 33, and 34.

cohorts; the other constituted by the similarly slower rates of decline in the two 'tails' between the earlier pre-war cohorts and between the later post-war cohorts. In other words, while the first two post-war cohorts moved rather sharply away from materialism, this seems, again, to be a short-term boost to a longer-term trend.

The post-war years of boom evidently made a difference to declining materialism and rising postmaterialism by speeding up developments already in train. But the steep drop in the postmaterialist rate of change and the levelling off in the materialist rate of change when we get to the two youngest cohorts suggest that this boost may be expended. It is particularly apposite in this instance to put the jury 'out' until the time series is extended to include the latest cohort, born 1980–90.

Intra-Generational Differences

According to postmaterialist theory, the shift to postmaterialist orientations is a generational development. Thus, inter-generational differences should be matched by intra-generational stability, with each generation broadly retaining its distinctive mix of materialist and postmaterialist orientations as it moves along its life course. In Table 5.3, we show the proportion of materialists and postmaterialists, as a mean for the EC-9 countries, in the same eight birth cohorts at three time points: 1973, 1981, and 1990. Spain, Greece, and Portugal are excluded in order to maintain a stable data base over the period.

These distributions show clear stability in inter-cohort differences: with only minor exceptions, the postmaterialist group is larger, and the materialist group is smaller, among each successive birth cohort at all three time points. More striking, however, is the intra-cohort variation. In 1981, every cohort is more materialist and less postmaterialist than in 1973; in 1990, every cohort is less materialist and more postmaterialist than in 1981; most cohorts are more postmaterialist and less materialist in 1990 than in 1973. The consistent direction of these variations suggests rather strong period effects.

We have already noted difficulties about explaining period effects in terms of inflation, but there may be other, unspecified, period effects. Whatever these may be, the important point is that period effects should influence each cohort in much the same way. Uncovering period effects among birth cohorts, however, is confounded by life-cycle effects: intra-cohort variations in the levels of materialism and postmaterialism may be due to either, or both, short-term period effects or changes in orientation as cohorts move through their life-cycle. But cohort effects, life-cycle effects, and period effects are linearly dependent on one another; any one of them is a linear function of the other two. Thus distinguishing between these effects—let alone measuring their impact on one another—is not readily done.

We can go some way in unpicking these intricacies by presenting standard cohort tables, and following a procedure proposed by Klecka (1971). His method is designed primarily to reveal the relative impact of cohort and life-cycle effects on social change, but we use it, initially, to estimate the inter-cohort uniformity, or otherwise, of changing levels of materialism and postmaterialism between the three times points. First, we calculate the overall proportion of change (P) between the first and second time points, and the second and third time points. On the assumption that each cohort changes by the same proportion, the value for P allows us, secondly, to estimate the expected level of materialism and postmaterialism within each cohort at the second and third time points, given the level at the previous time point. Then, thirdly, we calculate the proportion of the deviation (DP) from the general trend within each cohort at the second and third time points.[15] DP values close to zero indicate that the extent of change within a birth cohort reflects the general trend; values radically different from zero indicate intra-cohort change over and beyond the general period effect. These estimates of inter-cohort variation in intra-cohort change between 1973 and 1981, and 1981 and 1990, are shown in Table 5.4*a*.

In the next step, we focus on the relative contribution of cohort effects and life-cycle effects to changes in the level of materialism and postmaterialism at the second and third time points. First, we calculate, similarly, *DP* values among age groups, shown in Table 5.4*b*. Secondly, the *DP* values in each column are averaged to yield the average percentage difference (*ADP*) between two time points. Comparing the *ADP*s in the two tables allows us to estimate whether

TABLE 5.4. *Cohort and life-cycle matrices for materialists and postmaterialists, 1973, 1981, 1990*

Birth cohort	Percentage materialists					Percentage postmaterialists				
	1973	(DP)	1981	(DP)	1990	1973	(DP)	1981	(DP)	1990
(a) Cohort matrix										
1961–70	–		31.1	(−0.04)	16.1	–		14.8	(−0.17)	23.3
1951–60	22.6	(−0.06)	33.7	(−0.09)	19.9	19.8	(−0.16)	13.0	(−0.19)	19.6
1941–50	26.8	(+0.10)	39.5	(+0.03)	22.1	14.1	(−0.10)	10.0	(−0.01)	18.4
1931–40	34.8	(−0.04)	43.7	(+0.09)	25.9	8.4	(+0.02)	6.6	(+0.16)	14.5
1921–30	39.1	(−0.04)	50.3	(+0.18)	32.2	6.8	(+0.25)	6.6	(−0.24)	9.4
1911–20	42.4	(−0.12)	49.9	(+0.34)	36.3	6.3	(−0.23)	3.8	(−0.05)	6.8
pre-1911	47.9	(−0.18)	52.5	(+0.26)	35.7	3.6	(+0.09)	3.9	(−0.40)	4.5
Mean	37.5		47.7		25.8	12.6		9.8		18.5
N	4,601		10,586		6,096	1,291		2,383		4,100
ADP		*0.091*		*0.149*			*0.142*		*0.174*	
(b) Life-cycle matrix										
22 or younger	22.7	(+0.21)	32.1	(−0.24)	14.2	20.0	(−0.12)	14.6	(−0.07)	25.5
23–32	26.9	(+0.06)	33.4	(−0.09)	17.8	14.1	(+0.09)	12.8	(−0.11)	21.5
33–42	34.7	(+0.01)	40.9	(−0.14)	20.4	8.4	(+0.10)	7.7	(+0.39)	20.0
43–52	39.2	(−0.01)	45.4	(−0.14)	22.8	6.9	(+0.25)	7.2	(+0.26)	16.8
53–62	42.4	(−0.01)	49.1	(+0.01)	28.9	6.1	(+0.16)	5.9	(+0.06)	11.7
63–72	47.3	(−0.07)	51.8	(+0.07)	32.5	4.1	(−0.12)	3.0	(+0.68)	9.4
73 and older	57.7	(−0.23)	51.8	(+0.21)	36.7	1.6	(+1.80)	3.7	(−0.13)	6.1
Mean	36.9		43.3		25.3	12.9		10.3		19.2
N	4,348		11,681		6,436	1,263		2,456		4,672
ADP		*0.086*		*0.129*			*0.377*		*0.243*	

Note: The data for 1981 and 1990 are annualized averages.

Sources: European Community Survey (1973); Eurobarometer, Nos. 15, 16, 33, and 34.

cohort differences or life-cycle changes have the greater impact on intra-cohort variations. A lower *ADP* in the cohort table compared to the life-cycle table indicates greater consistency over time among birth cohorts than age groups—showing that change over time is primarily a cohort effect. Conversely, a lower *ADP* in the life-cycle table compared to the cohort table points to a life-cycle effect. This approach does not, of course, resolve the entanglement of period effects, cohort effects, and life-cycle effects in accounting for change, but it gives some purchase on the complexities of analysing generational differences over time.

Concentrating first on the *DP* values in Table 5.4*a*, we find two values close to zero and four values which are fairly close. Thus, for example, among the second post-war cohort (born 1951–60) the shift towards postmaterialism between 1981 and 1990 was just 1 per cent less than expected based on the general trend. Again, among the last pre-war cohort (born 1931–40), the shift towards materialism between 1973 and 1981 was 4 per cent less than expected. All the other *DP* values are quite sizeable, however, ranging from 0.5 to as high 0.40. In other words, most cohorts show some considerable deviation from the general trend. Moreover, the deviations vary between plus and minus to no evident pattern. Thus, although Table 5.3 suggested a general shift in value orientations between the time points, these results reveal that intra-cohort variations involve, as anticipated, influences other than period effects.

We move now to the second stage of the analysis, comparing the *ADP* values for the cohort matrix and the life-cycle matrix shown in Table 5.4. The results are rather startling.[16] Looking at the two matrices for the proportion of materialists, in both instances the *ADP* for the life-cycle matrix (0.086 and 0.129) is lower than for the cohort matrix (0.091 and 0.149). Thus, we conclude that changes in the proportion of materialists—between 1973 and 1981, and between 1981 and 1990—are primarily a cohort effect. Turning to the two matrices for the proportion of postmaterialists, however, we find that the *ADP* values for the cohort matrix (0.142 and 0.174) are lower than for the life-cycle matrix (0.377 and 0.243). In other words, changes in the proportion of postmaterialists between the three time points are primarily a life-cycle effect. Evidently, intra-cohort shifts into and out of materialist and postmaterialist priorities are underpinned by different dynamics—adding a further level of complexity to the interwovenness of cohort, life-cycle, and period effects.[17]

What conclusions can we draw from this review of aggregate-level trends? As our analysis is confined to the countries of the European Community, we should not generalize too broadly from our findings. None the less, three conclusions seem warranted. First, on the one hand, materialism has tended to decline and postmaterialism to have grown, overall, over the last twenty years; postmaterialism has progressed further among people in the more advanced industrial societies; materialism is more a feature of older generations, postmaterialism of younger groups. On the other hand, the incidence of materialism and post-materialism is not always widely different as between the more and less advanced societies. Again, the general trend towards postmaterialism is also evident among older groups, suggesting that the pre-war years, too, were conducive to a shift in value orientations. Moreover, the tide seems to have rather turned against further advances in post-materialism; whether this constitutes a temporary halt, a 'ceiling' effect, or a turning back to 'older' priorities we cannot tell until the data series is extended well into the 1990s.

Secondly, the Second World War marks a shift in value orientations in so far as the pace of change quickens among people coming to maturity during the years of the post-war boom. However, the pace slows again among people born later and goes into reverse among the most recent cohorts. Thus, the representation of the war as a 'watershed' is less persuasive than the effects of the post-war boom as a boost to longer-term trends. The boost seems to be exhausted.

Thirdly, over the long haul, the shift to postmaterialism shows a certain tenacity. Certainly, levels of materialism and postmaterialism lack the stability which might be expected of 'something pervasive and enduring in one's outlook' (Inglehart 1990: 131). None the less, the intra-generational retreat of materialist orientations and advance of postmaterialist orientations works in favour of the persistence, if not necessarily the further advance, of postmaterialism despite economic setbacks.

The ' Impact' of Social Antecedents

In the following sections, we drop down to the individual level to examine the social antecedents of postmaterialism. According to post-materialist theory, postmaterialism is primarily a phenomenon of the young, highly educated members of the 'new class'. Thus the micro-level propositions focus on age, education, and occupation. However, the relevance of these variables is not independent of the environmental argument, which means we have to be cautious about talking in terms of their 'impact' on the development of postmaterialism. So, before looking at the data, a word about the place of age, education, and occupation in postmaterialist theory.

Age is a matter of cohort differences: the distinctive outlooks of generations follow not from life-cycle effects but from the different environments in which individuals come to maturity. Hence, again, we have to draw comparisons across birth cohorts, and the definitive difference between cohorts is the enlarged structure of opportunities open to post-war generations—in particular, the expansion of higher education and shifts in the structure of employment. In other words, whereas the macro-level propositions in postmaterialist theory—in the West European context—emphasize the effects of peace and prosperity in generating a sense of security, the individual-level propositions relate not to differential perceptions of security but to the different life chances of pre- and post-war generations. Postmaterialism among younger birth cohorts is not a matter of 'youthful idealism' (Abramson and Inglehart 1992: 200), but of being young during an 'unprecedented' historical period.

Education is relevant in two rather different ways. In the first place, rising levels of education have generally promoted higher levels of 'cognitive mobilization'—a process entailing 'the dissemination of skills needed to cope with an extensive political community' (Inglehart 1990: 337). Higher education, in particular, stimulates values which emphasize the 'needs for belonging, esteem, and self-realization' (Inglehart 1977b: 5; 1990: fig. 0.1). In this sense, the influence of education reflects the significance of educational expansion in the post-war period—so tying it to changes in the societal environment. In the second place, experience of higher education is a reflection of 'formative security'; the children of well-off parents are the most likely to attend university. In this respect, the influence of education is tied to the socialization hypothesis. Neither account, however, points to a direct causal association between postmaterialism and education: what it is about cognitive mobilization which promotes postmaterialist orientations, rather than other possibilities, is not specified in postmaterialist theory; in interpreting higher education as a reflection of formative security, the causal work is done by formative security. Moreover, as it is well educated members of post-war cohorts who are most likely to be postmaterialists, the significance of education is tied in with birth cohort—reflecting enlarged educational opportunities after the war. At the same time, education is tied in with occupation by dint of the requirements of 'knowledge' occupations.

The relevance of occupation is oblique. Postmaterialist orientations are associated with the emergence of a 'new class' of highly educated young people employed in 'knowledge' occupations in advanced economies. Despite confusion about definitions of the 'new class', postmaterialist orientations are represented as constitutive of this new class: 'the rise of Postmaterialism and its subsequent penetration of technocratic and professional élites has been a major factor behind the emergence of the new class' (Inglehart 1990: 332). Postmaterialism is not a product of the 'new class' but, rather, shapes the career choices of 'young professionals, civil servants, managers and politicians' (Inglehart 1990: 67). Postmaterialist orientations are antecedent to, not consequent upon, occupation. Moreover, as the expansion of career opportunities is a function of welfare states and the emergence of advanced industrial economies, the significance of occupation is closely tied to both birth cohort and structural change. Thus, the significance of occupation lies not in promoting postmaterialism but in providing congenial employment for postmaterialists.

That postmaterialists are located in a social nexus constituted by the intertwining of generation, education, and occupation against a background of structural change is not a theoretical problem; many social phenomena are similarly complex. What is problematic, however, is that the individual-level variables lack independent causal force. That is, it is not when people were born and grew up, their education, or their occupation, as such, which explains whether or not they are post-materialists. Rather, these variables are the bearers, at the individual level, of the effects of macro-level changes in the economic and social environment—especially unprecedented security and opportunity. Thus, rather than explaining the emergence of postmaterialist orientations, generation, education, and occupation point to where postmateri-alists are to be found. In the next section, we examine whether or not postmaterialists are most likely to be found among the highly educated post-war recruits to the 'new class'.

Social Correlates of Postmaterialism

In Table 5.5, we present the results from multiple classification analysis of the relationship between birth cohort, education, and occupation and

TABLE 5.5. *Relationship between postmaterialism, birth cohorts, education, and occupation in EC-12 countries, 1973–91*

	eta	beta	N
Birth cohorts	0.22*	0.17*	
1901–10	−0.30	−0.26	15,101
1911–20	−0.21	−0.17	31,980
1921–30	−0.12	−0.08	45,932
1931–40	−0.08	−0.04	47,753
1941–50	0.02	0.03	56,714
1951–60	0.11	0.08	63,231
1961–70	0.20	0.14	48,875
post-1970	0.36	0.27	9,469
Education	0.24*	0.16*	
15 years or younger	−0.17	−0.11	137,617
16–19 years	0.03	0.01	108,149
20 years or older	0.25	0.19	46,775
Still studying	0.30	0.17	28,958
Occupation	0.20*	0.08*	
Executives and top managers	0.28	0.16	16,981
Professionals	0.18	0.04	4,681
White collar workers	0.10	0.03	52,505
Manual workers	−0.03	−0.02	53,852
Business owners	−0.03	−0.01	18,485
Farmers and fishermen	−0.15	−0.07	11,155
Retired	−0.14	0.07	47,511
Housewives; not employed	−0.13	−0.07	69,150
Students	0.28	−0.03	28,843
Unemployed	0.05	0.02	18,336
$R^2 = 0.080$			

* $p \leq 001$

Note: Entries are coefficients from multiple classification analysis.

Source: Eurobarometer cumulated data (1973–91).

the materialist–postmaterialist (percentage difference) index across the EC-12 countries. As before, we used the 1973–91 cumulated data, which smoothes out fluctuations and allows us to uncover underlying patterns. As the education variable records the age at which respondents completed full-time education, we assume that the most highly educated are those who are twenty years or older before completion. Note, too, that the occupational groups lack the ordering of an explicit class schema (cf. Erikson and Goldthorpe 1992: 35–46).

Looking first at their general relevance, all three variables show highly significant coefficients. Moreover, as singular characteristics, birth cohort, education, and occupation are of broadly similar relevance. But the beta values reveal that after controlling for the other two variables, occupation drops away compared to birth cohort and education which are of almost equal significance. Thus, although postmaterialist theory is primarily about generational differences, education emerges as a comparable discriminator. However, despite the high levels of significance, the net relationship is rather weak, accounting for only some 8 per cent of the variance in the index. According to these results, birth cohort, education, and occupation yield a rather fragile account of the social antecedents of postmaterialism. But this general picture conceals important differences between the subgroups.

Among the birth cohorts, both the eta and beta coefficients reveal the almost monotonic progress of postmaterialism as we move from the oldest to the youngest cohorts. In contrast to our earlier, more mixed, findings (see Table 5.2), this very clear pattern accords with the generational thesis of postmaterialist theory.[18] The significance of education similarly increases as we move up the education hierarchy. In particular, those remaining in education for longest—usually the university educated—are three times as likely to be postmaterialists as those whose education finished at secondary level, and twice as likely as those who had some three years of post-school education.

The data are less revealing about postmaterialism and the 'new class' as the occupational groupings do not allow us to distinguish between the 'old' middle class and the 'new class'. None the less, the beta coefficients for the occupational groups reveal some interesting contrasts. Most notable is the concentration of postmaterialism among 'executives and managers' as against materialism among 'farmers and fishermen'—apparently the poles of a continuum among the workforce. More surprising is the much weaker relationship between 'professionals' and postmaterialism compared to 'executives and top managers', and the very narrow difference between 'professionals' and 'white-collar workers'. This suggests that occupational sector may be more relevant than class in locating postmaterialism. The very narrow difference between manual workers and business owners points in the same direction. Finally, note that the relatively strong showing of postmaterialism among students disappears once birth cohort and education are taken into account.

Cross-National Differences

Does the general pattern emerging from Table 5.5 hold up across all the EC-12 countries? In Table 5.6, we set out the results from applying the same model to each of the EC-12 countries.

Looking first at the eta coefficients, we find a very mixed picture. In five countries (Germany, Britain, Ireland, Luxembourg, Spain) the principal—singular—discriminator is birth cohort; in five countries (Belgium, Denmark, France, Greece, the Netherlands) it is education; and in Portugal it is occupation. Moreover, in some instances, as in Greece, Italy, and the Netherlands, the eta coefficients for all three variables are of similar magnitude. The picture clears somewhat when we look at the beta values. After controlling for the other two variables, birth cohort is clearly the more revealing correlate in six countries (Germany, Britain, Ireland, Italy, Luxembourg, Spain), and marginally the more revealing in another four countries (France, Greece, Netherlands, Portugal). Education stands out as the most relevant variable only in Denmark and Belgium. Occupation emerges as the weakest correlate in every country except Portugal, although in several instances occupation lags behind less obviously than in the general case—for example, matching education in Spain and almost matching birth cohort in Portugal and Belgium. In short, as the core of postmaterialist theory proposes, cohort differences are generally more apt to locating post-materialists.

Even so, the combined influence of these individual-level attributes is weak. Taken together, the three variables capture 10 per cent or more of the variance in postmaterialism in three countries, and 8 per cent or so in a further six. Moreover, with these personal attributes accounting for some 5 per cent of the difference in outlooks in Britain and Ireland but around 12–13 per cent in Spain and Denmark, the significance of this social nexus evidently varies cross-nationally.

Differences between the birth cohorts, education groups, and occupational groups for each country (not shown here), are very similar to the general pattern evident in Table 5.5. Except in Spain, the relevance of birth cohort increases with each successive cohort—rising to a modest 0.15 (beta) in France and Denmark but an impresssive 0.42 in Italy and 0.49 in Ireland among the post-1971 cohort. Similarly, postmaterialism is almost invariably most in evidence among the university educated—but its relevance varies between 0.27 in Denmark to 0.06 in Ireland. Finally, postmaterialism is largely characteristic of 'executives and top

TABLE 5.6. *Relevance of birth cohorts, education, and occupation to materialism–postmaterialism in EC-12 countries, 1973–91*

	Birth cohorts	Education	Occupation	R^2	N
Belgium					
eta	0.19	0.25	0.22	0.076	38,246
beta	0.11	0.17	0.09		
Denmark					
eta	0.23	0.32	0.21	0.118	37,642
beta	0.16	0.26	0.08		
France					
eta	0.23	0.27	0.25	0.103	40,055
beta	0.18	0.17	0.12		
Germany					
eta	0.24	0.23	0.18	0.091	39,306
beta	0.24	0.16	0.12		
Britain					
eta	0.19	0.15	0.12	0.048	39,607
beta	0.20	0.09	0.07		
Greece					
eta	0.23	0.25	0.24	0.090	24,226
beta	0.16	0.15	0.11		
Ireland					
eta	0.23	0.15	0.15	0.059	37,448
beta	0.23	0.06	0.07		
Italy					
eta	0.25	0.25	0.23	0.092	40,464
beta	0.21	0.16	0.11		
Luxembourg					
eta	0.24	0.22	0.20	0.082	11,713
beta	0.22	0.12	0.10		
Netherlands					
eta	0.22	0.24	0.22	0.087	38,710
beta	0.17	0.15	0.11		
Portugal					
eta	0.19	0.21	0.23	0.071	14,000
beta	0.14	0.09	0.13		
Spain					
eta	0.32	0.27	0.29	0.128	14,067
beta	0.26	0.10	0.10		

Notes: Entries are coefficients from multiple classification analysis. All coefficients are significant at the 0.01 level at least.

Source: Eurobarometer cumulated data (1973–91).

managers', although professionals run them a close second in Germany and Italy. By contrast, farmers, fishermen, and those who are not employed—largely housewives—tend to be the most materialist groups. In short, postmaterialism is primarily sited among highly educated younger people.

The results of our analysis, then, depart from the postmaterialist account in two particulars. Whereas postmaterialism is identified as a distinctive phenomenon among young, well educated members of the 'new class', we find the net relationship between postmaterialism and birth cohort, education, and occupation to be rather weak. Capturing only around 8–10 per cent of the variance in postmaterialism in several countries—and notably less in Ireland and Britain—these variables supply a rather insubstantial account of postmaterialism.

Secondly, whereas highly educated young professionals and technocrats are regarded as the primary locus of postmaterialism, our findings indicate that occupation is a relatively marginal site of postmaterialism. Moreover, in so far as occupation is relevant, postmaterialism is more evident among executive and managerial groups than among professionals. The limitations of the occupational data preclude us from drawing any conclusions about the 'new class'.[19] At the individual level, then, more seems to be at work in the emergence of postmaterialism than the arrival of a new group of young, highly educated, relatively autonomous professionals.

Education and Postmaterialism

In pointing to the significance of generational differences, our findings for the social antecedents of postmaterialism accord with postmaterialist theory. However, we noted earlier that the significance of the generational factor lies in the greater security and opportunity—educational and occupational—enjoyed by post-war cohorts. There are no data about perceptions of security, and occupation provides a weaker account of postmaterialism than either generation or education. In Table 5.2, we saw that the incidence of postmaterialism generally rose steadily among successive birth cohorts—despite some falling off among the post-1970 cohort—but seldom exceeded the 25 per cent level in any cohort. In other words, postmaterialists are predominantly drawn from among post-war cohorts but post-war cohorts are not preponderantly postmaterialist in orientation. That leaves one last question to be addressed: postmaterialists are predominantly well educated, but are the well educated preponderantly postmaterialist?

In Table 5.7, we present the mean distribution of postmaterialism among three groups according to educational level for each of the EC-12 countries over the 1973–91 period. Those who left school at 15 or younger are in the 'low' group; those who had some years of schooling beyond the minimum school-leaving age are in the 'intermediate' group; and the 'high' group consists of those whose education continued beyond the age of twenty and those still studying. Again, we use the cumulated data in order to smooth out fluctuations; the standard deviation indicates the variation around the mean over the period.

In every instance, the proportion of postmaterialists is highest among the most highly educated. Moreover, there is an almost monotonic increase in the proportion of postmaterialists as we move up through the educational levels. The proportion of postmaterialists among the least educated reaches double figures only in the Netherlands; the proportion of postmaterialists among the 'intermediate' group comes close to the proportion among the highly educated only in Ireland, Italy, and Portugal. Moreover, the modest—in most instances, very low—standard deviations indicate that this is a fairly constant picture. Even so, the proportion of postmaterialists among the highly educated reaches above 25 per cent only in Germany, the Netherlands, and Spain. Indeed, in three countries (Ireland, Italy, and Portugal), over the period as a whole, less than one-sixth of the highly educated are postmaterialists. Thus, as with generation, higher education is indicative but not definitive of postmaterialists.

TABLE 5.7. *Postmaterialism among educational groups, 1973–91*

Educational level	BE	DK	FR	GB	GE	GR	IR	IT	LU	NL	PO	SP
Low	5	7	6	9	9	5	6	5	7	10	4	7
s.d.	1.7	3.8	2.6	3.7	4.5	1.7	2.6	1.8	3.6	2.5	1.6	2.0
Intermediate	11	13	12	12	15	12	8	12	11	17	10	18
s.d.	3.0	4.5	3.1	4.2	6.3	2.9	2.9	3.0	3.8	4.2	2.0	4.1
High	20	24	24	24	27	17	11	15	19	27	12	27
s.d.	4.4	6.3	4.5	8.2	9.6	3.2	4.0	3.9	5.1	6.5	2.2	3.3

Note: Entries are percentages and standard deviations.

Source: Eurobarometer cumulated data (1973–91).

That generation and higher education are the best predictors of postmaterialism yet not critical markers reflects the weakness of the postmaterialists' profile. Certainly, postmaterialists are preponderantly well educated young people in typically middle-class occupations, but the young and well educated members of the middle class are not preponderantly postmaterialists. Even in the more advanced countries, in environments conducive to re-evaluating value priorities, something more is involved before the well educated young come to postmaterialism. This conclusion does not necessarily undermine the role attributed in postmaterialist theory to the well educated young members of the 'new class' as the major vehicle of social and political change. However, it does imply that the individual-level propositions in postmaterialist theory are underspecified.

Conclusion

Indisputably, across much of Western Europe, value orientations are shifting. The fading of religious orientations, the weakening social bases of left–right materialism, the emergence of feminist, 'green', and 'postmodernist' outlooks, are all indicative of a general process of value change. This is not surprising, given the structural transformations characterizing the post-war period; the less advanced countries seem to be different only in coming later to these processes. And the concept of materialist–postmaterialist value shift evidently captures some part of this process of changing value orientations. However, our analysis suggests that postmaterialist theory is but an approximation of the social realities underlying contemporary value shifts. As becomes evident in later chapters, both the process of value change and the content of new value priorities are more complex, and more differentiated, than postmaterialist theory allows.

Finally, we should note the contrast between the compelling simplicity and parsimony of postmaterialist theory and the intricacies of the empirical evidence. While premised on two straightforward assumptions, postmaterialist theory gives rise to empirical propositions which are not readily amenable to definitive test. In part, this is due to the interweaving of macro-level propositions about structural changes in the economic and social environment and micro-level propositions about what kind of people are the principal agents of a general shift from materialist to postmaterialist value orientations. And in part it is due to the manifold nature of change over time—particularly pertinent in a theory which endeavours to explain societal change in terms of individual-level change within environments undergoing long-term change but with short-term interruptions. The potency of postmaterialist theory lies in providing us with one of the few explicated accounts of value change in contemporary West European societies. In subsequent chapters of this volume, the focus turns to examine the potency of postmaterialist value orientations in stimulating changes in political behaviour.

NOTES

1. Inglehart's position on the needs hierarchy remains ambiguous. He agrees with critics (see Lawler 1973) that the empirical evidence for 'higher order needs' is weak (Inglehart 1990: 152) but proposes that the notion is intuitively plausible: 'the idea of a need hierarchy would probably command almost universal assent' (1990: 68).

2. These are Eurobarometer, Nos. 1, 5–8, 13–20, and 23–35. The data are drawn from a cumulative Eurobarometer file, supplied by the Zentralarchiv in Cologne. Weights for the file allow the data to be used both as national cross-sectional data for country-specific analyses, and as pooled cross-sectional data for the EC countries as a whole. Unweighted data are used for comparisons within and between countries; data weighted according to population size are used in comparisons over time across the EC as a whole.

3. The coding of the value types is: materialists = 1; mixed = 2; postmaterialists = 3; missing = 0.

4. The sharp differences in economic development between the north and south, and extensive 'welfare clientalism' (Esping Anderson 1990: 39), might question placing Italy among the less advanced countries. However, the Italian data make only a marginal difference to the distributions in Fig. 5.1, depressing the index for the EC-9 by an average of 1.5 percentage points and raising it by 0.31 points for the EC-5 countries.

5. The addition of Spain, Greece, and Portugal makes little difference to the trend line for Italy and Ireland.

6. The percentage difference index can yield a misleading impression of the raw data in two ways. First, it can register an advance in postmaterialism when the raw data record only a decline in materialism. For example, 15% postmaterialists and 35% materialists yields an index score of −20; 15% postmaterialists and 25% materialists gives a score of −10, which indicates a 10 point advance in postmaterialism when, in fact, the proportion of postmaterialists has not changed. Secondly, the index can exaggerate the shift from materialism to postmaterialism. For example, a rise from 15% to 20% postmaterialists and a fall from 35% to 30% materialists

results in halving the index—from -20 to -10—when, in fact, the proportion of postmaterialists has increased by only one-third.

7. The size of the 'mixed' group falls to a low of 39.2% among the less advanced countries in 1980, and ranges between 40% and 45% in 1977, 1979, 1981, and 1983. These low points are accompanied by an increase in the size of the materialist group.

8. Clarke and Dutt (1991: 915–18) find very high turnover rates in responses to the individual items in the survey instrument between the first and second wave of the Political Action project. For example, 53% of the Dutch sample and 60% of the German sample changed their first priority; 38% of the Dutch and 48% of the German sample changed their materialist or postmaterialist classification.

9. Inglehart also finds Belgium a deviant case, which he attributes to 'a pervasive malaise in Belgian society during the 1980s' (1990: 96) following the introduction of severe austerity measures by the government (1990: 27).

10. Clarke and Dutt (1991), for example, argue that the apparent increase in post-materialism during the 1980s is an artefact of the survey instrument. The item 'fight rising prices' taps concern about inflation but there is no equivalent item to tap concern about unemployment, so people concerned about rising unemployment are likely to select the item 'give people more say in the decisions of government'. Thus, people who are concerned about unemployment are not only precluded from emerging as materialists but such concerns tilt the survey instrument towards postmaterialism.

11. See, for example, Clarke, Dutt, and Rapkin (1994).

12. It is unclear if the significance of economic growth rates (Inglehart and Abramson 1994: 351) applies in the case of the advanced industrial societies of Western Europe. However, Inglehart and Abramson concede that 'a resurgence of post-materialism was accompanied by a steep rise in unemployment' during the years 1981–5 but that, otherwise, 'the apparent causal linkage is spurious' (1994: 344, 346). It may also be that the three major periods of recession had a different specific character.

13. A first-order Cochrane–Orcutt correction yielded much improved d-values but also much lower b coefficients, non-significant t-ratios, and error terms close to 1 in every case except France. A second order correction provided a much improved fit, and a third order correction a pretty good fit, except for Denmark and Germany. At this point, the model becomes methodologically and substantively very complex.

14. An alternative, life-cycle, explanation for inter-generational differences (see e.g. Jagodzinski 1983) is no part of postmaterialist theory. Inglehart takes the view that 'belief in an ageing effect must depend on faith alone' (1990: 73), although Abramson and Inglehart (1992: 191) present data demonstrating that materialism increases with age. Even so, the postmaterialist argument remains that inter-cohort differences are due to generational effects (Inglehart and Abramson 1994). We concentrate on examining the empirical claims arising from postmaterialist theory.

15. The formulae used are: $P = \overline{Y} / \overline{X}$; $Y_{ei} = PX_i$; $DP = (Y - Y_{ei}) / Y_{ei}$, where Y_{ei} is the estimated value for group $_i$ derived from X_i.

16. But not altogether surprising; Van Deth (1983b) uncovered much the same pattern in analysing panel data from the two Political Action surveys.

17. In contrast to the cohort matrix, there is some suggestion of a systematic patterning

to intra-cohort change in the life-cycle matrix. However, whereas there is only one exception to a linear patterning to intra-age-group change among materialists, it does not hold up among postmaterialists.

18. Birth cohort is evidently more significant among the two oldest and two youngest cohorts compared with the pre- and post-war cohorts, which suggests, again, that life-cycle differences are relevant to postmaterialist orientations.

19. As Inglehart also uses the Eurobarometer data, the empirical bases of his claims about the 'new class' are unclear.

6

Left–Right Materialist Value Orientations

ODDBJØRN KNUTSEN

According to the traditional model of industrial society, class conflicts were central for political identities and political preferences. The value orientations associated with the political conflicts of industrial society reflected these class conflicts in terms of left–right polarization. The key issues underlying this conceptualization were conflicts related to economic inequalities, the ownership of the means of production, and conflict over the desirability of a market economy.

The ideology which supported emerging capitalism in the nineteenth century was economic and political liberalism. The value orientation associated with this ideology could also be called 'bourgeois' since these values were associated with the bourgeois class in the emerging capitalist society. Socialism and social democracy were the ideological response of the political forces of the left to the social and economic conflicts which characterized industrial society. At the mass level, these orientations grew out of the social experiences of industrial society and, in particular, the economic crises of the 1920s and 1930s. These value orientations will be labelled here—respectively—as *right materialism* and *left materialism*. Taken together they constitute the left–right materialist value orientation (cf. Von Beyme 1985: ch. 2; Lafferty and Knutsen 1984; Knutsen 1986*a*; Inglehart 1984: 25).

A central belief of right materialism is the supremacy of the market. This entails an emphasis on economic competition between independent enterprises, personal freedom, and the integrity of private property, including private ownership of the means of production. In political terms, these values imply a relatively weak state, resistance against government regulation, and opposition to notions of social and economic equality. A free market is socially desirable, both as the best way to organize the production and distribution of goods, and as a motivation system stimulating personal achievement. Moreover, in the long run, markets contribute to important collective interests. The market is also an effective information system for decentralizing decision-making, and an effective steering mechanism for distributing scarce resources.

Left materialism is based on the notion that governments have an active role to play in achieving overarching goals such as economic security, solidarity, and equality in income and living conditions between social classes and strata. According to this value orientation, government regulation of markets and private enterprises, societal planning, government redistribution via progressive taxation and welfare reforms are necessary for obtaining important goals such as full employment and social equality. Left materialism points to the failure of market mechanisms, which create social and economic inequalities, economic crises, and severe social conflicts. A regulated economy contributes to economic efficacy and individual work effort, and consequently to high productivity and economic growth. This clearly contradicts the bourgeois argument that there is an inevitable conflict between equality and strong government on the one hand, and efficiency and productivity on the other (cf. Castles 1978; Esping-Andersen 1985; Scharpf 1987).

Left materialism and right materialism also take a different view on the control of industry and the workplace. Left materialism emphasizes societal control 'from above' through state intervention, and participation and control 'from below' by workers and other employees through representation systems and industrial democracy. Right materialism emphasizes that ownership implies responsibility: it is a property right of owners to have the final word in the decision-making of firms. Thus the value conflicts incorporated in left–right materialism relate to power and control in the sphere of production and the degree of redistribution in the sphere of consumption. They centre around opposing ideas of workers' control and state regulation of the economy versus an emphasis on private enterprise and the market economy; an emphasis on economic and social equality versus the need for differentiated rewards to stimulate efforts. In brief, the political conflicts embedded in left–right materialism are, at heart, economic in nature, referring in particular to the role of government in the economy.

In this chapter, we focus on four aspects of left-materialist and right-materialist value orientations. First, the concepts of left and right materialism are compared to, and demarcated from, the more common notions of 'new' and 'old' politics and ideas referred to as the 'new right'. Secondly, we consider whether or not left–right materialism exists, empirically, at the mass level; that is, whether survey items which are assumed to tap left and right materialism are constrained at the level of the mass public. Thirdly, we examine the distribution of these value orientations over time and in comparative perspective. What are the long-term trends in the emphases on these values at the mass level? Which countries have the most leftist and most rightist population, and what explains the resulting comparative patterns? Finally, we look at the social structural antecedents of left and right materialism, again over time and comparatively. Are these value orientations primarily anchored in social class, as suggested by their association with the pattern of conflict in industrial society? And are there changes over time and between generations within countries with regard to these relationships?

Changing Value Orientations

Left–right materialism was a central political value orientation in industrial society, but is it characteristic of advanced industrial societies? New political values have been associated with advanced industrial society, primarily in the notion of 'new politics' and Inglehart's concept of materialist–postmaterialist orientations (see Chapter 5). Moreover, in the late 1970s and 1980s, there was a revival of conservative and libertarian ideas and movements, and increased support for political parties identified as 'new right'. How is the conceptualization of left and right materialism, as proposed in this chapter, related to these notions of 'new' and 'old' politics and the 'new right'?

The values incorporated in left–right materialism are central to the ideological polarization between the 'old' left and right. The term 'old politics' refers to the polarization patterns at the socio-structural and political level in typical industrial society and is based on the political conflicts between the 'old left' and the 'old right'. The class cleavage, focused on the labour market, was central in structuring the alignments of old politics, but old politics can also be conceptualized to include the pre-industrial cleavages related to religion (Dalton 1988: 133). Left–right materialism, together with religious and secular value orientations, can be considered as the central conflicting orientations of old politics (Inglehart 1984: 25–6; Dalton 1988: 133–49, 207–9).

The relationship between materialism–postmaterialism and left–right materialism can be conceptualized in several ways. From a developmental perspective, we can regard a materialist orientation as the common values of individuals with leftist and rightist materialist orientations in industrial society. However, with the emergence of advanced industrialism and postmaterialist values, a new and cross-cutting set of orientations has arisen which challenge the centrality of left–right materialism in the political belief systems of mass publics. This conceptualization, however, only partly accords with conceptualizations of value change from a materialist to a postmaterialist orientation as a change from the values of 'old' politics to the values of 'new' politics. In this literature, there is a tendency to characterize the shift from materialist to postmaterialist orientations as identical to a shift from old politics to new politics, without acknowledging the persisting divisiveness of the value orientations of old politics; these divisions do not necessarily disappear with a shift from materialism to post-materialism (cf. Dalton, Beck, and Flanagan 1984: 20; Dalton 1988: 82). According to our conceptualization, left–right materialism and materialism–postmaterialism are separate sets of value orientations. Hence, individuals of a postmaterialist orientation have to take a standpoint regarding left–right materialism because it still appears to be central to political conflict in most Western democracies.[1]

The conflict between the 'old' and 'new' left illustrates the relationship between the new and the older value orientations. In industrial societies, the left generally accepted a considerable degree of organizational discipline and hierarchy as necessary for effective political change. The left in advanced industrial politics is oriented more towards individual self-expression and tends to reject hierarchical organizations. Suspicious of the state, the new left tends to be more sympathetic to individualism, communalism, and variety in life-styles, while the old left tends to favour centralized, bureaucratic solutions, traditional life-styles and particularistic cultures—class culture, for example. The old left considers economic growth to be central for economic progress—to improve standards of living for the working class and other groups—to which the new left object. Even so, the new left also considers the traditions of the industrial left as central belief elements.

Distinct from the debate on 'old' and 'new' politics, the 1970s and

1980s have seen a revival of conservative and liberal ideas. This heterogeneous movement has been labelled the 'new right'. Although accounts of the new right vary, most authors agree that the core ideas are economic in character, with an emphasis on individualism, a free market, and a limited state. Hence, the ideas of the new right have challenged the post-war consensus on the welfare state, state intervention, and citizenship rights in the social domain—that is, central elements of left materialism which have been implemented in most West European polities. The new right emphasises the superiority of market mechanisms as a promoter of both economic prosperity and individual freedom, and stresses that state intervention does not work. Accordingly, new right thinking favours a minimal role for the state in both the economy and the social order (King 1987; Levitas 1985). Thus, although the new right can best be understood as emphasizing right materialist values, other 'conservative' moral and social beliefs are also involved, particularly reaction against the social and sexual liberation of the 1960s and 1970s (King 1987: 19–20)—that is, reaction against 'new politics' (Flanagan 1987; Flanagan and Lee 1988). However, according to King (1987: 17), 'conservatism is secondary to liberalism in New Right ideology'.

From this comparison of left and right materialism, on the one hand, and 'old' and 'new' politics and the 'new right' on the other, it becomes clear that the conflict of value orientations in advanced industrial societies in the 1970s and 1980s is related to divergent ideas grouped around our distinction between left and right materialism. There seems to be firm evidence that the shifts in value orientation in many countries can be understood in these terms. This brings us to the empirical part of our analyses.

Measuring Left–Right Materialism

Although the terminology is only rarely used, the empirical relevance of left and right materialist value orientations can be illustrated in many ways. For example, in Lijphart's study of twenty-one Western democracies, the 'socio-economic dimension' is the only one which is salient in all the countries examined. Moreover, compared to six other issue dimensions, the salience of the socio-economic dimension is 'high' in fourteen out of the fifteen West European countries examined (Lijphart 1984: 128–32). Thus, in a comparative perspective, this dimension is clearly the most salient. This dimension is identical to our left–right materialist orientation, comprising four sets of oppositions: state versus private ownership of the means of production; a strong versus a weak role for government in economic planning; support versus opposition on redistributing wealth from the rich to the poor; and support versus resistance on expanding social welfare programmes. Lijphart's discussion remains somewhat speculative and subjective, but the overall observation is confirmed in Budge and Farlie's (1983: ch. 2) study of political issue types in post-war elections in twenty-three democracies.[2]

Only a few of the available comparative data sets have satisfactory indicators of left–right materialism, and it is impossible to find comparative data containing the same indicators in several countries which span one decade or longer. Our strategy then is, first, to present findings from some of the West European countries where identical items covering left–right materialism have been asked systematically over time in national surveys. Then, secondly, we look at evidence from comparative surveys featuring such items.[3] Our aim is to trace the degree of constraint among the items which, we propose, tap left–right materialist orientations and to construct indices to measure these orientations. The indices are unweighted additive indices, and, with one exception, all have eleven categories, ranging 0–10. The alternative index constructed from the Danish Election Studies 1979, 1984, and 1987 has seven categories, ranging 0–6. An indication of these items is given in the tables.[4]

Country-Specific Evidence

We have country-specific data sets covering a time span of at least ten years for five countries: Denmark, Norway, Sweden, Britain, and the Netherlands. With only some exceptions, successive election surveys or other regular national surveys in these countries have posed the same items. In addition, we have data for Germany with items on left–right materialism which cover a period of six years. Our strategy is to include as many left–right materialist items as possible in each analysis so long as they are not 'narrow' issues related to particular political objects. Since the published work we refer to outlines results from factor analyses similar to our analyses using the country-specific data sets, the results from our analyses are presented without the tables.

The existence of left–right orientations consisting of items which tap

attitudes and values related to what we call left–right materialism, has
been documented in almost all election studies for the 1970s and 1980s
in Norway and Sweden. In Norway, analyses of some thirty to forty
items on 'political values' and 'issues' in the election surveys for 1977,
1981, and 1985 have established that conflict between notions of public
control and private initiative covers several elements of left–right
materialism (Valen 1981: 248–9, table 11.3; Valen and Aardal 1983:
164–5, table 7.2; Aardal and Valen 1989: 60–1, table 4.2). The same
applies to Sweden. Based on the 1979 election survey, Holmberg (1981:
262, table 12.8) found four factors: a left–right materialist factor which
explains most of the variance in the items; a nuclear energy factor; a
moral factor; and a factor related to social care. More recently, Gilljam
(1990: 275) reports that an economic left–right dimension is found in
every election survey since the first in 1956—altogether eleven studies
spanning thirty-two years.

Findings about constraint among traditional left–right values and
issues in Sweden are summed up by Bennulf and Holmberg (1990:
176). Discussing whether there exists a green versus economic growth
dimension among the Swedish mass public, they find that the strength
of the correlations between several green items are only moderate
compared to the strong correlations among left–right items (coefficients of 0.11–0.23 and 0.50–0.55 respectively). The authors doubt
the existence of a green dimension, but to doubt the existence of a
left–right materialist dimension would be absurd. Moreover, in a
comparative study of the 1976 and 1977 elections, Petersson and Valen
(1979) found an impressive similarity in the structuring of values
among the Swedish and Norwegian electorates. They identified four
dimensions, which they labelled government influence, energy and
environment, equality (related to gender issues) and cultural outlook
(related to religious and moral values). The first factor in both countries
was the left-right materialist dimension which, the authors concluded,
'takes on a striking predominance' (Petersson and Valen 1979: 319).
Finally, left–right items have frequently been used to analyse the
relationship between value orientations and party choice in Denmark.
Borre (1984: 160) found quite strong correlations between four items
among the Danish mass publics, of which three tap central elements of
left–right materialism in each election survey between 1971 and 1981.

To assess the structure of the items which, we anticipate, measure
left–right materialist orientations in the three Scandinavian countries,
we factor analysed data from election surveys conducted during the

1970s and 1980s.[5] Our results (not shown here) provide impressive support for the hypothesis that left–right materialism constitutes a major and distinctive value orientation among the mass public. In each survey, in each country, there is only one factor with an eigenvalue larger than 1.00, and the common factors have loadings of more than 0.50 on most of the items. In Norway and Sweden, the items which have a particularly high loading on the common factor are 'nationalization', 'risk of unemployment/public control', and 'societal control/ influence of leaders'. Our results for Denmark, too, provide strong support for the empirical reality of left–right materialism. Moreover, analyses of a more comprehensive series of items from the election surveys for the late 1980s reveal that left–right materialism remains a dominant orientation in all three countries; the number of factors differs but the first and major factor in each country is always our measure of left–right materialism. Despite this clear patterning, however, the left– right materialist indices for Denmark and Norway could not be based on the same items for the whole period as some items have been dropped from surveys conducted after 1985. Hence, two indices were developed for these two countries, one based on items from the older surveys (the main index) and one based on items from more recent surveys (the alternative index).[6]

In the case of Britain, the existence of left–right materialism at the mass level has been established by several scholars. The findings, however, are somewhat inconclusive when various types of social welfare issues are included in the analysis. Särlvik and Crewe (1983: 173–4) report five attitudinal dimensions for the 1974 (October) and the 1979 British Election Study. The dimensions are the same in the two surveys. The most important are, first, views on state control and other classic left–right issues, and, secondly, opinions on social welfare issues. These findings are confirmed by dimensional analyses of data from the 1974 (October) and 1983 election surveys by Rose and McAllister (1986: 119–21, 168, tables 7.1 and appendix D); Studlar and Welch (1981) present an even more convincing analysis of the structure of mass beliefs in Britain based on the British Election Study for 1974 (October).

In their analyses of the 1983 election, Heath, Jowell, and Curtice (1985: ch. 8) propose a two-dimensional map of the British electorate, one dimension represented by attitudes towards nationalization and the other by attitudes towards nuclear weapons. In their subsequent review of electoral change in Britain, this simple map is elaborated to include attitudes on other issues. The authors conclude that there is substantial evidence that political attitudes in Britain have a two-dimensional character (Heath *et al.* 1991: 172):

On the one hand there is the conventional left–right dimension which is concerned with economic issues such as equality, nationalisation and the welfare state. And on the other there is a liberal–authoritarian dimension which largely cross-cuts the left–right one and which is concerned more with social issues such as law and order.

We also used data from the British Election Study (1974 October, 1979, 1983, and 1987) to analyse left–right materialism in the British context. The analyses provide firm support for the notion of a single left–right dimension at the mass level. There is also a consistent pattern over time in the factor loadings.[7] A more comprehensive analysis of thirty items in the 1987 election survey reveals six factors. Left–right materialism is the first factor; support versus opposition to central aspects of the welfare state is the second factor (Knutsen 1991).

For the Netherlands, we review the findings reported by Middendorp (1978, 1991). Using data from the Dutch Cultural Change Survey, Middendorp (1978) examined the main dimensions of Dutch ideological controversies which he conceptualizes as a conflict between conservative and progressive ideology. In a more recent study, using data for 1970, 1975, 1980, and 1985, Middendorp analyses the indices tapping the philosophical and attitudinal levels. He finds that liberalism and socialism have opposite loadings on the economic left–right dimension at the attitudinal level, while conservatism has a high loading only on the libertarian–authoritarian dimension. The pattern is impressively stable across the four surveys (Middendorp 1991: 111, table 4.6), with the same two- and three-dimensional structure appearing in each survey. As regards the left–right dimension, Middendorp concludes (1991: 111):

The left–right dimension is 'truly ideological', not only in terms of the underlying basic value of equality, but also because the two 'opposed' philosophies of socialism and liberalism load consistently negatively and positively, respectively, on this dimension.

We selected five indicators from the data used by Middendorp, and our analysis revealed that left–right materialism clearly constitutes a common factor. No other factors emerged with an eigenvalue larger than 1.00 and all five indicators have loadings higher than 0.50 on the first factor in each analysis. Moreover, the factor structure and the loadings showed very high stability in the four surveys covering a period of sixteen years.

Finally, the situation in Germany. The 1984–9 IPOS studies contain several traditional left–right materialist items as well as items measuring materialist–postmaterialist orientations. Analyses of the data for 1984, 1985, 1988, and 1989 show an impressively similar structure. Three of the four items which, we anticipate, tap central elements of left–right materialism have high loadings on the first factor in each analysis, while two items tapping the authoritarian–libertarian aspect of materialist–postmaterialist orientations have a high loading on the second or third factor. The item 'social welfare', which we expected to have a high loading on the left–right materialist factor, constitutes— together with an item on environmental protection—a separate factor. The three items with consistently high loadings on the first factor were employed in constructing the left–right materialism index for Germany.

Comparative Evidence

In addition to the country-specific data, we can also examine data from comparative surveys. Items which might tap left–right materialism have been included in several Eurobarometer surveys and in the 1990 European Values Study.

Three surveys in the Eurobarometer series have items tapping left–right materialism: No. 11 (1979) has five items, and Nos. 16 (1981) and 19 (1983) have three items. Hence, because of the larger number of items, we use principally Eurobarometer No. 11, although the results obtained from Nos. 16 and 19 are referred to briefly. The results from the analysis of the five items tapping left–right materialism are presented in Table 6.1. These results show impressive support for the notion of a left–right materialist orientation. Only in Germany are there two factors with eigenvalues significantly higher than 1.00.[8] The left–right materialist factor explains 32–44 per cent of the variance in the eight countries, and has loadings higher than 0.45 on all variables in all countries. Most of the loadings are even higher than 0.60.

Similar factor analyses based on the three items in the other two Eurobarometers show the same pattern: a single factor which has loadings of 0.50 and higher on each item in each country (not shown here). In these analyses, the common factor explains 40–55 per cent of

TABLE 6.1. *Left–right materialist items in eight countries, 1979*

	DK	BE	GE		IR	NL	GB	FR	IT
			Unrotated	Rotated					
Economic equality	0.63	0.62	0.63	0.77	0.46	0.63	0.65	0.58	0.59
Public ownership	0.66	0.64	0.48	—	0.63	0.70	0.68	0.72	0.63
Government management of economy	0.55	0.68	0.55	0.79	0.60	0.60	0.61	0.59	0.70
Equal representation for employees	0.71	0.69	0.67	—	0.64	0.68	0.66	0.61	0.69
Public control of multinationals	0.47	0.58	0.58	0.81	0.48	0.71	0.66	0.49	0.61
Variance explained	37%	42%	34%	23%	32%	44%	43%	36%	42%
N	1,010	982	1,003		997	1,023	1,011	1,010	1,178

Notes: Entries are factor loadings. First factor unrotated solution; additionally, varimax rotation for Germany. Only factor loadings higher than 0.30 are reported.

Source: Eurobarometer, No. 11.

the variance in the variables. Eurobarometer, No. 19, includes data from Greece, and here too, there is strong support for the notion of a single left–right materialist dimension.

The existence of an economic left–right dimension, based on the five indicators from Eurobarometer, No. 11, has previously been documented by Inglehart (1984: 34–42; 1990: 290–300), employing pooled data from the nine European Community countries. Inglehart also included a series of new politics items, and found two factors: one reflecting the classic economic left–right dimension; the other a 'new politics' non-economic left–right dimension comprising items related to defence, penalties for terrorism, nuclear energy, and abortion. The same structure also appears in an élite sample of candidates to the European Parliament. Thus, the economic left–right dimension appears to be the predominant factor at both the mass level and the élite level.

The 1990 European Values Survey contains seven items directly relevant to tapping left–right materialism. These data cover thirteen countries, so giving a wide comparative base. In six countries (Britain, Italy, Spain, Portugal, Belgium, and Ireland), factor analysis of these seven items resulted in three factors with eigenvalues larger than 1.00; in the other countries, only two factors of this magnitude emerged. It appeared reasonable, therefore, to rotate only two factors for each country.[9] The factor loadings on the first rotated factor are presented in Table 6.2.

The items 'wealth accumulation' and 'individual freedom/healthy economy' do not load significantly on the first factor, but the other five items have consistently high loadings on the first factor across ten countries.[10] In the southern countries of Italy, Spain, and Portugal only three or four of these items have loadings higher than 0.30 on this factor. In Britain and Ireland the items 'nationalization' and 'individual/public responsibility' have much higher loadings than the other three items. Similar indices based on the five indicators were constructed for each country. Additional indicators based only on the three items 'nationalization', 'individual/private responsibility' and 'business management' were constructed for Italy, Spain, and Portugal since only these items loaded significantly on the first factor in these countries.

In all, then, our findings provide strong evidence of left and right materialist orientations among West European mass publics. The orientations emerge in all the surveys examined, and there is evidence from many countries that the items which tap these orientations are strongly constrained. Moreover, although many central left materialist values

TABLE 6.2. *Left–right materialist items in thirteen countries, 1990*

	DK	IC	NO	SV	BE	GE	IR
Economic equality	0.66	0.62	0.59	0.64	0.57	0.66	0.46
Nationalization	0.72	0.54	0.68	0.74	0.69	0.70	0.71
Individual/public responsibility	0.64	0.57	0.63	0.62	0.65	0.47	0.70
Business management	0.67	0.62	0.55	0.58	0.45	0.38	0.35
Social equality	0.52	0.58	0.43	0.58	0.30	0.51	—
Wealth accumulation	—	—	—	—	—	—	—
Individual freedom/healthy economy	—	0.34	0.36	—	—	0.33	—
Variance explained	31%	30%	27%	30%	23%	26%	21%
N	1,030	702	1,239	1,047	2,792	2,101	1,000

	NL	GB	FR	IT	SP	PO
Economic equality	0.69	0.34	0.48	0.51	—	—
Nationalization	0.62	0.77	0.71	0.66	0.55	0.70
Individual/public responsibility	0.61	0.77	0.69	0.56	0.71	0.68
Business management	0.60	0.34	0.65	0.63	0.46	0.49
Social equality	0.44	0.32	0.48	—	—	—
Wealth accumulation	—	—	—	—	0.55	—
Individual freedom/ healthy economy	—	—	—	—	—	0.48
Variance explained	26%	25%	27%	21%	22%	22%
N	1,017	1,484	1,002	2,018	2,637	1,185

Notes: Entries are factor loadings. First factor solution with varimax rotation. Only factor loadings higher than 0.30 are reported.

Source: European Values Survey (1990).

were under attack in the late 1970s and in the 1980s, our analyses show that left and right materialism are still constrained in the traditional way in the late 1980s and in 1990. There is no evidence supporting the idea of weakening constraint.

Change and Stability

We now turn to consider change and stability in left and right materialism. In particular, has there been a value shift in a right materialist direction from the 1970s to the 1980s—as suggested by both increased support for liberal and conservative parties and the literature on the new right? For Britain, Denmark, the Netherlands, Norway, and Sweden, we can trace developments from the early or mid-1970s to the late 1980s, but the period for Germany is shorter. The distributions from the comparative data can be used for investigating the priority of left and right materialism cross-nationally.

As a simple indicator of change, an 'opinion balance' was computed by subtracting the percentage of respondents with a right materialist orientation from the percentage with a left materialist orientation.[11] Positive scores indicate that there is a majority with left materialist priorities. Table 6.3 shows the opinion balance for the items which had high loadings on the left–right materialism factor; most items have appeared in at least two surveys but, for some countries, we also include items asked only once in the most recent surveys. In addition to the opinion balances, Table 6.3 presents the mean scores on the left–right materialist index.

The opinion balances confirm that there was a value shift in a right materialist direction around 1980 in most of these countries. In Denmark, there was a major shift from left materialist dominance among the mass public to more right materialist priorities. The major shift in the main index took place between 1979 and 1981, but there was some recovery in a left materialist direction between 1981 and 1984. According to the alternative index for Denmark, there was a marked tendency towards left materialism from 1984 to 1987. In all, then, by 1987, the Danish mass public was just as left materialist as in 1979.

Similar trends can be observed in the Swedish data, where there is a change in a right materialist direction between 1979 and 1985. However, the change is not as large as in Denmark. In Norway, there is generally no significant change from 1977 to 1981 towards right

TABLE 6.3. *Opinion balance in left–right materialism in six countries,*
1971–87

Denmark	1971	1975	1977	1979	1981	1984	1987
Main index							
Economic equality	19	14	11	11	−16	−22	
Investment control	31	19	43	46	−4	22	
Progressive taxes	13	25	25	40	9	14	
Mean	6.0	5.7	6.2	6.4	4.8	5.1	
N	1,302	1,600	1,602	1,989	968	1,035	
Alternative index							
Nationalization				−58		−63	−61
Income equalization				21		1	27
Public control over							
private enterprises				−11		−25	5
Mean				2.6		2.2	2.7
N				1,989		1,035	1,022

Norway			1977		1981	1985	1989
Main index							
Public control			−7		−20	−13	−14
Nationalization			−26		−35	−33	−46
Progressive tax			12		27	39	42
Societal control/							
influence of leaders			10		6		
Market economy							−30
Mean			4.4		4.3	4.7	4.7
Alternative index							
Risk of unemployment/							
government control			−25		−29	−25	
Mean			4.6		4.5	5.0	4.8
N			1,730		1,596	2,180	2,195

Sweden			1976	1979		1985	1988
Public control			−21	−12		−24	
Nationalization			−38	−35		−68	
Progressive tax			38	36		35	27
Societal control/ influence							
of leaders			33	41		27	47
Size of public sector							5
Private health care							−17
Market economy							−38
Mean			5.1	5.3		4.6	5.2
N			2,651	2,817		2,883	2,845

TABLE 6.3. *Cont.*

Netherlands	1970	1975	1980		1985
Nationalization	−14	−20	−2		−30
Progressive tax	32	39	60		53
Income equalization	63	68	72		47
Property equalization	55	56	52		37
Workers' say	63	51	49		42
Mean	6.6	6.4	6.5		6.1
N	1,905	1,803	1,859		1,759

Britain		1974	1979	1983	1985
Nationalization		10	−23	−25	−15
Redistribution		28	27	11	24
Workers' say		33	25	47	63
Reduction of poverty		80	75	75	81
Mean		6.6	6.0	6.4	6.8
N		2,365	1,803	3,955	3,826

Germany		1984	1985	1988	1989
Standard of living		−38	−37	−29	−40
Market economy		−48	−42	−43	−51
Economic equality		−39	−41	−40	−45
Mean		3.3	3.4	3.5	3.2
N		2,087	1,840	2,078	2,040

Notes: All opinion balances are reported. Blanks mean that the question was not asked in the survey. The main index for Norway 1989 includes one item that is different from the items used for 1977, 1981, and 1985. The alternative index for Norway is based only on the first three items which were asked in all surveys. The index for Sweden 1988 is based on two items from the earlier surveys and three new items.

Sources: National election surveys for Denmark, Norway, Sweden, and Britain; Cultural Change Survey for the Netherlands; IPOS surveys for Germany.

materialism. However, there is a shift towards the right on the items 'public control' and 'nationalization'. Between 1981 and 1985 there was a general shift to a more left orientation but between 1985 and 1989 there was stability. In general, Norwegians were more left materialist in the late 1980s than a decade earlier.

Shifts to the right can also be observed in the Netherlands between 1980 and 1985. In Britain, too, there was a rightwards shift between 1974 and 1979, but there was a gradual leftwards shift after 1979. According to the index, the British mass public was as leftist in 1987 as in 1974. Finally, Table 6.3 shows that there was a large and impressively stable right materialist majority during 1984–9 on each of the three items in the index for Germany.

In general, during the 1970s and 1980s, the mass public in all these countries were negative about the nationalization of industry and public control of private enterprises. However, opinion was generally positive about the further equalization of incomes and standards of living. Over time, there appear to be larger differences in the emphasis on the leftist position on nationalization and the leftist position on the other items.

We also computed the opinion balance using the comparative data. In Table 6.4, we present the opinion balance for the five items in Eurobarometer No. 11 (1979), the average opinion balance for the five items, and the mean scores on an additive index based on these items for each country.

The table shows that there was a leftist majority in all eight countries in the late 1970s on all the items except 'nationalization'. The average opinion balance for the individual items across the eight countries (not shown) are +70 for 'economic equality' and 'public control of multinationals'; +46 for 'equal representation for employees'; +39 for 'government management of the economy'; and −14 for 'nationalization'. However, there are rather large differences between the countries. The ranking of the countries according to the average opinion balance

TABLE 6.4. *Opinion balance in eight countries, 1979*

	IR	FR	BE	IT	NL	GE	DK	GB
Nationalization	40	3	11	−20	−37	−16	−58	−31
Economic equality	85	92	78	88	58	61	58	41
Government management	71	43	62	64	48	6	4	10
Public control of multinationals	88	77	75	71	64	62	89	35
Equal representation for employees	65	75	57	29	49	63	4	25
Average	70	58	57	46	36	35	19	16
Mean score on LRM index	7.4	7.2	7.1	6.7	6.5	6.2	5.7	5.4
N	997	1,010	982	1,178	1,023	1,003	1,073	1,011

Note: Entries are the opinion balance on each item, the average opinion balance, and the mean score on the left–right materialist index.

Source: Eurobarometer, No. 11.

based on the five items, reveals that the average opinion balance varies from +70 for Ireland and +58 for France, down to +19 and +16 for Denmark and Britain respectively.

Using the Euroweight variable which weights for the size of national populations,[12] the correlation between country and the left–right materialist index is 0.30 (eta). Analyses of the differences between countries on the individual items reveals that the correlation is largest for 'economic equality' (0.35), followed by 'government management of the economy' (0.28), 'equal representation for employees' (0.25), 'public control of multi-nationals' (0.21). It is notably smaller for 'nationalization' (0.15).

Two of the five items in Eurobarometer, No. 11—'nationalization' and 'economic equality'—also appear in Eurobarometer, No. 19 (1983), in the same format. So we can examine the development of priorities for these two items from 1979 to 1983. The average mean scores changed in the expected direction (data not shown), from −14 to −25 for 'nationalization', and from +70 to +64 for 'economic equality'. But this change was large in some countries: on 'nationalization', the change in Belgium was −41 (from +11 to −30), in France −37 (from +3 to −34), and in Ireland −22 (from +40 to +18). In Britain, however, the trend was in a leftist direction (+28). For 'economic equality', there were significant trends towards the right in Denmark (−20), Italy (−17), France (−14), and Britain (−13).

The next time point when we can make direct cross-national comparisons is 1990, using data from the European Values Study. The opinion balances and mean scores for the indicators of left and right materialism are shown in Table 6.5.

Although we cannot make direct comparisons between these results and those obtained for the 1979 Eurobarometer data, it is clear that the distributions in Tables 6.4 and 6.5 are very different. These differences are due—at least partly—to the fact that the question wordings are very different in the two surveys. Whereas all the items in Eurobarometer No. 11 invite respondents to 'agree' or 'disagree' with a left-worded statement, all the items in the European Values Survey are forced-choice questions. However, if we use a broader categorization of the countries, we find that our results for 1990 have much more in common with the Eurobarometer results than appears at first sight. In particular, the southern countries (Spain, Portugal, Italy, and France) have the most left-leaning populations, while the populations

TABLE 6.5. *Opinion balance in thirteen countries, 1990*

	Economic equality	National-ization	Individual/ public responsibility	Business management	Freedom/ equality	Average	Mean score on LRM index	N
SP	18 (6.0)	−33 (4.9)	7 (5.9)	−4	−6	−4	5.1	2,637
PO	29 (6.5)	−53 (4.2)	−24 (5.0)	−32	13	−13	4.6	1,185
IT	−13 (5.2)	−45 (4.3)	−4 (5.5)	−32	2	−18	4.2	2,018
FR	19 (5.7)	−54 (4.3)	−53 (4.2)	−9	−6	−21	4.2	1,002
IC	−12 (5.3)	−62 (3.9)	−28 (4.7)	−34	7	−26	4.0	697
IR	−31 (4.6)	−47 (4.1)	−26 (4.9)	−29	7	−25	3.9	1,000
BE	−14 (5.1)	−59 (4.0)	−29 (4.8)	−35	−14	−30	3.7	2,792
GB	−36 (4.5)	−33 (4.7)	−14 (5.2)	−32	−33	−30	3.6	1,484
NL	−27 (4.9)	−58 (4.3)	−36 (4.7)	−27	−8	−31	3.7	1,017
NO	−17 (5.0)	−55 (4.3)	−42 (4.5)	−27	−36	−35	3.4	1,239
DK	−30 (4.5)	−67 (3.7)	−52 (4.2)	−41	−30	−44	3.0	1,030
GE	−19 (4.8)	−68 (3.7)	−43 (4.2)	−38	−41	−42	3.0	2,101
SV	−53 (4.6)	−55 (4.3)	−71 (3.3)	−25	−39	−49	3.0	1,047

Notes: Entries are the opinion balance on each item, the average opinion balance, and the mean score on the left–right materialist index. Entries in parentheses are mean scores. 'Business management' and 'Freedom/equality' are dichotomous items.

Source: European Values Survey (1990).

in the economically more prosperous countries in the central and northern regions lean more to the right.

The cross-national differences are generally large on each item and the ranking of the countries is quite similar for the five items. The grouping of countries corresponds nicely to the three-fold typology developed by Van Deth (see Chapter 3) based on GDP per capita and employment in industry. According to this typology, Denmark, Norway, Sweden, Belgium, Britain, and the Netherlands belong to the group which can be labelled advanced industrial societies with a rising and high GDP per capita accompanied by a declining proportion of the labour force working in the industrial sector. These countries, and Germany, are the countries where the population has the most right-materialist orientations. Two of the three countries where industrialization is continuing (Spain and Portugal) have the most left-materialist population, while the middle-of-the-road countries (France and Italy) have a middle position on the left–right materialist index. The only two exceptions, which precludes a perfect correspondence between the index and the typology, are Ireland and Germany, where the population leans, respectively, more to the left and the right than expected.

There are two kinds of explanation for such differences. The substantive explanation is a variant of the *embourgeoisement* argument: people in affluent countries with advanced welfare states have more rightist orientations than people in less advanced societies due to their higher income, and their more differentiated occupations and life-styles.[13] The methodological explanation emphasizes the problems of explaining trends in one country because national situations change. For example, attitudes towards the nationalization of industry may depend on the extent of nationalization in a country at a particular time. Similar reasoning may apply to attitudes towards economic and social equality. People may retain the same orientation, but, as circumstances change or differ from one country to another, their response to survey questions may be different.

Social-Structural Antecedents

Left- and right-materialist value orientations are economic in character and refer, in particular, to the role of government in creating greater equality in society. We anticipate that the working class, those with low income, and those with less education are more inclined to emphasize left-materialist values, while employers, the self-employed, and the higher strata of the new middle class are likely to give the strongest support to right-materialist values. Consequently, we expect occupation and social class—the most direct indicators of economic interests—to be the strongest predictors of left and right materialism. In addition, as the most direct indicator of wealth, we expect income to be important. We expect these variables to be more important than education, which is less directly connected to economic values than the other hierarchical variables.[14]

These relationships, however, will change. We would expect the impact of left and right materialism to decline with the development of advanced industrial society and the rise of the welfare state in Western Europe. Most social groups in these societies have experienced increased prosperity, and the gap between the income and lifestyles of the middle class and the working class has narrowed. This reduction of objective class differences may modify class conflicts and reduce the differences between the classes concerning left- and right-materialist orientations.

Typically, industrial society was characterized by working-class and, to some extent, middle-class subcultures which were developed and strengthened by social networks structured along class lines. Left- and right-materialist orientations were largely derived from face-to-face contacts with family, friends, neighbours, and work colleagues. In contrast, advanced industrial society is characterized by residential mobility and increased residential heterogeneity, which tend to reduce the influence of group norms. Class-based social networks and community integration subsequently become less important for political orientations (Dalton, Beck, and Flanagan 1984: 17–18).

Institutional affiliations and loyalties have also declined in advanced industrial society. In industrial society, left-materialist values were 'learned', for example, in trade unions, and right-materialist values—to some extent—in the churches. But the type of attachment to unions has changed in advanced industrial societies (Goldthorpe *et al.* 1968). Particularly important for left materialism is the reduced sense of belonging and commitment to trade unions, the reduced sense of class solidarity, and reduced dependence on the unions for political information. But, more generally, the erosion of group ties has undermined the influence of the traditional socialization agents for left- and right-materialist orientations; and with the political and social heterogeneity of primary networks has come a decline in structured political cues.

In addition, the social mobility which characterizes advanced industrial societies tends to blur traditional class differences in value orientations. The rapid rise of the predominantly non-manual service sector has been accompanied by growing social mobility. Mobility from a working-class background to the new middle class is particularly relevant because it often implies moving from a left- to a right-orientated social environment. Some of these socially mobile individuals tend to keep their left materialist orientations, while others conform to their new environment, both of which tend to reduce the association between current socio-economic position and value orientations (Thompson 1971; Stephens 1981: 186–91).

The economic position of the new middle class is ambiguous, so probably we cannot expect to find that its members are decisively right-materialist in orientation. As a group with specialist knowledge and enjoying delegated authority in the workplace (Goldthorpe 1982: 168), the new middle class has economic interests in economic and social differentiation. At the same time, as employees, the new middle class shares some of the same interests and problems as the working class. Although there are several theories about the value orientations of the new middle class,[15] its emergence contributes to blurring the distinctiveness of the class-based value orientations which characterized industrial societies. In particular, the new middle class is probably fairly heterogeneous in terms of left- and right-materialist values, and consequently more left oriented than the old middle class.

The welfare state in advanced industrial society tends to produce more complex interests and value orientations than in typical industrial society. The income of a large segment of the population is a mixture of wage and welfare benefits, which often makes it difficult for individuals to define their political interests and their political value orientations. Thus, the welfare state also contributes to blurring class differences concerning left and right materialism (Janowitz 1976: ch. 5).

These factors imply that growing up in an advanced industrial society and a well-developed welfare state tends to reduce the impact of occupation, class, and income on left–right materialism. For example, coming to maturity during a period characterized by strong social tensions generated by economic and social differences generally leads to class and status differences with regard to materialist orientations, whereas being socialized during a less tense period tends to reduce these differences in values. Consequently, we anticipate that weakened correlations between the hierarchical variables and left–right materialism will be, in part, a consequence of generational replacement. Class-based differences will be greatest for generations which grew up during the pre-war period, and considerably less among post-war generations. However, period effects which influence all generations may also be present. In comparative terms, we expect these changes to be larger in the more advanced industrial societies of the northern and central regions of Western Europe because generational differences in experiences have been more evident in those countries.

Finally, gender is also a relevant socio-structural antecedent of left–right materialism. Various explanations have been advanced of the 'gender gap' in values and voting patterns among women and men (Hoel and Knutsen 1989). In relation to left–right materialism, we start from explanations which see changing values and attitudes among women as a result of economic and structural change. In particular, women have become increasingly independent economic actors. The earlier division of labour kept women in weaker positions in the education system and in the labour market, which has led to a concentration of women in the lower and middle levels in the education system and in the labour market. Thus, generally, we expect women to be more left materialist than men. Moreover, according to interest-based explanations, the effect of gender is likely to be indirect, making its impact via education and occupation. In a comparative perspective, we expect women to be more left materialist than men in the advanced industrial societies which are also characterized by high female labour participation.

The empirical relevance of this discussion is tested in the next section, in which we analyse the impact of age, gender, education, income, occupation, and social class on left- and right-materialist orientations.[16] First, we examine the bivariate correlations between these variables and the indices for left–right materialism. Secondly, we perform multivariate analyses, testing a model in which all these variables are included, and examine possible interaction effects.

Bivariate Analyses

We start by examining the bivariate relationships in the country-specific data. The product moment correlations are presented in Table 6.6; in addition, we present the eta coefficients for age and education when eta is significantly higher than r.[17]

Age and gender are seldom significantly correlated with the left–right materialist indices. Only in Germany and Britain (and Denmark on the alternative index) are there significant linear negative correlations, which indicate that the younger age groups are more leftist than older age groups. In Denmark, Norway, and the Netherlands, the eta coefficients are significantly higher than the product moment correlations in many instances. A closer examination shows that this is due to higher scores on the indices among the youngest and the older cohorts while the middle aged are more right materialist in all instances. The higher scores of the older cohorts may indicate the persistence of 'old left radicalism' among those who grew up in the 1920s and 1930s. The differences, however, are too small to analyse further. As to gender, the hypothesis that women are more left materialist than men in advanced industrial societies is not confirmed. Only in Norway and Germany do the most recent data show a modest correlation, in the expected direction, between gender and the left–right materialist indices. In these instances, women are more leftist than men, but this is not a general pattern.

The correlations are considerably larger for the status variables—occupation, class, education, household income—in all countries; and, apart from one exception, they are in the expected direction. Those with high income, high education, and those with middle-class occupations are more likely to be right materialist in orientation than those with lower income, less education, and those who belong to the working class. Except in the Netherlands, occupation and social class are the variables most strongly correlated with the left–right materialist indices. In the Netherlands, household income is somewhat more strongly correlated with the index than class and occupation. In the Scandinavian countries, education is generally more strongly correlated with left and right materialism than household income, although this changes over time in Denmark and Norway. On the whole, education is more strongly correlated with the index than we expected—but with Britain and Germany as clear exceptions. In Sweden and Germany, the correlation with household income is relatively low.

In general, the strength of the correlations between the three hierarchical variables and the left–right materialist indices have declined over time—which accords with our hypothesis. This is particularly evident in Denmark and Norway. In Denmark, between 1971 and 1984, the correlation with social class fell from -0.34 to -0.25; the correlation with education declined even more markedly, from -0.21 to

TABLE 6.6. *Correlates of left–right materialism in six countries*

	Age r (eta)	Gender r	Education r (eta)	Household income r	Occupation eta	Social class r
Denmark						
1971	(0.14)		−0.21 (0.22)	−0.11	0.36	−0.34
1975	(0.10)		−0.26	−0.21	0.35	−0.33
1977	(0.14)		−0.18 (0.23)	−0.14	0.35	−0.32
1979			−0.12 (0.16)	−0.18	0.27	−0.25
1981			−0.14 (0.17)	−0.17	0.38	−0.31
1984	(0.16)	−0.09	(0.13)	−0.20	0.30	−0.25
Alternative index						
1979	0.19 (0.22)		0.15 (0.18)		0.24	−0.16
1984	0.16 (0.22)		(0.18)		0.20	−0.09
1987	0.15 (0.18)				0.25	−0.15
Norway						
1977			−0.16 (0.18)	−0.18	0.31	−0.33
1981	(0.10)		−0.25	−0.19	0.26	−0.27
1985	(0.12)	0.11	−0.24	−0.21	0.29	−0.30
1989		0.09	−0.10 (0.13)	−0.13	0.16	−0.11
Sweden						
1976		−0.09	−0.16	−0.13	0.30	−0.30
1979			−0.16		0.29	−0.28
1985	(0.10)		−0.22	−0.07	0.31	−0.30
1988			−0.19		0.29	−0.24

Netherlands								
1970				−0.14	(0.16)	−0.32	—	—
1975				−0.18		−0.28	0.26	−0.26
1980		(0.14)		−0.17	(0.18)	−0.27	0.25	−0.26
1985		(0.11)		−0.17		−0.30	0.23	−0.18
Britain								
1974	−0.16			−0.09	(0.10)		0.25	−0.25
1979	−0.11			−0.08		−0.13	0.30	−0.29
1983	−0.10			−0.07		−0.15	0.27	−0.24
1987	−0.12	(0.13)			(0.11)	−0.21	0.25	−0.25
Germany								
1984	−0.11	(0.14)	0.11	−0.09	(0.13)		0.18	−0.16
1985	−0.11	(0.15)			(0.11)		0.12	−0.11
1988				−0.10			0.13	−0.12
1989	−0.08	(0.12)	0.12	−0.09	(0.13)		0.15	−0.14

Notes: Entries are correlations with the left–right materialism indices. Only coefficients of 0.07 and larger are reported. Middle-class respondents and women are assigned the highest values on the social class and gender variables, respectively. Those not in the workforce are excluded from the calculation of the coefficients for occupation and social class. For number of cases, see Table 6.3.

Sources: See Table 6.3.

−0.06. According to the alternative index for Denmark, based on the forced-choice items, the correlation with education is either positive but low, or not significant. In Norway, the decline in the correlations is largest for social class, which, between 1977 and 1989, fell by two-thirds (from −0.33 to −0.11), with most of the change occurring between 1985 and 1989.[18] The decline in the correlation for social class is somewhat smaller in the other countries, but still in the expected direction. Only in Britain do we observe more stability in the relationship.

Turning to the comparative data, the results of our analyses largely confirm our findings from the country-specific data. The results are shown in Table 6.7. In the 1979 Eurobarometer data, age correlates with the left–right materialist index only in Italy, and gender is not significantly correlated with the index in any country. Education, household income, occupation, and social class are either moderately or quite strongly correlated with the index. In comparative terms, social class is most strongly correlated with the index in the Netherlands (−0.30), followed by Denmark, Belgium, Britain and Italy (about −0.20). The correlation is very modest in Ireland and France (−0.10 and −0.13), and lowest in Germany.

Compared to these findings, the most important difference to emerge from the 1990 European Values data relates to gender. In seven of the thirteen countries, gender is significantly correlated with left–right materialism: in 1990, women are more left materialist than men. Moreover, as expected, this is most evident in the more northerly countries of Western Europe (Iceland, Norway, Sweden, Germany, and the Netherlands), but is also evident in Italy and Portugal. Age, however, is only very weakly correlated with the index in most countries.

There is some modest support for the hypothesis that the correlations between the hierarchical variables and left–right materialism are weakest in the advanced industrial democracies. The correlations with social class are weakest in the four Nordic countries (−0.11 to −0.18), and in Italy and Spain (−0.16). In the other countries, the correlations range between −0.20 and −0.26. For income there are larger and—according to our hypothesis—less systematic variations. Education is generally weakly correlated, and in some countries insignificantly correlated, with left–right materialism.

The eta coefficients for occupation and the *r* for social class indicate that there are distinctive differences between various occupational

TABLE 6.7. *Correlates of left–right materialism in comparative perspective,*
1979 and 1990

	Age	Gender	Education	Household income	Occupation	Social class
	r (eta)	*r*	*r*	*r*	eta	*r*
(a) Eight countries, 1979						
DE			−0.12	−0.13	0.30	−0.20
BE			−0.10	−0.10	0.27	−0.19
GB			−0.15	−0.13	0.23	−0.20
IR					0.14	−0.13
NL			−0.19	−0.23	0.36	−0.30
GE			−0.11		0.13	
FR			−0.11		0.19	−0.10
IT	−0.10			−0.14	0.27	−0.21
(b) Thirteen countries, 1990						
DK				−0.10	0.27	−0.11
IC		0.19		−0.16	0.15	−0.14
NO	(0.10)	0.10		—	0.18	−0.18
SV		0.10		0.17	0.24	−0.16
BE			−0.11	−0.20	0.26	−0.25
GB				−0.22	0.20	−0.20
IR			−0.10	−0.15	0.22	−0.22
NL		0.15	−0.10	−0.23	0.21	−0.20
GE		0.12		−0.19	0.22	−0.26
FR	(0.12)		−0.12	−0.20	0.25	−0.21
IT		0.10		−0.14	0.18	−0.16
SP				−0.16	0.16	−0.16
PO		0.11	−0.17	−0.26	0.23	−0.23

Notes: Entries are correlations with the left–right materialism indices. Only coefficients of 0.10 or higher are reported. Middle-class respondents and women are assigned the highest values on the variables social class and gender respectively. Those not in the workforce are excluded from the calculation of the coefficients for occupation and social class. For number of cases, see Tables 6.4 and 6.5.

Sources: Eurobarometer, No. 11; European Values Survey (1990).

groups, and between the working class and the middle class. But the fact that left–right materialist orientations follow the hierarchy of occupational positions cannot be detected directly from the eta coefficients since this indicator presupposes a nominal level measure for occupation. Thus a high coefficient can be obtained by large differences in orientation between any of the occupational categories. However, examination of the means for different occupational categories show that left-materialist orientations decline monotonically from workers, via lower-, medium-, and higher-level non-manual workers, to the two self-employed and employer categories. We do not present these tables but report findings from a simple model based on comparing the eta and *r* coefficients. We have assumed a rank order between the occupational categories, from workers (1) through the three levels of non-manual workers (2, 3, and 4 respectively) to both the self-employed and employers (5). We call this variable 'hierarchical occupation'. By comparing the eta coefficients between occupation (as a nominal level variable) and the left–right materialist indices and the correlation coefficients between hierarchical occupation and the indices, and testing whether the differences are significant, we can assess whether or not hierarchical occupation captures all the correlation with left–right materialism. And we find that, apart from a few weak exceptions, the *r* coefficients are almost equal to the eta coefficients in Tables 6.6 and 6.7. This indicates that it is hierarchical occupation which captures all the correlation which occupation accounts for in the left–right materialist indices.

Looking at all the surveys, there are two major exceptions to these models. The first relates to Denmark, Norway, and Sweden in surveys from 1985 to 1990. In these Nordic countries, middle-level non-manual workers are more left materialist than the model implies. For example, in the European Values data this group has the same mean score on the materialist index as workers in Denmark, while in Norway and Sweden the group approaches the lower-level non-manual workers in left-materialist orientation. This is an important finding which accords with previous research establishing that the radicalism of middle-level non-manual workers is generational, located primarily in post-war generations and related to public sector occupation (Goul Andersen 1984, 1989; Knutsen 1986*b*; Hoel and Knutsen 1989). The second significant deviation from a linear model emerges for Spain and Portugal in the 1990 European Values data. Here, the group consisting of employers and the self-employed, and partly also the higher-level non-manual workers, are just as left materialist as non-manual workers. However, it is not clear how to explain the deviant patterns in these instances.

Multivariate Analyses

Our next step is to test a multivariate model of the socio-structural antecedents of left- and right-materialist value orientations. The causal model we employ is outlined in Figure 6.1. As the model includes some nominal-level variables and we anticipate some non-linear correlations, we use multiple classification analysis to examine the effects of the five background variables on left–right materialism.[19] We do not present the results in tables, but discuss some general trends.

The analyses of the country-specific data show that the additive model generally explains 8–12 per cent of the variance in the left–right materialist indices. In Germany, however, the model explains only 3–4 per cent. There is no general trend towards the social background variables explaining less variance over time. As a rule, age and gender explain altogether about 1–3 per cent of the variance; the additional 6–10 per cent is explained by the three hierarchical status variables.

The patterns we found in the bivariate analyses of the hierarchical variables are generally little changed in these analyses. Since these variables are quite strongly intercorrelated, some part of the bivariate correlation of occupation and household income is spurious due to the prior education variable (and the prior occupation variable in the case of household income). Even so, the effects of age and education generally increase when education is included in the second step. This is related to the fact that younger groups in most countries are more left materialist than older groups, and that more highly educated people generally have a more right-materialist orientation than people

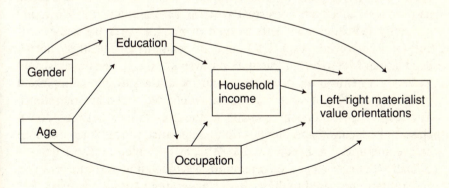

FIGURE 6.1. *Impact of socio-structural antecedents on left and right materialism*

with less education. At the same time, younger groups have higher education levels than older groups. When this education effect is controlled for, the direct effect of age increases. The same applies to the education variable when age is controlled for, which is more important since the controlled effect is the total effect of education. For example, in the British Election Study data, the bivariate correlations between left–right materialism and both age and education are around 0.10 (but 0.16 for age in 1974; see Table 6.6). The total effect of education increases to between 0.16 and 0.21 when age is controlled for, while the effect of age increases to between 0.17 and 0.27 when education is controlled for.

We conclude from these results that education stands out as a more important predictor of left–right materialism than the bivariate relationships indicate. Compared to occupation, the effect of education is generally of about the same magnitude or even somewhat larger in Norway, Sweden, the Netherlands, and in Denmark until the 1980s. Only in Britain and Germany are the effects of education generally smaller than for occupation. Education has generally a larger effect than household income in almost all analyses. Thus the hypothesis that education has less impact than income and occupation is not confirmed in the multivariate analyses.

Interaction Effects

As regards interaction effects, the interesting questions are whether there are similar patterns across surveys from different time points, and whether there are consistent patterns across countries. We found generally few interaction effects, and in most surveys the same variables are involved—especially, age in relation to education and/or occupation. Moreover, in line with our hypotheses, there is a consistent tendency for education, occupation, and social class to be less important predictors of left and right materialism among the post-war generations. This can be illustrated by looking at the correlations between social class and education and the left–right materialist indices for those born before and after the Second World War, as presented in Table 6.8.

Table 6.8 shows that the correlations are much higher for the pre-war generations compared to the post-war generations for all countries. For social class, the correlations for the pre-war generations are between −0.25 and −0.45 in most cases, while the correlations for the post-war

TABLE 6.8. *Correlations between left–right materialism indices, education, and social class in post-war and pre-war generations*

	Social class				Education			
	Pre-war	N	Post-war	N	Pre-war	N	Post-war	N
Denmark								
1971	−0.36	581	−0.21	75	−0.25	1,032		108
1975	−0.39	489	−0.10	201	−0.36	929		370
1977	−0.37	454	−0.14	222	−0.29	934		375
1979	−0.35	588	−0.10	285	−0.28	1,103		469
1981	−0.44	245	−0.11	142	−0.28	538		236
1984	−0.45	163	−0.13	307	−0.29	413	0.10	426
Index II								
1979	−0.26	588		285	−0.10	1,103	0.16	469
1984	−0.24	163		307	−0.13	413	0.27	426
1987	−0.28	186		433		378		550
Norway								
1977	−0.39	944	−0.23	229	−0.26	1,674		493
1981	−0.35	384	−0.20	334	−0.34	835	−0.14	646
1985	−0.34	376	−0.28	596	−0.31	955	−0.17	1,063
1989	−0.16	279	−0.10	751	−0.21	770		1,272
Sweden								
1976	−0.35	944	−0.16	509	−0.25	1,674		756
1979	−0.33	1,105	−0.17	678	−0.28	1,664		926
1985	−0.41	564	−0.23	905	−0.35	1,235	−0.11	1,276
1988	−0.33	469	−0.17	1,032	−0.33	1,073		1,375
Netherlands								
1970					−0.26	1,210		436
1975	−0.30	660	−0.18	271	−0.30	1,036		548
1980	−0.31	498	−0.15	338	−0.30	830	−0.10	784
1985	−0.28	383	−0.12	579	−0.28	603	−0.13	1,009
Britain								
1974	−0.28	1,209	−0.19	401	−0.13	1,635		548
1979	−0.30	737	−0.23	371	−0.11	1,133	−0.13	600
1983	−0.28	1,575	−0.19	1,235	−0.13	2,028		1,638
1987	−0.29	1,389	−0.23	1,450	−0.15	1,757		1,867
Germany								
1984	−0.21	305	−0.11	350	−0.18	1,168		752
1985	−0.13	258		406	−0.16	923		787
1988	−0.18	242	−0.10	503	−0.19	987		943
1989	−0.23	223	−0.10	521	−0.20	894		992

Notes: Entries are product moment coefficients (*r*). Only coefficients of 0.10 or higher are reported.

Sources: See Table 6.3.

generations are seldom more than −0.20. The pattern is even stronger for education. While there is a strong negative correlation between education and the left–right materialist indices among the pre-war generations, the correlation seldom reaches the limit of −0.10 for the post-war generations.

Denmark, however, appears to be an extreme case. Social class is very weakly correlated with the left–right materialist index among the post-war generations while quite strongly correlated among the pre-war generations. Education is not significantly correlated with the main index among the post-war generations but is quite strongly correlated among the pre-war generations. Moreover, in the 1984 data, education is positively correlated with the index in the post-war generations but shows a strong negative correlation in the pre-war generations. Opposite signs for the correlations in the two generations are also evident for the alternative index in both 1979 and 1984.

The other interaction effects which appear in many countries, especially in the more recent data, involve gender in combination with age and education. In Denmark, Norway, Sweden, and Britain, more highly educated women are more left materialist than men; and in the Scandinavian countries, younger women are more left materialist than men. Among the pre-war generations, there are either insignificant differences between the sexes, or men are somewhat more left materialist than women.

As to the comparative data, we report only results from the analysis of the 1990 European Values data. Generally, the results are very similar to those reported for the country-specific analyses. The five social background variables explain some 4–10 per cent of the variance in the left–right materialist index, and the three hierarchical variables explain most of this variance. The effect of education increases both absolutely and compared to the other hierarchical variables—and for the same reasons as explained above. However, the impact of education seldom approaches the impact of occupation and only approaches that of household income in about half the countries. In five countries, education has less effect than either occupation or income (Britain, Germany, the Netherlands, Iceland, Denmark), and in three of these countries education is a less important predictor than occupation or income (Denmark, Britain, and Germany). This is in line with our findings for the country-specific data.

In two countries, gender is among the two most important predictor variables (Iceland and the Netherlands). In Iceland, gender has the largest effect on the left–right materialist index compared to the other four background variables. This finding might be explained by the mobilization of Icelandic women by the Women's Alliance during the 1980s, which combined traditional demands for equality in the labour market and postmaterialist value orientations (Styrkarsdottir 1986). However, our hypothesis about interest-based explanations for the radicalism of women, as revealed in the 1990 data for several countries, is not confirmed. Almost all the effects of gender are direct effects in the multivariate analysis, not indirect effects via the three hierarchical variables. In the relevant countries, the direct effects of gender are changed insignificantly compared to the bivariate correlations in all countries. Most of the significant interaction effects in these data also involve age and either occupation or education.

We anticipated a generational pattern to the reduction of the correlations between the hierarchical variables and left–right materialism in advanced industrial societies. If this is correct, the differences between the generations in these countries should be distinctive. This hypothesis is partly confirmed. Significant differences between the pre-war and post-war generations are found in five advanced industrial societies (Denmark, Iceland, Norway, Sweden, Belgium, and Germany) but not in the Netherlands and Britain. However, such differences are not present in any country which has not reached the advanced industrial stage (Ireland, France, Italy, Spain, Portugal). In Portugal, the effects of education and social class are in the opposite direction to the findings for the advanced societies: social class and education are significantly more strongly correlated with left–right materialism among the post-war generations (-0.27 and -0.22 as against -0.16 and -0.08).

Conclusion

In this chapter we have brought together research findings on left–right materialism in order to further our understanding of the processes of value change in advanced industrial societies. First and foremost, we found strong evidence of left–right materialist orientations at the level of the mass public. Such orientations are manifest in all the surveys examined, and there is evidence from many countries that the items which tap left and right materialism are strongly constrained. There is no tendency for left–right materialist items to be less constrained in advanced industrial societies, although there is strong evidence for class de-alignment. In other words, left–right materialist orientations appear to be highly constrained in advanced industrial societies, although their anchoring in specific social groups seems to have declined.

Our findings with regard to trends provide some support for the notion of a shift to the right around 1980. However, there is also evidence that priorities among the public changed in a left-materialist direction during the 1980s. But these changes are small compared to the large differences between the most advanced and the less advanced countries in Western Europe. People in the less advanced countries are more left materialist than people in the more advanced countries. Analyses of the relationship between background variables and left–right materialism indicate that these value orientations are principally anchored in hierarchical variables such as social class, education, and income. However, these factors appear to be less important over time, particularly among the post-war generations. Gender, however, appears to be a predictor of moderate importance in some advanced industrial societies: women are more left materialist than men.

We can conclude, then, that left–right materialist value orientations are central features of political beliefs in West European societies. They mark out oppositions in the more advanced industrial societies no less than in the less advanced societies. This indicates a stability and continuity in political life in Western Europe which is often over-looked in studies of values and value change.

NOTES

1. This conceptualization differs from Flanagan's (1987: 1304–6) division of the mass public into materialists and non-materialists, emphasizing economic and non-economic issues. For materialists, the central political conflicts are related to the 'old' right and the 'old' left alignments of class politics. Non-materialists are divided along a 'new left–new right' cleavage related to libertarianism versus authoritarianism.
2. Issues about 'socio-economic distribution', 'government control and planning', and 'individual initiative and freedom' dominate the agenda in nearly all democracies. Almost half of all issues (43%) relate to these domains, and there is no tendency for these issues to decline in salience during the post-war period. These issue domains constitute about 50% of all issues in the periods 1945–54 and 1965–81; in the period 1960–75 their dominance was less pronounced (35–40%). See Budge and Farlie (1983: ch. 2).
3. Most of the data sets used were made available by the Norwegian Social Science Data Services (Bergen) from the ICPSR (Ann Arbor, Michigan), the Danish Data

Archives (Odense), the Swedish Social Science Data Service (Göteborg), and the ESRC Data Archive (Essex). The Norwegian Election Studies were made available directly from the Norwegian Social Science Data Services. The Dutch Cultural Change Studies were made available by Steinmetzarchief (Amsterdam). The German IPOS surveys were made available by Oscar Gabriel. Data from the 1990 European Values Study were made available by Ola Listhaug.

4. Details on the construction of the indices, and the wording of the questions used in the analyses, can be obtained from the author.

5. Only factors with an eigenvalue above 1.00 were rotated. This criterion was supplemented by the scree test, in which factoring stops when the graph of eigenvalues shows the eigenvalues beginning to level off (Kim and Mueller 1978: 44–5). In all analyses, units with missing values ('don't know' answers and 'not answered') have been included by assigning the mean score of the relevant variable. All variables have been recoded so that the presumed left- and right-materialist alternatives have been assigned high and low values, respectively.

6. For Denmark, the main index covers 1971–84; the alternative index, based on completely different items, covers 1979–87. The alternative index for Norway consists of three of the four items used in all the surveys; one of these four items was not used in the 1989 survey. The index for the 1988 Swedish survey consists of some items which are different from the index based on the previous surveys.

7. Items relating to the misuse of welfare benefits or that too many people rely on welfare benefits are deliberately excluded. The welfare items seem to tap a separate dimension.

8. The eigenvalue of the second factor in the German sample is 1.15. In Denmark there is more than one factor with an eigenvalue higher than 1.00, but the eigenvalue here is 1.04 for the second factor. In both countries all variables have quite high loadings in the expected direction on the first unrotated factor (the lowest loading in the German sample was 0.48).

9. The first factor in each of the six countries had eigenvalues of 1.46 or higher; the second factor had eigenvalues between 1.04 and 1.17; the third factor had eigenvalues slightly lower than the second. Graphs show that a two-factor model fits in each country.

10. The explanation for this deviation might be that these items are neither so clearly related to the economic domain nor are they prescriptive beliefs, i.e. values. The item 'people can only accumulate wealth at the expense of others' is evaluative rather than prescriptive; 'more freedom for individuals' is not directly related to the economic domain, although 'individual freedom' is an economic argument.

11. The calculations are based on relative distributions where 'don't know' answers and missing cases have been excluded. Neutral positions ('do not agree with either' or 'does not matter') were included in calculating the percentages but not in calculating the opinion balance. When the items are scales where respondents were asked to indicate their position, we present the mean as well as the opinion balance based on collapsing all categories to the left and to the right of the middle position. If a middle category exists, all categories to the left and all categories to the right are summed. The summed percentage for the right materialist responses are then subtracted from the summed percentage for the left materialist alternatives. The 'neutral' category is included in calculating the percentages. For scales where

the right-materialist alternatives have the highest value, the mean scores have been recalculated as if the leftist alternative had the highest score.

12. The Euroweight variable is used here because we consider the population of the eight countries as the universe, and examine how much of the total variance in the left–right materialist index and in the various items is explained by 'country'.

13. Inglehart has used a similar line of reasoning in analysing Eurobarometer, Nos. 11, 16, and 19. He explains the relatively large cross-national differences in left materialism on the grounds of diminishing marginal utility at both the societal and the individual level. See Inglehart (1990: 255–7).

14. Education may reflect cognitive factors in addition to class interests and value orientations to a larger extent than occupation and income.

15. The 'new middle class' refers to non-manual or white-collar workers. For a discussion of the structural characteristic of the new middle class, see Giddens (1973: ch. 10). For views about the political value orientations of the new middle class, see e.g. Bruce-Briggs (1979), Goldthorpe (1982), and Gouldner (1979). Ross (1978) presents a comprehensive review of influential French, Marxist-inspired, theories of the political orientations of the new middle class.

16. The variables occupation and social class are the respondent's own occupation and social class; income is household income. As occupation is coded differently in the several data sets, we constructed an occupation variable with the following categories: (1) workers; (2) lower-level non-manual workers; (3) middle-level non-manual workers; (4) higher-level non-manual workers; (5) self-employed in business and professions; (6) self-employed in primary sector (farmers, fishermen). The eta correlations between the value indices and occupation are based on these categories. The eta coefficient is based on the calculation of the total variance which occupation explains in the indices; i.e. occupation is treated as a nominal-level variable. In addition, we present the correlation between the value indices and a dichotomous variable for social class: (1) workers, (2) middle- and higher-level non-manual workers and the two self-employed groups. The lower-level non-manual group is deliberately not included since it is unclear whether it should be placed in the working class or the middle class.

17. Such deviation indicates that the relationship is non-linear.

18. Since an alternative item is included in the index based on data from the 1989 Norwegian election survey ('market economy'), it may be argued that the indices comprise different items in 1977, 1981, and 1985 compared with 1989. An alternative index containing only the three items asked in each survey (see Table 6.3) provides the following correlations with social class for 1977, 1981, 1985, 1989 respectively: -0.30, -0.24, -0.26, and -0.16. These results are weaker than for the main index, but they confirm the impression that a major reduction occurred in the strength of the correlation with social class between 1985 and 1989.

19. The method employed is the 'effect change design', not the traditional path or effect transmittance design (Hellevik 1989: ch. 5). The 'effect change design' means that the inclusion of variables starts with the prior variables and subsequently includes the intervening variables, but with the same dependent variable (here the left–right materialism index) in each step.

7

Religious Cognitions and Beliefs

KAREL DOBBELAERE AND WOLFGANG JAGODZINSKI

In Chapter 4, we focused largely on the behavioural aspects of church disengagement without analysing its internal aspects. We have shown only that some important indicators of religious cognitions and beliefs are highly correlated with church integration, as measured by church membership and frequency of attending services. Changes in the religious cognitions and beliefs of individuals during the process of secularization remain to be tackled. They are the concern of the present chapter. The global explanations for the process of secularization and its role in the decline of church integration, presented in Chapter 4, not only suggest explanations for the behavioural aspects of church engagement but also for its internal aspects.

Theoretical Considerations

The theories of secularization on which our research is based refer to broad socio-cultural trends to explain the decline of church religiosity. As these were summarized in Chapter 4, we shall recapitulate the major arguments only briefly. A popular hypothesis proposes a negative relationship between economic wealth and church religiosity (Inglehart 1990), although others have argued that religion will persist because, in the absence of other rewards, people look to religion as a form of compensation (Stark and Bainbridge 1985). According to a second approach, 'occidental rationalization' represents the world as calculable and controllable, leading to a disenchantment of the world (Weber 1975; Wilson 1976). Yet another approach stresses the contribution of functional or structural differentiation to secularization. It is claimed that the segmentation of institutional domains and the rationalization of these institutions (Luckmann 1967), which requires an educational system based on science and technical knowledge, has desacrilized the content of learning (Berger 1967; Wilson 1976). It is further argued that, as a consequence of functional rationalization, the growing impersonality of societal relationships (Dobbelaere 1988*b*), and the removal, by science, of anthropomorphism from our thinking, the traditional concept of God has been transformed, promoting agnosticism and atheism.

At first it was suggested that, since religion was excluded from the public sphere, it might survive in the private sphere (Berger 1967; Luckmann 1967), in the lifeworld of family, neighbourhood, and community. However, in the 1960s we witnessed a de-traditionalization of the lifeworld which led to individualization (Beck 1986). The reflexive self of advanced modernity (Giddens 1991) creates a 'bricolage' of the internal and behavioural aspects of church religiosity, contriving a 'patchwork' religion or 'religion *à la carte*'. However, since the Protestant creeds are not so extensively or dogmatically affirmed as the Catholic, Protestants were made personally responsible before God in religious matters, thus stimulating de-traditionalization and individualization much earlier in the Protestant world than in the Catholic world. These secularization theories, then, offer global explanations for changes in religious conceptions, the decline of religious beliefs, and the behavioural aspect of church religiosity.

All these theories point to structural changes in the wider society as the major cause of secularization—not to mental or psychological states, nor to hedonism, nor postmaterialism. However, several theoretically important variables, such as rationalization, functional differentiation, bureaucratization, and individualization, cannot be measured directly. Consequently, we have to rely on the standard socio-demographic variables which are related—theoretically—to the latent structural characteristics. In doing so, we postulate a number of relationships.

Two variables of particular interest are employment and education. If belief in a calculable and controllable world is a major cause of the disenchantment of the world—as we argued in Chapter 4—then church religiosity might be negatively related to employment (*Hypothesis 1*). This should be particularly true for those professions in which a high degree of technical knowledge and planning is required. The impact of education, however, is probably less straightforward. Remember that Inglehart (1990) considers church religiosity to be a consequence of unsatisfied security needs. Furthermore, he interprets education as an indicator of formative affluence (Inglehart 1977b). It follows from both assumptions that education has a negative impact on church religiosity. Our view is rather different, however. In the first place, we consider education to be an indicator of socialization; the value orientations in which individuals are socialized will differ from one educational system to another. In the Protestant and the religiously mixed countries of northern Europe, the influence of the churches on the educational system largely vanished before the Second World War. Since higher education in the natural and social sciences may have accelerated the disenchantment of the world, education in these countries should have only a small negative impact, if any, on religious cognitions and beliefs (*Hypothesis 2a*).

In Catholic countries, however, these developments occurred later. Consequently, even after the Second World War, important sections of the more highly educated were still effectively socialized into Catholicism, as studies on church religiosity in France and Belgium have shown (Pin 1956: 209–18; Dobbelaere 1966: 222–8). The situation changed during the 1950s and the 1960s when extensive educational reforms were enacted and increasing numbers of young people attained high levels of education. As a consequence, the position of religion was considerably weakened, and higher education was no longer so much influenced by the churches and religious teaching. This was the case even in Belgium, a so-called Catholic country—at least when measured by church membership and attendance (Dobbelaere 1984: 104–5; 1985a: 203–4). Thus, in Catholic countries we expect education to have a positive impact on the cognitive aspects of church religiosity among generations which finished school before the 1960s, and a negative impact on younger generations (*Hypothesis 2b*).[1]

Age and gender are also relevant socio-demographic variables. We showed in Chapter 4 that, in almost all countries, the behavioural aspects of church religiosity differ between age groups and generations. Thus we can safely assume that age is positively related to religious beliefs and cognitive aspects of church religiosity (*Hypothesis 3*). The fact that women are still more religious than men has been explained physiologically, psychologically, and psychoanalytically. However, we want to point to socio-cultural factors which suggest different patterns of role socialization according to gender

(*Hypothesis 4a*). Moreover, we predict that employed women are more akin to men rather than housewives in their religious beliefs, due to the disenchantment and the anonymity of the work sphere which conflict with a religious culture (*Hypothesis 4b*).[2] This hypothesis also refers back to our first hypothesis about the impact of employment.

We also anticipate that church integration exercises its own influence, in particular, that individuals who are integrated into an institutionalized church will be more resistant to the influences of secularization than others. High integration protects people from experiences which are detrimental to their religiosity. Therefore we postulate that church engagement has a positive impact on religious belief (*Hypothesis 5*). Unfortunately, since religious beliefs are frequently a precondition of participation in services and rites, the reverse causal ordering may also be true: a decline of religious belief may lead to disengagement from the church. It is almost impossible to disentangle empirically the direction of causality between these variables. We try to solve the problem not by estimating a feedback model, but by replacing church engagement with religious denomination. Our argument is that, in most instances, people's denomination is less influenced by religious beliefs than vice versa; that is, the dominant flux of causality is from denomination to church engagement. We have to admit that denomination becomes dependent on religiosity as soon as the possibility of leaving the church is considered, in which case religious belief or disbelief may become a decisive factor. On balance, we cannot offer a completely convincing solution to this problem.

Finally, we expect individuals to be less church religious the more rationalized is the country in which they live (*Hypothesis 6*). This hypothesis suggests that countries have attained different degrees of rationality and secularization. Even in modern Western Europe, persisting barriers of language and cultural tradition impede the rapid dissemination of secular ideas between countries. Since we have no optimal measure for the degree of rationality achieved in different countries, only a very crude test of this hypothesis is possible.

Research Design

The 1981 and 1990 European Values Surveys provide directly comparable data for ten West European countries. These surveys have several items enabling us to derive a fairly large set of religious cognitions and beliefs. These are not available in other surveys, which are usually limited to the behavioural aspects of religiosity. Since the relationships between religious cognitions and beliefs and the social variables are fairly similar in both data sets, we have combined the two surveys into a single data set. The first step in the empirical analysis is a country-by-country test of Hypotheses 1–5, using the combined data for each country. In a second step, we pool the data for the ten countries to obtain a very large data set, which allows us to test Hypothesis 6.

We operationalized three dependent variables. Throughout this chapter we are principally concerned with the extent of people's religious orientations, which is measured by the number of religious beliefs.[3] This variable was described in Chapter 4. A battery of items measures respondents' belief in God, the soul, sin, life after death, heaven, the devil, hell, and reincarnation. We exclude the last item because it might have been misunderstood by many respondents.[4] In answering the items respondents had to choose between 'believe', 'don't know', and 'don't believe'. Although the last two categories may indicate different philosophical positions—scepticism, agnosticism, or atheism—we decided to assign a code of zero to all respondents who did not chose the 'believe' category. Assuming that the extent of religious beliefs is larger the more of these beliefs an individual accepts, we constructed a cumulative index, ranging from 0 to 7.

From time to time, however, we also include two other aspects of church religiosity: the centrality and the abstractness of religious beliefs. The centrality of religious beliefs is measured by 'importance of God'.[5] The indicator for the abstractness of religious beliefs is 'type of God', reflecting a stepwise evaporation of belief in God; from God conceived as a person, to God conceived as a spirit or life force, to an agnostic position ('I don't know'), and, finally, to unbelief. We make the very strong assumption that these four positions constitute a metric scale.[6]

Since all three indicators—number of religious beliefs, importance of God, and type of God—are highly correlated (about 0.7 and more), one could treat them as multiple indicators of an underlying construct. However, in our view they reflect different properties of the religious belief system, therefore we keep them separate. Even so, we do not expect completely different relationships between these indicators and the structural variables. On the contrary, in general, these relationships should be fairly similar. Therefore, we include all three variables for these belief aspects of church religiosity only in those instances where we want to investigate their similarities or differences more closely.[7]

Three blocs of independent variables were constructed. The first bloc consists of the most suitable operationalizations of the socio-demographic variables relevant to Hypotheses 1–5. These variables are always included in the regression equations, whether or not they have a significant impact on church religiosity. To test Hypothesis 1, the employment variable distinguishes between, on the one hand, people who are partly or fully employed or self-employed and, on the other hand, all the others. No additional distinction was made within the employed category because the number of cases was too small.[8] However, we identified housewives separately by using a direct question.

Experience of work is poorly measured by employment, and education is not much better; the original variable only reports the school-leaving age of respondents. Hence, those who left school at the age of twelve or earlier were coded 1, those who left at age 13 coded 2, and so on. Since, according to our expectations, older and younger generations are affected differently by the educational system in the Catholic countries, this education variable was divided into two further variables. On the first, 'education young', all respondents who were born before 1945 and entered school before 1950 were assigned to zero, and all respondents who entered school after 1950 were assigned a numerical code corresponding to the number of years they had spent in education. Similarly, on the second variable, 'education old', all respondents who entered school after 1950 were assigned to zero, and all respondents who entered school before 1950 were coded according to the number of years of education they had received. If our hypotheses are correct, these two education variables should have approximately the same impact on the number of religious beliefs in Protestant and religiously mixed countries, but should have different impacts in Catholic countries. Finally, we include age and gender in testing Hypotheses 3 and 4a.

The second bloc consists of variables which might have an impact on religious beliefs and cognitions. Most variables in this bloc are related to employment status and education. We distinguish between respondents who have already retired from their job and others, and a further dummy variable differentiates between those who are unemployed and others. We identify students as a separate category, as they may be somewhat more secularized than other highly educated individuals.

Since we have no clear expectations about the impact of these variables, we report the respective regression coefficients only if they are significant after all the variables in the first bloc have been entered into the regression equation.[9]

We also constructed a dummy variable measuring change between 1981 and 1990,[10] in order to see whether there had been a change in the belief components of church religiosity even when the social background of respondents is held constant. For example, if any change between 1981 and 1990 was due only to the altered composition of the age or education variables, this variable would not be significant. Thus, the variable measures change in church religiosity which does not follow from social structural changes.

The third bloc of independent variables is designed to estimate the impact of church integration on church religiosity. For reasons already explained, we chose denomination and not church integration as the independent variable. Since denomination is a categorical variable, we represent all but one category by dichotomous variables (i.e. m categories are represented by $m - 1$ dummy variables).[11] These dummy variables were entered last in the regression equations because denomination has a dubious causal status. The combined effect of all the dummy variables in the equations will nevertheless overestimate the true influence of denomination because the reciprocal causal relationship is ignored.

Country Analyses

The results of the regression analyses shown in Table 7.1 by and large confirm our hypotheses. In almost all the countries under investigation age and gender are the most important social structural antecedents of church religiosity. While age consistently displays a strong positive effect, the regression coefficients for gender have a t-value larger than 2 in nine out of ten countries.[12] The exception is the Netherlands, where the effect of gender is insignificant but the effect of being a housewife is significant. Thus, only the Netherlands fits the hypothesis that differences in the belief component of church religiosity among women is solely due to differences in work experience. The results for the other countries point to differential socialization experiences: parents are still more likely to involve girls in church religion than boys. The experience of work may accentuate this difference, but the pattern is not unique. In

TABLE 7.1. *The impact of social structural variables on the number of religious beliefs, 1981 and 1990*

	Employ-ment	Education after 1950	Education before 1951	Gender: women	House-wife	Age	Change, 1981–90	R^2 (* 100) (%)	R^2 with denom-ination included (%)	N
Denmark										
beta	−0.04	−0.03	0.00	0.11	0.01	0.21	—	8.08	10.91	2,144
t	−1.84	−0.73	−0.07	4.86	0.37	6.01				
France										
beta	−0.02	0.01	0.12	0.12	0.06	0.11	—	6.19	24.40	2,077
t	−0.77	0.35	4.12	4.93	2.17	2.89				
Netherlands										
beta	0.02	−0.03	−0.03	0.01	0.08	0.16	−0.06	3.83	43.21	2,036
t	0.69	−0.62	−0.94	0.39	2.39	4.33	−2.40			
West Germany										
beta	−0.01	−0.11	−0.07	0.13	0.04	0.21	−0.05	10.07	19.76	3,361
t	−0.61	−3.24	−2.53	7.50	1.78	6.62	−2.42			
Belgium										
beta	−0.06	0.08	0.09	0.08	0.04	0.22	−0.09	8.24	29.68	3,491
t	−2.87	2.47	3.52	4.61	2.11	7.54	−5.43			

Norway										
beta	−0.01	0.02	−0.04	0.15	0.03	0.24	−0.10	7.76	13.70	2,381
t	−0.60	0.55	−1.20	7.35	1.56	6.79	−5.02			
Britain										
beta	0.02	−0.03	−0.03	0.15	0.01	0.13	—	4.41	17.68	2,642
t	0.66	−0.93	−0.87	7.33	0.27	3.98				
Spain										
beta	0.01	−0.02	0.10	0.14	0.12	0.21	−0.05	13.59	22.53	4,840
t	0.36	−0.74	5.88	8.10	5.31	9.60	−3.99			
Italy										
beta	−0.06	−0.06	−0.00	0.18	0.02	0.08	0.05	7.45	18.90	3,102
t	−2.85	−2.74	−0.10	9.33	0.88	3.68	2.75			
Ireland										
beta	−0.03	−0.02	0.10	0.08	−0.00	0.15	—	7.81	16.05	2,173
t	−0.77	−0.50	3.07	3.28	−0.10	4.06				

Notes: Entries in the first row of each cell are the standardized regression coefficients; entries in the second row show the *t*-value. In Spain, students also have a significant impact on number of religious beliefs (beta = 0.06; *t* = 3.04). In Ireland, unemployed people have significantly fewer religious beliefs than others (beta = −0.05; *t* = −2.03).

Sources: European Values Survey (1981, 1990).

four countries (West Germany, France, Belgium, and Spain) both variables—women and housewife—have an important effect on the internal component of church religiosity. In the remaining five countries (Denmark, Norway, Britain, Italy, and Ireland) only gender has a significant impact.

Employment does not have the impact we expected. The regression coefficient for employment has the expected sign in only six countries, and it becomes significant in only two out of these six cases. This disappointing result may be partly due to the fact that our theoretical arguments are not adequately reflected in their operationalization. Theoretically, we have distinguished between occupations in more or less rationalized industries or bureaucracies; empirically, we have only dichotomized between people with and without employment. A finer classification is not possible, partly because of problems with the number of cases, and partly because appropriate indicators are not available in the two European Values Surveys.

We performed two tests to estimate the impact of education. In Table 7.1 we have simply decomposed the effects of education into two components, the education of younger ('education after 1950') and of older generations ('education before 1951'). In Protestant and religiously mixed countries we expected both variables to have either no impact or a negative impact on the number of religious beliefs, and that both regression coefficients would have approximately the same magnitude (Hypothesis 2a). This hypothesis is confirmed consistently. In Denmark, Britain, the Netherlands, and Norway the impact of education has almost disappeared and the regression coefficients of 'education after 1951' and 'education before 1951' are fairly close to each other. In West Germany, education has a negative impact on religiosity but there are virtually no differences between older and younger generations.

According to Hypothesis 2b, we expected different results in Catholic countries. First of all, education should positively influence religiosity in the older generations. This is true in France (beta=0.12), Belgium (beta=0.09), Spain (beta=0.1), and Ireland (beta=0.1). The only exception is Italy where the standardized regression coefficient is almost zero. Secondly, the positive relationship should have disappeared in the younger generations. This hypothesis is also confirmed in four out of five cases: France, Spain, Italy, and Ireland. Only in Belgium do we observe—in spite of a negative bivariate correlation between 'education after 1950' and number of religious beliefs—that education has a positive impact on religiosity.

Hypothesis 2*b* implies an interaction effect between generation and education. Indeed, in most cases in Table 7.1, we observe noticeable differences between the effects of 'education after 1950' (or 'education young') and 'education before 1951' (or 'education old'). In order to test the interaction effect more rigorously, we have to replace the two interaction variables 'education young' and 'education old' by the linear terms 'education' and 'post-war generations'. The latter is a dummy variable which is set equal to 1 if respondents were born in 1945 or later, and zero otherwise. We have to estimate the common impact of these linear terms and the other social structural variables by means of the coefficient of determination. Then, in a further step, we have to enter the interaction term:

Education young = post-war generations * education.

If there is a significant increase in the amount of variance explained, we can be fairly confident that education has a different impact on older and younger generations. There is one exception to this procedure: 'post-war generations' and 'education young' are included stepwise in the same bloc of variables. If they both significantly increase the explained variance, they may both enter the regression equation. Yet it is also possible that only one of these variables or neither is included.

The results of this test are reported in Table 7.2. As can be seen, the theoretically postulated interaction effect is found in only two of the five countries: France and Spain. In Belgium and Italy, education seems to have similar effects in older and younger generations when all other variables are held constant. In Ireland, generation seems to have an impact, but not the interaction term.

On balance, Hypothesis 2*b* has to be modified. Apart from Italy, education has a positive impact on church religiosity in the Catholic countries. However, the differential effects of education in older and younger generations can be established only in France and Spain. These somewhat disappointing results may be due, again, to the poor measurement of education; they may also be due to the choice of the cutting point between older and younger generations. Had we chosen 1955 or 1960 as the watershed, we might have obtained different results. In any case, our findings clearly contradict the equation 'education = formative affluence'. If this equation were true, and if formative affluence contributed to the decline of church religiosity, we should observe a negative impact of education on the number of religious beliefs. In fact, we find this effect at best in some Protestant countries and Italy. In

TABLE 7.2. Interaction of age and education in Catholic countries, 1981 and 1990

	Step 1						Step 2			R² with denomination included (%)	N
	Employ-ment	Education	Gender: women	House-wife	Age	Change, 1981–90	R² (%)	PG	Education PG	R² (%)		
France												
beta	-0.01	0.06	0.12	0.08	0.20	—	5.57	—	-0.15	6.19	24.40	2,077
t	-0.19	2.57	4.86	2.78	7.65	—		—	-3.69			
Belgium												
beta	-0.06	0.06	0.08	0.04	0.24	-0.10	8.21	—	—		29.69	3,491
t	-2.80	3.48	4.58	2.23	12.24	-5.73		—	—			
Spain												
beta	0.02	0.05	0.13	0.13	0.28	-0.07	12.98	—	-0.16	13.59	22.53	4,840
t	1.08	2.87	7.65	6.15	16.70	-5.26		—	-5.80			
Italy												
beta	-0.06	-0.04	0.18	0.02	0.11	0.05	7.20	—	—		18.90	3,102
t	-2.69	-2.24	9.31	0.97	5.74	2.60		—	—			
Ireland												
beta	0.03	0.04	0.08	0.05	0.26	—	7.17	-0.14	—	7.73	16.14	2,173
t	1.07	1.69	3.27	1.52	10.93	—		-3.62	—			

Notes: Entries in the first row of each cell are the standardized regression coefficients; entries in the second row show the *t*-value. Listwise deletion. The post-war generations (i.e. born after 1944) are indicated by the variable *PG*. In Spain, students also have a significant impact on number of beliefs (beta = 0.05; *t* = 2.53).

Sources: European Values Survey (1981, 1990).

most Catholic countries education has a positive impact on church religiosity. In our view, this can only be explained by the position of the Catholic church in the educational system: as long as it had control over schools and universities, the well educated were socialized into Catholicism.

Among our second bloc of variables, only the measure of change 1981–90 has a significant impact in the majority of countries. Italy still remains a dubious case because the country has become slightly more church religious. Two variables become significant in only one country: unemployment has a negative regression coefficient in Ireland; students has a positive coefficient in Spain. While the former effect accords with our theoretical expectations, the latter at a first glance does not. However, in large part, this may reflect the influence of the old university system. In view of the the small and unsystematic effect of students, it was not worthwhile distinguishing between Catholic and Protestant countries as in the case of education. All the other variables in the second bloc consistently have no impact on the belief aspect of church religiosity.

As we know from many national surveys, the impact of social structure on attitudes and value orientations is not very impressive. In our data, the coefficient of determination varies between 3.8 per cent (Netherlands) and 13.6 per cent (Spain) if only the variables in the first two blocs are included. The variance explained is a bit higher in those countries where 'change 1981–90' has a significant impact. This might suggest that differences between social groups grow larger in times of rapid change. However, there are some exceptions from the rule. In Denmark, due to the strong impact of gender and age, the amount of variance explained is fairly high (8.1 per cent). And the Netherlands, with the lowest explained variance among all the countries, still experienced a significant decline in religious belief.

However, if we include denomination as an additional social structural antecedent, the coefficient of determination improves considerably. The change in the explained variance is most dramatic in the Netherlands where it climbs from 3.8 per cent to 43.2 per cent. However, we have repeatedly pointed to the problem that people's choice of denomination could also be due to the nature or the number of religious beliefs they hold. This seems to be particularly true in the Netherlands where a large part of the population has already left the churches. Therefore, the R^2 columns in Tables 7.1 and 7.2 should be interpreted with caution.

Pooled Analysis of Ten Countries

In this second step, we have pooled the data for all ten countries and both surveys. As before, we first ran the regression analyses with the two blocs of independent variables as in Table 7.1. The number of cases is now extremely large, nearly 30,000. The results for the number of religious beliefs are reported in the first three columns of Table 7.3.

These results fit beautifully with the figures in the previous tables. The variables age, women, and housewife now all have a substantial effect and the signs of their regression coefficients are in the expected direction. The influence of employment is still negligible. As far as education is concerned, in Table 7.1 we found almost no significant effect of 'education old' in the Protestant and mixed countries, and fairly strong positive effects in the Catholic countries. As a consequence, the effects in the Catholic countries become dominant in the pooled data set. Thus, 'education old' has a small positive effect. The effect of 'education young' is determined in a similar way: since the majority of countries display a negative effect, the pooled data set also yields a significant negative effect. The amount of variance explained (7.75 per cent) is almost an average of the explained variance in the country by country regressions.[13] We also want to know whether the two other measures of the belief aspect of church religiosity—importance of God and type of God—display a pattern similar to that for the number of religious beliefs. As we can see from the middle three columns and the last three columns in Table 7.3, the regression coefficients closely correspond to each other. In terms of explained variance, 'importance of God' performs best.[14]

The main purpose of the pooled analysis is to test the rationalization hypothesis (Hypothesis 6). Therefore we entered into the regression equation a set of country dummies as a third bloc of variables.[15] They are designed to measure the impact of the national context upon the individual. Spain is the reference category. If the rationalization hypothesis is true, we should observe not only a considerable increase in the explained variance when this bloc of variables is entered, but the unstandardized regression effects of the country dummy variables should also, by and large, be rank ordered according to the degree of rationality. The less rationalized a country, the lower the regression coefficient. Deviations from the rank order might be explained in terms of other socio-cultural factors, in particular by the existence of a religious cleavage. In those countries where a religious cleavage

TABLE 7.3. *Church religiosity and social structural antecedents, 1981 and 1990*

	Number of religious beliefs			Importance of God			Type of God		
	Unstandard. coefficient	t values	Standardized coefficient	Unstandard. coefficient	t values	Standardized coefficient	Unstandard. coefficient	t values	Standardized coefficient
Education young (after 1950)	-0.02	-2.71	-0.03	-0.04	-0.53	-0.05	0.01	2.93	0.03
Education old (before 1951)	0.02	2.76	0.02	0.01	1.78	0.01	-0.01	-2.98	0.02
Student	0.19	2.62	0.02	0.29	3.22	0.02	-0.09	-3.49	-0.02
Women	0.58	19.51	0.12	0.85	22.63	0.13	-0.22	-17.07	-0.11
Housewives	0.30	6.40	0.05	0.49	8.17	0.06	-0.09	-5.04	-0.04
Age	0.02	17.20	0.16	0.04	26.13	0.24	-0.01	-13.62	-0.14
Employment	-0.06	-1.39	-0.01	-0.03	-0.63	-0.05			
Change 1981–90	-0.01	-3.86	-0.02	-0.02	-6.38	-0.04			
(Constant)	(3.26)	(12.29)		(6.06)	(18.01)		(2.21)	(65.24)	
R^2 (2nd step equation)	7.75%			13.89%			6.41%		
R^2 (3rd step: countries incl.)	17.81%			22.94%			14.57%		
R^2 (4th step: denomination incl.)	28.54%			37.34%			25.73%		
Total N = 29,817									

Notes: The regression coefficients are taken from the third-step estimation where the country dummy variables are included. The pooled data set consists of twenty surveys (ten countries each in 1981 and 1990). The data are unweighted. In each model, about 2,000 cases are lost owing to listwise deletion.

Sources: European Values Survey (1981, 1990).

emerged during the process of nation building and where it still shapes the party system, we expect traditional religiosity to persist for longer than in countries without such a cleavage. Our results are presented in Table 7.4.

The first condition is met: the inclusion of the country dummy variables leads to a considerable increase in the explained variance. In the case of number of religious beliefs and type of God, the amount of variance explained is more than doubled. The explained variances now range between 14.6 per cent and 22.9 per cent. The second condition is also met. According to the level of economic performance we can roughly distinguish between two groups of countries, with the first seven countries in Table 7.4 belonging to the leading group and the last three countries (Spain, Italy, Ireland) belonging to the second (see also Chapter 3, Figures 3.2*a–c*).

Most scholars would probably agree that the classification which emerges from Table 7.4 also reflects different degrees of rationalization. However, as soon as we try to differentiate further between these countries, things become complicated. Is Denmark really more developed than the Netherlands, as the GDP per capita would suggest? Different economic indicators will lead to different rank orders. It might also be objected that a single indicator cannot reflect degrees of rationalization.

We take the view that the level of rationality within each group of countries is approximately the same, and that the different levels of church religiosity are better explained by the existence or absence of a religious cleavage. Thus, the two countries which are least church religious in terms of the internal, or belief, component—Denmark and France—either had no religious pillar or depillarized fairly early. In the Netherlands, West Germany, and Belgium, the dissolution of the religious cleavage started later, but probably rather earlier in the Netherlands than in the other two countries. A religious cleavage could also persist in Norway, centred around the Christian People's Party. The only country in the first group which does not fit the general pattern is Britain. However, as in the United States, church religion has penetrated much more into the lifeworld in Britain than in other Protestant or religiously mixed countries. This might also explain why the process of disengagement from the Anglican Church is more advanced than the transformation of the religious belief system. In our view, the rank order in Table 7.4 roughly reflects the degree of secularization at the macro level. This rank ordering will be used again in Chapter 8.

TABLE 7.4. *Church religiosity and the impact of the national context, 1981 and 1990*

	Average ranking	Importance of God		Number of beliefs		Type of God		Importance of God		Number of beliefs		Type of God: belief in a personal God	
	(1)	Regression coefficient (2)	Ranking (3)	Regression coefficient (4)	Ranking (5)	Regression coefficient (6)	Ranking (7)	Mean (8)	Ranking (9)	Mean (10)	Ranking (11)	% (12)	Ranking (13)
DK	1	−2.01	1	−1.70	1	0.75	1	4.03	1	1.76	1	21.7	1
FR	2	−1.66	2	−1.08	2	0.66	2	4.48	2	2.41	2	24.2	2
NL	4.3	−1.21	4	−0.81	4	0.42	5	4.66	3	2.77	6	31.3	4
GE	4.3	−0.90	5	−0.79	5	0.49	3	5.31	5	2.74	4	24.7	3
BE	4.6	−0.71	7	−0.85	3	0.44	4	5.45	7	2.64	3	35.3	7
NO	5	−1.35	3	−0.70	6	0.34	6	4.75	4	2.77	5	33.7	6
GB	7	−0.83	6	0.04	8	0.32	7	5.41	6	3.57	8	32.2	5
SP	7.6	0.00	8	0.00	7	0.00	8	6.21	8	3.53	7	53.3	9
IT	9	0.84	9	0.19	9	−0.05	9	6.55	9	3.64	9	49.6	8
IR	10	1.74	10	1.75	10	−0.35	10	7.95	10	5.28	10	71.7	10

Notes: Entries are unstandardized regression coefficients of the country dummy variables, means, and proportions. The regression coefficients in Tables 7.2a and 7.2b belong to the same regression equation. The first column in the table (average ranking) is the mean rank of columns (3), (5), and (7). The regression analysis is based on the four-point scale for church attendance (see Table 4.2).

Sources: European Values Survey (1981, 1990).

Our test of the combined effects of rationalization and the religious cleavage is admittedly crude. However, as long as no better indicators are available, country dummy variables give at least some indirect hints about the underlying causes of the decline of church religion. We should also point out that the rank orders of the regression coefficients for the three measures of the internal component of church religiosity differ slightly,[16] although they are highly intercorrelated[17] and are also highly correlated with the rank order of the respective means or proportions (see the right half of Table 7.4).

Conclusion

We have assumed that the decline of church religiosity is primarily caused by two processes, occidental rationality and the de-traditionalization of the lifeworld. Occidental rationality has resulted in the disenchantment of the world, in particular in the belief in a calculable and controllable world. De-traditionalization has made many more options available to modern individuals so that nowadays they can, or have to, choose among alternatives which formerly they either did not recognize or did not control—the so-called individualization process. The combined influence of these processes determines the degree of secularization which, in turn, has an impact on traditional religious beliefs.

At the individual level, the consequences of the secularization process become manifest in the significant effects of age, education, gender, and women's occupation. In accordance with the findings in Chapter 4, age primarily reflects differential cohort experiences and not life-cycle effects. This variable has the strongest effect, however, since it assimilates, to some extent, the impact of the other social-structural antecedents.

From a theoretical perspective, the interaction effect of country and education seems to be most important. As long as the educational system was under clerical control, it socialized people into traditional religion. This influence persisted in most Catholic countries after the Second World War. Accordingly, in Catholic countries highly educated older people are more church religious than the less educated. By contrast, education either has no effect or a negative effect in the Protestant world.

With only one exception, gender always has an impact on religious beliefs: women still display higher levels of church religiosity. Only in the Netherlands does the impact of gender become insignificant if we control for the employment of women. Housewives score somewhat higher on traditional religiosity than women in general. None the less, on the whole, women are considerably more religious than men. Differences in education and the socialization of men and women may be responsible for this result.

We have, then, to qualify the concluding remarks made in Chapter 4. Change in church religiosity is more nuanced than trends in the behavioural component—church membership and church integration—suggest. Trends in religious beliefs and cognitions point towards cultural lags between men, employed women, and housewives, and also between people according to their level of education. Our analysis also confirms the differences we registered earlier between young and old, and the country-specific differences due to different levels of secularization.

Finally, what political consequences might be anticipated to follow from these changes? We surmise that a large proportion of the more religiously conservative groups—housewives, the less educated, and the old—may still be geared to religious parties and may still accept a way of legitimizing programmes and policies which refer to religious beliefs and concepts. This may also be true, in general, for people living in less rationalized countries. The lags we detected may consequently lead to differences in trust in the political system and may also have an impact on participation in elections (see Chapter 16). However, if this may be true now, it might be a passing phenomenon since the effect of education and generational transitions will sooner or later eradicate these lags, and this trend will, of course, be faster in the economically more advanced countries. Consequently, the prevailing pluralism not only poses problems for the legitimation of politics in each country. Since religious orientations are gradually losing their dominant position in Western Europe, this might engender, for the time being, still greater problems of finding an adequate basis for the legitimation of certain kinds of policies.

NOTES

1. The relationship between church religiosity and education may be low in countries where the political struggle of the workers' movements was also directed against

the churches, in particular against the Catholic Church. We must not forget that the *Religionskritik* of the early materialists was very influential within the less educated working class.

2. For a critical overview of these hypotheses see Dobbelaere (1966: 170–94).

3. The 'number of religious beliefs' is almost as good an indicator as 'importance of God' but has no missing values.

4. For instance, in 1981, 20% of nuclear church members in Belgium claimed to believe in reincarnation.

5. The question is: 'How important is God in your life?' Answers are on a ten-point scale running from 1 = not at all important to 10 = very important.

6. The response categories, which are the same in both surveys, are: '[There is] a personal God', 'a sort of spirit or life force', 'I don't really know what to think', 'I don't really think that there is any sort of spirit, God, or life force'. We assign 1 to the first position (personal God) and 4 to the fourth (unbelief). We also tried to dichotomize the item, but the four-point scale performed best.

7. We know from other empirical analyses that 'importance of God' has the highest internal and external validity among all indicators of church religiosity. Nevertheless, we rely in the first instance on the number of religious beliefs and not on importance of God, for two reasons: number of religious beliefs has no missing values, while importance of God has quite a few. The latter variable has too many categories for the presentation of frequency distributions.

8. Moreover, we found no consistent cross-national differences between the three groups of employed people.

9. Stepwise inclusion was used.

10. All cases from the 1981 European Values Survey were coded 0; all cases from the 1990 European Values Survey were coded 1.

11. The reference category is 'no denomination'.

12. The *t* value is used as a crude criterion in order to distinguish between important and unimportant effects.

13. In Table 7.3 we have imputed the religious change between 1981 and 1990 to be approximately the same in all countries. Table 7.1 would suggest a quite different strategy, in order to allow for different changes within different countries. However, when we applied this alternative specification, the R^2 increased by less than 1 per cent in all three models. Furthermore, the regression coefficients we are interested in remained more or less the same. Since the presentation and description of the more complex models would require considerably more space, we report only the results for the simple models.

14. This is consistent with Inglehart's (1990: 184–5) finding that this variable is the best indicator of church religiosity.

15. Instead of country dummy variables, one could also introduce a country's economic performance (for instance, the GDP per capita) as a contextual property. However, we decided to proceed differently because the respective economic indicators are very crude measures of rationality. Furthermore, unlike GDP per capita, the dummy variables can also assimilate the influence of other factors such as the degree of pillarization.

16. Larger differences in the rank order occur only when the regression coefficients (or the means and proportions) are fairly similar. For instance, the rank order of

Belgium and West Germany changes from one variable to the next. However, these two countries have very similar regression coefficients in all three regression equations, as can be seen in Table 7.4

17. The correlations between the regression coefficients in columns (2), (4), and (6) of Table 7.4 are always larger than 0.95, and the correlations among the last three columns are only marginally smaller.

8

Religious and Ethical Pluralism

WOLFGANG JAGODZINSKI AND KAREL DOBBELAERE

The decline of church involvement during the last decades was documented in Chapter 4. There is also evidence that the process of disengagement has been accompanied or preceded by the erosion of religious beliefs. Unfortunately, the lack of longitudinal data makes it impossible to examine more closely the long-term transformation of religious beliefs or shifts in religious–secular value orientations. But we can gain some insight into changing individual levels of religiosity by means of cross-sectional analysis. This is the concern of the present chapter.

If we take religious beliefs, and not religious value orientations, as our starting point, it is not primarily on account of conceptual problems. Certainly, the notion of a religious value orientation is vague, and we do not see a straightforward strategy for operationalizing it.[1] However, in the present context, it is much more important that most of the hypotheses of interest are not stated in terms of religious value orientations but in terms of beliefs. For example, if the image of God is becoming more abstract (Durkheim 1960), then it is not an abstract value orientation which is changing but the content of a specific belief. And if traditional religiosity is assumed to contribute to a rigid interpretation of moral norms, then, again, we have a clear distinction between religious beliefs on the one hand, and moral convictions on the other. If all measures of church religiosity and all moral beliefs are seen as multiple indicators of the same latent value orientation, it would be impossible, or at least extremely difficult, to specify and test these hypotheses. Consequently, we avoid the term 'religious value orientation' in the present context.

Religious Beliefs Systems

Converse (1964: 207) defines a belief system as 'a configuration of ideas and attitudes in which the elements are bound together by some form of constraint or functional interdependence'. We adopt this definition. However, the notion of belief in the compound 'belief element' has to be distinguished from 'belief' in the usual sense; the latter can be equated to a more or less deep conviction, while the former refers to internal or mental states and processes.[2]

We are not so much interested in singular, isolated beliefs as in the interrelationships between a number of beliefs, in particular in the subtle interplay between religious beliefs and moral norms. Relationships among beliefs are usually established by individuals themselves. For instance, individuals may try to prove that some religious beliefs logically imply a particular position on an attitude continuum. In this sense, a priest may prove that the fundamental dogmas of Catholicism strictly prohibit any form of abortion. To laymen, logical implications are probably much less important than social and psychological sources of constraint (see Converse 1964; 1970); they simply know that a Catholic has to be honest, obedient to the Church, and must not support abortion. Even rudimentary forms of reasoning consciously generate relationships between religious beliefs and norms or obligations. Unfortunately, we are not able to measure these kinds of relationships with the available data. Rather, we have to restrict ourselves to statistical associations among belief system variables.

Since a system consists of a set of elements and relations among them, we call a set of belief elements and the relationships among these elements a belief system. A belief system is religious in a narrow sense if all the belief elements refer to supranatural beings, metaphysical entities, events, or states. We will use belief system variables to describe the properties of a religious belief system. These variables include both religious belief items—such as belief in a personal God—but also items concerning the centrality or intensity of these beliefs. In general, in Western Europe, the more traditional Judaeo-Christian beliefs people hold, the more intensively they believe, and the more important these beliefs are to them, then the more traditionally religious we judge them to be. A religious belief system in a broader sense also includes attitudes, evaluations, or cognitions which are assumed either to be dependent on religious belief elements or to influence them. We do not attempt to define the extended religious belief system more precisely since, in our view, determining the limits of religious or other belief systems is primarily a pragmatic matter.

Hypotheses

We do not elaborate on all changes to the belief systems which are expected to occur during the process of secularization. Rather, we concentrate on a few fundamental hypotheses which, to some extent, can be tested with the available data. In particular, it has been predicted that the diversification of religious beliefs and religious belief systems will increase in modern societies. As the churches have lost the power to interpret the content of belief authoritatively, religion has become a private matter (Luckmann 1991; Luhmann 1977). Numerous suppliers of religious goods have entered the religious market in order to satisfy metaphysical needs and individual religious tastes. Individuals can select their religion *à la carte* (Dobbelaere 1985b; Dobbelaere and Voyé 1990), creating their own *bricolage* (Luckmann 1979) of religious beliefs and value orientations.

As a consequence, we may observe, first, a large variety of religious belief systems in modern societies. Secondly, individual systems of religious beliefs and evaluations may become less consistent or coherent, partly because the religious consumer can buy from many different sources, and partly because the layman is unable to do the work of theologians in integrating the different orientations into a complex and coherent system. As a result, at the individual level, religion may become a patchwork of heterogeneous and frequently incompatible elements—what we call the *patchwork hypothesis*.[3] The same should apply to moral norms. Since religion no longer serves as a unifying and legitimizing fundament, a large number of competing moralities will emerge in modern societies. Accordingly, religious belief systems—in both the narrow and the broad sense—are likely to become more heterogeneous and less coherent.

In addition, obedience to moral norms is expected to decline. Remember that the Catholic Church and some of the smaller Protestant denominations have always stated clear and rigid rules for the guidance of their flock, particularly on sexual behaviour. People living outside these religious communities may either completely reject these moral norms, or, at least, treat them more flexibly. Moreover, people cannot be threatened with metaphysical sanctions. Again, to the extent that ethical pluralism is accepted as a normative principle, it implies a more tolerant and less unbending position on moral matters. If I accept that my neighbour has a different interpretation of moral norms and principles, I cannot require my own views to be valid for all persons and under all circumstances. Consequently, we may expect a rigid understanding of moral norms to disappear with the decline of church religiosity.

Analytic Design

We will first investigate the patchwork hypothesis. Since its precise meaning is not at all clear, we introduce two alternative interpretations. The first makes use of the well-known concept of constraint among beliefs. The second relates increasing value pluralism to heterogeneity: religious and moral beliefs, as well as religious belief systems, are becoming more heterogeneous in modern societies. To test this latter hypothesis, we define a new class of measures of constraint—measures of homogeneity.

Although the patchwork hypothesis applies to the religious belief system in the wider sense, we restrict the empirical analysis to a small number of religious and moral beliefs. The moral beliefs relate to some questions about sexual morality. At a first glance, such moral matters seem remote from politics in general, and from political trust and political support in particular. However, in almost all the countries under investigation, issues such as abortion, prostitution, and homosexuality are still highly salient in public debate; so too, until recently, was the issue of divorce in Catholic and religiously mixed countries. As matters of personal conviction, they may produce deeper conflicts within a society than most interest conflicts. Moreover, positions on such issues can readily be related to parties located on the religious cleavage since the Catholic and Protestant Churches have a clear stance on these matters. While the churches claim to defend Christian values and morality, opposing groups fight not only for liberalization, freedom, and emancipation, but also against the political power of traditional authority.[4] Thus, sexual norms still bear a high conflict potential even in more advanced societies. We examine the rigidity or moral norms in the last section of this chapter.

Both of our hypotheses imply dynamic relationships. The patchwork hypothesis predicts a long-term change in religious belief systems.

Similarly, the understanding of moral norms is assumed to undergo a slow and gradual change. Since the two comparative data sets at our disposal cover a period of only nine years (1981 and 1990), they do not allow us to study long-term change. Consequently, we are confined to cross-sectional analysis.[5] We compare the constraint and homogeneity of religious belief systems in less and more advanced industrialized societies, and we contrast the levels of homogeneity of moral beliefs in more and less church religious groups. We also investigate the relationship between the level of rigidity, the level of church religiosity, and social structural variables. It might be objected that empirical results derived from static analyses do not allow us to infer dynamic relationships: even if the level hypotheses hold, the dynamic hypotheses need not be true. However, the level hypotheses are an important part of secularization theories and therefore need to be tested. In addition, confirmation of the level hypotheses renders weak and indirect support for the dynamic hypotheses even though the latter cannot be mathematically deduced from the former.

The empirical analyses are based on the 1981 and 1990 European Values Study. Since the relationships between church religiosity and our other variables are fairly similar in both studies, we combine the data and perform a pooled analysis.

The Patchwork Hypothesis

Essential to the concept of a patchwork of religious beliefs is the assumption that even people in advanced societies cannot avoid transcendental experiences, thus they still hold religious beliefs. However, these beliefs are taken from different and frequently incompatible sources. A good example is belief in a personal God and, at the same time, in re-incarnation. This syncretism may not be logically inconsistent, but it is clearly incompatible with the tenets of traditional Christian theology. In this way, modern individuals hold to a system of loosely related transcendental beliefs which is fragile, unstable, heterogeneous, and, to an external observer, unpredictable.

It is this unpredictability which is elaborated here. Even if we know a smaller or larger part of a patchwork, it will nevertheless be difficult to anticipate the composition and colours of the other parts. And knowledge of these patchworks does not enable us to predict the composition of a new patchwork with much accuracy. The analogy in the field of religion is fairly obvious. If a multiplicity of religious belief systems co-exist in modern societies, then we can less accurately predict a person i's belief or belief system y_i, given the prior information about the distribution of Y within the population. Similarly, nowadays we may be much less successful in predicting a belief y_i, given the knowledge that i believes x_i. For example, while formerly those believing in God (belief x) may also have believed in a life after death (belief y), in modern societies this need not be true: given the knowledge that a person holds belief x_i, we can less accurately predict i's belief y_i.

Although it may be fruitful to consider both kinds of predictions as special cases of a general concept, we keep them separate. Both kinds of prediction can be tested by calculating the so-called PRE-measures of statistical association. The first error (E_1) is the smaller the better we can predict the beliefs y_i $(i = 1, \ldots, n)$ from the distribution of Y, and the second error (E_2) is the smaller, the better we can predict each y_i, given prior information about individual i's belief in x_i.[6] For the sake of brevity, let us speak of a first and a second prediction. Both prediction errors E_1 and E_2 should increase during the secularization process.

The second prediction also seems to enter the general definition of the static concept of constraint among a set of beliefs. The point is made by Converse (1964: 207): 'In the static case, "constraint" may be taken to mean the success we would have in predicting, given initial knowledge that an individual holds a specified attitude, that he holds certain further ideas and attitudes.' It follows that the constraint among two beliefs Y and X is the higher the better we can predict Y from X. According to the patchwork hypothesis, the less church religious an individual is, the lower is the constraint among his religious beliefs.

Straightforward operationalizations of the accuracy of predictions could be obtained from different PRE-definitions of the errors E_1 and E_2. As a general rule, the prediction of the religious beliefs y_i from the distribution of Y is the better, the smaller the proportion of errors E_1; and the prediction of y_i from x_i is the better, the smaller the proportion of errors E_2. However, Converse does not apply the latter measure but uses the correlation coefficient.[7] But the squared correlation coefficient does not reflect the success of prediction, only the improvement in prediction or the reduction of prediction error.[8] Thus, if the correlation coefficient is used, Converse's general definition has to be slightly modified. Constraint should not be equated to the success in prediction but, rather, to the improvement in the prediction of y_i, given the additional information that individual i holds certain further beliefs

x_{1i}, x_{2i}, . . ., x_{Mi}. However, this is a minor modification. Thus, in general, we distinguish three classes of measures for the goodness of prediction: the first is based on the prediction error E_1; the second on the prediction error E_2; and the third consists of the squared correlation coefficient and other PRE-measures. Subsequently, only a few selected measures from the first and the third class are considered. The former are measures of homogeneity, the latter are conventional measures of constraint. We elaborate on these measures in the next two sections.

Conventional Measures of Constraint

These measures do not require a lengthy discussion of their statistical properties. The correlation coefficient is used in the bivariate case, and in the multivariate case we use the proportion of variance explained by the first principal component. (The first eigenvalue divided by the number of belief system variables.) If 100 per cent of the variances are explained by the first principal component, the variables in the correlation matrix are perfectly correlated and are linearly dependent on each other. In this special case, the prediction error E_2 is zero and we can speak of maximum constraint.

What needs to be discussed, however, is whether these measures of constraint show decline during the process of secularization. We first examine religious beliefs in a narrow sense, and include in the analysis the three variables used in Chapter 4: the number of religious beliefs, the importance of God, and the type of God.[9] In traditional societies, the correlations among these variables can be expected to remain somewhat lower: if these societies were completely homogeneous, the correlation coefficients would not even be defined. If an overwhelming majority of citizens holds all seven Judaeo-Christian beliefs, considers God very important, and believes in a personal God, while a negligible minority is distributed more or less randomly on the three scales, the correlation coefficient would be close to zero. Clearly, if secularization results in religious pluralism and a more even distribution of all possible combinations of values on the variables, the correlation coefficient would not increase. However, we must bear in mind that during the first phase of secularization the antagonism between traditional Christians and an emerging group of agnostics and atheists may increase. To the extent that society then polarizes into camps of more or less equal size, constraint among religious beliefs will increase. If, at a later stage, atheists and agnostics became the majority, the constraint would decline to its former level. Thus, under these simplifying assumptions, we would predict a curvilinear development of constraint, with an increase in the early phase of secularization, and a decline in the later phase.

It is by no means clear that the real world takes the same developmental path. The patchwork hypothesis stresses religious pluralism more strongly than the antagonism between agnostics or atheists and orthodox Christians. Polarization may be mitigated or even neutralized by the emergence of a multitude of new religious belief systems. While antagonism will strengthen the correlations among the religious belief system variables, religious pluralism will prevent the relationships from becoming strong. Since the data do not permit longitudinal analysis, we have to compare the constraint among religious beliefs in a cross-section of contemporary West European societies. But here the situation is even more complicated. Even the most traditional societies cannot nowadays protect themselves against laïcization from abroad. Even these societies may therefore experience a certain amount of polarization, so differences between the less and more secularized societies become very small. However, the variables we include in the restricted religious belief system are much more sensitive to polarization than to religious pluralism. For this reason, we expect constraint among religious beliefs in a narrow sense to be the higher the more secularized a society (Hypothesis 1).

The extended religious belief system, besides the three religious variables, includes normative beliefs about sexual morality. Specifically, we include moral beliefs about under-age sex, homosexuality, prostitution, abortion, and extramarital affairs.[10] Respondents were asked to indicate their position on each of these topics on a ten-point scale running from 'can never be justified' (score 1) to 'can always be justified' (score 10). However, for several reasons, we expect no systematic variation between more or less secularized countries in the conventional measures of constraint on these items.

First of all, it is extremely difficult to find equivalent items for different countries. For instance, evaluations of under-age sex depends both on a country's laws and on the dominant meaning of the phrase 'sex under legal age'. If it is associated with sexual activities among young adolescents in one country and with child pornography in another, different response patterns would not be surprising. Secondly, we do not expect beliefs on all five items to change in the same direction during the process of secularization. While there might be more tolerance of homosexuality or divorce, that need not be true for under-age sex, particularly in the sense of child pornography. Thirdly, there may be differences between countries about sexual morality which have nothing to do with the extent of secularization. Even in highly secularized countries like Denmark and France evaluations of homosexuality may differ considerably. Clearly, most of these factors will affect the variable means. However, they will also alter, indirectly, the correlation coefficients and first eigenvalues in an unpredictable way. In any case, we do not expect constraint in the extended religious belief system to increase with the degree of secularization (Hypothesis 2).

Measures of Homogeneity

Since these measures have not been considered systematically in the analysis of belief systems, some definitions and explanations are required. In order to define some simple measures of homogeneity, we presuppose several measurement scales. The position of a person i on the scale will be called i's belief irrespective of whether or not beliefs in a narrow sense are investigated. We impute that beliefs can be measured without measurement error. If only a single belief system variable Y is considered and if only two beliefs y ($Y = 1$) and *non-y* ($Y = 0$) are possible, an intuitively meaningful definition of homogeneity can be given: a group is the more homogeneous, the more the percentage of persons believing y deviates from 50 per cent. Thus, a group is perfectly homogeneous if everybody believes y or nobody believes y. In the latter case, everybody necessarily believes *non-y*.

It follows that the variance of Y is the smaller the more homogeneous the group. Let p be the proportion of group members who believe y and n the number of all group members; then the variance is defined as $\pi*(1 - \pi)/n$, and the standard deviation is the square root of the variance. As can be easily verified, the variance and the standard deviations are the smaller the more p deviates from 0.5. This calculation suggests a straightforward generalization for belief system variables which are either dichotomies or metric scales: the homogeneity of a group is the larger, the smaller the standard deviation. As long as the same scale is applied in all groups, the standard deviation may be even more suitable as a measure of homogeneity than the variation coefficient.[11] The implications of this measure of homogeneity for the patchwork hypothesis is readily stated: the homogeneity of religious beliefs in a narrow sense should be lower the more secularized a society (Hypothesis 3).

As to national differences in the domain of sexual morality, we do not formulate a similar hypothesis for the extended religious belief system. However, we tentatively infer from the patchwork hypothesis that those moral norms which are firmly rooted in traditional religious beliefs will become more diversified with the de-institutionalization of religion. Accordingly, the more church religious a group is so the more homogeneous should be beliefs about sexual morality and divorce (Hypothesis 4). We now turn to the empirical analysis.

Levels of Constraint

As far as Hypothesis 1 is concerned, for the reasons already given, we do not expect large differences in constraint between countries. After all, in the societies under investigation the institutionalized churches still retain considerable influence. In Table 8.1, we have rank ordered the countries according to their degree of secularization—as empirically determined in Chapter 7. Denmark and France, at the top of the table, are most secularized, and the three Catholic countries Ireland, Italy, and Spain at the bottom are the least secularized. In Hypothesis 1, we anticipated lower constraint among the three religious variables in the more traditional societies, and higher constraint at middle levels of secularization. If the simple curvilinear model holds, constraint should also be somewhat lower in the most secularized countries than in the middle group.

Our findings for Hypothesis 1 are displayed in the left half of Table 8.1. The largest eigenvalue and the number of cases for the pooled sample are reported in the first column, for the 1981 European Values Survey in the second column, and the 1990 European Values Survey in the third column. If the largest eigenvalue is multiplied by 100 and divided by the number of variables (three), we obtain the explained variances in columns (4), (5), and (6). Therefore, Hypothesis 1 can most easily be examined by explained variances; the larger these variances, the higher the constraint.

By and large, the pattern of the explained variances fits our expectations. In the three most traditional countries constraint remains at a

TABLE 8.1. *Constraint among religious and moral beliefs in ten West European countries, 1981 and 1990*

	Nuclear religious belief system						Extended religious belief system					
	First eigenvalue			Explained variance			First eigenvalue			Explained variance		
	Pooled sample	1981	1990	Pooled sample	1981	1990	Pooled sample	1981	1990	Pooled sample	1981	1990
Total sample	2.32	2.30	2.34	77.3	76.5	77.9	3.72	3.80	3.66	46.5	47.5	45.7
N	27,546	12,135	15,411				24,170	11,132	13,038			
DK	2.30	2.35	2.24	76.6	78.4	74.7	—	3.43	—	—	42.9	—
N	2,005	1,015	990				—	976	—			
FR	2.22	2.27	2.16	74.0	75.7	71.8	3.46	3.61	3.29	43.2	45.2	41.1
N	2,018	1,099	919				1,873	1,023	850			
NL	2.40	2.43	2.38	80.1	80.9	79.2	3.91	3.95	3.85	48.9	49.3	48.1
N	2,080	1,087	993				1,870	931	939			
GE	2.36	2.34	2.37	78.7	78.0	79.1	3.81	3.88	3.78	47.6	48.5	47.2
N	3,064	1,139	1,925				2,677	1,124	1,553			
BE	2.30	2.13	2.35	76.6	71.0	78.3	3.58	3.43	3.60	44.8	42.9	45.0
N	3,434	919	2,515				3,010	831	2,179			
NO	2.42	2.40	2.44	80.8	80.0	81.4	3.15	3.23	3.09	39.4	40.4	38.6
N	2,389	1,198	1,191				2,211	1,092	1,119			

TABLE 8.1. *Cont.*

GB	2.22	2.17	2.26	74.1	72.4	75.4	3.22	3.28	3.17	40.3	41.1	39.6
N	2,606	1,162	1,444				2,435	1,066	1,369			
SP	2.12	2.05	2.16	70.5	68.5	72.2	3.91	4.16	3.72	48.8	52.0	46.5
N	4,603	2,113	2,490				4,224	1,926	2,298			
IT	2.20	2.09	2.30	73.3	69.6	76.7	3.68	3.66	3.79	46.0	45.8	47.3
N	3,192	1,240	1,952				2,952	1,170	1,782			
IR	2.08	2.14	2.01	69.3	71.3	66.9	3.40	3.58	3.22	42.5	44.7	40.2
N	2,156	1,164	992				1,942	993	949			

Notes: Entries are the results from principal components analyses with listwise deletion. Unweighted data.

Sources: European Values Survey (1981, 1990).

lower level than in the middle group of countries. To be sure, there are always exceptions from the rule. In 1981, the explained variance in Ireland is at the same level as in Belgium; in 1990, constraint in Italy is higher than in Denmark and France. However, the general tendency is fairly obvious: contrary to what, intuitively, might be expected, constraint among religious beliefs in a narrow sense does not decline during the process of secularization. Rather, the more advanced societies display higher degrees of constraint. In the 1990 survey and in the pooled sample, there is weak evidence for a curvilinear relationship with constraint being highest in the middle group of countries (Netherlands, West Germany, Belgium, and Norway), and somewhat lower at low and high levels of secularization. According to our explanation, the increase in constraint results from religious polarization: the more a society is divided between traditional Christians and agnostics or atheists, the higher constraint will become. Accordingly, the patchwork hypothesis cannot be translated into a hypothesis of declining constraint.

On the right side of Table 8.1 we report similar analyses for the extended religious belief system. This system includes five moral beliefs besides the three religious variables. Since the item on prostitution was not included in the 1990 Danish survey, the eigenvalue and explained variance for Denmark is displayed for 1981 only. Clearly, in the other countries, constraint has declined considerably because the correlations among the eight variables are, on average, much lower. Furthermore, as we anticipated in Hypothesis 2, constraint in the extended belief system does not vary systematically with the degree of secularization. Constraint is highest in the Netherlands, West Germany, Spain, and Italy—four countries at fairly different levels of secularization. Similarly, the countries with the lowest constraint differ very much with respect to secularization and rationalization. On balance, we do not observe a decline in the conventional measures of constraint. The secularization process seems not to reduce constraint, in this sense, among religious and moral beliefs.

Homogeneity of Beliefs

According to Hypothesis 3 we expect religious beliefs within a country to be less homogeneous the higher the level of secularization. To test the hypothesis, we report in Table 8.2 the standard deviations of the

TABLE 8.2. *Homogeneity of church religiosity by country, 1981 and 1990*

	Type of God			Importance of God			Number of religious beliefs			Pooled sample N
	Pooled sample	1981	1990	Pooled sample	1981	1990	Pooled sample	1981	1990	
DK	1.08	1.10	1.05	2.86	2.99	2.72	1.94	1.95	1.93	2,212
FR	1.05	1.09	1.01	3.06	3.08	3.03	2.32	2.32	2.33	2,202
NL	1.01	1.03	0.98	3.21	3.19	3.23	2.29	2.35	2.22	2,238
GE	0.96	1.00	0.94	3.05	3.07	3.04	2.16	2.18	2.15	3,406
BE	1.05	1.01	1.06	3.03	2.76	3.12	2.28	2.29	2.28	3,937
NO	0.98	0.99	0.97	3.22	3.24	3.20	2.49	2.48	2.49	2,485
GB	0.94	0.94	0.94	3.10	3.10	3.10	2.29	2.24	2.33	2,715
SP	0.93	0.92	0.94	2.82	2.77	2.86	2.44	2.46	2.41	4,940
IT	0.87	0.83	0.84	2.91	3.00	2.85	2.49	2.44	2.52	3,366
IR	0.68	0.68	0.69	2.40	2.48	2.30	1.96	2.02	1.88	2,217
Cochran's C	0.126	0.131	0.124	0.117	0.119	0.119	0.120	0.118	0.124	
Bartlett–Box F	71.60	43.43	35.48	32.21	15.84	21.03	40.04	16.77	23.94	

Notes: The country entries are standard deviations. Unweighted data. All coefficients are significant at $p < 0.000$.

Sources: European Values Survey (1981, 1990).

TABLE 8.3. *Homogeneity of sexual morality by levels of church religiosity, 1981 and 1990*

Number of religious beliefs	Sex under legal age			Homosexuality			Prostitution		
	Pooled sample	1981	1990	Pooled sample	1981	1990	Pooled sample	1981	1990
0	3.01	3.02	3.01	3.48	3.56	3.41	2.99	3.07	2.92
1	2.75	2.77	2.74	3.34	3.35	3.32	2.81	2.84	2.78
2	2.69	2.70	2.69	3.30	3.26	3.31	2.80	2.82	2.77
3	2.56	2.57	2.56	3.18	3.11	3.21	2.68	2.66	2.69
4	2.37	2.30	2.41	2.99	2.90	3.04	2.51	2.52	2.49
5	2.12	2.11	2.12	2.88	2.87	2.88	2.28	2.29	2.27
6	2.06	2.07	2.05	2.76	2.79	2.74	2.25	2.33	2.19
7	1.78	1.65	1.90	2.36	2.21	2.47	1.88	1.80	1.95
Total population	2.57	2.56	2.59	3.21	3.19	3.21	2.68	2.70	2.66
N	28,733	12,934	15,799	28,136	12,654	15,482	28,599	12,831	15,768
Cochran's C	0.19**			0.16**			0.17**		
Bartlett–Box F	237.95**			124.94**			180.34**		

	Abortion			Extramarital affair			Divorce		
	Pooled sample	1981	1990	Pooled sample	1981	1990	Pooled sample	1981	1990
0	2.92	3.10	2.74	2.63	2.76	2.50	2.77	2.89	2.68
1	2.91	3.15	2.66	2.46	2.57	2.36	2.83	2.93	2.74
2	2.78	2.99	2.60	2.35	2.42	2.29	2.75	2.87	2.66
3	2.66	2.84	2.47	2.30	2.41	2.20	2.75	2.85	2.64
4	2.57	2.73	2.44	2.12	2.17	2.08	2.69	2.75	2.65
5	2.47	2.50	2.43	1.85	1.89	1.83	2.72	2.80	2.64
6	2.45	2.54	2.34	1.88	1.90	1.87	2.70	2.75	2.64
7	2.12	2.01	2.18	1.62	1.56	1.68	2.51	2.45	2.54
Total population	2.90	3.09	2.73	2.69	2.39	2.23	2.90	3.01	2.81
N	27,752	12,911	14,841	28,673	12,892	15,781	28,738	12,949	15,789
Cochrans C	0.15**			0.18**			0.14*		
Bartlett–Box F	90.66**			208.12**			10.87**		

*$p < 0.001$ ** $p < 0.0001$

Notes: Entries are standard deviations of general attitudes measured on ten-point scales. Unweighted data.
Sources: European Values Survey (1981, 1990).

three measures of church religiosity for the 1981 survey, the 1990 survey, and the pooled data. Since it may be difficult to evaluate the relative size of the standard deviations, we report two well-known test statistics for variance homogeneity below each column. As can be seen, in all cases we can reject the assumption of equal variances. Accordingly, the standard deviations probably are not equal, yet they need not increase with the level of secularization.

In order to clarify this question, we again rank ordered the countries in the same way as in Table 8.1. Surprisingly, the variable with the lowest measurement quality fits Hypothesis 3 best. As predicted, the standard deviation of the variable 'type of God' increases with the level of secularization; the image of God seemingly diversifies at higher levels of secularization. However, although the variable 'importance of God' displays high levels of homogeneity in the three most traditional countries, the overall pattern does not fit the hypothesis. There is almost no difference in homogeneity with respect to the 'number of religious beliefs'. Only Ireland has a low standard deviation on all variables and in all surveys. Although the mean number of religious beliefs as well as the average values for 'importance of God' decline with the degree of secularization (see Table 7.4 above), homogeneity is not affected to any large extent. Accordingly, the content of religious beliefs seems to diversify to a larger degree than the more formal properties of the belief system, such as the centrality of the beliefs or the number of beliefs. Thus, we might have obtained rather different results if the content of beliefs had been taken into account.

Finally, turning to Hypothesis 4, we chose the number of religious beliefs as an indicator of church religiosity on pragmatic grounds.[12] We expect moral beliefs about sexual behaviour to be the more homogeneous the more these beliefs are integrated into a traditional Christian faith, or, in the operationalized version, the larger the number of religious beliefs. In Table 8.3, we have included divorce along with the five other items. Again, we display the standard deviations for both the 1981 and 1990 surveys and for the pooled sample. We distinguish eight groups. Those holding no traditional beliefs are displayed in the first row, those believing in God, the soul, sin, life after death, heaven, hell, and the devil, in the last row.

Apart from divorce, the pattern this time fits our expectations beautifully: the standard deviation becomes smaller as we move from the top to the bottom of the table. Highly church religious individuals are much more homogeneous with respect to the other five issues than non-believers. The differences between the standard deviations are so large that the assumption of equal variances can be rejected. The latter is even true in the case of divorce. However, this item does not display a strong relationship between homogeneity and church religiosity; only the most church religious group is somewhat more homogeneous than the others. Thus, church religiosity seems to have largely lost the power to homogenize the evaluation of divorce.

However, we must not be too quick to infer from these results that all attitudes towards issues of sexual morality become more heterogeneous in secularized societies. First, all six items may say more about verbal reactions to diffuse moral issues than about the true position of the respondent on the latent continuum. Since a rigid style of language in these matters is promoted by the institutionalized churches, especially the Catholic and some minor Protestant churches, highly church-integrated individuals may appear much more homogeneous than they really are. Secondly, heterogeneity will not only result if individuals subscribe to different norms but also if the norms implicitly refer to different situations. Some people may not have the cognitive ability to imagine a situation in which abortion is admissible, while others evaluate abortion in the light of the circumstances. They would probably choose different response alternatives even though they would not necessarily disagree in real life situations. Therefore, we want to know whether the group differences persist if behaviour in a more precisely circumscribed situation is evaluated.

The two European Values surveys allow us to examine this possibility. They include four items on abortion which refer to specified conflict situations. All four items present a conflict between the life of the embryo and a highly valued good: the health of the mother in the first case, avoiding the birth of a handicapped child in the second, and the freedom of the mother in the third and fourth cases. Each of the items has two response categories, approval and disapproval. To make interpretation easier, we report in Table 8.4 the percentages for the response category which corresponds most closely to the official doctrines of the Catholic Church. This time, the results for the pooled sample are presented in the upper half of the table, and the results from 1981 and 1990 surveys are contrasted in the lower half.

Apparently, heterogeneity does not always increase with the decline of church religiosity. Rather, the four items in the table can be evenly divided into two groups. In one group (woman not married and mother doesn't want a child), homogeneity increases with the number of

TABLE 8.4. *Homogeneity of sexual morality by levels of church religiosity: disapproval of abortion, 1981 and 1990*

(a) Pooled data

Number of religious beliefs	Child handicapped	Mother's health at risk	Mother not married	Mother does not want a child	N
0	11.9	3.8	48.9	42.9	5,386
1	14.3	4.8	61.1	55.1	4,567
2	16.7	5.3	67.5	62.4	3,822
3	22.0	7.0	72.9	69.6	3,473
4	28.9	11.5	79.1	77.0	3,178
5	36.4	15.8	81.8	80.9	2,795
6	41.8	19.9	83.9	82.3	1,691
7	54.8	29.7	89.6	89.3	4,806
Total sample	26.8	11.5	71.0	67.5	29,718
Missing values	1,316	624	1,460	1,317	

TABLE 8.4. *Cont.*

(b) Comparison between 1981 and 1990 surveys

Number of religious beliefs	Child handicapped		Mother's health at risk		Mother not married		Mother does not want a child		N	
	1981	1990	1981	1990	1981	1990	1981	1990	1981	1990
0	11.4	12.2	4.3	3.4	48.5	49.3	40.9	44.5	2,357	3,029
1	14.9	13.8	5.8	4.0	62.0	60.3	55.6	54.6	2,084	2,483
2	14.8	18.1	5.3	5.3	67.1	67.8	62.3	62.5	1,660	2,162
3	21.3	22.7	7.3	6.8	71.9	73.6	68.1	70.9	1,585	1,888
4	30.4	27.8	12.8	10.6	79.3	79.0	77.3	76.8	1,382	1,796
5	36.3	36.4	18.2	13.9	82.3	81.5	81.0	80.8	1,235	1,560
6	45.7	38.5	22.7	17.4	84.0	83.8	83.5	81.2	789	902
7	58.6	51.4	35.5	24.4	90.4	88.9	90.2	88.5	2,306	2,500
Total sample	27.9	25.9	13.6	9.9	71.4	70.4	67.6	67.4	13,398	16,320
χ^2	13.81		93.36		1.58		0.22			
p	0.00		0.00		0.21		0.64			
Missing values	688	628	413	211	763	697	715	602		

Notes: Entries are percentages disapproving of abortion in groups defined by the number of religious beliefs held. Unweighted data.

Sources: European Values Survey (1981, 1990).

religious beliefs; in the other group (mother's health at risk and child handicapped), just the opposite holds. Thus, a *bricolage* of moral attitudes cannot always be expected.

In our view, homogeneity will increase in secularized societies if this-worldly norms and values—such as the health or the life of a human being—come into conflict with the doctrines of the institutionalized churches. If these two conditions are met, church teaching will produce dissonance among its nuclear members which becomes manifest in a high degree of heterogeneity. It is for this reason that the first two items in Table 8.4 display the highest level of homogeneity in the least church religious groups. Remember that a group is the more homogeneous in this particular case the more the percentage of those (dis)approving deviates from 50 per cent. While abortion for the sake of mother's health is an old issue which has long since undermined the teachings of the churches, the abortion of a handicapped child has become salient only recently with improved methods of prenatal diagnosis. It is, therefore, not surprising that the population is more homogeneous with respect to the first than to the second issue.

That the first two items in Table 8.4 display a significant change between 1981 and 1990 (see the χ^2 test in Table 8.4*b*) nicely fits our explanation: church religious groups gradually adopt this-worldly norms, but the process of adaptation takes time. Even between 1981 and 1990 attitudes still homogenize more rapidly in the church religious groups when it comes to the old issue of risk to a mother's health than when it comes to aborting a handicapped child. This latter item yields a difference of about 7 percentage points in only two groups (those holding six or seven religious beliefs) but we obtain larger differences on the former item.

Things are completely different if this-worldly norms and values are not available or not undisputed. Then the church can provide its flock with guidance to resolve conflicts. This is why the remaining two items in Table 8.4 show a completely different pattern. Here, consensus among the church religious groups is much greater than among the other groups. This leads to the question of whether moral heterogeneity will be the rule or the exception in highly developed societies. On the one hand, we might argue that, apart from health and life, the stock of uncontroversial values has become quite small and it may shrink further. On the other hand, we must not overlook the possibility that institutions like schools, universities, or courts may generate a greater consistency of outlooks. There is also the danger of overestimating the homogeneity of traditional societies simply because we know almost nothing about the religious character and moral outlooks of former generations.

Rigidity of Moral Norms

It has often been argued that moral rigidity is promoted by traditional religion; religious people are usually assumed to be more rigorous and more inflexible on moral questions. Whether there are also differences between Catholics and Protestants is an open question. Catholics are often regarded as more dogmatic in stating a norm but more tolerant in applying it, but Protestants, too, are often accused of rigidity on questions of sexual morality. Finally, it has become part of popular mythology to assert differences between countries: sexual libertinism is considered to be widespread in the Netherlands, France, and Italy, but negligible in Ireland. Clearly, such assertations are prejudices rather than hypotheses. None the less, the possibility of differences between countries has to be taken into account.

Accordingly, we postulate two further hypotheses: that rigidity increases with traditional religiosity (Hypothesis 5); and, other things being equal, rigidity—if only verbal—is highest among Catholics, somewhat lower among Protestants, and lowest among unchurched individuals (Hypothesis 6). In the past, both churches have imposed severe restrictions on sexual behaviour. Furthermore, it is sometimes seen as an essential feature of postmodern individualism (see Chapter 11) that moral norms vary from one context to another and are more flexibly applied. Since our empirical analysis is based on verbal statements, we also expect Catholics to be rather more restrictive than members of dominant Protestant churches. We also expect differences between countries. However, unlike in Chapter 7, there are severe problems in explaining these differences. Explanations which refer to national character or specific national norms are almost always tautological (or nearly so): as soon as a difference between countries is observed, a national characteristic is invented to explain it. The explanation is as convincing as if we were to explain a thunderstorm by the rage of Jupiter.

Rigidity can be defined in many ways. We assume that a moral norm is understood more rigidly the less it is restricted to specific conditions and the fewer exceptions are admitted from the rule. For instance, if we consider that killing a human being is never admissible, we hold a fairly rigid view on this norm. Thus the six ten-point scales which have already been presented in Table 8.4 can also be seen as measures of moral rigidity. The lower the score on each variable the more rigidly the norm is understood by the respondent.

We test Hypotheses 5 and 6 by running similar regression analyses to that shown in Chapter 7, Table 7.3. There are only a few minor modifications. First, the dependent variable is the degree of rigidity with respect to a particular norm. Secondly, we enter the independent variables in different order. The three measures of church religiosity come first, then the social structural variables education, age, gender, housewife, and employment—operationalized in the same way as in Chapter 7—are entered next in a stepwise regression. Education, in particular, should have a direct impact on rigidity. The dummy variables for denomination are entered at the third step, with the unchurched group as the reference category. Fourthly, we include the country dummy variables in a stepwise regression, because we have no clear expectations about the rank order of their effects. Finally, we also take into account that rigidity might have changed in some countries between 1981 and 1990.

We know from Table 8.3 that the variance of the six dependent variables varies with the level of church religiosity. Usually, it is smaller the more church religious a group is. However, this clear relationship causes trouble in this regression because the assumption of homoscedasticity is violated, and this problem does not disappear even in the full model with all the independent variables. Since the elimination of heteroscedasticity is cumbersome, we have decided to perform the correction only on the fifth step.

The regression coefficients reported in Table 8.5 have been estimated by a weighted least squares estimation (WLS).[13] By contrast, the variance explained in steps 1–4 have been calculated from OLS regressions. The amounts of variance explained by the WLS regression and the OLS regression (in brackets) are reported in the last row of each regression in Table 8.5. As can be seen, the results differ only marginally in terms of explained variances. Although the differences in the *t*-values are a little higher, WLS estimation does not yield substantially different results. This is why we performed a WLS regression for Table 8.5 but not for Table 8.6.

Only those regression coefficients that are relevant in the present context are displayed in the table. Note that a negative sign implies a positive impact on rigidity. In all six regressions, church religiosity has the expected positive impact on rigidity. Among the three measures, importance of God consistently has the strongest impact, and number of religious beliefs comes second. The additional impact of type of God can usually be ignored. The effects are strongest in the case of abortion where the three measures of church religiosity alone—in step 1— explain 21 per cent of the variance in the dependent variable. In the other cases, the amount of variance explained by the first step is much smaller, varying between 6.9 per cent (sex under legal age) and 16.3 per cent (divorce). The differences may be partly due to intensive debate on the abortion issue in most of these countries, which probably makes it the most salient among these issues.

The social structural variables—with countries excluded—additionally explain between about 2 per cent (abortion) and 10 per cent (homosexuality) when they are entered at the second step. The respective regression coefficients are of secondary interest. However, we should note that increasing age is consistently related to greater rigidity, and increasing education, especially among young people, to less rigidity. Differences in the percentage variance explained are mainly due to the differential influence of these variables.

Apart from sex under legal age, the inclusion of denomination only marginally increases the explained variance: it rises from 12.7 per cent to almost 19 per cent for sex under age, but only increases by about 1 percentage point in the other cases. The differences between the churches are also small but usually in the predicted direction as far as Protestants and Catholics are concerned: Protestants are consistently slightly less rigid than Catholics. The most substantial difference is found in the equation for abortion where Protestants are not significantly different from unchurched individuals,[14] but Catholics display a highly significant standardized regression coefficient of -0.1. Although the additional contribution of denomination is not very strong, the standardized regression coefficients of the two large churches are almost of the same magnitude as those for church religiosity. In all, then, traditional religiosity, social structure, and denomination together explain a considerable proportion of the variance in the dependent variable. Accordingly, we conclude that there is weak evidence that rigidity will decline further if the de-institutionalization of churches and the decline of church religion continues and the level of education further increases.

Finally, turning to the differences between countries, the results are

TABLE 8.5. *Regression of rigidity of sexual morality on church religiosity, social structure, denomination, and country dummy variables, 1981 and 1990*

Independent variables	Sex under legal age (N=25,579)			Homosexuality (N=25,061)			Prostitution (N=25,495)		
	Unstandardized coefficient	*t* values	Standardized coefficient	Unstandardized coefficient	*t* values	Standardized coefficient	Unstandardized coefficient	*t* values	Standardized coefficient
Importance of God	−0.08	−13.42	−0.10	−0.13	−15.70	−0.13	−0.10	−14.81	−0.12
Number of religious beliefs	−0.05	−6.69	−0.05	−0.13	−12.64	−0.10	−0.09	−11.32	−0.09
Type of God	0.00	0.13	0.00						
Catholic	−0.77	−16.95	−0.16	−0.54	−9.16	−0.09	−0.46	−8.90	−0.09
Protestant	−0.54	−10.22	−0.10	−0.38	−5.75	−0.05	−0.44	−7.12	−0.07
Free	−0.62	−5.94	−0.03	−0.67	−4.64	−0.03	−0.99	−6.99	−0.04
Other	−0.83	−8.04	−0.05	−0.90	−6.43	−0.04	−0.82	−8.32	−0.05
Step 1: Indicators of church religiosity R^2	6.88%			10.79%			9.93%		
Step 2: Social structural variables R^2	12.53%			19.55%			12.90%		
Step 3: Denomination R^2	18.88%			20.39%			13.80%		
Step 4: Country dummy variables R^2	31.71%			25.14%			20.68%		
Step 5: Change 1981–90 within countries R^2	30.58% (32.17%)			25.53% (26.58%)			20.43% (21.11%)		

	Abortion (N=24,700)			Extramarital affair (N=25,528)			Divorce (N=25,568)		
	Unstandardized coefficient	t values	Standardized coefficient	Unstandardized coefficient	t values	Standardized coefficient	Unstandardized coefficient	t values	Standardized coefficient
Importance of God	-0.19	-23.34	-0.20	-0.10	-16.27	-0.14	-0.16	-20.80	-0.17
Number of religious beliefs	-0.19	-20.43	-0.16	-0.10	-13.60	-0.11	-0.18	-19.35	-0.15
Type of God	0.08	3.50	0.03						
Catholic	-0.60	-12.69	-0.10	-0.53	-11.76	-0.12	-0.55	-11.38	-0.11
Protestant	—			-0.46	-8.55	-0.09	-0.27	-4.84	-0.05
Free	-0.31	-2.58	-0.01	-0.64	-6.35	-0.04	-0.33	-2.42	-0.01
Other	-0.56	-4.73	-0.03	-0.52	-5.25	-0.03	-0.61	-4.58	-0.04
Step 1: Indicators of church religiosity R^2		22.08%			9.85%			16.34%	
Step 2: Social structural variables R^2		24.23%			13.01%			19.90%	
Step 3: Denomination R^2		25.26%			14.68%			20.26%	
Step 4: Country dummy variables R^2		28.77%			17.88%			22.72%	
Step 5: Change 1981–90 within countries R^2		29.69%	(29.77%)		18.17%	(18.42%)		23.60%	(23.89%)

Notes: The regression coefficients are taken from the WLS estimation (step 5). Pooled samples from 1981 and 1990 are used with listwise deletion. Unweighted data.

Sources: European Values Survey (1981, 1990).

disappointing. The respective dummy variables always lead to a considerable increase in the explained variance even though they were entered last in the regression equation; the increase in the variance explained varies between 2.5 per cent (divorce) and approximately 13 per cent (sex under legal age). But these findings are disappointing because we can give no convincing theoretical reason for the observed effects. We could try *ex post* explanations, but this is not as easy as one might expect: although sexual norms differ between countries, we cannot resort to statements like 'French people are typically more liberal in sexual matters.' The problem is manifest if we look at the means shown in Table 8.6, where the rank order closely corresponds to the rank order of the regression coefficients. For instance, Norway belongs to the most rigid countries on sex under legal age but is fairly liberal on abortion. Indeed, the rank order of sex under legal age is particularly puzzling. Perhaps different meanings are attributed to this issue in different countries.

On balance, then, church religiosity seems to have the expected positive effect on a rigid understanding of sexual norms. Sometimes, a rigid understanding is related to specific attitudes and behaviour. Conservatives frequently equate norm rigidity to a firm stand on all moral questions and obedience to the law. We can only warn against drawing such conclusions. For instance, among the respondents who say that abortion is never justified, only a minority is against an abortion if the mother's health is at risk. Thus, we cannot infer from the most rigid position on the ten-point scale a respondent's position on a two-point scale, even though the latter position seems to be logically implied. Much less can be said about the behaviour of individuals in real-life situations of conflict.

Conclusion

We argued in Chapter 4 that the decline of church religiosity is caused, primarily, by occidental rationality and the de-traditionalization of the lifeworld. The former resulted in the disenchantment of the world, particularly belief in a calculable and controllable world, while the latter has made available many more options to individuals in advanced societies. Nowadays they have to choose among alternatives which formerly they either did not recognize or which were thought not to be under human control.

TABLE 8.6. Regression of rigidity on social structural antecedents: impact of the national context, 1981 and 1990

Countries	Sex under legal age		Homosexuality		Prostitution		Abortion		Extramarital affairs		Divorce	
	Regression coefficient	Rank	Regression coefficient	Rank	Regression coefficient	Rank	Regression coefficient	Rank	Regression coefficient	Rank	Regression coefficient	Rank
DK	-1.83	2	0.85	9	0.64	8	1.43	10	-0.80	2	0.08	9
FR	0.91	9	-0.39	1	-0.01	4	0.61	8	0.89	10	-0.34	5
NL	1.97	10	2.57	10	2.06	10	0.41	7	-0.29	4	-0.34	6
GE	0.17	6	0.57	7	0.91	9	-0.07	2	0.01	8	-0.17	7
BE	0.91	8	-0.13	2	0.18	6	0.01	4	-0.19	6	-1.04	2
NO	-2.03	1	-0.11	3	-1.16	1	0.13	6	-0.97	1	-1.05	1
GB	-0.99	3	0.03	5	0.21	7	0.02	5	-0.27	5	-0.43	4
SP	–	5	–	4	–	5	–	3	–	7	–	8
IT	0.83	7	0.58	8	-0.12	3	1.19	9	0.70	9	0.47	10
IR	-0.80	4	0.16	6	-0.21	2	-0.90	1	-0.33	3	-0.84	3
Constant	4.94		4.58		4.32		5.50		4.31		7.29	
	Mean	Rank	Mean	Rank	Mean	Rank	Mean	Rank	Mean	Rank	Mean	Rank
DK	1.36	2	5.12	9	3.97	9	6.63	10	2.50	3	6.52	10
FR	3.91	9	3.66	6	3.21	7	5.07	9	3.95	10	5.58	9
NL	5.02	10	6.58	10	5.19	10	4.86	7	2.76	7	5.54	8
GE	2.94	6	4.20	8	3.83	8	4.26	4	2.87	8	5.53	7
BE	3.70	8	3.56	5	3.16	6	4.13	3	2.69	6	4.53	2
NO	1.03	1	3.93	7	2.01	1	5.04	8	2.16	2	5.09	3
GB	1.84	4	3.54	4	3.07	5	4.26	5	2.51	4	5.15	4
SP	2.49	5	3.28	2	2.75	4	3.63	2	2.55	5	5.16	5
IT	3.21	7	3.40	3	2.41	3	4.52	6	3.07	9	5.32	6
IR	1.40	3	2.99	1	2.20	2	2.02	1	1.87	1	3.68	1

Note: Entries are unstandardized regression coefficients of the country dummy variables, and means. Pooled data unweighted with listwise deletion. To obtain an average estimate of the country-specific component, regression coefficients were taken from the fourth step OLS regression in Table 8.4.
Sources: European Values Survey (1981, 1990).

Both of these processes are frequently assumed to lead to a pluralism of religious beliefs and ethical norms at the individual level. This development is sometimes seen as a menace to the political system because it is anticipated that it will lead to the breakdown of consensus about fundamental societal values and norms. It could be argued that ethical pluralism requires new kinds of political rules and different forms of legislation. Instead of prescribing or prohibiting particular behaviour, governments are confined to recommendations or the framing of procedural rules. As a consequence, the political process becomes more complicated and time consuming, and political control becomes more difficult, if not impossible.

In this chapter we have attempted to test the premiss of this argument. Is there really pluralism of religious beliefs and ethical norms in modern societies? In examining the question, we concentrated on a limited number of religious beliefs and a few normative beliefs about sexual morality. We focused on three aspects of religious and ethical pluralism: constraint among these beliefs, their heterogeneity, and a rigid understanding of norms. Using conventional measures of constraint revealed no hint of a decline in constraint. Rather, at the aggregate level, constraint among religious beliefs in a narrow sense seems to be curvilinearly related to the level of secularization: constraint increases as we move from lower to middle levels of secularization and declines moderately at upper levels. In this sense, religious beliefs are not less but more coherent in secularized societies. However, to gain a more complete picture of the ongoing process, we have to move from national aggregates to lower levels of aggregation, and we have to investigate other beliefs.

As for the homogeneity of religious beliefs, the image of God does, indeed, become more heterogeneous at higher levels of rationalization. This result fits nicely with the predictions of Durkheim and others. By contrast, variation in the number of religious beliefs does not systematically increase. Presumably, we have to investigate the content of specific sets or combinations of beliefs before general conclusions can be drawn. While the relationship between homogeneity and secularization is weak or non-existent, there is a clear tendency for some general beliefs about sexual morality to diversify with increasing distance from traditional religion. Even so, religious beliefs still unify positions on broadly defined moral issues. However, if sexual behaviour is less homogeneously evaluated among lay groups, this does not necessarily reflect the influence of incompatible moral norms.

Heterogeneity will almost certainly be observed if people are confronted with a general norm which they believe is valid only under specific conditions. The abortion items in our study are good examples: if all respondents believe abortion to be allowed in exceptional cases and they all agree upon the definition of these exceptions, then different estimates of the frequency of these exceptions alone will produce differences in the general evaluation of abortion. Accordingly, if ethical norms are relativized in their application and if absolute norms are replaced by conditional norms, the ethical evaluation of behaviour becomes much more complicated. The impression of ethical pluralism in advanced societies may partly be due to this complexity.

On balance, our study reveals a tendency towards increasing religious and ethical pluralism. However, the trend is by no means as universal as often suggested. Lay groups evaluate specific ethical conflicts more homogeneously than highly religious groups if uncontroversial this-worldly norms and values suggest a particular solution to a moral conflict and if this solution does not accord with the doctrines of institutionalized churches. Protestants in Scandinavia hold a more rigid and homogeneous view on under-age sex than people in the most traditional Catholic societies. Thus, in some domains, homogeneity and rigidity may even increase. Equally, consensus on other moral issues may diminish.

Finally, it seems possible that highly church religious individuals have more trust in political authorities and evaluate government outputs less critically. But these individuals are less pragmatic, and therefore may have more difficulty in compromising with other religious or ideological groups. Thus, the long-term consequences of religious change for West European political systems are ambiguous. What does seem clear is that there is no empirical evidence that the present problems of these systems stem from the growth of religious and ethical pluralism.

NOTES

1. First, we do not consider piety, modesty, humility, respect, honesty, and related concepts as religious value orientations even though they have played an important role in Judaeo-Christian religions. Secondly, we do not consider the principal components derived from factor analysis (cf. Inglehart 1990) of beliefs in a set

of dogmas, moral norms, and various attitudes to be evidence of a religious value. Rather, it is a measure of constraint for a complex belief system (see below).

2. The term 'belief' is used in both senses in this chapter. Since the meaning can be easily inferred from the context, different terms are not necessary.

3. Each belief element as well as systems of religious belief may also become unstable and volatile. The more open religious market produces its fashions, and religious consumers may be primarily concerned to keep up with the latest religious trends, whether or not these trends are consistent with their former beliefs.

4. Clearly, there may be exceptions from the general rule that these issues divide between a conservative, Christian camp, and anti-clerical camps. For example, on the issue of prostitution we may find an alliance between traditional Christians and proponents of the women's movement.

5. There seems to be no systematic change in our measure of consistency between 1981 and 1990. We suspect that the observed fluctuation is almost exclusively due to sampling error. Therefore it is not examined.

6. The general definitions refer to variables and not to beliefs.

7. The correlation coefficient is most frequently used (cf. Luskin 1987 for a critical discussion). Even if constraint is determined in more sophisticated structural equation models, the correlations or the covariances are the basic information (see Judd and Milburn 1980; Judd, Krosnick, and Milburn 1981; Converse 1980).

8. For illustration, let us assume that we could predict for each person whether she holds belief x or not (*non-x*). Suppose that 98% of the population share religious beliefs y and x; i.e. that the population is extremely homogeneous. The remaining 2% believe either y (1%) or x (1%), but not both. Then we will be extremely successful in predicting y, given the knowledge of x; 99% of the population will be correctly classified. However, we can make the same prediction on the basis of the distribution of Y alone. If we predict y for all individuals, we will also have 99% correct and 1% false predictions. Thus, the knowledge will not improve our prediction and the correlation coefficient is close to zero. It is not exactly zero because we do not predict class memberships but group means if this coefficient is used.

9. As all three indicators are highly correlated (about 0.7 and more), we could also treat them as multiple indicators of an underlying construct. Although we call them measures of church religiosity, they are kept separate because they reflect different properties of the religious belief system. In general their relationships with other variables should be fairly similar. Therefore, we include all three variables only where we want to investigate their similarities or differences more closely.

10. Divorce is not included in the principal component analysis because it is not directly related to sexual morality.

11. Things become more complicated if a large number of belief elements is considered because no measure of variability is available in the general case.

12. Other empirical analyses show that the variable 'importance of God' has the highest internal and external validity among all indicators of church religiosity. But we rely on the number of religious beliefs because it has no missing values, whereas 'importance of God' has quite a few missing values and has too many categories for frequency distributions to be presented.

13. The regression weights were calculated in several steps. First, an OLS regression

with the same independent variable was performed. Next, the squared residual of this regression was regressed on the best indicator of church religiosity; more precisely, it was regressed on the simple and quadratic term in order to admit curvilinear relationships. It was not necessary to correct using other measures of church religiosity. The predictor of this regression equation is then entered as a weight in the WLS regression (for details, see Greene 1991).

14. The unchurched is the reference group. The dummy for Protestants has not been entered into the regression equation because there is no significant difference between the two groups even at the 5% level. Clearly, faithful Protestants will differ from religiously indifferent unchurched people because the latter score lower on the measures of church religiosity.

9

Feminist Political Orientations

CARINA LUNDMARK

The roles of men and women have been extensively debated, particularly since the 1960s, when changing production patterns led to the wider recruitment of women into the workforce. The traditional division of labour became more diffuse as the state came to handle many former household tasks, for instance in education and health care. These developments made it possible for women to work in the paid economy and to retain responsibility for household work (Eduards, Gustafsson, and Jónasdóttir 1989). The result for women was a certain degree of economic independence, but at the price of a double workload. Economic developments coincided with a more liberal approach to family planning and the rise of a new women's movement protesting against inequalities between men and women. The process started earlier in some countries and later in others but the path it took was similar in most of the advanced industrial countries (see Chapter 3).

Moreover, over the period 1965–90, significant changes in political representation can also be identified. By the late 1980s, the proportion of women in Scandinavian parliaments and local assemblies commonly reached 30–40 per cent (Dahlerup 1988: 281). In the Netherlands and Germany it was 26 and 21 per cent respectively, in Luxembourg 16 per cent, and in Italy 13 per cent. Belgium, Ireland, Britain, France, and Greece formed a category of their own with only some 6–9 per cent of their members of parliament being women (Borchorst 1992).

A guiding hypothesis in this volume is that macro-level developments influence both value orientations and the actual behaviour of individuals (see Chapter 1). Orientations concerning the respective roles of men and women are thought to have formed part of a comprehensive value change in Western Europe in recent decades. Materialist, authoritarian, and religious orientations are mixed with, or even replaced by, for example, postmaterialism, postmodernism, environmentalism, and feminism. In brief, the shift implies the growth of orientations connected to self-realization and emancipation.

The starting point of this chapter is that the emancipation of women and other societal changes are likely to have resulted in altered outlooks about the distribution of power between men and women. Societal changes are also assumed to have altered preferences on how to abolish lingering gender inequalities, for instance by means of political participation and state intervention. In our analysis, feminist political culture is defined as a set of value orientations in its own right. Feminism is assumed to have specific implications for beliefs in government which cannot be explained by materialism–postmaterialism, left–right materialism, or religious–secular orientations—the three value orientations at the heart of this volume.

In studying political culture from the perspective of power relationships between men and women, at least two possible approaches may be identified. First, a focus on issues, illustrating the different opinions of men and women about a wide range of topics; and, secondly, a search for a fundamental feminist orientation with relevance for a political system in general and democracy in particular. As this chapter is primarily concerned with feminist theories, we adopt the second approach. It rests on the assumption that feminism is a set of fundamental orientations which can be identified no matter what issues are currently demanding political attention. The issue-orientated alternative would require us to search the political agenda of particular countries at different points in time. Even so, the issue approach is not completely overlooked. In a study of feminist political culture, gender is likely to be an important background variable along with, for instance, age and education. However, we do not explore empirical connections between feminist value orientations and standpoints on issues often associated with women, such as nuclear power, pollution, child care, and abortion. Although this kind of analysis would be very interesting, it is too extensive to pursue in a single chapter.

Over the years, the feminist movement has been a driving force in the emancipation of women. However, fundamental societal reforms require the engagement of more than a conscious few. It is reasonable to expect that a general improvement in the position of women has slowly begun to make its mark on people's fundamental orientations. In other words, we presume that feminist values were more widespread at the end of the 1980s than at the beginning of the 1970s.

In the next section the idea of a feminist political orientation is discussed from the perspective of feminist theories. We then propose an operationalization of feminist political culture which allows us to test the possibility of identifying a feminist orientation in a West European context. In the empirical sections, we present some analyses based on existing data sets for several West European countries. Finally, in the concluding sections, we discuss the interaction between a feminist value orientation and beliefs in government.

Feminist Political Orientations

Within the field of psychology, there is a vigorous debate about concepts such as masculinity and femininity. A so-called 'masculine male' is defined as an independent and assertive person, whereas a 'feminine female' is described as 'loving and helpful' (Feather 1984: 605). We adopt a different approach, disassociating feminist and—for want of a better term—'masculine' value orientations from personality traits. A feminist value orientation is linked to the concept of gender. This concept indicates male and female norms, which are social constructs. Female norms are not restricted to women but can also be held by men, although this is less likely.

In several respects, feminist theory is a reaction against the established ideologies of conflicts which can be located along the left–right continuum. Consequently, feminist thought has many variants. Nevertheless, a handful of common features can be distinguished, originating in a critique of present society from the perspective of women's subordination. These core aspects are a gender perspective, feminist cognition, and a wish to abolish gender-based inequalities.

It is argued here that a *gender perspective* is the most fundamental criterion for feminism. Feminist theorists stress the necessity of analysing men and women as basic categories in the distribution of goods and values in society. This is in contrast to mainstream political science which focuses instead on concepts such as class, citizens, or the individual, which are all assumed to be gender neutral. In line with feminist thought, asymmetric power relationships between the sexes exist at all levels in society (Eduards 1988). It is argued that society is shaped by men and in the interests of men, while women are perceived as an underprivileged group. Furthermore, it is claimed, 'masculine conceptions and actions form the norms and deviant feminine behaviour is punished by subordination and special treatment' (Eduards 1988: 210). Following Eduards, feminism includes both a gender perspective and a recognition of women's subordination in present society. This second criterion we label *feminist cognition* and it implies a negative perception of 'reality' for women.

Feminists recognize a gap between the democratic ideal and democratic practice (cf. Pateman 1983, 1988; Haavio-Mannila *et al.* 1985). Political rights are considered, for example, not to apply to women in the same way as they apply to men. Although women have attained a formal equality of status as citizens in most democracies, feminists argue that, in practice, women are still largely excluded from the corridors of power. Even in the 1990s, few women are found in top positions—whether in politics, administration, or business.[1] Furthermore, there is a general segregation of the sexes in modern society. Traditionally, men and women have different work tasks. When women entered the workforce, they often chose the same kind of work as they had previously performed in the household—caring roles, for example. This has led to occupational segmentation (Togeby 1985), and this segmentation remains when women enter politics. This pattern is clear in Sweden where women politicians are seldom found in traditionally male policy areas such as technical planning and national defence but, rather, in committees on health care, education, and culture. An explanation from a feminist point of view is that men actively seek to hold on to positions in policy areas which, by custom, are prestigious. A more traditional explanation is that women have personal experience of policy areas which involve caring and nurturing.

It is also held here that an awareness of women's subordination is a necessary but not a sufficient condition for an orientation to be classed as feminist. Besides cognition and a gender perspective, feminist political culture is also built around a wish to change the gender order where male norms are held to be more important, and where men and women are kept apart. Views on how to reach a society which is better for women diverge in feminist thought. The same is true regarding the construction of an ideal society.[2] To make these dividing lines visible, we introduce a scale of orientations relating to proposals for altering the present situation.

In theoretical terms, we can discern a continuum of orientations ranging from an optimistic to a pessimistic view concerning the possibility for change, and the state's ability to cope with issues related to gender equality. Both viewpoints propose stronger measures which could, and should, be taken to improve the condition of women, and so achieve a 'better' society for women and for men. However, advocates of the two 'poles' on the continuum have different measures in mind.

From the optimistic standpoint, the political systems of modern democracies are, by and large, legitimate. Not only is it possible to deal with women's issues within the present political order, but the state has shown some capacity for learning how to cope with new problems. Social security policies are seen as a classic example of how the state can help women, thereby demonstrating that women's issues should not prove to be irresolvable problems. At least in Scandinavia, political parties have included equality between men and women in their electoral platforms. In addition, women have been brought on to public boards and government committees. And now, in the 1990s, a party with few women representatives is regarded as presenting a poor image to the electorate.

Furthermore, according to the optimistic view, women should be active in political life, for instance through work in political parties. By doing so, conditions will gradually improve. It may take time, but, eventually, things will get better. This reformist direction of feminist thought, advocating reform of the political system from within, is commonly labelled 'state feminism' and is widespread across Scandinavia (Hernes 1987). In Hirschman's terminology (1970), the strategies for women are 'voice', combined with a certain amount of 'loyalty'.

From the pessimistic standpoint, radical solutions are required to change the status of women. Liberal representative democracies are deemed unable to meet women's demands. To improve the condition of women, society has to be changed completely (Pateman 1988). 'Loyalty' is replaced by 'exit'. According to this perspective, the state is just another patriarchal power structure, which makes it extremely difficult for women to work for change within the prevailing political system. If women try to do so, they become indoctrinated with its male rules and customs. The reforms women have obtained so far are held to be only minor concessions granted to undermine their demands. What is required is the transformation of society. How this is to be achieved is less clear, but one measure is quite explicit: all forms of hierarchical organization are to be replaced since situations involving subordination and superordination are detrimental to women. This line of thought is found among different shades of radical feminism.

In sum, a feminist political orientation is defined as consisting of three equally significant elements. First, a gender perspective, which implies the necessity of recognizing men and women as crucial categories in the distribution of goods and values in a society. Secondly, feminist cognition, which implies a recognition that women are disadvantaged. The third aspect relates to strategies for changing the present gender order; whether to accomplish change by means of political reforms and participation, or to insist on substantial changes in society.

Operationalization

Attempts have been made in oral history to document feminist cultures. Several researchers (cf. Anderson *et al.* 1990) used relatively unstructured interviews, and the results have been rather poor. So, what can we expect of data from structured surveys such as the ones we use in this chapter?

As was emphasized in Chapter 2, we—the researchers—apply the value concept as a way of enhancing our understanding of the evidence before us, and survey data provide a way of distinguishing generalized cultural patterns which are difficult to uncover through extended, qualitative interviews. Thus, the more pressing question is: what data sets are there which can be used to illustrate feminist political culture? We need survey data which include indicators measuring a gender perspective, feminist cognition, and support for reform or radical change.

Several European data sets include questions about women and their position in society. However, the questions are not framed from a feminist point of view. In fact, they are designed primarily to measure people's opinions about equality, or the proper scope of government, or to place people, objectively, along traditional (especially left–right) conflict lines. The best indicators, both in terms of quality and quantity, appear in the two Eurobarometer special surveys on the issue of women, No. 3 (1975) and No. 19 (1983). These two surveys have the additional advantages that the same themes recur, allowing for comparison over time, and they are truly comparative, involving ten West European countries: Denmark, Belgium, Germany, Ireland, Luxembourg, the Netherlands, Britain, France, Italy, and Greece. A

TABLE 9.1. *Six indicators of feminist, masculine, and traditional orientations*

Description	Masculine	Traditional	Feminist	
1. Is the situation of women in society a problem or not? (Degree of importance)	0–2	3–7	8–10	
2. Is the situation of women better or worse than that for men regarding job security?	Better for women	Same	Worse for women	⎫
3. Is the situation of women better or worse regarding prospects of promotion?	Better for women	Same	Worse for women	⎬ Cognition
4. Is the situation of women better or worse regarding wages in paid employment?	Better for women	Same	Worse for women	⎭
5. Politics should be left to men.	Agree strongly	Agree/disagree a little	Disagree completely	Reformist change
6. Women should organize into an independent movement to achieve radical transformation in society.	Disagree completely	Agree/disagree to some extent	Agree completely	Radical change

Sources: Eurobarometer, Nos. 3 and 19.

shortcoming is that there have been no Eurobarometer surveys with women as a special theme since 1983.[3]

Six indicators were selected, as shown in Table 9.1. They were selected from a larger number of variables about women and women's status in the two Eurobarometer surveys. These six variables are judged to be the most appropriate for capturing a feminist orientation.[4]

The gender perspective is problematized in each of the indicators here, since it is an inseparable aspect of both feminist cognition and strategies for change. Four variables were identified as a satisfactory operationalization of feminist cognition. They can be summarized as (1) whether the position of women in society is a problem, (2) whether women and men have equal opportunities concerning job security, (3) whether prospects of promotion are equal, and (4) whether wages paid in gainful employment are equal. We considered combining all four cognitive variables into an index but our initial analysis revealed that the variables are not one-dimensional. Whereas attitudes on wage differences, job security, and promotion prospects are positively associated (Kendall's tau-*b* about 0.4 in 1975 and 0.8 in 1983), responses to the question about the situation of women in society are not significantly related to the other variables (tau-*b* 0.1 at most). Accordingly, the three work-related variables—indicators 2, 3, and 4—were formed into a cognitive index. Attitudes towards women's position in society are analysed separately.

We should note that the sample size for the work-related indicators in Table 9.1 is not the same at the two points in time. These questions were put to all respondents in 1975, but in 1983 they were put only to respondents in paid employment. We have dealt with this problem by restricting the analysis of the cognitive index to employed people. Thus, although the indicators are directly comparable, the difference in sample size has some impact on our results.

Operationalizing the cognitive aspect is relatively uncomplicated as the same four variables appear in both surveys. However, the data situation is more problematic for indicators of strategies to improve the position of women in society. First, the questions are often general in character. Asking respondents whether or not they agree that 'There should be fewer differences between the respective roles of men and women in society' is just one example. Although this assertion indicates a commitment to change, it is diffuse in character and can mean anything from some redistribution of household responsibilities to positive discrimination policies to ensure that women occupy half the seats in elected assemblies. Consequently, this and similar questions cannot be treated as indicators of either reformist or radical strategies.

A second problem is that the relevant variables are often available in only one of the two Eurobarometer special issues on women. The fifth indicator in Table 9.1 is an exception. Respondents were asked to agree or disagree with a highly traditional statement: 'Politics should be left to men.' Disagreement implies a wish to see both women and men in political parties and in decision-making arenas. This is interpreted as an indicator of reformist feminism. Questions about the radical aspect of feminist strategy, however, seem to be a more recent development in survey research. In a comparative perspective, it is covered only in Eurobarometer, No. 19 (1983), in the item 'Women should organize into an independent movement to achieve radical transformation in society.' Thus, although the indicator is available for only one time point, it is retained in the analyses because of its importance.

Given the six variables presented in Table 9.1, it is easy to establish what attitudes reveal a feminist orientation. Our discussion of feminist political culture identified three common aspects of feminism: a recognition of the subordination of women in society, a wish to change this state of affairs, and a gender perspective. The third column in Table 9.1, labelled 'feminist', is in line with these criteria. Those viewpoints which stand in opposition to the feminist position—that the position of women in gainful employment is better than for men, for example—share a gender perspective but value it quite differently. Claiming that women enjoy advantages shows a touch of male chauvinism when compared with official statistics on wage differentials, and the acknowledged difficulties for women in combining a career with child-care responsibilities. This category is identified as 'masculine' in the following analyses.

After establishing strong masculine and feminist categories, a middle alternative remains. For the three cognition variables, at least, the most plausible interpretation is that respondents do not perceive any real differences in opportunities for men and women. In other words, this category is the only one lacking a gender perspective. As such, 'traditional' is an appropriate label. The fact that 'don't know' answers are grouped with missing observations in a separate category means that we are unlikely to be interpreting responses in the middle group as an expression of uncertainty.

The discussion in Chapter 2 emphasized that value orientations cannot be directly observed, so our empirical analysis focuses on attitudes. As in the chapters which examine the three central value orientations, we are looking for a patterning of attitudes which allows us to infer distinctively feminist, traditional, or masculine value orientations.

Cross-National Comparisons

The empirical analysis investigates whether we can identify a feminist political culture in Western Europe. If a feminist orientation can be distinguished, how does the distribution compare across countries, and how has it changed over time? Two time points are covered, 1975 and 1983. Our search for a feminist political orientation covers all the countries included in the two Eurobarometer surveys. We highlight similarities rather than country-specific differences, which may be related to historic, economic, and political factors.

Are women more feminist than men? It is easy to assume that this is the case. But it is also relevant to turn the question round, asking to what extent men share a feminist value orientation. Age and education may also be treated as background variables. According to theories of political socialization, age is important in explaining the content of value orientations. Feminism became very popular during the 1960s and 1970s, and political socialization research indicates that young people are more prone to absorb new phenomena and adjust more readily to social change (Niemi 1974). The persistence of value orientations, however, is open to discussion. There may be life-cycle effects (Cutler 1975), implying that young people tend to protest against their parent's generation. Yet we might note that, as they mature, younger generations tend slowly to adopt orientations similar to those of the older generation. Again, we could consider that shared experiences within a generation, combined with the spirit of the time during formative years, give rise to significant and persistent intergenerational differences.

We assume that rising levels of formal education since the Second World War have stimulated debate on the relationship between men and women in society. We also presume that generational differences in education influence all three aspects of a feminist value orientation: the gender perspective, the perceived position of women in society, and beliefs regarding political strategies for societal improvement. Direct measures on education are not available in the Eurobarometer surveys;

TABLE 9.2. *Feminist, traditional, and masculine cognition of women's situation, 1975 and 1983*

Cognition	DK	BE	GE	IR	LU	NL	GB	FR	IT	GR
Feminist										
1975	26	29	23	42	49	10	21	48	45	—
1983	18	12	16	16	17	8	13	23	34	28
Traditional										
1975	43	52	58	41	30	52	50	45	44	—
1983	50	54	56	56	57	56	52	58	50	50
Masculine										
1975	28	18	19	17	19	34	27	7	11	—
1983	30	24	23	26	23	35	31	14	16	12
d.k./n.a.										
1975	3	1	0	0	2	4	2	0	0	—
1983	2	10	5	2	3	1	4	5	0	10
N										
1975	1,073	1,554	1,039	1,000	324	1,093	1,328	1,156	1,043	—
1983	1,027	1,038	1,049	985	300	998	1,347	1,011	1,031	1,000

Notes: Entries are percentages of national samples based on responses to indicator 1 in Table 9.1. d.k./n.a. indicates 'don't know/not available'.

Sources: Eurobarometer, Nos. 3 and 19.

instead, the analysis of education is based on age of completing full-time study. Although this variable is not as accurate as a specific measure would be, the age groups provide an acceptable classification, ranking education from basic to advanced.[5] Furthermore, the indirect indicator for schooling is less sensitive to national differences in educational systems.

In Table 9.2 we present our findings for the first cognitive indicator, which stands on its own as a measure of feminist, traditional, and masculine 'awareness'. Respondents were asked whether they consider the position of women in society to be a problem. In 1975, Ireland, Luxembourg, France, and Italy ranked very high on this indicator: some 42–49 per cent of respondents in the national samples were located in the feminist category. In a middle group of countries, consisting of Denmark, Belgium, Germany, and Britain, about 20–30 per cent of the sample fell into the feminist category. The Netherlands stood on its own, with a notably low 10 per cent of respondents with a 'feminist cognition'.

Between 1975 and 1983, however, a considerable decline in feminist awareness is evident. For Ireland, Luxembourg, and France, the decline was quite dramatic, some 25–32 percentage points. In most of the other countries, the drop in feminist cognition, on average, was around 10 percentage points. The Netherlands was the only exception, showing little change between 1975 and 1983. Despite the general decline, there was still a sizeable proportion of the population in Italy, Greece, and France who recognized women as an underprivileged group in society in 1983.

Regardless of year and nation, the 'masculine' outlook was particularly frequent among respondents older than 55 years. Feminist cognition was slightly more common among younger West Europeans. In each of these countries, however, masculine and traditional orientations were overwhelmingly prevalent among those who completed their schooling aged 15 or younger.[6] However, the relationship between a feminist orientation and education is less clear. In 1983, in Belgium, Germany, and Britain, there were only marginal differences between educational groupings and a feminist value orientation. In Ireland, Luxembourg, the Netherlands, and France, a feminist orientation was most frequent among those leaving full-time education aged 16–19 (data not shown here).

To what extent did men in Western Europe, during the 1970s and 1980s, share a feminist cognition? In almost every country, it is possible to identify a clear pattern. As we might have expected, women were more likely to see the position of women in society as a problem, while men were overrepresented in the traditional and masculine categories. In 1975, as an average across the nine countries, the gap in feminist cognition between women and men was some 5–8 percentage points. The difference was largest in Germany, with a gap of 9 points. Denmark and the Netherlands proved to be interesting exceptions with practically no gender discrepancy. In 1983, a gap of some 5–11 percentage points was identified in most these countries. Denmark and the Netherlands continued to be the exceptions, revealing a comparably small divergence between the cognitive orientations of women and men. In 1983, the largest differences were found in Germany, Ireland, Britain, and Italy. Indeed, the pattern was at its clearest in Italy, where the gap between women and men in feminist cognition was fully 20 percentage points. These results strengthen the assumption that feminist cognitions are more common among women than among men.

As we can see in Table 9.2, about half the total sample recognized a gender perspective—either to the advantage of women or to the advantage of men. Merging the masculine and traditional categories, however, yields an impression of the general climate with regard to feminist cognition. The 'masculine' outlook is characterized by disapproval of the emancipation of women, while people in the traditional group do not perceive gender differences at all, which implies a preference for the status quo. Once we merge these two categories, it becomes evident that a patriarchal value orientation is overwhelmingly in the majority right across Western Europe, averaging approximately 80 per cent of national populations in 1983. The Netherlands led the field with 91 per cent displaying a patriarchal outlook; Greece was at the other extreme with 'only' 62 per cent in the patriarchal group.

In Table 9.3, cognition is measured by indicators 2–4 in Table 9.1. Respondents were asked their opinion about the position of women and men with respect to job security, promotion, and wages. As the three variables were found to be interrelated, the indicators were transformed into an index by adding together their values and dividing by three.[7] But before turning to the results, recall our earlier caveat about these data: the questions were put to the entire national sample in 1975, but only to people in paid employment in 1983. So the figures in Table 9.3 are restricted to people in gainful employment. Only for 1975 would it be possible to compare value orientations among the employed and those either outside the workforce or not in work.

TABLE 9.3. *Feminist, traditional, and masculine cognitions of women's employment, 1975 and 1983*

Cognition	DK	BE	GE	IR	LU	NL	GB	FR	IT	GR
Feminist										
1975	21	26	36	36	23	23	20	37	16	—
1983	34	24	37	18	13	31	15	32	13	17
Traditional										
1975	58	52	53	56	25	48	56	54	66	—
1983	47	61	47	64	70	60	67	56	77	59
Masculine										
1975	17	17	10	7	32	23	22	9	17	—
1983	14	12	11	15	16	8	15	11	9	19
d.k./n.a.										
1975	4	5	1	1	20	6	2	0	1	—
1983	5	3	5	3	1	1	3	1	1	5
N										
1975	605	722	645	453	170	431	771	518	527	—
1983	559	452	498	394	145	440	642	460	469	418

Notes: Entries are percentages among respondents in paid employment only. For details of the three categories, see n. 7. d.k./n.a. indicates 'don't know/not available'.

Sources: Eurobarometer, Nos. 3 and 19.

Ireland and France again show relatively high figures for the proportion with feminist cognition in 1975. The proportion is similarly high in Germany, while Italy ranks surprisingly low compared to the figures in Table 9.2. However, using the cognitive index brings the proportion with feminist cognition in the Netherlands more into line with the general picture across these countries. Evidently, the Dutch are more ready to acknowledge the specific difficulties which women experience in the labour market than to concede that these constitute a general problem.

Our first cognitive indicator—'the situation of women in society'—revealed a large drop in feminist awareness between 1975 and 1983. When measuring cognition with the cognitive index, six of the nine countries still displayed a decline in feminist cognition. But the fall is more modest. Since the number of women in paid employment increased during this period, this might lead us to infer that greater gender equality was being achieved. However, when inequalities are no longer formal in character but hidden in the structures of patriarchal society, they can be difficult to pinpoint. This might account for at least some part of the decline in feminist cognition between 1975 and 1983.

The differences in the results in Table 9.2 and Table 9.3 are not explained by varying sample size. In 1975, the discrepancy between employed people and the entire sample seldom exceeds 3 percentage points. We cannot make any judgement about which cognitive indicator accords most closely with 'reality' in these countries; both are regarded as acceptable measures of feminist and masculine awareness. However, in the analysis of feminist political orientations which follows in a later section, we return to the single indicator 'is the position of women in society a problem or not?' It allows us to increase the level of generality in our search for feminist political culture, for the position of women in society is a wider question than is captured by the work-related variables. In addition, using the first indicator means that we have data for the full national samples.

Feminist Strategies for Change

Respondents to the two Eurobarometer surveys were asked whether they thought politics should be left to men. Strong agreement is interpreted as a 'masculine' standpoint; repudiation implies a 'feminist' orientation along reformist lines; and the weaker responses 'agree'

TABLE 9.4. *Support for reformist change, 1975 and 1983*

Reformist strategies	DK	BE	GE	IR	LU	NL	GB	FR	IT	GR
Feminist										
1975	46	20	25	50	19	39	49	43	42	—
1983	65	28	29	45	37	61	54	55	53	66
Masculine										
1975	8	27	17	15	24	15	14	12	17	—
1983	3	12	6	10	16	8	10	8	11	11
Traditional										
1975	38	45	53	33	46	36	33	42	38	—
1983	22	48	59	41	47	29	34	35	35	20
d.k./n.a.										
1975	8	8	5	2	11	10	4	3	3	—
1983	10	12	6	4	0	2	2	2	1	3

Notes: Entries are percentages of national samples with a feminist, masculine, or traditional standpoint on reformist feminism. d.k./n.a. indicates 'don't know/ not available'. For *N*, see Table 9.2.

Sources: Eurobarometer, Nos. 3 and 19.

and 'disagree' represent a traditional position (see Table 9.1). In Table 9.4, we show levels of support for reformist feminism in nine countries in 1975 and ten countries in 1983. Clearly, people were much more prone to support reformist feminism in 1983 than in 1975, in spite of a decline in feminist awareness. In some countries—Denmark, Luxembourg, and the Netherlands—the increase was close to 20 percentage points. One possible explanation for this increase is that when people are uncertain about whether or not there is a problem, they are more likely to resort to modest instruments for change. Reforms stand for moderate changes which may benefit one group without limiting the options of another. When a reformist outlook is gaining ground, it is likely that fewer people prefer radical strategies for change. Yet trends in grass roots activism (see Chapter 15) suggest that the 1970s and early 1980s were not periods of quiet reformism.

From our earlier discussion of the three aspects of feminist political culture, reformist measures for change might be expected to predominate in Scandinavian countries. This is not the impression obtained from Table 9.4. Denmark was one of the top three countries in demonstrating support for reformism, but support was widespread across Western Europe. It seems that the basic ideas of 'state feminism', of incorporating women into the traditional political arena, were not exclusive to the Scandinavian countries during the 1970s and 1980s.

In both 1975 and 1983, some countries displayed considerable differences between women and men regarding reformist measures. Ireland headed the list, with a difference of 11 percentage points between women and men in the reformist category, followed by Germany with a 6–8 point difference. Most other countries showed a discrepancy of some 4–6 percentage points. Just a few countries diverge from this pattern; for example, in the Netherlands and Italy, for both time points, there was virtually no difference in the proportion of women and men supporting reformist change (data not shown here).

In the eyes of some feminists, political reforms are insufficient to achieve true equality between men and women. The radical end of the strategy scale is distinguished by a belief that women themselves have to take the initiative and work outside the traditional—male—political arena. Otherwise, change will either not occur, or the pace will be too slow. Although the question measuring support for a radical strategy was asked only in 1983, responses to the proposition 'Women should organize into an independent movement to achieve a radical transformation in

TABLE 9.5. *Feminist political culture in ten West European countries, 1975 and 1983*

	DK	BE	GE	IR	LU	NL	GB	FR	IT	GR
1975	15	9	9	25	11	6	14	24	24	—
1983	14	4	8	12	9	7	8	15	22	22

Notes: Entries are percentages of national samples with a feminist outlook on society and politics. For *N*, see Table 9.2.

Sources: Eurobarometer, Nos. 3 and 19.

society' give us some idea about levels of support for radical feminist strategies.

Only very small proportions in each country were in complete agreement with the need for women to organize independently to achieve societal transformation (data not shown here). In most of these countries no more than a hard core of some 4–8 per cent supported radical feminism. However, this was not the case in Greece, where as many as 32 per cent supported the idea of a radical feminist movement. Italy did not even faintly resemble its neighbour, but was positioned within the group of 'modest' nations. In most countries, disapproval of a radical women's movement was most pronounced among men: in Italy there was a gap of 24 percentage points between men and women in disagreeing with the proposal. In most other countries, the difference remained around 10 percentage points. As for differences by age, radical opinions were most frequent among the two youngest age groups (up to the age of 34).[8] This is in line with the findings about protest activity in most surveys for the early 1980s.

Feminist Political Culture

In Table 9.5, feminist cognition and preference for a reformist strategy are combined, giving us a measure of feminist political culture. Only two indicators are used: feminist cognition, based on the question 'Is the position of women in society a problem or not?', and support for a reformist strategy, based on the question 'Should politics be left to men?' Both questions were asked in 1975 and 1983 (except in Greece in 1975).

An identifiable feminist political culture emerges in each of the ten countries. However, developments between 1975 and 1983 suggest a division of the countries into two distinct categories. On the one hand, Denmark, Germany, Luxembourg, the Netherlands, and Italy display little change over the period. On the other hand, there is a significant decline in feminist culture in Belgium, Ireland, Britain, and France. At the end of this short period, feminist political culture seems most robust in Italy and, perhaps, in Greece.

It is easy to establish cross-national differences, but what do they mean? Is the relatively high incidence of feminist political culture in Italy and Greece an indication of an advanced feminist movement or, perhaps, a reflection of more obvious differences in the position of men and women? To explain the ranking of nations, we need to know more about the actual position of women in these countries during the 1970s and 1980s.

Formal statistics about employment rates and wage differentials between men and women can give us some indication. However, this background information does not quite follow the cultural patterns found in our data. In the case of employment, the situation in 1975 was that about 75–80 per cent of men aged 15 to 64 were in full-time employment. The corresponding figure for women was only 30–63 per cent, with the highest levels in Denmark, Germany, Britain, and France.[9] Part-time work was, and is, significantly more common among women, especially among married women.[10] About half the working women were engaged in public sector service work, except in Denmark and the Netherlands, where the corresponding figure was three-quarters. Regardless of the type of employment and the country, women earned considerably less than men. In 1975, the largest wage gaps were found in Germany, Britain, and the Netherlands, the narrowest in France and Italy.

To interpret fully the results of our analyses, the findings should be placed in a wider cultural context. History, tradition, religion, and fluctuations in the economy are likely to be important factors in explaining national differences in feminist value orientations. Formal statistics concerning the number of women in the workforce and the provision of child-care facilities provide some guidance. Ideally, close examination of the actual position of women in each country would allow us to interpret the meaning of a sudden drop in, for example, feminist cognition. Detailed country-specific analyses, however, cannot be pursued in this chapter. The discussion here only concerns broad trends and cross-national differences. None the less, in all, a feminist political culture can be traced right across Western Europe. Some variation can probably be explained by country-specific factors, but the cross-national comparison hints at a common pattern which goes beyond national frontiers.

Beliefs in Government

A feminist orientation not only implies a perception of women as an underprivileged group, but also a desire to see present society transformed. Different versions of feminist thought propose different ways of proceeding to this goal. For lack of data about attitudes towards radical strategies, we have emphasized reformist courses of action. According to reformist arguments, women themselves should take the initiative to increase their power by working within the prevailing political order, by being active in a political party or through influencing public opinion, for example. Reformist feminism thus implies fairly positive feelings about government and its capacity for managing issues related to the emancipation of women.

Men and women of 'masculine' orientation disapprove of the emancipation of women. The arguments can vary from statements such as 'a woman's place is in the home' to a wish to preserve clear male–female roles in society. Biology is likely to be part of their way of reasoning. Just as with feminists, people with a masculine orientation have different perspectives on government. We have assumed that the masculine ideal type adopts a traditional conception of politics, according to which political activities are associated with men and shaped by male perceptions of society.

Adherents of the large traditional group are expected to be satisfied with the present situation, in which inequalities and political conflicts are gender-neutral. According to this ideal type, political participation is modest and hardly directed towards any form of system change. The fact that inequalities between men and women, in terms of power and influence, linger behind the formal façade of equality is either not recognized or simply meets with acquiescence.

Let us again turn our attention to the actual types of gender-related orientations derived from the Eurobarometer data, but this time exploring their relationship with political interest. Our general hypothesis is that political interest and political behaviour are positively related to both masculine and feminist orientations. Differently phrased, strong opinions and firm goals are expected to result in activity and interest. To

TABLE 9.6. *Gender orientations and political interest, 1975 and 1983*

	Masculine		Traditional		Feminist	
	1975	1983	1975	1983	1975	1983
Low political interest	55	51	41	37	31	28
Medium political interest	32	37	39	41	35	35
High political interest	13	12	20	22	34	37
N	2,115	2,035	5,510	6,166	1,439	1,181

Note: Entries are percentages of national samples.

Sources: Eurobarometer, Nos. 3 and 19.

test this hypothesis, we constructed two indexes: one for feminist political culture, by adding together the values for indicators 1 and 5 in Table 9.1 and dividing by two; and the other for political interest, measured by the frequency of discussing politics and attempts to persuade friends in political discussion,[11] again adding the values together and dividing by two. As our sample sizes now fall quite substantially, in Table 9.6 we focus on gender-based differences and leave aside differences between countries.[12]

It is clear from the table that a high level of political interest is more common among people of feminist orientation than among either traditionalists or those of masculine orientation. Moreover, in both years, relatively fewer feminists show little interest in politics than people in either of the two other groups. Thus, while our general hypothesis that firm, gender-based orientations—whether feminist or masculine—stimulate greater interest in politics is not supported, there is support for the more limited hypothesis that a feminist orientation stimulates political interest. In other words, whereas, as we would expect, feminists are eager to argue for the rightness of their opinions, a masculine orientation appears not to promote a strong, perhaps even defensive, interest in politics. Furthermore, there is some increase in high political interest among feminists between 1975 and 1983, which, although modest, is consistent with the assumption that the influence of feminism is spreading steadily.

Most studies of political participation find that men are more interested in politics than women (see Chapter 14). However, we anticipate that a feminist orientation stimulates interest in politics, hence we would expect levels of political interest among women with a feminist orientation to—at least—match levels of interest among men in general.

TABLE 9.7. *Gender cultures among men and women, 1975 and 1983*

	Masculine		Traditional		Feminist	
	Men	Women	Men	Women	Men	Women
1975						
Low political interest	42	68	33	50	26	36
Medium political interest	38	25	41	37	32	37
High political interest	20	7	26	13	42	27
N	1,083	1,030	2,679	2,826	643	795
1983						
Low political interest	41	63	30	44	26	30
Medium political interest	42	31	43	39	30	38
High political interest	17	6	27	17	44	32
N	1,115	919	3,015	3,148	495	686

Note: Entries are percentages of national samples.

Sources: Eurobarometer, Nos. 3 and 19.

In Table 9.7 we look at gender differences in political interest among people of masculine, feminist, and traditional orientation.

Our expectation is clearly surpassed. In both years, high political interest is much more often found among feminist women than among men of masculine orientation and easily matches that among traditionalist men. Morover, and particularly interestingly, a feminist orientation goes along with higher levels of political interest among both men and women. However, whether this is because a feminist orientation stimulates a greater interest in politics, or because the politically interested are more responsive to feminist arguments, we cannot tell from these data. Even so, regardless of orientation, political interest remained higher among men, indicating that differences between men and women continue to play a significant part in the political culture of Western Europe.

Perhaps suprisingly, people adhering to a masculine orientation were less interested in politics than the traditionalists. Political passivity can be either an indication of trust—or, at least, consent—or a belief that one's activities do not matter. In line with Almond and Verba (1963), we prefer the first interpretation. Thus, we interpret the relatively low levels of political interest among people of masculine orientation as an indication of satisfaction with the status quo, suggesting that they believe their interests are dealt with effectively by decision-makers. Maybe people with a masculine orientation do not perceive the emancipation of women as a threat to their interests.

Finally, we should note the change in the levels of political interest among feminist women between 1975 and 1983. Although an increase of 5 percentage points in high interest, and a similar drop in low interest, is still modest, it points in the direction we would anticipate. The women's movement is a relatively recent influence in politics but, in view of the feminists' case, we would expect its influence to spread, bringing more women into the political arena. This process seems to have been under way by the early 1980s, although the advance is slow. But clearly, feminism and an active political role go together, boosting political involvement among both men and women.

Neglected Aspects of Political Culture

The choices about strategy made by feminists have clear implications for beliefs in government in terms of trust and legitimacy. What about government itself? The findings in this chapter indicate that a feminist value orientation is more common among women than among men. So what happens to politics when women enter this traditionally male arena? In Scandinavia, the reformist strategy of integrating women into the decision-making process has long been official policy. Although changes are often subtle and difficult to verify, the consequences are beginning to emerge. Some examples are to be found in the greater informality of meetings and the conduct of politics in a different, less male-dominated language (Hedlund-Ruth 1985). The actual content of politics can also change. Studies referred to by Dahlerup (1988) show that women tend to focus on such issues as family matters, health care, child care, and environmental protection. With the greater involvement of women in policy-making arenas, these issues are being brought to the top of the political agenda.

Even so, many factors prevent women from pursuing political careers. Dahlerup (1988) lists several obstacles that women encounter in male-dominated organizations such as political parties: the lack of allies, exclusion from informal networks, lower promotion rates. It is also important to stress the implications of an active life in politics for their private lives. It is more difficult to pursue a political career when carrying a double or even a triple workload, encompassing employment, political commitments, as well as primary responsibility for children and a household (Lundmark 1990).

The position of women in advanced industrial societies has changed significantly in the period since the Second World War, both in terms of their status and the related value transformations about the respective roles of women and men. We have limited knowledge about the actual content of gender-related orientations. Even less information is available to analyse possible changes in feminist political culture. Existing data sets, such as the Eurobarometer series, provide only a limited insight on the subject. Surveys in line with feminist criteria would be essential to examine these neglected aspects of political culture.

NOTES

1. See e.g. Lovenduski (1986). For a case study on the Netherlands, see Leijenaar (1991).
2. Feminist writers have made countless attempts to picture a better and more humane society. The ideal society is often characterized as being free from oppression, war, and poverty, as well as creating new conditions for production and reproduction, and new relations between public and private spheres of activity. In every feminist Utopia, reproductive values are given a central position, but claiming female supremacy is not a common argument.
3. The explicit intention of the Beliefs in Government project was to use existing data sets rather than to collect new data. If the data had been specifically collected in a search for feminist political culture, the indicators would, of course, differ from the ones used in this chapter. There are always difficulties in applying new perspectives to old data. Nevertheless, the data used here are judged to be sufficient to permit a meaningful analysis of feminist value orientations. The British data include Northern Ireland.
4. It may seem odd that membership in the women's movement, actual as well as potential, is not included among the indicators tapping feminism. All women in the 1983 sample were asked about their sentiments towards the women's movement. Since this measure is restricted to women and only found in Eurobarometer, No. 19, membership in the women's movement is treated as a sort of check digit to verify the percentage of women classified as holding a feminist orientation according to the definition used in the chapter. The empirical analysis revealed that, in most countries, the gap between membership in the women's movement and feminist orientation was no more than 10 percentage points.
5. The categories are: 15 years and younger; 16–19 years; 20 years and older; and still studying.
6. These results refer to the total Eurobarometer sample. Country-specific analysis on the education variable is distorted by the small number of respondents in the

categories 'still studying' and '20 years or over' when finishing full-time schooling. This led to the results being non-significant.

7. The index ranges from 1 (low) to 3 (high). This ideal type approach for classifying respondents as feminist or masculine results in a mixed category approximating 90% of the national samples. To obtain more manageable groups without compromising feminist theory too much, the following recodes were used: 1–1.66 = masculine, 1.67–2.99 = mixed, 3 and over = feminist. Note that for the 1983 data, there is a discrepancy between the number of respondents in the data file and the number reported in the codebook. This concerns half the countries and accounts for a maximum of 50 people.

8. Italy proved to be an exception. Italians aged 55–64 were more supportive of radical feminist change than younger cohorts. A similar pattern appeared in Luxembourg, although less pronounced.

9. For details, see OECD (1991: tables 2.7 and 2.8.).

10. See Commission of the European Communities (1980: tables 11.1–11.7 and 12.2).

11. The political interest index was recoded to 0.5 = 0, 1–1.5 = 1, and 2.5–3 = 3. The index for gender-related value orientations was constructed from the frequencies in Table 9.2 and recoded to 1–1.49 = masculine, 1.50–2.99 = traditional, 3 and over = feminist.

12. The sample sizes fall owing to, first, the high consistency required for answers to be classified as feminist or masculine; secondly, numbers fall off rapidly when the national samples are further divided by gender and levels of political interest. Several cells had fewer than 10 cases. The percentages in Tables 9.6–9.7 were calculated excluding the categories 'don't know' and 'no answer'; they amount to under 5% of the samples.

10

Green, Greener, Greenest

MASJA NAS

Interest in environmental pollution surged ahead in the late 1960s and 1970s. Before then, various groups and organizations were already engaged in the protection of the environment, but these organizations were mainly conservationist in outlook and largely defensive in character. At the end of the 1960s, and especially at the beginning of the 1970s, environmental movements changed their orientation from conservation to a critique of prevailing methods of production and patterns of consumption. The *Rome Report* and the energy crisis had the effect that more and more people questioned the sustainability of ever-growing rates of production. In most West European countries, the 1970s was a period of steady expansion for the ecology and anti-nuclear movements. During the same period, several accidents with far-reaching consequences for the natural environment received world-wide attention: the escape of a toxic defoliant in Seveso in Italy, 1976; the *Amoco Cadiz* spillage of 228,000 tons of oil on the French coast in 1978; the accident in the nuclear plant on Three Mile Island, Pennsylvania, in 1979. These and various other national incidents and scandals made the heritage of rapid industrialization after the Second World War ever more clear. With the emergence of green parties at the end of the 1970s, and notably at the beginning of the 1980s, environmental issues became part of the political agenda. The series of scandals and accidents continued, and ever more alarming reports were published about the deterioration of the natural environment and the direct threats to human life.

Most literature on green parties and their electorates deals with a particular type of 'greens'; that is, those parties representing 'new politics' issues (see Müller-Rommel 1989; Poguntke 1987a). Together with 'new left' parties, green parties are treated as representatives of these new politics issues in most studies. Because green parties with a conservative background do not meet the assumptions of new politics, they are often excluded from the analysis of 'green' politics. Furthermore, without going into detail, the most striking aspect of almost all analyses of green party members and voters, is that precisely that theme which is central to green political thinking tends to be neglected. With a few exceptions (see Cotgrove and Duff 1980, 1981; Rohrschneider 1988), ecology takes a very modest place compared to the other issues of new politics. Only occasionally are attitudes towards nuclear energy or—even more rarely—environmental protection included. Always putting green parties and their voters in the wider context of new politics carries the risk of forgetting why they are called 'green' in the first place: the priority given to the ecological system and its protection.

In this chapter, we try to gain an insight into the relationship between changing value orientations and the rise of 'greenness'. Unfortunately, there are no data which allow us to examine green attitudes along with religious–secular orientations or left–right materialism. Of the three value orientations central to this volume, only data for materialism–postmaterialism are available in combination with indicators about green attitudes. So, when examining the significance of value change for green attitudes, we concentrate on materialist–postmaterialist orientations. A brief summary of green political thinking is presented in the next section, and, then, in the following section, the notion of 'greenness' is operationalized, allowing us to construct a typology of green attitudes. In the third section, we discuss the relationship between greenness and postmaterialism, at the aggregate as well as the individual level.

Green Beliefs

The term 'green' is used to describe a heterogeneous group of people and organizations, varying from those protecting wildlife to those who believe that society should be fundamentally changed. In order to differentiate between the various positions, we can follow Dobson (1990: 3–5) in making a more or less arbitrary distinction between ecologists or Greens (capital G) and environmentalists or greens (lower-case g).[1] Both ecologists and environmentalists worry about the environmental crisis, but their strategies to solve it differ markedly. In essence, environmentalists try to solve environmental problems within the existing social, political, and economic system, while ecologists are convinced that a fundamental change of the dominant way of thinking, living, and producing is needed (Dobson 1990: 3; Cotgrove and Duff 1980: 333–4). In what follows, the major themes of ecologism are described. Later on we point out some differences between ecologists and environmentalists.

One of the most important sources of inspiration for ecologists is the *Limits to Growth* (Meadows *et al.* 1972) report of the Club of Rome, and its conclusions based on computer simulations. Central to Green political thought is the idea that 'infinite growth in a finite world is impossible' (Dobson 1990: 13). The earth itself sets 'limits to growth', simply because its capacity to carry an ever-expanding population, its productive capacity (use of resources), and its capacity to absorb pollution are finite. It is this idea of the finitude of the earth's 'carrying capacity' which is the framework of Green thought. Moreover, ecologists argue that the growth rates sought by industrial societies are exponential, and therefore might turn very suddenly into a catastrophe. If there are limits to growth, there must be limits to consumption. Ecologists not only argue that an ever-growing rate of consumption is impossible, but also that human needs are not best satisfied by continuous economic growth. This 'limits to growth' thesis, then, is closely connected to the concept of a sustainable society. In order to achieve a sustainable society, a fundamental change in human values and ideas, towards adopting an ecological consciousness, is needed. This implies an accommodation to the earth's finitude and giving up attempts to overcome these limits. It goes beyond the scope of this chapter to describe the different concepts of the sustainable society in terms of political institutions, but these vary from authoritarian to anarchistic proposals (see Dobson 1991; O'Riordan 1981).

From an ecological perspective, environmental problems all have the same nature and are interrelated. Consequently, solving one problem does not mean solving all the others; in fact it may even aggravate them. This, together with the idea of adjusting to the limits of growth—rather than trying to surmount them—makes ecologists highly suspicious of technological solutions. As Irvine and Ponton point out: 'Technological gadgets merely shift the problem around, often at the expense of energy and material inputs and therefore more pollution' (1988: 36). Thus, although new techniques may be part of the new society, they do not change the fact that there are limits to production and consumption, and therefore will not bring a sustainable society any nearer. The holism of ecologists is reflected in their belief that a solution to one problem carries the risk of forgetting others. So, although ecologists may be in favour of pollution taxes, they emphasize, for example, that energy consumption should be reduced anyway because of the earth's finitude.

Ecologists often claim that they stand outside conventional left–right politics because they see more similarities than differences between communism or socialism and capitalism. As Porrit declares: 'Both are dedicated to industrial growth, to the expansion of the means of production, to a materialistic ethic as the best means of meeting people's needs, and to technological development' (1986: 44). Furthermore, underlying both capitalism and socialism is a human-centred ethic. This anthropocentrism is seen as the basic cause of environmental decay. In its strong version, nature is perceived instrumentally, as a means to human ends. Weak anthropocentrism, by contrast, is human-centred. From an ecological perspective the natural world has an intrinsic—or independent—value. Humans should stand within, or live in harmony with, and not apart from, or even above, nature. Every human intervention endangers the delicate balance of nature. Thus, instead of instrumental or human-centred arguments, ecologists give biocentric or earth-centred reasons to protect the environment.[2] Sometimes the recognition of this oneness with nature, or ecological consciousness, is seen as an important component of the political change needed (Dobson 1990: 49–50).

Although ecologism criticizes current production and consumption practices and outlines a future sustainable society, it does not present a ready-made plan for social change. Dobson (1990: 130–1) suggests that this could be due to the belief of some ecologists that the necessary change is so fundamental that it will only coincide with a global catastrophe, while others think that the prediction of this calamity will suffice to convince people of the necessity of political and value change. As a consequence, there is little theorizing about the agents of social change. This could be explained by the claim that the deterioration of the environment is global. Thus the answer to the question of who should bring about social change is simple: everybody. It is often claimed that this universalism of its goals is the strength of ecologism, and most ecologists dislike, for example, class-based theories, precisely because they might undermine its universal appeal. But some ecologists reflect on which class might generate the social change required. Porrit (1986: 116), for example, considers the middle classes to be the instigators, while others (e.g. Spretnak and Capra 1985) put new social movements at the centre. Yet another line of thought suggests that the initiators of change are those who are marginalized in the present society (e.g. Porrit and Winner 1988: 156), and thus are more or less isolated. In this perspective, the unemployed are the hope for the future.

Both ecologists and environmentalists are concerned about environmental degradation, but differ in their approach. Whereas ecologists deal with the causes of environmental pollution and find these in politics and economics, environmentalists fight against the symptoms and the consequences. One could say that environmentalists have a more 'managerial' approach towards nature (Dobson 1990: 13). Environmentalists do not necessarily subscribe to the 'limits to growth' thesis, nor do they think that the only sustainable society is one where material standards of living are seriously reduced. Like the ecologists, environmentalists may believe that there are limits to resources or that there may be scarcity. The major difference is that ecologists argue that there are natural limits, while environmentalists say that these limits are merely temporary—because, for example, technology is not yet sophisticated enough.

How the limits to growth are evaluated has consequences for the strategies ecologists and environmentalists prefer. Green political thought has little to say about the strategy for bringing about a sustainable society, but Greens do have ideas about strategies which will certainly not lead to a green Utopia. Most of the discussion centres on whether a sustainable society is to be achieved through reforms or radical strategies. The debate between fundamentalists (*Fundis*) and realists (*Realos*) within the Green Party in Germany captures the contrast between the approaches of ecologists and environmentalists. There are three related reasons why fundis are against the reforms supported by the realos. First, in the light of the oncoming catastrophe, the changes resulting from reforms are too little and too slow, or too late. Secondly, industrial society is destroying itself by destroying nature. This is immanent in the system and cannot be changed by reforms, because they do not alter the fundament of industrial society. Finally, reforms will stabilize the system. Reforms improve conditions temporarily, but they also create the undesirable impression that fundamental change is not urgent. Consequently, the political will to change is weakened (Siegert and Ulrich *et al.* 1986). In other words, the more visible the catastrophe, the more willing people are to change.

Contrary to ecologists, environmentalists favour 'technological gadgets' such as catalytic convertors in cars, a strategy which ecologists regard as patchwork solutions (Dobson 1990: 18). So-called green consumerism ('help nature, buy green') illustrates the difference between Green and green strategies. Although both favour growing and buying organic food, green consumerism as a strategy to solve environmental problems is green but not Green. In fact, given the centrality of reducing consumption in Green political thought, green consumerism stands to some degree in contradiction with a Green position.

Environmentalists are unlikely to say that nature has an intrinsic value. Yet they do not evaluate nature only as an economic resource. Instead, they put people at the centre of the argument (weak anthropocentrism), saying that it is in the interests of human beings to protect nature. They argue, for example, that the deterioration of the ozone layer has to be halted because it puts people's health at risk. Ecologists agree, but primarily because the destruction of the ozone layer endangers the precarious natural balance (biocentrism), not because of the exclusive interests of mankind. Thus the border between Greens and greens is not strict; in reality different shades of green and Green exist.

Measuring Greenness

Having outlined some of the major themes of Green political thought, the distinction between Greens and greens makes it possible to detect various nuances in 'greenness'. However, as there are no data sets available which contain questions on all these themes, only a tentative empirical account of the different shades can be given. The data used here are from Eurobarometer, Nos. 25 (1986) and 29 (1988).[3] Two sets of items are used to develop a typology of attitudes towards the environment. The first consists of seven questions about 'how worried' respondents are about various forms of environmental pollution: air pollution, water pollution, damage to the sea, disposal of chemical waste, loss of natural resources, extinction of plants and animals, and damage to the atmosphere. The other set of items comprises eight questions about 'activities already done to improve the environment': being careful not to throw rubbish on the ground, not wasting tap water, equipping a car with a catalytic convertor, contributing money to environmental associations, recycling household products, getting involved in local action, or personally involved in an environmental association, and joining a demonstration. The same questions were asked in both years.

Our first step was to apply principal component analysis to test whether these items measure one or more latent variables which might account for attitudes towards the environment. The results of this analysis were then used to develop a typology. The method used in the analysis is the identity-equivalence procedure (Van Deth 1986; 1990). Instead of searching for identical indicators of attitudes towards the environment for all the countries, this method allows country-specific items to enter the analysis. The identity-equivalence procedure starts with a search for a solution within a pooled cross-national sample. The next step is to find an 'identity set'; that is, a set of core items which form a scale regardless of differences in political culture. Subsequently this identity set is tested among the countries, while adding country-specific items to the identity scale.[4]

This method enables us first to compare country-specific attitudes towards the environment; secondly, to compare the level of the scores for the variable(s); and, thirdly, to compare the relationship between the items in the identity set for the various countries (Van Deth 1986: 265). In the case of attitudes towards the environment, the cultural and political context is particularly important, especially with regard to various activities. In some of the countries under consideration, recycling bottles, for example, has become everyday practice; hardly anyone sees a connection between bringing glass to a bottle bank and saving the environment. In other countries, it is perceived specifically as an environmental issue.

First, we analyse the pooled data for eleven countries. In order to capture the most favourable or greenest attitudes towards the environment, responses to the items measuring concern were dichotomized as between respondents who are 'very worried' and those who were only 'worried' and 'not (at all) worried'. Table 10.1 shows a three-factor solution for both time points.[5] In both 1986 and 1988 the same set of items loads on the three factors, which can easily be interpreted: the first as concern about pollution, the second and the third as activities in the private and public sphere respectively. The other three items (equipping your car with a catalytic convertor, contributing money to

TABLE 10.1. *Attitudes towards the environment, 1986 and 1988*

	1986			1988		
	Factor 1 concern	Factor 2 private	Factor 3 public	Factor 1 concern	Factor 2 private	Factor 3 public
Water	0.82			0.81		
Sea life	0.83			0.83		
Air pollution	0.80			0.81		
Industrial waste	0.76			0.77		
Species extinction	0.76			0.74		
Natural resources	0.75			0.75		
Atmosphere damage	0.75			0.75		
Rubbish		0.65			0.68	
Water		0.72			0.74	
Noise		0.75			0.75	
Local action			0.68			0.71
Demonstration			0.67			0.70
Personally involved			0.69			0.71
Eigenvalues	4.32	1.51	1.32	4.38	1.53	1.44
Variance explained	33.3	11.6	10.2	33.7	11.8	11.1
Total variance explained		55.1			56.8	
Correlation factors		0.18			0.15	
Number of cases		11,208			11,098	

Notes: Entries are factor loadings and eigenvalues of selected items from principal components analysis of pooled data for eleven countries; oblique rotation.

Sources: Eurobarometer, Nos. 25 and 29.

environmental associations, and recycling household products) showed communalities below 0.40 and were excluded. An explanation for this latter result might be the different cultural and political settings mentioned above. In some countries, for example, catalytic convertors are obligatory, while in others only some types of cars or only new cars have convertors. Thus, in one country installing a catalytic convertor is seen as an environment-saving activity, while in another it simply belongs to standard car equipment.

The second step is to find an identity set; that is, a factor solution which is the same in all eleven countries. Although Table 10.1 shows a three-factor solution in both 1986 and 1988, it was impossible to find an identity set with three factors. Most of the problems are due to the second factor, identified as private activities. In several countries we find a solution similar to that found for the pooled data set, but in some countries one or more of the activities undertaken in the private sphere do not have a sufficiently high loading. This, in itself, shows that there are cross-national differences with regard to environment-saving activities in the private sphere—and stresses the usefulness of the identity-equivalence procedure. As a result, as we show in Table 10.2, only two factors are identical in all eleven countries at both time points: concern and public activities. Thus, the item 'local action' has to be dropped from the identity set for both 1986 and 1988. In addition, because of the results for Italy and the Netherlands, concern about 'industrial waste' could not be included for 1988. The resulting two-factor solution, however, is satisfactory in all eleven countries: the communalities of the items are all above 0.40, the factor loadings are sufficiently high, and the total variance explained varies between 54.5 per cent (France) and 70.5 per cent (Portugal) in 1986, and between 57.2 per cent (Denmark) and 72.8 per cent (Portugal) in 1988.

TABLE 10.2. *Cross-national identity sets, 1986 and 1988*

	1986		1988	
	Factor 1 concern	Factor 2 action	Factor 1 concern	Factor 2 action
Water	0.82		0.80	
Sea life	0.83		0.82	
Air pollution	0.80		0.80	
Industrial waste	0.76			
Species extinction	0.75		0.77	
Natural resources	0.74		0.78	
Atmosphere damage	0.75		0.77	
Demonstration		0.78		0.79
Personally involved		0.77		0.79
Eigenvalues	4.30	1.16	3.80	1.21
Variance explained	47.8	12.8	47.5	15.1
Total variance explained	60.6		62.6	
Correlation factors	0.17		0.15	
N	11,208		11,098	

Notes: Entries are factor loadings and eigenvalues of selected items from principal components analysis of pooled data for eleven countries; oblique rotation.

Sources: Eurobarometer, Nos. 25 and 29.

In Tables 10.3 and 10.4 we present the results from extending the identity set by adding country-specific items for 1986 and 1988, respectively. Because both identity sets yield a two-factor solution, country-specific items were allowed to be part of the final solutions only if they loaded on one of these two factors. None of the items loading on the second factor (private actions) in the analyses of the pooled data set (see Table 10.1) could be included in the country-specific analyses. It seems that the kind of activity (private versus public) is more important than its goal. In 1986, the item 'local action' can be added to the second factor in Denmark, Ireland, Greece, Spain, and Portugal (see Table 10.3). In Britain and Spain 'money contributions' are part of the final scale. In five of the eleven countries, no items at all were added to the final scale. In 1988, 'concern about industrial waste' again loads on the first factor in all countries except Italy and the Netherlands (see Table 10.4). One of the reasons for the exclusion of this item in Italy and the Netherlands might be that about 60 per cent of the population in both instances is very concerned about industrial waste, in contrast to about 40 per cent for the other items. Only in Belgium and France were no items added to the final scale. The item 'local action' can be added to the identity set in more countries than in 1986; only in Belgium, France, and Britain does this item not load on the second factor. Again, the final scale for Britain includes the item 'money contributions'.

The results of the country-specific analyses allow us to create an empirical typology of attitudes towards the environment. However, with the data available to us, it is not really feasible to measure the ecologist position but only the slightly darker shades of green. The first step is to separate those who are very concerned about all types of pollution from those who are not concerned. The items measuring concern include several forms of pollution. For example, the extinction of plant and animals is more a conservationist concern, whereas 'loss of natural resources' comes close to Green ideas of the finitude of the world and the limited carrying capacity of the earth. Because of the interrelatedness of environmental problems and their exponential character, we would expect greens to be very worried about most or even all forms of pollution. But being very concerned is only a minimal condition of greenness. In the light of an oncoming catastrophe, greens should not only be very concerned, but should also be prepared to act to avert this disaster. We noted earlier that ecologists do not say much about the strategies which should be followed to bring

TABLE 10.3. *Identity sets and country-specific additions, 1986*

	DK		BE		GE		GB		IR		NL		FR		GR		IT		SP		PO	
	a	b	a	b	a	b	a	b	a	b	a	b	a	b	a	b	a	b	a	b	a	b
Identity set																						
Water pollution	0.80		0.86		0.75		0.82		0.82		0.79		0.79		0.82		0.80		0.86		0.86	
Sea life	0.84		0.88		0.77		0.80		0.81		0.78		0.82		0.84		0.82		0.87		0.90	
Air pollution	0.78		0.84		0.74		0.80		0.78		0.76		0.77		0.82		0.81		0.83		0.86	
Industrial waste	0.73		0.82		0.67		0.77		0.79		0.61		0.71		0.72		0.77		0.84		0.86	
Species extinction	0.75		0.82		0.76		0.68		0.71		0.74		0.72		0.76		0.68		0.84		0.82	
Natural resources	0.78		0.86		0.71		0.68		0.73		0.67		0.63		0.78		0.62		0.83		0.82	
Atmospheric damage	0.75		0.79		0.73		0.72		0.72		0.68		0.67		0.78		0.66		0.82		0.83	
Demonstrate		0.71		0.73		0.62		0.67		0.73		0.80		0.73		0.70		0.66		0.67		0.78
Personally involved		0.69		0.73		0.80		0.78		0.74		0.74		0.78		0.80		0.77		0.72		0.68
Nation-specific additions																						
Rubbish																						
Tap water																						
Noise																						
Car equipment																						
Money contribution																				0.65			
Recycling								0.63															
Local action		0.73								0.68					0.72					0.67		0.66
Eigenvalues	4.29	1.44	4.93	1.08	3.93	1.13	4.06	1.41	4.30	1.42	3.68	1.16	3.81	1.10	4.45	1.57	3.89	1.06	5.03	1.76	5.10	1.46
Variance explained	42.9	14.4	54.7	11.9	43.7	12.5	40.6	14.1	43.0	14.2	40.9	12.9	42.3	12.2	44.5	15.7	43.3	11.8	45.8	16.0	51.0	14.6
Total variance explained	57.4		66.7		56.2		54.8		57.2		53.8		54.5		60.3		55.0		61.8		65.6	
Factor correlations	0.17		0.05		0.17		0.20		0.23		0.15		0.19		0.18		0.18		0.17		0.16	
N	1,043		1,003		987		1,055		1,000		1,001		1,003		1,000		1,102		1,008		1,000	

Notes: Entries are factor loadings; oblique rotation. Entries for *a* are concern items; entries for *b* are activity items.
Source: Eurobarometer, No. 25.

TABLE 10.4. *Identity sets and country-specific additions, 1988*

	DE a	DE b	BE a	BE b	GE a	GE b	GB a	GB b	IR a	IR b	NL a	NL b	FR a	FR b	GR a	GR b	IT a	IT b	SP a	SP b	PO a	PO b
Identity set																						
Water pollution	0.82		0.81		0.76		0.82		0.79		0.77		0.78		0.82		0.79		0.86		0.83	
Sea life	0.85		0.83		0.80		0.86		0.81		0.75		0.78		0.83		0.82		0.88		0.89	
Air pollution	0.79		0.82		0.77		0.80		0.81		0.76		0.77		0.84		0.79		0.88		0.86	
Natural resources	0.76		0.78		0.66		0.77		0.79		0.67		0.70		0.70		0.65		0.85		0.85	
Species extinction	0.71		0.77		0.73		0.75		0.80		0.74		0.72		0.68		0.69		0.86		0.84	
Atmospheric damage	0.78		0.75		0.74		0.74				0.70		0.70		0.71		0.71		0.83		0.83	
Demonstrate		0.75		0.79		0.64		0.66		0.72		0.78		0.78		0.76		0.63		0.74		0.77
Personally involved		0.65		0.76		0.73		0.76		0.74		0.67		0.82		0.70		0.75		0.74		0.79
Nation-specific additions																						
Industrial waste	0.72		0.80		0.72		0.75		0.79				0.73		0.77				0.87		0.88	
Rubbish																						
Tap water																						
Noise																						
Car equipment							0.64															
Money contribution																						
Recycling																						
Local action		0.71		0.71		0.68				0.70		0.76				0.71		0.69		0.71		0.76
Eigenvalues	4.31	1.41	4.46	1.17	3.90	1.41	4.44	1.29	4.59	1.49	3.25	1.59	3.92	1.26	4.17	1.56	3.39	1.39	5.20	1.59	5.14	1.80
Variance explained	43.1	14.1	49.6	13.0	39.0	14.1	44.4	12.9	45.9	14.9	36.1	17.7	43.5	14.0	41.7	15.6	37.7	15.5	52.0	15.9	51.4	18.0
Total variance explained	57.2		62.6		53.1		57.4		60.9		53.7		57.5		57.3		53.2		67.9		69.4	
Factor correlations	0.18		0.16		0.11		0.26		0.19		0.12		0.15		0.13		0.15		0.08		0.09	
N	1,009		1,022		1,007		1,014		992		1,023		993		1,000		1,021		1,017		1,000	

Notes: Entries are factor loadings; oblique rotation. Entries for *a* are concern items; entries for *b* are activity items.

Source: Eurobarometer, No. 29.

about a sustainable society. They are not in favour of technical gadgets; some ecologists are even against reforms. Even so, it is safe to assume that greens are more active than other people. Demonstrations, local actions, and personal involvement in environmental associations all add up to the increasing visibility of environmental problems without necessarily being directed towards reform.

In order to construct a typology of attitudes towards the environment, two additive scales based on the country-specific factor solutions were constructed. The number of positive responses were counted, and, for comparability, divided by the total number of items in the factor analyses. This results in two scales for each country; one for concern and one for action. Both scales range from zero to one. The means of these country-specific scales serve as breakpoints to distinguish four different types of attitudes towards the environment:

1. 'Grey' or non-green are respondents whose scores on both scales are below the mean scores for their country.
2. 'Contemplatives' are those who show above average concern but are not more active than the average activity level for their country (the minimal condition of greenness).
3. 'Apparently impetuous' are respondents who have been more active than the average level in their country, but who are as worried or less worried than average about pollution (both types 2 and 3 can be considered particular types of environmentalists).
4. 'Greens' are both more concerned and more active than average.

In the next section, we use this typology of shades of greenness to examine the relationship between attitudes towards the environment and postmaterialist value orientations.

Postmaterialism and Greenness

The connection between growing concern with the environment and materialist–postmaterialist value orientations is often seen as straightforward: environmental issues are mere reflections of postmaterialist concerns. The theory of value change, as developed by Inglehart, states that class-based issues will lose their relative importance and that, instead, 'quality-of-life' issues will have increasing significance (Inglehart and Rabier 1986: 456). The environment is part of people's assessment of the 'quality of life'. This line of reasoning is criticized on several grounds: one related to the nature of environmental problems in general; another is more closely connected to Greenness. A further reason addresses the items in Inglehart's postmaterialism index.

First of all, the perception of environmental problems as a higher order, or remote and abstract concern (Inglehart 1979c: 345), can be questioned. Offe (1987) noted that advanced industrial societies not only give rise to new values but also to new problems, such as environmental pollution. The high priority given to the environment can then be understood as 'a rising urgency to defend existing needs whose conditions of fulfilment have deteriorated' (Offe 1987: 84). According to this line of reasoning, the salience of environmental concern is rooted in actual objective conditions rather than in a post-materialist orientation: people became more concerned because the extent of pollution has increased, not because their value orientations have shifted. Furthermore, one could argue that increasing pollution affects a growing number of people personally: their health is in jeopardy or their houses are built on polluted soil. In other words, it is at least debatable to claim that environmental pollution is a remote and abstract concern (see also Chapters 14 and 15). However, although there were some serious accidents at about the same time as environmental concern became significant, there had been major pollution events before, but without a similar effect.[6] These arguments are not mutually exclusive. Rohrschneider (1988), for example, analysed whether favourable attitudes towards environmental issues spring from postmaterialism or complaints about the condition of the environment, and found that both contribute to the salience of environmental issues.

The second reason to question representing environmental issues as a postmaterialist concern, is more directly linked with the discussion on greenness. Although postmaterialists 'tend to give relatively high priority to nonmaterial goals' (Inglehart 1979c: 308), this does not automatically imply that material goals are unimportant to them. The term 'priority' says nothing about the relative strength of preferences, and does not imply anything about the absolute importance attached to postmaterialist and materialist goals. Moreover, that postmaterialists give priority to nonmaterial goals is not to say that all nonmaterial goals are equally unimportant. Given the conceptualization of values as 'features of domains of behaviour' (see Chapter 2), the importance of particular nonmaterial goals may vary according to different domains. In other words, it is not self-evident what will happen when postmaterialists are confronted with a choice between a cleaner environment and their own mobility, such as losing their car or giving up their holiday flight to the tropics. This makes it at least questionable to assume a direct link between ecologism and postmaterialism, and makes it more likely that postmaterialists are a light shade of green rather than Green.

Finally, Inglehart's four-item or twelve-item index can hardly be said to capture attitudes towards the environment. The only item which comes close to measuring something of the kind, and is often interpreted as such, is 'trying to make our cities and countryside more beautiful'. Besides the well-known problems caused by this item,[7] it is a rather ambiguous way to capture environmental concerns. In fact, Inglehart places this item as the highest order need on the continuum of needs, labelling it as an aesthetic need (1977*b*: 313–18). This indicates that to Inglehart, at least in the 1970s, environmental concerns mean something different from the concept which 'green' tries to capture.

In the following sections, the direct relationship often presumed between environmentalism and a postmaterialist orientation is tested. It goes beyond the scope of this chapter to examine whether the objective condition of the environment is a stimulus to green attitudes. However, testing the connection between greenness and postmaterialism provides some insight into whether or not the growing salience of environmental issues can be explained by a shift in value orientations. On the one hand, if greenness is a reflection of the shift from materialist to postmaterialist goals, we would expect relatively high levels of greenness among postmaterialists, as opposed to the grey position taken by those with materialist orientations. At the aggregate level, we expect that countries with a less materialist population are at the same time less grey, that is, greener. On the other hand, if the link between postmaterialism and greenness is not as straightforward as often presumed, we expect to find only a weak relationship or no relationship at all between positions in the typology and postmaterialism at the individual and at the aggregate level. Since a possible relationship between greenness and postmaterialism could be the result of common background variables, these background variables are introduced in the last section.

Greenness of Countries

The distributions of the four attitudinal types in both 1986 and 1988 are shown in Figure 10.1. Not surprisingly the greys form the largest group in all countries. Yet we notice that, whereas in 1986 more than 50 per cent of the population was grey in five of the eleven countries, in 1988 this was only the case in Belgium and Ireland, both with about 55 per cent greys. In other words, the figure shows that almost all countries, with the exception of Portugal and Greece, were greening during the later 1980s. The proportion of people with green, contemplative, or impetuous attitudes increases, while at the same time the proportion with grey attitudes declines. Moreover, in the majority of these countries, the gap between the proportion of greys and contemplatives diminishes. In the Netherlands, the grey group is somewhat smaller in 1988 (38 per cent are grey, 40 per cent are contemplative). If we compare the types across the countries, we see that, in both 1986 and 1988, the highest proportions of people with green attitudes are found in Denmark (14 and 16 per cent respectively), Britain (12 and 14 per cent), the Netherlands (10 and 15 per cent), and Italy (11 and 12 per cent). In

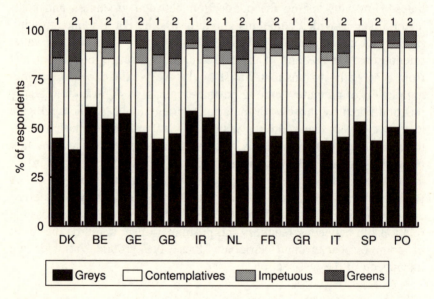

FIGURE 10.1. *Distribution of attitudes towards the environment in 1986 (1) and 1988 (2)*

Sources: Eurobarometer, Nos. 25 and 29.

1986, Spain and Belgium had the smallest proportions of greens; in 1988, Spain, Portugal, and Greece had the smallest proportions.

The relationship between greenness and postmaterialist orientations in each country for both 1986 and 1988 is presented in Figure 10.2. For the vertical axis, the percentage of greys in a country is subtracted from the percentage of greens; for the horizontal axis, the percentage of materialists is subtracted from the percentage of postmaterialists. Thus, moving to the right of the figure indicates an increasingly postmaterialist outlook, while moving up along the vertical axis indicates increasing greenness.

For 1986 we have a rather vague picture. At first sight, there seems to be no relationship between the greenness of national populations and the extent of postmaterialism.[8] However, a closer look reveals that there are actually three groups of countries, although not along regional lines. On the right side of the figure is one group consisting of Germany and the Netherlands; a second group, in the centre, is made up of Denmark, Britain, France, Ireland, Spain, and Belgium; and on the left side we find the third group comprising Italy, Greece, and Portugal. Among these three groups, countries with a more postmaterialist population also tend to be greener. The pattern for 1988, however, seems to support the idea that the more postmaterialist are the value orientations of a population, the greener it will be.[9] Germany and Denmark, however,

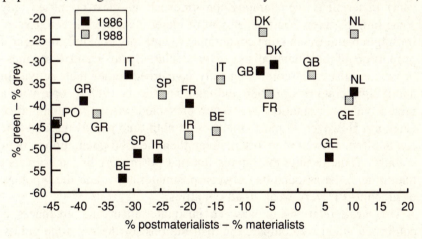

FIGURE 10.2. *Relationship between postmaterialism and greenness in West European countries, 1986–8*

Sources: Eurobarometer, Nos. 25 and 29.

deviate from this general rule: in terms of postmaterialism among their populations, Germany is too grey and Denmark is too green.

The Greenness of Postmaterialists

At the individual level, we find a clear pattern in all countries with respect to the grey and green types. As we show in Figures 10.3*a* and 10.3*b*, materialists are clearly overrepresented among the greys at both points in time. The most extreme examples are Belgium in 1986, where 73 per cent of the materialists are grey (compared with 61 per cent of the population as a whole), and Germany in 1988 where 65 per cent are grey (compared with 48 per cent of the population). Moreover, with the exception of Denmark and the Netherlands in 1988, more than 50 per cent of the materialists in all these countries are also grey. Postmateri-alists, on the other hand, are more often green than people with mixed or materialist value orientations in both 1986 and 1988. This is espe-cially clear in the case of Danish postmaterialists: in 1986 and 1989, 29 and 39 per cent, respectively, of postmaterialists are green whereas only 14 and 16 per cent of all Danes were green. In Belgium, Germany, and Ireland, however, 50 per cent and more of the postmaterialists were grey in 1986; this was no longer the case in 1988. Compared with others, Danish (9 per cent), British (9 per cent), and Dutch (13 per cent) materialists were among the greenest; in most countries only something between 2 and 7 per cent of materialists were green. Except in Belgium and Ireland, the contemplative category contains the highest proportion of postmaterialists. In particular, Spanish and Portuguese postmaterialists are more often only concerned rather than active. In about eight countries in 1986 and ten countries in 1988, people with a mixed value orientation are overrepresented in the contemplative category. However, in most countries, at both time points, these people are as often, or even more often, green than the total population in their country. Thus, despite the impression that postmaterialists are greener than others, the association between postmaterialism and the typology of greenness is very weak in all countries.[10]

The weak relationship between postmaterialism and greenness is confirmed when we compare the distributions for the two time points. In all countries where the proportion of greens increases (which excludes Greece and Portugal), all three groups—materialist, mixed, and postmaterialist—can be seen to be greening. For example, in

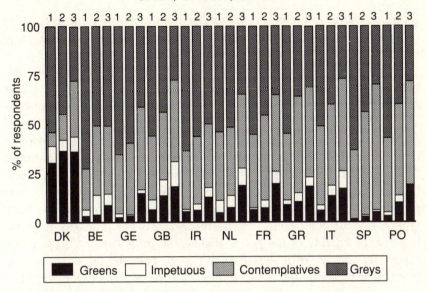

FIGURE 10.3*a*. *Materialist (1), mixed (2), and postmaterialist (3) value orientations and greenness in West European countries, 1986*
Source: Eurobarometer, No. 25.

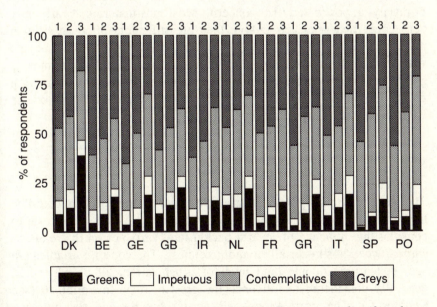

FIGURE 10.3*b*. *Materialist (1), mixed (2), and postmaterialist (3) value orientations and greenness in West European countries, 1988*
Source: Eurobarometer, No. 29.

Denmark there is only a 1.6 percentage point increase in the proportion of greens in the general population whereas there is a 10.3 point increase in the proportion of postmaterialists who are green. Only in the Netherlands does the position change most among the materialists; between 1986 and 1988, greenness increases by 8 percentage points among materialists but by only 3 percentage points among postmaterialists. At the other end of the spectrum, the change in the proportion of greys cannot be clearly attributed to materialists or postmaterialists. In three countries, the proportion of materialists with grey attitudes declines disproportionately—markedly so in Belgium where the proportion of grey materialists declines by 12 percentage points while the proportion of greys among the Belgium population only drops by 6 points. In four other countries, postmaterialists are primarily responsible for the decline of the greys; that is, the proportion of greys drops especially among postmaterialists. When we consider the growth in the proportion of contemplatives, we see that materialists especially have become more concerned about the environment. In Belgium, for example, the proportion of contemplatives increased by 2.2 percentage points, whereas the percentage of concerned materialists rose by 7.1 points.

It seems, then, that, in the later 1980s, the environment was not primarily a postmaterialist concern. Most postmaterialists are only very concerned—not active—but they are still more often green than materialists or people of mixed orientation. But we also see that people with mixed value orientations are more concerned and sometimes as green as the population at large in their countries. In addition, a growing proportion of materialists is very concerned about the state of the environment in many countries.

A Common Background?

The weak relationship between greenness and postmaterialism could be the result of common background variables. So, we now turn to consider the influence of several background variables on the relationship between postmaterialism and greenness. The control variables are age, education, income, and level of urbanization, all of which are generally considered to influence the growth of postmaterialism (see Chapter 5). The correlations and partial correlations for our two scales—concern about the environment and environment-saving action—are presented in Tables 10.5 and 10.6.

TABLE 10.5. *Concern about environmental pollution and materialism–post-materialism, controlling for background variables: eleven West European countries, 1986 and 1988*

	Correl.	Controlling for					N
		Education	Age	Income	Urban	All	
Denmark							
1986	0.18	0.16	0.14	0.16	0.17	0.14	735
1988	0.12	0.08	0.11	0.11	0.11	0.08	787
Belgium							
1986	0.17	0.14	0.15	0.14	0.11	0.11	735
1988	0.14	0.14	0.16	0.16	0.16	0.14	652
Germany							
1986	0.17	0.17	0.18	0.19	0.19	0.16	703
1988	0.22	0.19	0.23	0.25	0.24	0.18	761
Britain							
1986	0.14	0.14	0.14	0.13	0.14	0.14	757
1988	0.11	0.14	0.15	0.14	0.14	0.15	743
Ireland							
1986	0.07	0.08	0.10	0.10	0.09	0.10	552
1988	0.12	0.10	0.12	0.10	0.07	0.08	525
Netherlands							
1986	0.10	0.12	0.12	0.11	0.11	0.11	791
1988	0.10	0.10	0.11	0.09	0.10	0.10	782
France							
1986	n.s.	n.s.	n.s.	n.s.	n.s.	n.s.	859
1988	n.s.	n.s.	n.s.	n.s.	n.s.	n.s.	837
Greece							
1986	0.14	0.13	0.12	0.13	0.13	0.10	801
1988	0.12	0.08	0.11	0.09	0.11	0.07	804
Italy							
1986	0.10	0.10	0.10	0.09	0.09	0.09	928
1988	0.12	0.07	0.11	0.08	0.09	0.06	825
Spain							
1986	0.20	0.20	0.14	0.15	0.19	0.11	599
1988	0.15	0.12	0.12	0.13	0.13	0.10	734
Portugal							
1986	0.14	0.11	0.11	0.09	0.13	0.09	680
1988	0.17	0.12	0.12	0.11	0.13	0.06	836

Notes: Entries are first-order correlations and partial correlations. Only significant correlations are shown ($p \leq 0.05$). The first column shows the correlation between concern about environmental pollution and a three-point postmaterialism index. The entries under 'All' are the partial correlation between materialism–postmaterialism and concern about environmental pollution after controlling for all background variables. Education is measured by school-leaving age. Income is measured in quartiles. The degree of urbanization is measured by the size of the community.

Sources: Eurobarometer, Nos. 25 and 29.

TABLE 10.6. *Environment-saving activities and materialism–postmaterialism, controlling for background variables: eleven West European countries, 1986 and 1988*

| | Correl. | Controlling for | | | | | N |
		Education	Age	Income	Urban	All	
Denmark							
1986	0.17	0.07	n.s.	0.08	0.07	n.s.	735
1988	0.18	0.16	0.19	0.19	0.19	0.16	787
Belgium							
1986	0.11	0.09	0.06	0.07	0.10	0.7	735
1988	0.08	n.s.	0.08	0.08	0.08	n.s.	652
Germany							
1986	0.09	n.s.	n.s.	0.07	0.07	n.s.	703
1988	0.15	0.12	0.13	0.15	0.15	0.12	761
Britain							
1986	0.14	0.13	0.12	0.13	0.14	0.11	757
1988	0.11	0.07	0.08	0.09	0.09	0.07	743
Ireland							
1986	n.s.	n.s.	n.s.	n.s.	n.s.	n.s.	552
1988	0.06	0.09	0.09	0.09	0.11	0.10	525
Netherlands							
1986	0.17	0.14	0.14	0.15	0.15	0.13	791
1988	0.10	0.11	0.11	0.11	0.11	0.11	782
France							
1986	0.14	0.14	0.13	0.13	0.14	0.13	859
1988	0.14	0.13	0.14	0.15	0.14	0.13	837
Greece							
1986	0.10	0.10	0.10	0.11	0.11	0.08	801
1988	0.16	0.14	0.16	0.15	0.16	0.14	804
Italy							
1986	0.14	0.14	0.13	0.14	0.14	0.12	928
1988	0.11	0.07	0.08	0.10	0.10	0.06	825
Spain							
1986	0.08	0.11	0.08	0.08	0.10	0.08	599
1988	0.21	0.12	0.14	0.16	0.18	0.12	734
Portugal							
1986	0.13	0.10	0.09	0.11	0.10	0.09	680
1988	0.10	0.09	0.09	0.11	0.11	0.09	836

Notes: Entries are first-order correlations and partial correlations. Only significant correlations are shown ($p \leq 0.05$). The first column shows the correlation between environment-saving activities and a three-point posmaterialism index. The entries under 'All' are the partial correlation between materialism–postmaterialism and environment-saving activities after controlling for all background variables. See also notes to Table 10.5.

Sources: Eurobarometer, Nos. 25 and 29.

The first column in both tables shows that the correlations between the two scales and postmaterialism, although significant and in the expected direction, are very weak in all countries. In the case of concern about environmental pollution (Table 10.5), the partial correlations show that the influence of the background variables on this relationship is limited at both points in time. In France there is no significant association at all. The influence is strongest in Spain (1986) and Portugal (1988); after introducing the background variables, the partial correlations between postmaterialism and concern about environmental pollution drop from 0.20 to 0.11 and from 0.17 to 0.06 respectively. In both countries, age and income have relatively the strongest impact. In Portugal, education level and urbanization are also of some importance. In most countries, then, the positive correlation between postmaterialism and environmental concern is somewhat attenuated when we control for background variables. None the less, the relationship remains significant.

In the case of environment-saving activities (Table 10.6) the influence of background variables is also weak. In Denmark, in 1986, the weak correlation (0.17) between postmaterialism and activities disappears when we control for the background variables. However, the impact of postmaterialism on the level of activity turns out to be especially dependent on age. In 1988 the influence of background variables is strongest in Spain where, in particular, the level of education is relevant. In six countries, the correlation between postmaterialism and activities depends more on educational level and on age than on the other variables. The influence of background variables on the relationship between activism and postmaterialism seems to be somewhat stronger than in the case of environmental concern. With the exception of Denmark, West Germany, Ireland, and Belgium in 1986, the weak impact of postmaterialism on activism remains statistically significant.

Our test to see if the more postmaterialist countries are, indeed, also greener yields mixed results. In 1986, this was the case but only within the three groups of countries identified in Figure 10.2, whereas in 1988 the relationship between greenness and a postmaterialist outlook was much clearer. Even so, there is only a weak association between postmaterialism and greenness at the individual level. In most cases, this correlation, although weakened, remains significant when we control for various background variables. Postmaterialists are, then, in most instances, more often green, active, or more concerned about the environment than materialists, indicating that greenness does spring to some extent—albeit small— from a postmaterialist orientation. In most countries, postmaterialists are largely responsible for the increase in the proportion of people with green attitudes. However, it seems that the decline of the greys, or the greening of the population, cannot be attributed solely to postmaterialism. In general, materialists and people with a mixed value orientation are also developing a greater concern about the environment. Moreover, most postmaterialists are only concerned—rather than active—about environmental questions, and the gap between their concern and that of people with a mixed value orientation has narrowed.

Beliefs in Government and Greenness

We started out by questioning the widespread understanding of environmental attitudes as merely a reflection of postmaterialist value orientations. The discussion on green beliefs showed that there are several major themes within green political thinking, which gave some indication that it might be too simple to reduce greenness to postmaterialism. However, as we have seen in this analysis, the relationship between postmaterialism and greenness turned out to be weak. Environmentalism cannot be construed as a mere reflection of postmaterialist concerns. Furthermore, it might be the case that environmental concerns have gradually lost, or are losing, their 'new politics' characteristics: the protection of the environment is no longer an issue exclusively for green parties.

Nowadays, hardly anyone doubts that there is an environmental crisis. Increasing numbers of people are concerned about, and personally affected by, the deterioration of nature. However, at the same time, the environment seems to be losing its potential to mobilize people against a political and economic system which, according to Green thinking, causes its destruction. The issue is no longer whether the environment should be a political issue, but rather how to deal with the issue. This basic consensus seems to induce a depoliticization of environmental problems in favour of a more managerial approach. This implies stressing reforms rather than aiming at fundamental change.

Governments find themselves in an ambiguous situation: on the one hand, they need to find some kind of answer to this issue; on the other hand, most solutions seem to ask for sacrifices which people may not always be willing to make. Johansson's findings for Germany and Britain (see Volume iii, Tables 11.7–11.9) illustrate the point. In both countries a large majority says that government spends too little on protecting the environment but, at the same time, about 50 per cent are not willing to pay more taxes for environmental protection. Thus, both action and inaction may influence a government's credibility.

As early as the 1970s, governments and established parties tried, more or less, to deal with environmental problems. The most obvious signs of their interest were the creation of ministries of the environment and the signing of several national and, to a lesser extent, international agreements to regulate pollution. During this period, the common view was that environmental protection and economic growth are inextricably linked: more protection would entail less growth; more growth would entail further environmental degradation.

During the 1980s, the focus moved to 'nature first–economy first' debate. Increasingly, political parties and governments turned to 'ecological modernization' (Weale 1992); the protection of the environment as a necessary precondition for long-term economic growth. Instead of having to deliver the unpopular message that consumption levels have to be reduced if the oncoming catastrophe is to be avoided, ecological modernization seems to offer governments a way out of the growth versus environmental protection dilemma.

Nevertheless, a serious response to the environmental crisis demands more than rhetoric and good intentions. The experience of the 1970s was that policies aimed at reducing specific forms of pollution are like cutting off the heads of a hydra: solving one problem aggravates others. Over the years, there has been a growing insight that coping with pollution requires coping with the specific character of the environment—its interconnectedness and international scope (Weale 1992: 23–33). National governments, confronted with the limits of their power and effectiveness, thus face a profound challenge.

NOTES

1. Several other labels distinguish between ecologists and environmentalists: e.g. 'deep ecology and shallow ecology' (Næss 1973); 'utopian environmentalists' (Cotgrove and Duff 1980).
2. Ecologists might use human-centred but never human-instrumental arguments. Human-centred arguments are more convincing and attractive to most people

than pure biocentred ones, and therefore strategically more convenient (see Dobson 1990: 19–21).

3. The fieldwork for Eurobarometer, No. 25, was carried out during March and April 1986. On 26 April the nuclear reactor in Chernobyl exploded, and nuclear fallout was detected outside the Soviet Union between 28 April and 2 May (Affigne 1990). The influence of this accident on the results of this study, however, should be minor.

4. One of the most important reasons to use identity-equivalent instead of identical measures is given by Van Deth (1992: 305): 'Since the relevant phenomena obtain their meaning in a specific cultural context, we cannot rely on identical instruments. . . . In this way (identity-equivalence), the search for structure in distinct aspects of a concept like participation is combined with the need to obtain reliable information for cross-national analyses. This kind of approach seems to be much more attractive than the virtual endless speculations on the cultural meaning of our instruments in distinct settings.'

5. At first, cumulative (Mokken) scale analysis seemed to be a more attractive method to measure attitudes towards the environment. As it turned out, the 'difficulties' of the items differed only slightly, and the assumption of holomorphism was violated too often to regard these (relatively strong) scales as acceptable. In the factor analyses, only items that have a communality of 0.40 or higher were accepted.

6. For some examples of earlier accidents, such as smoke pollution in Pennsylvania (1948) and London (1952), see Weale (1992: 10).

7. The item is known to cause problems to the underlying structure when entered in factor analysis. See Inglehart (1977*b*: 45; 1979*c*: 313–16).

8. The Pearson correlation between the extent of greenness and the level of post-materialism in countries is not significant at the 0.05 level.

9. The Pearson correlation is 0.59 (significant at the 0.05 level).

10. For example, in 1986 Cramer's *V* varies between 0.09 in Ireland (1988) and 0.21 in Germany (1988).

11

Postmodernism

JOHN R. GIBBINS AND BO REIMER

A long-term process of value pluralization and de-alignment, accompanied by realignments along more local and transnational, group and individual lines—reflecting wider and deeper economic and social change—has produced fluidity and complexity in politics, as well as problems in the management of self and society, economy and government. Postmodernist value change has altered the way governments, institutions, and politicians are evaluated, and has challenged old ideas and expectations about government.

This chapter has two aims. The first is to show that postmodern theory helps us to understand and perhaps explain contemporary value change in Western Europe and its impact on beliefs about the role and legitimacy of government. The second is to demonstrate that the concept of postmodernism can be operationalized and put to empirical use. We hypothesize the emergence of new 'structures of feeling' and new formations of values which are united by little else than a common concern of individuals and groups for the right to be and to express themselves. Those who accept this reality and seek to open spaces for the exercise of their diversity, difference, and identity, are postmodernists. Postmodernists are characterized by a high level of cultural capital, and they are directed towards leisure, life-style, and image. *Expressivism* is the core notion of postmodernism, measured by such indicators as the high priority given to individual development and restlessness. But expressivists seek to realize themselves in two different ways, either through the accumulation of material goods and objects (instrumentalists), or through cultural accumulation (humanists).

Our hypothesis implies that, rather than moving in patterns structured around traditional socio-economic groupings, people move in a multitude of both individual- and group-based directions. This may be discerned in work as well as in leisure, and at all levels—from local to global. New patterns of value orientations affect the behaviour of people, and, as these affect both beliefs about government and government behaviour, traditional allegiances and interests are being transcended.

Postmodernism and Postmaterialism

There are some very obvious similarities between the theory of postmodernism and the theory of postmaterialism, the main 'contender' in this context (Inglehart 1977*b*; 1990). Both seek to explain shifts in political inputs and outputs through the examination of value change. Both detect the emergence of new values, and both endeavour to relate these to the development of new selves seeking realization, which are brought into being through generational socialization. Both identify new young cohorts as educated, activist, and prone to belong to new movements. Also, as Inglehart agrees, both pinpoint new issues and axes of conflict; postmaterialism 'seems to be an important factor contributing to the evolution of the postmodernist culture' (Inglehart 1989*a*: 251). Here the similarities end.

A postmaterialist seeks self-realization while the postmodernist seeks self-expression; fulfilment on a developmental scale as against hedonist enjoyment. The postmaterialist is teleological, future orientated, and concerned with progress, whereas postmodernists are concerned with the immediate, the present, and have no agreed narrative for the future. Postmaterialists seek the natural, the real, and authentic, while postmodernists relish the simulated, the image, and the representation. Postmaterialists consider the self to be stable once socialized, while postmodernists see the self as being constantly constructed, deconstructed, and reconstructed throughout their lifetime. The value orientation of postmaterialists is homogeneous while the orientations of postmodernists are pluralist and heterogeneous. For postmaterialists, the conditions spawning the new values are largely economic and military, with a common stress upon growing security; postmodernists, by contrast, stress technology and the media with a growing awareness of existential and social insecurity and risk. Postmaterialists stress the impact of education, especially higher education, while postmodernists stress exposure to everyday culture, the mass media, and travel. Ultimately, postmaterialists attack the canons of materialism, and postmodernists attack the canons of modernism. Unlike a postmaterialist, a postmodernist can be materialist; unlike a postmodernist, a postmaterialist can be modernist. The two orientations cannot be collapsed into one, for postmodernist and postmaterialist theory are competitors to explain political change in the Western world.

Why then prioritize the postmodern account? Two interrelated insights form the central strand of the answer. First, the world of politics is changing. Secondly, conventional approaches in political science seem unable to account for these changes, while great strides have been made in other related disciplines. We look into both these factors.

A Changing Political World

In brief, postmodernists claim that many of the practices and preconditions of politics in the modern world are being undermined by technological, organizational, social, and above all cultural changes which create discontinuities, incongruity, dissonance, fragmentation, and dissensus. The key changes include the transfer to a post-industrial information and consumer society; the disorganization of capitalism, socialism, and bureaucracy; transnationalism and globalization processes; the reorganization of employment along post-Fordist lines; the arrival of new classes or segments within classes; heightened conflict between the public and private worlds; and the emergence of a postmodern culture. The latter involves the emergence of hyper-differentiation and de-differentiation; the reorganization of leisure, the life world, and habitus; the commodification and mass production of a plurality of images, cultures, and life-styles. These developments entail the creation of new expressive selves which are mosaics of subjectivities and new attitudes, both local and universalized, stressing immediate gratification, novelty, play, hedonism, consumption, and style (Gibbins 1989a: Reimer 1988; 1989; Featherstone 1991; Crook, Pakulski, and Waters 1992).

Although the political system as a whole has shown a certain stability within the advanced industrial societies of Western Europe (see Chapter 3), there are indications of an increasing 'uncoupling' of political divisions from socio-economic structures. In the political sphere, observers note the de-alignment of class and party choice, and increasing electoral volatility; peculiar realignments around figures and issues in new movements, new behaviours and styles of participation called new politics. They note, too, new types of challenge and opposition to the state and parties; and weakening loyalties, trust, and confidence in the state (Gibbins 1989*b*: 15–16; Crook *et al.* 1992: 138–57).

We can also observe the changing functions, architecture, and status of the modern state. States seem less able to perform traditional functions: technology and the costs of defence have forced states out of sovereign control into transnational defensive groupings; transnational financial and corporate realities no longer allow states to have control of financial and economic management within their territories. Political and legal sovereignty is melting and reforming in federated structures; the rights of citizens have increasingly come to be seen as universal 'human rights' to be defended and promoted by international bodies. Internally, the bureaucratic and centrally organized state is releasing power and responsibility to local and regional bodies, quasi-political bodies such as hospital and housing trusts, and to the market, in a process now widely called 'the restructuring of the central and local state' (Aglietta 1979; Johnson 1990; Jessop *et al.* 1991). The interpenetration of public and private spheres—or 'imbrication' (Cerny 1990)—reduces the ability of the state to manage public life, and interest intermediation now often bypasses the state (Gibbins 1991; Crook *et al.* 1992).

The self and society, citizen and state, have thus changed—sometimes dramatically. The rate of change demands reflection and reformulation. We use the concept of postmodernism to account for these changes and try to show how postmodern value change affects political behaviour and beliefs in government.

Political Science and a Changing Political World

Profound shifts which find mirrors and connections in postmodern theory have taken place within many disciplines. These shifts include underlying assumptions, the selection of subject matter, the choice of methods, evaluations of the relationship between paradigms. They may be found in disciplines as diverse as literary theory, sociology and cultural studies, geography, art history, intellectual history, philosophy and political theory. But these shifts do not seem to have had resonances in political science.

Among the underlying assumptions (which also inform our thinking) are anti-essentialism, anti-foundationalism, and anti-rationalism; and changes hinging upon re-evaluating the role of language and discourse in the creation of meaning, the self, behaviour, and order (Rorty 1979; 1990; Bernstein 1985; Oakeshott 1962). Subject matters are becoming more diverse and are uncovering previously unrecognized or under-valued factors. The deviant, the odd or querky, the forgotten or suppressed, or the relatively ignored—all now attract attention in their own right as well as for their capacity to throw light on the normal (Foucault 1977; 1981; Cousins and Hussain 1984; Featherstone 1991). Attention is given to the everyday; to popular rather than to élite culture; to alternative rather than to dominant ideologies; to divergent life-styles rather than to the dominant social order; and to the emerging power of the mass media in constructing and maintaining them (Fiske 1989; Turner 1990; Curran and Seaton 1985; Curran and Gurevitch 1991; Silverstone 1991).

Among new methodologies, the most pertinent are the reflexive analysis of theoretical and practical discourses, especially in-depth study of everyday accounts and popular media representations (Lawson 1985; Lindlof 1987); the deconstruction of popular narratives and the uncovering of the power/knowledge dynamics behind their construction; contextualism invoked by the recognition of the reality of historical contingency (Cohen and Scull 1983; Baron 1988); and the multiplicity of methods for providing understanding as opposed to finding explanations (Giddens 1976). Finally, the increasing multiplicity of paradigms and the uncovering of their incommensurability also characterize many contemporary social sciences, as does argument over their moral, political, and epistemic status (Rosenau 1992). Post-modernism as a theoretical construct is a response to many of these changes in scholarship, which poses the question: how, if at all, is social and especially political science possible if such developments are entertained seriously?

Identities of Postmodernism

What conditions should a postmodern value orientation try to meet? To date, no surveys have been conducted with the aim of analysing such an orientation. In order to grasp a postmodern value oriention four conditions must be met. First, the value orientation must be conceptually and theoretically coherent. Secondly, it must be grounded in arguable historical, economic, social, and political contexts. Thirdly, it must be definable with appropriate indicators. And, finally, hypotheses must be framed about change which may be tested and supported by empirical evidence. While our analysis is preliminary, we aim to satisfy these conditions in the following discussion.

What, then, is postmodernism? Since coined by Frederico de Onis in 1934 to describe Spanish and Latin American poetry between 1905 and 1914 which reacted against modernism, the term 'postmodernism' has had a volatile history. Six kinds of accounts or usages can be identified, although they sometimes overlap. Postmodernism may refer to aesthetic and architectural movements or cultures (Onis 1934; Jenks 1986); or to a cultural *avant garde* or élite movement whose cry was 'anything goes' (Heller and Feher 1989: 138–40; Bauman 1987). It may also refer to popular phenomena in which consumer life-styles and mass consumption dominate taste and fashion, and in which groups stress difference and distinction in their attempt to accumulate cultural capital (Howe 1971; Turner 1990; Featherstone 1988; Bourdieu 1984). Postmodernism may also refer to a general cultural orientation with special recognition of the new self and groups rooted in the economic and political context of late modernity, with significant expressions in political culture as well as life-styles (Etzioni 1968; Bauman 1988; Gibbins 1989*b*; Reimer 1989; Hall 1989; Turner 1989). Again, postmodernism may refer to a *Zeitgeist* or the spirit of the age (Mills 1959; Lyotard 1984; Huyssen 1984; Forbes 1989), or to an historical period, variously described as starting around 1875 (Toynbee 1939; Somervell 1946) and prevailing until some unspecified future time (Giddens 1990).

All these usages are meaningful in their own context, but we must be careful to avoid 'category mistakes' or conflation. For our purposes here, we argue for a special application based on postmodernism as a general cultural orientation, which emerges from the wider contextual arguments provided by interpreting postmodernism as referring to the phenomena of mass popular culture and the spirit of the age. We regard the expression of postmodernism in aesthetic or architectural movements, or among the cultural *avant garde*, as exemplars. Our approach focuses on the sociological—or intermediary—level between micro- and macro-theories; what we can term the meso-level.

The process of transformation from modernity to postmodernity, is postmodernization (Crook *et al.* 1992: 32–41). In economic terms, modernity was characterized by two rational forms of production and distribution: capitalism and communism. Both were materialist in ethos and embraced the logic of mass industrial production. The division of labour in both was functional, but one was driven by private and corporate capital, the other by state bureaucracy. In late capitalism and in communism, serious problems arose in managing and organizing both systems, to the point where even their architects posited terminal crisis (Brittan 1977; 1988; O'Connor 1973; Jameson 1984; 1989).

Corporatism, bureaucracy, and even belief in any state or mixed economy solutions have come in for radical critique (Saunders 1979; Cawson 1982; 1989). The globalization of capitalism and the interpenetration of national capitalisms by transnational bodies, including multinational corporations, have undermined national economic units and the ability of the sovereign state to control them (Cerny 1990). The postmodern picture of transformation is affirmed in Bell's account of the effects of technology in creating a post-industrial economy; Baudrillard's account of the new economy of simulation and signs where the logic of reproduction replaces production, and correspondence declines between signs and meanings, system and outcome, market and value; the accounts of Featherstone and others of the new consumer economy; and Bourdieu's recognition of the encroachment of cultural capital into areas formerly dominated by capital. The byproducts of these economies are unpredictable and often dangerous, producing pollution, unemployment, social dislocation, and de-skilling. Thus the broad postmodernist picture is of modern economies becoming unwieldy, unworkable, unpredictable, and disorganized (Lash and Urry 1987; Offe 1985*a*).

Just as modernity invoked the decline of a feudal form of life, so late modernity has witnessed the fragmentation of the newer form. Old class allegiances have fragmented; social de-alignments and realignments have emerged. The most obvious are the growth of new distinctions and differences within the middle classes, including the growth of the 'new class' of professional public sector workers and the emergence of a new working class whose members are owner-occupiers, non-unionized, and employed in the 'high-tech' private sector (Bourdieu 1984; Offe 1985*b*; Veen 1989; Ignatieff 1992; Betz 1991). New groups with new life-styles have been spawned, creating a mosaic society, in which location has proved so disruptive and confusing that it has called for a new breed of psychologists, counsellors, and social engineers to manage it (Featherstone 1991; Polsky 1991).

The key dynamic of postmodernity is not economic or social but cultural. Modernity saw the spawning of new imperatives in culture—centrally, the drive towards mass popular culture and the attendant decline of élite culture. The 'civilizing process' which created modern selves descended to the masses through new forms of education and communication (Elias 1978; 1982). Alongside ran the development of the consumer society and culture (*Theory, Culture & Society*, 1/3 (1983)), targeting new consumer segments such as women, children, and the working classes. Cleavages based on culture and life-style are replacing traditional class divisions, further nurtured by new forms of media and advertising. Cultural competition is fought over distinction and difference, with the ironic results that new differences are accentuated while old ones are levelled, creating more fluid political constituencies.

Postmodernists have criticized these processes and observed their internal dislocation. Despite attempts to create dominant ideologies, the failures have been signified by the emergence of alternative, oppositional, and counter cultures, and the explosion of new cultures around women, youth, leisure, the aged, ethnic, religious, and other groups. The characteristic features are the creation of difference and distinction: on culture located in a shared life-style and habitus (Bourdieu 1984); a stress on signs and simulation (Baudrillard 1983); an emphasis on the immediate and the cathartic experience and full exchange of feelings, as in the emergence of new evangelical Christian movements and Buddhist movements (Bellah 1989: 101–2, 333–4); and on narcissistic representation and self-expression (Hebdige 1979; Reimer 1989).

Spatial developments which disrupt continuities by shortening or lengthening distances—emigration, proximity to immigrants, travel, and tourism—promote postmodern value orientations. So does time distanciation, encouraged by high technology travel and by new technologies (facsimile machines and computers) which speed up work. Concepts such as 'time–space compression' (Harvey 1989) and 'time–space distanciation' (Giddens 1991), question traditional conceptions of time and space. The world is shrinking, and activities taking place in other parts of the world tend to become more important for everyday lives than activities taking place in local communities (Beck 1992; Giddens 1990).

Exposure to television, video, film, and other mass media—not forgetting music—are crucial in the mediation of the private and public spheres, as well as in the mediation of the local and the global (Meyrowitz 1985; Reimer 1994; Silverstone 1991). The relationships between high and popular culture, and between individual and collective cultural spheres, are also affected by the mass media. Although it is incompatible with postmodern theory—and the evidence—to ascribe a controlling power to the mass media, or through them to the ruling class, their role in encoding, producing, and promoting messages for decoding, consumption, and use can be regarded as fundamental (Curran and Seaton 1985; Morley 1986; Turner 1990: 183–5).

The postmodern self is constructed in environments mediated by the mass media. But this postmodern self is an unfinished project: an identity is a role and a performance in the making, and public and private life are restless searches for self-knowledge and self-production for public consumption and recognition. Being incomplete, the self is restless, thus the postmodernist's search for identity is relentless. Political behaviour follows these developments by encouraging the decline or radical transformation and reorientation of traditional parties and the growth of new social and political movements on the one side, and apathy on the other. Old movements and groups are recycled with, and into, the new, as are the old with the new in values, beliefs, ideologies, and attitudes. The mixings and remixings which arise and the strange new alignments have no definite lasting shape (Betz 1991). Faced with such turmoil, parties and governments have turned to information and image management in attempts to create common narratives from discontinuous and incommensurable political forces and to fashion allegiances around personality and charisma. The political careers of Ronald Reagan, Margaret Thatcher, Ross Perot, and Silvio Berlusconi are cases in point (Jamieson 1984; Pekonen 1989; Hall 1988*a*; 1988*b*). Politics increasingly becomes about presentation and representation. The mass media, in turn, deconstruct and reconstruct these representations, leaving the consumer free to ferret in the wreckage to fashion their own reality.

Finally, the modern state and its bureaucratic structures have ceased to work effectively or to deliver on promises of progress, welfare, and security for citizens. The literature is littered with debates about government overload, fiscal crisis, the erosion of sovereignty, the retreat from welfare, deregulation, devolution, and privatization. Hence, we might ask whether the nation state is in terminal decline, or whether it is being transformed into a 'new state' and the world into a postmodern political order (Cerny 1990; Gibbins 1991; Rennger 1989; Connolly 1991: 49–51). According to some observers, the new state will take the form of a revived civil society, with government as umpire rather than provider (Keane 1984; 1988*a*; 1988*b*; Oakeshott 1975; Hirst 1993). Filling the space left by the nation state and hoping to negotiate the 'anarchical society' (Bull 1977) are a conglomeration of new international, multinational, and transnational political formations which have not yet created the security lost by the decline of Europe and America as the foci of the old international order (Rengger 1989; Cerny 1990; Brown 1988; Heller and Feher 1989).[1]

Expressivism: The Postmodern Identity

How can we define and operationalize postmodernism? A postmodern value orientation must be grasped in relation to modern value orientations. We need to capture the transfer from a rational, instrumental, and materialist culture stressing roles to one stressing life-styles and signifying feeling, expression, and cultural capital. Whereas modernists are committed to status and class segments, to means–ends rationality and teleology, postmodernists are committed to the logic of the now and the immediate. At the heart of this distinction lies the belief that the modern self is being replaced by a more inner-directed postmodern self. Originally a psychological concept, this is now neatly captured in the recent work of Connolly (1984; 1991), Giddens (1990; 1991), Bellah *et al.* (1985), and Taylor (1985; 1989). They have in common a preoccupation with a dramatically different kind of self—one who thinks, feels, and acts in very different ways to the modern norm.

Having embraced the reality of anti-foundationalism and essentialism, Connolly has revealed our theoretical ejection from the garden of modernity (as signified by Nietzsche) and presented an in-depth analysis of the new self and its implications for liberalism, democracy, and the world order. Connolly argues that the modern self identifies itself by stressing contrast and difference. This self finds security by fixing and opposing those differences at all levels, including the political. As every self is particular, constructed, and relational, and all feel the drive to 'naturalize' or objectify themselves, society is a battle ground for identities and differences (Connolly 1991: 64–6). The only possible form of democracy would be the opening of political spaces for agonistic relations of adversarial respect. The paradigm shift is of the self which is not fixed, with essential elements, but is 'both historically contingent and inherently relational' (1991: 48).

While Giddens contends that postmodernity is not yet fully upon us, his diagnosis of the late modern self also stresses the 'discontinuities' of late modernity (Giddens 1990: 2–7, 46–53). His 'radicalized modernity' downgrades the attack on foundations and rejects the notion of the dissolved, fragmented self, and the emptying of social life stressed by postmodernists. His notion of late modernity stresses a self which is empowered to generate new identities, which sees social life as 'an active complex of reactions to abstract systems, involving appropriation as well as loss' (1990: 150). In addition, radicalized modernity exhibits 'the dissolution of evolutionism, the disappearance of historical tele-ology, the recognition of thoroughgoing, constitutive reflexivity, together with the evaporating of the privileged position of the West' (1990: 52)—a disturbing universe of experience which shares many features we characterize as postmodern.

Two other features of the late modern identified by Giddens may be useful indicators of postmodernity: the stress on the here and now (immediate space and time), and growing scepticism about science and its capacity to create progress (1990: 2, 172; cf. Topf 1993). We might also seek to tap the tensions he sees as typical of the late modern: the growth of security and danger, trust and risk (1990: 7, 34–5, 100; cf. Beck 1992). But, for Giddens, a truly postmodern society would transcend these tensions, providing a growth of ontological security, a re-embedding of the self in tradition, a loss of concern for the future, and a reunification of the global and local levels (1990: 178). For us, these are possible goals but not the only goals of contemporary post-modernists.

Bellah and his colleagues present a critical assessment of contem-porary values and society with particular clarity. Expressivist indi-vidualism, the belief that each individual has a unique set of feelings and intuitions which have to be expressed if the individual is to be realized, is held to be the central and unifying feature of contemporary American cultural life (1985: 333–4). Intensely romantic relationships, cathartic religious experiences, and the shared world of life-style enclaves are expressions of new postmodern value orientations (1985: 101–2, 291; cf. Taylor 1989: 508).

Finally, Taylor presents the self as framed in language, so generating different selves in different discourses. This self is less a set of powers or capacities, not a machine or natural entity, nor regarded in terms of origins or ends, but is signified by 'openness to certain matters of significance' (Taylor 1985: 105). The self is signified by the effort to understand itself, to reflexivity, to establish what it wants and ought to do (1985: 112). The subject is self-defining, and its attitudes and behaviour are located in this process. All actions are expressions and self-definitions, but the logic of action is to construct a narrative of self-expression—an authentic, real or 'self-realized self' in the sense suggested by Hegel and Heidegger. From Hegel is also derived the notion that, despite its self-expression, the self is essentially a social self and actions are group expressions (Taylor 1985: 93–6). There is both the drive to identify and to differ; the self is established in both (Bourdieu 1984).

Taylor identifies three sources of the self: theistic, with roots in Christianity; naturalistic, grounded in scientific or instrumental rationality; and expressive, or romantic self-expression (Taylor 1989: 495–6). Our contemporary crisis arises from secularization and the triumph of instrumentalism. Expressivism and community, whether secular or not, offers an alternative morality and politics (1989: 500–5). Hence the dilemma which Taylor poses: how can expressive value orientations be compatible with communal identity, society, and the state?[2] Our reply is that the postmodern self seeks to fix its ever-changing identity in expression—at all levels from the private to the public, from the body to politics. Thus, at the centre of the postmodern self is a value orientation which can collectively be called expressivism. Such a self feels free and confident in most areas of social life, yet is restless and unhappy about the present, and seeks arenas for change.

Expressivism distinguishes our analysis from other accounts of cultural change. By expressivism we mean the desire to actualize self-constructions or identities. Pure expressivism is this desire focused as close to the self as possible—in the body, clothing, possessions, and domestic things. As it extends beyond the body, expressivism takes the form of social self-expression, with realization located in relationships, life-style, groups, and movements. Alongside expressivism, we have the notions of *instrumentalism* and *humanism*. At one extreme, self-expression can focus on private life, and, being more means–ends oriented, focuses largely on material goods and objects; at the other extreme, it may realize itself in public life, focusing largely on social goods and interactions.

We distinguish between instrumental and humanist postmodernists.

Instrumental postmodernists focus on private life and material goods; humanist postmodernists focus on the public world and social goods. In essence, modernists seek capital accumulation while postmodernists prioritize cultural capital. To instrumental postmodernists, this means accumulating the material signs of culture, whereas humanist post-modernists seek cultural accumulation in social activities such as dance, holidays, and politics. In our conceptualization, then, there are two kinds of postmodernists: instrumental postmodernists, who combine expressivism with instrumentalism, and humanist postmodernists, who combine expressivism with humanism.

Hypotheses

We can now advance some hypotheses concerning humanist and instrumental postmodernists and their relationship to politics. The components of expressivism, humanism, and instrumentalism are by no means new, but we argue that it is only now that their specific articulations as humanist and instrumental postmodernism may be seen as value orientations in everyday life. However, as value change is a slow process, we do not expect these value orientations to be widespread. Moreover, as values are shaped through complicated socialization processes, post-modern value orientations will be more likely among certain parts of the population rather than as a general development across an entire society.

We would expect to find postmodern value orientations among people who are most involved with the experience of late modernity; among the highly mobile, both socially and geographically, and among those who take full advantage of the mass media. Moreover, late modernity is a phase characterized by contradictions, fluidity, and continuous change. In order to negotiate one's way through its complexities and uncertainties, one needs competence and confidence. Thus, we would expect postmodern value orientations to be more common among people occcupied in parts of the service sector (Abercrombie and Urry 1983). Again, people with higher levels of education and, thus, higher economic and especially cultural capital, are more likely to have postmodern orientations (Bourdieu 1984). We also expect younger people to be more postmodern than older people. On the one hand, this is due to life-cycle differences: young people have more contacts with other people in everyday life, travel more, and use the media more (Ziehe 1986). But there is also a cohort effect: having been accustomed to a life full of contacts and experiences, it is not unlikely that the young generation of today will keep their postmodern orientations even in later years. We do not expect gender to be important. But to a certain extent men and women live in different realities, one more oriented towards the public sphere, the other towards the private sphere. We would therefore expect differences when it comes to the type of postmodern value orientation. So we expect instrumental postmodernists to be more common among men and humanist postmodernists to be more common among women.[3]

Like any other value orientation, a postmodern orientation is relevant for the whole of everyday life, not just political practices. Among other things, we expect postmodernists to be involved in a multitude of everyday life practices, to be consumer oriented, and to be frequent users of the mass media (Mort 1989; Nava 1991). In line with the notions of fluidity and change, we expect postmodernists to rearrange their everyday practices frequently and maybe even unsystematically. Their activities may or may not be tied to memberships in organizations; if they are, we would expect these memberships to be short-lived. Postmodernists are more likely than others to join an organization for a while and then move on.

Postmodernists are unlikely to differ from others in conventional political behaviour. The normal repertory of political activities is not in any way tied to late modernity. Even though postmodernists are more likely than others to change party orientation, we would expect them to vote and belong to political parties to the same degree as non-post-modernists. We do hypothesize, however, that postmodernists are more positive than others towards unconventional political activities, and more willing to participate in demonstrations, for example. We hypothesize also that postmodernists are more directed towards expressive political behaviour which typifies what postmodernists stand for—activities which signify immediacy and change. We would expect to find these patterns among both humanist and instrumental postmodernists. They would be natural ingredients in the life-styles of humanist postmodernists; and although not as important for instrumental post-modernists, they would at least accept their importance. We do not expect postmodernists to distrust either government or democratic processes more than other citizens; postmodernists depend upon the security provided by the state to facilitate expressive activities and life-styles. However, being more socially orientated, we would expect humanist postmodernists to be more supportive and trusting than instrumental postmodernists.

Finally, we bring time into the picture. As we see postmodern value orientations as tied to late modernity, we expect the proportion of postmodernists to be rising in all West European countries over time. We also expect the proportion of postmodernists to be highest in countries which are most involved with the experience of modernity—that is, in the most advanced industrial societies. This means that we expect postmodern value orientations to be more common in Central and northern Europe than in southern Europe.

Analytic Strategy

A postmodern value orientation is based on the articulation between, on the one hand, expressivism and, on the other hand, humanism or instrumentalism. Those individuals whom we have characterized as truly postmodern share a certain 'structure of feeling' (Williams 1961; Reimer 1989), which makes it meaningful to group them together. However, as they can be divided on the grounds of other values—humanism and instrumentalism—postmodernists are not a homogeneous group. Thus, as we have outlined, we arrive at our central concepts: humanist postmodernism and instrumental postmodernism.

Our data sources are the 1981 and 1990 European Values Survey, conducted among representative national samples in twelve West European countries. We use a number of items from each survey to operationalize the concepts of expressivism, humanism, and instrumentalism. On the basis of these three variables, we then constructed the variables 'humanist postmodernism' and 'instrumental postmodernism' which are used throughout the analysis. We should note, however, that the surveys did not include questions specifically framed to capture our concepts. This is obviously a disadvantage. However, if we obtain results in line with our hypotheses despite the limitations of the data, this strengthens our argument.

We use two items to operationalize expressivism, our core concept. The first concerns an emphasis on the development of the individual, which we regard as crucial for expressivism. Respondents who do not regard individual development as important cannot be classified in the expressive category. The second item is drawn from a question about 'the way people are feeling these days'; the feeling of 'restlessness' taps a different aspect of expressivism. Therefore, to get the maximum value of two on the expressivism variable, respondents have to be both concerned about individual development and be restless; those who are concerned only about individual development are assigned the value one. All others are assigned zero.

As we noted, expressivism in itself does not constitute a postmodern value orientation; it has to be articulated with either humanism or instrumentalism. Humanism is constructed using two items. To be a humanist, one must either believe that most people can be trusted or that an important aspect of a job is that it is useful for society. Similarly, to be an instrumentalist, one must either believe that an important aspect in a job is that it is well paid or that less emphasis on money and material possessions in our ways of life would be a bad thing. Thus, each respondent is assigned a value between zero and two on expressivism and a value of zero or one on humanism and instrumentalism. The variables 'humanist postmodernism' and 'instrumental postmodernism' were then constructed by combining, on the one hand, expressivism with humanism and, on the other hand, expressivism with instrumentalism. Finally, the two constructed variables were transformed into a three-point scale (0–2).

Our earlier discussion makes clear that the two types of postmodern value orientations—humanist postmodernism and instrumental postmodernism—are conceptually distinct. Empirically, however, they overlap to some extent due to the measures we use. But as the relationship between instrumentalism and humanism is very weak, this problem is minor. However, the weak relationship between instrumentalism and humanism must be distinguished from the relationship between humanist postmodernism and instrumental postmodernism, which, due to the inclusion of expressivism in both variables, is somewhat stronger. And so it should be: expressivism is the common element in our conceptualization of postmodern value orientations.

Thus, on the one hand, we want to highlight the common element in postmodern value orientations which makes it meaningful to see them as intimately related. On the other hand, we want to highlight that this common element may be articulated with different elements, making it meaningful to separate them. In our empirical analysis, we focus on the second aspect. That is, we do not start the analysis by showing, empirically, how postmodern value orientations as such differ from non-postmodern value orientations. Those differences may be gleaned from the analysis presented, and it would make the analysis unnecessarily repetitive. Nor do we explore the relationship between instrumental postmodernism and humanist postmodernism. Suffice it to state that these variables, owing to the inclusion of expressivism, are related, but that the relationship, due to the articulation with either instrumentalism or humanism, is not particularly strong.

In the empirical analysis, we describe, first, the spread of postmodern value orientations in West European countries, and outline how their distribution is structured by socio-economic characteristics. Secondly, we relate these value orientations to other central value orientations. We then analyse the relationship between postmodern value orientations and political behaviour. Finally, we examine the relationship between postmodern orientations and confidence in societal institutions, a confidence which we see as an indicator of people's beliefs in government.[4]

Of the three value orientations central to this volume, we focus on religious–secular orientations and materialist–postmaterialist orientations. The indicator for left–right materialism which can be constructed with data from the European Values Survey is rather limited, so interpretation of the relationship between left–right materialism and postmodern value orientations is troublesome.

Postmodern Value Orientations in Western Europe

An initial impression of the spread of postmodern value orientations in West European countries, and how they are structured by socio-economic characteristics, is given in Table 11.1. The first thing to note is that there are, indeed, differences between countries. The mean value for humanist postmodernism is highest in countries characterized as industrially more advanced. The pattern is clearer for 1990 than for 1981. For instrumental postmodernism, West Germany has a notably high mean at both time points. On the whole, however, the pattern for instrumental postmodernism is not as clear cut as for humanist post-modernism.

If we look at changes in the distribution of postmodern orientations between 1981 and 1990, the pattern is in line with our hypothesis: in almost all countries, postmodern value orientations seem to have become more important in 1990 than they were in 1981. The means for humanist postmodernists increased in ten countries and fell in only one, whereas the means for instrumental postmodernists increased in

TABLE 11.1. Postmodernist orientations by age, education, and gender, 1981 and 1990

	1981					1990				
	Mean	Age	Education	Gender	N	Mean	Age	Education	Gender	N
	(a) Humanist postmodernism									
DK	0.77	-0.10*	0.12*	0.02	1039	0.80	-0.16*	0.20*	-0.01	965
NO	0.87	-0.11*	0.15*	-0.06	1118	0.88	-0.11*	0.13*	-0.03	1,143
SV	0.66	-0.07	0.17*	-0.05	865	0.86	-0.08*	0.09*	0.02	943
BE	0.53	-0.09*	0.20*	-0.06	964	0.56	-0.04	0.12*	0.01	2,537
GB	0.55	0.04	0.17*	-0.09*	1184	0.63	0.04	0.14*	0.02	1,430
GE	0.70	-0.20*	0.16*	-0.03	1080	0.75	-0.04	0.17*	0.05	1,720
IR	0.58	-0.03	0.17*	0.02	1169	0.69	0.02	0.14*	0.03	982
NE	0.70	-0.07	0.15*	-0.04	1020	0.90	-0.03	0.13*	0.02	955
FR	0.45	0.01	0.11*	-0.05	1081	0.48	0.02	0.14*	-0.10*	902
IT	0.68	-0.02	0.11*	-0.03	1302	0.73	0.01	0.01	0.05	1,921
PO	—	—	—	—	—	0.66	0.02	0.01	0.07	1,122
SP	0.72	-0.11*	0.17*	0.04	2130	0.66	-0.02	0.08*	0.00	2,439

(b) Instrumental postmodernism

DK	0.61	-0.21*	0.05	-0.17*	1146	0.70	-0.26*	0.08*	-0.18*	988
NO	0.77	-0.15*	0.01	-0.12*	1216	0.72	-0.14*	0.09*	-0.14*	1,223
SV	0.61	-0.07	0.10*	-0.14*	937	0.81	-0.13*	-0.02	0.08*	1,042
BE	0.66	-0.08*	0.04	-0.05	1076	0.76	-0.06*	0.01	-0.05	2,792
GB	0.61	-0.09*	0.00	-0.09*	1222	0.78	-0.06*	-0.01	-0.05	1,473
GE	0.93	-0.20*	0.05	-0.07*	1296	1.01	-0.16*	0.05*	0.00	2,090
IR	0.71	-0.05	-0.01	-0.02	1211	0.86	-0.08*	0.07	-0.01	994
NL	0.55	-0.04	-0.03	-0.10*	1135	0.87	-0.08*	0.01	-0.05	1,005
FR	0.61	-0.11*	-0.03	-0.01	1104	0.64	-0.11*	0.01	-0.01	925
IT	0.79	0.02	-0.13*	-0.01	1348	0.82	-0.08*	0.03	-0.02	2,005
PO	—	—	—	—	—	0.75	-0.02	0.01	0.03	1,155
SP	0.88	-0.10*	0.03	0.00	2271	0.86	-0.01	0.00	0.00	2,595

* $p < 0.01$

Note: Entries are means and product moment coefficients of scores on the postmodernist index with age, education, and gender.

Sources: European Values Survey (1981, 1990).

nine countries and fell in two.[5] The change seems to have been sharpest in the Netherlands and Sweden.

Our hypotheses anticipate that postmodern orientations are most common among young people and the well educated. We further hypothesized that women are more likely to be humanist postmodernists and men to be instrumental postmodernists.[6] Although by no means conclusive, on the whole the data point in the right directions. As we can see from Table 11.1, humanist postmodernism is related to both age and level of education. Younger people and people with higher levels of education are more likely to be humanist postmodernists than other people. The relationship to age is somewhat stronger in the northern countries and Germany than in the rest of Western Europe, whereas education shows roughly the same impact throughout Western Europe. Age is by far the most important characteristic when it comes to instrumental postmodernism; in all countries, and in both years, younger people are more likely to be instrumental postmodernists than older people. The pattern is stronger in the northern and central countries than in southern Europe. Gender is also important. Men are, at both time points, more likely than women to be instrumental postmodernists. This pattern is especially strong in the northern countries. More unexpectedly, the level of education is very weakly related to instrumental postmodernism.[7]

Postmodernism and Other Orientations

In seeing postmodern value orientations as something distinctly new and tied to late modernity, these orientations are far removed from the much older distinction between religious–secular value orientations. We do not consider postmodern orientations to be necessarily linked to the secularization process. Indeed, the humanist component of postmodern orientations is clearly compatible with religious value orientations. It is evident from Table 11.2, however, that postmodern orientations are, on the whole, very weakly related to religious–secular orientations. Even so, there is a difference between humanist and instrumental postmodernism. People with humanist postmodern orientations are somewhat more likely to be religious, whereas people with instrumental postmodern orientations are somewhat more likely to have a secular outlook on life.[8]

Postmaterialist orientations, like postmodern orientations, are

TABLE 11.2. *Religious–secular orientations by humanist and instrumental postmodernism, 1981 and 1990*

	Humanist postmodernism		Instrumental postmodernism	
	1981	1990	1981	1990
DK	0.00	0.06	0.08	0.07
NO	−0.01	0.00	0.00	0.08*
SV	−0.02	−0.02	0.12*	0.00
BE	−0.07	−0.06	0.03	0.01
GB	−0.08	−0.11*	0.12*	0.00
GE	0.00	−0.04	0.05	0.09*
IR	0.00	−0.05	−0.06	0.04
NL	−0.07	−0.05	0.03	0.08*
FR	−0.07	−0.02	0.10	−0.03
IT	−0.03	−0.03	0.08*	0.07*
PO	—	0.01	—	0.02
SP	−0.02	−0.04	0.04	0.03

*$p < 0.01$

Note: Entries are product moment coefficents.

Sources: European Values Survey (1981, 1990).

relatively new phenomena. We discussed earlier the differences between these two types of value orientations. As we can see in Table 11.3, instrumental postmodernism is practically unrelated to material-ism–postmaterialism—as measured by the original Inglehart four-item battery. Humanist postmodernism, however, is related to postmaterial-ism: in most countries, humanist postmodernist orientations are significantly correlated with postmaterialist orientations.

The relationships are not strong, however. Postmaterialists tend to have a higher level of education than humanist postmodernists, and they are younger. In that respect, postmaterialists are a more distinctive group than humanist postmodernists. How much of this distinctiveness is due to our operationalizations is difficult to gauge. Clearly, here we are up against the limitations of the data. Thus, a more detailed empirical analysis could be misleading. However, it is by using these value orientations in relation to political practices and beliefs in government that we get an idea of how well our operationalizations work. After examining that aspect, we return to the relationship between postmodern value orientations and materialism–postmaterialism.

TABLE 11.3. *Materialist–postmaterialist orientations by humanist and instrumental postmodernism, 1981 and 1990*

	Humanist postmodernism		Instrumental postmodernism	
	1981	1990	1981	1990
DK	0.12*	0.18*	0.06	0.04
NO	0.12*	0.09*	−0.03	0.02
SV	0.15*	0.10*	0.05	0.02
BE	0.17*	0.13*	0.07	0.02
GB	0.07	0.06	0.00	−0.02
GE	0.20*	0.15*	0.09*	0.09*
IR	0.03	0.11*	0.00	0.07
NL	0.15*	0.06	0.03	−0.12*
FR	0.27*	0.22*	0.03	0.01
IT	0.14*	0.10*	−0.11*	−0.07*
PO	—	0.00	—	−0.02
SP	0.08*	0.04	−0.02	−0.03

* $p < 0.01$

Note: Entries are product moment coefficients.

Sources: European Values Survey (1981, 1990).

Postmodern Orientations and Political Behaviour

In looking at postmodern value orientations and political behaviour, we first look briefly at conventional political behaviour, and then move on to expressive and unconventional political behaviour. The aspect of conventional political behaviour we consider concerns party membership. Being a party member means assigning great importance to the traditional political game, so party membership is an indicator of whether 'postmodern times' may mean a weakening of this form of traditional political behaviour.

The data (not shown here) do not support such a conclusion. The relationship between party membership and postmodern values varies quite considerably between countries, but, if anything, it is slightly positive. The result is not surprising. We did not expect postmodernists to differ significantly in their conventional political behaviour from non-postmodernists. But do they differ in their political views?

Using a question on left–right self-placement, we see in Table 11.4 that humanist postmodernists are, on the whole, positioned more to the left of centre than non-postmodernists. Only in Belgium, Britain, and Portugal do we find exceptions to this pattern. The pattern is stronger in 1981 than in 1990, but at both time points the relationship between left–right self-placement and humanist postmodernism is strongest in Denmark. Instrumental postmodernists, on the other hand, are more heterogeneous in their placements. With the exception of Norway in 1990, the relationship to the left–right scale is insignificant for all countries at both time points.

Turning to unconventional political behaviour, it is here, according to our hypotheses, that postmodern value orientations are most crucial. If we are right, postmodernists are more positive towards unconventional political behaviour and participate more frequently in such activities than others. This should be the case even when we control for factors such as age and education. We look first, in Table 11.5, at a question which taps what may be called expressive political behaviour. The question concerns how often respondents discuss politics (never, occasionally, or frequently).

As the table shows, there is a modest relationship between humanist postmodernism and the frequency of discussing politics. Controlling for

TABLE 11.4. *Left–right self-placement by humanist and instrumental post-modernism, 1981 and 1990*

	Humanist postmodernism		Instrumental postmodernism	
	1981	1990	1981	1990
DK	−0.15*	−0.14*	−0.07	−0.05
NO	−0.07	−0.02	0.01	0.09*
SV	−0.01	−0.04	0.04	0.01
BE	0.06	0.02	0.08	0.02
GB	0.04	0.01	−0.04	0.01
GE	−0.11*	−0.07*	−0.05	0.05
IR	−0.02	0.05	−0.03	0.01
NL	−0.08	−0.03	0.04	0.02
FR	−0.07	−0.16*	−0.02	0.01
IT	−0.09*	−0.03	0.03	0.02
PO	—	0.04	—	0.02
SP	−0.05	−0.01	−0.02	0.02

* $p < 0.01$

Note: Entries are product moment coefficients.

Sources: European Values Survey (1981, 1990).

TABLE 11.5. *Discussing politics by humanist and instrumental postmodernism, 1981 and 1990*

	Humanist postmodernism		Instrumental postmodernism	
	1981	1990	1981	1990
DK	0.09*	0.12*	0.03	0.02
NO	0.04	0.13*	0.02	0.05
SV	0.11*	0.04	0.02	0.03
BE	0.11*	0.09*	0.07	0.07*
GB	0.09*	0.04	0.06	0.02
GE	0.18*	0.10*	0.05	0.04
IR	0.11*	0.03	0.03	0.05
NL	0.14*	0.11*	0.02	0.04
FR	0.12*	0.10*	0.04	0.06
IT	0.11*	0.16*	0.05	0.04
PO	—	0.11*	—	0.04
SP	0.11*	0.11*	0.06*	0.01

* $p < 0.05$

Note: Multiple classification analysis controlling for age and education.

Sources: European Values Survey (1981, 1990).

both education and age, the relationship is significant in ten of the eleven countries in 1981 and nine of the twelve countries in 1990. Furthermore, there are no major differences between the different parts of Western Europe. Although instrumental postmodernists are some- what more inclined to discuss politics than non-postmodernists, the relationship is much weaker than for humanist postmodernists.

The questions we use as indicators of unconventional political behaviour take into account both actual behaviour and attitudes towards behaviour. Several activities associated with politics were presented to respondents who, for each type, answered whether they had engaged in such activities, and if not, if they might do so, or if they would never do so. Here, we present data on two types of political action: signing petitions and participating in lawful demonstrations. Both should be seen as unconventional political behaviour, although the first is less demanding, so more frequently undertaken, than the second.

Regardless of value orientation, roughly half the population in most countries have signed a petition. And in most countries, it is corre- lated—although not strongly—with humanist postmodernism. As we can see from Table 11.6, after controlling for education and age, the higher the value on humanist postmodernism, the higher the probability of having signed a petition. However, whereas the relationship is significant in most countries in 1981, it is significant in only seven of the twelve countries in 1990.

Instrumental postmodernism, by contrast, seems almost unrelated to signing petitions. Indeed, in some countries (Germany and the Netherlands, for example), non-postmodernists are more likely to have signed petitions than instrumental postmodernists. Yet instrumental postmodernism is not totally unrelated to signing petitions: attitudes towards signing petitions among those who have never done so are more positive among instrumental postmodernists than among non-postmodernists. In fact, the proportion of respondents who claim that they would never sign a petition is lower among instrumental post-modernists than among non-postmodernists in all countries except Spain and Portugal.

Participation in lawful demonstrations is, on the whole, undertaken by only a minority in any of the countries examined. But when this type of activity is undertaken, it seems to be related to postmodern orientations,

TABLE 11.6. *Signing petitions by humanist and instrumental postmodernism, 1981 and 1990*

	Humanist postmodernism		Instrumental postmodernism	
	1981	1990	1981	1990
DK	0.10*	0.14*	0.07	0.04
NO	0.03	0.12*	0.02	0.06
SV	0.11*	0.12*	0.01	0.04
BE	0.09*	0.04	0.04	0.05
GB	0.03	0.05	0.06	0.09*
GE	0.10*	0.11*	0.02	0.03
IR	0.10*	0.06	0.06	0.03
NL	0.13*	0.14*	0.05	0.01
FR	0.12*	0.06	0.04	0.03
IT	0.12*	0.09*	0.04	0.01
PO	—	0.03	—	0.03
SP	0.06*	0.17*	0.02	0.05

$* p < 0.05$

Note: Multiple classification analysis controlling for age and education.

Sources: European Values Survey (1981, 1990).

TABLE 11.7. *Attending demonstrations by humanist and instrumental postmodernism, 1981 and 1990*

	Humanist postmodernism		Instrumental postmodernism	
	1981	1990	1981	1990
DK	0.13*	0.17*	0.09*	0.12*
NO	0.09*	0.09*	0.02	0.01
SV	0.10*	0.10*	0.05	0.01
BE	0.11*	0.10*	0.06	0.06*
GB	0.12*	0.11*	0.08*	0.05
GE	0.14*	0.09*	0.04	0.03
IR	0.06	0.06	0.03	0.11*
NL	0.21*	0.15*	0.05	0.05
FR	0.15*	0.16*	0.05	0.02
IT	0.14*	0.09*	0.05	0.02
PO	—	0.04	—	0.06
SP	0.11*	0.11*	0.02	0.05

* $p < 0.05$

Note: Multiple classification analysis controlling for age and education.

Sources: European Values Survey (1981, 1990).

particularly humanist postmodernism. As shown in Table 11.7, with the exceptions of only Ireland and Portugal (1990), at both time points humanist postmodernists are more likely to have attended demonstrations than other people.

Instrumental postmodernists, however, are not more likely to have attended demonstrations than non-postmodernists. Even so, on the whole, they tend to be more positive towards the idea of doing so. Moreover, a comparison of Tables 11.6 and 11.7 reveals that the relationship between attending demonstrations and instrumental postmodern orientations is somewhat stronger than between signing petitions and instrumental postmodernism.

Postmodern Orientations and Confidence in Institutions

Finally, we examine the relationship between postmodern value orientations and beliefs in government. The indicator we use for beliefs in government is drawn from a question on people's confidence in societal institutions. In the European Values Survey, respondents were asked to state, on a four-point scale, how much confidence they had in ten different institutions. Three of them are particularly relevant to people's beliefs in government: parliament, the education system, and the civil service. Summarizing replies about these three institutions, we have a variable ranging from 3 to 12, where 12 means having a great deal of confidence in all three institutions and 3 means having no confidence whatsoever in any of these institutions. In the first four columns of Table 11.8, we present the correlations between the two postmodern orientations and the scale for confidence in institutions.

As the table shows, there is some relationship, although slight, between humanist postmodernism and confidence in these three institutions. The relationship is somewhat stronger in the countries of Central and northern Europe than in southern Europe. Except in the occasional instance, however, instrumental postmodernism is either weakly or negatively related to confidence in these institutions.

Earlier, we examined the relationship between postmodern and postmaterialist value orientations by looking at their socio-economic antecedents. We did not bring in materialism–postmaterialism when

TABLE 11.8. *Confidence in institutions by humanist and instrumental postmodernism, and materialism–postmaterialism, 1981 and 1990*

	Humanist postmodernism		Instrumental postmodernism		Materialist–postmaterialist value orientations	
	1981	1990	1981	1990	1981	1990
DK	0.09*	0.07	−0.06	−0.01	−0.05	0.01
NO	0.06	0.00	0.05	0.03	−0.03	−0.03
SV	0.04	0.12*	−0.10*	0.02	−0.09*	−0.02
BE	0.00	0.03	0.04	0.02	−0.12*	−0.09*
GB	0.05	0.07*	0.01	0.01	−0.03	0.11*
GE	0.02	0.05	−0.02	−0.07*	−0.16*	−0.15*
IR	0.05	0.09*	−0.01	−0.06	−0.14*	−0.13*
NL	0.04	0.09*	0.01	0.04	−0.06	−0.01
FR	0.01	0.04	−0.05	0.04	−0.19*	−0.16*
IT	−0.03	0.04	0.04	−0.07	−0.14*	−0.08*
PO	—	0.06	—	0.05	—	−0.12*
SP	−0.05	0.03	−0.05	0.02	−0.25*	−0.12*

* $p < 0.01$

Note: Entries are product moment coefficients.

Sources: European Values Survey (1981, 1990).

looking at political practices because the topic is taken up in several other chapters. Here, we only need to note that materialist–postmaterialist orientations are more strongly related to political practices than postmodern orientations. What is more interesting is to compare the relationship between these two value orientations and beliefs in government. Thus, we have included the materialist–postmaterialist value orientation in the final two columns of Table 11.8.

The differences between these value orientations now become quite clear. Whereas humanist postmodernism is, by and large, positively related to beliefs in government and the picture for instrumental postmodernism is very mixed, there is a clear negative relationship between a postmaterialist orientation and confidence in the three institutions. This is so in every country at both time points—except Denmark in 1990. That is, on the whole, materialists in every country express more confidence in parliament, the civil service, and the education system than postmaterialists. Almost consistently, and often very significantly, postmaterialists express relatively little confidence in these institutions.

Postmodernism and Beliefs in Government

Our data suggest that it is possible to discern something which we may call a postmodern value orientation in all West European countries. It is not widespread, but it is spreading slowly and perceptibly. As our hypothesis predicts, postmodernism is on the rise, although not to the extent we anticipated. However, with data for only two time points, we are not in a position to observe longer-term change. None the less, our evidence does suggest that both the humanist and instrumental components of postmodernism are empirical phenomena.

We discovered little overlap between postmodern value orientations and other value orientations. Humanist postmodernists are marginally more likely to share religious value orientations and instrumentalists to share secularized value orientations. This is explained by the compatibility of religion and humanism, and secular value orientations with instrumentalism. With a few national exceptions, humanist postmodernism is strongly related to postmaterialism as both groups share the goal of self-realization. Instrumental postmodernism, however, is only weakly related to postmaterialism.

Of more interest is the finding that humanist postmodernists have more confidence in societal institutions than postmaterialists. Instrumentalists would be expected to favour private solutions to social problems and humanists to prefer public solutions. The explanation for the difference in confidence is more likely to lie in the postmodernist's preference for doing things for themselves, which also extends to politics. Postmodernists believe in their own capacities.

When it comes to politics generally, humanist postmodernists are remarkably different both from other groups and from instrumental postmodernists. They discuss politics frequently, and they sign petitions and attend demonstrations to a much greater extent. Humanist postmodernists diverge more from non-postmodernists than instrumental postmodernists when we look at political practices such as party membership, discussing politics and persuading others, attending meetings, participating in demonstrations, or signing petitions.

We face, then, a conundrum: how can we explain that predictions about postmodernists turning their back on government and conventional politics are not borne out by our study? Some writers, especially Rosenau (1992: 138–44), have identified a section of postmodernists as 'sceptical'. But Rosenau also claims that 'affirmative postmodernists' exist, which we have identified among the humanist postmodernists with their confidence in societal institutions. But we cannot identify the 'dark side' of the postmodernists whose scepticism draws them into apathy and 'ironic detachment', or preoccupations with death or nihilism. In our view, Rosenau's sceptics are latent affirmatives and activists who see withdrawal as a temporary response to a situation, especially in a representative democracy, which is ritualistic and corrupt. Among postmodernists, scepticism about politics arises as much from confidence in the self's ability and judgement as from doubts about others and political systems. The response to doubt is likely to be a temporary suspension of belief and a redirection of effort and support into other, more effective, activities rather than wholesale abandonment of democratic practices.

Indeed, our evidence suggests that lack of action among postmodernists is an affirmation of their views, feelings, and priorities, and not a withdrawal from politics or a vote for chaos (Edelman 1988: 7–8; Ferry and Renault 1985: 100, 164). As Rosenau observes, sceptical postmodernists 'avoid judgement' when discussing conventional politics, and refuse labels such as right or left, good or bad, distorted or oppressive. They call less for disruption and deconstruction rather than overthrow and opposition. Like humanist postmodernists, sceptical postmodernists prefer to seek expression in some alternative innovative production—in the spirit and practice of carnival festivity—rather than negative political practice (1992: 53–61).

Finally, what can we say about the political impact of postmodernist value orientations? Obviously, in view of the limitations of the data, this has to be speculative. However, as the analysis largely conformed with our general argument, we take that line of thought further. We see the movement from pre-modern to modern and then to postmodern society as a developmental process in which trust, confidence, and loyalty change. It is not that postmodernists do not trust government and the state, but they do so in a more diffuse and less dependent way. Thus, as the needs and capacities of citizens change, both governments and citizens will have to experiment with a multiplicity of accommodations and settle for looser bonds (Bernstein 1991).

We might expect postmodernists to trust governments not from deference or in exchange for protection, but in response to the state's ability to provide the conditions for diversity to flourish. Confidence will depend less on the delivery of security and more on generating a sense of well-being, continuity, and existential freedom. Loyalty will probably only come into question if the state seeks to reinstitute paternalism. Also, in postmodernity, the state and other political bodies will have to trust citizens more, with the open circulation of information, and the devolution of power and responsibility. Governments of states and regions, and international bodies, will have to behave more as civil associations, holding the ring between exclusive groups rather than as inclusive and all embracing sovereign powers.

NOTES

1. In a keynote lecture to the British Sociological Association Conference in 1992 on Europe, Alain Touraine proposed that the 'new Europe is post-national and post-modern'.
2. According to Taylor, 'A society of self-fulfillers, whose affiliations are more and more seen as revocable, cannot sustain the strong identification with the political community which public freedom needs' (1989: 508).
3. Although we discuss four factors of importance for postmodern value orientations, we can deal only with education, age, and gender in the empirical analysis. There are no appropriate indicators for occupational sector in the data we use.
4. As relevant variables are not available in either European Value Study, nor in other

comparative surveys, we are not able to deal with the role of the mass media in relation to postmodern value orientations.

5. Portugal was not included in the 1981 survey.

6. The socio-demographic variables were recoded as follows. Age: 18–29 years = 1; 30–49 years = 2; 50 years and older = 3. Education: age when left school: younger than 16 = 1; 17–20 = 2; 21 years and older = 3. Gender: male = 1; female = 2.

7. One reason for the lack of significance is the measure applied, the product moment correlation. The actual pattern is curvilinear; the value orientation is somewhat more common among people with medium levels of education than among people with low or high levels of education. The relationship is not strong, however.

8. Following the evidence presented in Ch. 4, religious–secular value orientations are measured by frequency of church attendance: attends church at least once a week = 1; attends church less than once a week = 2.

12

Status Tensions

ETIENNE SCHWEISGUTH

The changes which have come about in the advanced societies of Western Europe during the post-war period have led scholars to hypothesize a declining role for social class in shaping political orientations. In analysing the development of postmaterialism, for example, Inglehart has suggested that West European societies are in the process of shifting from a 'class-based to a value-based political polarization' (1984: 26). Decline is not synonymous with disappearance, however, so people's social position may still be a tangible influence on their political attitudes. But a more serious flaw in the decline case is that it conceptualizes the relationship between social status and political attitudes only in terms of socio-economic conflicts. With the rise of a 'new' political agenda, however, the influence of social status on political attitudes needs to be examined in relation to issues such as ecology, women's rights, sexual morality, attitudes towards immigrants, and such like.

During the three decades since 1960, Western Europe has experienced a shift in value priorities—away from tradition and respect for authority and towards a concern for self-fulfilment, independence, and the quality of life (see Chapter 1). In Inglehart's (1977b) terms, this constitutes a shift from materialist to postmaterialist values. According to others (Flanagan 1987; Middendorp 1991), the process amounts to a shift from authoritarianism to libertarianism. But whatever the terms employed, the important point is that the shift in value orientations has gone hand-in-hand with major socio-structural change, particularly the expansion of the well-educated middle class. Such people are more likely to adhere to postmaterialist or libertarian value orientations than members of the working class. Moreover, Inglehart (1987) has shown that postmaterialist orientations are linked to pro-ecologist and left-wing political attitudes; others (Flanagan and Lee 1988; Grunberg and Schweisguth 1981; 1990; Middendorp 1978; 1991) have reached similar conclusions with regard to what they prefer to call libertarian orientations. It thus makes sense to represent members of the middle class as progressive or left-wing in political outlook—in terms of their adherence to libertarian or postmaterialist values. In short, outside the domain of socio-economic concerns, the middle class can be seen to be associated with a leftist or progressive outlook.

Against this background we can formulate our central hypothesis: that members of the middle class are conservative on socio-economic issues but progressive on cultural issues, while members of the working class are progressive on socio-economic issues but conservative on cultural issues. Within the framework of this hypothesis, we shall argue that the various components which, together, make up socio-economic status can have contradictory effects on an individual's political orientations—some fostering a left-wing orientation, others fostering a right-wing orientation. Thus, to analyse the effects of social status on political attitudes, it is necessary to examine value orientations along two dimensions, and to investigate how these two dimensions are related to social status. But, first, before embarking on the empirical analysis, we say rather more about the concepts of social class and social status and, secondly, clarify the relationship between the concepts postmaterialism and libertarianism.

Conceptual Questions

So far, we have used the terms social class and socio-economic status synonymously to refer to locations in the social structure. But the notions of class and status emerge from different theoretical traditions which have direct implications for our study. In order to make clear our own position, we review these traditions briefly.

In the classic Marxist tradition (Poulantzas 1979; Wright 1985), social class identifies the place of individuals in the production process with implications for their attitudes towards the social order. The concept of class engages the notion that the central political conflict in society is opposition, along a single vertical axis, between exploiters and the exploited, between dominant and dominated groups—or, simply, between those at the top and those at the bottom. There is little room for the idea that location at the upper end of the axis could generate progressive political attitudes; any show of libertarianism among those at the upper end is often interpreted as pseudo-progressivism to conceal genuine conservatism (Bourdieu 1979). Similarly, being at the bottom end is seldom associated with conservative attitudes, except as evidence of the cultural hegemony of the dominant class (Parkin 1972) or the 'manipulative socialization' (Mann 1978) practised via schools, the media, and the state. This approach is too narrow, and too rigid, to match the complexity of social structure, or the subtle connections between social position and attitudes, in advanced industrial societies.

Theorists in the Weberian tradition take a more differentiated and less conflictual view of social structure, portraying individuals as ranked on several vertical dimensions—wealth, prestige, power, education. The relatively homogenous groups arrived at by these rankings are referred to as classes or strata, which are evaluated in terms of a status hierarchy. Occupation is the principal criterion used in some schema (Goldthorpe and Hope 1974); others have combined income levels and education into a socio-economic index (Blau and Duncan 1967); yet others have combined all three criteria (Warner, Meeker, and Eells 1949). Some studies include class self-images as a reflection of class consciousness (Marshall, Rose, Newby, and Vogler 1988). The problems with this approach, for us, are that defining groups *a priori* on the basis of multiple criteria precludes analysis of the specific effects of the separate components constituting a status group. In other words, we are less interested in the social homogeneity implied in the notion of class or strata but, rather, in the way in which the specific elements which go to make up social status serve to differentiate between members of a status group.

Our approach, then, differs from most conventional approaches. We are interested in the components of structured social differences because we anticipate that they can give rise to 'inconsistencies' in value orientations—to economic conservatism along with social libertarianism among high status groups, to economic egalitarianism along with social conservatism among low status groups. Thus, rather than adopting the notions of class or strata, we use the concept of socio-economic status, and focus on the impact, on value orientations, of income, education, and occupation.

Our second task is to clarify, for our purposes, the concepts postmaterialism and libertarianism, which, despite originating in two different research traditions, are often brought together in values research. The notion of a libertarian–authoritarian dimension dates back to *The Authoritarian Personality* (Adorno *et al.* 1950), which showed that anti-semitism, ethnocentrism, moral conventionalism, and the like are correlated in such a way as to constitute a defining attribute in people's outlook. However, by underlining the correlations between authoritarianism and conservatism, Adorno and his colleagues, almost unwittingly, helped to bring to light the two-dimensional structure of attitudes. Lipset (1959; 1960), too, distinguished between a libertarian–authoritarian dimension and a left–right dimension, but argued that the former was secondary to the latter. According to Lipset, one can be an authoritarian of the left, the centre, or the right, but being an authoritarian or a libertarian is not a decisive factor in choosing between the parties of the left or the right.

Middendorp (1978; 1991) is one of the first to have uncovered a two-dimensional structure in these kinds of political attitudes. Factor analysing Dutch data about political and social goals, he found two distinct dimensions to voters' political choices. The first is socio-economic in nature, referring to the role of government in promoting greater economic equality in society—with economic liberalism standing opposed to state intervention. The second dimension consists of elements such as tolerance, internationalism, permissiveness, unconventional gender roles, and non-authoritarian parent–child relationships. Middendorp (1978) originally termed the dimension libertarianism—traditionalism, but in a second study (1991) adopted authoritarianism in place of traditionalism. Grunberg and Schweisguth (1981; 1990) distinguish between 'economic liberalism' and 'social libertarianism'; Knutsen and Lafferty (1985) distinguish between materialist–postmaterialist orientations and left–right materialist orientations (see also Chapter 6). Heath and Topf (1987: 59) go further, proposing that economic egalitarianism and values relating to the moral order represent the two most important ideological principles in contemporary society. Thus, although the terms vary, the common critical distinction is between concerns within and outside the socio-economic domain.

By contrasting a 'class-based' against a 'value-based' pattern of political polarization, Inglehart also implies that political attitudes are structured along two dimensions. But, as several scholars point out (Flanagan 1987), the opposition between materialism and postmaterialism can be interpreted in two different ways. In one sense, it represents opposed opinions on the same issue, such as supporting or opposing freedom of speech. In this case, materialist–postmaterialist orientations are very similar to libertarian–authoritarian orientations. In the other sense, materialist–postmaterialist opposition means having different priorities, such as regarding inflation as more important than freedom of speech. In this second sense, Inglehart's thesis is that the postmaterialist concerns of 'new politics' are gaining the edge over the materialist concerns of 'old politics'. Here again, then, the critical distinction is between the socio-economic domain and other domains. As the concepts of materialism–postmaterialism and authoritarianism–libertarianism are underpinned by quite different theoretical arguments and evidenced in different empirical measures, we use an indicator for libertarianism as well as an indicator of postmaterialism in our analysis.

Empirical Analysis

In the empirical analysis we concentrate on examining, separately, the effect of the three main components of social status—income, education, and occupation—on the three major value orientations studied in this volume: religious–secular value orientations, left–right materialism, and materialism–postmaterialism. We also introduce a scale of social libertarianism comprising items emphasizing individual freedom or tolerance toward sexual behaviour.[1]

Our data source is the 1990 European Values Study which contains all the indicators we need and covers twelve countries: Denmark, Iceland, Norway, Belgium, Germany, Ireland, the Netherlands, Britain, France, Italy, Spain, and Portugal. The three major value orientations—the dependent variables—are operationalized in the same way as in Chapters 4, 5, and 6 in this volume. The independent variables are education, income, and occupation. Income is measured as household income, and educational level by the respondent's school-leaving age. As to occupation, we first distinguished between inactive and working people and then settled on a four-fold classification: managers and professionals; white-collar employees; manual workers; the self-employed, but excluding professional groups. However, as it is difficult to locate the self-employed on the social ladder, occupation is not treated as a linear variable. Instead, the four occupational categories are treated as dummy variables with inactive individuals forming the constant. Moreover, as the independent impact of occupation on value orientations tends to be relatively weak, we only comment on these findings. Thus, most of our tables report findings for the effects of education and income.

According to Inglehart (1990), the younger one is, the more likely it is that one subscribes to secular, postmaterialist, and libertarian value orientations. Moreover, with rapid developments in education over the past forty years, the average level of education is higher among younger people than among their elders. Thus, for each of the value orientations, we began by performing a regression analysis by age, and then, using the residuals method, created a new variable eliminating the effect of age. The regression analysis focuses on this age-adjusted variable.

We report three different statistics in the tables. The first column reports the correlation (Pearson's r) between the independent variable and the value orientation, unadjusted for any other effects. The second column gives the correlation between the independent variable and the value orientation after adjusting for age; that is, using the new variable created by the residuals method. The third column reports the beta coefficient for the independent variable after controlling for the effects of all the other independent variables in a multivariate model.

We also use an additional method to analyse the effect of occupation. One difficulty when using the dummy variables method is that regression analysis indicates that the score of one group is higher or lower than the mean, but does not indicate whether the difference between the two groups is significant. Therefore, we completed the regression analysis using the group comparison method, calculating for each pair of groups whether the difference of means is statistically significant. Again to adjust for the effects of age, income, and education, we used the residual method to create for each value orientation a new variable eliminating the effect of these three variables. We retained our four occupational categories and added four categories of inactive individuals: the unemployed, students, housewives, and retired people.

Religious–Secular Value Orientations

An understanding of the relationship between social status and religious–secular value orientations can be derived from more general ideas about how religious values are linked to representations of the

TABLE 12.1. *Religious practice by education, income, and left–right materialism, 1990*

	Education			Income			Left–right materialism	
	r Uncontrolled	r Controlled by age	beta	r Uncontrolled	r Controlled by age	beta	r Uncontrolled	beta
DK	—	—	—	—	—	0.08	-0.13	0.08
IC	-0.10	—	—	-0.13	-0.11	-0.12	—	-0.12
NO	—	0.11	0.10	—	—	—	—	—
BE	-0.09	—	—	—	0.05	0.08	-0.06	0.08
GE	-0.16	-0.09	-0.11	-0.06	—	0.07	—	0.07
IR	-0.12	—	—	-0.12	—	—	-0.09	—
NL	-0.10	—	—	—	—	0.08	—	0.08
GB	0.06	0.15	0.13	0.07	0.07	—	-0.13	—
FR	-0.07	0.07	—	-0.07	0.09	0.11	—	0.11
IT	-0.07	—	—	—	—	—	—	—
SP	-0.12	—	—	-0.10	—	—	-0.11	—
PO	-0.25	-0.14	-0.08	-0.21	-0.14	—	—	—

Note: Only coefficients significant at the 0.05 level or higher are reported.

Source: European Values Survey (1990).

social order. In an analysis of the conservative religious ideology of practising Catholics, Michelat and Simon (1977*a*) show that these beliefs rest on the idea of a natural order, presumed to be fair, good, and harmonious, and of divine origin. It is wrong to perturb or try to change this natural order, to believe that reason and human will are capable of bringing about a better order of things. In practice, these ideas constitute a legitimation of the traditional order, prescribing the acceptance of existing social hierarchies, deference to established authorities and institutions, and respect for moral values passed down through tradition.

This general description enables us to pose two contradictory hypotheses. First, that tradition weighs more heavily on the uneducated working class, whereas social élites more easily escape the grips of tradition. Hence, we would expect secular orientations to be more widespread among the better educated and higher income groups. The second hypothesis relates to the place of socio-economic inequality in structuring value and representation systems. In this case, religious orientations are perceived to justify inequality, suggesting that members of the middle class are more religious than members of the working class.

Looking at the first column for education and for income in Table 12.1, we find that the correlations with religious practice are almost invariably negative.[2] These results would seem to support the hypothesis of religious scepticism among the social élite. Looking at the second columns, however, where we have controlled for the effects of age, almost all the negative correlations disappear and few significant correlations remain. Moreover, the beta coefficients for the multivariate model show that education has relatively little impact on religious activity. In eight of the twelve countries the impact of education, after controlling for age, income, and occupation, is not statistically significant. Indeed, the hypothesis of a link between high education and secular orientations is confirmed only in Germany and Portugal, and is directly contradicted by the results for Norway and Britain where high education goes along with religious orientations. (For a closer analysis of this point, see Chapter 4.) In all, then, our findings for the effects of education on religious–secular orientations are inconclusive.

The beta coefficients for income show that, again, after controlling for the effects of age, education, and occupation, a positive impact on religious practice is evident only in some countries: Denmark, Belgium, Germany, the Netherlands, and France. In these countries, low income is conducive to secular orientations while high income is conducive to religious orientations. In Iceland, the coefficient is significant but negative. Elsewhere, the beta values are not significant.

The positive correlation between income and religious practice suggests that, at least in these five countries, adherence to religious or secular orientations reflects social inequalities. This suggests that the social élite shares a vision of the world in which religious beliefs help to legitimate social inequality, whereas the less privileged have turned away from values which appear to justify inequality. If that is the case, then we would expect to find, in these countries, negative correlations between religious practice and left–right materialism—that not attending church tends to be associated with left-materialist orientations. This hypothesis is supported by the results shown in the final two columns of Table 12.1. With the exception of Belgium, the correlation between religious practice and left–right materialism is negative in the countries under observation.

Finally, occupational differences have little impact on religious–secular orientations (data not shown). Rather, the key feature here is the relatively high rate of religious practice among housewives. In most countries, housewives are more religious than any group among the employed population—which has the effect of rendering religious observance among most groups of the working population relatively low compared to the national average. The exceptional cases are Iceland, Norway, and Britain.

Left–Right Materialist Value Orientations

In Chapter 6, left–right materialism is presented as an indicator of two major, intertwined conflicts: between economic liberalism and state intervention in the sphere of production; over socio-economic inequality in the sphere of distribution. Historically, this kind of conflict was related to notions of social class in which classes were represented as struggling collective actors, whose members are possessed of class identity, class consciousness, a sense of class opposition, and an image of an alternative society (Mann 1978). This traditional conception held that the working class was struggling against the bourgeoisie in order to achieve a more egalitarian society, especially with the intent of abolishing the private ownership of the means of production.

Whatever the historical reality of class struggle, this account hardly fits present realities in Western Europe. Several empirical studies bear this out. The British working class of the 1960s was shown to engage in 'instrumental collectivism' aimed at raising their standard of living rather than any design to overturn the social structure (Goldthorpe *et al.* 1968). Again, Butler and Stokes (1969: 80–94) showed not only that a spontaneous link between political choice and class membership was rare among British middle-class voters in the 1960s, but also that even working-class supporters of the Labour Party who held a class conflict conception of party choice did not demand a radical change in the socio-economic system. Qualitative interviews conducted in 1983 among French workers revealed the persistence of a strong class identity but no real notion of social transformation beyond the idea that 'the rich ones should have to pay' (Schweisguth 1986; 1988), and recent British studies, also based on qualitative data, echo this kind of analysis (Pahl and Wallace 1988: 129). More recently, Marshall acknowledges that the disappearance of capitalism is not at stake in class conflict, and that social justice within capitalism is a valid alternative goal (Marshall 1988). Indeed, a group of scholars not known for their conservatism have only recently concluded that the central life interests of members of the working class are home centred (Rose 1988).

The findings in Chapter 6 suggest that attachment to egalitarian values remains strong in West European societies, but that support for a radical restructuring of ownership—or nationalization—has lost ground. It seems that majority opinion has rallied to the idea of combining a market economy with social interventions by the state. Thus the differences between left and right materialists no longer represent, except in extreme and rare cases, opposition between conflicting conceptions of economy and society, but relative preferences for tilting the balance towards more economic liberalism or more state intervention. Several factors might account for these preferences. Awareness of inequality alone can account for left-materialist orientations—and is less binding than the class conflict model. Thus, generally, we expect a negative correlation between left materialism and income. However, if the opposition is between upper and lower positions, rather than between major social groups, we can expect to observe a negative correlation with income within a single social group. As for education, we can anticipate two contradictory effects. In so far as income is tied to educational level, its effect should be cumulative with income. Alternatively, since education is generally

Value Orientations and their Antecedents

TABLE 12.2. *Left–right materialism by income and education, 1990*

	Education			Income		
	r Uncon-trolled	r Controlled by age	beta	r Uncon-trolled	r Controlled by age	beta
DK	—	—	—	−0.13	−0.15	−0.16
IC	—	—	—	−0.17	−0.17	−0.19
NO	−0.08	−0.07	—	−0.19	−0.20	−0.18
BE	−0.12	−0.13	−0.07	−0.19	−0.19	−0.14
GE	—	—	0.06	−0.19	−0.20	−0.18
IR	−0.11	−0.13	—	−0.15	−0.16	−0.10
NL	−0.09	−0.09	—	−0.23	−0.23	−0.22
GB	−0.06	−0.07	—	−0.24	−0.25	−0.24
FR	−0.13	−0.17	−0.12	−0.20	−0.21	0.17
IT	−0.08	−0.10	—	−0.14	−0.15	−0.10
SP	−0.08	−0.09	—	−0.17	−0.17	−0.14
PO	−0.17	−0.14	—	−0.22	−0.20	−0.16

Note: Only coefficients significant at the 0.05 level or higher are reported.

Source: European Values Survey (1990).

thought to foster humanist attitudes, these may translate into a certain sensitivity to egalitarian values. Occupational sector is also relevant, with the public sector embracing interventionist values while the private sector tends to foster the idea that state regulation inhibits economic activity. Unfortunately, while our data allow us to distinguish between salaried employees and the self-employed, the public–private variable is available only for the Scandinavian countries.

Our findings, presented in Table 12.2, reveal that in all twelve countries there is a negative correlation between income and left–right materialist orientations.[3] The effect is strikingly uniform, and controlling for age makes no noticeable difference to the correlations. Age is not a relevant variable here.[4] Moreover, in each case, the beta coefficient is scarcely different from the correlation coefficient. At most, we see a reduction of 0.04 or 0.05 in some countries (Belgium, Ireland, France, Italy, Spain, Portugal), demonstrating that the impact of income holds up after controlling for the effects of education and occupation. The impact of education, however, is almost negligible. All the significant bivariate correlations are negative but these only represent the link between income and education. In other words, once adjusted for the effects of income and occupation, the impact of education almost totally disappears—except for negative effects in Belgium and France, and a positive impact in Germany. Thus, in most countries, education as a component of social status does not translate into attitudinal differences about socio-economic equality.

The bivariate results for occupation show a high level of right materialism among the self-employed in all countries (data not shown). Similarly, right materialist orientations are always more widespread among members of the middle class than among members of the working class. But do these results merely reflect differences in income as between the middle class and the working class, or do they represent value orientations related to specific occupational characteristics irrespective of their income?

Our analysis of the impact of occupation after controlling for income levels confirms that the self-employed remain significantly more right materialist than the rest of the population in all the countries except Iceland, the Netherlands, and Portugal. Running one's own business, whatever the size, increases support for economic liberalism; feeling personally responsible for one's successes or failures does not foster adherence to egalitarian values. The other occupations rarely show such a clear association with either left or right materialism. Only in Iceland and Portugal are workers more left-materialist than the population as a whole; managers and professionals are significantly more right-materialist than the population as a whole only in Italy, Spain, and Ireland. However, the public–private sector variable is significant in the three Scandinavian countries. A more refined operationalization of occupational categories, taking into account, for instance, workplace autonomy or the exercise of authority, might have revealed certain effects specific to occupation. However, although increasing the number of relevant explanatory variables, it would not have allowed us to define some major social groups characterized by contrasting positions on socio-economic issues.

The second method used to assess the impact of occupation, the comparison of means, confirms that, with the exception of the self-employed, occupation has little effect on left–right materialist orientations (data not shown). The analysis of workers is particularly revealing: they are not significantly more left-materialist than managers and professionals except in Spain and Italy. Thus the difference in outlook between members of the middle class and the working class which emerges when no adjustment is made for income, appears to be due mainly to the effect of income alone. Nor are workers significantly different from housewives or retired people in any country. In other words, there is not a specific working-class outlook apart from what follows as an effect of differential income when it comes to left–right materialist orientations.

To complete the analysis in this section, we calculated the correlation coefficient between income and left–right materialism within each of the three major occupational categories. The results are presented in Table 12.3. Among the managers and professionals income differences translate as considerable differences in the level of left materialism: significant negative correlations are observed in eight countries. This suggests that the group forms a pyramid, the tip of which constitutes a small, right-wing élite, while the much larger numbers at the base are more inclined to left materialism. Among white-collar and manual workers, however, the correlations are weak and very rarely significant; among lower status groups, apparently, income differences have little effect on economic values.

Thus, an overly atomistic account of the effect of income would be misleading. It appears that income, especially, serves as a criterion for making inter-group—rather than inter-personal—comparisons. In other

TABLE 12.3. *Left–right materialism by income among occupational groups, 1990*

	Managers and professionals	White-collar employees	Workers
DK	−0.10	−0.08	−0.19**
IC	−0.18*	−0.19	−0.13
NO	−0.24**	—	—
BE	−0.21**	−0.07	−0.08
GE	−0.15*	−0.14**	−0.07
IR	−0.17	—	—
NL	−0.21**	−0.22	−0.13
GB	−0.18**	−0.09	−0.12*
FR	−0.27**	—	—
IT	−0.20	—	—
SP	−0.12	—	−0.08
PO	−0.30*	−0.19**	−0.06

*$p < 0.05$ **$p < 0.01$

Note: Entries are correlation coefficients (Pearson's r) between income and left materialism.

Source: European Values Survey (1990).

words, people seem to assess their social position in terms of the income of people in their social group rather than by strict comparisons between individual incomes. Accordingly, they accept social inequalities more or less readily. The bulk of these results, then, are compatible with our view that an 'inequality consciousness' is better able to account for political value orientations than 'class consciousness' in the traditional sense.

Libertarian Value Orientations

Flanagan sums up the overlap between libertarian and postmaterialist value orientations in the overarching concept of 'self-actualization' (Flanagan and Lee 1988: 3–4). Empirical evidence accumulated in recent years suggests that the three major elements of self-actualization identified by Flanagan—autonomy, openness, and self-betterment—do, indeed, tend to cluster together (Hildebrandt and Dalton 1978; Calista 1984; Grunberg and Schweisguth 1983; Inglehart 1977*b*; 1990; Lafferty and Knutsen 1984; Middendorp 1978; 1991). But there is less agreement about the nature of the relationship between social status and these new value orientations.

One type of explanation engages various interpretations of class effects. A common theme is the authoritarianism of the middle class. Adorno *et al.* (1950) emphasized the conformism of the middle class, while for Kristol (1972), the apparent libertarianism of the middle class is merely a cloak for resentments against hierarchical authority. The classic 'resource mobilization' approach (McCarthy and Zald 1977) similarly emphasizes that the libertarian value orientations of the middle class mask their interests in attaining privileged social positions. More radically, for Bourdieu it is not even admissible that the middle class can hold libertarian views: the 'new ethic' is a set of hedonistic attitudes spread by the new business bourgeoisie in order to create needs for new products which are part of the 'new mode of domination' (Bourdieu 1979: 172). But, in parallel, there are accounts of working-class authoritarianism. Lipset's (1959) explanation is rooted in the psychological concept of ego insecurity, attributable to the poor education, economic insecurity, and authoritarian family patterns which characterize working-class life. Middendorp offers a similar explanation for the observed relationship between authoritarianism and low levels of income and education—such circumstances engender insecurity and uncertainty, leading people to 'abide by the rules of the existing social system, and to adhere to traditional norms and habits' (Middendorp 1978: 263).

A second type of analysis underlines the role of education. Lipsitz (1965) demonstrated that, after adjusting for education, members of the working class are not significantly more authoritarian than members of the middle class—except for attitudes towards punishment. Similarly, Dekker and Ester (1987) observed a strong negative correlation between educational level and authoritarianism in Dutch data for the period 1975–85; a finding endorsed by Middendorp (1991). Grunberg and Schweisguth (1990) find similar results in a 1988 French survey. But what is the specific contribution of education to libertarian values? According to Gabennesch (1972), the 'breadth of perspective' provided by education broadens, multiplies, and diversifies the individual's socio-cultural perspectives—prompting an awareness of alternative definitions, assessments, and viewpoints. Again, education helps to avoid the reification of social phenomena (Berger and Luckmann 1967), and fosters the ability to take a complex view of social and political structures (Lipset 1964). The absence of the larger perspective underpins the less complex and less tolerant orientations of the working class.

So, what are our findings for social libertarianism? Looking at the entries in the first column for education and for income in Table 12.4, we find relatively high correlations with social libertarianism in all countries, especially for education. However, in the second column, after adjusting for age, the coefficients diminish noticeably, confirming that, generally, younger people are more libertarian. In this sense, in being largely a generational phenomenon, the shift towards libertarianism looks very much like the shift to postmaterialist orientations. However, when analysed in a multivariate model, the effects of education and income are very different. As the beta coefficients reveal, the effect of education holds true in all but three countries (Spain, Ireland, and Norway), whereas the impact of income on social libertarianism holds true in only four of the twelve countries.

Evidently, then, education exerts an independent influence on libertarianism regardless of any links with age, income, or occupation. This result is compatible with the 'breadth of perspective' interpretation of education. The impact of income is less straightforward. According to accounts of working-class authoritarianism, as suggested by Lipset and Middendorp, the four countries in which the impact of income holds up

TABLE 12.4. *Social libertarianism by education and income, 1990*

	Education			Income		
	r Uncon-trolled	r Controlled by age	beta	r Uncon-trolled	r Controlled by age	beta
DK	0.26	0.20	0.16	0.18	0.10	—
IC	0.32	0.25	0.23	0.13	0.10	—
NO	0.15	0.06	—	0.13	0.07	—
BE	0.21	0.12	0.09	0.15	0.09	—
GE	0.27	0.19	0.19	0.15	0.06	—
IR	0.26	0.15	—	0.37	0.24	0.19
NL	0.30	0.19	0.15	0.13	0.12	—
GB	0.22	0.13	0.08	0.25	0.12	0.09
FR	0.26	0.15	0.10	0.14	0.13	—
IT	0.18	0.13	0.07	0.23	0.18	0.14
SP	0.20	0.05	—	0.21	0.10	0.07
PO	0.30	0.17	0.11	0.23	0.14	—

Note: Only coefficients significant at the 0.05 level or higher are reported.

Source: European Values Survey (1990).

in the multivariate model—Ireland, Britain, Italy, Spain—should be countries where low income and low education interact. Ordering the twelve countries by the average age at which respondents finished their schooling, Spain, Ireland, Britain, and Italy do, indeed, emerge (along with Portugal) as the countries with the lowest educational levels. However, the correlation between income and social libertarianism at comparable educational levels in these four countries, reported in Table 12.5, is statistically significant for both low and high levels of education (except high level in Britain)—and not as a conjunction of low income and low education.

We can suggest an alternative explanation. To the extent that educational levels are relatively low in these countries, it might be that, for many people, high social status has been achieved regardless of educational level. We might then assume that this social ascent has been accompanied by an increase in cognitive skills through exposure to information networks and widened social relations. The culture acquired in this way would have the same 'breadth of perspective' function as formal education. In these circumstances, the effect of income substitutes, to some extent, for the effect of education.

TABLE 12.5. *Social libertarianism by income and educational level in four countries, 1990*

	Mean school-leaving age	Educational Level		
		Low	Middle	High
GB	16.44	0.18**	0.13**	0.04
IT	—	0.19**	0.17**	0.17**
SP	16.87	0.19**	0.18**	0.20**
IR	16.52	0.26**	0.30**	0.35**
Average for EC-12 countries	17.55			

** $p < 0.01$

Notes: Entries are means and correlation coefficients (Pearson's r). The mean school-leaving age for Italy is missing, but all the available data show a low school-leaving age for Italy.

Source: European Values Survey (1990).

Materialist–Postmaterialist Value Orientations

Inglehart's theory of postmaterialism focuses principally on the effects of education and income, but with some additional comments about occupation. Although education may nurture cognitive and communicative capacities, its explanatory power lies in signifying 'formative security' in pre-adult years. That is, in the context of a generational theory, postmaterialist value orientations are more likely among people brought up in socially advantaged families. As to income, Inglehart (1990: 175) finds some tendency for postmaterialists to have lower household incomes than materialists which he interprets as indicating that, in their career, postmaterialists seek to maximize prestige, interesting experiences, or the quality of life in general, rather than sheer income. They are voluntarily economic under-achievers. Finally, although Inglehart refrains from specifying any direct effects of occupation on postmaterialism, he anticipates a relatively high incidence of postmaterialism among members of the 'new middle class' of young professionals (1990: 332).

As in the case of libertarianism, we find major differences between the effect of income and the effect of education on postmaterialism.[5] But the surprising finding from this analysis was a dichotomy between countries with a Catholic tradition (Belgium, France, Italy, Spain,

Portugal, and Ireland) and, on the other hand, Protestant or religiously mixed countries (Denmark, Iceland, Norway, Germany, the Netherlands, and Britain). In part, the difference concerns the effect of educational levels, but in the main it concerns, quite astonishingly so, the effect of income.

In Table 12.6, before introducing the age adjustment, the correlation between postmaterialism and education is positive and significant in all countries. But after adjusting for age, the correlations in the second column of Table 12.6 decline markedly in Ireland, France, Spain, and Portugal. In these countries, all with strong Catholic traditions, a large portion of the bivariate effect is thus due to the link between young age and high education. On the other hand, the correlation scarcely declines at all in Denmark, Iceland, Norway, Germany, and the Netherlands— which are either Protestant or religiously mixed countries. Moreover, controlling for the effects of income and occupation only slightly reduces the correlation between postmaterialism and education. The beta coefficients remain positive and significant in all countries except Ireland and Italy. From this standpoint, then, postmaterialism seems

TABLE 12.6. *Postmaterialism by income and education, 1990*

	Education			Income		
	r Uncontrolled	*r* Controlled by age	beta	*r* Uncontrolled	*r* Controlled by age	beta
DK	0.23	0.21	0.17	—	—	—
IC	0.29	0.26	0.25	—	—	−0.16
NO	0.22	0.18	0.16	—	—	−0.10
BE	0.15	0.11	0.09	0.09	0.05	—
GE	0.27	0.21	0.22	—	—	−0.09
IR	0.18	0.07	—	0.16	0.07	—
NL	0.29	0.23	0.20	—	—	−0.13
GB	0.15	0.09	0.14	—	−0.07	−0.13
FR	0.22	0.14	0.09	0.10	0.10	—
IT	0.13	0.08	—	0.07	—	—
SP	0.16	0.06	0.06	0.10	—	—
PO	0.28	0.16	0.13	0.17	0.10	—

Note: Only coefficients significant at the 0.05 level or higher are reported.

Source: European Values Survey (1990).

TABLE 12.7. *Comparison of Catholic and non-Catholic countries, 1990*

	Materialism–postmaterialism by education	Libertarianism by education	Materialism–postmaterialism by income	Materialism–postmaterialism by left–right materialism
	B	*B*	*B*	*r*
DK	0.08	0.10	—	0.34
IC	0.10	0.11	−0.12	0.25
NO	0.07	—	−0.07	0.24
GE	0.14	0.13	−0.09	0.28
NL	0.10	0.09	−0.13	0.22
GB	0.10	0.07	−0.13	0.29
BE	0.05	0.06	—	0.13
FR	0.05	0.06	—	0.14
IT	—	0.05	—	0.17
SP	0.02	0.05	—	0.16
PO	0.05	0.06	—	0.08
IR	—	—	—	0.14

Notes: Only coefficients significant at the 0.05 level or higher are reported. *B* is the unstandardized regression coefficient.

Source: European Values Survey (1990).

very similar to libertarianism: once the age effect is eliminated, education emerges as the dominant influence.

To highlight the difference between Catholic and non-Catholic countries, in Table 12.7 we first list the six Protestant or mixed countries, then the six Catholic countries. And instead of the beta coefficient, we used the unstandardized *B* coefficient, which eliminates the effect of possible differences in variance between countries and is more appropriate to cross-national comparison. The results, shown in the first two columns of the table, reveal that the impact of education is always greater in non-Catholic countries than in Catholic countries, on both postmaterialist orientations and libertarian orientations (except in Norway). This suggests a real cultural difference between these countries—perhaps in the emphasis on individual freedom which is characteristic of Protestantism and which has an affinity with libertarian values.

Analysis of the effect of income reveals a totally different pattern. Returning to Table 12.6, before adjusting for age, a rather weak positive relation between postmaterialism and income is observed but only in

Catholic countries. The correlations diminish considerably when the age adjustment is introduced, and it disappears completely in the multivariate model. Thus the positive correlations appear to represent simply the combined effects of age and educational level in these Catholic countries. However, the multivariate model—controlling for the effects of the other independent variables—reveals negative beta coefficients for the Protestant or religiously mixed countries. Only Denmark is an exception, but the coefficient there is nearly significant, and a highly significant coefficient appears among the post-war generation. In fact, in all these non-Catholic countries, the negative relation between income and postmaterialism is particularly strong in the post-war generation.

Here, then, we have a case in point where postmaterialism is quite different from libertarianism. In most countries, income has a positive but weak and insignificant impact on libertarian orientations. It can be interpreted as a cultural indicator, the effects of which are added to the effects of educational level—producing significant coefficients in countries where school enrolment rates are lowest. In the case of postmaterialism, these two aspects of social status—income and education—have effects in the opposite direction: in Protestant or religiously mixed countries, education has a strong positive impact whereas income has a negative impact. Moreover, the pattern holds up after removing students from the sample.

This last result is worth a pause. In one sense, the result can be read as confirming, as Inglehart claims, that postmaterialists are economic under-achievers, genuinely indifferent to acquiring material goods. It is nevertheless puzzling that this relationship is evident only in non-Catholic countries. One possibility is that this reflects yet again the ambiguities associated with the materialist–postmaterialist measure (see Chapter 5). That is, the negative relationship observed between income and postmaterialism, shown in the third column of Table 12.7, suggests that the measure may serve, to some degree, as an indicator of egalitarianism. Some items in the extended index certainly have an egalitarian connotation: 'giving people more say in the decisions of the government', 'giving people more say in how things are decided at work and in their community', and 'move towards a friendlier, less impersonal society'. To test this possibility, we calculated the correlation between materialism–postmaterialism and left–right materialism in each country. The results, shown in fourth column of Table 12.7, both support our interpretation and complicate it. On the one hand, the correlation between postmaterialism and left–right materialism proves to be positive in all countries. But, on the other hand, there remains a clear distinction between Catholic and non-Catholic countries: in the former the correlation is always considerably lower than 0.20, whereas in the latter it is always considerably higher than 0.20.[6]

Finally, is postmaterialism a particular feature of certain occupational groups? The bivariate results invariably reveal that postmaterialism is most widespread among managers and professionals. Regression analysis confirms that, in many countries, this is not simply a consequence of their high educational level, but also consitutes a specific effect of their social location. Such people are significantly more postmaterialist than the average population in Denmark, Iceland, Norway, Belgium, the Netherlands, France, and Italy. Similarly, social libertarianism is much more widespread among this group in Denmark, Ireland, Belgium, the Netherlands, France, Italy, and Spain. These results are consistent with findings from other studies showing that libertarian orientations are characteristic of members of the middle class, especially civil servants and teachers (Dekker and Ester 1987; Schweisguth 1983).

Conclusion

In order to understand the relationship between social location and value orientation in contemporary Western Europe, we need to distinguish between orientations relating to the socio-economic domain and orientations relating to other domains—notably more general social and cultural concerns. The changed character of this relationship is due, in part, to the social changes which have taken place during the post-war period and, again in part, due to the emergence of new issues on the political agenda.

The data examined in this chapter indicate that the three value orientations at the heart of this volume are subject to considerable social tension. Whereas high income, high educational level, and high occupational status tend to go together, they have contradictory effects on value orientations: high income tends to foster non-egalitarian socio-economic orientations, while high education and high occupational status tend to foster libertarian orientations. Thus we conclude that progressive and conservative attitudes are arrayed along two, rather than one, dimension—reflecting the intrinsically contradictory effects of social status on political attitudes in contemporary West European societies.

The fact that there is not a single progressive–conservative dimension but at least two independent dimensions is not without consequence for understanding people's beliefs in government. If a single dimension could be assumed, the major lines of political conflict would be clear and predictable, giving voters and parties, and governments and oppositions, a certain well-defined common purpose. That the 'progressive–conservative' label can be applied to two dimensions makes for a considerable loss of predictability in these relationships. We can anticipate that some parts of the electorate have a 'coherent' stance on both dimensions: some being both left materialist and libertarian may thus be called 'progressive'; some being right materialist and authoritarian may be regarded as 'conservative'. But, by our account, there are bound to be fractions of national electorates whose value orientations lack such clarity. If their contradictory positions on the two major dimensions prevent them defining themselves as either progressive or conservative, they may have greater difficulty identifying with a party. This alone makes it more difficult for parties to build electoral coalitions, and more difficult for governments to create the critical mass of support for legislative innovation.

NOTES

1. The social libertarian scale was extracted from factor analysis of a large set of items, ranging from 'avoiding a fare on public transport' to 'killing in self-defence', in which respondents were asked to respond on a scale runinng from 1 (never justified) to 10 (always justified). Seven items were finally selected, relating to extramarital affairs, homosexuality, prostitution, abortion, divorce, suicide, and euthanasia. All had loadings of 0.30 or higher on the first factor which had an eigenvalue of 4.53 or higher (more than 7.00 in some countries). A high score on the scale indicates libertarianism.

2. The indicator is frequency of church attendance. The four categories are: 1 = never; 2 = once a year or less; 3 = monthly and on holy days; 4 = once a week or more.

3. We have used the same indicator for left–right materialism as in Ch. 6. A high score indicates left materialism, a low score, right materialism.

4. The influence of income remained constant when we performed a regression analysis for the three age groups 18–44 years, 45–64 years, and over 65. The beta coefficient remained negative and nearly always significant, except in some cases among the over 65 group, probably owing to the small number of cases.

5. We used the 12-item materialism–postmaterialism battery, operationalized as described in Ch. 17. A high score indicates a postmaterialist orientation.

6. A regression analysis, comparing the unstandardized *B* coefficient, is a more rigorous test of the relationship between left–right materialism and materialism–postmaterialism. In this way, too, the correlation between the two variables is always higher in Protestant than in Catholic countries.

PART III

The Impact of Values

13

Political Efficacy and Trust

OSCAR W. GABRIEL

According to several observers, a wave of political discontent seems to
be spreading over the Western world. Apparently disappointed by the
conduct of public affairs, increasing numbers of people cast ballots in
favour of protest parties, and, more generally, refrain from participation
through conventional channels. At the same time, various types of
protest behaviour serve as conduits for articulating political demands.
While conventional political activity seems to be declining, political
disengagement and disruptive activities have apparently become more
widespread. Changes in the prevailing modes of political behaviour are
due, among other things, to increasing political alienation among
Western publics, manifested in critical attitudes towards politics
among large segments of the public.

A rich body of literature has dealt with political alienation in
advanced industrial societies, giving special attention to feelings of
political inefficacy (powerlessness) and distrust (normlessness). The
prominence of these features in research on political alienation is
largely due to their impact on people's political behaviour. While
political inefficacy or incompetence will eventually lead to political
inactivity, the behavioural implications of political self-consciousness
largely depend on the way this interacts with political distrust. According to some authors, feelings of political efficacy joined with political
distrust are powerful predictors of disruptive activities. According to
others, when political efficacy goes along with political trust, it is an
important antecedent of reformist activity. In political alienation theory,
changing patterns of political behaviour may be attributed to shifts in

the way political (dis)trust and (in)efficacy interact (Finifter 1970; Mason, House, and Martin 1980; Wright 1976; 1981).

Although explanations of political alienation vary, a change in value orientation is thought to be influential in the shifting relationship between people and the political system. The role of value orientations in a country's politics deserves attention because these orientations are core elements in a more encompassing belief system, integrating and steering a larger set of specific attitudes. Consequently, shifting value orientations probably induce related changes in more 'peripheral' attitudes such as political trust and efficacy (Maag 1990).

In public opinion research, only meagre attention has been given to the impact of value orientations on trust and efficacy. Whereas the implications of materialist and postmaterialist orientations have been examined extensively (cf. Gabriel 1986; Inglehart 1977*b*; 1990; Klages 1984; Klages and Herbert 1983), the impact of religiosity, secular values, egalitarianism, and libertarianism has been almost completely ignored. Hence, in this chapter we investigate some neglected problems in empirical research on the impact of value orientations. After clarifying the concepts of trust and efficacy, some hypotheses are proposed and tested for a set of West European democracies.

Political Efficacy and Political Trust

Since first introduced in the 1952 and 1958 American National Election Study, the concepts of trust and efficacy have frequently been investigated in international research. Most studies have interpreted the concepts as referring to relatively stable, deep-seated, fundamental attitudes towards politics, and as key properties of a democratic political culture (cf. Abramson 1983: 135ff., 193ff.). However, despite their prominence in public opinion research and in democratic theory, the conceptual status of political trust and efficacy remains unclear. There is confusion about the definition and the operationalization of the concepts, the adequacy of the measurement instruments, the dimensionality of the attitudes under observation, and their relationship to other elements of an individual's belief system. Moreover, there is uncertainty about the consequences of varying levels of trust and efficacy for the performance and stability of the political system. According to Craig (1979: 229), 'we are increasingly well informed about what efficacy and trust are not, yet we remain unable to agree what they are'.

The concept of political efficacy was introduced into empirical research by Campbell, Gurin, and Miller (1954: 187) with only a short definition:

Sense of political efficacy may be defined as the feeling that individual political action does have, or can have, an impact upon the political process, i.e. that it is worth while to perform one's civic duties. It is the feeling that political and social change is possible, and that the individual citizen can play a part in bringing about this change.

A core element in this definition is the individual's self-image as an active and influential participant in politics. Politically efficacious citizens are seen as comprehending, controlling, and mastering their political environments. Hence, the concept of political efficacy relates to the input component of the political system, regarding citizens as able and willing to participate. Almond and Verba's concept (1963: 136 ff.) of subjective political competence similarly taps the citizens' self-image as active participants in political processes.

In criticizing these interpretations for confounding two aspects of citizens' attitudes towards politics, Lane (1959: 149) proposed distinguishing between *internal* efficacy (political competence) and *external* efficacy (political responsiveness). This distinction parallels Almond and Verba's (1963: 16) distinction between people's perception and evaluation of their own role in politics and the way they look at their political environment. This entails separating, analytically, the self-image of citizens as effective actors from their perception of the political system and the incumbent administration as responsive to the public's demands. As Prewitt (1968: 225) puts it:

The efficacious person views his political self with respect. He feels powerful, competent and important. He holds a corollary set of expectations with respect to political officials; they are concerned about his vote and heed his demands. The self evaluations and orientations toward political authorities are related to a generalized set of attitudes about the political system—for example, that elections matter or that leadership circles can be influenced and even penetrated.

According to this conceptualization, feelings of internal political efficacy entail an individual's self-image as a competent political actor, broadly similar to Almond and Verba's (1963: 136 ff.) notion of civic or political competence. In addition, external efficacy implies perceiving and evaluating the political system and the government as open and responsive to the average citizen's demands (cf. Abramson 1983: 141 ff.).

How to measure political efficacy has been vigorously debated. The instruments developed by Campbell *et al.* (1954) and Almond and Verba (1963) were not validated empirically, but rested on plausibility. However, several attempts to validate the concept of efficacy have ended in inconclusive results. Asher (1974) found efficacy items rather unreliable in general, but other researchers presented evidence supporting the distinction between internal and external efficacy. However, the relationship between the scale items and the efficacy scale varied between different analyses (see Acock and Clarke 1990; Acock, Clark, and Stewart 1985; Balch 1974).[1] In part, this may have resulted from using different data sets and applying different validation strategies. Nevertheless, the research situation, particularly with regard to the measurement instruments, turns out to be confusing.

One of the tests of the validity and reliability of the standard efficacy items carried out by Acock, Clark, and Stewart (1985), using the 1973–6 Political Action data, demonstrated that decomposing political efficacy into internal and external efficacy makes sense analytically and empirically. Moreover, this conclusion was valid for all West European democracies except Italy. Accordingly, we apply Acock's concept of political efficacy when analysing data from the Political Action studies.

The analyses presented in this chapter focus on internal efficacy[2] and civic competence.[3] We disregard the concept of external efficacy because neither the concept nor its measurement can be readily disentangled from internal efficacy and political trust: the stimulus objects and the evaluative considerations underlying trust and external efficacy are very similar. Theoretically, this involves no substantial loss of information about people's beliefs in government. Thus, when we use the term political efficacy, it is to be understood as internal efficacy.

Many discussions of political trust start out from Easton's (1975; 1979: 153 ff.) concept of political support. Although political support may be behavioural as well as attitudinal, we are interested only in the latter—defined by Easton (1975: 436) and, more precisely, by Muller (1970: 1151), as a set of positive attitudes to (political) objects. Easton further distinguishes between specific and diffuse support, referring to the *objects* and the *content* of support respectively. Moreover, this theoretical distinction is supported by empirical analyses (Fuchs

1989; Gabriel 1986: 232 ff.; 1989). Political trust, then, can be understood as a form of diffuse support with regard to both the political regime and the incumbent political authorities. In Easton's words (1975: 447):

the presence of trust would mean that members would feel that their own interests would be attended to even if the authorities were exposed to little supervision or scrutiny. For the regime, such trust would reveal itself as symbolic satisfaction with the processes by which the country is run . . . It may be not the results of authoritative actions that count so much as the processes which lead to such results.

Positive feelings of this type are largely independent of the advantages people obtain from particular policy outputs. Rather, they stem from a favourable perception of the conduct of political affairs in general. Owing to these general properties of political institutions and processes, trusting people expect the political system to produce preferred outcomes 'even if left untended' (Gamson 1968: 54). Moreover, political trust refers to the qualities—not the performance—of the people occupying authoritative positions at a certain time (Easton 1975: 449). Political leaders are trusted because they are perceived as open minded, fair, responsive, and acting in the best interests of the political community. In contrast, cynics think of political leaders as élitist, corrupt, unresponsive, and primarily intent on pursuing their own interests or benefiting a narrow segment of the public. In the long run, distrust of political leaders may become generalized and eventually attributed to political institutions and processes (see Volume i, Chapters 9 and 11). In short, political trust springs from the perceived properties of political institutions or processes and the personal attributes of powerholders.

In the first survey featuring trust measures—the 1958 American election study—five items were designed to examine how much Americans trust their government (Abramson 1983: 193 ff.). Although the validity of these standard items has been a matter of debate (Abramson and Finifter 1981; Citrin 1974; Craig, Niemi, and Silver 1990; Miller 1974), we have largely to rely on them.[4]

Research Strategy and Hypotheses

In the explanatory model tested in this chapter, political efficacy, civic competence, and trust in government are the dependent variables. As only a few data sets have indicators for these attitudes, we also use civicness—an attitude similar to both (personal) efficacy and trust—as a surrogate variable.[5] Materialism–postmaterialism[6] and religious–secular orientations[7] are the central explanatory variables in all the analyses. Where possible, libertarianism will also be added as an explanatory factor.[8] Each of these variables can be considered a relevant predictor of beliefs in government, although their relationship to efficacy, trust, and civicness is not the same. However, in contrast to other chapters in this volume, left–right materialism is not included in our model. Appropriate indicators of left–right materialism are not available in the surveys we use, nor are there convincing reasons to expect people who favour 'big government' and an extended welfare system to be more trusting or feel politically more efficacious than those favouring a restricted role for government.

In the first step of the analyses, we assess the appropriateness of a value orientations model of beliefs in government. Using multiple regression analyses, we investigate how much value orientations contribute to explaining political efficacy, civic competence, trust in government, and civicness. However, since the value orientations may be interrelated and, additionally, influenced by background variables, it may be misleading to focus exclusively on the impact of values. Thus, to avoid overestimating the impact of values, the multivariate analyses are controlled for the influence of relevant background variables: education, age, gender, social status, political involvement, and party preference.[9] Although our model contains both background variables and value orientations, we focus on interpreting the coefficients for the value orientations; the background variables are only of concern as control variables.

We noted earlier that research, to date, has largely neglected the impact of value orientations on trust, efficacy, and related attitudes. Therefore, hypotheses about the relationships between the relevant variables have to be inferred from the general properties attributed to value orientations or from specific aspects of an individual's value orientations. Our first hypothesis is derived from conceptualizing value orientations as more or less fundamental and central elements of an individual's belief system. Value orientations can then be supposed to have a genuine impact on beliefs in government—that is, an independent effect after the relevant political and social background variables are held constant.

Our second hypothesis is that the impact of value orientations is stronger and more consistent for political efficacy than for political trust. This is due to the varying role of situational factors: political efficacy is a general and relatively stable personality trait, whereas feelings of political trust are influenced by the actual performance of the incumbent government which may vary over time. Hence, we do not expect value orientations to contribute uniformly to explaining variance in beliefs in government. Rather, the explanatory power of the value orientations probably differs on account of their different components.

Thirdly, we anticipate that postmaterialism and libertarianism have a particularly strong impact on feelings of political efficacy. Postmaterialism and libertarianism share a participatory component which is part of people's self-evaluation as competent political actors. Although participation and self-expression are not elements in feelings of trust in government, deference to authority is a common component in religious value orientations, authoritarianism, and trust in government. Thus, fourthly, we anticipate that secular orientations and authoritarianism are strongly related to political trust.

However, before examining the impact of particular value orientations on beliefs in government, we have to consider the general suitability of a value-based explanatory model. So, first, we investigate whether a model containing only value orientations contributes significantly to explaining variance in trust and efficacy, and whether, and how much, a value model can be improved by including background variables. Only after value orientations have been shown to influence, in general, the way people relate to politics does it make sense to examine the impact of particular value orientations on beliefs in government.[10] The data we use are drawn from five comparative surveys: Civic Culture, conducted in 1959–60 (Germany, Italy, and Britain); the Political Action studies carried out in 1973–6 (Austria, Switzerland, Finland, Germany, Italy, the Netherlands, and Britain) and 1979–80 (Germany and the Netherlands); and, finally, Eurobarometer, Nos. 24 (1985), 26 (1986), and 30 (1988) covering all EC member countries.

Civic Competence and Political Efficacy

Although value orientations contribute to reducing variance in civic competence in Britain, Germany, and Italy, the explanatory power of the initial model is by no means impressive and is substantially improved by including social and political background variables.

Only in Italy could more than 5 per cent of the variance in civic competence be attributed to value orientations, but the proportion of variance explained increased to about 20 per cent in Germany and Italy when age, education, political involvement, and the like were included in the model. Much the same picture emerges from the two Political Action studies: as we show in Table 13.1, the proportion of variance attributable to value orientations alone ranges from 2 per cent (Finland, 1973–6) to 8 per cent (Netherlands, 1979–80), but increases to range between 11 per cent (Finland) and 24 per cent (Switzerland) in the 1973–6 data, when the more encompassing model is applied. Clearly, then, value orientations play some role in explaining citizen competence, but including additional factors yields a better account of the forces leading people to perceive themselves as effective political actors.

Largely the same applies to political efficacy, shown in Table 13.2. The impact of the total set of value orientations on political self-consciousness is statistically significant in all seven countries for which data are available. However, the proportion of the variance in political efficacy attributable to value orientations differs considerably from one country to another. The model fits best in Germany and Austria, where up to 9 per cent of the variance in internal efficacy is attributable to value orientations. However, in Finland, Switzerland, and Britain, although value orientations are statistically significant predictors, they are rather poor determinants of efficacy. Including social and political background variables leads to a substantial improvement in the explanatory power of the model in all countries except Italy. By far the largest part of the additional variance explained by the model can be attributed to education and political involvement.

Although a few German and Dutch surveys carried out in the 1980s contain political efficacy items, the measurement instruments were not always the same as in the Political Action studies, which raises problems about comparisons over time. None the less, the conclusion to be drawn from the national surveys is that the explanatory power of a value model of political efficacy varies over time. Generally, value orientations have an impact on political efficacy, but this is not always the case (data not shown here).

To summarize, although the models developed to explain internal efficacy are often useful, a pure value model is less adequate than a more encompassing model for explaining political efficacy and civic competence. Including variables related to social status and socialization

TABLE 13.1. *Impact of value orientations on civic competence in seven countries, 1959–60 to 1979–80*

Value orientations	FI	AU	GE	NL	SW	GB	IT
1959–60							
Materialism–non-materialism			0.12* 0.04			0.13* 0.07	0.23* 0.15*
Religious–secular			−0.10* −0.03			−0.03 −0.06	0.07 −0.01
Libertarianism–authoritarianism			0.06 0.04			−0.04 −0.06	0.11* 0.09*
R^2							
Values model			0.024*			0.017*	0.062*
Full model			0.190*			0.121*	0.225*
N			955			963	995
1973–6							
Materialism–postmaterialism	0.07* 0.05	0.17* 0.08*	0.16* 0.05*	0.12* 0.05	0.09* 0.01	0.03 0.02	
Religious–secular	0.02 0.00	−0.02 −0.07*	0.01 −0.05*	0.07* 0.05	0.06 −0.01	−0.13* −0.10*	
Libertarianism–authoritarianism	0.12* 0.05	0.17* 0.11*	0.11* 0.06*	0.11* 0.09*	0.13* 0.05	0.12* 0.07*	
R^2							
Values model	0.022*	0.065*	0.047*	0.043*	0.037*	0.028*	
Full model	0.111*	0.221*	0.161*	0.125*	0.237*	0.124*	
N	1,224	1,585	2,307	1,201	1,290	1,483	
1979–80							
Materialism–postmaterialism			0.12* 0.04	0.25* 0.20*			
Religious–secular			0.08* 0.03	−0.01 −0.01			
Libertarianism–authoritarianism			0.15* 0.11*	0.11* 0.07			
R^2							
Values model			0.057*	0.084*			
Full model			0.131*	0.139*			
N			912	780			

* $p \leq 0.05$

Note: The first row shows the beta weights for value orientations in the values model; the second row shows beta weights for values in the complete models after including social and political background variables.

Sources: Civic Culture (1959–60); Political Action (1973–6); Political Action (1979–80).

TABLE 13.2. *Impact of value orientations on political efficacy in seven countries, 1973–6 to 1979–80*

Value orientations	FI	AU	GE	NL	SW	GB	IT
1973–6							
Materialism–	0.07*	0.16*	0.20*	0.20*	0.12*	−0.01	0.20*
postmaterialism	0.01	0.09*	0.07*	0.11*	0.04	−0.01	0.16*
Religious–	0.04	0.12*	0.07*	−0.03	0.03	−0.12*	0.05
secular	0.01	0.07*	0.00	−0.04	−0.01	−0.09*	0.03
Libertarianism–	0.11*	0.12*	0.13*	0.02	0.08*	0.08*	−0.04
authoritarianism	0.01	0.06*	0.09*	0.01	−0.02	0.02	−0.07*
R^2							
Values model	0.021*	0.072*	0.089*	0.040*	0.027*	0.015*	0.039*
Full model	0.205*	0.195*	0.285*	0.238*	0.270*	0.171*	0.053*
N	1,224	1,585	2,307	1,201	1,290	1,483	1,779
1979–80							
Materialism–			0.14*	0.23*			
postmaterialism			0.04	0.16*			
Religious–			0.04	−0.09*			
secular			−0.02	−0.07			
Libertarianism–			0.20*	0.02			
authoritarianism			0.14*	−0.02			
R^2							
Values model			0.076*	0.051*			
Full model			0.211*	0.240*			
N			912	780			

* $p \leq 0.05$

Note: The first row shows the beta weights for value orientations in the values model; the second row shows beta weights for values in the complete models after including social and political background variables.

Sources: Political Action (1973–6); Political Action (1979–80).

enables us to explain some 20 per cent or more of the variance in political efficacy and civic competence in all the countries under observation except Italy. It seems appropriate, then, to go into more detail when looking at the impact of particular value orientations.

Value Orientations and Trust in Government

Trust in government refers to the way people perceive their political environment, and, particularly, the actors responsible for the conduct of public affairs. Since values are used as standards in evaluating political situations and objects, a strong relationship can be expected between value orientations and feelings of trust. How much people trust the government will depend on the correspondence between their political value orientations and interests on the one hand and the government's actions on the other. The more the conduct of government conforms to people's political convictions, the more they will trust the government new. Feelings of distrust will emerge when there is a perceived discrepancy between people's normative expectations and the conduct of public affairs.

Normative standards, however, are not the only criteria applied when people evaluate governments. Public perceptions are also influenced by particular circumstances, such as the state of the economy. Short-term influences of this kind will reduce the explanatory power of long-term value orientations. Moreover, party affiliation and incumbency effects have to be taken into account: supporters of governing parties are generally more trusting of the political élite than supporters of opposition parties (Gabriel 1987; 1989; Miller and Listhaug 1990). So party-related variables may have a double impact on trust in government: on the one hand, reducing the impact of value orientations; on the other hand, improving the performance of an explanatory model.

In Table 13.3, we present the results of applying our model to the determinants of trust in government. We have data for four time points but only Germany is covered at each time point. Although the wording of the items in these surveys is not exactly the same, they are sufficiently similar to be comparable.

In 1959–60, except in Italy, where about 7 per cent of the variance in trust can be attributed to value orientations, the explanatory power of a value model is rather poor. Adding background variables does not alter the position substantially. Much the same holds true when we apply the value model to the Political Action data. Again, it worked best in Italy, but trust was also strongly influenced by value orientations in Britain. Apart from Italy and Britain, including party-related variables substantially improves the model only in Austria. The additonal data for 1985 underline the limited role of value orientations for trust in government in most West European countries. Apart from Britain, where the results are roughly similar to 1973–6, the model performs poorly—even in Italy. Party-related variables, however, are approximately as influential in explaining trust in 1985 as in 1959–60 and 1973–6.

Clearly, then, contrary to the assumption that the emergence of new

TABLE 13.3. *Impact of value orientations on trust in government in nine countries, 1959–60 to 1985*

Value orientations	FI	AU	GE	NL	SW	GB	FR	IT	SP
1959–60									
Materialism–non-materialism			−0.01			0.01		0.02	
			−0.02			−0.01		0.01	
Religious–secular			−0.13*			−0.10*		−0.26*	
			−0.10			−0.09*		−0.17*	
Libertarianism–authoritarianism			−0.18*			−0.03		−0.06	
			−0.16*			−0.04		−0.06	
R^2									
Values model			0.046*			0.008		0.066*	
Full model			0.054*			0.010		0.091*	
N			955			963		995	
1973–6									
Materialism–postmaterialism	−0.02	−0.05	0.01	−0.03	−0.12*	−0.12*		−0.12*	
	−0.05	−0.02	−0.01	−0.03	−0.13*	−0.09*		−0.06*	
Religious–secular	−0.09*	0.10*	0.05	−0.13*	−0.14*	−0.16*		−0.19*	
	−0.08*	0.01	−0.01	−0.11*	−0.12*	−0.11*		−0.15*	
Libertarianism–authoritarianism	0.07	0.00	0.02	0.02	−0.08*	−0.14*		−0.15*	
	0.05	0.01	0.00	0.01	−0.10*	−0.11*		−0.13*	
R^2									
Values model	0.006*	0.009*	0.002	0.016*	0.055*	0.073*		0.108*	
Full model	0.042*	0.084*	0.028*	0.036*	0.066*	0.214*		0.156*	
N	1,224	1,585	2,307	1,201	1,290	1,483		1,779	

1979–80		
Materialism–postmaterialism	−0.06	0.02
	−0.07	0.02
Religious–secular	0.04	−0.00
	0.02	−0.05
Libertarianism–authoritarianism	0.04	−0.05
	0.03	−0.07
R^2		
Values model	0.002	0.000
Full model	0.000	0.011
N	2,307	1,201

1985					
Materialism–postmaterialism	−0.09*	−0.07*	0.07	−0.03	−0.01
	−0.06	−0.06*	0.03	−0.03	−0.01
Religious–secular	−0.17*	−0.24*	0.08*	−0.17*	0.00
	−0.08*	−0.30*	0.02	−0.12*	−0.06
R^2					
Values model	0.043*	0.065*	0.009*	0.030*	0.000
Full model	0.143*	0.120*	0.125*	0.111*	0.112*
N	1,029	1,382	1,006	1,047	1,003

* $p \leq 0.05$

Note: The first row shows the beta weights for value orientations in the values model; the second row shows beta weights for values in the complete models after including social and political background variables.

Sources: Civic Culture (1956–60); Political Action (1973–6); Political Action (1979–80); Eurobarometer, No. 24.

value orientations leads to declining trust in government (Inglehart 1977*a*; Klages and Herbert 1983: 106 ff.; Klages 1984: 45 ff.), only a small proportion of trust in government in all the countries under observation can be attributed to value orientations. This is primarily because trust in government is more dependent on party preferences than political value orientations. None the less, we should take a closer look at the role of the value orientations in the model. In particular, do weak religious–secular orientations or postmaterialist orientations have a negative impact on trust in government; and which of these variables is more important as a predictor of people's attitudes towards incumbent authorities?

Value Orientations and Civicness

More recent comparative surveys have not used the standard efficacy and trust items in a large set of countries, so we have to turn to data from surveys using less than optimal instruments. Eurobarometer Nos. 26 (1986) and 30 (1988) include data on materialism–postmaterialism, religion, and a set of items referring to people's perception of their social and political environment as trustworthy and open to their influence. These items tap several aspects formerly attributed to the concepts of trust and efficacy. However, factor analysis of the five items revealed one single dimension in all the countries examined (data not shown here), demonstrating that a distinction between a trust component and an efficacy component in people's attitudes towards their socio-political environment is not supported by the Eurobarometer data. Hence, the items were combined into a single additive index, labelled 'civicness'. A roughly similar measurement instrument is also available in the Civic Culture data.[11]

As the data in Table 13.4 clearly show, our conclusion about the impact of value orientations on trust is also valid for civicness. A pure value model explains at best 5 per cent of the variance in civicness (Germany 1959–60), but normally the joint impact of value orientations on civicness, although statistically significant, is substantively weak. Only after party-related variables are included does the explanatory power of the model increase substantially in several instances.

Impact of Materialism–Postmaterialism

According to Inglehart (1977*b*: 5), changing value orientations are closely related to cognitive mobilization. The relationship assumed by Inglehart is particularly relevant here since both postmaterialism and internal efficacy include a participatory component. This argument was stressed by Bell in discussing the axial principles of post-industrial society: the axial principle of the cultural system is 'self-fulfilment', and the axial principle in the political sphere is 'participation' (Bell 1973: 12, 36ff., 114ff., 376ff., 475ff.). A similar argument is advanced by Klages (1984: 39ff., 51ff., 56ff.; Klages and Herbert 1983: 32ff.), who assumes that the distinction between traditional (conformist) and new (non-conformist) values centres around the goals of self-actualization and participation, with non-conformists giving a high priority to participative goals. In line with these arguments, Inglehart (1990: 342) expects postmaterialism to lead to high rates of political involvement and participation, which, in turn, presuppose stronger feelings of internal political efficacy. The more emphasis people place on post-materialist values, the more efficacious they presumably feel, even if education and political involvement are held constant.

There are no indicators for materialism–postmaterialism in the Civic Culture data but the materialism–nonmaterialism measure is a near equivalent,[12] indicating the relative priority of non-material values compared with bread-and-butter themes. In line with our theoretical expectation, materialism–nonmaterialism has a substantial positive impact on civic competence, in 1959–60, in Britain, Germany, and, particularly, Italy (see Table 13.1). The evidence from the Civic Culture data is confirmed for Germany by the data from both Political Action surveys, but postmaterialism was not relevant to civic competence in Britain in 1973–6. More recent data on civic competence are not available for Italy. Postmaterialist orientations had a positive impact on civic competence in Finland, Austria, Switzerland, and the Netherlands in 1973–6. However, if social and political background variables are held constant, the effects of non-material or postmaterialist orientations become statistically insignificant in most instances. The exceptions are Italy in 1959–60, Germany and Austria in 1973–6, and the Netherlands in 1979–80.

Looking again at Table 13.2, the hypothesis that postmaterialism has a positive impact on internal efficacy is supported in all countries except Britain. Even so, beta coefficients of substantial strength which

Table 13.4. *Impact of value orientations on civicness in eleven countries, 1959–60 to 1988*

Value orientations	DK	BE	GE	IR	NL	GB	FR	IT	GR	SP	PO
1959–60											
Materialism–non-materialism			0.22* 0.13*			0.13* 0.05		0.16* 0.08			
Religious–secular			0.11* 0.06			−0.08* −0.10*		−0.02 −0.01			
Libertarianism–authoritarianism			−0.03 0.01			0.01 −0.01		−0.04 −0.06			
R^2											
Values model			0.053*			0.024*		0.023*			
Full model			0.189*			0.136*		0.119*			
N			955			963		995			
1986											
Materialism–postmaterialism	−0.03 −0.05	−0.06 −0.01	−0.05 −0.06	−0.13* −0.13*	−0.03 −0.04	−0.14* −0.12*	0.05 0.02	0.14* 0.10*	0.01 −0.05	0.15* 0.08	0.03 −0.02
Religious–secular	−0.03 −0.06	−0.12* −0.08	−0.18* −0.17*	−0.07 −0.08	−0.07* −0.04	−0.09* −0.09*	−0.11* −0.09*	−0.10* −0.09*	0.11* 0.03	−0.05 −0.09	0.01 0.00

R^2											
Values Model	0.000	0.017*	0.035*	0.020*	0.005*	0.026*	0.010*	0.020*	0.009*	0.016*	0.000
Full model	0.065*	0.054*	0.084*	0.043*	0.057*	0.156*	0.068*	0.074*	0.075*	0.039*	0.092*
N	997	999	1,085	1,007	1,026	1,000	995	1,098	1,000	1,010	1,000
1988											
Materialism–postmaterialism	−0.08*	0.01	−0.04	−0.00	0.01	−0.12*	0.02	0.06	0.03	0.01	−0.10*
	−0.07*	−0.02	−0.07*	−0.02	−0.01	−0.09*	−0.05	0.01	0.03	0.00	−0.11*
Religious–secular	−0.12*	−0.05	−0.09*	−0.07*	−0.09*	−0.07*	−0.03	−0.04	0.06	−0.01	0.11*
	−0.10*	−0.06	−0.12*	−0.05	−0.07*	−0.02	−0.07*	−0.08*	0.04	−0.06	0.06
R^2											
Values model	0.020*	0.000	0.009*	0.003	0.005*	0.020*	0.000	0.002	0.002	0.000	0.021*
Full model	0.104*	0.037*	0.089*	0.073*	0.057*	0.134*	0.072*	0.085*	0.045*	0.047*	0.072*
N	1,006	1,024	1,051	1,012	1,006	1,017	1,001	1,058	1,000	1,013	1,000

* $p \le 0.05$

Note: The first row shows the beta weights for value orientations in the values model; the second row shows beta weights for values in the complete models after including social and political background variables.

Sources: Civic Culture (1959–60); Eurobarometer, Nos. 26 and 30.

remained statistically significant after controlling for background variables emerged only in Austria, Germany, and Italy in 1973–6, and in the Netherlands for both 1973–6 and 1979–80. In several cases—Finland, Switzerland, and Germany (1979–80)—the impact of postmaterialism fades when background factors are held constant. Only in Britain were political efficacy and postmaterialism completely unrelated. Although postmaterialism seems to enhance political self-consciousness in several cases, in other instances its impact is due, in part, to the fact that postmaterialists are more educated and politically involved than other people.[13]

In general, then, hypotheses about the impact of materialist–postmaterialist value orientations on political efficacy and civic competence—more or less explicitly stated by Inglehart and Klages—are supported by the data. However, several reservations are necessary with respect to the influence of social and political background variables, as well as particular political circumstances. Why the impact of postmaterialism on efficacy varies over time and between countries is by no means obvious. Neither the diffusion of postmaterialist orientations within these societies, nor factors such as education levels or media use account for the differences in the relationship observed between postmaterialism and political efficacy.

Next, we examine the impact of materialism–postmaterialism on trust in government. According to Inglehart (1977*a*; 1977*b*; 1990), postmaterialists living in a predominantly materialist environment and confronted with political institutions and leaders pursuing primarily materialist goals tend to be more distrusting than materialists and people with mixed priorities. Since materialists are more numerous than postmaterialists, and have better access to established channels of interest articulation, politicians will normally be more responsive to their demands than to postmaterialist concerns. On the other hand, postmaterialists feel politically more competent, have a stronger interest in political affairs, think of politics as an important domain of social life, and participate more actively in politics than materialists (see Chapters 14, 15, and 16).

Thus, the properties attributed to materialists and postmaterialists can lead to contradictory expectations about their impact on trust in government. Accordingly, we propose three different hypotheses. First, according to an issue-oriented, 'new politics' explanation closest to Inglehart's view, materialists will show high levels of trust because they perceive good opportunities to transmit their demands to the political élites by regular political channels, or they consider political élites responsive to their interests. Postmaterialists will not show a high level of trust because they perceive political leaders as unresponsive. The second hypothesis proposes that there is no relationship between materialism–postmatcrialism and trust. The reasoning here is that, whereas politicians might act according to the preferences of materialists because they represent a large segment of the electorate, they might also be responsive to postmaterialists because they are politically more active. The third hypothesis proposes that the highest level of trust is found among people with mixed preferences—since political élites, in order to maximize their success in elections, tend to offer a policy mix of materialist and postmaterialist issues. This is particularly likely when people with mixed value orientations are the most numerous among the electorate, and the proportions of materialists and post-materialists are approximately equal.

The data presented in Table 13.3 clearly indicate, however, that there is no instance of a statistically significant, positive relationship between postmaterialist value orientations and trust in government. On the one hand, when postmaterialism impinges on trust at all, it goes along with cynical rather than trusting attitudes towards the government. On the other hand, the null hypothesis is more often supported by the data than the expectation that materialists are particularly trusting. However, in a few instances, postmaterialism has a negative impact on trust in government: in Britain in 1973–6 and 1985, and in Italy and Switzerland in 1973–6. Additionally, postmaterialism is a determinant of trust in government in Germany in 1985, but only so long as party-related variables are excluded.

In view of these modest relationships, we might question whether our analytic strategy fits our theoretical assumptions. This caveat is particularly relevant to the third hypothesis proposing that political trust will be highest among people with mixed value orientations. As ordinary regression analysis is not sensitive to non-linear relationships, we modified our strategy in order to test this assumption. However, a non-linear effect of materialism–postmaterialism on trust emerged only in Germany in 1973–6 and 1985. In both instances, materialists did not deviate from the public at large nor from the mixed group, but postmaterialists were clearly more distrusting than the general public. In all other instances, controlling for non-linear effects did not lead to new insights.

Finally, we examine the impact of materialism–postmaterialism on civicness. Since civicness contains elements of both trust and efficacy, the effect of postmaterialism is rather difficult to predict. This is largely attributable to hypothesizing that postmaterialism is positively linked to efficacy but negatively to trust. Hence, in the case of civicness, influences stemming from postmaterialist orientations could easily cancel out. This assumption is partially supported by the data in Table 13.4, showing that the relationship between materialism–postmaterialism and people's perceptions of the responsiveness and trustworthiness of their social environment does not follow a uniform pattern. Whereas in 1959–60 people with nonmaterialist orientations were the most civic group—at least so long as background variables are disregarded—the position is very different in 1986 and 1988. In 1986, civicness was positively related to postmaterialism in Spain and Italy, but negatively in Britain and Ireland. Two years later, the position remained the same in Britain, but the relationship between postmaterialism and civicness had become insignificant in the other three countries. Moreover, postmaterialism had a negative impact on civicness in Denmark and Portugal, and in Germany after background variables are held constant.

The picture becomes even more variable when we look at non-linear relationships. In 1986, postmaterialists were least civic in Germany and Denmark, whereas in 1988 materialists were least civic in Spain and Italy—although that relationship faded after controlling for background factors. Thus, instead of uncovering some general relationship between materialism–postmaterialism and civicness, we found very different constellations which are probably better explained by situational rather than structural factors.

To sum up, although the measurement instruments are not always the same, the survey data for fourteen countries over a span of some thirty years allow us to draw some general conclusions about the impact of materialism–postmaterialism on attitudes towards politics and government. In most instances, postmaterialist orientations have a significant, positive, and consistent impact on the way people define their role as political actors. In line with Inglehart's understanding of the political consequences of the 'silent revolution', people holding postmaterialist orientations are the most efficacious and subjectively competent among the respondents in all the countries examined, except Britain. This can be seen most clearly in countries where relevant data have been collected in several surveys: Germany, the Netherlands, and Italy. We can conclude, then, that the theory of the 'silent revolution' contributes markedly to understanding the participatory orientations of citizens in Western Europe.

Even so, the relationship between postmaterialism and political self-consciousness is, at least partially, due to the higher educational attainment and political involvement of postmaterialists. However, the strength of these relationships varies considerably over time and between countries. The variation over time is not incompatible with Inglehart's discussion of the impact of the 'silent revolution', but the variation between countries cannot be explained with the models used here (see also Gabriel 1986: 211 ff.; 1987).

Our assumptions about the relationship between materialism–postmaterialism and trust are more often disconfirmed than supported by the data. Value orientation makes a difference to attitudes towards the government only in Britain. Postmaterialists are clearly the most cynical among the electorate—but this does not apply to non-materialists in 1959–60. Moreover, whenever postmaterialist orientations make a substantial impact on trust in government, the British pattern is confirmed. But since this is the exception rather than the rule, materialism–postmaterialism can be seen, more often than not, as irrelevant in the explanation of trust in political leaders. Instead, for the most part, situational and party-related variables account for the differences in trust in government.

Impact of Religious Orientations

Hypotheses about the impact of religion on civic competence and political efficacy are not easily formulated. Although a few core values typical of the Judaeo-Christian tradition are usually thought to be important preconditions for the emergence of a democratic political culture, different religious denominations stress some values while de-emphasizing others. As Inglehart (1990: 53 ff.) supposes, the Lutheran Reformation was the first step in the modernization of the Western world, undermining control of social life by the hierarchically organized Catholic Church and finally ending in a process of cultural secularization. Similarly, Lipset (1960: 152, 165, 168 ff.) pointed to the different contributions which Catholic and Protestant doctrines have made to the development of democracy: while Protestantism stresses individual autonomy, even in one's relationship to God, Catholicism is conducive to the ideas of hierarchy, subordination, and allegiance. Hence, religiosity may be assumed to have a negative impact on political efficacy in predominantly Catholic societies and among the Catholic segment of religiously heterogeneous societies. Since individualism and autonomy are incorporated in Protestant doctrine, Protestants in Western societies can be expected to manifest much the same degree of internal efficacy as secular people.

Apart from different historical heritages, the meaning of religion in political life has changed to some degree during the last decades. The nature of the religious cleavage has been transformed from conflicts between different religious denominations to conflicts between religious and secular groups. People of strong religious conviction tend to be conservative, irrespective of their affiliation to the Catholic or Protestant churches (see Chapters 4, 7, and 8; Inglehart 1990: 185ff.). Hence, religious values tend, generally, to encourage political attitudes typical of subject and parochial political cultures, which, among other things, implies weak political self-confidence. Attitudes considered typical of a modern, participant civic culture are probably more often found among the secularized segments of a society.[14]

Compared to materialism–postmaterialism, religious–secular orientations are clearly less important as a determinant of civic competence and political efficacy. As we saw in Tables 13.1 and 13.2, statistically significant and substantively meaningful relationships between these variables are found only occasionally. However, contrary to the parochialism hypothesis assuming a negative impact of religion on civic competence and internal efficacy, the evidence here is inconclusive. Although religious–secular orientations turn out to be largely unrelated to political self-consciousness in most instances, there are some—but contradictory—deviations from this general pattern. While people who are highly integrated into religious communities felt politically most competent in Germany (1959–60), Britain (1973–6), and the Netherlands (1979–80), the opposite was true in the same countries at other times (Germany 1973–6 and 1979–80, the Netherlands 1973–6), and in Austria.

Even more confusingly, inconsistencies emerge not only between different points in time but also when the results for civic competence and internal efficacy, using the same data, were compared. Controlling for background variables yielded even more ambiguous results. Consequently, a clear statement about the impact of religion on political self-consciousness is virtually impossible. Thus, the hypotheses about the effect of religious–secular orientations on people's self-image as competent political actors can generally be rejected. The same holds true for the assumption that religious–secular orientations have a different impact in different cultural settings.

Next, we assess the impact of religion on trust in government. Here, party competition has to be taken into account as an intervening variable. The role of religion in the political life of West European countries differs considerably (Lijphart 1984: 127ff.; see also Chapter 17), so the influence of religious orientations on the way people relate to political élites may be expected to vary. Some countries have been characterized by extreme cultural fragmentation stemming from the religious cleavage as in Germany, Switzerland, and the Netherlands; other countries have been split by antagonisms between Catholic and secular subcultures as in France, Austria, and the Mediterranean countries. Until recently, the party systems of these countries have reflected these religious cleavages, thus religion can be assumed to have an impact on trust in government. Depending on the partisan composition of the government, people with religious convictions are expected to feel trusting or cynical—showing positive attitudes towards governments led by conservative parties, and negative attitudes when secular parties control the administration. The opposite may hold true for people of secular outlook. By contrast, in countries where religious cleavages do not shape party competition, trust will not be influenced by religious beliefs. This applies, in our sample, to Britain, Finland, Denmark, Ireland, and Greece.

Looking back to Table 13.3, we can see that religious–secular orientations exert a moderate to sizeable influence on trust in government in most countries at several points in time. The only exceptions were Germany (1973–6, 1979–80) and Spain (1985). In Austria and France, the impact of religion on trust disappears when party-related variables are held constant. More striking, however, is the observation that distance from organized religion often goes along with critical attitudes towards the government, whatever its partisan composition. This clearly runs counter to the expectation that the impact of religion on trust will vary, depending on the cleavage structure of a given society. Instead, the process of secularization in Western Europe seems to be accompanied by declining trust in government. Moreover, this decline is not confined to societies where religion has traditionally been important in politics but, rather, seems to be occurring in most West European societies. However, as demonstrated by the Austrian and

French data, control of the government by secular parties may reduce cynicism among the secular strata of a political community. None the less, the partisan composition of the government never converts cynicism into trust. We conclude, then, that religious–secular orientations do influence trust in government, and that the influence is only partially attributable to party effects.

For theoretical and empirical reasons the impact of religion on civicness is less clear. Different approaches suggest rather contradictory hypotheses. If religion is interpreted as an integrative force while secularization is thought to promote social fragmentation, religion may be expected to be positively linked to civicness. From a modernization perspective, however, religion can be thought of as a correlate of parochialism. Then, the emergence of civicness becomes probable only after religious ties have weakened and people have become free to adopt the orientations typical of a modern, secularized, political culture. From this perspective a religious orientation would go along with rather weak civicness.

That religion is an integrative force is, empirically, more strongly supported than the competing view that secularization promotes civicness. As we saw in Table 13.4, the evidence from the 1959–60 Civic Culture data is contradictory; in the 1986 and 1988 Eurobarometer data, we found only two positive relationships between secular orientations and civicness, in Greece (1986) and Portugal (1988). But controlling for party-related variables in these deviating cases produced insignificant coefficients. Yet there are several instances of statistically significant, consistently negative relationships between religious–secular orientations and civicness—so long as incumbency effects are ignored. Even if they are taken into account, the singular impact of value orientations on civicness survives in a sizeable number of cases. This, again, demonstrates that civicness is closer to trust in government than to internal efficacy. Once more, too, the negative impact of religious–secular orientations on trust is largely independent of the cleavage structure in these societies and, moreover, of the partisan composition of the government.

We have to conclude, then, that the evidence of the impact of religious–secular value orientations is rather mixed. There are clear indications that the influence of religion on social and political life is not entirely channelled by party competition. As most of our findings show, religious people are generally more trusting while secular people are more distrusting than the public at large, even after incumbency effects are taken into consideration. On the one hand, postmaterialism has a marked effect in encouraging people's sense of political efficacy and civic competence, and religious orientations generally lead people to become more trusting while secularization is linked to political cynicism. On the other hand, feelings of political competence are usually unrelated to secular orientations.

Religion, then, may be viewed as an important integrative mechanism, and the continuing decline of religion in most West European countries may eventually lead to a more cynical view of the governing process. Moreover, the positive impact of religion on trust in government was evident regardless of varying historical and socio-structural conditions—in predominantly Catholic Italy, in the religiously mixed Netherlands, and in Protestant Norway and Britain. This pattern is not completely independent of incumbency effects, but the impact of religious–secular orientations on social and political trust can by no means be attributed entirely to the particularities of party competition.

Impact of Libertarianism

In contrast to religion, libertarianism and authoritarianism can be conceived as a set of orientations and attitudes specifically referring to the political realm. According to Lipset (1981: 89 ff.), libertarianism is especially weak among the lower strata, since their socialization patterns and life circumstances do not favour open-mindedness and tolerance. This working-class authoritarianism hypothesis is supported by several studies demonstrating that tolerance and libertarianism increase with social status (Erikson, Luttbeg, and Tedin 1988: 101 ff.; Topf 1989: 70 ff.). However, empirical evidence about the impact of libertarianism on beliefs in government is more limited than for post-materialism or religious–secular orientations. So is the attention given to it in the theoretical debate.

The theory of political alienation (Finifter 1970; Mason, House, and Martin 1980; Wright 1976; 1981) and Almond and Verba's concept of the 'civic culture' converge in concluding that, in a democratic polity, holding authoritarian values indicates estrangement from the political community. People who do not conform to the values and norms institutionalized in some domains may also fail to do so in other domains; values and attitudes corresponding to the requirements of a democratic polity are typical of a 'civic culture' (Almond and Verba

1963: 5ff., 16ff., 337ff.), implying adherence to libertarianism, rejection of authoritarianism, and leading to strong political ego-strength.
Thus, feelings of efficacy should increase with libertarianism. Finally,
taking participation and self-actualization as typical of a libertarian
image of the political order, it is plausible to assume that holding
libertarian values has a positive impact on internal efficacy.

It is evident from Tables 13.1 and 13.2 that this hypothesis is
confirmed in most instances. In 1959–60 libertarianism is positively
related to feelings of civic competence in Italy, but not in Germany and
Britain. The 1973–6 and 1979–80 data, however, convey a very
different picture: libertarianism enhances people's feelings of civic
competence in all countries. However, this relationship fades after
controlling for political involvement, education, and the like, in
Finland and Switzerland in 1973–6, and the Netherlands in 1979–80.
Similarly, except in the Netherlands and Italy, libertarianism was a
significant predictor of political efficacy, but in almost all instances
this relationship disappeared when factors such as education and
political involvement were taken into account.

Understanding how libertarianism influences trust in government
may be derived from the images of society and politics typical of
authoritarian and libertarian orientations. Hierarchy, strong leadership, order, and social control are essential elements in an authoritarian
model of state and society. Authoritarians attribute a prominent role to
political leaders who are perceived as the true representatives of a
common good which, if necessary, has to be put into effect against
the wishes of individuals and interest groups. To do so, political leaders
need some kind of unconditional reserve of good will, usually defined
as political trust (Gamson 1968: 32; Topf 1989: 68ff.; Wright 1976:
13ff.). Libertarianism, on the other hand, with its emphasis on
individualism, self-determination, and limited government, implies a
critical view of authority in general and authority figures in particular
(Döring 1990: 74ff.). Libertarians think of individuals as the best
promoters of their own interests and values, and are sceptical of the
public-regardingness of political leaders.

Looking at Tables 13.3 and 13.4, a close relationship between the
variables under scrutiny is evident in only a few instances: Germany in
1959–60, Switzerland, Italy, and Britain in 1973–6. However, without
exception, whenever political libertarianism has an impact on trust in
government, the relationship is negative and remains so after the background variables are held constant. Civicness, however, was generally

unrelated to libertarianism in 1959–60. Unfortunately, survey data including indicators for civicness and libertarianism are not available for later time points.

In all, then, libertarianism is primarily related to perceptions of the input component of a nation's political system. In most instances, the assumption that libertarian orientations enhance people's sense of civic competence and political efficacy is supported—so long as education and political involvement are not taken into consideration. Thus, it is valid to conclude that self-fulfilment, participation, and libertarianism cluster together as elements of a civic culture, which is more or less firmly institutionalized in the political communities of Western Europe. The evidence about libertarianism and trust in government is more mixed. The hypothesis that libertarianism undermines trust, due to a sceptical view of authority, is supported in some instances, but not all. Nevertheless, libertarianism helps to explain the way people relate to the government of the day, and the evidence is broadly consistent with the liberal doctrine of limited government.

Changing Orientations and Attitudes

The analysis so far has focused on the relationship between value orientations and beliefs in government at particular points in time. This is in line with most literature on the impact of value change among Western publics, but, strictly speaking, arguments about value change require dynamic analysis. Generalizing from our previous discussion, the important point is not so much that people differ in their value orientations but, rather, that the spreading of postmaterialist, secular, and libertarian orientations leads to people becoming more self-confident political actors and, thus, to taking a more critical stance towards political authorities. Entailed in this description is the assumption that value orientations and beliefs in government shift simultaneously.

To examine whether or not a dynamic account fits political reality, we need panel data. The data from the German and Dutch panels in the two waves of Political Action, covering a span of five to six years (1974 to 1979–80), include indicators of postmaterialism, secularization, and libertarianism as well as political efficacy and trust in government.

Since discussion about the impact of values centres around the influence that increasing postmaterialism, secularization, and libertarianism exerts on beliefs in government, our focus is on the way in which the shift to 'modern' value orientations influences people's attitudes towards their governments. Consequently, only developments in the political attitudes of people who are becoming more postmaterialist, secularized, or libertarian are addressed. The hypothesis underlying the analyses is simple: people who shift from traditional (materialist, religious, authoritarian) to modern (postmaterialist, secular, libertarian) value orientations between 1974 and 1979–80 are expected to become more efficacious but less trusting in government. At least, people with modernizing value orientations should show a clearer shift

TABLE 13.5. *Changing value orientations and changing sense of political efficacy: Germany and the Netherlands, 1974–80*

	Shift in mean values for political efficacy	
	Germany	Netherlands
More materialist	−0.242	0.236
Stable	−0.123	−0.111
More postmaterialist	−0.081	0.044
All	−0.139	0.003
Pearson's *r*	0.022	0.037
Eta	0.051	0.088
Less secularized	−0.140	0.131
Stable	−0.151	−0.080
More secularized	−0.115	0.102
All	−0.141	0.011
Pearson's *r*	0.005	0.005
Eta	0.008	0.040
Less libertarian	−0.233	0.166
Stable	−0.072	0.158
More libertarian	−0.131	−0.240
All	−0.128	0.014
Pearson's *r*	0.017	0.070
Eta	0.036	0.079
N	912	780

Notes: Entries are differences in the group means as measured in the first and second wave of the Political Action panels. All coefficients are statistically insignificant at the 0.05 level. A negative score means a decline in political efficacy; a positive score, an increase in political efficacy.

Sources: Political Action (1973–6); Political Action (1979–80).

towards greater efficacy but less trust than people with stable or less modern value orientations.

The analysis to test this hypothesis is also simple. First, we grouped people, according to their responses to the respective value items, into stable (no change at the individual level), more modernizing (post-materialist, secular, libertarian) and, correspondingly, less moderniz-ing strata. Secondly, for each group, we computed the shift in the mean values for trust and efficacy from 1974 to 1979–80 by subtracting the 1974 mean scores from the 1979–80 mean scores. Positive scores indicate that feelings of trust and efficacy have increased, negative scores indicate decline, and zero indicates stability. Comparing the means across the groups gives us an impression of whether changes in value orientations are accompanied by changes in trust and efficacy. Our findings are presented in Tables 13.5 and 13.6.

The data in these tables clearly indicate that changing value orienta-tions normally do not induce pronounced shifts in political trust and efficacy. By and large, the development of beliefs in government among the various groups follows the general trend among the electorate. The only exception concerns the relationship between secularization and trust in government in Germany, where the increase in trust in govern-ment was clearly strongest in the secularizing group. Presenting any plausible explanation of this finding is not easy. Since only this single result deviates from the general trend, situational rather than structural factors are probably at work. We can conclude, then, that despite the several relationships found between value orientations and beliefs in government, these elements change rather independently of each other, at least in the short term.

Conclusion

At the beginning of this chapter, we posed questions about whether, and how much, value orientations contribute to explaining beliefs in gov-ernment. Obviously, on the evidence we presented, no simple answers can be given. Rather, we have to distinguish between the several facets of a complex relationship. In particular, we have to address three further questions: (1) Which aspects of beliefs in government are best explained by value orientations? (2) Which orientations are most important to beliefs in government? (3) Do value orientations have a

TABLE 13.6. *Changing value orientations and changing trust in government: Germany and the Netherlands, 1974–80*

	Shift in mean values for political trust	
	Germany	Netherlands
More materialist	−0.087	0.465
Stable	0.000	0.609
More postmaterialist	−0.451	0.608
All	−0.057	0.624
Pearson's r	−0.075	0.023
Eta	0.121	0.068
Less secularized	−0.132	0.595
Stable	−0.217	0.648
More secularized	0.490	0.497
All	−0.028	0.603
Pearson's r	0.102*	−0.014
Eta	0.133*	0.027
Less libertarian	−0.328	0.665
Stable	0.063	0.610
More libertarian	0.031	0.554
All	−0.031	0.606
Pearson's r	0.051	−0.022
Eta	0.069	0.022
N	912	780

* $p \leq 0.05$

Notes: Entries are differences in the group means as measured in the first and second wave of Political Action panels. A negative score means a decline in political trust; a positive score, an increase in political trust.

Sources: Political Action (1973–6); Political Action (1979–80).

uniform effect on beliefs in government, strengthening rather than weakening a political culture conducive to liberal democracy?

We have examined the impact of materialism–postmaterialism, religious–secular orientations, and libertarianism–authoritarianism on political efficacy, civic competence, trust in government, and civicness. Our findings suggest a complex picture. Apart from failing to establish, empirically, a homogeneous syndrome of modern value orientations (data not shown here), the relationship between the three value orientations and beliefs in government is far from consistent or coherent. Libertarianism and postmaterialism emerge as important antecedents of civic competence and internal efficacy, but this is not the case with religious–secular orientations. Moreover, whereas trust in government and civicness are strengthened by religiosity, they are largely unrelated to postmaterialism. Libertarianism has an impact on trust in some instances, but not in others.

Consequently, we cannot give a simple answer to the first two questions posed above. Rather, which value orientation best explains beliefs in government depends on which attitude is being examined. The spread of modern orientations does not have a uniform impact on beliefs in government: some are strengthened while others are weakened. Generally, the explanatory power of the value models is modest, the statistical relationships are rather weak, and they often fade away when background variables are included. Finally, the relationships are far from stable across time or between countries.

When we interpret our hypotheses as statements asserting that value orientations have a uniform impact on people's beliefs in government, we have to reject them. However, although value orientations are far from having a strong and consistent impact on beliefs in government, they are none the less important in understanding how people relate to their political environment. Moreover, predictions derived from theories of value change are—at least partially—correct in many instances. Even so, the processes of value change do not uniformly impinge on people's attitudes towards government, nor is their impact clearly established. The national differences evident in our analyses suggest that this may be due, at least in part, to the influence of country-specific situational factors. Maybe also we have to go much further in uncovering the social forces mediating the processes of value change and their impact on beliefs in government.

Returning to our opening remarks, the growing sense of political alienation among publics in Western Europe noted by several observers cannot be attributed directly to the impact of value change. As we have emphasized, the position is highly variable and few relationships are robust. In so far as general conclusions can be drawn, it is that postmaterialism and libertarianism seem to enhance people's feelings of political efficacy while declining religiosity induces growing political distrust. This suggests that, as the numbers of people with postmaterialist, secular, or libertarian orientations grow, enlarging the politically mobilized and distrusting segment of the public, political authorities will be subject to more scrutiny and questioning than used to be the case some decades earlier.

NOTES

1. For analyses using a rather different set of items, see Craig, Niemi and Silver (1990); Niemi, Craig, and Mattei (1991).
2. Internal political efficacy is measured by three variables in the Political Action survey: V136, V138 and V139 in Political Action I; V1173, V1175 and V1176 in Political Action II (agree strongly = 1, disagree strongly = 4). An additive index was computed ranging from 1 (low efficacy) to 10 (high efficacy). A missing value on one variable led to a missing value on the index.
3. Measures of civic competence are available from the Civic Culture survey (V52 and V59), Political Action I, except in Italy (V18 and V19), and Political Action II (V1039 and V1042); any activity mentioned = 1, none = 0. An additive index was computed ranging from 0 (no competence) to 2 (competent in local and national politics). A missing value on one variable led to a missing value on the index.
4. Two of the standard trust items were included in Political Action I (V144 and V145) and Political Action II (V1181 and V1182). The coding for the first item is: 'a few big interests' = 1, 'all the people' = 4; for the second item, 'almost never' = 1, 'just about always' = 4. An additive index was formed out of both variables ranging from 1 (low trust) to 7 (high trust). The second trust in government item (V145/V1182) was included in Eurobarometer, No. 24. Since the standard items were not included in the Civic Culture survey, a substitute variable was constructed consisting of V41 (agree = 1; agree in part = 2; disagree = 3) and V67 (better without government = 1; in part better/no difference = 2; better with government = 3). A missing value on one variable led to a missing value on the index.
5. The variables are V62–V66 in Eurobarometer, No. 26, and V55–V59 in Eurobarometer, No. 30 (yes = 1; no = 2). Additive indices were computed from these variables ranging from 1 (low civicness) to 5 (high civicness). Two missing values were allowed without leading to a missing value on the index. The variables from the Civic Culture are: V37 (agree = 1; it depends = 2; disagree = 3); V165, V169 (agree = 3; disagree = 1); V166, V168, V170, V172 (agree = 1; disagree = 3). A missing value on one variable led to a missing value on the index.
6. Materialism–postmaterialism is measured as follows; for Political Action I and II, see Evans and Hildebrandt (1979: 564 ff.); for Eurobarometer, Nos. 24, 26, and 30, see V20/V21, V45/V46, and V60/V61 in the respective codebooks. The index was constructed in the same way as for the Political Action data. As an identical measure was not available in the Civic Culture survey, a near-equivalent measure labelled 'materialism–nonmaterialism' was used (see V22 and V23 in the codebook). The materialist items on this measure are 'making ends meet', 'government control and regulation of business', 'foreign affairs/national defence', 'improving conditions for your family'; the non-materialist items are 'spiritual and moral betterment', 'eliminating inequality and injustice'. The codings are: materialist = materialist items mentioned as first and second priority; mixed = any combination of materialist and non-materialist items; non-materialist = non-materialist items mentioned as first and second priority.
7. Religious–secular orientation is measured using the following variables. Civic Culture, V197 (at least once a week = 1; sometimes = 2; special days only = 3;

never/not member of a religious community = 4). Political Action I and II, V207/ V1195 (every week = 1; almost every week = 2; once or twice a month = 3; few times a year = 4; never = 5; not a member of a religious community = 6). Eurobarometer, No. 30, V703 (several times a week = 1; once a week = 2; several times a year = 3; once a year or less = 4; never = 5; not a member of a religious community = 6. Eurobarometer, No. 24, V59 (importance of God, 0 = very important, 10 = absolutely unimportant). Eurobarometer, No. 26, V200 (religious affiliation, 1 = very close, 4 = not member of a religious community). In all instances, high numbers were given to low church integration. Arguments for using frequency of church attendance as a measure of religious–secular orientations are set out in Chapter 4.

8. For measuring libertarianism in the Political Action data, the index of repression potential was used (V331 and V1289); see Evans and Hildebrandt (1979: 555 ff.). In the Civic Culture data, the relevant variables are V167 and V171 (agree = 1; disagree = 2). An additional index of libertarianism was constructed ranging from 1 to 3.

9. The measurement of these variables is as follows. Education: Civic Culture, V148 (no school = 0; Volksschule, Scuola Elementare, elementary school = 1; Scuola Media = 2; Höhere Schule, high school, Liceo = 3; Universität, university, universita = 4); Political Action, V384/V1311. Age: Civic Culture grouped data V198; age in exact years in all other surveys. Sex: male = 1, female = 2. Social Status/Class: Civic Culture, V205; Political Action, V124/V1201. Political Involvement: Civic Culture, V28 and V32 (regularly/almost daily = 3, from time to time/once a week = 2, never = 1); Political Action V13/ V1018 (very interested = 4, somewhat interested = 3, not much interested = 2, not at all interested = 1) and V126/ V1157 (often = 4, sometimes = 3, seldom = 2, never = 1). An additive index was formed out of both variables. A missing value on one variable led to a missing value on the index.

10. The criteria for determining that value orientations are important determinants of beliefs in government are: (i) the value model has to be statistically significant at the 0.05 level; (ii) the beta weights of a particular value orientation should be statistically significant at the 0.05 level and not weaker than 0.10 in a pure value model, and not weaker than 0.05 in a model including other social and political background variables.

11. Another difference between this civicness variable and the concepts of trust and efficacy refers to the object of the attitudes: the standard trust and efficacy items refer to the political system, whereas the civicness variable has broader reference, tapping individual orientations towards society as well as politics. Details of the construction of the instrument in the Civic Culture study are given in n. 5.

12. See n. 6.

13. These relationships also become apparent when analysing some national data. Several other surveys conducted in Germany during the 1980s showed that materialism–postmaterialism is an important determinant of efficacy; cf. Gabriel (1986: 211 ff.; 1987). A similar pattern is evident in a Dutch sample for 1981.

14. The assumption of a link between religion and parochialism was partially confirmed by Almond and Verba (1963: 308 ff.), who found people holding strong religious beliefs to be the most parochial in Italian society.

14

Political Interest

OSCAR W. GABRIEL AND JAN W. VAN DETH

One of the best established findings in empirical research on the impact of value orientations is the positive relationship between new values and political involvement. Indeed, some of the most prominent theories about value orientations and value change have been advanced with the explicit goal of explaining the wave of political participation which swept the advanced industrial world in the late 1960s (cf. Inglehart 1971a; Marsh 1977). The assumptions underlying these theories are simple. The populations of advanced industrial societies are demonstrating an increasing emphasis on non-material and emancipatory goals, shifting away from tradition, deference, and material well-being, and moving towards self-fulfilment, independence, and emancipation. These new priorities imply that people no longer unquestioningly accept political authority or confine their participation in politics to voting or other forms of conventional behaviour. With some exaggeration one might say that the whole thesis of 'new politics' is no more than the idea that ever growing numbers of people are becoming more interested in politics. The appearance, in many countries, of new orientations in the early 1970s and the increasing—although still limited—number of people indicating they are very interested in politics, suggests a clear link between these two phenomena.

In spite of all manner of differences—historical, economic, social, and political—between the countries of the Western world, the ongoing increase in political interest seems to be a universal development. In his overview of the changes in political culture in the United States, Britain, West Germany, and France, Dalton notes (1988: 22): 'The available evidence is often incomplete, and different survey questions are used in each nation, but the trend of increasing political interest is unmistakable.' A decade earlier, in *Political Action*, the 'increasing political involvement of the citizenry' was observed 'unambiguously' (Kaase and Marsh 1979: 36). These findings are in sharp contrast to the portrait of the average citizen as not particularly active and certainly not deeply involved in politics which can be found in the traditional voting studies of the 1950s (cf. Berelson, Lazarsfeld, and McPhee 1954: 305 ff.; Campbell, Converse, Miller, and Stokes 1960: 539 ff.).

How is this shift in political interest to be explained? Is it a consequence of a shift in value orientations among the mass publics of Western democracies? Or are we dealing with, say, two distinct phenomena which are related only by a common background factor such as a general increase in the level of education? Straightforward explanations of changing levels of involvement in terms of new value orientations frequently obscure several serious problems. For example, new value orientations are often defined or operationalized in terms of involvement, and so explanations or predictions become simply tautologies. Moreover, it is not always clear how the relationship between value orientations and involvement should be understood, and how the different modes or dimensions of involvement can be distinguished.

In this chapter we consider, first, some interpretations of the link between 'new' value orientations and increasing political interest. Secondly, we discuss various operationalizations of the complicated concept 'interest in politics'. We present the empirical results in the third section, starting with multivariate analyses of the impact of value orientations on political interest. In addition, we examine the relationship between political interest and attitudes towards specific issues. In the final section, we discuss the relevance of our findings for beliefs in government in Western Europe.

Theoretical Notions and Explanations

The bulk of empirical research on the relationship between value orientations and political interest in the last two decades seems to have been inspired by Inglehart's notion of a 'silent revolution' with the rise of postmaterialism (Inglehart 1971*a*; 1977*b*; 1990). It is not easy to find alternative interpretations which might be used as fruitful additions to Inglehart's seminal work. For instance, there has been virtually no attempt to explain political involvement in terms of libertarian values or the effects of secularization. Although there is a general consensus about the relevance of postmaterialist value orientations for political interest, the flipside is a rather uncritical acceptance of the interpretations offered. Indeed, Inglehart's account of the factors and processes involved seems to be one of the most frequently quoted in the literature. According to Inglehart (1979*a*: 345), value orientations play a particularly important role in shaping predispositions towards political involvement for three reasons:

(1) Materialists tend to be preoccupied with satisfying immediate physiological needs and their derivatives. Postmaterialists feel relatively secure about these needs and have a greater amount of psychic energy to invest in more remote concerns. This may lead to involvement in a wide variety of activities, among which politics is one possibility.

(2) As a recently emerging minority whose highest priorities tend to be slighted, Postmaterialists are apt to be relatively disaffected from the established social order.

(3) The disruption or property damage that may result from unconventional political action may seem less negative to Postmaterialists, since they threaten things they value less than Materialists do.

This is a strange mixture of arguments in terms of needs, preferences, priorities, social positions, and interests. However, the third point can readily be rejected as an inadmissible intersubjective comparison of preferences. Postmaterialists give priority to non-material goals above their own material goals, but nothing is implied about the relative strength of these preferences as compared with other individuals.[1] That leaves us with two types of interpretations of the relationship between value orientations and political involvement. Although not exactly in line with Inglehart's distinctions, we discuss briefly these types of approaches—first, in terms of the content of value orientations and, secondly, in terms of the social position of people with new value orientations.

The content of new value orientations can easily, and misleadingly, be used to explain different levels of involvement. When people are identified as adherents of new value orientations by favouring, among other things, people having 'more say in government', it is hardly surprising to find relatively high levels of political interest among such people. There has not been, and should not be, much emphasis in the literature on these almost tautological interpretations. A second straightforward link between the content of value orientations and involvement is based on what Inglehart labels as 'remote concerns'. This interpretation has been repeated in almost exactly the same words as used more than a decade earlier: 'being raised with a sense of economic and physical security apparently encourages one to devote a larger share of attention to relatively remote and abstract concerns, such as politics' (Inglehart 1990: 369).

Aside from the Maslovian heritage underlying the first part of this statement, the weak and disputable points are, first, that politics is a remote and abstract concern and, second, the admission that involvement in politics is only one specimen of this type of concern. The argument is invalid if, for instance, people perceive politics as a threat to their immediate interests. Moreover, people can achieve emancipation and self-fulfilment in non-political environments. It is not self-evident that people with new value orientations turn to politics instead of turning to other 'relatively remote and abstract' spheres like, for instance, literature and art.

The most acceptable interpretation of the relationship between value orientations and involvement in terms of the content of value orientations seems to be the introduction of a shift in issue priorities. People with deviant issue priorities are urged to introduce these wishes into the political arena. In this way, values—as conceptions of the desirable— stimulate people to express their views and to look for coalitions with other people with the same views. However, the crucial factor in this line of reasoning is that the rise of new value orientations introduces distinctions between the adherents of traditional value orientations and people with these new orientations. The specific content of these value orientations is less relevant than the fact that changing value orientations contribute to social differentiation. This depiction of people with new value orientations as a minority brings us close to interpretations in terms of social position.

Inglehart's second argument for predicting a relatively high level of political involvement among postmaterialists is based on the idea that postmaterialists are a 'rising minority'. It is not self-evident, however, that rising minorities have a predisposition towards politics. At least one additional assumption is required: this particular minority is set upon improving its situation by political means. An almost infinite number of minorities, such as stamp-collectors or orthodox Calvinists, seldom enter the political arena to improve their position. Looked at from this perspective, postmaterialists are a specimen of the well-known phenomenon that, to achieve their own aims, some minorities present themselves as the spokesman of a 'common interest' or a 'better world'. In this way, with their high levels of education and intellectual skills, postmaterialists can be compared to political entrepreneurs looking for opportunities to invest their intellectual capital. Entry to élite positions can be facilitated by deploying value orientations in an ideological way—as a mask to hide other interests or motives—to gain entry into élite positions.

This kind of interpretation of the behaviour of minorities is usually linked to the 'resource mobilization' approach (cf. McCarthy and Zald 1977). That is, the behaviour of postmaterialists can easily be identified with this emphasis on their social position instead of the content of new values. From this perspective, it becomes clear that involvement based on postmaterialist value orientations does not necessarily have to be seen as a consequence of grievances or dissatisfaction.

Interpretations of the impact of value orientations in terms of the content of value orientations or the social position of adherents are not mutually exclusive. The missing link between these two lines of reasoning seems to be the ideological way in which value orientations can be used. People can be convinced of the moral superiority of new values, observe that the relevance of some issues is underestimated, and become increasingly involved in political activity. Thus, they acquire information about their situation, deliberate about efficient strategies, and come to comprehend what is going on. At the same time, however, their competence and behaviour places them in an élite position with excellent opportunities to use their intellectual skills. New values, then, function as the ideological vehicle to realize a seamless connection between public goods and private interests.

Before we turn to the empirical aspects of these approaches, we have to consider a different explanation of the link between value orientations and political interest. In Chapter 3 we described the main macro-level trends in West European societies, pointing especially to increasing levels of welfare, education, mobility, communication, and the like. These developments may all result in the emergence of new value orientations favouring self-fulfilment and emancipation, which, in turn, has consequences for the level of interest in politics among mass publics. However, an increase in the level of political interest can also be a direct effect of the process of modernization, irrespective of a change in values. The frequently observed relationship between value orientations and interest is not necessarily that of cause and effect, but could be the outcome of a change in both value orientations and political interest which are separately but simultaneously stimulated by the same underlying developments in advanced industrial societies.

At the individual level, education has been shown to be relatively strongly correlated with both new value orientations and with political interest. The relationship between new orientations and political interest might, then, be spurious—with rising education levels a serious candidate to account for both developments. Analysing the connections in this instance brings us close to interpretations of high levels of involvement in terms of social position. Moreover, the effects of the modernization process may not affect every individual in the same way: some people might become more interested in politics while others may adopt new values. In this case, too, the outcome will be a rise in levels of political interest as well as a rise in adherence to new values at the aggregate level. This last line of reasoning, however, takes us rather away from our goal of studying the impact of value orientations on political interest, so we concentrate on the possibility of a spurious correlation at the individual level.

Measuring Political Interest

In this chapter, our concern is to test the simple proposition that levels of political interest are changing over time owing to the impact of new value orientations. Hence, we are not particularly interested in individual social characteristics nor in the behavioural consequences of different levels of political interest. Our first task, then, is to settle on an indicator of interest in politics which captures the phenomenon we are interested in and for which time series data are available.

Terms such as 'interest in politics', 'political interest', 'political involvement' have often been used both as synonyms and as specifications of each other.[2] But, basically, what we are looking for is a sense of curiosity about political matters. This can be measured in two ways. The first is to measure subjective political interest by asking people directly how interested they are in politics. Some variant of this question has been used in several surveys since the early 1950s (see Lazarsfeld, Berelson, and Gaudet 1944: 24–5; Barnes, Kaase, *et al.* 1979: 264–85). The question is not identical in every study; sometimes only three response categories are allowed, and sometimes there is an additional sentence or so in the introduction. But these are minor differences, which do not violate the equivalence of the instrument across different surveys.

A second way to measure political interest is to look for some utterance which embodies a behavioural component. That is, rather than relying on what people say about themselves in the politically 'cold' circumstances of a survey, we need an indicator in which what people say reflects how they behave, and the behaviour is indicative of their interest in politics. The behaviour does not have to be directly related to what we normally regard as political activity but can appear in informal ways according to the particular concerns of individuals. A question that fulfils these conditions is: 'When you get together with your friends, would you say that you discuss political matters frequently, occasionally, or never?' This question, too, has been used in electoral research in several surveys over many years. Berelson, Lazarsfeld, and McPhee (1954) refer to it as a 'behavioural manifestation of interest', which makes the point that, in using this instrument, we have crossed the borderline between predispositions and behaviour. However, the informal context of this behaviour limits spoiling effects. While discussions about politics with friends might result from social processes and pressures which have nothing to do—directly—with political phenomena, it is unlikely that someone who is very interested in politics would not say 'frequently' in answer to the question. Thus, people who say they 'frequently' discuss politics with friends are considered to be interested in politics; all other responses are taken as indicating a lack of interest in politics (cf. Van Deth 1991: 204).

Our two indicators of political interest, then, are subjective political interest and frequency of political discussion. Both measures can be used to describe developments in the level of political involvement among citizens in West European countries. Although subjective political interest is available in many national surveys and several cross-national data sets, the Eurobarometers provide for many countries a long time series for the frequency of political discussion. Rather than combining the results obtained with measures of subjective political interest from national surveys, the cross-national trends and differences can be described directly by using the Eurobarometer data. Moreover, we regard frequency of discussion about politics to be the most unambivalent indicator of interest in politics. So, what is the trend in political interest in West European countries over the last twenty years or so?

In Figure 14. 1, we plot the proportion of people who frequently talk with friends about politics in the twelve member states of the European

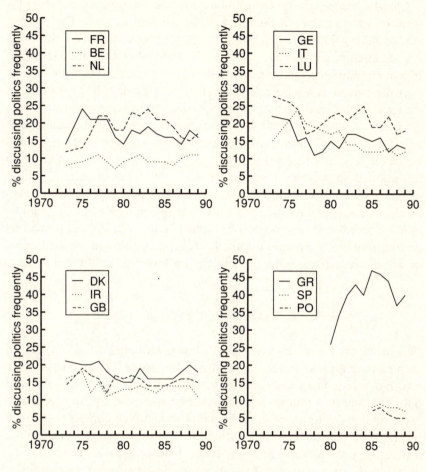

FIGURE 14.1. *Proportion of people who frequently discuss politics with friends, EC countries, 1973–89*

Sources: European Community Study (1973); Eurobarometer, Nos. 3–32.

Community. Although this is not the full array of West European countries, the trends shown here make the general point at the heart of this chapter. Obviously, whether we interpret the impact of new value orientations in terms of content or social position, we expect to find a generally rising trend in every country over this period. So we would, too, if new orientations and increasing interest are the simultaneous but separate outcomes of modernization processes in advanced industrial societies.

Clearly, the trends shown in Figure 14.1 do not support any straightforward statement about rising levels of political interest. The proportion of people interested in politics seems to have increased slowly in several countries in the late 1970s, as in the Netherlands and Germany. In other countries, as in Britain and Italy, there seems to be little change over the period as a whole. The most striking finding, however, is that the level of political interest appears to decline in many countries. This is clearly at odds with Dalton's claim, noted earlier, of the 'unmistakable' evidence of a trend towards increasing political interest. On the contrary: generally increasing levels of political interest cannot be taken for granted in advanced industrial societies. The situation is more complex, and more puzzling, than is suggested by representing rising levels of political interest as a universal phenomenon. So it requires more detailed analyses to uncover what is going on. We approach this puzzle from the two angles outlined earlier, concentrating on the impact of value orientations and value change on levels of political interest.

Value Orientations and Political Interest

Following on from the discussion above, we perform two types of empirical analyses. First, we evaluate the evidence that there is a positive relationship between new value orientations and levels of political interest among mass publics. Secondly, we try to disentangle these findings in terms of the arguments about value content and social position by examining the distinction between private and public aspects of involvement. In both types of analyses, we investigate the question of cross-national differences in the development of political interest as summarized in Figure 14.1.

Our main independent variables, as in other chapters in this volume, are postmaterialism, left–right materialism, and religious–secular orientations. But we also include political libertarianism, which was defined and discussed in the previous chapter, and introduce two further value orientations: new egalitarianism and social libertarianism. Whereas political libertarianism relates to the limitations of political authority, new egalitarianism refers to questions of political and social equality such as the unequal distribution of wealth and the rights of women. The concept of social libertarianism taps the broader aspect of social life in so far as people's behaviour is regulated by norms of personal conduct and social order.

Our starting point is the simple proposition that there is a positive relationship between adherence to new value orientations and levels of political interest. However, the test of this proposition cannot be restricted to bivariate analyses. At least four further factors have to be taken into account. The first three are the socio-economic factors traditionally relevant for the explanation of political interest: gender, age, and education.[3] These factors, of course, have also been identified as major correlates of new value orientations, so we have to control for the spurious effects of these complex relationships. The fourth factor is nation or nationality. This is a far more troublesome factor: almost every comparative analysis in this field reveals that cross-national differences far outweigh any other source of differentiation. As many studies are restricted to single-nation studies, the significance of nationality is not always evident. But when operationalizing political interest in a more restricted way—by the frequency of political discussion—the findings from multivariate analyses with pooled data lead to a clear conclusion: 'Nationality proves to be the strongest predictor of political discussion, and large cross-national differences persist even when we control for differences in education, values, occupation, and other variables' (Inglehart 1990: 352).

The prominence of 'nationality' as a surrogate variable for some set of unidentified structural and cultural differences between countries can be found in debates about every aspect of the relationship between value orientations and political interest (Dalton 1988; Van Deth 1990). This underlines the importance of presenting our findings in both longitudinal and cross-national terms.

Three questions are addressed in this section. First, we investigate whether or not value orientations—or these particular orientations—stimulate people's interest in public affairs. According to the value content approach, modern value orientations like postmaterialism, secular orientations, social and political libertarianism as well as new egalitarianism can be expected to have a positive impact on political interest. An assumption of this kind is implicit in Inglehart's (1977*b*; 1990) description of the association between the spread of postmaterialist orientations and cognitive mobilization. A second question relates to the background variables noted earlier. As several studies have demonstrated that political involvement is strongly dependent on people's social background, we have to assess the impact of value orientations after controlling for the effects of gender, age, and education. Thus the impact of value orientations have to be examined in a second stage in which the effects of the background variables are held constant. Finally, we have to assess the power of a value-based explanation of political interest.

Taking up some of the arguments more or less explicitly presented in the literature, postmaterialism, secular orientations, new egalitarianism, social and political libertarianism are all assumed to have a positive impact on people's involvement in the political process. This assumption has been most clearly formulated with respect to postmaterialism. But formulating a convincing hypothesis about the impact of left–right materialism on political interest is not easily done. So we assume that left–right materialism is unrelated to political interest. As to the impact of particular national influences, evident enough in Figure 14.1,[4] it is not sufficient simply to assume that the impact of value orientations is mediated by national political and social settings. Rather, political and social modernization seem to be global processes influencing peoples' political involvement in a similar fashion in all countries. Consequently, although the strength of the association between the variables under observation will vary between countries, the direction of the relationships should be the same in all the countries examined.

The data we use are from the first Political Action survey (1973–6), the two European Values surveys (1981 and 1990), and Eurobarometer, Nos. 26 and 31 (1986 and 1989). However, not all the indicators in which we are interested are available in every one of these data sets. The two measures included in all our analyses are materialism–postmaterialism and religion. We also have measures for left–right materialism and political libertarianism, but indicators of new egalitarianism are available only in the Political Action data, while social libertarianism is available only in the European Values data. The indicator used for social libertarianism is attitudes towards homosexuality. Analyses using the Eurobarometer data relate only to postmaterialism and religiosity. Finally, as our two indicators of political interest are related to the three main value orientations in roughly the same way (data not shown here), collapsing them into a single additive measure of political interest seems appropriate.

We present three tables in which the impact of value orientations on political interest is described in terms of multiple regression measures. Table 14.1 reveals the picture for seven countries in the early 1970s;[5] Tables 14.2 and 14.3 reveal the picture for twelve countries in 1981 and 1990.[6]

The data in these tables clearly demonstrate that the modernization

TABLE 14.1. *Impact of value orientations on political interest in seven countries, 1973–6*

	Materialism– postmaterialism	Religious– secular	Left–right materialism	Political libertarianism	New egalitarianism	R^2 adj.
FI	0.02	−0.06	0.02	0.24	−0.04	0.052*
	0.02	−0.05	0.07*	0.23	−0.03	0.133*
AU	0.13*	0.09*	0.01	0.16*	0.04	0.063*
	0.08*	0.05*	0.05	0.11*	0.04	0.168*
GE	0.23*	0.07*	−0.06*	0.08*	0.12*	0.105*
	0.14*	0.02*	−0.01	0.05*	0.09*	0.251*
NL	0.14*	−0.04	0.03	0.01	0.07*	0.027*
	0.09*	−0.03	0.08*	0.01	0.03	0.195*
SW	0.11*	0.05	−0.13*	0.17*	0.04	0.070*
	0.09*	0.03	−0.05	0.11*	0.04	0.208*
GB	0.00	−0.03	−0.06*	0.13*	0.10*	0.026*
	0.00	−0.03	−0.01	0.13*	0.10*	0.098*
IT	0.30*	0.15*	−0.03	0.11*	0.04	0.174*
	0.18*	0.08*	0.01	0.08*	0.07*	0.300*

*$p \leq 0.05$

Note: The first row shows beta weights before social background variables have been included in the model; the second row shows beta weights for the final models.

Source: Political Action (1973–6).

hypothesis is confirmed in some instances, but refuted in others. Not surprisingly, the variable most consistently and strongly related to political interest is postmaterialism. Only in a few instances is adherence to postmaterialist value orientations not a significant predictor of political interest. The exceptions are Finland and Britain in 1973–6, and Ireland in 1990. The size of the beta weights, shown in the first column of the three tables, indicates that postmaterialist value orientations are important determinants of political interest in almost every instance. It should be noted, however, that the impact of postmaterialism differs somewhat from one country to another, and at different points in time. Since the incentives to become politically involved are not independent of the peculiarities of particular political circumstances, this result is by no means surprising. None the less, Inglehart's assumption of a close relationship between postmaterialism and political involvement is clearly in line with the data reported in these tables.

TABLE 14.2. *Impact of value orientations on political interest in twelve countries, 1981*

	Materialism–postmaterialism	Religious–secular	Left–right materialism	Political libertarianism	Social libertarianism	R^2 adj.
DK	0.16*	−0.12*	0.04	0.02	0.17*	0.071*
	0.13*	−0.14*	0.07	0.04	0.15*	0.124*
IC	0.22*	−0.03*	−0.06	−0.06	0.07	0.062*
	0.18*	−0.02	−0.02	−0.04	0.09*	0.150*
NO	0.22*	−0.06*	−0.03	0.02	0.14*	0.075*
	0.17*	−0.09*	0.02	0.01	0.12*	0.154*
SV	0.11*	−0.08*	−0.01	0.02	0.11*	0.020*
	0.09*	−0.06	0.03	0.01	0.11*	0.042*
BE	0.19*	−0.10*	−0.06	0.03	0.13*	0.061*
	0.15*	−0.10*	−0.01	0.05	0.11*	0.105*
GB	0.13*	−0.12*	−0.07*	0.00	0.13*	0.048*
	0.12*	−0.12*	−0.04	0.00	0.17*	0.134*
GE	0.28*	−0.05	−0.05	0.07*	0.15*	0.108*
	0.24*	−0.06	−0.01	0.08*	0.14*	0.188*
IR	0.13*	0.03	−0.10*	−0.05	0.10*	0.049*
	0.11*	0.02	−0.04	−0.04	0.13*	0.160*
NL	0.28*	−0.14*	−0.04	0.07*	0.25*	0.165*
	0.23*	−0.14*	−0.01	0.06*	0.23*	0.194*
FR	0.27*	−0.08*	0.02	−0.03	0.10*	0.098*
	0.20*	−0.07*	0.05	−0.01	0.08*	0.140*
IT	0.23*	0.07*	−0.01	−0.08*	0.13*	0.113*
	0.17*	0.00	0.02	−0.07*	0.13*	0.221*
SP	0.23*	0.04	−0.06*	0.02	0.17*	0.117*
	0.16*	0.01	−0.01	0.03	0.11*	0.219*

*$p \leq 0.05$

Note: See Table 14.1.

Source: European Values Survey (1981).

In contrast to postmaterialism, religious–secular value orientations provide a rather poor explanation of political interest. Looking at the second columns in the tables, it is clear that religious–secular orientations and political interest are unrelated to each other. When a statistically significant relationship appears at all, the data more often refute rather than confirm the hypothesis that low church integration stimu-

TABLE 14.3. *Impact of value orientations on political interest in twelve countries, 1990*

	Materialism– postmaterialism	Religious– secular	Left–right materialism	Political libertarianism	Social libertarianism	R^2 adj.
DK	0.24*	−0.06	−0.09*	−0.13*	−0.03	0.097*
	0.19*	−0.08*	−0.06	−0.12*	−0.02	0.154*
NO	0.19*	0.04	−0.10*	−0.09*	−0.06*	0.061*
	0.16*	0.04	−0.06*	−0.08*	−0.06*	0.104*
SV	0.13*	−0.10*	−0.05	−0.16*	−0.08*	0.059*
	0.12*	−0.09*	−0.02	−0.15*	−0.07*	0.082*
BE	0.19*	−0.12*	−0.10*	−0.07*	0.10*	0.081*
	0.15*	−0.12*	−0.06*	−0.06*	0.09*	0.128*
GB	0.11*	−0.12*	−0.08*	−0.04	0.13*	0.047*
	0.11*	−0.11*	−0.04	−0.03	0.15*	0.097*
GE	0.20*	−0.04	−0.08*	−0.08*	0.02	0.056*
	0.17*	−0.07*	−0.04	−0.06*	0.04	0.156*
IR	0.05	−0.03	−0.06	−0.09*	0.10*	0.025*
	0.05	−0.06	−0.03	−0.09*	0.13*	0.115*
NL	0.14*	−0.13*	−0.05	−0.06	0.19*	0.089*
	0.13*	−0.14*	−0.03	−0.06	0.21*	0.128*
FR	0.23*	−0.12*	−0.02	−0.12*	0.06	0.095*
	0.19*	−0.10*	0.02	−0.11*	0.08*	0.140*
IT	0.18*	0.03	−0.05	−0.03	0.09	0.051*
	0.17*	−0.02	−0.02	−0.04	0.12*	0.111*
PO	0.20*	0.12*	−0.16*	−0.04	−0.09*	0.092*
	0.17*	0.07	−0.12*	−0.01	−0.07	0.172*
SP	0.12*	0.04	−0.07*	−0.08*	0.10*	0.056*
	0.10*	−0.01	−0.05*	−0.08*	0.10*	0.089*

*$p \leq 0.05$

Note: See Table 14.1.

Source: European Values Survey (1990).

lates political interest. Only in a few instances is the expected positive association between religious–secular orientations and political interest manifest in the data: in Austria, Germany, and Italy in 1973–6, Italy in 1981, and Portugal in 1990. Interestingly, all the observations confirming the hypothesis are recorded in predominantly Catholic or religiously mixed countries. But these latter, positive findings should not be overestimated. The beta weights are normally of a modest size, and in all instances except Austria and Italy in 1973–6, the impact of religious–secular orientations on political interest fades away after controlling for education, gender, and age. Moreover, there are more disconfirming than confirming observations. Finally, looking across the three tables, the general pattern of the relationship is highly inconsistent over time and between countries; in many countries weak church integration coincides with low political interest.

Of the remaining variables, only left–right materialism was included in all three surveys. Looking at the third column in the tables, the assumption that left–right materialism is not an important determinant of political interest is consistent with most of our findings. Although the null hypothesis is disconfirmed in some instances, the pattern of the relationship is very inconsistent. We can conclude, then, that left–right materialism is not a necessary element in an empirical model explaining political involvement.

Indicators of new egalitarianism were available only in the Political Action study. At first glance, the impact of this variable is very similar to the impact of postmaterialism. However, as we can see from the fifth column of Table 14.1, in several instances, new egalitarianism has an impact of its own on political interest—notably in Germany and Britain. Otherwise, its impact is very uneven. In the Netherlands, new egalitarianism becomes statistically insignificant when social background variables are included in the model, but in Italy it has a statistically significant impact only after controlling for social background. Generally, the beta weights are lower than for postmaterialism or political libertarianism.

Measures of political libertarianism were included in all three surveys, although the items used for measuring this attitude were not the same. While support for libertarian political values comes close to postmaterialism as a determinant of political interest in 1973–6 (Table 14.1), this was by no means the case in 1981 and 1990. As Tables 14.2 and 14.3 show, in most countries the relationship between political libertarianism and political interest is weak and inconsistent. As to the impact of social libertarianism, the pattern is less clear and consistent than for postmaterialism. Even so, social libertarianism turns out to be particularly involved in political life in Belgium, Ireland, the Netherlands, Italy, and Spain (see Tables 14.2 and 14.3). In contrast, the relationship evident in Norway and Sweden in 1981 is reversed in 1990. Thus, apart from postmaterialist value orientations and political libertarianism (as measured in 1973–6), adherence to libertarian social values seems to be the most important of the predictors of political involvement included in our analyses.

To sum up: some value orientations are clearly relevant for involvement in political life. Postmaterialism stands out as a variable closely associated with political interest, and social libertarianism comes close to it. But the role played by the other orientations is, at best, ambiguous—even irrelevant—in determining levels of political interest. Consequently, the joint impact of value orientations on political interest—as measured by the adjusted coefficient of determination shown in the last column of the three tables—varies considerably. On the one hand, in Britain, Ireland, and Sweden, value orientations can be discounted as determinants of political interest. On the other hand, except in 1990, value orientations are important for understanding why people become politically involved in Italy and Germany. In other words, the results clearly diverge between countries, and the models do not seem very impressive in identifying the major explanatory factors in levels of political interest. In all, when we take into account the total variance explained, the joint impact of value orientations on political interest appears to be modest in every country.

Private and Public Aspects

We noted earlier that the positive relationship between value orientations and political interest can be interpreted either in terms of the content of these value orientations or in terms of the social position of the people adhering to these particular values. These two interpretations cannot be disentangled empirically in a straightforward way. Instead, we will examine the consequences of a distinction between private and public aspects of involvement to see whether or not political interest is associated with different types of social involvement.

The assumption that postmaterialism enhances political involvement is not the only hypothesis implied in Inglehart's concept of value change. In modern societies, politics is a domain of social life competing with other life interests for people's attention and engagement. Owing to its initial foundation in Maslow's (1954) theory of a needs hierarchy, entailing more or less precise assertions about the relative priority of several life domains for individuals, we can derive some hypotheses from Inglehart's discussion of the primacy of private and public concerns among people with different value orientations. According to the Inglehart/Maslovian hypotheses, postmaterialists will generally be more interested in public affairs than materialists. This refers not only to political life in the narrower sense, but also to a greater concern with public affairs such as social problems, environmental protection, Third World problems, and science, for example. Materialists, on the other hand, will be more concerned about private concerns like income, family life, and so on. Hypotheses about other life domains, particularly leisure activities such as sports, arts, and culture, are less readily formulated. These kinds of activities, although in part private in nature, may also engage self-fulfilment aspirations and, consequently, may be positively related to postmaterialist values.

Since the available data are not well fitted to the distinction between public and private—political and non-political—areas of social life, we might approach this question from a different direction, examining the impact of value orientations on interest in the issues of 'old politics' and 'new politics'. As several authors have shown, value orientations are linked to issue preferences in a way which distinguishes between the domains of new and old politics (cf. Baker, Dalton, and Hildebrandt 1981; Kunz, Gabriel, and Brettschneider 1993). Consequently, post-materialists can be expected to be preoccupied with the concerns of new politics, such as the environment and the Third World.

Data for testing our hypotheses are available for all EC countries from Eurobarometers, Nos. 26 and 31 (1986 and 1989), in which respondents were asked to report their concern about several areas of social and political life. However, since the items were not the same in both surveys, the results cannot be directly compared. Attempts to cluster the life domains using factor analysis and discriminant analysis proved unsatisfactory as none of the results could be interpreted in any theoretically meaningful way. As these efforts to reduce the information to a few important dimensions failed, the data presented in Table 14.4 are based on ordinary multiple regression analyses, using the various types of interests as dependent variables with postmaterialism as the explanatory variable.[7] In the first step of the analysis, only postmaterialism was included as an explanatory variable. After computing the results for a pure value model, we again introduced age, gender, education, and—where possible—social class as control variables.

The first assumption to be tested is that postmaterialists are generally more interested in public life, whatever the matter might be. As a look

TABLE 14.4. *Impact of postmaterialism on interest in several life domains in eleven countries, 1986 and 1989*

	DK	BE	GB	GE	IR	NL	FR	GR	IT	PO	SP
1986											
National politics	+	o	+	o	o	+	+	(+)	(+)	+	+
Social problems	+	+	+	+	o	+	+	o	+	+	(+)
Environmental protection	+	o	o	+	o	+	o	o	(+)	+	(+)
International politics	+	o	+	o	o	+	+	+	+	+	+
Third World	+	+	+	+	o	+	+	+	+	+	(+)
Science and technology	+	(+)	(+)	o	o	o	(+)	(+)	+	(+)	(+)
Arts and entertainment	o	o	o	o	o	(+)	o	+	o	(+)	+
Sports	o	o	o	−	<−>	<−>	o	(+)	o	o	o
1989											
Political news	+	+	+	+	+	+	+	o	+	+	+
New inventions	(+)	+	(+)	+	+	+	+	(+)	+	+	+
New discoveries	+	(+)	o	+	+	+	(+)	(+)	+	(+)	+
New medical discoveries	o	o	o	+	+	o	o	o	(+)	(+)	+
New films	+	o	(+)	+	(+)	(+)	(+)	(+)	(+)	+	+
Sports, news	−	o	o	o	o	o	o	o	(+)	+	(+)

o	Not significant at the 0.05 level
+/−	Statistically significant positive or negative relationship
(+)	Statistically significant positive relationship even when social background variables are held constant
<−>	Statistically significant negative relationship only when social background variables are held constant

Note: Unstandardized regression coefficients are used for assessing the impact of postmaterialism.

Sources: Eurobarometer, Nos. 26 and 31.

at Table 14.4 makes obvious, this hypothesis is largely supported by the data. There are only four instances in which materialists are more interested in a particular matter than postmaterialists, and all these instances relate to sports—a life domain that is largely nonpolitical. Materialists showed above average interest in sport in Germany, Ireland, and the Netherlands in 1986, and Denmark in 1989. However, in Ireland and the Netherlands the relationship became statistically insignificant only after social background variables were held constant.

Turning to the domains more evidently related to politics and public life, national politics was clearly a focus of attention for postmaterialists. Apart from a few exceptions, postmaterialist value orientations are positively related to interest in national politics in both 1986 and 1989. This is consistent with the data presented earlier showing the impact of value orientations on political interest. Exceptions from that general pattern, where postmaterialist value orientations made no difference to people's involvement in politics, are found in Belgium, Germany, and Ireland in 1986, and Greece in 1989. In 1986, in Greece and Italy, postmaterialism only impinged on interest in politics when education, gender, and age were excluded from the model.

Much the same applies to other life domains. In 1986, postmaterialists were clearly more interested in social problems, international politics, and Third World problems than other people. Nevertheless, the assumption that this pattern reflects the salience of new politics issues to postmaterialists is not unambiguously supported by the data. While postmaterialists show above average interest in Third World problems in all countries except Ireland—and Spain when social background is held constant—this does not apply to environmental issues. Perhaps this rather surprising result reflects the fact that environmental protection has become an issue relevant to almost everyone in the Western world, so the new politics aspect originally evident in environmentalism has increasingly faded away over the years (cf. Kunz, Gabriel, and Brettschneider 1993).

Several items in both Eurobarometer surveys refer to scientific and technological progress, discoveries, and inventions. However, the way attitudes to science and technology are related to postmaterialism is not self-evident. On the one hand, as people of progressive outlook, postmaterialists might be expected to be strongly in favour of innovation and the rational, scientific organization of social life. On the other hand, postmaterialism also entails scepticism about several aspects of science, and protest against nuclear energy and other developments detrimental to the natural environment are a major feature of the new social movements. These movements, in turn, have their ideological roots in postmaterialism (see Chapter 15). Thus, as we might expect, the evidence about the impact of postmaterialism on the salience of science, inventions, and discoveries is mixed. Returning to Table 14.4, in 1986 there is a statistically significant relationship between postmaterialism and the 'science' variables in all countries except Germany, Ireland, and the Netherlands, but in most instances it disappears after the social background variables, particularly education, are included in the analysis. The impact of postmaterialism is more marked in 1989, but again, in several countries, this is attributable to the higher levels of education among postmaterialists compared to the population at large. Interestingly, although postmaterialism is clearly linked to attitudes to science and inventions, this does not apply to medical discoveries.

Finally, the way value orientations relate to cultural matters deserves some attention. According to the Maslovian needs hierarchy—in which postmaterialism originates conceptually—postmaterialism is rooted in higher-order needs which have a cultural component; thus, postmaterialists might be expected to be particularly attentive to cultural life. The data, however, support this assumption only in part: interest in the arts and entertainment is largely unrelated to postmaterialism in 1986, while interest in new films is only exceptionally linked to postmaterialist value orientations in 1989.

A large number of comparative surveys conducted at various times in several different countries supports the general claim that postmaterialism is an important factor in explaining why people become involved in politics (cf. Van Deth 1990; Gabriel 1986: 186ff.). Inglehart (1977*b*; 1990) has made this point frequently and our evidence does not contradict him on this point. Moreover, postmaterialism is related not only to interest in politics but, more widely, to interest in public affairs in general. Nevertheless, some caution is required when asserting which of these processes is to be regarded as the independent variable. Postmaterialism might equally well be considered a consequence rather than a determinant of involvement in politics and public affairs. The data presented here, however, do not refute interpretations in terms of the effects of value orientations on involvement, so we do not pursue recursive interpretations.

In contrast to postmaterialism, religious–secular orientations can be largely ignored as a determinant of interest in politics or wider social and political concerns (data not shown here). The relationship between religion and interest in national as well as international politics is inconsistent, and the different patterns cannot be evidently attributed to structural factors.

Conclusion

In this chapter we examined the claim that a rising level of political interest is a universal phenomenon in Western society. This claim cannot be accepted unconditionally. The empirical evidence shows that there are widely divergent levels of political interest as between different countries and that the level of interest within countries changes between time points. No general rise in political interest can be observed over the last two or three decades, although this trend can be found in some countries. Yet we also found that the impact of value orientations on political interest appears to be more or less similar across most countries in Western Europe. Postmaterialism, in particular, proves to be a clear predictor of involvement in politics in several countries. This specific value orientation is also highly relevant for the issues which concern people.

What are the implications of these findings for beliefs in government among people in Western Europe? Except for the evident relevance of postmaterialism, no general statement can be based on our empirical results. There does not seem to be a continuous increase in political interest as many observers seem to have expected. Equally, the data do not point towards a decline in political involvement. In other words, if there are substantial changes in beliefs in government they will not be the result of a general change in political interest among the citizens of West European countries. However, the data do contain some clear clues about the impact of the spread of postmaterialism. Since post-materialists tend to be more interested in politics than other people, the impact of postmaterialism on the political agenda is likely to be much greater than suggested by the number of postmaterialists in the population (cf. Van Deth 1991). Postmaterialists are strongly interested in social problems, international politics, and Third World problems. Combining the numerical size of postmaterialists with the relative intensity of their interests in politics leads to the conclusion that governments will be confronted by the specific claims of a passionate minority.

It is particularly situations in which governments confront a passionate minority in the midst of a citizen body only moderately concerned about politics which could give rise to problems about beliefs in government. If governments are inclined to meet the loudly voiced demands of a minority, this might lose them the loyalty—or at least the relative silence—of the majority. However, we are dealing with relative differences in levels of political interest, and it is by no means clear that materialists are opposed to paying more attention to wider social and political problems; they merely have other priorities. In this sense, then, the higher levels of political interest shown by postmaterialists will probably have only modest effects on the nature of political regimes in Western Europe.

NOTES

1. The fact that Inglehart presents an argument like the third one is rather remarkable if one notices that he—for very good reasons!—introduced the term 'postmaterialist' instead of 'non-materialist', and ranking procedures instead of rating instruments.
2. See Van Deth (1990: 276 ff.) for a concise overview of the literature.
3. See Van Deth (1990: 301 ff.) for a discussion of these factors.
4. See also Dalton (1988), Van Deth (1990), or Gabriel (1994).
5. The indices reported in Table 14.1 are the same as in Ch. 13. Details of their construction can be found there in nn. 6 (materialism–postmaterialism), 7 (religious–secular), 8 (libertarianism), and 9 (political interest and involvement). New egalitarianism is an additive index based on V347 and V354. Left–right materialism is an additive index based on V348, V251, and V354. For details of the coding procedure, see Political Action Codebook.
6. The indices reported in Tables 14.2 and 14.3 are constructed as follows. Political interest is an additive index of V244 and V298 (1981), and questions 122 and 471 (1990). Items in V244 and question 122 were recoded as 1 = 4, 2 = 3, 3 = 2, 4 = 1; variable 298 and question 471 were recoded as 3 = 1, 1 = 3. To obtain the value 1 as the lowest point on the scale, one point was subtracted from the resulting index values. The materialism–postmaterialism index is the same as in Chapter 13. Frequency of church attendance is based on V124 (1981) and question 336 (1990) and recoded as 1, 2 = very high; 3 = high; 4, 5, 6 = moderate; 7 = low; 8, 9 = none. Left–right materialism is an additive index of V101 (2 = 4), 102 (3 = 4, 4 = 3) , and 252 (3 = 2.5, 2 = 4) (1981), and questions 277, 278, and 477 (1990), respectively. Recoding, shown in parentheses, follows the variable descriptions for 1981. To obtain value 1 as the lowest point on the scale, two points were subtracted from the resulting index. Social libertarianism is based on V276 (1981) and 6221 (1990), tapping attitudes to homosexuality. Political libertarianism is V262 (1 = 3, 2 = 1, 3 = 2) (1981), and question 541e (1990) tapping respect for authority. Education is measured by school-leaving age; age is measured in exact years; sex is coded 1 = male, 2 = female. For details, see Ch. 13, n. 9.
7. Details of the items used for measuring domains of interest reported in Table 11.4 can be found in the codebooks for Eurobarometer, Nos. 26 and 31 (V20–V25 and V50–V59).

15

Grass-Roots Activity

PETER GUNDELACH

In Western Europe, as in the United States, the relatively stable social and political life of the 1950s and early 1960s was replaced by social unrest, political protest, and social movements during the late 1960s and 1970s. As social scientists responded to these developments, theories of post-industrialism were advanced, claiming that a new society was emerging with new types of values and political conflicts (Bell 1973; Touraine 1974). Offe (1985*b*) distinguishes between the 'old' and 'new' paradigms of politics along four dimensions: actors, issues, values, and modes of action. The old collective actors are class-based organizations, focusing on issues of economic growth and distribution; the projects of the new actors, typically the environment and peace, are unrelated to class. The old values, according to Offe, relate to consumption and material progress, the new to personal autonomy and identity; the old modes of action are centred around pressure groups and corporatist practices while the new can be characterized as protest politics (Offe 1985*b*: 832).

The same kind of characterization of new and old politics can be found in much of the recent political science literature (cf. Dalton 1988; Inglehart 1990). Some theories suggest that a new kind of politics is being created by new value orientations; for example, Inglehart finds strong correlations between a postmaterialist orientation and protest behaviour. But uncovering the difference between old and new politics cannot be confined to the influence of materialist–postmaterialist orientations. Lipset and Rokkan's (1967) account of political development in Western Europe pointed to the prominence of class and religious cleavages in shaping modern party systems. The analysis of class conflicts has revealed the significance of left–right materialism (see Chapter 6), but the influence of religion has been either ignored or incorporated into a general characterization of traditional politics (see Chapter 7). As a traditional orientation, religiosity is often considered to inhibit protest but empirical studies show that religiosity may also inspire political activism, even protest (Marx 1967; Gurth and Green 1990).

In short, the importance of demographic characteristics for political behaviour has changed. In the old paradigm, there was a supposed identity between positions in the social structure and value orientations, so individual political behaviour could be adequately described by social—usually socio-economic—variables. In the new politics paradigm, value orientation is a better predictor of political behaviour than social position. Thus, as the relationship between social position and values has been modified, both demographic and values data have to be included in the analysis of political behaviour.

The aim of this chapter is to examine the significance of social factors and value orientations for people's involvement in protest activity and social movements. We use the standard social variables—gender, age, education, and occupation—and both old and new value orientations. The old orientations are left–right materialism and religious–secular orientations. Materialism–postmaterialism is the principal new orientation. However, in face of criticism of Inglehart's index, we supplement those data with two other value orientations: political libertarianism and social libertarianism. If 'new politics' theory is correct, two findings should follow: first, that materialism–postmaterialism (or political and social libertarianism) is the best predictor of protest behaviour; secondly, that social factors provide a weaker explanation of involvement in social movements and protest than value orientations.

Theories of Protest Behaviour

The analysis of protest behaviour in the broadest sense can be divided, broadly, into three approaches. They are more or less identical with three subdisciplines within social science and are closely related to different measurement techniques. The differences, however, are not just matters of methodology: they concern different aspects of protest behaviour.

The *social movement approach* focuses on membership in a

movement. However, what constitutes a social movement varies. Most early accounts represented social movements as the outcome of class conflict (Heberle 1951) or other sources of social tension (Smelser 1962; Parsons 1942: 1960) or, more specifically, as a response to relative deprivation (Gurr 1970). With the emergence of new social movements in the 1970s, the traditional role of the working class as the agent of social change was replaced by new social movements, represented as collective actors who aim to transform social consciousness. European scholars such as Touraine (1974) retained the notion of class, re-interpreted in terms of knowledge, and focused on the objectives of movements. Melucci (1980) understood the new phenomena as cultural rather than political movements. By contrast, research on new social movements in the United States was dominated by the notion of resource mobilization. The focus was on the leadership and the strategies of organizations which mobilize citizens to influence decision-makers (Jenkins 1983; Zald and McCarthy 1979). More recently, several attempts have been made to mediate between the social movement and resource mobilization approaches (Klandermans 1991; Klandermans and Tarrow 1988).

Methodologically, the social movement and resource mobilization approaches are similar. Data are usually collected from local case studies, or, but rarely, from a study of one movement in different countries, or several movements in a particular area. This makes cross-national comparison difficult, although there are a few such studies (e.g. Kitschelt 1986). In survey-based research, the individual is the unit and the sample is a cross-section of the national population, hence surveys cannot tap the local networks which are characteristic of social movements. The only measure of an individual's relationship to a social movement available from survey data is membership. However, as we shall see below, membership is a problematic variable.

With the *protest event approach*, by contrast, comparisons across time and between countries are fairly easy. The best known historical studies are by Tilly and his associates (see Tilly 1978; Tilly and Tilly 1981). In several of these studies, collective violence (Tilly and Rule 1965; Tilly and Schweitzer 1982) is the dependent variable and the data cover some two or three centuries. Tilly sees collective violence as 'normal' in the modernization of societies, as a consequence of structural change that creates conflicts between groups and classes which organize collectively to gain influence. Tilly regards these events as the way ordinary people rationally try to pursue their common interests.

Some political scientists (Eisinger 1973; Kitschelt 1986) have tried to account for protest events in terms of the characteristics of political systems.

In the *political activity approach*, the individual is the unit of analysis. This makes it much easier to use survey research methods. The first comparative study of individual protest behaviour was Political Action (Barnes, Kaase, *et al.* 1979). After determining the characteristics of protest behaviour, the researchers concluded that respondents evaluated the principle of the behaviour rather than the context in which it occurred (Barnes, Kaase, *et al.* 1979: 67). The various kinds of protest behaviour, together with the affective ('do you approve of . . . ?') and cognitive ('do you think it is efficient . . . ?') components of this behaviour, can be placed on a protest potential scale. However, the study revealed that only actual behaviour and approval of the behaviour could be analysed on one dimension.

Political Action examined a range of protest behaviours: petitions, lawful demonstrations, boycotts, rent strikes, unofficial strikes, occupying buildings, blocking traffic, painting slogans, damaging property, personal violence. The study also included Inglehart's materialist–postmaterialist index, a measure originally devised to explain the protests of the late 1960s in terms of changing value orientations. The study revealed strong correlations between postmaterialism and protest potential (Inglehart 1979*a*). Several national studies have replicated the Political Action items as well as the materialist–postmaterialist instrument and found that postmaterialists are more active in protest behaviour, or have higher protest potential, than materialists (Inglehart 1990).

This brief review points up some of the differences in the major approaches to the study of social movements and political protest. For the purposes of this chapter, it is especially important to note differences in the dependent variable and the research method. In the social movement approach, the dependent variable is the organization or—less usefully—some measure of organizational involvement. The other approaches use the protest event or individual protest activity as the dependent variable. As the analysis in this chapter uses cross-national survey data, the protest event approach is not appropriate.

Measuring Individual Involvement

The social movement and the political action approaches focus on different dependent variables: membership and unconventional political activity. Although both approaches highlight the significance of values, both dependent variables are problematic. Before deciding on the dependent variable for this study, we need to consider the different properties, and the methodological implications, of movement membership and unconventional political action.

Membership is often the only indicator of individual involvement available in survey research on social movements. However, membership is relevant only when the boundaries of a movement are clear and fixed. This is rarely the case with new social movements; indeed, some movements do not have members at all, only participants. For example, the number and variety of consciousness-raising groups in the early women's movement make it extremely difficult to specify the boundaries of the movement. Again, many people contribute money to support the goals of Greenpeace and Amnesty International, for example, but are not involved in their activities.

In an attempt to solve these problems, Pappi (1990) used the notion of 'psychological membership', measured by asking survey respondents whether they were supporters (*Anhänger*) of certain movements. However, comparing Pappi's 1987 figures (1990: 152) with 1986 Eurobarometer data on membership (Gabriel 1992: 580) illustrates the problems with this approach. Whereas Pappi found that, among West Germans, 28 per cent supported the peace movements and 22 per cent supported the anti-nuclear power movement, the Eurobarometer data reveal membership levels of 2 per cent in both instances. These findings suggest that formal membership and psychological membership in new social movements are different. This in itself is an important finding. But it also means that interpreting survey questions about membership is complicated, which, in turn, raises doubts about the reliability of the data. For the same reason, questions about approval of a social movement (Fuchs 1990; Fuchs and Rucht 1994) yield a problematic measure.

Two further problems are the limited number of cross-national surveys with membership data and the small numbers of members. In effect, the only data sources are some of the Eurobarometer surveys, and the 1981 and 1990 European Values surveys. The best operationalization of social movement membership is found in Eurobarometer, Nos. 17 (1982), 21 (1984), 25 (1986), and 31a (1989), in which respondents were asked if they are members of the ecology, anti-war, or anti-nuclear social movements. These data reveal that only some 1–4 per cent of national populations are members of one or more of these movements. Clearly, new social movements do not have a large membership. This does not necessarily imply that these movements have few activists or low mobilization potential, but it does mean that sample numbers are too small to permit subgroup analysis.

The two European Values surveys, however, allow the most comprehensive comparisons of social movement membership over time and between countries. Both studies have data on membership of human rights organizations, and conservation, environmentalist, and animal protection groups. However, this operationalization of new social movements is ambiguous because it does not distinguish clearly between movements and voluntary associations (cf. Gundelach 1984; Rothschild-Whitt 1979). Hence, people who are members of, for instance, nature protection societies count as members of social movements. None the less, for lack of better data, in Table 15.1 we present the membership levels for this mixture of movements and associations at two time points in twelve West European countries.

TABLE 15.1. *Membership of new social movements and voluntary associations, 1981 and 1990*

	1981	1990
Denmark	8	15
Iceland	6	7
Norway	7	8
Switzerland	6	17
Belgium	4	11
Britain	6	7
Germany	5	6
Ireland	4	4
Netherlands	13	29
France	2	5
Italy	2	4
Spain	2	2

Notes: Entries are percentages who are a member of one or both of the following: (1) organizations concerned with human rights at home or abroad; (2) conservation, environmentalist, or animal protection groups. The total N for the 1981 survey is 14,837; for the 1990 survey, 17,913.

Sources: European Values Survey (1981, 1990).

These data show that, generally, membership levels are fairly low and have changed little between 1981 and 1990. There are relatively high levels in Denmark, Sweden, and the Netherlands in 1990, but these are largely due to increased memberships in nature protection associations. In the rest of Western Europe, membership in new social movements or associations seems to be stagnating. It might, of course, be objected that a major problem with the data from the two European Values surveys, as with the Eurobarometer surveys, is that membership in the women's movement is not included. However, data from Eurobarometer, Nos. 8 (1978) and 19 (1983), and from the 1990 European Values Survey, reveal that very few women say they are members of the women's movement.

Clearly, then, movement membership is a problematic variable. New social movements do not have fixed boundaries, and it is difficult to distinguish, empirically, between membership in voluntary associations and new social movements. Moreover, when this variable is used in surveys, we find few members. Thus, purely as a matter of sample numbers, the analysis of membership data is unsatisfactory. These difficulties do not challenge the social movement approach theoretically, but they show that survey methods are not well suited to the study of new social movements.

Unconventional political action is an attractive alternative as the dependent variable for scholars interested in social protest and values. Several surveys have replicated the activity items from the Political Action study, and most studies of the impact of values on unconventional action have followed in the tradition, also established in Political Action, of concentrating on materialist–postmaterialist orientations. However, closer analysis reveals a number of problems with Inglehart's approach.

According to Inglehart, postmaterialists are particularly likely to be involved in politics because they are well fitted to dealing with remote concerns and because their priorities tend to be neglected (1979*a*: 345; see Chapter 14). The first difficulty with Inglehart's argument is why the postmaterialist's quest for self-realization should lead to involvement in politics—and not, say, in art or philosophy. Life-style analysis (Bourdieu 1979) indicates that highly educated people—and postmaterialists tend to be well educated (see Chapter 5)—engage in several self-realization activities. Thus, to validate his claim, Inglehart needs to show the full range of self-realization investments made by postmaterialists, not just their involvement in politics. The second difficulty is Inglehart's representation of politics as a remote concern. This suggests a narrow construction of politics, whereas what takes place in everyday life in the family and the work-place can be seen as politics just as much as the workings of the formal political system. When individuals talk about environmental problems or gender roles they are discussing matters closely linked to their everyday lives.

None the less, if Inglehart's arguments are correct, materialists should be less involved in unconventional political activity than post-materialists. Moreover, if materialists do engage in unconventional behaviour, they should be concerned with issues quite different from those which concern postmaterialists. Broadly, postmaterialists should be interested in general, cosmopolitan goals while materialists should be concerned with more limited, local goals. We can test these inferences with data from the second Political Action study (Jennings, Van Deth, *et al.* 1989) about the goals of unconventional action. Selecting only respondents who have signed a petition or participated in a demonstration, we have divided them according to their value orientation and the goal of the activity. The results are presented in Table 15.2.

These distributions suggest that Inglehart's arguments are generally correct. Political action among materialists, according to these data, is largely concerned with community goals whereas postmaterialists tend to be concerned about general societal goals. But the data do not support Inglehart's hypotheses unambiguously: whereas postmaterialists are apparently uninterested in ecology, they are fairly evenly distributed between concern for community goals, concern for disadvantaged groups, and general societal goals. Moreover, post-materialists appear to be the most active on behalf of disadvantaged groups. Our other worry about these data, however, is whether the findings are still valid. A comparison of Danish data for the late 1970s and the late 1980s (Svensson and Togeby 1991) indicates that there is increasing activity focused on small-scale everyday-life interests while responses to larger social and political problems are declining. This finding questions Inglehart's general hypothesis of an increase in postmaterialism and cosmopolitanism.

Other aspects of Inglehart's assumptions can be criticized,[1] but we are concerned principally with operationalizing unconventional political action. A major difficulty is that the protest potential scale developed in the Political Action study combined actual behaviour with readiness to take unconventional action. Later analyses, however, show that both past and potential behaviour are strongly related to

TABLE 15.2. *Grass-roots activity by goal of the activity and value orientation: Netherlands and West Germany, 1980*

Activity goal	Value orientation		
	Materialist	Mixed	Postmaterialist
Ecology	8	5	1
Community	45	41	30
Disadvantaged groups	19	30	33
General societal goals	28	24	36
N	130	356	264

Notes: Entries are percentages. Goals other than those shown here are excluded from the table.

Source: Political Action (1979–80).

situational and institutional contexts; petitions, demonstrations and boycotts were usually initiated together with others, seldom by the respondent alone (Kaase 1989: 57). Contextual factors are difficult to estimate with traditional survey techniques and, as we noted above, it is unsatisfactory to mix actual behaviour and potential behaviour. As Inglehart comments: 'A drawback was that the scale appeared to be heavily attitudinal in nature' (1989*b*: 93). It follows, then, that analysis of unconventional political action has to concentrate on actual protest action, not protest potential.

A second problem is the selection of protest activities, particularly the item 'joining unofficial strikes'. As only the employed can participate in a strike, this item effectively excludes many groups, especially young people. Moreover, strikes are related to economic conflicts, which makes them part of the action repertory of the labour movement. In contrast to old movements, new social movements are concerned with cultural and political goals. If we accept Ingehart's distinction between materialism and postmaterialism, the inclusion of strike activity in the dependent variable would distort the analysis.

The third problem concerns reliability in the measurement of unconventional political activity. Pierce and Converse (1990) show substantial differences between 'before' and 'after' measurements of protest activity. Similarly, Togeby (1989) demonstrates massive differences in the number of positive answers obtained by personal interviews as against telephone interviews. In all, then, we have to be cautious in using survey data to estimate levels of unconventional political activity.

Even so, protest activity rather than movement membership brings us closer to the kind of measure we need. So we have settled on a modified form of the unconventional action scale as our dependent variable. We focus on actual behaviour and four protest actions: signing a petition, attending lawful demonstrations, boycotts, and occupying buildings or factories. However, these modifications mean that we need a different term to ensure that our measure is not confused with the terms 'unconventional political action' or 'protest activity' used in much of the literature. In keeping with the Scandinavian tradition, we use the term 'grass-roots activity'.

Grass-Roots Activity

On two grounds, we can propose the general hypothesis that the number of people engaged in grass-roots activity would increase between 1981 and 1990. General modernization arguments suggest that, in response to increased state involvement in society, new arenas of conflict will emerge (Offe 1985). Moreover, as Thomassen shows (Volume i, Chapter 13), individualist and libertarian values have become more widespread. Hence people may wish to participate in organizations in which there are more opportunities for expressive activity than in traditional political parties (Dalton 1988).

In Table 15.3, we combined the data from the first Political Action study and the two European Values surveys to show the percentage of respondents who say they have participated in two or more grass-roots activities. Thus, we have observations over a period of some fifteen years for the four countries included in the Political Action study. The data were dichotomized into one activity or none versus two or more activities; this dichotomy is retained throughout the chapter in order to have sufficiently high numbers for subgroup analysis.[2] The four items on grass-roots activity form a scale (measured by a Mokken technique) and, since signing a petition is the most common activity in all countries,[3] the dichotomization generally means that respondents who have only signed a petition have performed no other grass-roots activity. They are classified in the low activity category. People who have performed two or more activities are in the high-activity category.[4]

The expected increase in grass-roots activity from the mid-1970s to around 1990 is evident from the table. For most countries, the increase is so large that it cannot be due to noise in the data. There are only two

T ABLE 15.3. *Trends in grass-roots activities in twelve countries, 1974–90*

	1974	1981	1990
Denmark	–	15	25
Iceland	–	14	24
Norway	–	19	21
Switzerland	–	16	28
Belgium	–	10	22
Britain	6	12	20
Germany	9	13	20
Ireland	–	11	16
Netherlands	7	11	23
France	–	24	31
Italy	8	18	27
Spain	–	14	11

Notes: Entries are percentages who have done two or more of the following: signing a petition, attending lawful demonstrations, joining boycotts, occupying buildings or factories. The scale is controlled by a Mokken analysis. The total *N* for the 1974 survey is 6,721.

Sources: Political Action (1973–6); European Values Survey (1981, 1990).

exceptions to the general trend: the 1981 and 1990 levels in Norway are almost identical, and there is a clear decline in the level of activity in Spain. However, these deviations may be due to specific methodological problems.[5] In all, we can safely conclude that levels of grass-roots activity have increased over the last fifteen years or so.

Protest and Membership

The findings in the previous section stand in sharp contrast to the apparent stagnation of movement membership shown in Table 15.1. They also contrast with the implication in the social movement approach that people who are members of new social movements also engage in grass-roots activity (Inglehart 1990). The relationship between the two is seldom analysed empirically, but, as Melucci (1985) has argued, several social movements emphasize symbolic processes rather than overt action. To get a handle on the relationship between membership of new social movements and grass-roots activity, we have to expand the discussion to include the relationship between membership of other political associations and new social movements.

The general hypothesis of the Political Action Study leads us to expect significant correlations between membership of a political party and a trade union, and between a new social movement and grass-roots activity. That is, following the findings of *Political Action* that political activity is cumulative, we expect to find significant differences in levels of activity between members and non-members of such organizations. Mann-Whitney tests of differences on our data (not shown here) show that, for all countries, there are the expected significant differences (5 per cent level) in grass-roots activity among members and non-members of new social movements, political parties, and trade unions. Thus grass-roots activity is not more often found among members of new social movements; it is also found among members of other political organizations. In other words, grass-roots activity is not a special characteristic of new social movements. Rather, it is part of a repertory of action which is used by members of all kinds of political organizations. Indeed, Pappi (1990: 155) found that only about a quarter of the supporters of a movement had participated in a demonstration organized by the movement.[6]

Clearly, then, the relationship between movement membership and grass-roots activity is complicated. This reinforces our earlier discussion about the difficulty of identifying the dependent variable. Since there is no meaningful way to combine movement membership and grass-roots activity, the choice of grass-roots activity as the dependent variable is strategic. Thus, in investigating the relationship between grass-roots activity and various independent variables, in the rest of this chapter we follow the political activity approach, but also use insights from the social movement approach.

Explanations of Grass-Roots Activity

We saw in Table 15.3 the general increase in grass-roots activity across Western Europe during the 1980s. More precisely, by 1990 markedly more people had engaged in two or more grass-roots activities than before 1981. As we noted earlier, according to the old paradigm this greater activism might be explained by changing social circumstances whereas according to the new paradigm it might be explained by changing value orientations. In this section, we analyse the relationship between grass-roots activity and two kinds of independent variable: socio-economic characteristics and value orientations.

Since the outbreak of protest in the 1960s, grass-roots activity has

TABLE 15.4. *Grass-roots activity among socio-economic groups in twelve countries, 1981 and 1990*

	Denmark		Iceland		Norway		Sweden		Belgium		Britain		W. Germany		Ireland		Netherlands		France		Italy		Spain	
	1981	1990	1981	1990	1981	1990	1981	1990	1981	1990	1981	1990	1981	1990	1981	1990	1981	1990	1981	1990	1981	1990	1981	1990
Gender																								
Men	20	27		25	24	24	17	26	13	29	21	25	19	23	17	20	14	27	31	36	24	35	22	14
Women	14	22		30	15	18	13	28	8	16	11	16	9	17	8	12	8	20	17	26	11	20	9	8
Age																								
–29	27	28	17	28	28	23	18	28	12	26	18	22	23	31	16	19	15	28	29	26	21	33	26	15
30–49	17	32	17	35	21	21	20	32	13	27	20	24	11	24	11	19	11	29	25	41	20	34	14	15
50–	6	12	6	12	10	13	12	21	7	15	9	16	7	9	8	11	5	13	16	24	11	16	9	4
Education																								
Low	8	12	3	10	14	8	12	20	7	14	10	13	5	9	11	11	4	6	13	14	15	24	9	5
Middle	12	21	8	19	12	14	15	23	10	18	14	19	8	19	9	14	6	18	19	28	23	40	17	12
High	24	30	23	37	27	28	24	31	18	34	33	38	24	43	31	34	25	38	51	50	21	42	26	24
Occupation																								
Self-employed	6	13	5	21	13	21			14	25	16	19	16	23	7	17	12	14	27	23	11	32	12	13
White-collar	20	35	23	38	24	29			16	33	20	27	17	28	17	23	17	41	39	43	34	42	26	20
Blue-collar	22	28	10	19	22	21			8	23	18	18	10	16	14	17	10	18	20	30	19	30	21	13
Pensioner	5	11	4	4	8	9			10	17	9	14	7	8	8	9	8	13	14	22	11	16	8	3
Housewife	1	10	6	12	6	7			2	10	7	15	6	10	6	6	4	11	10	18	4	8	5	5
Student	42	29	24	54	42	33			12	30	26	44	40	55	29	35	23	27	33	37	31	34	25	18
Other	23	18	14	20	22	15			14	21	17	27	13	26	15	21	8	20	29	23	27	30	34	11

Notes: Entries are percentages in the group who have performed two or more grass-roots activities. The sample size for the 1981 survey varies between 912 (Iceland) and 2,295 (Spain); for the 1990 survey the samples size varies between 637 (Iceland) and 2,637 (Spain). Owing to coding problems, the percentages for occupational groups cannot be computed for Sweden.

Sources: European Values Survey (1981, 1990).

been associated with young people. The young engaged in new kinds of political behaviour, it seemed, as a protest against society. Moreover, the most prominent protests occurred among students, and many subsequent studies have shown that highly educated young people have the highest level of protest activity (Bolton 1972; Kriesi 1989; McAdam 1986). Women have generally been less active than men, but the growing mobilization of women (Svensson and Togeby 1991; Westle 1994) leads us to expect that the gap is closing. Finally, occupational differences suggest, first, that students are more active than the rest of the population and, secondly, that grass-roots activity is relatively high among white-collar workers (cf. Parkin 1968; Offe 1985*b*; Kriesi 1989).

In Table 15.4 we show the incidence of grass-roots activism among various social groups in twelve West European countries in 1981 and 1990. In order to concentrate on activism, people who have been inactive or have been engaged in only one activity—usually signing petitions—are excluded from the table.

The differences between men and women are fairly straightforward. In both years, grass-roots activism is higher among men in all countries, confirming the hypothesis that there are gender differences in political activity. Yet there is also a slight tendency towards narrowing differences, especially in the Scandinavian countries and in Germany, France, and Spain. Similarly, educational differences yield a fairly clear picture. Although activism does not in every case increase monotonically with the level of education, there is a positive correlation between higher education and grass-roots activity in every country at both time points.

The differences by age and occupation are less clear. Grass-roots activity increases in all age groups. This is most likely due to a period effect. The exceptions are France, Norway, and Spain, where there is a decline in activity among the youngest group. However, we noted earlier that the Norwegian and Spanish data may not be very reliable and the difference in France is not significant. But what is particularly interesting is that the rank order of the level of grass-roots activity among the age groups has changed in several countries. In 1981 the youngest age group was the more active, but in 1990 the more active in many countries are people aged 30–49 years. This may indicate a change in political activism, with grass-roots activity being more attractive to the middle aged than to the young. As to occupation, in all countries (except Denmark and Belgium in 1981) the highest levels of grass-roots activity are found among students and white-collar workers and the lowest levels among housewives and pensioners. However, there are many national variations which are not easily explained. The decline in activism among students in Denmark, Norway, and Spain is particularly puzzling.

The findings in Table 15.4 confirm the results of many studies. Men are more active than women, the better educated more active than the less educated, students and white collar workers generally more active than other groups. But the findings with regard to age are unexpected. That the young are more involved in grass-roots activity is a well established finding in the literature, but there are indications in Table 15.4 that in 1990 middle-aged people were the more active. This suggests that people who were engaged in grass-roots activism when young continue to be active as they grow older, whereas young people are less active. In other words, grass-roots activism seems to be a generational phenomenon. To test this explanation requires cohort analysis. However, as we shall see, the relationship between age and grass-roots activity depends quite strongly on value orientations. Hence, before discussing age-related effects, we examine the relationship between grass-roots activity and value orientations.

We examine the effects of five value orientations: religious–secular, left–right materialism, materialism–postmaterialism, social libertarianism, and political libertarianism. In general, it must be expected that respondents with traditional values are less inclined to participate in grass-roots activity. Traditional values may be religious or political. Although Inglehart (1990) found low correlations between religious values and political activism, we noted earlier that other studies have found some positive relationships. Traditional political values are related to left–right materialism. According to the new politics paradigm, we would expect negative correlations between left-materialism and new political values. Several studies, however, indicate that people on the left are more inclined to hold new values than people on the right (Inglehart 1989*b*; 1990)—perhaps because they similarly challenge the dominant values in society.

Inglehart's (1990) analyses clearly show a correlation between materialism–postmaterialism and grass-roots activity. Many critics, however, have questioned the one-dimensionality of Inglehart's conceptualization of new values. Flanagan (1982; 1987) distinguishes between authoritarian–libertarian values on the one hand and material–non-material values on the other. Klages (1984) has shown that self-realization, duty, and acceptance values are important to understanding political activity. Thus, we use two related value orientations: social libertarianism and political libertarianism. Social libertarianism concerns attitudes towards behaviour which has traditionally been considered immoral (suicide, euthanasia, homosexuality); political libertarianism concerns attitudes towards authority.[7]

The relationship between these value orientations and grass-roots activity in 1981 and 1990 is reported in Table 15.5. Although the correlations show considerable variation, it is clear that political

TABLE 15.5. *Value orientations and grass-roots activity in twelve countries, 1981 and 1990*

	Political libertarianism	Social libertarianism	Materialism– postmaterialism	Left–right materialism	Religious– secular
1981					
DK	0.20*	0.22*	0.22*	0.13*	0.08*
IC	0.01	0.17*	0.18*	0.05	0.08*
NO	0.16*	0.14*	0.19*	0.09*	0.05*
SW	0.09*	0.08*	0.09*	0.10*	−0.01
BE	0.03	0.04	0.09*	−0.06*	0.00
GB	0.08*	0.13*	0.06*	0.05	0.01
GE	0.21*	0.18*	0.24	0.06*	0.11
IR	0.10*	0.15*	0.15*	0.02	0.07
NL	0.22*	0.18*	0.22*	0.05*	0.09*
FR	0.24*	0.14*	0.32*	0.11*	0.04
IT	0.16*	0.17*	0.20*	0.05*	0.07*
SP	0.14*	0.20*	0.17*	0.05	0.16*
1990					
DK	0.18*	0.19*	0.21*	0.08*	0.04
IC	0.07	0.20*	0.14*	0.03	0.08*
NO	0.18*	0.13*	0.15*	0.06*	0.04
SW	0.20*	0.19*	0.15*	0.02	−0.03
BE	0.15*	0.13*	0.22*	−0.01	0.06*
GB	0.08*	0.10*	0.15*	0.04*	−0.00
GE	0.29*	0.15*	0.27*	0.02*	0.12*
IR	0.07*	0.17*	0.17*	0.02	0.10*
NL	0.20*	0.18*	0.26*	0.06*	0.13*
FR	0.14*	0.18*	0.24*	0.00	0.09
IT	0.14*	0.20*	0.24*	−0.03	0.18*
SP	0.09*	0.13*	0.14*	−0.01	0.10*

* $p \leq 0.05$

Note: Entries are tau–*c* correlations.

Sources: European Values Survey (1981, 1990).

libertarianism, social libertarianism, and materialism–postmaterialism have higher correlations with grass-roots activity than left–right materialism and religiosity. This is in line with our expectation that grass-roots activity is related to new values. Traditional value orientations evidently have a much smaller part to play. These findings support the idea of a new politics paradigm.

However, as we are interested in the relative impact of the several independent variables, we need to perform multivariate analyses. Data on grass-roots activity have often been analysed using regression techniques despite their methodological weakness for nominal or rank order data. Moreover, using regression models in comparative analysis assumes that the same kind of model fits all countries. To avoid such problems, a log-linear approach is used here.

The first step in the analysis was to analyse, separately, the impact of the socio-economic variables and the value variables on grass-roots activity (dichotomized). A stepwise deletion of variables allowed us to drop the less important variables. The second step was to analyse a model in which only the relevant socio-economic and value variables are included. The procedure yields two results. First, it shows which variables are important for grass-roots activity in 1981 and 1990. Secondly, the parameters indicate the strength of each category of the independent variables. Thus, the final results are fairly complex. They are shown in a simplified form in Table 15.6, in which only the logit parameters for the theoretically most important category of the independent variables are shown. For materialism–postmaterialism, for instance, postmaterialists are included but not materialists. The blank cells indicate that the relationships were too weak to be included in the combined analysis. As is clear from the table, the variables which are relevant vary for the two time points and from country to country.

The logit analysis does not provide a conventional measure of explained variance but the fraction $(\chi^2/(\chi^2 + N))$ is often used to evaluate this kind of model. These values, shown in the last column of the table, indicate that the models yield rather low levels of explained variance. Even so, we have fairly unambiguous results for the more important independent variables. Clearly, materialist–postmaterialist orientations play the more important role in grass-roots activity. This accords with the new politics paradigm. Education is the more important of the socio-economic variables. This is also expected from the literature. However, it is interesting to note that, although protests were originally associated with the 1960s' student rebellions, occupation plays a lesser role than the general level of education. Moreover, the students of the 1980s only rarely show higher levels of grass-roots activity compared with other groups. The exception is Italy, where education has a minor role compared with occupation in both 1981 and 1990.

Among the other value orientations, neither religious–secular values nor left–right materialism have much of a place in explaining grass-roots activity. Protesters have often been accused of being left-wing but these findings show that, apart from Denmark, this is not the case. Materialism–postmaterialism is clearly more important, and it emerges as a better predictor of grass-roots activity than social libertarianism or political libertarianism. Although this finding accords with Inglehart's theory, it still leaves us with the problem of interpretation. In other words, the finding makes sense only if we accept Inglehart's theoretical arguments—but, as we indicated earlier, we have serious reservations, both conceptual and methodological, about Inglehart's claims.

Protest Generations?

Earlier we suggested that the impact of age on grass-roots activity might be a generational phenomenon. Separate analyses following on from Table 15.6 allow us to investigate that possibility. The proportion of materialists and postmaterialists engaging in two or more activities among different age cohorts in 1981 and 1990 are plotted in Figure 15.1. As we would expect, postmaterialists are more active than materialists, in both 1981 and 1990. The surprising result, however, is the curvilinear relationship between grass-roots activity and the age cohorts. Young postmaterialists have much lower levels of grass-roots activity than people born in the 1940s or 1950s. Levels of activism among the current generation of young people are more like that of their grandparents rather than their parents. This suggests either that grass-roots activism may decline in the coming years, or that it will become limited to certain cohorts.

We can only speculate about the reasons for these generational differences. One explanation could be differences in political socialization. Among older cohorts, grass-roots activity is perhaps less acceptable because these people grew up accustomed to channelling political activity through traditional organizations, such as parties and interest groups. Among younger cohorts, low levels of activism may be due to

TABLE 15.6. Logit parameters for independent variables on grass-roots activity in twelve countries, 1981 and 1990

	High education	Age >29	Male	Student	White-collar	Post-materialist	High polib.	High soclib.	Secular	Left-mat.	$\frac{\chi^2}{(\chi^2 + N)}$
Denmark											
1981	0.29			0.42	−0.06	0.36		0.27		0.27	0.08
1990	0.06	0.12				0.41		0.11		0.17	0.09
Iceland											
1981	0.43			0.09	0.22	0.42		0.10			0.07
1990	0.27	0.08				0.33		0.18			0.07
Norway											
1981	0.21	0.18				0.52		0.12		0.14	0.08
1990	0.23			0.07	0.08	0.32	0.11				0.05
Sweden											
1981	0.21	−0.03				0.36		0.08		0.21	0.10
1990	0.06	0.02				0.20	0.18	0.22			0.07
Belgium											
1981	0.22	0.09	0.11			0.37					0.05
1990	0.20	−0.05				0.34	0.14				0.07
Britain											
1981	0.54		0.15	−0.05	0.18	0.30	0.09	0.10			0.05
1990	0.31		0.12			0.31	0.15				0.07

West Germany											
1981	0.27	0.24	0.20			0.49	0.18	0.17	0.16		0.08
1990	0.35	0.15				0.46					0.04
Ireland											
1981	0.41		0.20			0.36		0.21	0.13		0.07
1990	0.34		0.17			0.28		0.07	0.08		0.10
Netherlands											
1981	0.46			0.12	0.41	0.47		0.19	0.25	0.19	0.06
1990	0.36	−0.31		−0.11		0.43					0.07
France											
1981	0.44		0.15			0.55	0.18			0.20	0.03
1990	0.36					0.32					0.09
Italy											
1981	0.03		0.17	0.28	0.25	0.18	0.16	0.15	0.26		0.09
1990			0.12	0.05	0.25	0.39					0.09
Spain											
1981	0.38	0.11	0.21			0.46	0.19	0.24			0.06
1990		−0.11				0.39		0.13			0.03

Notes: Grass-roots activity was dichotomized into (0–1), (2+) actions. The variable 'polib' is political libertarianism; 'soclib' is social libertarianism; 'left-mat' is left materialism.

Sources: European Values Survey (1981, 1990).

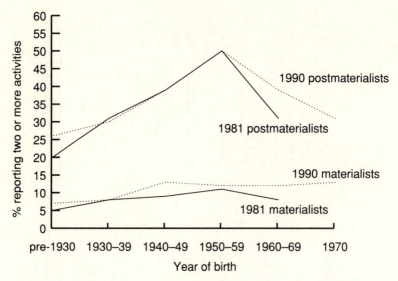

FIGURE 15.1. *Grass-roots activity by year of birth and value orientation, 1981 and 1990*

Sources: European Values Survey (1981, 1990).

growing individualism, generally associated with modernization processes (see Chapter 4). Moreover, postmaterialists who were born
during the 1940s and 1950s had their first political experiences in the
1960s and 1970s, a period when demonstrations, sit-ins, and other kinds
of grass-roots activity became widespread. They were socialized into a
political culture characterized by protest and have maintained this
pattern of activity. Later generations, however, may not consider
grass-roots activity as protest activity. As activism has become normal
politics, grass-roots activity may have lost some of its significance as a
form of political protest. This interpretation, of course, suggests that
grass-roots activity depends less on particular value orientations and
more on the character of a political culture.

Our general finding, then, is that postmaterialism plays a notable role
in stimulating grass-roots activity, but it is most important among
generations born in the 1940s and 1950s. For these generations,
grass-roots activity seems to be part of their general understanding of
politics. Even though there are more postmaterialists among younger
generations, grass-roots activity seems to be less attractive—and perhaps less unconventional—to them. If the level of such activity is in
decline, as our analysis suggests, this questions not only the relationship

between value orientations and grass-roots activity but Inglehart's whole formulation of a 'silent revolution'. Among the youngest generations, the 'silent revolution' may entail value change which is not accompanied by overt change in political behaviour. Or, to put it more provocatively, the 'silent revolution' is becoming more silent.

Our findings so far largely accord with most of the literature on grass-roots activity and value orientations. However, the generational differences question the conventional assumption of a causal relationship between activism and value orientations. Rather, they suggest that grass-roots activity follows from a learning process. The following section examines this interpretation in more detail.

Grass-Roots Activity and Value Change

So far, we have assumed that value orientations are key independent variables in explaining political behaviour. Parkin's classic study of the British Campaign for Nuclear Disarmament in the early 1960s suggested that participants subscribed to a particular constellation of 'deviant' values: their participation 'depended . . . on their having the kind of value orientation which made this case psychologically appealing' (1968: 30). Several studies, however, suggest that the new values associated with protest do not necessarily exist prior to participation but are created or strengthened in the process of participation. According to Gerlach and Hine (1970), recruitment into activism is not explained by prior values or individual motivation but by people's location in certain networks, and learning processes are an integral part of participation. Others have found that participation in a movement can create critical attitudes about society (Myers 1973), or protest can radicalize people who are already critical (Ball-Rokeach and Tallman 1979). Engaging in action creates a feeling of belonging to the movement and shows that the participants' values differ from the rest of the population (Gerlach and Hine 1970; Paris 1989). In some movements, there is a form of socializing agency in which change in the values of participants is an intended, organized process; other studies indicate that participation always has socializing effects (Pitts 1976*a*, 1976*b*).

Without panel data, it is difficult to establish the causal direction between values and participation. Instead, we have to rely on an indirect measure of the prior existence of the relevant values. Inglehart's (1990) explanation is that values are created during the socialization process.

He shows that the causal relation is: socialization → values → protest. Inglehart uses the education of the respondent's father to operationalize socialization, treating it as a measure of the affluence enjoyed by respondents during their formative years.

Both the 1981 and 1990 European Values surveys had a question which can be used as an alternative operationalization. Respondents were asked whether or not they hold the same political opinions as their parents. This makes it possible to test whether respondents who say they have the same values as their parents are less likely to protest than those who have different values. These data do not tell us anything about the direction of change from parent to child. However, in the light of Inglehart's findings it should be safe to assume that, in general, children will be more postmaterialist than their parents. Thus, people who say they have different values from their parents are more likely to have developed a postmateralist orientation. If a socialization hypothesis is correct, we can expect people with different value orientations from their parents to have higher levels of grass-roots activity.[8]

In Table 15.7 we present four sets of correlations. The first two columns show the bivariate correlations between the variable same or different views as parents and materialist–postmaterialist orientations and grass-roots activity respectively. The third column gives the partial correlations for the relationship between grass-roots activity and materialist–postmaterialist orientations among people with the same views as their parents, and the fourth column the partial correlations for people with views different from their parents. Only the findings for the 1990 data are shown here but the results for the 1981 data are almost identical.

The findings in the table are clear. The bivariate correlations are low and the correlations between materialism–postmaterialism are high and of the same magnitude when the relation between the political views of respondents and their parents is held constant. Thus, the relationship between the political opinions of respondents and their parents has no impact on materialism–postmaterialism or grass-roots activity, or on the relationship between these two variables. These data, then, do not support a socialization hypothesis. But neither do these data totally refute a socialization hypothesis: the operationalization is problematic, and socialization may take place other than in the family. What these data do indicate is that a mobilization hypothesis may challenge a socialization hypothesis. Such a mobilization hypothesis would suggest that there is a strong relationship between activity and

TABLE 15.7. *Materialism–postmaterialism, grass-roots activity, and whether respondent has same or different political views as parents, 1990*

	Bivariate correlations		Partial correlations	
	Same or different views MPM	Same or different views activity	Same view MPM/activity	Different view MPM/activity
DK	0.04	0.14*	0.51*	0.38*
IC	−0.05	0.00	0.37*	0.19*
NO	0.07	0.03	0.27*	0.31*
SW	0.02	0.00	0.25*	0.29*
BE	0.04	−0.04	0.35*	0.39*
GB	0.10	−0.05	0.36*	0.25*
GE	−0.03	−0.17*	0.51*	0.50*
IR	0.02	0.11	0.41*	0.24*
NL	0.16*	0.17*	0.38*	0.49*
FR	0.13*	0.07	0.35*	0.41*
IT	0.01	−0.01	0.33*	0.42*
SP	0.13*	0.10*	0.33*	0.42*

* $p \leq 0.05$

Note: The entries are gamma coefficients.

Source: European Values Survey (1990).

value orientation irrespective of the relationship between the values of parents and child. This is exactly what is shown in Table 15.7.

So we can conclude that the childhood socialization hypothesis cannot be taken for granted. Grass-roots activity may lead to changes in individual value orientations. Such an understanding of protest is in line with the resource mobilization approach to the study of social movements (cf. Jenkins 1983). According to this perspective, social movements do not occur just because of the existence of certain attitudes in the population, such as a sense of relative deprivation. Such attitudes always exist. For a social movement to develop, there must be organizational and structural factors which facilitate the movement. Once established, the movement creates new experiences and ways of thinking among its participants as well as in other parts of the population. Similarly, grass-roots activity may stimulate new insights and new value orientations. If so, identifying value orientations as independent variables and grass-roots activity as a dependent variable is not the only way to represent the relationship between values and activism. The direction of causality may run the other way, or there may be processes of mutual reinforcement. However, a more precise analysis of the relationship is difficult with the available survey data.

Beliefs in Government

Finally, we address the question: what is the role of social movements and grass-roots activity in relation to beliefs in government? Ever since de Tocqueville's observation about America as a nation of joiners, social scientists have been interested in the integrative effects of voluntary associations. One of the best known studies is Almond and Verba's *The Civic Culture* (1963). They found that a political culture where the individual is active but not too involved was characteristic of a stable liberal democratic political system (1963: 262):

Democracy depends on citizen participation and it is clear that organizational membership is directly related to such participation. The organizational member is likely to be a self-confident member as well as an active one. Membership in a politically oriented organization appears to lead to greater political competence than does membership in a nonpolitical organization, and active membership in an organization has greater impact on political competence than does passive membership.

Almond and Verba's conclusion has been widely criticized for, among other things, its cultural bias (cf. Topf 1989) and the failure to take account of the dispersion and integration of conflicting interests (Siisiäinen 1985). None the less, it raises the question of whether social movements and, similarly, grass-roots activity, as special kinds of voluntary associations, can be understood as integrative forces.

As we have seen, the frequency of grass-roots activity has increased in Western Europe during the last ten years. It is now a familiar feature of advanced industrial societies. Whereas such activity was earlier considered as unconventional 'protest behaviour', it is now part of the regular repertory of political activity (Fuchs 1990). The objectives of protest have also changed. In the 1970s, protest was directed towards general societal goals; the aims of the new social movements, such as the women's movement, the peace movement, or the environmental movement, were to secure major changes in society. Judging from Danish data (Svensson and Togeby 1991), these movements have largely been assimilated into 'routine politics'. The goals of social movements no longer represent a radical break in society. Their aims have been more or less integrated into normal political decision-making and it appears that movement membership is not expanding.[9]

What are the effects of these developments for beliefs in government? We might surmise that, as the increase in collective consumption associated with welfare states has created many more possibilities for conflict between citizens and political decision-makers, politization has taken place. Protest has expanded, directed towards almost all aspects of society. But just as increased levels of protest may be a learning process for citizens, decision-makers too have learnt to cope with protest. Such an assimilation would mean that protest does not threaten the stability of the political system but, rather, functions as 'warning signals' to political élites. This argument can be formulated in two hypotheses. First, since grass-roots activity expresses protest against society, the correlation between grass-roots activity and confidence in the political system is negative. Secondly, with the normalization of protest, grass-roots activists have become less negative about government during the last ten years.

There are no direct measures of beliefs in government in either European Values Study but there is a set of items about confidence in

TABLE 15.8. *Confidence in institutions and grass-roots activity in twelve countries, 1981 and 1990*

	1981	1990
Denmark	−0.08*	−0.06*
Iceland	−0.05*	−0.06*
Norway	−0.08*	−0.06*
Switzerland	−0.00	−0.05*
Belgium	−0.03*	−0.02
Britain	−0.06*	−0.08*
Germany	−0.08*	−0.04*
Ireland	−0.09*	−0.10*
Netherlands	−0.04*	−0.06*
France	−0.09*	−0.06*
Italy	−0.05*	−0.06*
Spain	−0.08	−0.03*

* $p < 0.05$

Note: Entries are tau–c correlations.

Sources: European Values Survey (1981, 1990).

institutions. So we use an index of confidence in government institutions as a surrogate for beliefs in government. In Table 15.8 we present the correlations between grass-roots activity and confidence in public institutions such as parliament, the civil service, courts, and the like.[10] The low negative correlations here indicate a slight tendency for grass-roots activists to have less confidence in the institutions of government, but there are no important changes between 1981 and 1990. Evidently, grass-roots activity is not a particularly accurate reflection of people's confidence in government.

To examine this finding more fully, we analyse the relationship between approval of new social movements and grass-roots activity. The data allow this analysis only for 1990. Although approval of a social movement cannot be compared directly to confidence in institutions, we anticipate a rather strong relationship between approval of movements and grass-roots activity. What we find, however, is a positive but very low correlation (data not shown here). Combining this finding with the findings shown in Table 15.8 indicates that protest cannot be represented either as staunch support for social movements or as antipathy towards government or the political system.

If protest is understood as a critique of governing institutions, our findings indicate that, at least since the early 1980s, grass-roots activity cannot adequately be described as protest behaviour. Rather, protest has become a 'political manifestation of a general process of societal differentiation' (Fuchs 1990: 18). The results shown in Table 15.8 confirm the impression that, even if grass-roots activity was protest activity in the late 1960s and early 1970s, it soon became a standard part of the repertory of political activity. Political systems have not been seriously threatened by the mushrooming of grass-roots activity and new social movements. Rather, political systems seem to have absorbed and adjusted to the new forms of political activity, and citizens seem to consider grass-roots activity as additional ways of influencing political systems in specific matters.

It may be that we shall witness a decline in grass-roots activities in the coming years. Not only is this kind of political activity more characteristic of specific cohorts but it may be that, with the normalization of grass-roots activity, it will lose its significance as political protest. If this is true, then whereas the concern of the 1960s and 1970s was to understand the emergence of grass-roots activity, the problem of the coming years may be to interpret political systems with much less political activity.

NOTES

1. Among others, some of the problematic assumptions are that the traditional political agenda does not include postmaterialist goals; that postmaterialists see protest as the only way to reach their political goals; that lack of power is a sufficient explanation for protest activity among postmaterialists, disregarding social networks, organization, and other structural preconditions; and that engaging in protest activity is the same as participation in new social movements.

2. For a different approach, see Vol. i, Ch. 3.

3. Except in Spain in 1990, where almost identical proportions of respondents claimed to have signed a petition and to have taken part in a demonstration.

4. As signing a petition is a rather undemanding kind of activity, which in many countries is not considered as a form of protest and is often unrelated to social movements, this dichotomization of the dependent variable is justifiable.

5. A comparison of the data from Eurobarometer, No. 31 (1990), and the 1990 European Values Survey shows rather large differences in levels of grass-roots activity. This is partly due to the phrasing of the questions, but the Spanish Eurobarometer figures suggest that there is something wrong with the Spanish data. Norway, too, deviates from the general trend, which may be explained by the peaking of activity in Norway around 1980. Research for 1975 (Olsen and Sætren 1980) hint in that direction.

6. An alternative to the assumption that members of old and new collective actors engage in different grass-roots activity is a mobilization hypothesis (Olsen and Sætren 1980), asserting that certain groups in the population, such as young people and women, are mobilized through social networks. Such networks are important characteristics of new social movements (Klandermans and Oegema 1987; Melucci 1985; Snow *et al.* 1980) and are relevant for both recruitment and activity (Pappi 1990). This hypothesis cannot be tested with the available data.

7. Political libertarians were identified as people who said it would be a bad thing if a future change in our way of life were to be greater respect for authority. Social libertarianism was constructed as an additive index from questions about homosexuality, euthanasia, and suicide which asked: 'Please tell me for each of the following statements whether you think it always can be justified, can never be justified or something in between'. Any answers except 'Never be justified' were classified as social libertarian. Factor analysis showed that these items are one-dimensional. Left–right materialism was constructed as an additive index from three questions. (1) 'One of two secretaries who do practically the same job finds out that the other one earns £10 more than she does. She complains to her boss. He says, quite rightly, that the other secretary is quicker, more efficient and more reliable at her job. In your opinion is it fair or not fair that one secretary is paid more than the other?' Answer: Fair. (2) 'There is a lot of discussion about how business and industry should be managed. Which of these four statements comes closest to your opinion?' Answer: The owners should run their business or appoint the managers. (3) 'Which of these two statements comes closest to your own opinion: A: I find that both freedom and equality are important. But if I were to make up my mind for one or the other, I would consider personal freedom more

important, that is, everyone can live in freedom and develop without hinderance. B: Certainly both freedom and equality are important. But if I were to make up my mind for one of the two, I would consider equality more important, that is nobody is underprivileged and that social class differences are not so strong.' Answer: A. Three positive answers to these questions are classed as a right-materialist orientation; no positive answers as a left-materialist orientation. Factor analysis showed that these items are one dimensional.

8. This interpretation assumes that political values actually are rather similar between parents and children. Studies by Glass, Bengtson, and Dunham (1986) and Jennings and Niemi (1981) suggest that there is a moderate similarity but this declines with age. Glass *et al.* (1986: 695) also show that the child influences the political attitudes of the parents, but this influence, although substantial, is smaller than the influence from parent to child. This is true for all age groups but does not hold for other, non-political values. The direction of the influence between parent and child cannot be tested with data from the 1981 and 1990 European Values Survey.

9. Except in the Scandinavian countries and the Netherlands, see Table 15.1. As noted, this may be due to a weakness in the formulation of the questionnaire.

10. Confidence in institutions is an additive index constructed from the answer 'a great deal' to a multi-item question asking how much confidence the respondent has in the following: parliament, civil service, armed forces, educational system, legal system, police. Factor analysis showed that these items are one-dimensional.

16

Electoral Participation

SAMI BORG

For the overwhelming majority of citizens in Western democracies, casting a vote is the most regular and the most frequent mode of political participation. The rise of unconventional types of political action in recent decades has not altered this observation. On the contrary: most citizens still use their right to vote as the principal way of expressing their political preferences.

In many West European countries universal suffrage was adopted after the First World War. In France, Italy, and Belgium, however, women were enfranchised only in the late 1940s, while in Switzerland they had to wait until 1971. Universal suffrage turned out to be a key factor in building nation states in Western Europe, because it recruited the mass of the population to political parties and brought them into the national political arena (cf. Rokkan 1970). Voting is, or has been, compulsory in several countries, but most citizens probably would have exercised their suffrage rights without legal constraints. Already, at the beginning of the 1950s, four out of five voters in Western Europe went to the polls in national elections. As described in Chapter 3, during the post-war decades, the proportion of the electorate casting a vote in national elections was well above 75 per cent in every country except Switzerland.

Closer inspection of aggregate turnout data, however, reveals a decline in average participation levels over the post-war period as a whole. The fall is modest but, none the less, discernible and, even more to the point, almost entirely confined to the late 1980s. In France, for example, turnouts averaging 80 per cent and more over the 1965–79 period fell to 66 per cent in 1988; in Germany, turnouts averaging 90 per cent during 1970–84 fell to 77.8 per cent in 1990. Although turnout has not declined in every West European country—in Spain and Britain, for example, turnout was quite stable during the 1980s—such change in an apparently well-established aspect of democratic politics in Western Europe merits examination. This is particularly so as the timing coincides with the 'normalization' of unconventional political action.

In this chapter, we look at the relationship between value orientations and voting turnout from an individual or micro perspective. The primary aim is to evaluate the impact of value orientations on the decision to vote, and to compare this with the impact of traditional socio-economic factors. Obviously, the choice of which party to support with one's vote is a related question but, as we are interested in electoral participation *per se*, that question is not dealt with here (see Chapter 17).

Most of the available comparative data cover the period from the late 1970s to the late 1980s—the most interesting period for considering change in electoral turnout. Of the three value orientations which are central to this volume, we focus on the impact of materialist–postmaterialist and religious–secular value orientations. Left–right materialist orientations could not be included owing to the lack of comparable data.

Framework for Analysis

Elections have special social features, particularly the notion that voting is a form of action with high social desirability. Thus, although the institutional and legal settings vary from country to country, the ubiquity and normative status of elections in Western democracies separates voting from other forms of political participation. Moreover, voting does not require the relatively high political skills or specialist resources needed for other, more demanding, forms of participation (Dalton 1988: 36; Crewe 1981: 216–17).

Several scholars have focused on the meaning of the decision to vote, rather than the choice of party. Some have interpreted voting as a form of action based on a sense of 'civic duty' (Milbrath 1981: 201). Furthermore, election surveys reveal that 'civic duty' is the reason most often given for turning out to vote, and voting seems to correlate positively with different kinds of patriotic acts (Powell 1986; Milbrath 1968).

Other scholars have interpreted electoral participation as an instrumental form of political action. Verba, Nie, and Kim (1978: 1), for example, defined political participation as action aimed at influencing the process of government, thus representing electoral participation as a particular form of instrumental political behaviour. Clearly, this is an overly restrictive view, neglecting the manifold motives which may inform voting and glossing over the complex relationship between election outcomes and the behaviour of governments. Milbrath offers a more inclusive view, in which political participation may be understood 'as those actions of private citizens by which they seek to influence or to support government and politics' (Milbrath 1981: 198). But this definition, too, in our view, focuses too narrowly on the connection between voting and government outputs.

Instead of conceptualizing electoral participation as, by definition, instrumental political action, we stress the expressive aspects of electoral participation. By participating in elections, voters may be expressing their solidarity with their families or status group, or their loyalty to a party or to the state as a political regime, without necessarily any thoughts about influencing particular policy outcomes. Moreover, whereas the variety of economic or issue-based models of electoral behaviour may be appropriate to explaining voting choice—to vote for one party rather than another—an expressive account seems more appropriate to explaining the decision to vote at all.

Even so, the distinction between the expressive and instrumental aspects of voting is not always clear-cut, nor is it meant to be in our analysis.[1] Our intention is not to reject all instrumental interpretations of voting but, rather, to provide a more inclusive perspective on electoral behaviour. This, then, is our point of departure for examining the impact of values on electoral participation.

Hypotheses

After noting the stagnation of electoral turnouts in Western democracies, Inglehart (1990: 336) goes on to discuss the potential for rising levels of participation. In the context of advanced economic development, increasing mass political participation can be expected for three reasons: generally rising levels of education; social norms concerning women's participation have become more permissive; and, thirdly, the shift to postmaterialist values encourages people to devote more time and energy to politics. On these grounds, we might anticipate a general increase in participation among the electorates of advanced industrial societies. Moreover, in view of Inglehart's more general argument about the generational nature of value change, we would expect the third reason—the shift to postmaterialist orientations—to stimulate participation especially among younger people.

In addition, Inglehart (1990: 312) and others (Dalton 1988: 92–3) have linked the shift from materialist to postmaterialist value orientations to a shift from conventional to unconventional political participation. But if we take into account that postmaterialists not only possess relatively high political resources but are also usually young and potentially disaffected from the social order, then there seems to be no good reason to assume that postmaterialism has any remarkable influence on electoral participation. Indeed, this is explicitly what Inglehart argues about the meaning of party choice for postmaterialists. Voting is dominated by long-term party loyalties, and issues of social change—of particular concern to postmaterialists—are not closely tied to voting for parties (Inglehart 1990: 306).

So far, then, we do not expect to find that materialist or postmaterialist value orientations have much influence on electoral participation. But we need to modify this hypothesis in two respects. First, we assume that the influence of postmaterialism is stronger in countries where electors have the opportunity to vote for a party which represents postmaterialist value orientations. Green parties, in particular, offer such an opportunity, mobilizing postmaterialists who might otherwise have stayed home at election time. Secondly, we assume that postmaterialism has more influence on participation in European elections than in national elections. This is in the line with the argument that postmaterialists are more internationally minded than materialists (Inglehart 1977b: 5). Furthermore, we can relate this assumption to our emphasis on expressive motivations for participation; the lack of international loyalties may be one of the key reasons for the low turnout rates in elections for the European Parliament.

Hypotheses about the impact of religious–secular value orientations on electoral participation are less readily formulated. However, we can turn over the coin, as it were, to focus on assumptions about the impact of religiosity—that is, church attendance. In the first place, practically all institutionalized forms of Christianity embrace the idea of respecting the state. Certainly this is the case in the Catholic and Protestant churches of Western Europe. Thus, the social environment of 'church integrated' (see Chapter 4) electors is conducive to voting, especially in the sense of internalizing the norms connected to electoral participation. Moreover, an environment in which notions of duty and deference are strong may serve as a form of external mobilization. The obverse of this reasoning is that electors who are 'disengaged' from church activity are less likely to vote.

Along with this general assumption, we can further distinguish between members of Catholic and Protestant communities. The reasoning here parallels the hypothesis about the impact of postmaterialism: electors who are integrated in church communities have political alternatives which are better fitted to their outlook than church goers in countries without Christian parties. This applies most obviously to electors in countries which are predominantly Catholic (Belgium, France, Ireland, Italy, Luxembourg, Portugal, and Spain in our analysis) or have strong Catholic segments (Austria, Germany, Switzerland, the Netherlands).

Finally, we assume that differences in church teaching (see Chapter 4) affect turnout levels. Among Catholics, the emphasis on common fellowship in a universal church suggests that they are more likely to regard voting as a form of collective behaviour; whereas Protestants, in line with the emphasis on personal responsibility, are more likely to regard voting as an individual act. By adding to this argument the assumption that expressive reasons for electoral participation are more appropriate to collectivism than to individualism, we can expect the association between religious–secular value orientations and voting to be particularly negative in Catholic countries.

Data and Analytic Strategy

In most countries, citizens have the right to vote in elections at different levels of the political system. From a comparative perspective two types of elections might be equivalent. First, there are the general elections for the national parliament in each country held at more or less regular intervals. Secondly, citizens of the member states of the European Union are eligible to vote for the European Parliament every five years. All other elections—presidential, regional, provincial, municipal, and the like—are too dissimilar to warrant systematic cross-national comparisons of electoral participation. Besides, at least postmaterialism is expected to have a specific impact on turnout in European Union elections. Focusing on national and European elections, then, enables us to compare nations without being restricted to a single type of election.

The hypotheses set out above are tested using data from four large-scale comparative surveys: Political Action, 1973–6, and Eurobarometer, Nos. 8 (1977), 19 (1983), and 31 (1989). However, these data sets include four different measures of the dependent variable—electoral participation:

1. voting in the last national elections (Political Action, 1973–6; Eurobarometer, No. 31);
2. voting in past elections to the European Parliament (Eurobarometer, No. 19);
3. intention to vote in the next national elections (Eurobarometer, No. 19);
4. intention to vote in the forthcoming elections to the European Parliament (Eurobarometer, Nos. 8 and 31).

The first two variables are dichotomies, and both are subject to problems of reliability. This is particularly relevant to European elections, in which turnout is considerably lower than in national elections. The third and fourth variables are based on the usual pre-election question about the likelihood of participating in the forthcoming elections.[2]

Whenever possible, value orientations were operationalized by using conventional measures. For materialism–postmaterialism, we used the standard index, and we treated church (non-) attendance as an indicator of adherence to secular values (see Chapter 4). As church attendance was not available in Eurobarometer, No. 19, secular value orientations were measured by a three-point scale of religiosity.[3] Unfortunately, there are no indicators at all for secularization in Eurobarometer, No. 31.

Our socio-economic indicators are age, gender, education, and income. However, income was not available in Eurobarometer, No. 19; and, on account of the number of missing cases, we excluded income from the analysis for Belgium and Ireland when using Eurobarometer, No. 31. The socio-economic variables were selected on the grounds that previous research has shown them to be important correlates of political participation in general. Moreover, age and education have been found to correlate significantly with the value orientations used in this analysis (Inglehart 1977*b*: 72–84).

Our analytic strategy is to compare the results from two multivariate models. The first is the *values model*, in which the two

TABLE 16.1. *Turnout in European and closest national election in twelve countries, 1979–89*

	BE	DK	FR	GB	GE	GR	IR	IT	LU	NL	PO	SP
1979												
European	91.4	47.8	60.7	32.2	65.7	78.6	63.6	84.9	88.9	58.1	—	—
National	94.8	85.6	82.8	76.0	88.6	78.6	76.2	93.4	89.9	87.0	82.9	68.0
Difference	3.4	37.8	22.1	43.8	22.9	0.0	12.6	8.5	1.0	28.9	—	—
1984												
European	92.2	52.2	56.7	31.8	56.8	77.2	47.6	83.4	87.0	50.6	72.4	68.9
National	93.6	88.4	78.3	72.7	89.1	79.1	73.8	89.0	88.8	85.8	71.6	70.8
Difference	1.4	36.2	21.6	40.9	32.3	1.9	26.2	5.6	1.8	35.2	-0.8	1.9
1989												
European	90.7	46.2	48.7	35.9	62.3	79.9	68.3	74.4	87.4	47.2	51.2	54.8
National	94.1	85.7	65.7	75.3	77.8	78.7	68.5	88.7	87.4	80.3	71.6	69.9
Difference	3.4	39.5	17.0	39.4	15.5	-1.2	0.2	14.3	0.0	33.1	20.4	15.1
Year of national elections	1978	1979	1978	1979	1980	1981	1981	1979	1979	1981	1979	1979
	1985	1984	1986	1983	1983	1985	1982	1983	1984	1986	1987	1986
	1987	1988	1988	1987	1990	1989	1989	1987	1989	1989	1987	1989

Notes: Voting is compulsory in Belgium, Luxembourg, Greece, and Italy. European and national elections were held concurrently in Greece 1981, Portugal 1987, Greece and Ireland 1989, and in all three years in Luxembourg. The first European elections in Greece were held in 1981; in Spain and Portugal in 1987.

Sources: Gabriel (1994: table 79); *Keesing's Record of World Events*, 35 (Longman, 1989), 36873–7; *Elections since 1945: A Worldwide Reference Compendium* (Longman, 1989).

value orientations—materialism–postmaterialism and religious–secular orientations—are the only independent variables. The second is the *complete model* in which both the two value orientations and the socio-economic variables are predictors.[4] The complete model allows us to estimate the impact of the value orientations after controlling for the impact of the socio-economic variables—usually the major predictors of turnout.

Value Orientations and National Elections

Before examining the survey data, we look at the official turnout data for the period in question. In Table 16.1, we present the turnout levels for three elections to the European Parliament and the nearest national elections for each member country of the European Community.

The table shows, not suprisingly, that the highest turnouts were achieved in countries with compulsory voting—in Belgium, Luxembourg, Italy, but, curiously, not in Greece. This is broadly the case for both national and European elections. Setting aside the countries with compulsory voting, turnout at European elections is markedly lower than for national elections. The differences are generally about 20 percentage points or more. Moreover, on the face of it, the existence of a party associated with postmaterialist values does seem to make a difference to turnout. Again excluding the countries with compulsory voting, turnouts are generally lower in both national and European elections in countries where no party offers a postmaterialist alternative: Ireland, Britain, Portugal, and Spain.[5] Furthermore, the most postmaterialist countries—the Netherlands, Germany, Denmark (see Chapter 5)—also rank highest in turnout in national elections. However, these data are too preliminary for us to draw any firm conclusions. So we turn directly to our findings from the multivariate analyses of the individual-level data.

In Table 16.2, we present the results from applying the value model and the complete model to the data on participation in national elections for the period 1970–5. The dependent variable is voting in the last election.

In general, the results reveal a mixed picture. Looking at the first two rows in the table, materialism–postmaterialism evidently has little impact on voting. As the beta weights show, the impact of postmaterialism is significant, and positive, in the values model and the complete

TABLE 16.2. *Impact of value orientations on voting in national elections in seven countries, 1970–5*

	AU	FI	GB	GE	IT	NL	SW
Materialism–postmaterialism							
Values model	−0.03	−0.05	−0.06*	−0.00	0.02	0.04	0.09**
Complete model	−0.03	−0.03	−0.03	−0.01	0.01	0.06	0.08**
Religious–secular							
Values model	0.00	−0.03	−0.10***	−0.05*	−0.07**	−0.10**	−0.12***
Complete model	0.01	−0.01	−0.08**	−0.04*	−0.09**	−0.08**	−0.13***
R^2 (values model)	0.03	0.06	0.11	0.05	0.07	0.11	0.15
R^2 (complete model)	0.11	0.13	0.25	0.12	0.09	0.26	0.31
N	1,464	1,020	1,362	2,194	1,417	1,071	1,287
Voting/secular (r)	−0.00	−0.04	−0.11***	−0.05*	0.07*	−0.12***	−0.12***
Voting/MPM (r)	−0.04	−0.05	−0.06*	−0.01	0.01	0.04	0.09**

*$p < 0.05$ **$p < 0.01$ ***$p < 0.001$

Notes: Entries for the multivariate models are beta weights. Voting is compulsory in Italy and some parts of Austria and Switzerland. National elections were held in Britain in 1970, in Austria in 1971, in Finland, Germany, Italy, and the Netherlands in 1972, and in Switzerland in 1975.

Source: Political Action (1973–6).

model only in Switzerland. In Britain the impact is significant, but negative, in the values model but disappears in the complete model. The correlation coefficients (*r*), shown in the lower part of the table, confirm that the relationship between postmaterialism and voting is generally either negative or weak—except in Switzerland. Religious–secular orientations, however, do have an impact. With the exception of Austria, the signs for all the beta weights—shown in the second and third rows—are negative; and the betas are significant at or above the 0.01 level in four of the seven countries, and the 0.05 level in the fifth country. Although controlling for the socio-economic variables had some effect in weakening the impact of religious–secular orientations, the impact remained strikingly significant in four of the seven countries. Turnout in Finland and Austria appears immune to the influence of these two value orientations.

In the case of the values model, the proportions of the variance explained are modest, except in Switzerland. Moreover, the proportion of the variance in electoral participation accounted for by the values model varies considerably between countries, falling as low as 3 per cent in Austria. However, except in Italy, the explanatory power of the complete model is notably higher—ranging between 11 per cent in Austria to 31 per cent in Switzerland.

The countries examined in the second electoral period, 1985–8, are the member states of the European Community. The dependent variable is, again, voting in past elections; that is, voting in national elections sometime after the 1984 European elections. However, as Eurobarometer, No. 31, does not include a question on church attendance, we can examine only the impact of materialism–postmaterialism on turnout in this period. The general pattern of the coefficients presented in Table 16.3 again supports the no impact hypothesis. Only in the Netherlands can we see that postmaterialist values have a significant impact on turnout. Moreover, this impact did not fade when we controlled for the socio-economic variables.

Even in the Netherlands, however, materialism–postmaterialism explains only a very modest proportion of the variance in turnout (9 per cent). In Belgium, materialist and postmaterialist values explain virtually none of the variance. However, except in Belgium, the variance explained improves markedly with the inclusion of the socio-economic variables; the complete model explains 12 per cent and upwards to 24 per cent of the variance in participation.

So far, then, we have found little evidence that postmaterialist value

TABLE 16.3. *Impact of postmaterialism on voting in national elections in twelve countries, 1985–8*

	BE	DK	FR	GB	GE	GR	IR	IT	LU	NL	PO	SP
Materialism–postmaterialism												
Values model	0.00	0.01	−0.06	−0.04	0.02	−0.05	−0.03	0.03	−0.08	0.09*	−0.05	−0.06
Complete model	−0.00	0.02	−0.04	−0.02	0.03	−0.00	−0.01	0.02	−0.05	0.09*	−0.03	−0.01
R^2 (values model)	0.00	0.01	0.06	0.04	0.02	0.05	0.03	0.03	0.08	0.09	0.05	0.06
R^2 (complete model)	0.02	0.12	0.18	0.24	0.15	0.21	0.24	0.14	0.17	0.19	0.19	0.14
N	919	960	928	1,167	981	886	867	911	253	944	904	848

*$p < 0.05$

Note: Entries for the multivariate models are beta weights. Voting is compulsory in Belgium, Luxembourg, Greece, and Italy. National elections were held in Luxembourg in 1984; in Greece in 1985; in the Netherlands and Spain in 1986; in Belgium, West Germany, Britain, Ireland, Italy, and Portugal in 1987; and in Denmark and France in 1988. Owing to the number of missing cases, income was not entered in the complete model for Belgium and Ireland.

Source: Eurobarometer, No. 31.

orientations have an impact on turnout. However, according to Table 16.2, religious–secular orientations do have the predicted negative effect on turnout in several countries. But that observation is based on only one data point. We can firm up the picture by examining data about voting intention. The dependent variable is the intention to participate in the next national general election, which would be sometime in the mid-1980s (see Table 16.1). We present the results, using the same models, in Table 16.4.

The results for materialist–postmaterialist value orientations are again fairly mixed. Except in Ireland, all the signs for the beta weights are positive, and statistically significant in five countries—albeit, except in Belgium, at a modest level. However, in four countries the betas in the values model are not significant, and postmaterialism remains significant in only four countries after controlling for the background variables. Even then, the association is not particularly strong. This is confirmed by the correlation coefficients, showing that the direct association between postmaterialism and voting is significant only in Belgium. Thus, all in all, the evidence about postmaterialism in these data tends to support the no impact hypothesis.

There is far greater consistency in the results for the impact of religious–secular values. With the exception of the Netherlands, all the signs for the beta weights and the correlation coefficients, in line with our hypothesis, are negative. In six of the nine countries, the size of the beta weights are statistically significant, and, except in Luxembourg, their strength is little changed in the complete model. Moreover, as the r values show, secular values had a direct, and significant, impact on voting intention in five countries. These findings accord with the hypothesis that secular values depress turnout especially in Catholic countries or religiously mixed countries with large Catholic segments.[6]

Value Orientations and European Elections

We now turn to the role of value orientations in a European electoral context. Recall that we expect turnout in European elections to be more influenced by postmaterialism than in national elections—owing to the relatively international outlook of postmaterialists. Our expectation about the influence of religious–secular orientations remains the same as for national elections: namely, that secular orientations are

TABLE 16.4. *Impact of value orientations on intention to vote in next national election in nine countries, 1983*

	BE	DK	FR	GB	GE	IR	IT	LU	NL
Materialism–postmaterialism									
Values model	0.11***	0.07*	0.01	0.06*	0.07*	−0.05	0.07*	0.12	0.06
Complete model	0.08*	0.07*	0.01	0.05	0.06	−0.05	0.07*	0.16*	0.04
Religious–secular									
Values model	−0.12***	−0.02	−0.09**	−0.12**	−0.10**	−0.09**	−0.05	−0.13*	0.00
Complete model	−0.13***	−0.01	−0.07*	−0.10***	−0.10***	−0.10***	−0.05	−0.09	0.00
R^2 (values model)	0.15	0.07	0.09	0.13	0.11	0.11	0.08	0.15	0.06
R^2 (complete model)	0.22	0.16	0.16	0.20	0.17	0.18	0.09	0.26	0.13
N	1,010	1,007	986	1,310	1,015	942	991	287	975
Voting/secular (r)	−0.11***	−0.01	−0.09**	−0.11***	−0.09**	−0.11**	−0.04	−0.10	0.02
Voting/MPM (r)	0.10**	0.06	−0.01	0.04	0.06	−0.06	0.06	0.08	0.06

*p < 0.05 **p < 0.01 ***p < 0.001

Notes: Entries for the multivariate models are beta weights. Voting is compulsory in Belgium, Luxembourg, and Italy.

Source: Eurobarometer, No. 19.

TABLE 16.5. *Impact of value orientations on voting in European elections in nine countries, 1979*

	BE	DK	FR	GB	GE	IR	IT	LU	NL
Materialism–postmaterialism									
Values model	0.04	−0.02	−0.06	−0.00	0.05	−0.06	0.06	−0.08	0.06
Complete model	0.04	−0.01	−0.03	−0.00	0.09**	−0.03	0.07*	−0.07	0.05
Religious–secular									
Values model	−0.00	−0.06	−0.09*	−0.14**	−0.06	−0.17***	−0.06	−0.06	−0.08*
Complete model	0.01	−0.05	−0.06	−0.11***	−0.03	−0.13***	−0.06	−0.05	−0.07*
R^2 (values model)	0.04	0.07	0.12	0.14	0.07	0.19	0.08	0.11	0.09
R^2 (complete model)	0.14	0.21	0.20	0.18	0.25	0.30	0.10	0.14	0.12
N	945	948	891	1,196	938	842	899	264	907
Voting/secular (r)	0.00	−0.08*	−0.13**	−0.15***	−0.06	−0.21*	−0.06	−0.08	−0.08*
Voting/MPM (r)	0.05	−0.03	−0.10*	0.03	0.04	−0.10*	0.05	−0.10	0.04

$*p < 0.05$ $**p < 0.01$ $***p < 0.001$

Notes: Entries for the multivariate models are beta weights. 'Don't know' responses (10–30% of national samples) were excluded. Voting is compulsory in Belgium, Luxembourg, and Italy.

Source: Eurobarometer, No. 19.

negatively associated with turnout, especially in Catholic countries. Using the same models, we examine data relating to the European elections held in 1979, 1983, and 1989.

In Table 16.5, we present the results for the 1979 elections. The dependent variable is past participation in elections to the European Parliament. As the data are from Eurobarometer, No. 19 (1983), respondents were being asked to recall whether or not they had voted in the elections held four years earlier. In this instance, postmaterialism is clearly a very poor predictor of turnout: none of the beta weights in the values model is significant; in the complete model, the only significant beta weights are found in West Germany and Italy. Thus, the hypothesis that postmaterialism would have a stronger impact in European elections gains virtually no support at all. Indeed, the several negative correlation coefficients—for Denmark, Britain, Ireland, Luxembourg, and France—point in the opposite direction.

Consistent with our earlier findings, the impact of religious–secular value orientations is fairly uniform. Except in Belgium, the signs of the beta weights and the correlation coefficients are negative in every instance. Although the size of the beta weights fades somewhat in the complete model, the influence of secular values remains statistically significant in three countries. However, here we find that religious–secular orientations play a significantly independent role in countries of different religious character—in Catholic Ireland, Protestant Britain, and in the religiously mixed Netherlands.

In Tables 16.6 and 16.7, the independent variable is voting intention in the forthcoming European election—in 1979 and 1989 respectively. In both instances, we find rather stronger support for the hypothesis that postmaterialism has more influence in European elections than in national elections.

The table shows positive beta weights for materialism–postmaterialism in each instance, and they are statistically significant in six of the nine countries. But the size of the beta weights tends to be smaller in the complete model—except in Ireland—indicating that much of the effect of postmaterialism is carried by the background variables. Moreover, looking at the correlation coefficients (r) in the bottom part of the table, we find that postmaterialism has a direct and significant impact on turnout in only four countries (Belgium, Germany, Ireland, and the Netherlands).

The findings for religious–secular orientations confirm the general picture that disengagement from church communities tends to depress

TABLE 16.6. *Impact of value orientations on intention to vote in European elections in nine countries, 1979*

	BE	DK	FR	GB	GE	IR	IT	LU	NL
Materialism–postmaterialism									
Values model	0.07*	0.05	0.07*	0.01	0.10**	0.10**	0.07*	0.10	0.10**
Complete model	0.02	0.02	0.06	0.01	0.08*	0.10**	0.05	0.08	0.08*
Religious–secular									
Values model	−0.07*	0.01	−0.09**	−0.10**	−0.02	−0.09**	−0.08*	−0.05	−0.07*
Complete model	−0.06	−0.00	−0.08*	−0.08*	−0.04	−0.11**	−0.10**	−0.08	−0.06
R^2 (values model)	0.10	0.05	0.10	0.10	0.10	0.12	0.09	0.10	0.12
R^2 (complete model)	0.24	0.20	0.16	0.21	0.18	0.19	0.19	0.22	0.25
N	987	970	985	1,010	964	947	1,112	343	928
Voting/secular (r)	−0.07*	0.01	−0.08*	−0.10**	−0.01	−0.07*	−0.06*	−0.04	−0.06
Voting/MPM (r)	0.07*	0.05	0.05	0.00	0.11**	0.08*	0.05	0.09	0.10**

*$p < 0.05$ **$p < 0.01$

Notes: Entries for the multivariate models are beta weights. Voting is compulsory in Belgium, Luxembourg, and Italy.

Source: Eurobarometer, No. 8.

turnout. Except in Denmark, all the signs for the beta weights are negative, and they are statistically significant in six countries. Moreover, in four instances, the impact of these value orientations remains significant in the complete model. The direct impact of religious–secular orientations on turnout is significant, but at fairly modest levels, in six countries. The results for Belgium, Ireland, and Italy support the assumption that secular orientations depress turnout in Catholic countries; the results for France and the Netherlands support the argument that secular orientations depress turnout in religiously divided countries. The results for Britain are less straightforward—until one remembers that the focus on class has tended to underestimate the impact of religion on electoral behaviour in Britain (Heath, Jowell, and Curtice 1991: 204).

What is particularly noticeable about the findings in Table 16.6, however, is the difference in the explanatory power of the two models. The values model explains some 5–12 per cent of the variance in turnout—very modest by any standards. However, the proportion of the variance accounted for by the complete model averages 20 per cent—ranging from a low of 16 per cent to a high of 25 per cent. This suggests that socio-economic background variables are doing much of the work in stimulating or inhibiting turnout.

The findings for postmaterialism are reinforced by the results in Table 16.7 reporting the intention to vote in the 1989 European elections. With the exception of Portugal, all the beta weights are positive and they are significant in six countries. But, with the partial exception of Britain, the strength of the beta weights fades in the complete model—although remaining significant in five countries.

Thus, as shown by the amount of variance explained, postmaterialism had a noticeably direct impact on turnout intentions in West Germany, the Netherlands, and Belgium, accounting for some 15–17 per cent of the variance. Postmaterialism had a similar but less decisive impact in Britain, Italy, and Luxembourg. In the other six countries, however, postmaterialism had only a weak impact on voting intentions—even no impact whatsoever in Greece. However, the amount of variance explained by the complete model is consistently more impressive, although ranging widely from 8 to 26 per cent. In other words, the impact of postmaterialism on turnout—or intended turnout—even when largely positive, tends to vary quite widely; and when it is fairly impressive, owes much to the influence of background variables.

TABLE 16.7. *Impact of value orientations on intention to vote in European elections in twelve countries, 1989*

	BE	DK	FR	GB	GE	GR	IR	IT	LU	NL	PO	SP
Materialism–postmaterialism												
Values model	0.15***	0.08	0.06	0.09**	0.17***	−0.00	0.05	0.11**	0.13*	0.17***	−0.02	0.03
Complete model	0.12***	0.06	0.06	0.09**	0.14***	0.00	0.05	0.08*	0.08	0.14***	−0.04	0.04
R^2 (values model)	0.15	0.08	0.06	0.09	0.17	0.00	0.05	0.11	0.13	0.17	0.02	0.03
R^2 (complete model)	0.19	0.16	0.20	0.21	0.25	0.08	0.16	0.17	0.26	0.26	0.12	0.08
N	969	980	952	1,210	1,003	951	916	969	284	997	942	923

*$p < 0.05$ **$p < 0.01$ ***$p < 0.001$

Notes: Entries for the multivariate models are beta weights. Voting is compulsory in Belgium, Luxembourg, Greece, and Italy. Owing to the number of missing cases, income was not entered in the complete model for Belgium and Ireland.

Source: Eurobarometer, No. 31.

Conclusion

We have looked at the impact of changing value orientations on electoral participation. Clearly other factors, such as the mobilization capacity of parties and the conflicts of the day, also have effects for turnout. Thus, our conclusions remain at a rather general level. Recent developments in Western Europe indicate some decline in turnout levels. This is contrary to what we might expect, given rising education levels and greater participation among women—and even the participative aspect of postmaterialist values. In the event, in the light of our findings, it appears that postmaterialist values have little impact on turnout levels. By contrast, at least some part of the decline during the 1980s is attributable to the weakening of religious orientations in Western Europe.

NOTES

1. The 1991 Finnish election study investigated motives for voting in some detail. One group (46 %) gave primarily expressive reasons such as duty, habit, 'the right thing to do'; a second group (38 %) gave both instrumental (benefits, influencing government or policy) and expressive reasons. A very small third group (6 %) gave only instrumental reasons (Borg 1995).
2. The five response options for this question are the same in all three Eurobarometer surveys. They were recoded as follows: certainly not = 0; probably not = 1; it depends = 2; probably = 3; certainly = 4.
3. This indicator is based on Variable 245 in Eurobarometer, No. 19, which was recoded as: religious = 0; not religious = 1; convinced atheist = 2.
4. For an approximately similar treatment see, for example, Kaase (1992). It might be argued that prior causal status should have been given to the socio-economic variables, entering the ascriptive variables (age and gender) first and then the achieved status variables (education and income) before the value variables. However, as the study is about the impact of values, our purpose was to estimate how much the effects of the socio-economic variables reduce the effects of the value variables. The betas presented for the socio-economic variables in Tables 16.2–16.7 show their direct effects on electoral participation; the total effect of the socio-economic variables would have been stronger if they had been entered in the model prior to the value variables.
5. There is a Green Party in Britain but the dominance of the two major parties, encouraged by the electoral system, renders it a minor player. However, it did gain 15% of the vote in the 1989 European election.
6. The negative impact of secular values in Britain and the absence of any impact at all in the Netherlands, however, rather speaks against the hypothesis. The position in

the Netherlands is particularly puzzling, contrasting sharply with the earlier results from the Political Action data (see Table 16.2). Whether this is due to differences in the wording of the dependent variable or represents a real change in the importance of religion, we cannot say. In the case of West Germany and Britain, however, the results in the two tables are broadly similar.

17

Party Choice

ODDBJØRN KNUTSEN

The impact of value orientations on party choice has not been given much attention compared to the impact of social structure, organizational affiliations, or belongingness in subcultures. Two reasons for this might be put forward. First, the relationship between value orientations and party choice may be considered spurious; that is, the relationship can be explained, to a large extent, by prior variables such as social structure, community networks, or organizational affiliations. Secondly, the focus on political issues may be more fruitful, particularly in election studies, since issues are often used to explain the outcome of elections by focusing on floating voters. Our reason for using value orientations as explanatory variables for party choice is to explore the long-term relationship between people's political outlooks and an important aspect of their political behaviour. Examining the impact of value orientations on party choice enables us to understand the more permanent choices about party—even identification with a party—which electors typically make.

The most systematic attention to the impact of value orientations on party choice is to be found in the 'new politics' literature, the contributions of Inglehart in particular. According to Inglehart's developmental model, political conflict variables can be grouped under three headings (Inglehart 1977b: 181–2): (i) pre-industrial variables, which are more or less ascriptive variables such as religion, language, ethnicity, and the like; (ii) industrial variables, or achieved variables such as occupation, income, education, and membership in trade unions; (iii) post-industrial variables which reflect individual-level value orientations, 'particularly those based on post-economic needs'. In this last instance, political

conflict arises between materialist and postmaterialist value orientations. These three types of variables are related in a developmental
sequence because of their origins. However, Inglehart emphasizes that
the model does not imply that the pre-industrial and industrial variables
necessarily will become less important. Rather, he tends to see a
gradual change from the first two types of variables to the third, and
particularly from the second type to the third. The process of change is
characterized as a shift from a 'class-based to a value based pattern of
political polarization' (Inglehart 1984: 26–33).

The emphasis on value orientations as a new feature of mass politics
is not unchallenged. Lipset and Rokkan hinted that the religious,
territorial, and linguistic conflict lines which were the consequences
of the national revolution were conflicts over values and cultural
identities, while the conflicts arising with the industrial revolution
were primarily struggles between economic interests more directly
anchored in structural variables (Lipset and Rokkan 1967: 18–19).
Following their argument, we would not expect conflicts centred
around value orientations to be exclusively associated with advanced
industrial societies.

The focus of this chapter is the impact on party choice of the three
value orientations central to this volume: religious–secular, left–right
materialism, and materialism–postmaterialism. These value orientations might be thought of as representing, although not exclusively,
the pre-industrial, industrial, and post-industrial stages of development
in West European societies. We do not compare the impact of value
orientations with the impact of other types of variables (see Chapter
18). Hence the approach is bivariate. Our first research task is to
evaluate, comparatively, the extent to which the three sets of value
orientations have an impact on party preference across Western Europe.
Our second task is to explore how voters for different party families are
arrayed according to the three sets of value orientations.

Data and Research Strategy

The dependent variable is party choice which has been measured by
rather different questions in the various data sources.[1] We used three
types of question: voting intention 'if a general election was held
tomorrow'; or actual vote if using data from national election studies;
or, if these questions were not available, respondents' closest party.

We use mean scores on the scales for the three sets of value orientations among voters for different parties. The strength of the relationships between value orientations and party choice are measured by the eta coefficient from analysis of variance, and multiple classification analysis. This coefficient is obtained by reversing the causal order between party preference and the independent variables, treating party preference as the independent variable. The eta coefficient is identical to Pearson's *r* between party preference and the value orientation scales when the categories on the party choice variable are given their mean scores on the scales. In formulating the hypotheses and in presenting the results, we first discuss the anticipated impact of the three value orientations over time and cross-nationally. We then analyse the placement of various party families.

Religious–Secular Value Orientations

The religious cleavage is primarily a conflict over values and cultural identities, although it is firmly rooted in institutional forces, such as affiliation to a church and various member organizations. Conflicts over religion defined the structure of élite conflicts and political alliances in the late nineteenth century, and the emerging political parties often defined themselves in relation to religious interests—Catholic or Protestant, religious or secular. The religious cleavage was institutionalized early in the twentieth century and became a dominant feature of the alignments of 'old politics' (Dalton 1988: 160–1).

Empirical research on voting behaviour has underscored the importance of the religious cleavage. In an early study of seventeen Western democracies Rose and Urwin (1969) showed that religion provided the basis of cohesion in a greater number of parties than any other cleavage variable, including social class. Contrary to Lipset's (1960: 220) claim for the primacy of the class factor in democratic politics, Rose and Urwin concluded: 'religious divisions, not class, are the main social basis of parties in the Western world today' (Rose and Urwin 1969: 12). The persisting importance of the religious cleavage in Catholic and religiously mixed countries has been documented subsequently in national, cross-national, and longitudinal studies (see Books 1980; Dalton 1988: 160–9; Pappi 1984; Michelat and Simon 1977*b*; Lewis-Beck 1984: 436–9). Using the 1970 European Community Survey, Inglehart (1977*b*: ch. 9) found that religion was more important than any other structural cleavages in all Catholic and religiously mixed countries; only in Britain was class more important than religion. However, these studies dichotomized party choice into two broad categories, 'right' and 'left'. Consequently, they seldom allow for examining whether or not the religious cleavage cuts across the left–right division of parties.

In formulating hypotheses about the changing impact of religious value orientations, our point of departure is the secularization process which has affected all Western European countries. There is no doubt that the secularization process has resulted in a smaller religious segment in all West European societies (see Chapter 4), but the process has not had the consequences one might expect. There are basically two different hypotheses about the impact of religious–secular orientations over time; one predicting that such value orientations have become less important (the *declining correlation hypothesis*), and one predicting a stable impact (the *stable correlation hypothesis*). Both hypotheses take the secularization process for granted.

The difference between the two perspectives, however, is more intricate. On the one hand, according to the declining correlation hypothesis, the secularization process may have disrupted religious alignments in the same way as the impact of social class has become blurred. In this perspective, increasing social and geographical mobility, changes in leisure patterns, and the like, have undermined community integration and social bonds of all kinds, including religious networks. The Catholic Church no longer intervenes in politics, ceasing to campaign actively against parties of the left; and in the 1970s and 1980s many Catholic clergy and organizations expressed sympathy with left causes (Berger 1982). Thus the secularization process has reduced potential support for religious parties in the sense that the proportion of the electorate which is likely to vote for a religious party has declined. This implies that religious–secular orientations have become less consequential for voting. On the other hand, the stable correlation hypothesis suggests that people of religious orientation, although a smaller proportion of the electorate, are still well integrated into a religious network and maintain distinctive voting patterns. The secularization process has reduced the proportion of voters with a religious orientation, but there is nevertheless a stable correlation between religious–secular value orientations and party choice.

In comparative terms, we expect religious–secular value orientations to have the strongest impact on party choice in Catholic and religiously mixed countries. Conflicts between the Catholic Church and secular forces have historically been strongest in these countries. In Protestant countries, we expect religious–secular orientations to be most significant in countries with Christian parties which specifically articulate religious values, as in Denmark, Norway, and Sweden.

As to the distribution of voters of different orientation across party families, we anticipate that the religious parties predominantly attract voters of religious orientation. Conservative parties, too, have emphasized religious values. In Britain, for example, historically there has been a close association between the Conservative Party and the Church of England, and in the Scandinavian countries high church clericalism and the conservative parties have been closely allied. Agrarian parties also generally uphold religious values, and their predominantly rural support suggests that their voters have a religious outlook.

The parties which articulate a secular value orientation are principally the socialist and left-wing socialist parties, as well as liberal and radical 'bourgeois' parties. Traditionally, socialism, liberalism, and radicalism have been the main opponents of the church and Christian political interests. In the late nineteenth and early twentieth centuries, in many countries, liberal and radical bourgeois forces engaged in strong anti-clerical opposition, especially against the Catholic Church. After the Second World War these parties largely dropped their anti-clerical image (Von Beyme 1985: 35–6). To some extent, the same can be said about the socialist parties. However, the liberal parties in Protestant countries have traditionally been associated with religious dissenters, as with the Liberal Party in Britain, or members of the low church as in the Scandinavian countries. We expect these parties to have a relatively religious electorate. Although the Christian People's parties have absorbed most of the low church voters in Scandinavia, we expect the liberal parties in Britain and the Nordic countries to have a more religious electorate than the liberal and radical parties in Catholic and religiously mixed countries.

For the empirical analyses, we rely mainly on comparative data from the Eurobarometer series and the 1990 European Values Survey. Following Jagodzinski and Dobbelaere (Chapter 4), we use church attendance as the indicator for religious integration or religious–secular orientations. The correlation coefficients between religious integration and party choice are reported in Table 17.1.

The results shown here confirm previous findings about the strong impact of religious–secular orientations in Catholic and religiously

TABLE 17.1. *Religious–secular orientations and party choice in fourteen countries, 1973–90.*

	1973	1978	1981	1990
DK	0.30	0.40	0.37	0.35
N	870	740	588	839
BE	0.54	0.51 (0.53)	0.54 (0.55)	0.44 (0.45)
N	741	539	487	1,876
GB	0.14	0.14	0.09	0.16
N	1,550	851	858	1,216
GE	0.35	0.22	0.30	0.34
N	1,341	819	765	1,719
IR	0.21	0.23	0.21	0.25
N	848	712	629	850
NL	0.65 (0.65)	0.57	0.58	0.51
N	1,150	853	747	884
FR	0.39	0.37	0.34 (0.034)	0.37 (0.037)
N	1,497	848	718	600
IT	0.47	0.48	0.34	0.46
N	1,153	740	640	1,234

	1957	1965	1969	1973	1977	1981	1985	1989
NO	0.21	0.41	0.34	0.47	0.32	0.31	0.39	0.41
N	1,132	1,471	1,376	1,976	1,447	1,338	1,829	1,833

	1985	1988	1990
SW	0.36	0.34	0.28
N	2,495	2,317	830
IC			0.24
N			446
SP			0.43
N			1,566
PO			0.29
N			694

	1981
GR	0.28
N	627

TABLE 17.1. *Cont.*

Notes: Entries are correlation coefficients (eta). The first entry for Belgium is based on collapsing the Flemish and Francophone Christian Social, Socialist, and Liberal parties; the second entry (in parentheses) is based on analysing the Flemish and Francophone parties separately. The first entry for the Netherlands is based on collapsing the Catholic People's Party, Anti-Revolutionary Party, and Christian Historical Union into one party; the second entry (in parentheses) is based on treating them as separate parties. The first entry for France is based on collapsing the three parties in the UDF alliance (Republican Party, Christian Democrats, and Radical Party) into a single group; the second entry (in parentheses) is based on treating them as separate parties.

Sources: European Community Study (1973); Eurobarometer, Nos. 10 and 16; European Values Survey (1990); Norwegian election surveys (1957–89); Swedish election surveys (1985, 1988).

mixed countries. The correlations between church integration and party choice are above 0.50 for Belgium (except in the 1990 data) and the Netherlands, and around 0.47 in Italy (except in 1981). The correlations are somewhat lower for France, averaging around 0.36, and for Germany, averaging 0.33 over three surveys. Among the Protestant countries, the correlations are generally strongest, above 0.30, in Denmark, Norway, and Sweden,[2] and considerably weaker in Britain and Iceland. The low correlations between religious–secular orientations and party choice in Ireland reflects the high incidence of religious orientation among voters for all parties. Thus our expectations about the comparative impact of religious–secular orientations are largely borne out.

As regards the hypothesis about developments over time, the stable correlation hypothesis receives most support from the analyses. For most of the countries for which we have time series from the 1970s to 1990, there is an impressive stability. However, the exceptions are important. In Belgium and the Netherlands, where the impact of religious–secular orientations is strongest, there is a tendency for their impact to decline. Compared to the early 1970s, the impact is reduced by 0.10–0.14 in 1990. This is consistent with other findings about the declining impact of religion on electoral politics in Belgium and the Netherlands (Eijk and Niemöller 1985: 352–3; Mughan 1985: 328–37). These countries have traditionally had the strongest *verzuiling* structures in Western Europe: that is, religious (and secular) organizations performing societal functions which have kept religious and secular groups separate in many areas of life. But a process of *ontzuiling* or 'depillarization' has been taking place in both countries, so weakening the once very strong organizational structures. This process is reflected in our findings.

Our hypotheses about the distribution of voters of different orientation across party families are generally confirmed. Examining the average score of voters for different parties on the church attendance variable (data not shown here), we find that the Christian democratic parties and the Christian people's parties in the Nordic countries have the most religious electorate. Moreover, there is generally a large difference in the index scores between voters for these parties and other parties. In many countries the difference is larger between these parties and the second (or third) party than between all the other parties. Among the countries examined, the impact of religious–secular orientations is weakest of all in Britain. The Conservative Party does not have very religious voters; and Liberal and Conservative voters have very similar scores on religious involvement. Moreover, there is only a small, but quite stable, difference between these voters and Labour Party voters.

In the Nordic countries, however, voters for centre parties—descended from older agrarian parties—are well integrated into church communities. The same applies to some extent to the liberal parties, in accordance with our hypothesis. The conservative parties do not have a very religious electorate, although conservative voters are somewhat more religious in orientation than voters for socialist parties. Indeed, there is a much larger difference in terms of religious orientation between voters for the religious parties and the conservative parties than between voters for conservative, liberal, and socialist parties.

In Catholic and religiously mixed countries there is a much stronger tendency, compared to Protestant countries, for socialist voters to be secular in orientation. Voters for liberal parties are generally more religious than voters for socialist parties, but in Belgium, the Netherlands, Germany, and Italy, the differences between the index scores for Christian democratic voters and liberal voters are generally larger than the differences between liberal voters and socialist voters. The largest differences are found between the Christian democratic parties on the one hand and the liberal and socialist parties on the other. In France, however, voters for both the large 'bourgeois' parties—the conservative Rally for the Republic (RPR) and the liberal alliance Union for French Democracy (UDF)—are the most religious; so are supporters of the three parties in the UDF coalition. In other words, the religious–secular divide follows the left–right divide much more closely in France than in other Catholic countries. The position in Spain and Portugal is similar: the conservative parties of the right (Partido Popular in Spain, the Partido Social Democrata in Portugal) have more religious voters than the centrist parties (Centre Social Democrats and Democratic Centre Union, respectively).

Looking to the smaller parties, the moderate regionalist parties in Spain, particularly the Basque nationalists, also have very religious voters. The same applies to the Volksunie in Belgium and, to some extent, to the regionalist parties in Britain. The new green parties, and especially the 'new left' parties, in all countries where they exist, have a largely secular electorate. Supporters of the parties of the extreme right in Germany (Republican Party) and France (National Front), as well as supporters of the Progress parties in Denmark and Norway, are more secular than the average voter.

For some countries, national time series data are available for examining changes over time in the impact of church integration on party choice. Although church attendance is measured rather differently in these data, they yield basically the same results as reported above. The British election studies data reveal barely significant correlations between church attendance and party choice, varying from 0.13 and 0.12 in 1974 and 1979 to 0.08 and 0.09 in 1983 and 1987. In the Dutch Cultural Change Study, the correlations decline from 0.67 in 1970 to 0.60 in 1980 and 1985. In the German IPOS studies, the correlations are stable (0.30–0.33) across the relatively short time span for which we have data (1984–9). In those Danish election studies when a question on church attendance has been asked, the correlations are 0.39 in 1971, 0.40 in 1979, and 0.29 in 1987.

Left–Right Materialist Value Orientations

According to the classic model of industrial society, political polarization was a direct reflection of class conflict (Inglehart 1984: 25). However, value orientations were not absent from the political struggle. The conflicts underlying the 'left–right' polarization of industrial politics were over ownership of the means of production, the distribution of income, and public regulation and control in relation to private enterprises. In accord with this model, left–right materialist orientations incorporate value conflicts related to control and power in the sphere of production and the degree of redistribution in the sphere of distribution (see Chapter 6).

Our hypotheses focus on longitudinal change and the placing of supporters of different parties on the left–right materialist index. There are two contradictory hypotheses about developments over time. According to the first hypothesis, left–right materialism will decline in importance as a consequence of socio-economic and political change. Although left–right materialism was important in structuring the polarization pattern in industrial society, this conflict will become less important with the emergence of a post-industrial society. The issues coupled to left–right materialist orientations have become less central to the political agenda and, at the individual level, the experiences which gave rise to these value orientations have become less fundamental. The second hypothesis predicts a transformation of traditional left–right conflicts in which left–right materialism will remain an important predictor for party choice in post-industrial society. Regulation and control of private enterprises versus *laissez-faire* policies and conflicts over economic inequality are still important on the political agenda, and in the formative experiences of individuals. For example, according to issue salience theory, voting is determined by those value orientations and issues which dominate the political agenda and party conflicts in given political systems. Several studies indicate that socio-economic and related issues are still highly salient in most West European countries (Knutsen 1988: 339–40).

Left–right materialist orientations are expected to group party supporters according to the placement of parties along the conventional left–right spectrum. We expect communist and socialist parties to have voters with the most left-materialist orientation. These parties have traditionally emphasized state intervention in the economy, economic planning, public ownership of the means of production, industrial democracy, and a large public sector (Von Beyme 1985: 68–71). Left materialism has also been emphasized by small left socialist parties in some countries. Although these parties advance 'new left' values, they also put great store by economic redistribution and worker control of the same kind as the traditional left (Kitschelt 1988: 195).

On the right-materialist side and in the centre of the spectrum we expect to find voters for the 'bourgeois' party families. First and foremost, we expect voters for the liberal, conservative, and Christian democratic parties to be predominantly materialist in orientation. We also expect that to be the case among voters for right-wing extremist parties, agrarian parties, and most regional parties. The Christian democratic parties underlined class integration and their broad-based *Volkspartei* nature when they were set up after the Second World War; and they have advocated only moderate state intervention and redistribution (Irving 1979). In the Scandinavian countries, Christian people's parties have also placed themselves to the left of the conservative parties. Although traditionally conservative parties tended to oppose liberal economic ideas, many modern conservative parties have overtaken liberal parties as the standard-bearers of the free market economy, hostility to economic intervention, and opposition to the welfare state (Von Beyme 1985: 50, 52). Again, whereas liberal parties traditionally elevated the concepts of a free market economy and private property, in the post-war period many post-war liberal parties have moved to emphasizing social liberalism, accepting the welfare state and moderate economic redistribution (Von Beyme 1985: 37, 39). It is not always easy to distinguish between liberal-conservative and liberal-radical parties,[3] but we anticipate that voters for liberal-conservative parties give more emphasis to right materialism than voters for other bourgeois parties.

To test our comparative hypotheses we use data from Eurobarometer, Nos. 11 (1979), 16 (1981), and 19 (1983), and the 1990 European Values Survey. To examine change over time, we use data from national surveys. The same items are used for the left–right materialism index as we used in Chapter 6; the index ranges 0–10.

The average correlations between the index and party choice in the Eurobarometer data (not shown here) reveal that left–right materialist orientations generally have the strongest impact on voting intention in France, the Netherlands, Denmark, and Greece. In these countries, the average eta coefficient—across the three surveys—ranges between 0.45 and 0.47. The average correlations are weaker in Italy (0.34), Britain (0.29), Belgium (0.24), and West Germany (0.20), and notably weak in Ireland (0.09). To examine the relationship more closely, in Table 17.2 we present the results from analysing the 1990 European Values data.

Looking at the mean scores on the left–right materialist index in Table 17.2, we find that in all countries the socialist and communist parties have the most left-materialist electorates. Voters for the left-socialist parties are more left-materialist than voters for the traditional socialist parties. On the 'bourgeois' or right-materialist side, the picture is less consistent, as predicted. The electorates of the liberal parties are the most right-materialist in each country in continental Europe. In France, RPR voters are somewhat more right-materialist than UDF voters, but the differences are small. There are no consistent or significant differences between voters for the three parties in the UDF alliance. In Italy, the Republican Party and the Liberal Party have the

TABLE 17.2. *Left–right materialist orientations and party choice in thirteen countries, 1990*

Denmark

	Mean	N
Socialist People's	5.0	143
Greens	5.0	17
Social Democrats	3.7	277
Radical Liberals	3.1	32
Christian People's	2.6	17
Centre Democrats	2.2	49
Progress	1.9	52
Conservatives	1.3	126
Agrarian Liberals	1.2	109
Overall mean	3.0	840
eta	0.55	

Sweden

	Mean	N
Left Party	5.0	57
Social Democrats	4.1	242
Green	3.4	79
Centre	2.6	74
Liberals	2.4	159
Christian Democrats	2.2	26
Moderate	1.4	205
Overall mean	2.9	842
eta	0.47	

Iceland

	Mean	N
People's Alliance	6.1	43
Women's Alliance	5.6	44
Progress	4.4	85
Social Democrats	3.7	57
Independence	2.5	228
Overall mean	3.7	465
eta	0.47	

Belgium

	Mean	N
Socialist	4.6	466
Ecolo/Agalev	4.1	311
Christian Social	3.9	614
Volksunie	3.4	85
Flemish Block	3.3	34
FDF/Rass. Wallon	2.9	37
Liberal	2.2	304
Overall mean	3.8	1,879
eta	0.32 (0.34)	

Norway

	Mean	N
Socialist Left	5.0	130
Labour Party	4.2	343
Liberal	3.6	35
Christian People's	3.1	78
Christian Centre	3.0	60
Progress	2.1	128
Conservatives	2.1	197
Overall mean	3.5	983
eta	0.44	

Britain

	Mean	N
Labour	4.8	571
Nationalists	4.1	67
Social Democrats	3.9	12
Green	3.4	54
Liberal Democrats	3.0	68
Conservatives	2.3	444
Overall mean	3.7	1,219
eta	0.46	

Germany

Party		N
Greens	4.6	122
Social Democrats	3.4	700
Republican	2.8	41
Christian Democrats	2.4	697
Free Democrats	2.0	146
Overall mean	2.9	1,772
eta	0.30	

Ireland

Party		N
Workers'	5.5	33
Labour	5.1	72
Green	3.8	34
Fianna Fáil	3.8	446
Fine Gael	3.6	200
Progressive Democrats	3.0	33
Overall mean	3.9	851
eta	0.21	

Netherlands

Party		N
Green Left	5.5	70
Labour	5.0	218
Christian Democrats	3.3	289
D'66	3.1	164
Calvinist Fund	3.0	37
VVD Liberal	1.7	94
Overall mean	3.7	887
eta	0.46	

France

Party		N
Communist	7.3	32
Socialist	4.7	250
Ecologist	4.2	97
UDF	3.1	119
National Front	3.0	31
RPR	2.4	58
Overall mean	4.2	604
eta	0.42 (0.43)	

Italy

Party		N
Proletarian Democrat	5.9	14
Communist	5.5	218
Radical	4.8	16
Green	4.4	165
Socialist	4.2	151
Socialist Democrat	4.1	18
Christian Democrat	4.0	451
Movimento Sociale	3.4	32
Republican	3.2	37
Regional lists	2.9	75
Liberal	1.9	20
Overall mean	4.3	1,233
eta	0.30	

Spain

Party		N
Radical Basques	6.8	39
Left Coalition	6.3	168
Green	6.0	57
Socialist	5.7	573
Nationalist Parties	5.1	65
Moderate Basques	4.8	27
Democratic Centre	4.6	106
Catalan Nationalist	4.5	82
Partido Popular	3.8	447
Overall mean	5.1	1,569
eta	0.36	

Note: Table 17.2 continues on p. 474.

TABLE 17.2. *Cont.*

	Mean	N
Portugal		
Democratic Coalition	6.6	56
Socialist	5.0	279
Social Democrats	4.2	321
Democratic Centre	3.7	39
Overall mean	4.7	712
eta	0.27	

Notes: Entries are mean scores and correlation coefficients (eta). The double entries for Belgium and France are explained in Table 17.1.

Source: European Values Survey (1990).

most right-materialist electorate. Indeed, voters for the Liberal Party are even more right-materialist than supporters of the far right MSI. In Britain and in the Scandinavian countries, in particular, the conservative parties have the most right-materialist electorate. Voters for the Liberal Party in Britain are to the left of Conservative Party voters; but, on average, Liberal voters are closer to Conservative rather than Labour voters. In the Scandinavian countries, too, voters for the liberal parties are to the left of voters for conservative parties, although the patterns in these countries are rather different. Voters for the Agrarian Liberals in Denmark and the Liberal People's Party in Sweden are closer to voters for the conservative parties, while voters for the Radical Liberals in Denmark and the Liberal Party in Norway are closer to the socialist parties than to the conservative parties.

The analysis, then, generally confirms that, in terms of left–right materialism, Christian democratic voters tend to be centrists leaning towards the centre right. In most instances, voters for these parties are grouped at about the same distance from voters for conservative and liberal parties on the one hand, and socialist parties on the other. This is the case in Denmark, Norway, Belgium, and the Netherlands. But voters for the Christian Democratic Party in Germany are closer to voters for the (liberal) Free Democrats than the Social Democrats, whereas in Sweden Christian Democratic voters are closer to the (conservative) Moderate Party. By contrast, voters for the Italian Christian Democrats are much closer to the Socialist Party than to either the Liberal Party or the Republicans. In Norway, Denmark, and Sweden, the centre parties occupy a position at the middle of the left–right materialist index, together with the Christian parties, and partly together with the radical liberal parties and other small centrist parties. It is interesting to find that voters for the right-wing, populist Progress Party in Denmark and Norway are not extremists in terms of right materialism. Rather, in both countries, they are placed somewhat to the left or have much the same score on the left–right materialist index as voters for conservative parties. This pattern is even more consistent in the country-specific data (not shown here).

The new green parties appear to have rather different electorates. In Germany, Denmark, and Iceland (Women's Alliance) their voters are more left materialist than voters for socialist parties, whereas they are more right materialist than socialist voters in Sweden, Belgium, and Britain. These findings correspond nicely with Müller-Rommel's (1985*b*: 491) classification of green parties into 'pure green reformist'

TABLE 17.3. *Trends in left–right materialism and party choice in six countries, 1970s and 1980s*

Denmark	1971	1975	1977	1979	1981	1984
	0.48	0.49	0.46	0.49	0.52	0.60
N	1,160	1,241	1,241	1,632	776	854

Alternative index	1979	1984	1987
	0.57	0.60	0.61
N	1,632	854	876

Norway	1977	1981	1985	1989
	0.68	0.64	0.62	0.51
N	1,465	1,349	1,840	1,837

Sweden	1976	1979	1985
	0.63	0.69	0.64
N	2,409	2,569	2,609

Britain	1974 (Oct.)	1979	1983	1987
	0.53	0.49	0.53	0.54
N	1,948	1,558	3,203	3,204

Germany	1984	1985	1988	1989
	0.29	0.34	0.27	0.29
N	828	1,617	1,794	1,762

Netherlands	1970	1975	1980	1985
	0.55 (0.55)	0.52 (0.52)	0.52	0.56
N	1,294	1,369	1,380	1,290

Notes: Entries are correlation coefficients (eta). The double entries for the Netherlands are explained in the notes to Table 17.1.

Sources: Election studies for Denmark, Norway, Sweden, and Britain; Culture Change Survey of the Netherlands; IPOS surveys for Germany.

and 'alternative green radical' parties, based on programme and strategy. Only the latter group of green parties has a leftist programme; according to our findings, they also have a left-materialist electorate.

In Table 17.3, we report the eta coefficients from the analysis of the time-series data we have for six countries. With one exception

(Germany), these are countries where we have seen that, in comparative terms, left–right materialist orientations have a large impact on party choice. Those findings are generally confirmed by the national data, although cross-national comparisons are more uncertain since the indicators are not identical. The relationship between left–right materialism and party choice is remarkably strong throughout the 1970s and 1980s in Sweden and Norway (except in 1989), with correlations above 0.60. For Britain and the Netherlands, the coefficients are rather lower, ranging between 0.49 and 0.56. They are considerably lower in Germany (0.29–0.34). The results for Denmark, ranging between 0.46 and 0.60, indicate rather large variations (see below). The results for Britain confirm our earlier findings, reported in Table 17.2, which placed Britain in the group of countries where left–right materialist orientations have a large impact on party choice.

There is a remarkable steadiness in the correlations between left–right materialist orientations and party choice in Sweden, Britain, Germany, and the Netherlands—which accords with the stability hypothesis. Moreover, the placing of party supporters on the left–right materialist index is very similar to our findings in the comparative surveys (not shown here). However, the results for Britain indicate that voters for the Liberal Party were placed midway between Labour and Conservative voters in the 1970s, whereas voters for the Alliance parties were closer to Labour than to Conservative voters in the 1980s. The data for Germany show no consistent differences between voters for the Christian Democrats and the Free Democrats.

In Denmark, there is an increase in the impact of left–right materialist orientations from the 1970s to the 1980s, from around 0.50 to around 0.60 in the 1980s. This is due to the strong support for left-wing parties in Denmark. These parties have the support of most voters with a left-materialist orientation, and in the 1980s the gap increases between the index scores among these voters and among voters for the socialist parties. Only in Norway is there a marked decline in the correlation between left–right materialist orientations and party choice, from 0.68 in 1977 to 0.62 in 1985, and down again to 0.51 in 1989. It is evident from the mean scores that this decline is largely attributable to voters for the Labour Party and, especially, the Socialist Left who become distinctly less left materialist. Thus, the degree of overall polarization on the left–right materialist index drops. The Norwegian pattern, especially the substantial drop from 1985 to 1989, is exactly what is expected according to the declining correlation hypothesis.

Materialist–Postmaterialist Value Orientations

According to 'new politics' theory, materialist–postmaterialist value orientations will become an increasingly important conflict line in advanced industrial society. Within a developmental framework, value orientations are gradually replacing the traditional socio-structural cleavages as posited by Lipset and Rokkan. The rise of materialism–postmaterialism as a source of political conflict suggests a realignment in mass politics. Materialist–postmaterialist value orientations will become an important cleavage by contributing to the ideological re-orientation of party profiles, the creation of new parties, and the emergence of a new political space in which voters, social groups, and parties are aligned in terms of materialist–postmaterialist opposition. This new alignment is expected to cut across traditional left–right materialist alignments. More specifically, former left–right materialist orientations are anticipated to split between the new postmaterialist left parties as against traditional left parties (socialists and communists) which have a more materialist electorate (Inglehart 1984: 28).

Thus, as materialist–postmaterialist opposition takes hold, parties will become aligned according to a materialist–postmaterialist conflict line. According to Müller-Rommel (1982: 69), the parties which will be located near the postmaterialist pole can be grouped into three types. The first group consists of small left-wing socialist, or new left, parties founded in the late 1950s or 1960s before the appearance of the environmental movement. They have defined themselves as alternatives to the established socialist and communist parties. From the beginning, these parties have been committed to international disarmament and have demanded the withdrawal of West European countries from NATO. They have also gradually adopted some key perspectives from the environmental movement. The second group consists of green parties which were established in the late 1970s and 1980s. These parties were formed because of the perceived failure of the established parties to come to grips with fundamental environmental issues. Their ideology incorporates ecological concerns, disarmament, alternative life-styles, and self-determination through grass roots democracy.[4] The third group consists of established parties from the political centre—along the left–right spectrum—which have incorporated environmental concerns into their political profile since the 1970s.

According to new politics theory, the impact of materialism–postmaterialism on party choice will vary cross-nationally according to certain criteria: the strength of current alignments; whether or not existing parties express a postmaterialist orientation; the spread of postmaterialism (Inglehart 1977*b*: 258); the number of parties in the political system; and the nature of the electoral system (Inglehart 1984: 28). However, new politics theory has been criticized for not being able to explain the lags and cross-national variations between value change and party realignments, and for not being able to predict the conditions under which value change will lead to the formation of, and support for, green or 'left-libertarian' parties (Kitschelt 1988: 208). A comparative analysis of nine countries, for example, found no correlation between levels of materialism and postmaterialism in different countries and the impact of materialism–postmaterialism on party choice (Knutsen 1988: 344). That postmaterialism is more widespread in one country than another does not entail that its impact on party choice is greater in the one country than the other. Thus, comparative analysis of the distribution of materialist–postmaterialist orientations is not very fruitful for testing hypotheses about the comparative impact of materialism–postmaterialism on voting.

Instead, our hypotheses about the impact of materialist–postmaterialist orientations on voting are directed towards those countries where parties which articulate a postmaterialist orientation exist and garner support from a significant part of the electorate. In other words, we take as given the emergence of parties articulating a postmaterialist orientation, treating that development as an independent variable. Thus, in comparative terms, the impact of materialist–postmaterialist orientations on party choice, in each country and over time, can be explained by the emergence and persistence of left-wing socialist, green, or centre parties with a post-materialist profile. In those countries where such parties existed around 1970, they have contributed to polarizing the electorate as between materialists and postmaterialists. Further, the impact of materialism–postmaterialism is expected to increase most in countries which had no significant postmaterialist party in the early 1970s but in which green or new left parties have been established and gained support in elections since the late 1970s and 1980s.

Next, we consider hypotheses about the distribution of materialists and postmaterialists among party families. Left-wing socialist parties are the oldest of the postmaterialist parties, appearing around 1970. These parties appeared, primarily, in the Netherlands and the Nordic countries: the Pacifist Socialist Party in the Netherlands, the Socialist People's Party in Denmark, the Socialist Left Party in Norway, Left

Party Communists (VPK) in Sweden, and the People's Alliance in Iceland. In the late 1960s and 1970s, these parties incorporated green standpoints into their political profiles. In addition, several established centre parties embraced green issues during the 1970s, as in the case of the centre parties in Sweden and Norway and the Liberal Party in Norway (Knutsen 1990: 262).

Most parties in the other party families have traditionally had a predominantly materialist profile. This applies in particular to the conservative, Christian democratic, and liberal parties. The socialist parties are perhaps the most interesting of the traditional party families in relation to new politics. Both their electorates and the party élites have traditionally emphasized old left concerns for physical and economic security and stability. However, postmaterialist forces have emerged within many socialist parties which have tried to change the traditional preoccupation with materialist concerns. Therefore, we hypothesize that the electorates of these parties are closer to the post-materialist pole compared to traditional 'bourgeois' party families. In sum, we expect materialist–postmaterialist orientations to have had an impact on party choice, particularly in the Netherlands and the Nordic countries. Italy and France are borderline cases; electoral support for the United Socialists (PSU) in France and for the Radicals and Proletarian Democrats in Italy suggests that materialist–postmaterialist orientations may have had some impact in those countries during the 1970s.

In several countries new green parties articulated postmaterialist orientations from the late 1970s and gained significant support in elections during the 1980s. In countries where no clear postmaterialist alternatives existed previously, we expect the impact of materialist–postmaterialist orientations on party choice to have increased from the 1970s to the 1980s. The relevant countries here are Austria, Belgium, Finland, Germany, and, in some measure, Italy and Sweden. In other countries, where parties with a postmaterialist profile already existed, the new green parties became significant among new politics parties. The relevant countries here are Iceland,[5] Sweden, Italy, and France. In countries with no significant postmaterialist alternatives, we expect the impact of the materialist–postmaterialist orientations to have remained modest during the 1980s. This applies to Britain and Ireland, and to the southern European countries of Spain, Portugal, and Greece.

To measure materialist and postmaterialist orientations we used the three batteries comprising twelve items developed by Inglehart (1977*b*: 39–53). The index, based on the ranking of the items, ranges from 1 to

10. We have data from the first half of the 1970s for some countries, but data for a number of other countries are available only for the 1980s. In Table 17.4, we present the correlations between the materialist–postmaterialist index and party choice for all available data sets. We then go on, in Table 17.5, to examine the placing of voters for party families. As the data for the first half of the 1970s cover only the European Community countries, Austria, and Finland, our comments about developments over time are limited to these countries.

Our hypothesis about the countries in which materialist–postmaterialist orientations have the largest impact in the early 1970s is generally supported by the data. Based on the average coefficients from the 1970s data, the impact is largest (higher than 0.30) in Denmark, France, the Netherlands, and Italy. The coefficients are considerably weaker in Belgium, Germany, Ireland, Britain (0.18–0.24), and Austria (0.13).

There are several patterns to developments over time. In the four countries where materialism–postmaterialism has the largest impact in the 1970s, there are two trends. In Denmark and the Netherlands the impact remains high and even increases. In France and Italy the coefficients decline somewhat. While materialist–postmaterialist orientations played an important role for party choice in these countries during the 1970s, their impact is below average during the late 1980s. In Austria, Belgium, Britain, and Germany the impact of materialism–postmaterialism increases significantly, while the correlations are constantly low in Ireland and Finland. The increase is particular large in Britain and Germany. These findings largely support our hypotheses, but there are some deviations. Particularly noticeable is the remarkable increase in the coefficients for Britain and their low values in Finland, despite the electorally significant Green List in Finland but a rather marginal Green Party in Britain.

In the late 1980s, the impact of materialism–postmaterialism on party choice[6] is largest in Denmark, Iceland, Germany, and the Netherlands (above 0.40). Their impact is rather lower in Norway, Britain, and Greece (0.35–0.37), followed by Belgium, France, Italy, and Spain (0.30–0.31). Their impact is lower again in Sweden, Finland, and Austria (0.21–0.27), and lowest of all in Ireland and Portugal (0.16–0.17). Whereas we expected materialism–postmaterialism to play a rather minor role in party choice in all three southern countries, it is evident that there are significant differences between these countries. In Portugal, materialism–postmaterialism has only a small impact while in Spain and Greece the relationship is quite strong.

TABLE 17.4. *Trends in materialist–postmaterialist orientations and party choice, 1973–90*

	1973	1974–6	1978	1979–81	1987–8	1990
Denmark	0.34		0.56	0.45	0.47	0.46
N	871		699	1,158	746	799
Finland		0.24			0.21	
N		986			641	
Iceland					0.41	0.43
N					670	457
Norway				0.47	0.37	0.34
N				1,013	1,072	947
Sweden					0.26	0.28
N					893	777
Austria		0.13			0.23 (1985)	
N		1,014			2,959	
Britain	0.23	0.23	0.17		0.51	0.35
N	1,532	1,275	830		767	1,189
Belgium	0.23		0.13		0.38 (0.39)	0.23 (0.25)
N	733		511		588	1,786
Germany	0.19	0.28	0.22		0.49	0.41
N	1,341	1,505	737		804	1,567
Ireland	0.19		0.19		0.13	0.20
N	847		702		637	845
Netherlands	0.35 (0.36)	0.37 (0.37)	0.40		0.39	0.44
N	1,109	1,036	837		788	855
France	0.38		0.38 (0.38)		0.33 (0.34)	0.28 (0.30)
N	1,466		831		776	595
Italy	0.31	0.36	0.38		0.32	0.28
N	1,150	1,269	740		640	1,190
Greece					0.37	
N					536	
Spain					0.28	0.32
N					535	1,471
Portugal					0.18	0.16
N					453	657

Notes: Entries are correlation coefficients (eta). The double entries for France, Belgium, and the Netherlands are explained in the notes to Table 17.1.

Sources: European Community Study (1973); Political Action (1973–6); Eurobarometer, Nos. 10 and 29; European Values Survey (1990); Political Values in Denmark (1979); Democracy in Norway; Participation and Basic Values (1981); Postmaterialism and Political Action in the Nordic Countries (1987–8); Value Change and Political Orientations in Austria (1985).

Our hypotheses about the distribution of voters among party families according to materialist and postmaterialist orientations are generally confirmed although there are also some clear deviations from our expectations. Looking at the means in Table 17.5, it is evident that green parties and left-wing socialist parties have the most postmaterialist electorates in most countries. In Italy and Sweden there is a tendency for the left-wing parties to have an even more postmaterialist electorate than the 'pure' green parties. One important explanation for the declining impact of materialism–postmaterialism from the 1970s to the 1980s in France and Italy is that the left-wing parties of the 1970s (PSU and Proletarian Democrats, respectively), on average, have more postmaterialist electorates than the 'pure' green parties which emerged in the late 1970s and 1980s.

A notable departure from our expectations is that support for the Nordic centre parties has nothing to do with postmaterialism. Voters for these parties, including the Agrarian Liberals in Denmark and the Progressive Party in Iceland, are among the most materialist electorates in all countries.[7] The Liberals in Norway, the Radical Liberals in Denmark, the regionalist Volksunie in Belgium, and D66 in the Netherlands also have predominantly postmaterialist electorates.

As expected, the conservative and Christian democratic electorates in most countries are predominantly materialist. In the Nordic countries, the conservative parties (with Finland as an exception) and the Progress Party in Denmark and Norway have clearly materialist electorates. So do the Agrarian Liberals in Denmark and the Centre Party in Finland. The conservative parties in Austria (ÖVP), France (RPR), Britain, Greece (New Democracy), and Spain (Partido Popular) have the most materialist electorate in their country. The Christian democrats also have a materialist electorate in Belgium, the Netherlands, Germany, and Italy. The same applies to the liberal parties in Belgium, France (UDF), Italy, and the Netherlands (VVD). In Belgium, Italy, and the Netherlands, the differences between voters for the Christian democrats and the liberal parties are small, whereas in Germany, Christian Democrat voters are clearly more materialist than voters for the Free Democrats. The same applies when we compare voters for the conservative parties in France (RPR) and Britain with their respective liberal parties.

In general, the socialist parties have a more postmaterialist electorate than the bourgeois parties. However, in most countries socialist voters are closer to the materialism of voters for the conservative, liberal, and Christian democratic parties than to the postmaterialism of supporters

TABLE 17.5. *Materialist–postmaterialist orientations and party choice in Western Europe, 1990*

	Mean	N		Mean	N		Mean	N
Denmark			**Iceland**			**Norway**		
Green	7.5	15	Women's Alliance	6.7	44	Socialist Left	6.0	122
Socialist People's	7.1	139	People's Alliance	5.8	43	Liberal	5.9	35
Radical Liberals	6.0	30	Social Democrats	5.2	57	Christian People's	4.7	71
Social Democrats	5.1	261	Progressive	4.2	82	Labour Party	4.5	333
Centre Democrats	5.1	48	Independence	4.2	223	Centre Party	4.4	58
Christian People's	4.6	17	Overall mean	4.8	457	Conservatives	4.1	192
Conservatives	4.4	122	eta	0.43		Progress	3.9	124
Progress	4.2	52				Overall mean	4.6	947
Agrarian Liberals	4.1	97				eta	0.34	
Overall mean	5.2	799						
eta	0.46							
Sweden			**Belgium**			**Britain**		
Left Party	6.5	52	Ecolo/Agalev	6.7	300	Green	6.6	51
Green	6.1	73	Flemish Block	5.8	34	Liberal Democrats	5.8	65
Christian Democrats	5.8	23	Socialist	5.6	433	Labour	5.5	533
Liberals	5.6	147	Social Christian	5.5	433	Nationalists	5.3	66
Centre	5.5	68	Volksunie	5.3	80	Social Democrats	5.2	12
Social Democrats	5.2	226	Liberal	5.1	287	Conservatives	4.1	437
Moderates	4.4	188	FDF/Rass. Wallon	5.0	36	Overall mean	5.0	1,186
Overall mean	5.3	777	Overall mean	5.6	1,769	eta	0.35	
eta	0.28		eta	0.23 (0.25)				

Germany

Greens	7.8	112
Social Democrats	6.0	635
Free Democrats	5.8	139
Republican	4.5	35
Christian Democrats	4.4	632
Overall mean	5.4	1,568
eta	0.41	

France

Ecologist	6.4	96
Communist	6.0	32
Socialist	5.8	245
UDF	5.0	117
National Front	4.7	30
RPR	4.4	58
Overall mean	5.6	595
eta	0.28 (0.30)	

Ireland

Green	5.8	34
Labour	5.8	72
Workers'	5.2	33
Progressive Democrats	5.0	33
Fine Gael	4.8	199
Fianna Fáil	4.6	441
Overall mean	4.9	845
eta	0.20	

Italy

Proletarian Democrat	7.6	14
Green	6.6	161
Social Democrats	6.1	18
Communist	6.0	212
Radical	5.9	16
Republican	5.8	36
Socialist	5.2	149
Liberal	5.1	19
Christian Democrat	5.0	418
Regional lists	4.8	72
Movimento Sociale	4.7	31
Overall mean	5.5	1,182
eta	0.28	

Netherlands

Green Left	8.2	69
D66	6.3	157
Labour	6.1	211
Christian Democrats	5.1	276
Calvinist Fund	4.8	34
Liberal	4.7	94
Overall mean	5.8	855
eta	0.44	

Spain

Radical Basques	7.9	36
Green	7.1	56
Left Coalition	6.3	163
Nationalist parties	5.8	62
Moderate Basques	5.7	27
Socialist	5.4	533
Democratic Centre	5.0	99
Catalan Nationalist	4.9	75
Partido Popular	4.9	420
Overall mean	5.4	1,476
eta	0.32	

Note: Table 17.5 continues on p. 486.

T ABLE 17.5. *Cont.*

	Mean	N		Mean	N		Mean	N
Portugal			Finland (1987)			Austria (1985)		
Democratic Coalition	4.9	53	Green List	7.7	35	Alternative List	5.9	30
Socialist	4.4	257	Christian People's	6.2	13	Green	5.1	54
Democratic Centre	4.2	36	Swedish People's	5.9	18	Christian Social	3.6	1,245
Social Democrats	4.0	292	Democratic League	5.8	57	Socialist	3.5	1,550
Overall mean	4.2	655	Conservative	5.7	135	Freedom	3.2	75
eta	0.16		Rural	5.6	39	Overall mean	3.6	2,959
			Social Democrats	5.4	179	eta	0.23	
			Centre	5.3	120			
			Overall mean	5.7	641			
			eta	0.21				

Notes: Entries are mean scores and correlation coefficients (eta). The double entries for France and Belgium are explained in the notes to Table 17.1.
Sources: European Values Survey (1990); Postmaterialism and Political Action in the Nordic countries (1987); Value Change and Political Orientations in Austria (1985).

of green or new left parties. There are also generally much larger differences in materialism–postmaterialism than in left–right materialism between voters for the socialist parties and the left socialist parties in the relevant countries—Denmark, France, Italy, Norway, and Sweden.

Relative Impact of Value Orientations

We have found that the three value orientations are moderately to strongly correlated with party support. We also found that the value orientations group party electorates in different ways, constituting cross-cutting conflict lines.

We formulated two hypotheses about the relationship between party choice and, first, religious–secular orientations, and, secondly, left–right materialism. The stable correlation hypothesis implied their persisting significance; the declining correlation hypothesis implied that their significance is fading. For both sets of orientations, the stable correlation hypothesis fitted the data in most countries. There is an impressive stability in the correlations over time in most countries. Similarly, the impact of materialism–postmaterialism is highly stable in most countries. However, for those countries where we have data going back to the early 1970s, there is a tendency for the impact of these orientations to increase.

To sum up our findings, the correlations between the three sets of value orientations and party choice are presented for five-year periods in Table 17.6. The results from the 1990 European Values Survey are presented separately as this is the only comparative survey which contains all three value orientations.

The table reveals three basic patterns. In France, Britain, and the Nordic countries (Denmark, Iceland, Norway, and Sweden) left–right materialism consistently has the largest impact on party choice. Among these countries, materialism–postmaterialism is consistently the second most important orientation in Denmark, Iceland, and Britain, whereas religious–secular orientations have more impact than materialism–postmaterialism in Catholic France and in Protestant Norway (although the relative impact of materialism–postmaterialism and religious orientations changes in Norway during the 1980s). Religious–secular orientations have the largest impact in most Catholic

TABLE 17.6. *Value orientations and party choice in Western Europe, 1970–90*

Value orientations	1970–5	1976–80	1981–5	1986–90	1990
Denmark					
Religious–secular	0.30	0.40	0.37	0.35	0.35
Left–right materialism	0.49	0.48	0.56	0.61	0.55
Materialism–postmaterialism	0.34	0.51	–	0.47	0.46
Norway					
Religious–secular	0.47	0.32	0.35	0.41	0.41
Left–right materialism	–	0.66	0.63	0.51	0.44
Materialism–postmaterialism	–	–	0.47	0.36	0.34
Sweden					
Religious–secular	–	–	0.36	0.34	0.28
Left–right materialism	–	0.66	0.64	0.64	0.47
Materialism–postmaterialism	–	–	–	0.27	0.28
Belgium					
Religious–secular	0.54	0.51	0.54	0.44	0.44
Left–right materialism	–	0.23	0.25	0.36	0.36
Materialism–postmaterialism	0.23	0.13	–	0.31	0.24
Britain					
Religious–secular	0.14	0.14	0.09	0.16	0.16
Left–right materialism	0.53	0.49	0.53	0.54	0.46
Materialism–postmaterialism	0.23	0.17	–	0.45	0.38
Germany					
Religious–secular	0.35	0.22	0.30	0.34	0.34
Left–right materialism	–	0.13	0.24	0.30	0.30
Materialism–postmaterialism	0.24	0.22	–	0.45	0.41
Ireland					
Religious–secular	0.21	0.23	0.21	0.25	0.25
Left–right materialism	–0	0.15	(0.06)	0.21	0.21
Materialism–postmaterialism	0.19	0.19	–	0.13	0.20

Netherlands					
Religious–secular	0.65	0.57	0.58	0.51	0.51
Left–right materialism	0.55	0.52 (1975)	0.52 (1980)	0.56 (1985)	0.45
Materialism–postmaterialism	0.36	0.40	–	0.42	0.44
France					
Religious–secular	0.39	0.37	0.34	0.37	0.37
Left–right materialism	–	0.40	0.49	0.42	0.42
Materialism–postmaterialism	0.38	0.38	–	0.31	0.28
Italy					
Religious–secular	0.47	0.48	0.34	0.46	0.46
Left–right materialism	–	0.45	0.28	0.30	0.30
Materialism–postmaterialism	0.34	0.38	–	0.30	0.28
Iceland					
Religious–secular					0.24
Left–right materialism					0.47
Materialism–postmaterialism					0.43
Spain					
Religious–secular					0.43
Left–right materialism					0.36
Materialism–postmaterialism					0.32
Portugal					
Religious–secular					0.29
Left–right materialism					0.27
Materialism–postmaterialism					0.16

Notes: Entries are correlation coefficients (eta). For the period 1986–90 the results from national data have been used for religious–secular orientations and left–right materialism if the data are a continuation of a time series. For other countries, the results from the 1990 European Values Survey have been used. For materialism–postmaterialism, the average coefficient is based on the 1987–8 and 1990 data from Table 17.4.

countries (Belgium, Ireland, Italy, Spain, and Portugal) and in the Netherlands. In all these countries, with Ireland as a somewhat deviant case, left–right materialism has a stronger impact than materialism–postmaterialism, although the impact of materialism–postmaterialism approaches that of left–right materialism in Belgium and the Netherlands. Germany is the only case where materialism–postmaterialism has taken over as the most important orientation for explaining party choice. In the early 1970s, religious–secular orientations were more important but by the later 1980s materialism–postmaterialism had come to have the larger impact.

Beliefs in Government

Finally, what do our findings reveal about the mass public's beliefs in government? The relationship between people's value orientations and the structure of political institutions are decisive for the functioning of representative democracy; and political parties are crucial intermediaries between the public and their government since parties transform interests and values into 'inputs' to the political system. Thus, shifts in the value orientations of electors may be expected to work their way through to the 'outputs' of governments.

The conflict lines of 'old politics', largely rooted in religious–secular and left–right materialist orientations, have been institutionalized in most West European democracies through regular channels of representation and interest articulation. The role of parties in this institutionalization has been supplemented by various corporatist or 'consensual' arrangements (Lijphart 1984), giving all groups a stake in the political system. Therefore, the general stability we have found in the political impact of the value orientations associated with 'old politics' implies no immediate change in the mass public's more general beliefs in government.

The stable impact of left–right materialist orientations are particularly important in this respect. The failure of political élites to attend to the value conflicts relating to economic inequalities, reflected in left–right materialism, would generate severe disjunctures between political élites and the mass public. However, it is the rise of materialist–postmaterialist orientations which may pose the greater challenge to the politics of West European democracies. In promoting fissures in established institutional arrangements, particularly in challenging the dominance of the 'old' parties, the political influence of materialism–postmaterialism augers the fragmentation of politics. Far from incorporating all major interests, the reach of existing institutional arrangements has to be extended to include the new value orientations and interests which postmaterialist values represent yet without weakening political loyalties founded in traditional value orientations.

NOTES

1. The data sets used in Ch. 6 are also used in this chapter. Most of the additional data have been made available by the Norwegian Social Science Data Services (NSD). The Austrian data were supplied by Christian Haerpfer.
2. Generally, the standard deviations for the indices used in this chapter are similar but this is not the case for religious–secular orientations. In the Nordic countries, the distributions on the church attendance variable are very skewed because only a small proportion of voters attend church regularly; in Belgium and the Netherlands, there are large religious and non-religious segments in the population. Thus, the standard deviations are larger in the latter countries; and the relative impact of religious–secular orientations are somewhat larger than the correlations indicate.
3. A division of this kind is made by Smart (1989: 380) and Von Beyme (1985: 45), although the divisions are different. In the liberal–conservative group are: the Italian, Belgian, and Dutch liberal parties, Agrarian Liberals in Denmark, Liberal People's Party in Sweden, Austrian Freedom Party, Radical Democrats in Switzerland, and the Republican and Radical parties in the French UDF. In the liberal–radical group are: the British Liberal Party, German Free Democrats, Italian Republicans, D66 in the Netherlands, French left radicals (MRG since 1978), Radical Liberals in Denmark, and the Liberal Party in Norway.
4. For empirical evidence that these groups of parties have a 'new politics' orientation related to 'programmatic features' and 'political style', see Poguntke (1988).
5. In Iceland the 'green' party is the Women's Alliance. Although the Women's Alliance does not explicitly consider itself a green party, its ideology and issue orientation indicate that it comes the closest to being the Icelandic equivalent of a green party (Hardarson and Kristinsson 1987: 222–3).
6. These results are based on the correlations for the periods 1987–88 and 1990 in Table 17.4. Where there are two surveys, the average correlations are used.
7. These findings are supported by evidence of the 'programmatic orientation' of 'new politics' parties by Poguntke (1988), who concludes that these parties have few of the programmatic orientations required for classification as 'new politics' parties. Müller-Rommel (1990: 212–18) classifies the 'new politics' parties into two streams, the left-wing socialist and green groups, omitting the centrist group but adding another category of 'other small parties'.

18

Cleavage Politics

ODDBJØRN KNUTSEN AND ELINOR SCARBROUGH

Two broad patterns can be discerned in electoral politics across Western Europe during the post-war decades. The 1950s and 1960s were marked by a general political quietude, with electors supporting the major parties in fairly predictable numbers—reflected in Rose and Urwin's conclusion that, since 1945, 'the electoral strength of most parties has changed little from election to election, from decade to decade, or within the life span of a generation' (1970: 295). During the 1970s, with the appearance of new parties, protest groups, and new social movements, a growing restiveness was evident. By the 1980s, such manifestations of 'new politics' (Baker, Dalton, and Hildebrandt 1981: 141) were regular features of many West European polities (Poguntke 1987; Müller-Rommel 1989). In place of continuity and stability, there was talk of 'volatility' (Pedersen 1979; Crewe and Denver 1985), 'dealignment' (Särlvik and Crewe 1983), 'unconventional' political behaviour (Barnes, Kaase, *et al.* 1979), and the 'unfreezing' of party systems (Maquire 1983; Shamir 1984). In all, the latter decades of electoral politics in Western Europe have been characterized by a sense that far-reaching political change is afoot: 'Virtually everywhere among the industrialized democracies, the old order is changing' (Dalton, Flanagan, and Beck 1984: 451).

Although claims about change are not uncontested (cf. Bartolini and Mair 1990), our starting point is the assumption that the old order of cleavage politics is being displaced by conflicts centred around value orientations (Inglehart 1984; Inglehart and Rabier 1986). The relationship between party choice and the shifting salience of our three central value orientations—religious–secular, left–right materialism,

materialism–postmaterialism—was examined in the previous chapter. In this chapter we explore claims about the changing dynamics of mass politics by posing a confrontation between a 'cleavage model' and a 'values model' of electoral behaviour. First, we clarify what we mean by 'cleavage politics' and, secondly, examine the notion of 'value cleavage'. Then, thirdly, we set out a model of party choice which, in the empirical analysis, we test using national and comparative data covering the period from the early 1970s through to 1990. Our purpose is to assess the relative impact of cleavage politics and value conflicts on electoral behaviour over the last twenty years or so.

Cleavage Politics

According to Lipset and Rokkan's classic account, the underlying structure of politics throughout the period of mass mobilization is to be found in the interaction of four cleavages generated by two 'revolutions' under way during the nineteenth century. The state–church and centre–periphery cleavages reflect conflicts arising from the drive to build nation states; the land–industry and employers–workers cleavages reflect conflicts consequent on the industrial revolution. Subsequent empirical studies have updated the content of Lipset and Rokkan's four cleavages (Lybeck 1985), commonly operationalizing the class cleavage as middle class–working class, reformulating the state–church cleavage in terms of religiosity, and recasting sectoral conflicts as an urban–rural cleavage, while the centre–periphery cleavage is understood to capture subnational resistance to the state, often based on ethno-linguistic conflicts (Lane and Ersson 1991: 75).

In contrast to the representation of parties as the 'outgrowths' of social forces, Lipset and Rokkan portray parties as the principal agents in transforming societal conflicts into political divisions. It was the work of parties, with the advent of adult suffrage, to translate group conflicts into political oppositions—by crystallizing and articulating conflicting interests, constructing political alliances, creating organizational networks, and devising electoral strategies. In short: 'cleavages do not translate themselves into party oppositions as a matter of course' (Lipset and Rokkan 1967: 26). Secondly, although Lipset and Rokkan tend to talk of cleavages as engaging clashes of 'interests', their understanding of interests is clearly wider than simply economic advantage or social privilege. They note the 'strong elements of cultural opposition and ideological insulation' engaged in the class cleavage, and represent church–state conflicts as, at heart, a question of values, of conflict about 'the control of community norms' (1967: 18, 15). Similarly, they interpret the land–industry cleavage in nineteenth century Britain as 'an opposition between two value orientations' (1967: 19) relating to status legitimation. Indeed, and a point much neglected in conventional accounts of cleavage politics, Lipset and Rokkan saw parties as engaging '*value commitments within the larger body politic*' (1967: 5; emphasis original). For them, the group conflicts and accompanying ideological confrontations typical of mass politics in Western Europe are less about the 'specific gains and losses' of particular groups than about 'conceptions of moral right and interpretations of history and human destiny' (1967: 11).

In place of the general notion of cleavages as deep-seated socio-structural conflicts with political significance, our concept of cleavage encompasses three distinct but intertwined phenomena. First, a cleavage is rooted in a relatively persistent social division which gives rise to 'objectively' identifiable groups within a society—according to class, religion, economic, or cultural interests, or whatever. Secondly, a cleavage engages some set of values common to members of the group; group members know a 'common life' in so far as they share the same value orientation. Thirdly, a cleavage is institutionalized in some form of organization—most commonly a political party, but also in churches, unions, and other associational groups. Our focus is confined to parties. According to our conceptualization, the political party transforms social divisions into cleavages by giving coherence and organized political expression to what are otherwise inchoate and fragmentary beliefs, values, and experiences among members of some social group or some cluster of groups. Thus our concept of cleavage is more extensive than the notion of societal division and more exclusive than the notion of political division: cleavages are more than simply social conflicts, and cleavages constitute a particular form, rather than any form, of political division. If we use the term 'cleavage' for any and every kind of social or political division, the concept loses its analytic power; we are left unable to distinguish between 'cleavage politics' and any other kind of politics.

Our concept of cleavage, then, takes in three dimensions: social structure, value orientations, party support. This renders 'cleavage politics' a particular kind of politics; its distinctiveness follows both from the relatively stable relationship between some social group(s) and a particular party, and from the way value orientations inform the relationship between parties and voters. Thus voting for a party out of 'objective' group interests without sharing the values of the party does not constitute cleavage politics; nor does voting for a party out of shared values without being a member of the associated social group. Structural variables or value orientations may yield intelligible accounts of voting, but they do not amount to accounts of 'cleavage politics'.

The account of electoral change which speaks most directly to our concerns, however, comes from the proponents of 'new politics'. Almost immediately in the wake of the 1968 'student events', Inglehart (1971a) suggested that traditional cleavage politics is being displaced by the emergence of new intergenerational conflicts between 'acquisitive' and 'post-bourgeois' values—subsequently recast as 'materialist' and 'postmaterialist' value orientations. According to Inglehart, as industrial society gives way to advanced 'post-industrial society', the weakening of class and—but more ambiguously—religious divisions[1] is accompanied by the emergence of a new 'value cleavage' rooted in materialist–postmaterialist orientations (1977: 182; 1984: 53; 1985: 486; 1990: 263). Inglehart is not alone in claiming that postmaterialism is changing the face of mass politics as portrayed in the cleavage model (cf. Baker, Dalton and Hildebrandt 1981: 2; Dalton 1988: 169; 1989: 117), but he is more insistent on the notion that 'new politics' constitutes a 'value cleavage'.

These claims raise two questions. First, can the political conflicts arising from materialist–postmaterialist opposition properly be termed a new cleavage? Secondly, is materialist–postmaterialist opposition symptomatic of a general shift from 'cleavage politics' to 'value politics'? That is, given the persistence of the 'old' parties despite the declining salience of class and religious differences, we might anticipate that the values associated with class and religious cleavages have an independent effect on party choice comparable to the impact of materialist and postmaterialist values as posited by Inglehart. In other words, does the appearance of 'new politics' mean a reformulation of cleavage politics, as suggested by the notion of a value cleavage, or is mass politics more generally coming to centre around value conflicts?

A 'Value Cleavage'?

The notion of a 'value cleavage' is, of course, a diminution of our conceptualization of cleavage. None the less, empirically, Inglehart links materialist–postmaterialist opposition to party choice in two ways. The 'issue polarization' hypothesis links materialists to 'old' parties and postmaterialists to 'new' parties, while the 'group polarization' hypothesis implies that support for parties espousing postmaterialist values comes from post-war generations, the highly educated, and the 'new middle class' (Inglehart 1984, 32). By contrast, pre-war generations, the less educated, and members of the 'old' middle class and working class are more likely to support parties upholding materialist values. Thus, materialist–postmaterialist polarization is expressed in party choice and is underpinned by distinctive social characteristics. What is important here, however, is that social location is less important than value orientations in shaping party choice. In place of cleavage politics, in which party choice is portrayed as the outcome of social structure and value orientations working together, materialist–postmaterialist conflicts are seen to create divisions between and, in the case of the middle class, among social groups. To put it another way: whereas the dynamics of cleavage politics are rooted in social structure and engage value oppositions, the dynamics of the 'new cleavage' are to be found in value oppositions which result in social and political conflicts.

On other grounds, too, materialist–postmaterialist opposition is different in kind to the oppositions characteristic of cleavage politics. On the social dimension, the generational, educational, and class differences associated with postmaterialist orientations lack the degree of 'closure' (Bartolini and Mair 1990: 93) which marks class and religious groups. Age constitutes an open frontier, so does higher education—unless underpinned by class differences.[2] Likewise, in recruiting from among the university educated, the composition of the 'new middle class' appears too fluid to constitute the kind of persistent social divisions which support cleavage politics. That postmaterialists tend to be concentrated among 'social and cultural specialists' (Kriesi 1989) or 'symbol specialists' (Kitschelt and Hellemans 1990: 105) within the new middle class—rather than technocrats and entrepreneurs (Cotgrove 1982: 95)—suggests that postmaterialism flourishes within middle-class strata distinguishable by their skills and values rather than their location in the 'structure of positions' (Goldthorpe 1983: 467). Indeed, according to Inglehart (1990: 332), postmaterialist orientations serve to shape career choices among the new middle class rather than following from the location of postmaterialists in the class structure. Thus, postmaterialism has a less rooted place in structural differences than the values associated with class and religious conflicts.

On the institutional dimension, neither materialism nor postmaterialism enjoys the institutionalization characteristic of cleavage politics. The 'old' parties associated with materialist orientations are divided not about the priority of materialist goals but about which materialist goals should have priority. Materialists, in other words, have no natural party 'home'. Postmaterialists, on the other hand, may be 'at home' supporting 'green' or 'new left' parties but these parties are about more than postmaterialist values (see Chapters 10 and 17). New social movements also provide a 'home' for postmaterialists (Inglehart 1990: 378; Chapter 15 above) but these movements lack an institutional form comparable to parties. Thus, on this dimension, too, materialist–postmaterialist conflicts lack the embeddedness characteristic of cleavage politics.

The putative new 'value cleavage', then, lacks two features of what constitutes a cleavage: grounding in a relatively enduring social division and institutional organization. Thus, in our view, materialist–postmaterialist opposition is unlikely to result in a new cleavage. On the contrary, materialist–postmaterialist opposition is about value conflict unencumbered by the immobilities of cleavage politics. Whereas the cleavage model suggests a relatively robust structuring of mass politics, the 'new politics' perspective points to the more fluid, volatile relationships between social groups, value orientations, and party preferences which might be expected of a politics unanchored in cleavages. A more appropriate description for this kind of politics would seem to be 'politics without cleavages'—or 'post-cleavage conflicts'.[3]

Value Conflicts

What of the more general idea that political conflicts are increasingly coming to centre around value orientations? If that were the case, it would go some way to resolve a paradox posed by the cleavage model: the tenacity of the 'old' parties despite the social transformations of the post-war period. Although the major parties founded in religious and class conflicts have lost the commanding position they enjoyed in the 1950s and 1960s, they remain dominant in most party systems[4]—yet with widespread secularization and the weakened salience of class differences, social identities are waning as a source of political cues

(Särlvik and Crewe 1983; Franklin *et al.* 1992). But on what grounds might we expect support for the parties associated with religious and class cleavages to be sustained now by values alone?

With respect to voters, we might draw on the notion of 'cognitive mobilization', by which electors come to 'possess the level of political skills and resources necessary to become self-sufficient in politics' (Dalton 1988: 18). With the arrival of new media, especially television, and the expansion of education, citizens have become better informed and more sophisticated. Hence, rather than relying on the 'external mobilization' provided by social norms or party cues (Dalton *et al.* 1984: 18–19, 461), electors are increasingly independent in their political judgements. With respect to parties, they possess considerable ideological and organizational resources enabling them to adjust to structural change. Since the 1960s, shifts in what they stand for are evident among the parties associated with religious and class cleavages: Christian democratic parties have broadened their appeal to become 'catch-all' parties; conservative parties have assimilated neo-liberal economic values; and social democratic parties have foresworn most of their Marxist heritage (Von Beyme 1985: ch. 2). However, the process of de-alignment—the loosening of ties between social groups and parties—is slow, so there may be very long lags before the effects of structural change are manifest. Moreover, even when 'objective' positions change, well-established voting habits are not readily altered (Franklin 1985). Indeed, putting aside the assumptions of the cleavage model, there are no good grounds for presupposing that the values embedded in class and religious cleavages have faded in tandem with the blurring of class differences and declining religious affiliation. Unanchored in social structures, these value orientations may be less robust but, none the less, remain a potent basis for party choice.

To sum up: our concern is to assess whether or not the place of value orientations in electoral politics is changing. Drawing from 'new politics' arguments, we anticipate that the capacity of the cleavage model to explain party preferences is declining, and we expect value orientations, especially materialist–postmaterialist conflicts, to play a larger part in explaining party preference. That is, in general, over time, the growing influence of values should be reflected in a declining relationship between social structure and party preference but a strengthening relationship between values and party choice. Our next task is to specify a model of party choice which allows us to quantify the relative influence of social structures and value orientations, over time, in several West European countries. We then pose more specific hypotheses arising from our discussion of the cleavage model and 'new politics' claims.[5]

A Conflict Model of Party Choice

Our model of party choice, set out in Figure 18.1, consists of three types of conflict variables and three types of voting. The conflict variables are drawn from our earlier discussion of socio-structural, cleavage, and 'new values' accounts of voting; the voting types operationalize the explanations of voting offered by those accounts.

We specify, first, the conflict variables. Religious denomination denotes the structural dimension of the religious cleavage. Social class is the structural dimension of the class cleavage which is measured using three hierarchical status variables: occupation, education, and household income.[6] Our measures of value conflicts are the three value orientations central to the studies in this volume: religious–secular orientations, measured by frequency of church attendance (see Chapter 4); left–right materialism based on the indicators used in Chapter 6; and

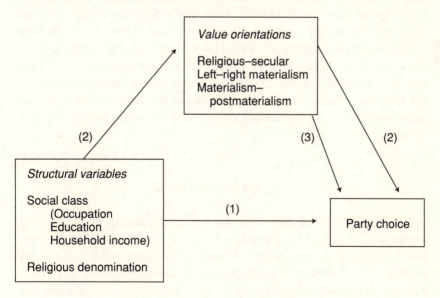

FIGURE 18.1. *A conflict model of party choice*

materialism–postmaterialism based on the twelve-item variant of Inglehart's standard instrument, or some equivalent measure. However, in contrast to previous chapters, we examine the joint—rather than separate—impact of the three value orientations.

The arrows in Figure 18.1 indicate three pathways representing different types of voting. Path 1 represents structural voting;[7] electors taking this path are members of some social group with long-standing ties to a party although they do not share the values informing that tie. Nominal Catholics who vote for a Christian democratic party would be a case in point. Path 2 represents cleavage voting: members of a structurally defined social group adhere to the value orientation associated with the group and support the party giving political voice to those values. Voting of this kind is typified by working-class supporters of social democratic parties. Path 3 represents values voting; party choice is accounted for by value orientations, with structural variables having little explanatory power. We might expect voting of this type among postmaterialists supporting green parties or middle-class supporters of left parties. Thus, the independent variables—social structure and value orientations—have a different role in the three voting paths. Social structure has a direct effect on party choice in path 1 but an indirect effect, via value orientations, in path 2. Value orientations have mediating and reinforcing effects in path 2, but direct effects in path 3.

In operationalizing the model, note that the impact of the structural variables equals the combined impact of 'structural' and 'cleavage' voting since the impact of structural variables is the total impact of these variables, both direct and indirect via value orientations. Consequently, 'structural' voting and the impact of the structural variables are not identical. 'Value voting' is the impact of the three value orientations since both effects are net associations based on controlling for the prior structural variables.

Hypotheses and Data

Our hypotheses are drawn from the earlier discussion of the cleavage model and 'new politics' literature. First, we specify general hypotheses about trends over time within countries. We anticipate that the proportion of the variance in party choice explained by structural variables has declined absolutely (*Hypothesis 1.1*) and relative to the proportion of the variance explained by value orientations (*Hypothesis 1.2*).

Structural voting is declining; that is, the direct effects of social class and religious denomination on voting is declining (*Hypothesis 2*). Cleavage voting is declining. However, this expectation is not unambiguous; a larger portion of the impact of structural variables may be transmitted via value orientations. Cleavage voting may therefore increase relative to structural voting (*Hypothesis 3.1*) but, as the total effect of structural variables is declining, the impact of cleavage voting is declining absolutely (*Hypothesis 3.2*). Value voting is increasing; that is, the impact of value orientations is increasing absolutely (*Hypothesis 4.1*) and relative to structural variables (*Hypothesis 4.2*). Finally, we expect these changes to be reflected in generational differences. In particular, that structural and cleavage voting is more common among pre-war generations (*Hypotheses 5.1–5.3* respectively) while 'pure value' voting is more common among post-war generations, both absolutely (*Hypothesis 5.4*) and relative to structural and cleavage voting (*Hypothesis 5.5*).

Secondly, we specify comparative hypotheses which relate to the effects of economic and social developments on cleavage politics. We expect the decline in the impact of structural variables to have progressed further in the more advanced industrial societies than in the less advanced industrial societies (*Hypothesis 6.1*). At the same time, we expect the impact of value orientations on party choice to be larger in the more advanced than in the less advanced industrial societies (*Hypothesis 6.2*); that the impact of value orientations on party choice has grown most in the more advanced countries (*Hypothesis 6.3*); and that both structural voting and cleavage voting is more significant in the less advanced industrial societies (*Hypotheses 7.1 and 7.2* respectively). However, some West European countries have been characterized by 'segmented pluralism' (Lorwin 1971), giving rise to a particularly robust—'pillarized'—form of cleavage politics which might be longer-lived than in other societies. Thus, we expect 'cleavage voting' to be at its strongest in countries which have a history of 'segmented pluralism' (*Hypothesis 8*).

We used data from cross-national surveys to test the comparative hypotheses and country-specific time series for testing the hypotheses about trends. Despite an extensive search we found only three suitable cross-national surveys: the 1973 European Community Survey; Eurobarometer, No. 16 (1981); and the second European Values Survey (1990). All three surveys cover eight countries: Denmark, Belgium, Britain, Ireland, Germany, France, Italy, and the Netherlands. The

1990 European Values Study provides data on a further five countries: Norway, Sweden, Iceland, Portugal, and Spain. All three data sets record church attendance, but the indicators for the other two value orientations are not the same. Both the 1973 European Community Survey and the 1990 European Values Study contain the twelve-item battery for materialism–postmaterialism; an equivalent index was constructed from the 1981 Eurobarometer data.[8] There are no indicators for left–right materialism in the 1973 European Community Survey, and the indicators in the 1981 Eurobarometer data and 1990 European Values Study data are quite different (see Chapter 4). Thus, since only two of the three value orientations are available in the 1973 data, we can examine changes in the impact of value orientations only between 1981 and 1990. This means we have to be careful about interpreting changes within countries over the 1973–90 period.

The country-specific data are from national election studies for Denmark (1971–87), Norway (1977–89), Sweden (1976–88), and Britain (1974–87), and the Cultural Change Surveys for the Netherlands (1970–85).[9] With only minor exceptions, these surveys contain the relevant structural variables and church attendance.[10] They also contain identical or very similar indicators of left–right materialism for the 1970s. However, the twelve-item materialist–postmaterialist battery is not available in any of these surveys. Thus the country-specific analysis for Denmark, Britain, and the Netherlands is limited to two value orientations: religious–secular and left–right materialism. For Norway and Sweden, however, indices have been constructed based on 'green' values versus economic growth and technocratic orientations. As these indices are different from those for the other countries, data from the 1990 European Values Study are used to make cross-national comparisons for these countries.

In countries of mixed denominations, we use separate categories for the different denominations; they are relevant only in Germany, Britain, and the Netherlands.[11] In addition, all denominations in these three countries were collapsed to obtain a dichotomous variable—religious denomination/no denomination—which can be used for direct comparisons. Most of our comments relate to the denomination variable, except in the case of Britain. No denominational data are available for the Nordic countries, but more than 80 per cent of these populations are members of the state Protestant Church and, as data from the 1990 European Values Survey show, religious denomination has only a minor effect on party choice in these countries. Finally, the dependent variable, party choice, includes parties supported by at least 2 per cent of those indicating a party preference. All parties are treated as separate categories;[12] respondents who have not indicated a party choice are excluded from the analysis.

The total impact of the several conflict variables on party choice is estimated using the coefficient Wilks's lambda from discriminant analysis (Klecka 1980: 38–40). To avoid confusion, we transform Wilks's lambda by the simple formula $1.00 - W$. We then employ discriminant analysis, entering party choice as a group variable and the conflict variables as discriminating variables.[13]

The first part of the analysis which follows examines the impact on party choice of the three types of conflict variables. Then we go on to assess the relative growth or decline of the three voting types. In a final section, we report the main findings from examining generational differences.

The Impact of Conflict Variables

In this section we examine the absolute and relative impact of the three types of conflict variables, with particular attention to the impact of value orientations after controlling for the prior structural variables. We adopt a comparative perspective first: in which countries do religious denomination, class, and value orientations have the largest impact? In Table 18.1*a–c* we present the results from stepwise discriminant analysis (with forced inclusion) in which religious denomination—as a more or less ascriptive variable—is entered first, followed by the three status variables. The results are ranked according to the impact of the conflict variables in the data from the 1990 European Values Survey.

The rankings show that religious denomination has the largest impact on party choice in Catholic and religiously mixed countries—as we might expect (cf. Rose and Urwin 1969: 13–20; Rose 1974: 16–19). This is most evident in the Netherlands, but is also the case in Belgium, Italy, France, Spain, and Portugal. In Britain the impact of religious denomination fades away when the dichotomous variable is used; closer analysis reveals that membership of the Church of Scotland contributes almost all the difference between the two measures. Thus, denomination in the British case reflects not religious conflict as a structural factor but regional differences between England and Scotland. Religious denomination has the least impact in the Nordic countries.

TABLE 18.1. *Effects of structural variables on party choice in Western Europe, 1970–90*

(a) Religious denomination

	Comparative surveys		
	1973	1981	1990
NL	0.33 (0.25)	0.31 (0.28)	0.39 (0.30)
IT	0.11	0.14	0.13
BE	0.15	0.13	0.12
FR	0.15	0.12	0.11
SP			0.10
PO			0.10
IR	0.01	0.00	0.04
GE	0.07 (0.01)	0.09 (0.07)	0.04 (0.03)
GB	0.08 (0.01)	0.17 (0.01)	0.07 (0.03)
DK	0.05	0.08	0.03
SV			0.02
NO			0.02
IC			0.01

	National surveys			
	1970–4	1975–9	1980–3	1984–7
GB	0.17 (0.02)	0.02 (0.01)	0.05 (0.00)	0.07 (0.01)
NL	0.46 (0.38)	0.34 (0.29)	0.32 (0.27)	0.29 (0.24)

(b) Social class

	Comparative surveys		
	1973	1981	1990
DK	0.26 (0.28)	0.29 (0.33)	0.24 (0.24)
NO			0.20 (0.20)
SV			0.15 (0.15)
BE	0.13 (0.16)	0.17 (0.19)	0.14 (0.16)
IC			0.13 (0.14)
GE	0.09 (0.09)	0.12 (0.13)	0.13 (0.13)
IT	0.14 (0.16)	0.19 (0.23)	0.13 (0.16)
FR	0.05 (0.07)	0.14 (0.17)	0.12 (0.14)
SP			0.12 (0.14)
NL	0.11 (0.16)	0.14 (0.20)	0.12 (0.20)
GB	0.08 (0.09)	0.06 (0.07)	0.10 (0.11)
IR	0.07 (0.07)	0.06 (0.06)	0.09 (0.10)
PO			0.06 (0.06)

T ABLE 18.1. *Cont.*

	National surveys				
	1970–4	1975–9	1980–3	1984–7	1988–9
DK	0.23 (0.23)	0.22 (0.22)		0.20 (0.20)	
NO		0.30 (0.30)	0.29 (0.29)	0.25 (0.25)	0.22 (0.22)
SV		0.23 (0.23)		0.19 (0.19)	0.21 (0.21)
GB	0.12 (0.12)	0.09 (0.09)	0.13 (0.13)	0.12 (0.12)	
NL	0.14 (0.26)	0.13 (0.14)	0.14 (0.15)	0.14 (0.16)	

(*c*) *All structural variables*

	Comparative surveys		
	1973	1981	1990
NL	0.44 (0.38)	0.45 (0.42)	0.48 (0.42)
DK	0.31	0.37	0.27
BE	0.28	0.30	0.26
IT	0.25	0.33	0.26
FR	0.20	0.26	0.23
NO			0.22
SP			0.22
GE	0.16 (0.10)	0.21 (0.18)	0.17 (0.15)
SV			0.16
PO			0.16
IC			0.15
GB	0.16 (0.10)	0.23 (0.08)	0.17 (0.13)
IR	0.08	0.06	0.13

	National surveys				
	1970–4	1975–9	1980–3	1984–7	1988–9
DK	0.23	0.22		0.20	
NO		0.30	0.29	0.25	0.22
SV		0.23		0.19	0.21
GB	0.27 (0.14)	0.11 (0.10)	0.17 (0.13)	0.19 (0.13)	
NL	0.60 (0.53)	0.47 (0.43)	0.46 (0.42)	0.44 (0.40)	

Notes: The variables are religious denomination and the three measures of social class. Entries are Wilks's lambda (transformed). In parts (*a*) and (*c*) the figures in parentheses for the Netherlands, Germany, and Britain are based on a dichotomous religious denomination variable (member/not member of a denomination). Denomination is not available in the Danish, Swedish, or Norwegian election studies. Social class is measured by occupation, education, and household income. In part (*b*) the bivariate effects are shown in parentheses. N varies between 715 (Belgium) and 1,516 (Britain) in the 1973 data; between 416 (Belgium) and 855 (Britain) in the 1981 data; and between 439 (Iceland) and 1,740 (Belgium) in the 1990 data. The average N in the national data is Denmark 1,205; Norway 1,563; Sweden 2,474; Britain 2,467; the Netherlands 1,269.

Sources: European Community Survey (1973); Eurobarometer, No. 16; European Values Survey (1990); Danish, Norwegian, Swedish, and British election surveys; Dutch Cultural Change Survey.

Although comparative data for Scandinavia are only available for 1990, the impact of denomination is very similar in Denmark, Norway, and Sweden; the rather higher coefficients for Denmark in 1973 and 1981 suggest further decline from a low base. The coefficient for Ireland is similarly low, but not surprising in an overwhelmingly Catholic country. More surprising is the low coefficient for Germany with its mixed denominations and history of religious divisions.

Table 18.1*b* presents the coefficients for both the bivariate (in parentheses) and the 'controlled' effects of social class on party choice. The rank ordering shows that these conflicts are generally most important in Scandinavia, where, with only one exception, the bivariate coefficients are above 0.20. The bivariate coefficients are also relatively high in the Netherlands, Belgium, and Italy but considerably smaller in Germany, Britain, Ireland, Spain, and Portugal. The relative position of the countries is little changed when the controlled effects are compared. The only exception is the Netherlands, where the impact of class is considerably reduced owing to the prior impact of the religious denomination.

Comparing the impact of religious denomination and social class, we see that only in the Netherlands (and Portugal in 1990) is religious denomination clearly more important than class. In Belgium, France, Italy, and Spain (in 1990) the class variables have a somewhat larger impact than denomination, although the differences are not large. In brief, in most countries, social class is more important than religious denomination for explaining party choice—especially in the Nordic countries but also in Britain and Germany. This is also the case in the controlled model.

The total impact of the structural variables, shown in Table 18.1*c*, is generally largest in the Netherlands, followed by Denmark, Belgium, and Italy, and then by Norway, France, Sweden, and Britain. Their impact is generally lowest in Ireland, Germany, and Iceland. This general pattern holds. for all three data sets, but is clearest in the 1990 data where the indicators are the same for all countries.

What of changes over time? The hypothesis that the proportion of the variance in party choice explained by structural variables has declined absolutely over time (Hypothesis 1.1) is not confirmed by the findings from the comparative data. Of the eight countries for which we have data for 1973, 1981, and 1990, only Denmark shows a modest decline. The general pattern is of trendless fluctuation, not steady decline, in the impact of class and religion on party choice. Even so, in the five countries for which we have national data, the discriminating power of structural variables does tend to decline. This is notably the case in the Netherlands and Norway, but there are weak tendencies in the same direction in Britain, Denmark, and Sweden. Thus the national data, which are more reliable for comparisons over time, provide some—although not strong—support for the hypothesis. But, since all these countries are advanced industrial societies, we cannot test the hypothesis that the reduced impact of social structure is largest in advanced industrial societies (Hypothesis 6.1). The comparative data, however, lend no support for this hypothesis.

The impact of value orientations on party choice is examined in Table 18.2a–b. Looking first at the bivariate effects, shown in Table 18a, the coefficients are generally largest for the Netherlands and the Nordic countries; 0.40 or higher except for Denmark during the 1970s and Sweden in the 1990 data. Value orientations have their weakest impact in Ireland and Portugal with coefficients lower than 0.20. With coefficients in the range 0.29–0.35 for 1990, Belgium, Italy, France, Britain, Spain, and Germany are in an intermediate position.

The results in Table 18.2b are based on stepwise discriminant analysis (forced inclusion) with the structural variables entered before the three value orientations. We can see that the controlled impact of value orientations likewise varies considerably. Their effects are largest in the Nordic countries and Britain; in the 0.24–0.28 range in the European Values data, and more than 0.30 in the election studies data for Norway and Sweden. Again, their impact is quite low in Ireland and Portugal, and in a broadly similar middle range (0.16–0.20) in most other countries. In the 1973 and 1981 comparative data, Britain belongs to the intermediate group, but by 1990 Britain has moved to the group in which value orientations are most important—owing to a considerable increase in the both the absolute and relative importance of value orientations.

Hypothesis 6.2, predicting that the impact of value orientations is larger in the more advanced industrial societies, receives strong support from the analysis reported in Table 18.2b. We correlated the three-fold classification of countries along the more advanced–less advanced dimension developed by Van Deth (see Chapter 3) with a three-fold classification of countries according to the impact of value orientations (high, intermediate, and low) for 1981 and 1990. The correlations for the eight countries in the 1981 data are modest: 0.21 in the bivariate analysis and 0.14 for the controlled impact (tau-b). In 1990, however,

TABLE 18.2. *Effects of value orientations on party choice in Western Europe,*
1970–90

(a) Bivariate effects

	Comparative surveys		
	1973	1981	1990
NL	0.47	0.53	0.52
DK	0.16	0.46	0.45
NO			0.38
IC			0.35
BE	0.32	0.35	0.35
SV			0.34
IT	0.26	0.41	0.33
SP			0.33
GB	0.06	0.14	0.31
FR	0.27	0.40	0.30
GE	0.14	0.21	0.29
PO			0.17
IR	0.07	0.05	0.13

	National surveys				
	1970–4	1975–9	1980–3	1984–7	1988–9
DK	0.34	0.35		0.41	
NO		0.54	0.58	0.54	0.44
SV		0.42		0.46 (0.52)	0.47 (0.52)
GB	0.29	0.25	0.28	0.30	
NL	0.66	0.53	0.52	0.56	

(b) Controlled effects

	Comparative surveys		
	1973	1981	1990
IC			0.28
NO			0.28
DK	0.08	0.25	0.28
SV			0.25
GB	0.04 (0.05)	0.09 (0.11)	0.22 (0.24)
SP			0.20
GE	0.09 (0.12)	0.11 (0.13)	0.19 (0.20)
IT		0.14	0.20	0.18

TABLE 18.2. *Cont.*

	Comparative surveys		
	1973	1981	1990
BE	0.14	0.17	0.18
NL	0.15 (0.18)	0.20 (0.21)	0.17 (0.20)
FR	0.16	0.23	0.16
IR	0.06	0.05	0.09
PO			0.09

	National surveys				
	1970–4	1975–9	1980–3	1984–7	1988–9
DK	0.21	0.22		0.31	
NO	0.36	0.38	0.37	0.32	
SV		0.28		0.33 (0.38)	0.33 (0.37)
GB	0.18 (0.21)	0.19 (0.19)	0.19 (0.20)	0.19 (0.21)	
NL	0.14 (0.19)	0.16 (0.18)	0.16 (0.18)	0.21 (0.23)	

Notes: Entries are Wilks's lambda (transformed). For Sweden, the first entry is for left–right materialism and materialism–postmaterialism; the results for all three orientations are shown in parentheses. For Britain and the Netherlands, the first entry is for religiosity and left–right materialism. The entry in parentheses, for Germany, is based on the dichotomous religious denomination variable. For N, see notes to Table 18.1.

the correlations are much stronger: 0.46 for the same eight countries for both the bivariate and controlled effects. For the thirteen countries in the 1990 data the correlations are 0.51 and 0.52 respectively. A comparison of the results from 1981 and 1990 indicates, then, that the impact of value orientations has increased most in the advanced industrial societies—in accord with Hypothesis 6.3.

In most countries, the three value orientations explain party choice better than all the structural variables taken together. But this finding applies only to the bivariate case; the controlled case reveals a rather different picture. Estimates of the relative effects of value orientations and structural variables can be derived from dividing the controlled impact of value orientations by the impact of the structural variables.[14] Our results are shown in Table 18.3.

In the 1973 and 1981 data, the structural variables have the largest impact in all countries—except Britain when religious denomination is

TABLE 18.3. *Impact of value orientations compared with the impact of all structural variables in Western Europe, 1970–90*

	Comparative surveys		
	1973	1981	1990
IC			1.87
GB	0.25 (0.50)	0.39 (1.38)	0.95 (1.85)
SV			1.56
NO			1.27
GE	0.56 (1.20)	0.52 (0.72)	1.12 (1.33)
DK	0.26	0.68	1.04
SP			0.91
FR	0.80	0.88	0.70
IT	0.56	0.61	0.69
BE	0.50	0.57	0.69
IR	0.75	0.83	0.69
PO			0.56
NL	0.34 (0.47)	0.44 (0.50)	0.35 (0.48)

	National surveys				
	1970–4	1975–9	1980–3	1984–7	1988–9
DK	0.91	1.31		1.45	
NO		1.20	1.31	1.48	1.45
SV		1.22		1.74 (2.00)	1.57 (1.76)
GB	0.67 (1.50)	1.73 (1.90)	1.12 (1.54)	1.00 (1.62)	
NL	0.23 (0.36)	0.34 (0.42)	0.35 (0.43)	0.49 (0.58)	

Notes: Entries are the controlled effects of value orientations divided by the effects of the structural variables. For Britain, Germany, and the Netherlands, the entries are based on a dichotomous variable for religious denomination. See also notes to Table 18.2.

Source: See Table 18.1.

dichotomized. The impact of the value orientations is about 50–80 per cent of that of the structural variables in most countries. But the position changes somewhat in the 1990 data: value orientations now have a larger effect than the structural variables in Denmark, Norway, Sweden, Iceland, Britain, and Germany. The relative impact of value orientations, compared with the structural variables, ranges from 1.87 for Iceland to 0.35 for the Netherlands. Thus, the Netherlands shows the sharpest reduction in the impact of value orientations—principally because of the relatively large impact of structural variables and the reduced impact of church attendance when controlling for religious denomination.[15]

The longitudinal national data allow us to draw fairly firm conclusions about trends over time in five countries. These data show no clear support for the hypothesis that the impact of value orientations is increasing absolutely (Hypothesis 4.1). But in the controlled analysis, a substantial increase in the effect of value orientations is evident in Denmark and the Netherlands, a small increase in Sweden, and stability in Britain and Norway. In the case of Norway, the impact of value orientations actually drops from the mid-1980s to the late 1980s.

The discriminatory power of all the conflict variables, taken together, varies considerably from country to country (data not shown here). The Netherlands stands out as the country where the full model has the largest discriminatory power: 0.59 in 1973 and 0.65 in 1981 and 1990. Based on the comparative data for 1973 and 1981, Denmark, Belgium, France, and Italy constitute a second group with coefficients above 0.35; Britain and Germany form a third group with coefficients of about 0.20 in 1973 and 0.30–0.32 in 1981. In both 1973 and 1981, the total conflict model has least explanatory power in Ireland with, respectively, coefficients of 0.11 and 0.14. In the 1990 data, the discriminatory power of the total conflict model varies from 0.65 for the Netherlands, 0.55 for Denmark and 0.50 for Norway to 0.25 for Portugal and 0.22 for Ireland. For the remaining eight countries the coefficients are in the range of 0.36–0.44.

These data, then, suggest a general trend for the impact of value orientations to increase relative to the impact of structural variables. But the pattern is not sufficiently consistent across all countries for us to conclude that Hypotheses 1.2 and 4.2 are confirmed. The pattern is most consistent in Denmark and the Netherlands, where the impact of value orientations has increased and the impact of structural variables has declined. The same patterns are found in Norway and Sweden over the longer term, but the impact of value orientations is either constant or declines somewhat from the mid- to late 1980s. The pattern in Britain is the least consistent. These findings accord with the hypothesis that the impact of value orientations on party choice has increased most in the advanced industrial countries (Hypothesis 6.3). However, as all the countries for which we have longitudinal data fall into the advanced category, we cannot refute the alternative hypothesis that the impact of value orientations on party choice is increasing at about the same rate across all West European countries.

Three Voting Types

In Figure 18.1 we distinguished between three voting 'paths' or types of voting: structural voting based on membership of a structurally defined group in which values play little part; value voting based on value orientations in which structural locations are of little consequence; and cleavage voting in which structural locations and value orientations, taken together, underpin party choice. The analyses above suggest considerable variation in the absolute and relative impact of structural variables and value orientations across Western Europe over the last twenty years. Now we consider how these changes are reflected in different voting paths.

The total effects of our model of party choice are decomposed into structural voting, value voting, and cleavage voting. The results from the three comparative surveys are presented in Table 18.4*a–c*.

In 1973, structural voting had the largest effects in Denmark, Britain, and Germany; cleavage voting the largest effect in Belgium and the Netherlands; and value voting the largest effect in France. The results for Ireland and Italy are more ambiguous. However, these findings must be set against the absence of left–right materialist orientations in the 1973 data. In 1981, structural voting had the largest impact only in Britain—and then only when the full religious denomination variable is used. Cleavage voting is most important in the Netherlands, but only marginally so in Belgium. Value voting has its largest impact in Denmark and France, and also in Britain when using the dichotomous denomination variable. All voting types are about equally important in Germany. In Belgium and Italy, value voting and cleavage voting have about the same impact. Structural voting and value voting have some weak effects in Ireland, but there is no trace of cleavage voting. The rather mixed picture becomes much clearer in the 1990 data: value voting is dominant in most countries. In nine out of thirteen countries (the Nordic countries, Britain, Germany, France, Italy, and Spain), the significance of value voting clearly outstrips structural and cleavage voting. Cleavage voting is dominant only in the Netherlands. In Belgium, Ireland, and Portugal no voting type emerges as dominant.

What is the magnitude of these developments? The average impact in the 1981 data is 0.11 for structural voting, 0.15 for cleavage voting, and 0.17 for value voting. The average impact in the 1990 data is 0.09 for structural voting, 0.13 for cleavage voting. and 0.20 for value voting.[16] The relative significance of these three voting types on party choice can

TABLE 18.4. *Effects of the three voting types in Western Europe, 1973–90*

	Structural voting	Value voting	Cleavage voting	Total conflict model
(a) 1973				
Denmark	0.23	0.08	0.08	0.39
Belgium	0.10	0.14	0.18	0.42
Britain	0.14 (0.09)	0.04 (0.05)	0.02 (0.01)	0.20 (0.15)
Germany	0.11 (0.08)	0.09 (0.12)	0.05 (0.02)	0.25 (0.22)
Ireland	0.07	0.06	0.01	0.14
Netherlands	0.12 (0.09)	0.15 (0.18)	0.32 (0.29)	0.59 (0.56)
France	0.09	0.16	0.11	0.36
Italy	0.13	0.14	0.12	0.39
Average	0.11	0.11	0.11	0.33
(b) 1981				
Denmark	0.17	0.25	0.20	0.62
Belgium	0.12	0.17	0.18	0.47
Britain	0.18 (0.05)	0.09 (0.11)	0.05 (0.03)	0.32 (0.19)
Germany	0.11 (0.10)	0.11 (0.13)	0.10 (0.08)	0.32 (0.31)
Ireland	0.06	0.05	0.00	0.11
Netherlands	0.12 (0.10)	0.20 (0.21)	0.33 (0.32)	0.65 (0.63)
France	0.09	0.23	0.17	0.49
Italy	0.12	0.20	0.21	0.53
Average	0.11	0.17	0.15	0.43
(c) 1990				
Denmark	0.10	0.28	0.17	0.55
Iceland	0.08	0.28	0.07	0.43
Norway	0.12	0.28	0.10	0.50
Sweden	0.07	0.25	0.09	0.41
Belgium	0.09	0.18	0.17	0.44
Britain	0.08 (0.06)	0.22 (0.24)	0.09 (0.07)	0.39 (0.37)
Germany	0.07 (0.06)	0.19 (0.20)	0.10 (0.09)	0.36 (0.35)
Ireland	0.09	0.09	0.06	0.22
Netherlands	0.13 (0.10)	0.17 (0.20)	0.35 (0.32)	0.65 (0.62)
France	0.09	0.16	0.14	0.39
Italy	0.11	0.18	0.15	0.44
Spain	0.09	0.20	0.13	0.42
Portugal	0.08	0.09	0.08	0.25
Average	0.09	0.20	0.13	0.42

Notes: Entries are Wilks's lambda (transformed). For Britain, Germany, and the Netherlands, the results for the dichotomous denomination variable are shown in parentheses.

Sources: European Community Survey (1973); Eurobarometer, No. 16; European Values Survey (1990).

be summarized in proportional terms: of the total impact of our model, on average, structural voting accounts for some 21–26 per cent of its explanatory power, cleavage voting for about 30–35 per cent, and value voting for some 40–50 per cent. So we can conclude that value voting and cleavage voting are, generally, more widespread than structural voting in Western Europe. Moreover, according to the latest comparative data, the 1990 European Values Study, value voting is the most widespread of all three voting types.

For a more systematic comparison of the impact of the three voting types, we estimated the proportion of the discriminating power of the total conflict model accounted for by each voting type in each country in 1981 and 1990. For the eight countries in the 1981 data, we took the average percentages for 1981 and 1990; for the other five countries, we use only the 1990 data. The results are presented in Table 18.5.

Clearly, then, structural voting accounts for a large part of the discriminating power of our model only in Ireland and Portugal, two of the least advanced societies in Western Europe. Elsewhere, structural voting accounts for less than 25 per cent of the total explanatory power of our model. This finding, although based on only two cases, tends to support our expectation that structural voting is more significant in less advanced countries (Hypothesis 7.1). Values voting accounts for more than half of the explanatory power of our model in Iceland, Norway, Sweden, and Britain, and accounts for some 40–49 per cent in another six countries; it accounts for less than 40 per cent only in Belgium, Portugal, and, notably, the Netherlands. As to cleavage voting, the Netherlands stands out as the only country which comes near to the stereotype of cleavage politics: fully 53 per cent of the explanatory power of our conflict model is accounted for by cleavage voting. In Belgium, Italy, and France, cleavage voting accounts for 35–39 per cent of the explanatory power of our model. Cleavage voting is less important in Denmark, Germany, Spain, and Portugal; and particularly unimportant, around 14–22 per cent, in Iceland, Norway, Sweden, Britain, and Ireland. The appearance of Portugal and Ireland in the lower ranking of cleavage voting suggests that, contrary to our expectation (Hypothesis 7.2), cleavage voting is not significant in less advanced societies.

We suggested that cleavage voting would be more widespread in 'segmented' or 'plural' societies (Hypothesis 8), particularly in the Netherlands and Belgium. However, according to Lijphart (1984: 43–4), Italy and France are 'semi-plural' societies; the remaining countries,

TABLE 18.5. *Total effects of the three voting types in Western Europe*

% of total discrimination power	Structural voting	Value voting	Cleavage voting
60–65		IC, SV, GB	
50–59		NO	NL
40–49	IR	DK, GE, IR, FR, IT, SP	
35–39		BE, PO	BE, IT, FR
30–34	PO		DE, GE, SP, PO
20–29	DK, NO, BE, GB, GE, FR, IT, SP	NL	SV, NO
10–19	IC, SV, NL		IC, GB, IR

Notes: The total effects are decomposed into the portions of the total discriminating power of the conflict model accounted for by the three voting types. The average for 1981 (Eurobarometer, No. 16) and 1990 (European Values Survey) is shown for eight countries. For five countries, only results from the 1990 European Values Survey are shown.

by the same classification, are non-plural societies. That the Netherlands, Belgium, France, and Italy appear in the upper ranking on cleavage voting broadly confirms our hypothesis. The distinction between non-plural, semi-plural, and plural societies seems to correlate highly with the distribution of cleavage voting.

It is also evident from Table 18.5 that value voting is most widespread in the four Nordic countries, Germany, Britain, and Spain, whereas cleavage voting dominates in the Netherlands while structural voting is the most widespread type in Ireland. Value voting and cleavage voting are about equally important in Belgium, France, and Italy, and all voting types are about equally important in Portugal. We conclude, then, that value voting is the more common path in the more advanced industrial countries in Western Europe, while structural voting has a larger role in the less advanced countries. Cleavage voting is principally associated with plural and semi-plural societies.

The findings for the countries for which we have truly longitudinal data are presented in Table 18.6. Clearly, there is a fairly stable pattern over time in all five countries. Value voting has the largest effect in all these countries apart from the Netherlands, where cleavage voting dominates. In the other four countries, value voting accounts for 50

TABLE 18.6. *Developments in three voting types in five countries, 1970–89*

	Structural voting	Value voting	Cleavage voting	Total conflict model
Denmark				
1971	0.10	0.21	0.13	0.44
1979	0.12	0.25	0.10	0.47
1987	0.10	0.31	0.10	0.51
Norway				
1977	0.10	0.36	0.20	0.64
1981	0.11	0.38	0.18	0.67
1985	0.08	0.37	0.17	0.62
1989	0.10	0.32	0.12	0.54
Sweden				
1976	0.09	0.28	0.14	0.51
1985	0.06 (0.05)	0.33 (0.38)	0.13 (0.14)	0.52 (0.57)
1988	0.07 (0.06)	0.33 (0.37)	0.14 (0.15)	0.54 (0.58)
Britain				
1974	0.16 (0.06)	0.18 (0.21)	0.11 (0.08)	0.45 (0.35)
1979	0.05 (0.04)	0.19 (0.19)	0.06 (0.06)	0.30 (0.29)
1983	0.08 (0.05)	0.19 (0.20)	0.09 (0.08)	0.36 (0.33)
1987	0.08 (0.04)	0.19 (0.21)	0.11 (0.09)	0.38 (0.34)
Netherlands				
1970	0.10 (0.08)	0.14 (0.19)	0.50 (0.45)	0.74 (0.72)
1975	0.10 (0.08)	0.16 (0.18)	0.37 (0.35)	0.63 (0.61)
1980	0.10 (0.08)	0.16 (0.18)	0.36 (0.34)	0.62 (0.60)
1985	0.08 (0.07)	0.21 (0.23)	0.35 (0.33)	0.64 (0.63)

Notes: Entries are Wilks's lambda (transformed). For Britain, Germany, and the Netherlands results for the dichotomous denomination variable are shown in parentheses.

Sources: European Community Survey (1973); Eurobarometer, No. 16; European Values Survey (1990); Danish, Norwegian, Swedish, and British election surveys; Dutch Cultural Change Survey.

per cent or more of the total effects of the conflict model. Structural voting is the least important type in all these countries, but the Danish case is borderline. Structural voting accounts for some 10–20 per cent of the explanatory power of the conflict model in four countries, but about 20–26 per cent in Denmark. Among these countries, value voting increases relative to the other types only in Denmark, where it accounts for about 50 per cent (0.21 of 0.44) of the total effect in 1971, increasing to about 61 per cent (0.31 of 0.51) in 1987. In Norway and Sweden, the relative impact of value voting is notably stable, accounting for about 60 per cent of the impact of the conflict model.

The pattern is also very stable in Britain provided we overlook the effect of religious denomination in 1974. This stability should be seen against the fact that materialist–postmaterialist orientations are not included in the British election data: in the 1981 and 1990 comparative data, however, we have seen that the impact of value orientations increases in Britain due to the considerable increase in the impact of materialist–postmaterialist orientations.

Although cleavage voting is dominant in the Netherlands for the whole period, its impact on party choice falls absolutely and relative to the other types, and value voting has increased. In 1970, cleavage voting accounted for 68 per cent (0.50 of 0.74) of the total effects of the conflict model, which declined to 55 per cent (0.35 of 0.64) in 1985. In parallel, the impact of value voting has increased from 19 per cent (0.14) to 33 per cent (0.21). Cleavage voting also declines somewhat in Denmark and Norway (from about 30 per cent to 20 per cent of the total impact of the conflict model), but not in Sweden or Britain. The impact of structural voting remains quite low and constant in all these countries. In all, then, apart from the overall tendency to stability, the main trends are that value voting has increased, cleavage voting has declined, and structural voting is constant but at a relatively low level.

Thus, our expectation that structural voting is declining (Hypothesis 2) is not borne out. The trends for Denmark, Norway, and the Netherlands support our expectation that cleavage voting is declining (Hypothesis 3.2), but not our expectation that structural voting is declining relative to cleavage voting (Hypothesis 3.1). In Norway and the Netherlands, cleavage voting is declining but structural voting remains almost constant. According to the national data, value voting is increasing in Denmark and the Netherlands (Hypothesis 4.1), but is fairly stable in the other countries. Hence, although the position is not always clear cut, on balance our expectations about the changing impact of value voting are not confirmed by the longitudinal data.

Pre-War and Post-War Generations

Our hypothesis about generational differences anticipate that structural variables are less significant among the post-war generations (Hypothesis 5.1); that value orientations have a larger impact on party choice, both absolutely and relative to structural variables, among post-war generations (Hypotheses 5.4 and 5.5); and that structural voting and cleavage voting are stronger among pre-war generations (Hypotheses 5.2 and 5.3). Moreover, we expect generational differences in the impact of value orientations to be larger when the prior structural variables are controlled for than in the bivariate case since the anchoring of value orientations in structural variables is more typical of an older politics. Thus, a larger proportion of the bivariate effects of value orientations may be spurious among the earlier generations due to stronger correlations with the prior structural variables. To test for generational differences we use the 1990 European Values Survey data and the 1985–9 national data. The generations are defined as those born before 1940 and those born after 1945. A significant difference between the generations is a difference of 0.05 or more in Wilks's lambda, reported in parentheses.

The main findings (details not shown here) support the five hypotheses, and they are in the same direction for both sets of data. The impact of the structural variables is reduced among the post-war generation in seven of the thirteen countries: Norway (−0.24), Iceland (−0.19), the Netherlands (−0.16), Portugal (−0.14), Sweden, France, and Ireland (between −0.07 and −0.10). The impact of value orientations is larger among the post-war generation only in Iceland (0.16), Norway (0.10), Denmark and the Netherlands (both 0.05),[17] although in eight countries, the relative impact of value orientations is larger among the post-war generation than among the pre-war generation. Moreover, in Iceland, Norway, and Sweden, structural variables have a larger impact than value orientations among the pre-war generation, while the relative impact of these variables is quite the opposite among the post-war generation. Iceland and Norway are extreme cases in this respect: the relative impact of value orientations compared to structural variables, in both countries, is about 0.50 among the pre-war generation but about 1.90 among the post-war generation.

In addition, structural voting is less widespread among the post-war generation in Iceland (0.15), Norway (0.13), Ireland (0.11), France (0.07), and the Netherlands (0.5). Cleavage voting declines among the post-war generation in Iceland (0.16), Portugal (0.12), Norway and the Netherlands (both 0.11), Sweden and Belgium (0.05–0.06). Only in four countries are there no significant differences between the generations: Britain, Germany, Italy, and Spain. So, all five hypotheses are confirmed in several—between four and eight—of the thirteen countries in the comparative data, and there is no significant trend in the opposite direction in any of the countries.

Analysis of the longitudinal national data largely confirm the comparative findings. That is, the hypotheses are supported in some countries but the tendencies are not uniform. The only exception is the hypothesis about the decline of structural voting: this is not supported by the longitudinal data from any of the five countries. However, structural voting is less widespread among the post-war generation in the five countries. Thus, although the picture is not uniform, the direction of generational trends largely accords with our expectations.

Conclusion

Our starting point in this chapter was the assumption that the basis of party choice is changing and that much of the change is attributable to the growing salience of value conflicts. We tested this assumption by posing a confrontation between a 'cleavage' account and a 'new politics' account of party choice, comparing the impact of structural variables and value orientations over time and across countries.

Our findings are mixed. Generally, value orientations are more important than structural variables and, in some countries, the significance of value orientations has grown over the period 1973–90. Value voting is generally more widespread than structural voting or cleavage voting, and the incidence of value voting has grown in some countries. Yet we did not find either a general decline in the impact of structural variables or a general increase in the impact of value orientations. Rather, the overriding impression is of stability—both in the impact of the conflict variables and in the incidence of the voting types. Some of the change from one time point to another appeared as trendless fluctuation.

None the less, these findings point to an important general conclusion: the basis of party choice is more stable than suggested by 'new politics' accounts. The structural basis of political conflict, rather than being eroded, appears quite resilient. This leads us to suggest that much of the force of arguments about the changing basis of party choice stems from comparisons with socio-structural accounts of cleavage politics in which value orientations played little part. At the same time, we should note that the impact of structural variables is less significant, and the independent impact of value orientations more significant, than is implied by the cleavage model.

Our more specific findings, however, yield a more varied picture. The

most consistent evidence for the increasing influence of value orientations on party choice relates to the impact of the conflict variables.
According to the comparative data, the impact of value orientations is
largest in the more advanced industrial societies and this impact has
increased most, during the 1981–90 period, in the more advanced
industrial societies. But the hypotheses most strongly supported by
the data relate to the voting types: structural voting is most significant
in the less advanced industrial societies (Ireland and Portugal); cleavage
voting is strongest in countries with a history of 'segmented pluralism'
(the Netherlands and Belgium); value voting is most significant in the
more advanced industrial societies (Britain, Germany, and the Nordic
countries).

In the five countries for which there are national data, the controlled
impact of value orientations accounts for more discriminating power
than the structural variables in both the earlier (1970–7) and the later
period (1980–9). This implies that value orientations and value voting
have been important since the early 1970s, leading us to speculate that
value orientations may also have had important effects on party choice,
independently of social structure, in the 1950s and 1960s. The data do
not allow us to investigate this possibility. In the previous chapter,
however, the impact of class and religious value orientations on party
choice was found to have remained fairly constant in most countries,
while the impact of materialist and postmaterialist orientations
increased. Those findings imply that where the overall impact of value
orientations has increased, much of it is due to the growing influence of
materialist–postmaterialist orientations. That we have not found the
same pattern in the national data sets may be due to the lack of time-
series data with indicators for all three value orientations.

Support for other hypotheses is more inconclusive. But there is some
evidence: the proportion of the variance in party choice explained by
structural variables has declined both absolutely and relative to the
proportion of the variance explained by value orientations; cleavage
voting is declining relative to value voting; and value voting is increasing in some countries. However, there is only limited evidence of a
general increase in value voting and a general decline of cleavage
voting. Even so, both the national data and the 1990 comparative
data reveal that value voting is the most widespread type in most
West European countries.

Clearly, we have not found the kind of general change in the basis of
party choice which would bear out the claim that value conflicts are

superseding the old order of cleavage politics. That appears to be the case in some of the more advanced countries—but, even in those cases, there is not, overall, a steady trend towards value voting accompanied by a steady trend away from cleavage voting. In the absence of clear trends in any direction, we conclude that West European electorates seem to be short of the kind of shift in the basis of party choice suggested by 'new politics'. Equally, these electorates seem to be less straightjacketed by social structures than implied by cleavage politics.

Finally, as our data are about voters and their party preferences, our findings have implications for the relationship between electors and parties—the principal agents of government. Whereas the cleavage model suggests that political conflicts are rooted in socio-structural conflicts with normative implications, the primacy of value voting suggests that value conflicts are the real stuff of mass politics. This implies that the 'old' parties erected on the class and religious cleavages still enjoy the advantages of institutional entrenchment. Moreover, given the primacy of value conflicts, the advantages are not merely a matter of organizational capacity. Rather, we suggest, the institutional resources of entrenched parties allows for ideological elasticity as the environment of politics changes; when parties and voters are out of joint, the abstract and generalized nature of values permits the re-articulation of the voter–party relationship. This makes for the resilience of electoral politics.

The primacy of value orientations in party choice, however, also implies that values constrain parties: recasting what a party stands for is circumscribed by what its supporters believe is 'morally desirable'—as values were defined in Chapter 2. This involves a degree of ideological stasis which, we suggest, limited the capacity of the 'old' parties to respond to concerns outside the established repertory of value conflicts. From this perspective, the political irruptions of the 1970s were less about a long-term change in the basis of party choice and more about extending the repertory of politically relevant values. With the emergence of postmaterialist orientations, we find a certain pluralization of the values informing party preferences without undermining the potency of class and religious value orientations. As political values are not readily unmade and remade, the basis of party choice among West European electorates has remained largely unchanged over the last two decades, and perhaps longer, due, principally, to the centrality of values in political conflicts.

NOTES

1. Inglehart is ambivalent about developments in the religious cleavage, noting that 'religious cleavages remain astonishingly durable' (1990: 15) but also anticipating that the emergence of post-industrial society may lead to 'a renewed concern for spiritual values'—although 'a simple reprise of traditional religion does not seem likely' (1990: 180).

2. If university entry is differentiated by class, postmaterialism would be rooted in a form of social closure, so strengthening the claim that materialism–postmaterialism constitutes a 'value cleavage'. That is not an argument made by Inglehart.

3. Regarding ecology and new left parties, Inglehart comments: 'They have not yet developed strong voter loyalties or party organization. Whether they ever will is an open question' (Inglehart 1990: 263). Dalton (1988: 174) elaborates on the same point: 'Electoral politics is moving from cleavages defined by social groups to value and issue cleavages that identify only communities of like-minded individuals . . . The new politics value cleavage is unlikely to provide a basis of mobilization into exclusive, cohesive associational frameworks.'

4. See Lane, McKay, and Newton (1991: tables 7.5*a*, 7.5*b*, 7.6, 7.11*a*, 7.11*b*).

5. We have said nothing about centre–periphery or urban–rural cleavages, in part because 'new politics' arguments are largely addressed to developments in the class and religious cleavages and in part because this focus fits our comparative framework. The class cleavage has been ubiquitous in Western Europe, although recent in Ireland, and the religious cleavage has been dominant in much of Catholic Europe and not irrelevant in Protestant Europe. The political significance of the centre–periphery and urban–rural cleavages is more patchy (Lijphart 1981; 1984: ch. 8).

6. Religious denomination is based on the following questions: 'Do you belong to a religious denomination? If yes, which one? (European Community Survey 1973, European Values Study 1990); 'Do you regard yourself as belonging to a religion? If so, to which one?' (Eurobarometer, No. 16). Education level is measured by school-leaving age. Household income is based on reported income before deductions. The occupational categories in the European Community Survey and Eurobarometer, No. 16, are: skilled and unskilled workers; white-collar workers; professionals, higher-level white-collar workers; employers and self-employed in primary industries; other employers and self-employed. In the European Values Survey, non-manual workers are divided into lower, medium, and higher groups. Since there are so few cases in the employer/self-employed categories, these were collapsed.

7. Structural voting is similar to Parisi and Pasquino's 'vote of *appartenenza*' in Italy, based on 'an organic liaison with the social group to which the voter belongs', which is 'manifested by the exclusion of any assessment of the programmatic position of parties' (1979: 14–18).

8. In Eurobarometer, No.16, in addition to Inglehart's standard four-item battery, the following agree/disagree items were used: 'Western Europe should make a stronger effort to provide adequate military defence'; 'More severe penalties should be introduced for acts of terrorism'; 'Nuclear energy should be developed to meet future energy needs'; 'Stronger measures should be taken to protect the environment against pollution'; 'Regions of [our country] should be given more freedom to handle their own affairs'.

9. Most of the data sets were made available, via the Norwegian Social Science Data Services (NSD), from the ICPSR (Ann Arbor, Michigan), the Danish Data Archive (Odense), the Swedish Social Science Data Service (Göteborg), and the ESRC Data Archive (Essex). The Norwegian election studies were made available directly from NSD. Data from the 1990 European Values Study were made available by Ola Listhaug. The Dutch Cultural Change Surveys were provided by Steinmetzarchief (Amsterdam). We thank Ola Listhaug and the archives for their assistance.

10. Church attendance is not included in the 1976 Swedish election survey. During this period, only the 1971, 1979, and 1987 Danish election surveys record church attendance.

11. Religiously mixed countries, as a rule, are those in which more than 5% of the population belong to a denomination other than the dominant religion. For Germany, the relevant denominations are Protestant and Catholic; for the Netherlands, Catholic, Dutch Reformed, and Calvinist; for Britain, Anglican, Church of Scotland, Presbyterian, Methodist, and Catholics.

12. For Belgium, the Flemish and Francophone wings of the Christian Social (CVP and PSC), Socialist (BSP and PSB), and Liberal (PVV and PRL) parties are collapsed into one party. Similarly, the three parties in the UDF alliance (Republican, Christian Democrats, and Radicals) in France are treated as one. The three parties which merged as the Christian Democratic Appeal in the Netherlands (Catholic, Anti-Revolutionary, and Christian Historial Union) are treated as one party prior to 1977. Separate analyses show that treating these parties singly makes little difference to our findings: the explanatory power of the total model increases by 0.02–0.04. Our conclusions are not altered in any way.

13. The categories for occupation and religious denomination (for the three countries with more than one significant denomination), are recoded as dummy variables. Those not in the workforce and those who declare no denomination are reference categories.

14. Both the numerator and the denominator in this calculation are the transformed Wilks's lambda. For example, based on the comparative surveys, the estimate for Denmark 1973 (0.26) is derived from dividing 0.08 from Table 18.2*b* by 0.31 from Table 18.1*c*.

15. Similar conclusions emerge from analysing the data from Eurobarometer, No. 16, the 1990 Europan Values Survey, and the national data using the so-called *F*-to-remove statistic. This partial multivariate *F*-statistic in discriminant analysis indicates the relative contribution of a set of value orientations after controlling for all prior structural variables as well as the other value orientations (Klecka 1980: 57–8). From these analyses, it is evident that the impact of class and religious value orientations on party choice has remained fairly constant in most countries while the impact of materialism–postmaterialism has increased. These findings imply that where the overall impact of value orientations has increased, much of it is due to the growing influence of materialism–postmaterialism. Further details can be obtained from the authors.

16. The average effects in the 1990 data for the eight countries in the 1981 data are very similar: 0.09, 0.19, and 0.15 respectively.

17. According to the 1988 election data, Sweden also belongs in this group (0.11).

PART IV

In Conclusion

19

Perspectives on Value Change

JAN W. VAN DETH AND ELINOR SCARBROUGH

Along with our colleagues, we started out with the notion that, by now, rapid political change in Western Europe is a platitude. Following the general thrust of much recent literature, we expected the populations of these countries to be increasingly intent on pursuing non-material and emancipatory goals. In place of an emphasis on material well-being, respect for authority, or traditional norms, we thought to find a flowering of orientations which might be classed as expressions of self-fulfilment, independence, or emancipation. This is what terms such as 'individualization', 'post-conventional norms', 'de-traditionalization', or the spread of 'postmaterialism' and the arrival of 'postmodern society' would lead us to expect. Yet in many discussions about social and political change, emphasis on the independent individual is combined with the observation that, for most people, connectedness to others is essential for happiness and self-esteem.

This combination of fading traditional values, increasing self-reliance, yet the need for belongingness in modern society, presents several puzzles. But it was not fascination with the process of shifting values which led us to focus on the impact of changing values. Rather, as we emphasized in the introductory chapter, it is the *analytic primacy* of values in explanations of political change. The idea of changing values is at the heart of interpretations of almost every aspect of political change in Western Europe. Although the nature and impact of such change are much disputed, many researchers have felt compelled to use some value concept in understanding political change in these societies. At the simplest, most direct level, shifts in value orientations are seen to induce change in the modes and levels of political involvement. In a more complex way, value shifts may modify the nature of support and legitimacy, alter the content of ideological conflict and party competition, and redraw the contours of party systems. This analytic primacy of the value concept is the first reason for focusing on value change.

The *substantive primacy* of the value concept follows from another rather paradoxical observation: the wide-ranging changes which affect many aspects of life in Western Europe seem to have touched the national state only lightly. Satisfaction with the way democracy works, trust in government, attachments to the status quo—none of these touchstones of democratic politics appear to have declined any further after the late 1960s. Thus the shifts in value orientations evident over recent decades seem to have missed one of their major targets: the national state. In the light of fashionable debates about the 'crisis of the welfare state', the revival of neo-liberal ideology, and attempts to redefine the state, this makes a study of the impact of value change even more appealing. Hence, our second reason for focusing on the value concept.

The previous chapters have addressed aspects of changing value orientations, and their consequences, in Western Europe during the last twenty years or so. Do the results justify concentrating on value change in our explanation for political change? Or are our results to be seen primarily as evidence that the concern with values is an exaggeration based on trendy notions like 'individualization' and 'self-fulfilment'? Before we address these questions, we look, first, at how our results relate to the research questions set out in the introductory chapter.

Research Questions and Answers

Based on the broad lines of reasoning outlined in Chapter 1, we posed five questions. Our findings can be summarized by setting out the answers to those questions which emerge from our research.

1. *What is the meaning, status, and relevance of the value concept in perspectives on social and political change?*

Terms such as 'values', 'value change', 'value orientations', 'value dimensions', or 'value patterns' seem to be applied in widely divergent ways. As a first step, in Chapter 2, we specified a conceptualization of values as conceptions of the desirable. Our conceptualization recognizes that values are not directly observable but are relevant to the formulation of attitudes. This approach places attitudinal measures at the core of the empirical analyses presented in this volume. Uncovering 'real' values was not our objective; rather, our aim was to uncover underlying patterns, as evidence of constraint, among attitudes. To underline the heuristic purposes of the concept, we used values as a hypothetical construct which constrains attitudes. Thus, the empirical relevance of values requires evidence of some systematic patterning among attitudes. We termed these patterns 'value orientations'.

Working with the notion of value orientations had several implications for our research strategy. First, as values are not directly observable, it became clear that we would have to rely on uncovering the patterns, or constraint, underlying attitudes. This strategy soon ran up against the limitations of the data. For the most part, the available data were not collected for the purpose of explicating the political implications of value orientations. Thus, in several instances, the data base was put together by specifying the content of particular orientations and then searching for appropriate indicators. Indeed, in view of the readiness of some commentators to appeal to value change as the explanation for political change, the often fragmentary nature of the available data came as a suprise. So our strategy of focusing on value orientations implied that it was for us, the researchers, to give structure and meaning to the evidence.

The second implication is that, while we had good grounds for identifying certain key value orientations, our task could not be confined to tracing their development. If value orientations are characterized as heuristic devices, then the relevant evidence for accepting specific interpretations of underlying patterns follows from testing these concepts against other relevant variables. Hence, the empirical analyses had to go beyond establishing the value orientations as empirical phenomena to explore their social antecedents and their import. However, while our objective was to examine the impact of value orientations on beliefs in government, the limitations of the data meant that sometimes we had to settle for delineating their impact on political behaviour, leaving us to infer the implications for beliefs in government.

Conceptualized in this way, value orientations can perform a dual task in examining the linkage between social change and political change. On the one hand, value orientations are affected when changes in the economic and social environment work their way through to influence people's attitudes. On the other hand, value orientations can be used as explanatory variables in dealing with political change. This was the central message of the simple scheme set out in Figure 1.1.

2. *What are the major characteristics of West European societies, and to what extent is a process of value change actually taking place?*

We described the processes of industrialization and economic growth, the rise of the welfare state, and the stability of their political systems as the major characteristics of West European societies. These distinctive but related developments set the macro-level context for the micro-level developments examined in this volume. Despite many differences between countries, especially in levels of economic development, West European countries have much in common. In particular, advanced industrial societies have developed in several West European countries, and are developing in others, during the last decades. Parallel to this process, the position of government has expanded, and rising levels of government intervention and regulation have become characteristic of everyday life in Western Europe.

Although economic advance and social change have generally characterized Western Europe during the post-war period, the pattern of change is not uniform. The 1960s and the 1970s were clearly different from each other and different again from the previous decades. The largely uninterrupted experience of economic growth, especially during the 1960s, stimulated the idea that economy and society were manageable and that all economic and social problems could—and should—be approached by government intervention. The economic stagnation of the 1970s revealed that unemployment had not been banished and brought to light constraints on the further development of welfare states. On the one hand, the post-war period can be seen as the culmination of the very successful efforts to overcome the destruction of the Second World War, erecting societies of unprecedented prosperity and security for the average citizen. Expanding government intervention played an important role in this process. On the other hand, the period also exposed limits to further expansion of both the economy and government, heralding the arrival of changed economic, social, and political constellations.

The very general idea of the advance, first, from pre-industrial to industrial society, and, secondly, from industrial to advanced industrial society, suggested the kinds of value orientations which should be the core variables in our research. The first transition is more or less complete in most of Western Europe, but pre-industrial value orientations will be fading away only very slowly. Similarly, we expected to find the value orientations associated with industrial society beginning to wane as advanced economic and social forms take hold. The three sets of value orientations we selected were most likely to reveal, at the individual level, the influence of changes evident at the macro level. Thus, religious orientations as against secular orientations reveal the remnants of pre-industrial society; left–right materialist orientations are markers of industrial society; and postmaterialist orientations, as against materialist orientations, are seen as most relevant to advanced industrial society.

The empirical record on changing political value orientations is not easy to interpret unequivocally. All three measures reveal evidence of value change: the populations of Western Europe are becoming less religious, somewhat more left-materialist, and rather more postmaterialist in orientation. Only for religious–secular orientations, however, is the picture unambiguous: in every country, and especially among the young, there has been a very substantial decline of religious orientations. There is a certain steady decline of materialist orientations, but it is not fully matched by the advance of postmaterialist orientations. The significance of left–right materialism, however, persists even in the most advanced societies. In brief: pre-industrial orientations seem to have lost much of their hold, but the left–right materialist orientations typical of industrial societies endure while the materialist–postmaterialist orientations anticipated of advanced industrial society seem to be poised in the wings.

3. *What distinctive value orientations can be documented empirically, what traces of newly arising value orientations are available, and what are the major socio-structural antecedents of specific value orientations?*

The three central value orientations were documented, empirically, by using several different comparative and national data sets. Materialist–postmaterialist orientations were readily detected using the standard instrument, or its variants, in the Eurobarometer series. Uncovering left–right materialism, however, entailed detecting underlying structures among a number of attitudes. For documenting religious–secular orientations, it turned out that the straightforward question on church attendance can be taken as a valid indicator. So although establishing some of the indicators raised initial problems, we have been able to show that the value orientations of substantial proportions of the populations of West European countries can be characterized by variants of our three instruments.

In addition to the three central value orientations, other approaches to the question of new value orientations have been explored. First, we have shown that changes in religious–secular orientations are closely linked to changes in specific norms, especially in relation to sexual morality. The general direction of change is towards ethical pluralism. We have also shown the emergence, if very slowly, of a feminist political culture in every West European country during the 1970s, albeit that by 1983 further advance was halted in the southern countries. Similarly, we have shown that 'green' political ideas are a mass phenomenon in every country, irrespective of actual levels of environmental pollution. Moreover, quite clearly a 'green' orientation cannot be reduced to a postmaterialist orientation: the two orientations are conceptually and empirically distinct. We have also examined the empirical basis for perhaps the newest value orientation to emerge in the literature—postmodernism. It appears that postmodernist value orientations, based on the notions of expressivism, instrumentalism, and humanism, can be found in all advanced industrial countries in Western Europe. Finally, we used a crude measure of authoritarian and libertarian orientations to flesh out tensions, at the individual level, when the traditional links between social status and value orientations start to unravel.

Looking at the socio-structural antecedents of the three central value orientations, and the five additional orientations, we find a more or less similar pattern. In general, secularized orientations, left materialism, postmaterialism, sexual permissiveness, ecologism, feminism, postmodernism, and libertarianism are more evident among young people and the highly educated. This general pattern tends to support a generational model of changing value orientations: the young and highly educated are exposed most intensively to new social arrangements and show the greatest willingness to accept new ideas. A lack of longitudinal data for most of the value orientations, however, precludes a more conclusive evaluation of these processes in terms of birth-cohort, life-cycle, and period effects.

4. *What is the impact of value orientations on political orientations and behavioural intentions among the populations of Western Europe?*

Value orientations are not simply or only shaped by economic and social change; equally, value orientations may lead to specific modes of behaviour which reflect changes in the environment. Value orientations, then, can provide a link between the macro-level characteristics of advanced, and advancing, industrial societies on the one hand, and individual behaviour on the other.

We analysed the impact of the three central value orientations on a number of political orientations related to involvement, participation, and preferences. Levels of political interest, and interest in specific issues, can be ascribed, especially, to the spread of postmaterialism. A religious orientation tends to lead to greater concern about matters of sexual conduct, but otherwise to have ambiguous effects for political behaviour. These patterns are more or less similar across the countries of Western Europe. We also examined the impact of value orientations on grass-roots activity. Here, again, we found that postmaterialism plays a notable role in predicting behaviour; those involved in local, grass-roots political activity tend to be postmaterialist in orientation.

While informal political activities have become common in much of Western Europe, voting is still the most frequent mode of political participation. We found that postmaterialism has little influence on electoral turnout, but turnout tends to weaken with the decline of religious orientations. But the three central value orientations are clearly relevant to party preference. People of religious orientation tend to vote for parties of the right, whether Christian or conservative parties; parties of the left garner much of their support from among left materialists and postmaterialists. The influence of postmaterialism is most evident among voters for green parties and parties of the new left. However, the relative impact of these value orientations varies across countries, with left–right materialism having the strongest relationship with party preference in most countries. Finally, from examining a traditional cleavage model of party preference, we found that value orientations have a larger impact on party choice than variables reflecting social differences.

Nevertheless, our research suggests that the behaviourial consequences of value orientations are rather modest. Moreover, their influence is not uniform across countries. Postmaterialism seems to be especially relevant for political interest and grass-roots activities, while the effects of left–right materialism are most evident when it comes to party preference. But variations in these patterns between national populations showed that the influence of left–right materialism and materialism–postmaterialism are far from definitive. Furthermore, it became evident that the political influence of value orientations has changed little during the twenty years or so covered by our study. Religious orientations have clearly declined and secular orientations are widespread, but they emerged as the least relevant for explaining political behaviour at the individual level. Thus, apart from the general dwindling of religous orientations, our analyses revealed a rather stable picture in which left–right materialism and materialism–postmaterialism are the most relevant orientations for political behaviour. However, their influence on different forms of political behaviour and in different countries varies too much to allow us to go beyond broad generalizations.

5. *What are the implications of our findings about changing value orientations for beliefs in government among citizens in West European countries?*

We anticipated that the process of value change would affect beliefs in government in two closely related ways. On the one hand, as rising cognitive mobilization—in line with ongoing modernization—goes along with the emergence of 'new' value orientations, the general consequence would be increasing levels of political self-confidence. Citizens would develop greater political efficacy and civic competence. On the other hand, 'new' value orientations imply more critical attitudes towards traditional values and political authorities. In which case, they would have consequences for levels of political trust and civicness.

Our analysis of the consequences of the three central value orientations shows that these two general expectations are not borne out. The process of value change does not have a more or less uniform impact on beliefs in government. Postmaterialism is an important antecedent of civic competence and efficacy; the relatively high levels of post-materialism among grass-roots activists, too, suggest that postmaterialists are self-confident political actors. However, whereas trust in government and civicness are strengthened by religious orientations, postmaterialism is virtually unrelated to these two aspects of beliefs in government. In other words, while postmaterialism seems to promote civic competence and efficacy, it does not imply a loss of trust in government and a decline of civicness. The conclusion has to be that while value orientations are clearly relevant for beliefs in government, their specific relevance depends on both the type of value orientation and the particular aspects of beliefs in government at issue.

The direct impact of shifts in value orientations on beliefs in government is not all that counts, however. Political interest, grass-roots activity, electoral turnout, and party choice are influenced by 'new' orientations. Moreover, we found that sizeable segments of West European societies hold ecological, feminist, and postmodernist orientations. Thus, we have to conclude that the political landscape in Western Europe is highly differentiated. There are many more value orientations—of political relevance—influencing people's attitudes and behaviour than we would have expected to find in the pre-war years, or even in the early post-war years. Moreover, the influence of both 'new' and 'old' value orientations on political behaviour and beliefs in government is less predictable than often supposed.

In this landscape, the job of modern government is becoming more difficult. The 'new' value orientations bring new issues on to the political agenda while the persistence of 'old' orientations indicates that many of the old issues, especially the classic issues of inequality, are still not resolved. Modern governments have thus to wrestle with a much enlarged agenda. Some of the new value orientations, especially ecologism and feminism, specifically engage notions of political activism; the spread of postmaterialism carries with it a greater sense of political efficacy; the decline of religious orientations undermines deference and the habits of political obedience. Modern governments thus face electorates which are better prepared, in terms of outlooks, to challenge their power and performance. Moreover, modern governments have to find support among electorates which are more diverse in orientation. This makes it more difficult to put together the kind of broad consensus necessary to mount major policy initiatives. In this way, the impact of changing value orientations goes well beyond their direct effects on beliefs in government.

Value Pluralism and Analytical Primacy

The process of value change as described in this volume is intricate and complex. By no means is it possible to summarize developments over the last decades as a monotonic or singular change in a specific direction. What is most striking about our results is that traces of changing value orientations seem to be everywhere, while at no point or place can we show a dominant or unequivocal pattern. Rather, the populations of West European countries can be depicted, in our terms, as more or less postmaterialist, more or less left-materialist, more or less secular, more or less taken with ecological or feminist ideas, and more or less well described as instrumental or humanist postmodernists. Even this characterization is not an exhaustive account of the value orientations which influence political attitudes and behaviour among these populations. But even from this account, it is clear that the dominant themes are dispersion, fragmentation, and heterogeneity.

This picture of dispersion and heterogeneity is even more convincing when we see that the orientations of large numbers of citizens do not fit some simple classification of unambivalent value orientations. The distribution of postmaterialism is the readiest example: most of the analyses in this volume focused on the 'pure' postmaterialists and 'pure' materialists, yet we saw that about half the respondents in the survey data do not fit in either category. That these respondents are characterized as 'mixed' in value orientation makes the point. Again, while religious orientations—and green and feminist orientations for that matter—have some fairly clear effects for attitudes and behaviour, they characterize minorities among national populations. In all, the constraint or coherence between attitudes which allowed us to apply the concept of value orientations hid from view substantial numbers of people.

Moreover, when all three of our central value orientations were brought together into a single perspective, to explain grass-roots activity, voting, or political efficacy, for example, the heterogeneity of 'value types' increases spectacularly. This is consistent with findings from other research. Klages (1993) reports that a major distinction among materialists depends on whether or not they have hedonistic preferences. In his view, the most interesting new type of value orientation is found among 'hedomats': people who are both materialist and hedonist in orientation. Similarly, Flanagan (1987) has urged a distinction between authoritarian and non-authoritarian materialists. These multi-dimensional approaches to the problem of describing value orientations reinforce the conclusions we have come to: for the most part, value orientations are dispersed and fragmented; where clear 'value types' can be identified, value orientations define relatively small groups. What we observe, then, are multifaceted and varying combinations of specific orientations. Each of the value orientations we identified unravelled important aspects of the distribution of value orientations among West European populations. Equally, none of them can be used to delineate these populations in a simple, straightforward way.

Similar conclusions follow from looking at the evidence of value change. We cannot identify a clear, general direction in the development of value orientations. Certainly, some of our findings are in line with the idea of a general shift away from traditional orientations, evidenced by declining religiosity and declining materialism. The shift towards postmaterialist and other 'new' value orientations, however, while evident, looks less decisive. Moreover, the persisting influence of left–right materialist orientations, even in the most advanced industrial societies of Western Europe, indicates that changing value orientations is not a general process. Further, it became evident that we are not witnessing the rise of completely 'new' values, but more complex processes in which less prescriptive, individualistic interpretations of long-standing values are intertwined with the extension of core values to 'new' groups, such as women, and the reformulation of old values to address 'new' problems such as environmental pollution. From this perspective, too, we do not find some dominant development which could account for most of the patterns observed. Value change does not follow a single developmental path; rather the picture is of divergence, fragmentation, and diversity.

Two conclusions can be derived from this dual characterization of the process of value change as both heterogeneous and subject to varying forms of fragmentation. First, the term 'value change', in the singular, should be abandoned. It is not only misleading but is based on the rather unrealistic notion that changes in value orientations can be summarized in a simple way. Instead, we would prefer to refer to changes in value orientations among particular populations in specific national contexts in order to stress that, in this matter, we are dealing with distinctive orientations which are characterized by specific processes of change and persistence. In these processes, 'new' value orientations arise by combining familiar values in new ways. So fragmentation provides the basis for both value pluralization and value synthesis. This observation leads to a second conclusion.

The processes of changing value orientations are not characterized by a rather straightforward replacement of existing value orientations by new orientations. Rather, elements in traditional value orientations are gradually losing their authority or relevance, while other elements retain their force. At the same time, the fading old elements are slowly, but only partly, being replaced by elements from new value orientations. Few people adopt a new value orientation—with its coherent and integrated set of values—in its entirety, but take up parts of available orientations. The reconfiguration of values in new constellations is an intrinsic part of more general processes of social change. Klages (1993: 33) refers to this development as the 'potential for differentiation and individualization' which is inherent in the processes of change in advanced industrial societies.

The empirical findings presented in this volume underline the complexities of analysing political change in terms of value orientations. The analytical primacy of the value concept proved to be a very fruitful starting point for examining developments in Western Europe over recent decades. Using the concept of value orientation as a heuristic device has enabled us to link changes at the societal level to specific attitudes and modes of political behaviour at the individual level. But the prominence accorded to value orientations in our account does not imply that the concept of value orientations can be used as a template for describing every aspect of social and political change in a systematic way. There is, indeed, something like a 'megatrend' in the developmental processes associated with value orientations, and in that sense the concept has proved its empirical usefulness. At the same time, we have shown the particularized nature of the social antecedents and the specific developmental trajectories of our three central value orientations. We have also underlined value pluralization and value synthesis. From this it follows that the analytic primacy of the value concept should be taken for what it is: the recommendation to use value orientations as a starting point for explaining individual behaviour and attitudes in rapidly changing societies.

Government in a Fragmented World

The final question is to assess the substantive primacy of the value concept, as demonstrated by the findings presented in this volume. From our perspective, the substantive primacy of the value concept was based on the observation that the position of the national state is affected by changing value orientations in a complex way (see Chapter

1). While the several changes which have occurred over the last decades seem to have affected many aspects of West European societies, the authority of the national state has not been endangered. On the contrary: with the fall of the Berlin Wall and the collapse of the communist regimes, representative democracy appears to be virtually unchallenged as a vital and attractive way to organize political life. But the populations of West European states did not wait until 1989 to draw this conclusion. Whatever changes have occurred in people's value orientations, the national state has not been rejected by large majorities in Western Europe.

Our findings go a long way towards understanding this paradox. In the first place, the processes of fragmentation and pluralization we emphasized render most value orientations minority phenomena. Even if we had uncovered a value orientation hostile to the national state, it would be unlikely to have adherents among a large section of the population. Secondly, it turned out that none of the value orientations we documented can be characterized as rejecting the power of the national state. Some might lead to demands for more institutional openness, for citizens to have a more direct input to government decision-making. But modern governments appear able to handle these kinds of demands, making marginal but incremental adjustments to institutional procedures. Moreover, some 'new' value orientations specifically look to governments for intervention—to regulate against pollution or to realize equal rights for men and women, for instance. While 'new' value orientations put governments under pressure, the position of the national state is strengthened when citizens rely on governments to handle salient issues. The processes of changing value orientations we have documented, then, do not lead to a direct challenge to the national state. That citizens are more critical about what governments do, and how they go about it, should not be confused with a rejection of political power in the traditional sense.

We noted above that the job of national governments in Western Europe is becoming more difficult. The pluralism and fragmentation of value orientations alter the terms of mass politics and the basis of public policy-making. Governments are confronted by a much wider variety of demands put forward by a larger range of different groups. Governments seem to respond to these pressures by either adopting short-term *ad hoc* policies, or withdrawing as active arbiters in societal conflicts. Confronted with the diversity of values and the divergence of demands, governments tend to settle for establishing procedures by which conflicts might be resolved—thereby leaving the battlefield to citizens and their organizations. The effects of this development in statecraft are ambiguous: on the one hand, governments appear to be open to any manner of demand; on the other hand, the institutions of government become a much weaker vehicle for effecting social transformations.

Examining the degree of openness among West European governments is beyond the scope of this volume. What is relevant here is that these governments do not exclude alternative value orientations by adopting some 'official' position, as with governments dominated by, for example, a communist creed. In this sense, there is little point in citizens rejecting government as the power centre in modern states; it is altering the political agenda or the nature of government power which is relevant for 'new' value orientations. It is in this dynamic, inclusionary relationship between the pluralization of value orientations on the one hand, and the reactions of governments on the other, that we have to place the 'beliefs in government' of citizens in Western Europe. And it is this relationship which demonstrates the substantive primacy of the concept of value orientations in analysing political change.

Our quest started from the idea that rapid political change in Western Europe has become a platitude. By using the concept of value orientations we showed that the processes of change are much more differentiated and complicated—and much more interesting—than we would expect of a platitude. Only a monomaniac approach could yield unidirectional or determinist interpretations of developments in the advanced societies of Western Europe. It is not the case that changing value orientations entails the erosion of beliefs in government. People are adjusting their value orientations to changing environments, and, in turn, their shifts in value orientations influence the political nature of these environments. Political decision-making is more complicated in a fragmented world, but coping with societal complexity is one of the tasks of government. From the citizen's viewpoint, changing value orientations might be looked upon as an enrichment of their societies, elevating individuality and independence of thought above traditional norms and social conformity. This richness is also reflected in the rather short brushstrokes which characterize our account.

REFERENCES

Aardal, B. O., and Valen, H. (1989). *Velgere, partier, og politisk avstand*. Oslo and Kongsvinger: Statistisk Sentralbyrå.

Abercrombie, N., and Urry, J. (1983). *Capital, Labour and the Middle Classes*. London: Allen and Unwin.

Abramson, J. B., Arterton, F. C., and Orren, G. R. (1988). *The Electronic Commonwealth: The Impact of New Media Technologies on Democratic Politics*. New York: Basic Books.

Abramson, P. A. (1983). *Political Attitudes in America: Formation and Change*. San Francisco: W. H. Freeman.

—— and Finifter, A. W. (1981). 'On the Meaning of Political Trust: New Evidence From Items Introduced in 1978'. *American Journal of Political Science* 25: 297–307.

—— and Inglehart, R. (1992). 'Generational Replacement and Value Change in Eight West European Societies'. *British Journal of Political Science* 22: 183–228.

Acock, A. C., and Clarke, H. D. (1990). 'Alternative Measures of Political Efficacy: Models and Means'. *Quality and Quantity* 24: 87–105.

—— —— and Stewart, M. C. (1985). 'A New Model for Old Measures: A Covariance Structure Analysis of Political Efficacy'. *Journal of Politics* 47: 1062–84.

Adler, F. (1956). 'The Value Concept in Sociology'. *American Journal of Sociology* 62: 272–9.

Adorno, T. W., Frenkel-Brunswick, E., Levinson, D., and Sanford, R. N. (1950). *The Authoritarian Personality*. New York: Harper and Row.

Affigne, A. D. (1990). 'Chernobyl and the Swedish Greens'. In *Green Politics One*, ed. W. Rüdig. Edinburgh: Edinburgh University Press.

Aglietta, M. (1979). *A Theory of Capitalist Regulation*. London: New Left Books.

Albert, E. M. (1956). 'The Classification of Values: A Method and Illustration'. *American Anthropologist* 58: 221–48.

—— (1968). 'Value Systems'. In *International Encyclopedia of the Social Sciences*, xii, ed. D. L. Sills. Glencoe, Ill.: Free Press.

Almond, G., and Verba S. (1963). *The Civic Culture: Political Attitudes and Democracy in Five Nations*. Boston: Little, Brown.

Anderson, K., and Armitage, S., et al. (1990). 'Beginning Where We Are: Feminist Methodology in Oral History'. In *Feminist Research Methods: Exemplary Readings in the Social Sciences*, ed. J. M. Nielsen. Boulder, Colo.: Westview.

Apter, D. E. (1965). *Rethinking Development: Modernization, Dependency, and Postmodern Politics*. Beverly Hills, Calif.: Sage.

Asher, H. B. (1974). 'The Reliability of the Political Efficacy Items'. *Political Methodology* 1: 45–72.

Baker, K., Dalton, R. J., and Hildebrandt, K. (1981). *Germany Transformed: Political Culture and New Politics*. Cambridge, Mass.: Harvard University Press.

Balch, G. I. (1974). 'Multiple Indicators in Survey Research: The Concept "Sense of Political Efficacy"'. *Political Methodology* 1: 1–43.

Ball-Rokeach, S., and Tallman, I. (1979). 'Social Movements as Moral Confrontations: With Special Reference to Civil Rights'. In *Understanding Human Values*, ed. M. Rokeach. New York: Free Press.

Barnes, S. H., Kaase, M., et al. (1979). *Political Action: Mass Participation in Five Western Democracies*. Beverly Hills, Calif.: Sage.

Baron, C. (1988). *Asylum to Anarchy*. London: Free Association Books.

Bartolini, S., and Mair, P. (1990). *Identity, Competition, and Electoral Availability*. Cambridge: Cambridge University Press.

Baudrillard, J. (1983). *Simulations*. New York: Semiotext.

Bauman, Z. (1987). *Legislators and Interpreters: On Modernity, Postmodernity, and Intellectuals*. Cambridge: Polity Press.

—— (1988). 'Is There a Postmodern Sociology?' *Theory, Culture and Society* 5: 217–37.

Beck, U. (1986). *Risikogesellschaft: Auf dem Weg in eine andere Moderne*. Frankfurt: Suhrkamp.

—— (1992). *Risk Society: Towards a New Modernity*. London: Sage.

Becker, G. S. (1981). 'Altruism in the Family and Selfishness in the Market Place'. *Economica* 48: 1–15.

Bell, D. (1960). *The End of Ideology*. Glencoe, Ill.: Free Press.

—— (1973). *The Coming of Post-Industrial Society: A Venture in Social Forecasting*. New York: Basic Books.

—— (1976). *The Cultural Contradictions of Capitalism*. London: Heinemann.

Bellah, R. N. (1967). 'Civil Religion in America'. *Daedalus* 96: 1–21.

—— (1989). *Postmodern Theology*. New York: Harper and Row.

—— Madsen, R., Sullivan, W. M., Swidler, A., and Tipton, S. M. (1985). *Habits of the Heart: Individualism and Commitment in American Life*. New York: Harper and Row.

Bengtson, V. L., and Lovejoy, M. C. (1973). 'Values, Personality, and Social Structure'. *American Behavioral Scientist* 16: 880–912.

Bennulf, M., and Holmberg, S. (1990). 'The Green Breakthrough in Sweden'. *Scandinavian Political Studies* 13: 165–84.

Berelson, B. R., Lazarsfeld, P. F., and McPhee, W. N. (1954). *Voting: A Study of Opinion Formation in a Presidential Campaign.* Chicago: University of Chicago Press.

Berger, P. L. (1967). *The Sacred Canopy: Elements of a Sociological Theory of Religion.* Garden City, NY: Doubleday.

—— and Luckmann, T. (1967). *The Social Construction of Reality.* Garden City, NY: Doubleday.

Berger, S. (1982). 'Introduction: Religion in West European Politics'. *West European Politics* 5: 1–7.

Bernstein, R. (1985). *Philosophical Profiles: Essays in a Pragmatic Mode.* Cambridge: Polity Press.

—— (1991). *The New Constellation: The Ethical and Political Horizon of Modernity and Postmodernity.* Cambridge: Polity Press.

Betz, H.-G. (1991). *Postmodern Politics in Germany: The Politics of Resentment.* Basingstoke, Hants.: Macmillan.

Billig, M. (1987). *Arguing and Thinking.* Cambridge: Cambridge University Press.

—— (1988). *Ideological Dilemmas.* London: Sage.

Blau, P., and Duncan, O. (1967). *The American Occupational Structure.* New York: John Wiley.

Bolton, C. D. (1972). 'Alienation and Action: A Study of Peace Group Members'. *American Journal of Sociology* 78: 537–61.

Books, J. W. (1980). 'Class and Religious Voting in Three European Nations: Political Changes in the 1960s'. *Social Science Journal* 17: 69–87.

Borchorst, A. (1992). 'EF, Kvindeinteresser, og velfaerdsstatsregimer'. Presented at the Nordic Symposium Kvinnorna och Europa, Stockholm.

Borg, S. (1995). 'Electoral Participation: Survey Results.' In *The Finnish Voter*, ed. S. Borg and R. Sänkiaho. Tampere: Finnish Political Science Association.

Borre, O. (1984). 'Træk af den danske vælgeradfærd 1971–84'. In *Valg og vælgeradfærd: Studier i dansk politik*, ed. J. Elklit, and O. Tonsgaard. Århus: Politika.

Bourdieu, P. (1979). *La Distinction.* Paris: Éditions de minuit.

—— (1984). *Distinction: A Social Critique of the Judgement of Taste.* Cambridge, Mass.: Harvard University Press.

Brittan, S. (1977). *The Economic Consequences of Democracy.* London: Temple Smith.

—— (1988). *A Restatement of Economic Liberalism.* Basingstoke, Hants.: Macmillan.

Brown, S. (1988). *New Forces, Old Forces and the Future of World Politics.* Glenview, Ill.: Scott, Foresman.

Bruce-Briggs, B. (ed.) (1979). *The New Class?* New York: McGraw-Hill.

Bruntland, G. H., *et al.* (1987). *Our Common Future: World Commision on Environmental Development.* Oxford: Clarendon Press.

Budge, I., and Farlie, D. J. (1983). *Explaining and Predicting Elections: Issue Effects and Party Strategies in Twenty-Three Democracies*. London: Allen and Unwin.

Bull, H. (1977). *The Anarchical Society: A Study of Order in World Politics*. London: Macmillan.

Butler, D., and Stokes, D. (1971) (1st edn. 1969). *Political Change in Britain*. London: Macmillan.

Calista, D. (1984). 'Postmaterialism and Value Convergence'. *Comparative Political Studies* 16: 529–55.

Campbell, A., Gurin, G., and Miller, W. E. (1954). *The Voter Decides*. Evanston, Ill.: Row and Peterson.

—— Converse, P., Miller, W., and Stokes, D. (1960). *The American Voter*. New York: John Wiley.

Carnap, R. (1936). 'Testability and Meaning; I–III'. *Philosophy of Science* 3: 419–71.

Castles, F. G. (1978). *The Social Democratic Image of Society: A Study of the Achievements of Scandinavian Social Democracy in Comparative Perspective*. London: Routledge and Kegan Paul.

Catton, W. R. (1959). 'A Theory of Values'. *American Sociological Review* 24: 310–17.

Cawson, A. (1982). *Corporatism and Welfare*. London: Heinemann.

—— (1989). *Corporatism and Political Theory*. Oxford: Basil Blackwell.

Cerny, P. (1990). *The Changing Architecture of Politics*. London: Sage.

Citrin, J. (1974). 'Comment: The Political Relevance of Trust in Government'. *American Political Science Review* 68: 973–88.

Clarke, H. D., and Dutt, N. (1991). 'Measuring Value Change in Western Industrialized Societies'. *American Political Science Review* 85: 905–20.

—— —— and Rapkin, J. (1994). 'Conversations in Context: The Case of the Eurobarometer Values Battery'. Unpublished paper.

Cohen, S., and Scull, A. (1983). *Social Control and the State*. Oxford: Martin Robertson.

Commission of the European Communities (1980). *Women and the European Community: Community Action, and Comparative National Situations*. Luxembourg: European Commission.

—— (1992). *Panorama: Statistical Data Concerning the Participation of Women in Political and Public Decision-Making*. Luxembourg: European Commission.

Connolly, W. (ed.) (1984). *Legitimacy and the State*. Oxford: Basil Blackwell.

—— (1991). *Identity/Difference: Democratic Negotiations of Political Paradox*. Ithaca, NY: Cornell University Press.

Converse, P. E. (1964). 'The Nature of Belief Systems in Mass Publics'. In *Ideology and Discontent*, ed. D. Apter. New York: Free Press.

—— (1980). 'Comment: Rejoinder to Judd and Milburn'. *American Sociological Review* 45: 644–6.

Cotgrove, S. (1982). *Catastrophe or Cornucopia: The Environment, Politics, and the Future*. Chichester, Sussex: John Wiley.

—— and Duff, A. (1980). 'Environmentalism, Middle-Class Radicalism, and Politics'. *Sociological Review* 2: 333–51.

—— —— (1981). 'Environmentalism, Values, and Social Change'. *British Journal of Sociology* 32: 92–107.

Cousins, M., and Hussain, A. (1984). *Michel Foucault*. Basingstoke, Hants.: Macmillan.

Craig, S. C. (1979). 'Efficacy, Trust, and Political Behavior: An Attempt to Resolve a Lingering Conceptual Dilemma'. *American Politics Quarterly* 7: 225–39.

—— Niemi, R. G., and Silver, G. E. (1990). 'Political Efficacy and Trust: A Report on the NES Pilot Study Items'. *Political Behavior* 12: 289–314.

Crewe, I. (1981). 'Electoral Participation'. In *Democracy at the Polls: A Comparative Study of Competitive National Elections*, ed. D. Butler, R. Howard, and A. Ranney. Washington, DC: American Enterprise Institute.

—— and Denver, D. (eds.) (1985). *Electoral Change in Western Democracies: Patterns and Sources of Electoral Volatility*. London: Croom Helm.

Crook, S., Pakulski, J., and Waters, J. (1992). *Postmodernization: Change in Advanced Society*. London: Sage.

Curran, J., and Gurevitch, M. (eds.) (1991). *Mass Communication and Society*. London: Edward Arnold.

—— and Seaton, J. (1985, 2nd edn.). *Power without Responsibility: The Press and Broadcasting in Britain*. London: Methuen.

Cutler, N. E. (1975). 'Toward a Generational Conception of Political Socialization'. In *New Directions in Political Socialization*, ed. D. C. Schwartz and S. K. Schwartz. New York: Free Press.

Daalder, H. (1974). 'The Consociational Democracy Theme'. *World Politics* 26: 604–21.

Dahlerup, D. (1988). 'From a Small to a Large Minority: Women in Scandinavian Politics'. *Scandinavian Political Studies* 4: 275–98.

Dalton, R. J. (1988). *Citizen Politics in Western Democracies: Public Opinion and Political Parties in the United States, Great Britain, West Germany, and France*. Chatham, NJ: Chatham House.

—— (1989). *Politics in West Germany*. Glenview, Ill.: Scott, Foresman.

—— (1991). 'The Dynamics of Party System Change'. In *Eurobarometer: The Dynamics of European Public Opinion*, ed. K. Reif and R. Inglehart. London: Macmillan.

—— Beck, P. A., and Flanagan, S. C. (1984). 'Electoral Change in Advanced Industrial Democracies'. In *Electoral Change in Advanced*

546 References

Industrial Democracies: Realignment or Dealignment? ed. R. J. Dalton, S. C. Flanagan, and P. A. Beck. Princeton: Princeton University Press.

Dalton, R. J., Flanagan, S. C., and Beck, P. A. (eds.) (1984). *Electoral Change in Advanced Industrial Democracies: Realignment or Dealignment?* Princeton: Princeton University Press.

Dekker, P., and Ester, P. (1987). 'Working-Class Authoritarianism: A Re-examination of the Lipset Thesis'. *European Journal of Political Research* 15: 395–415.

Deutsch, K. W. (1960). 'Towards an Inventory of Basic Trends and Patterns in Comparative and International Politics'. *American Political Science Review* 54: 34–57.

Dobbelaere, K. (1966). *Sociologische analyse van de Katholiciteit.* Antwerp: Standaard Wetenschappelijke Uitgeverij.

—— (1984). 'La Religion en Belgique'. In *L'Univers des Belges: Valeurs anciennes et valeurs nouvelles dans les années 80,* ed. R. Rezsohazy and J. Kerkhofs. Louvain-la-Neuve: Ciaco.

—— (1985a). 'La Dominante catholique'. In *La Belgique et ses dieux: Églises, mouvements religieux et laïques,* ed. L. Voyé *et al.* Louvain-la-Neuve: Cabay.

—— (1985b). 'Secularization Theories and Sociological Paradigms: A Reformulation of the Private–Public Dichotomy and the Problem of Societal Integration'. *Sociological Analysis* 46: 377–87.

—— (1988a). 'Secularization, Pillarization, Religious Involvement, and Religious Change in the Low Countries'. In *World Catholicism in Transition,* ed. T. M. Gannon. New York: Macmillan.

—— (1988b). *Het ' Volk-Gods' de mist in? Over de Kerk in België.* Leuven: Acco.

—— (1989). 'The Secularization of Society? Some Methodological Suggestions'. In *Religion and the Political Order,* iii, *Secularization and Fundamentalism Reconsidered,* ed. J. K. Hadden and A. Shupe. New York: Paragon House.

—— and Voyé, L. (1990). 'From Pillar to Postmodernity: The Changing Situation of Religion in Belgium'. *Sociological Analysis* 51: 1–13.

—— —— (1991). 'Western European Catholicism since Vatican II'. In *Religion and the Social Order: Vatican II and US Catholicism,* ed. H. R. Ebaugh. Greenwich, Conn.: JAI Press.

Dobson, A. (1990). *Green Political Thought.* London: Harper Collins.

—— (ed.) (1991). *Green Reader.* London: André Deutsch.

Döring, H. (1990). 'Aspekte des Vertrauens in Institutionen. Westeuropa im Querschnitt der Internationalen Wertestudie 1981'. *Zeitschrift für Soziologie* 19: 73–89.

Dukes, W. F. (1955). 'Psychological Studies of Values'. *Psychological Bulletin* 52: 24–50.

Durkheim, E. (1912). *Les Formes élémentaires de la vie religieuse*. Paris: Presses Universitaires de France.

—— (1960). *De la division du travail social*, 7th edn. Paris: Presses Universitaires de France.

Easton, D. (1965) (2nd edn. 1979). *A Systems Analysis of Political Life*. New York: John Wiley.

—— (1975). 'A Re-assessment of the Concept of Political Support'. *British Journal of Political Science* 5: 435–57.

Edelman, M. (1988). *Constructing the Political Spectacle*. Chicago: University of Chicago Press.

Eduards, M. (1988). 'Att studera politik ur ett könsperspektiv'. *Statsvetenskaplig Tidskrift* 3: 207–21.

—— Gustafsson, G., and Jónasdóttir, A. (1989). 'Könsmakt och maktlöshet i nationalstaten'. *Kvinnors makt och inflytande*. Stockholm: JÄMFO.

Eijk, C. van der, and Niemöller, B. (1985). 'The Netherlands'. In *Electoral Change in Western Democracies: Patterns and Sources of Electoral Volatility*, ed. I. Crewe and D. Denver. London: Croom Helm.

Eisinger, P. K. (1973). 'The Conditions of Protest Behaviour in American Cities'. *American Political Science Review* 67: 11–28.

Elias, N. (1978, 1982). *The Civilizing Process,* i, ii. Oxford: Basil Blackwell.

Erikson, R., and Goldthorpe, J. (1992). *The Constant Flux: A Study of Class Mobility in Industrial Society*. Oxford: Clarendon Press.

—— Luttbeg, N. R., and Tedin, K. L. (1988). *American Public Opinion: Its Origins, Content, and Impact*. New York: Collier-Macmillan.

Esping-Andersen, G. (1990). *Three Worlds of Welfare Capitalism*. Cambridge: Polity Press.

Etzioni, A. (1968). *The Active Society: A Theory of Societal and Political Processes*. London: Collier-Macmillan.

Eurostat (1987, 1991, 1992). *Statistische Grundzahlen der Gemeinschaft: Vergleich mit verschiedenen europäischen Ländern, Kanada, den USA, Japan und der UdSSR*, 24, 28, and 29, ed. Statistical Office of the European Communities. Luxembourg: Eurostat.

Evans, S., and Hildebrandt, K. (1979). Technical Appendix. In S. H. Barnes, M. Kaase, *et al.*, *Political Action: Mass Participation in Five Western Democracies*. Beverly Hills, Calif.: Sage.

Fallding, H. (1965). 'A Proposal for the Empirical Study of Values'. *American Sociological Review* 30: 223–33.

Farr, R. (1990). 'Social Representations as Widespread Beliefs'. In *The Social Psychological Study of Widespread Beliefs*, ed. C. Fraser and G. Gaskell. Oxford: Clarendon Press.

Feather, N. T. (1984). 'Masculinity, Femininity, Psychological Androgyny, and the Structure of Values'. *Journal of Personality and Social Psychology* 47: 604–20.

Featherstone, M. (1988). 'In Pursuit of the Postmodern'. *Theory, Culture, and Society* 5: 195–216.

—— (1991). *Postmodern Sociology*. London: Sage.

Fenn, R. K. (1972). 'Toward a New Sociology of Religion'. *Journal for the Scientific Study of Religion* 11: 16–32.

Ferry, L., and Renault, A. (1985). *French Philosophy of the Sixties*. Amherst, Mass.: University of Massachusetts Press.

Finifter, A. W. (1970). 'Dimensions of Political Alienation'. *American Political Science Review* 64: 389–410.

—— (ed.) (1972). *Alienation and the Social System*. New York: John Wiley.

Fiske, J. (1989). *Understanding Popular Culture*. London: Unwin Hyman.

Flanagan, S. A. (1982). 'Changing Values in Advanced Industrial Societies: Inglehart's Silent Revolution from the Perspective of Japanese Findings'. *Comparative Political Studies* 14: 403–44.

—— (1987). 'Changing Values in Industrial Society Revisited: Towards a Resolution of the Values Debate'. *American Political Science Review* 81: 1303–19.

—— and Lee, A.-R. (1988). 'Explaining Value Change and its Political Implications in Eleven Advanced Industrial Democracies'. Paper presented at the 14th World Congress of the International Political Science Association, Washington, DC.

Flora, P., and Heidenheimer, A. J. (1981). *The Development of Welfare States in Europe and America*. New Brunswick, NJ: Transaction Books.

Folsom, J. K. (1937). 'Changing Values in Sex and Family Relations'. *American Sociological Review* 2: 717–26.

Forbes, I. (1989). 'Nietzsche, Modernity, and Politics.' In *Contemporary Political Culture: Politics in a Postmodern Age*, ed. J. R. Gibbins. London: Sage.

Foucault, M. (1977). *Discipline and Punishment: The Birth of the Prison*. London: Allen and Unwin.

—— (1981). *The History of Sexuality*, i. Harmondsworth, Middx: Penguin.

Franklin, M. N. (1985). *The Decline of Class Voting in Britain*. Oxford: Clarendon Press.

—— Mackie, T. T., Valen, H., *et al.* (1992). *Electoral Change: Responses to Evolving Social and Attitudinal Structures in Western Countries*. Cambridge: Cambridge University Press.

Fuchs, D. (1989). *Die Unterstützung des politischen Systems der Bundesrepublik Deutschland*. Opladen: Westdeutscher Verlag.

—— and Rucht, D. (1994). 'Support for New Social Movements in Five Western European Countries'. In *A New Europe? Social Change and Political Transformation*, eds. C. Rootes and H. Davis. London: University College London Press.

Gabennesch, H. (1972). 'Authoritarianism as World View'. *American Journal of Sociology* 77: 857–75.

Gabriel, K., and Kaufmann, F.-X. (eds.) (1980). *Zur Soziologie des Katholizismus*. Mainz: Matthias-Grünewald.

Gabriel, O. W. (1986). *Politische Kultur, Postmaterialismus und Materialismus in der Bundesrepublik Deutschland*. Opladen: Westdeutscher Verlag.

—— (1987). 'Wahrnehmung der Politik durch den Bürger als Herausforderung für die Politikvermittlung'. In *Politikvermittlung: Beiträge zur politischen Kommunikationskultur*, ed. U. Sarcinelli. Stuttgart: Bonn Aktuell.

—— (1989). 'Regierungswechsel und politische Unterstützung: Implikationen des Parteienwettbewerbs für die Struktur politischer Unterstützung in der Demokratie'. *Politische Vierteljahresschrift* 30: 75–93.

—— (1994) (2nd edn.). 'Politische Einstellungen und politische Kultur'. In *Die EU-Staaten im Vergleich: Strukturen, Prozesse, Politikinhalte*, ed. O. W. Gabriel and F. Brettschneider. Opladen: Westdeutscher Verlag.

—— and Brettschneider, F. (ed.) (1994) (2nd edn.). *Die EU-Staaten im Vergleich: Strukturen, Prozesse, Politikinhalte*. Opladen: Westdeutscher Verlag.

Gamson, W. A. (1968). *Power and Discontent*. Homewood, Ill.: Dorsey.

Gastelaars, M. (1987). 'Niets zo modern als een mens alleen'. In *Dagelijks leven in Nederland: Verschuivingen in het sociale leven na de Tweede Wereldoorlog*, ed. T. van der Kampt and H. Krynen. Amsterdam: De Populier.

Gerlach, L. P., and Hine, V. H. (1970). *People, Power, Change: Movements and Social Transformation*. Indianapolis: Bobbs–Merrill.

Gibbins, J. R. (ed.) (1989a). *Contemporary Political Culture: Politics in a Postmodern Age*. London: Sage.

—— (1989b). 'Contemporary Political Culture: An Introduction'. In *Contemporary Political Culture: Politics in a Postmodern Age*, ed. J. R. Gibbins. London: Sage.

—— (1991). 'The New State'. Paper presented to the European Science Foundation Project on Beliefs in Government, Berlin.

Gibbs, J. P. (1965). 'Norms: The Problem of Definition and Classification'. *American Journal of Sociology* 70: 587–94.

Giddens, A. (1973). *The Class Structure of the Advanced Societies*. London: Hutchinson.

—— (1976). *New Rules of Sociological Method*. London: Hutchinson.

—— (1990). *The Consequences of Modernity*. Stanford, Calif.: Stanford University Press.

—— (1991). *Modernity and Self-Identity: Self and Society in the Late Modern Age*. Cambridge: Polity Press.

Gilljam, M. (1990). 'Sex förklaringar till valet av parti'. In *Rött, Blått, Grönt:*

En bok om 1988 års riksdagsval, ed. M. Gilljam and S. Holmberg. Stockholm: Bonniers.

Glass, J., Bengtson, V. L., and Dunham, C. C. (1986). 'Attitude Similarity in Three-Generation Families: Socialization, Status, Inheritance, or Reciprocal Influence?' *American Sociological Review* 51: 685–98.

Glenn, N. D. (1980). 'Values, Attitudes, and Beliefs'. In *Constancy and Change in Human Development*, ed. O. G. Brim and J. Kagan. Cambridge, Mass.: Harvard University Press.

Goldthorpe, J. (1982). 'On the Service Class, its Formation and Future'. In *Social Class and the Division of Labour*, ed. A. Giddens and G. Mackenzie. Cambridge: Cambridge University Press.

—— (1983). 'Women and Class Analysis: In Defence of the Conventional View'. *Sociology* 17: 465–88.

—— and Hope, K. (1974). *The Social Grading of Occupations: A New Approach and Scale*. Oxford: Oxford University Press

—— Lockwood, D., Bechoffer, F., and Platt J. (1968). *The Affluent Worker Series*. Cambridge: Cambridge University Press.

Goul Andersen, J. (1984). 'Decline of Class Voting or Change in Class Voting? Social Class and Party Choice in Denmark in the 1970s'. *European Journal of Political Research* 12: 243–59.

—— (1989). 'Social klasse og parti'. In *To folketingsvalg: Vælger-holdninger og vælgeradfærd i 1987 og 1988*, ed. J. Elklit and O. Tonsgaard. Århus: Politica.

Gouldner, A. W. (1979). *The Future of Intellectuals and the Rise of the New Class*. London: Macmillan.

Greene, W. H. (1991). *Econometric Analysis*. New York: Macmillan.

Greenstein, F. I. (1975). 'Personality and Politics'. In *Macropolitical Theory: The Handbook of Political Science*, ii, ed. F. I. Greenstein and N. W. Polsby. Reading, Mass.: Addison-Wesley.

Grunberg, G., and Schweisguth, E. (1981). 'Profession et vote'. In *France de gauche, vote à droite*, ed. J. Capdevielle *et al.* Paris: Presses de la Fondation Nationale des Sciences Politiques.

Gundelach, P. (1984). 'Social Transformations and New Forms of Voluntary Associations'. *International Social Science Review* 23: 1049–81.

Gurr, T. R. (1970). *Why Men Rebel*. Princeton: Princeton University Press.

Gurth, J. L., and Green, J. C. (1990). 'Politics in a New Key: Religiosity and Participation Among Political Activists'. *Western Political Quarterly* 13: 153–79.

Haavio-Mannila, E., *et al.* (1985). *Unfinished Democracy: Women in Nordic Politics*. Oxford: Pergamon Press.

Habermas, J. (1976). *Legitimation Crisis*. London: Heinemann.

Hall, S. (1988a). 'The Toad in the Garden: Thatcherism among the Theorists'.

In *Marxism and the Interpretation of Culture*, ed. C. Nelson and L. Grossberg. Basingstoke, Hants.: Macmillan.

———— (1988*b*). *The Hard Road to Renewal: Thatcherism and the Crisis of the Left*. London: Verso.

———— (1989). 'The Meaning of New Times'. In *New Times: The Changing Face of Politics in the 1990s*, ed. S. Hall and M. Jacques. London: Lawrence and Wishart.

Halpern, S. (1986). 'The Disorderly World of Consociational Democracy'. *West European Politics* 9: 181–97.

Hardarson, O., and Kristinsson, G. (1987). 'The Icelandic Parliamentary Election of 1987'. *Electoral Studies* 6: 219–34.

Harvey, D. (1989). *The Condition of Postmodernity: An Enquiry into the Origins of Cultural Change*. Oxford: Basil Blackwell.

Heath, A., Jowell, R., and Curtice, J. (1985). *How Britain Votes*. Oxford: Pergamon Press.

———— ———— ———— (1991). *Understanding Political Change: The British Voter 1964–1987*. Oxford: Pergamon Press.

———— and Topf, R. (1987). 'Political Culture'. In *British Social Attitudes*, ed. R. Jowell, S. Witherspoon, and L. Brook. Aldershot, Surrey: Gower.

Hebdige, D. (1979). *Subculture: The Meaning of Style*. London: Methuen.

Heberle, R. (1951). *Social Movements: An Introduction to Political Sociology*. New York: Appleton Century.

Hedlund-Ruth, G. (1985). 'Kvinnorörelsens påverkan på lokal politik'. *Kvinnovetenskaplig Tidskrift* 6: 36–53.

Heidenheimer, A. J., Heclo, H., and Adams, C. T. (1983). *Comparative Public Policy: The Politics of Social Choice in Europe and America*. New York: St Martin's Press.

Heller, A., and Feher, F. (1989). *The Post-Modern Political Condition*. Cambridge: Cambridge University Press.

Hempel, C. G. (1965). *Aspect of Scientific Explanation and Other Essays in the Philosophy of Science*. New York: Free Press.

Hernes, H. M. (1987). *Welfare State and Woman Power: Essays in State Feminism*. Oslo: Norwegian University Press.

Hildebrandt, K., and Dalton, R. J. (1978). 'The New Politics: Political Change or Sunshine Politics'. In *Elections and Parties*, ed. M. Kaase and K. von Beyme. Beverly Hills, Calif.: Sage.

Hilliard, A. (1950). *The Forms of Value*. New York: Columbia University Press.

Hirschman, A. O. (1970). *Exit, Voice, and Loyalty: Responses to Decline in Firms, Organizations, and States*. Cambridge, Mass.: Harvard University Press.

Hirst, P. (1993). *Associative Democracy*. Cambridge: Polity Press.

Hoel, M., and Knutsen, O. (1989). 'Social Class, Gender, and Sector Employment as Political Cleavages in Scandinavia'. *Acta Sociologica* 32: 181–201.

Holmberg, S. (1981). *Svenska väljare*. Stockholm: LiberFörlag.

Howe, I. (1971). 'Mass Society and Mass Fiction'. In *Decline of the New*, ed. I. Howe. London: Gollancz.

Huyssen, A. (1984). 'Mapping the Postmodern'. *New German Critique* 33: 5–52.

Ignatieff, M. (1992). 'How the Glitz Turned to Ashes'. *The Observer*, 12 April, p. 23.

Inglehart, R. (1971*a*). 'The Silent Revolution in Europe: Intergenerational Change in Post-Industrial Society'. *American Political Science Review* 65: 991–1017.

—— (1971*b*). 'Revolutionnarisme post-bourgeois en France, en Allemagne et aux Etats-Unis'. *Il Politico* 36, 2: 209–36.

—— (1977*a*). 'Political Dissatisfaction and Mass Support for Social Change in Advanced Industrial Societies'. *Comparative Political Studies* 10: 455–72.

—— (1977*b*). *The Silent Revolution: Changing Values and Political Styles among Western Publics*. Princeton: Princeton University Press.

—— (1979*a*). 'Political Action: The Impact of Values, Cognitive Level, and Social Background'. In *Political Action: Mass Participation in Five Western Democracies*, ed. S. H. Barnes, M. Kaase, *et al*. Beverly Hills, Calif.: Sage.

—— (1979*b*). 'Wertwandel in den Westlichen Gesellschaften: Politische Konsequenzen von materialistischen und postmaterialistischen Prioritäten'. In *Wertwandel und gesellschaftlicher Wandel*, ed. H. Klages and P. Kmieciak. Frankfurt and New York: Campus.

—— (1979*c*). 'Value Priorities and Socio-economic Change'. In *Political Action: Mass Participation in Five Western Democracies*, ed. S. H. Barnes, M. Kaase, *et al*. London: Sage.

—— (1981). 'Postmaterialism in an Environment of Insecurity'. *American Political Science Review* 75: 880–900.

—— (1984). 'The Changing Structure of Political Cleavages in Western Society'. In *Electoral Change in Advanced Industrial Democracies: Realignment or Dealignment?* ed. R. J. Dalton, S. C. Flanagan, and P. A. Beck. Princeton: Princeton University Press.

—— (1985). 'New Perspectives on Value Change: Responses to Lafferty and Knutsen, Savage, Boltken, and Jagodzinski'. *Comparative Political Studies* 17: 485–532.

—— (1989*a*). 'Observations on Cultural Change and Postmodernism'. In *Contemporary Political Culture: Politics in a Postmodern Age*, ed. J. R. Gibbins. London: Sage.

—— (1989*b*). 'Political Value Orientations'. In *Continuities in Political*

Action: Mass Participation in Five Western Democracies, ed. M. K. Jennings, J. W. van Deth, *et al*. Berlin: de Gruyter.

—— (1990). *Culture Shift in Advanced Industrial Society*. Princeton: Princeton University Press.

—— and Abramson, P. A. (1994). 'Economic Security and Value Change'. *American Political Science Review* 88: 336–54.

—— and Klingemann, H.-D. (1976). 'Party Identification, Ideological Preference and the Left–Right Dimension among Western Mass Publics'. In *Party Identification and Beyond*, ed. I. Budge, I. Crewe, and D. Farlie. London: John Wiley.

—— and Rabier, J.-R. (1986). 'Political Realignment in Advanced Industrial Society: From Class-Based Politics to Quality-of-Life Politics'. *Government and Opposition* 21: 456–79.

Irvine, S., and Ponton, A. (1988). *A Green Manifesto: Policies for a Green Future*. London: Macdonald Optima.

Irving, R. E. (1979). 'Christian Democracy in Post-War Europe: Conservatism Writ Large or Distinctive Political Phenomenon?' *West European Politics* 2: 53–68.

Jagodzinski, W. (1983). 'Materialism in Japan Reconsidered: Towards a Synthesis of Generational and Life-Cycle Explanations'. *American Political Science Review* 77: 887–94.

—— (1991). 'The Transformation of Religious Belief Systems'. Paper presented at the autumn meeting of subgroup IV of the BiG Project, Vienna.

—— and Weede, E. (1981). 'Testing Curvilinear Propositions by Polynomial Regression with Particular Reference to the Interpretation of Standardized Solutions'. *Quality and Quantity* 15: 447–63.

Jameson, F. (1984). 'Postmodernism, or the Cultural Logic of Capitalism'. *New Left Review* 146: 53–92.

—— (1989). 'Marxism and Postmodernism'. *New Left Review* 176: 31–45.

Jamieson, K. H. (1984). *Packaging a President*. Oxford: Oxford University Press.

Janowitz, M. (1976). *Social Control of the Welfare State*. New York: Elsevier.

Jaspers, J., and Fraser, C. (1984). 'Attitudes and Social Representations'. In *Social Representations*, ed. R. M. Farr and S. Moscovici. Cambridge: Cambridge University Press.

Jenkins, J. C. (1983). 'Resource Mobilization and the Study of Social Movements'. *Annual Review of Sociology* 9: 527–53.

Jenks, C. (1986). *What is Post-Modernism?* New York: St Martin's Press.

Jennings, M. K., and Niemi, R. G. (1974). *The Political Character of Adolescence: The Influence of Families and Schools*. Princeton: Princeton University Press.

—— —— (1981). *Generations and Politics: A Panel Study of Young Adults and Their Parents*. Princeton: Princeton University Press.

Jennings, M. K., Van Deth, J. W., *et al.* (1989). *Continuities in Political Action: A Longitudinal Study of Political Orientations in Three Western Democracies*. Berlin: de Gruyter.

Jessop, B., Kastendiek, H., Nielsen, K., and Pederson, O. (eds.) (1991). *The Politics of Flexibility: Restructuring State and Industry in Britain, Germany, and Scandinavia*. Aldershot, Surrey: Edward Elgar.

Johnson, N. (1990). *Restructuring the Welfare State: A Decade of Change 1980–1990*. Brighton: Harvester Wheatsheaf.

Jónasdóttir, A. G. (1985). 'Kvinnors intressen och andra värden'. *Kvinnovetenskaplig Tidskrift* 6: 17–33.

Judd, C. M., and Milburn, M. A. (1980). 'The Structure of Attitude Systems in the General Public: Comparisons of a Structural Equation Model'. *American Sociological Review* 45: 627–43.

———— Krosnick, J. A., and Milburn, M. A. (1981). 'Political Involvement and Attitude Structure in the General Public'. *American Sociological Review* 46: 660–9.

Kaase, M. (1989). 'Mass Participation'. In M. K. Jennings, J. W. van Deth, *et al.*, *Continuities in Political Action: Mass Participation in Five Western Democracies*. New York: de Gruyter.

———— (1992). 'Direct Political Participation in the EC Countries in the Late Eighties'. In *From Voters to Participants*, ed. P. Gundelach and K. Siune. Århus: Politica.

———— and Marsh, A. (1979). 'Political Action: A Theoretical Perspective'. In *Political Action: Mass Participation in Five Western Democracies*, ed. S. H. Barnes, M. Kaase, *et al.* Beverly Hills, Calif.: Sage.

Katz, D. (1960). 'The Functional Approach to the Study of Attitudes'. *Public Opinion Quarterly* 24: 163–204.

Kaufmann, F.-X. (1979). *Kirche begreifen: Analysen und Thesen zur Gesellschaftlichen Verfassung des Christentums*. Freiburg: Herder.

Keane, J. (1984). *Public Life in Late Capitalism*. Cambridge: Cambridge University Press.

———— (ed.) (1988a). *Civil Society and the State*. London: Verso.

———— (1988b). *Democracy and Civil Society*. London: Verso.

Kim, J.-O., and Mueller, C. W. (1978). *Factor Analysis: Statistical Methods and Practical Issues*. London: Sage.

Kinder, D. R., and Mebane, W. R., Jr (1983). 'Politics and Economics in Everyday Life'. In *The Political Process and Economic Change*, ed. K. R. Monroe. New York: Agathon.

King, D. S. (1987). *The New Right: Politics, Markets, and Citizenship*. Basingstoke, Hants.: Macmillan.

Kitschelt, H. P. (1986). 'Political Opportunity Structures and Political Protest: Anti-Nuclear Movements in Four Democracies'. *British Journal of Political Science* 16: 57–86.

—————— (1988). 'Left-Libertarian Parties: Explaining Innovation in Competitive Party Systems'. *World Politics* 40: 194–234.

—————— and Hellemans, S. (1990). *Beyond the European Left: Ideology and Political Action in the Belgian Ecology Parties.* Durham, NC: Duke University Press.

Klages, H. (1984). *Wertorientierungen im Wandel: Rückblick, Gegenwartanalyse, Prognosen.* Frankfurt: Campus.

—————— (1988). *Wertedynamik: Über die Wandelbarkeit des Selbstverständlichen.* Zürich: Edition Interform.

—————— (1993). *Traditionsbruch als Herausforderung: Perspektiven der Wertewandelsgesellschaft.* Frankfurt: Campus.

—————— and Kmieciak, P. (eds.) (1979). *Wertwandel und gesellschaftlicher Wandel.* Frankfurt: Campus.

—————— and Herbert, W. (1983). *Wertorientierung und Staatsbezug; Untersuchungen zur Politischen Kultur in der Bundesrepublik Deutschland.* Frankfurt: Campus.

Klandermans, B. (1991). 'New Social Movements and Resource Mobilization: The European and the American Approach Revisited'. In *Research on Social Movements*, ed. D. Rucht. Boulder, Colo.: Westview.

—————— and Oegema, D. (1987). 'Potentials, Networks, Motivations, and Barriers: Steps Towards Participation in Social Movements'. *American Sociological Review* 52: 519–31.

—————— and Tarrow, S. (1988). 'Mobilization into Social Movements: Synthesizing the European and American Approaches'. *International Social Movement Research* 1: 1–38.

Klecka, W. R. (1971). 'Applying Political Generations to the Study of Political Behaviour: A Cohort Analysis'. *Public Opinion Quarterly* 35: 358–73.

—————— (1980). *Quantitative Applications in the Social Sciences*, xix, *Discriminant Analysis.* Beverly Hills, Calif.: Sage.

Kluckhohn, C. (1951). 'Values and Value-Orientations in the Theory of Action: An Exploration in Definition and Classification'. In *Towards a General Theory of Action*, ed. T. Parsons and E. A. Shils. Cambridge, Mass.: Harvard University Press.

Kmieciak, P. (1976). *Wertstrukturen und Wertwandel in der Bundesrepublik: Grundlagen einer interdisziplinären empirischen Wertforschung mit einer Sekundäranalyse von Umfragedaten.* Göttingen: Schwartz.

Knutsen, O. (1986a). 'Political Cleavages and Political Realignment in Norway: The New Politics Thesis Re-Examined'. *Scandinavian Political Studies* 9: 235–63.

—————— (1986b). 'Sosiale klasser og politiske verdier i Norge: middelklassen i den offentlige sektor som "den nye klasse"'. *Tidsskrift for samfunnsforskning* 27: 263–87.

—————— (1988). 'The Impact of Structural and Ideological Party Cleavages in

West European Democracies: A Comparative Empirical Analysis'. *British Journal of Political Science* 18: 323–52.

Knutsen, O. (1990). 'The Materialist–Postmaterialist Value Dimension as a Party Cleavage in the Nordic Countries'. *West European Politics* 13: 258–74.

——— and Lafferty, W. (1985). 'Postmaterialism in a Social Democratic State'. *Comparative Political Studies* 17: 411–30.

Kolb, W. L. (1957). 'The Changing Prominence of Values in Modern Sociological Theory'. In *Modern Sociological Theory in Continuity and Change*, ed. H. Becker and A. Boskoff. New York: Holt.

Kriesi, H. P. (1989). 'New Social Movements and the New Class in the Netherlands'. *American Journal of Sociology* 94: 1078–1116.

Krippendorff, K. (1970). 'The Expression of Value in Political Documents'. *Journalism Quarterly* 47: 510–18.

Kristol, I. (1972). *On the Democratic Idea in America*. New York: Harper and Row.

Kunz, V., Gabriel, O. W., and Brettschneider, F. (1993). 'Wertorientierungen, Ideologien und Policy-Präeferenzen in der Bundesrepublik Deutschland'. In *Wahlen in Zeiten des Umbruchs*, ed. O. W. Gabriel and K. G. Troitsch. Frankfurt: Lang.

Laermans, R. (1992). *In de greep van ' De moderne tijd'. Modernisering en verzuiling: Evoluties binnen de ACW-vormingsorganisaties*. Leuven and Appeldoorn: Garant.

Lafferty, W., and Knutsen, O. (1984). 'Leftist and Rightist Ideology in a Social Democratic State: An Analysis of Norway in the Midst of the Conservative Resurgence'. *British Journal of Political Science* 14: 345–67.

Lane, J.-E., and Ersson, S. O. (1991). *Politics and Society in Western Europe*. London: Sage.

——— McKay, D., and Newton, K. (1991). *Political Data Handbook: OECD Countries*. Oxford: Oxford University Press.

Lane, R. E. (1959). *Political Life: How and Why Do People Get Involved in Politics*. New York: The Free Press.

Lash, S., and Urry, J. (1987). *The End of Organized Capitalism*. Cambridge: Polity Press.

Lasswell, H., and Kaplan, A. (1952). *Power and Society: A Framework for Political Inquiry*. London: Routledge and Kegan Paul.

Lawler, E. (1973). *Motivation, Work, Organization*. Monterey, Calif.: Brooks Cole.

Lawson, H. (1985). *Reflexivity: The Post-Modern Predicament*. London: Hutchinson.

Lazarsfeld, P. F., Berelson, B. R., and Gaudet, H. (1944). *The People's Choice*. New York: Columbia University Press.

Leijenaar, M. (1991). 'Women in Public Administration in the Netherlands'. In *Women and Public Administration*, ed. J. H. Bayes. New York: Haworth.

Lepsius, R. M. (1990). *Interessen, Ideen, und Institutionen*. Opladen: Westdeutscher Verlag.

Levitas, R. (ed.) (1985). *The Ideology of the New Right*. Oxford: Polity Press.

Lewis-Beck, M. S. (1984). 'France: The Stalled Electorate'. In *Electoral Change in Advanced Industrial Societies*, ed. R. J. Dalton, S. C. Flanagan, and P. A. Beck. Princeton: Princeton University Press.

Lijphart, A. (1969). 'Consociational Democracy'. *World Politics* 21: 207–25.

—— (1981). 'Political Parties: Ideologies and Programs'. In *Democracy at the Polls: A Comparative Study of Competitive National Elections*, ed. D. Butler, H. Penniman, and A. Ranney. Washington, DC: American Enterprise Institute.

—— (1982). 'The Relative Salience of the Socio-Economic and Religious Issue Dimensions: Coalition Formations in Ten Western Democracies, 1919–1979'. *European Journal of Political Research* 10: 201–11.

—— (1984). *Democracies: Patterns of Majoritarian and Consensus Government in Twenty-One Countries*. New Haven: Yale University Press.

Lindlof, T. R. (ed.) (1987). *Natural Audiences: Qualitative Research of Media Uses and Effects*. Norwood, NJ: Ablex.

Lipset, S. M. (1959). 'Democracy and Working-Class Authoritarianism'. *American Sociological Review* 30: 103–9.

—— (1960). *Political Man: The Social Basis of Politics*. Garden City, NY: Doubleday.

—— (1964). 'The Changing Class Structure of Contemporary European Politics'. *Daedalus* 93: 271–303.

—— (1981) (expanded and updated edn.; 1st edn. 1959). *Political Man: The Social Bases of Politics*. Baltimore: Johns Hopkins University Press.

—— and Rokkan, S. (1967). 'Cleavage Structures, Party Systems, and Voter Alignments: An Introduction'. In *Party Systems and Voter Alignments*, ed. S. M. Lipset and S. Rokkan. New York: Free Press.

Lipsitz, L. (1965). 'Working-Class Authoritarianism: A Re-evaluation'. *American Sociological Review* 30: 103–9.

Lorwin, V. R. (1971). 'Segmented Pluralism: Ideological Cleavages and Political Cohesion in the Smaller European Democracies'. *Comparative Politics* 3: 141–75.

Lovenduski, J. (1986). *Women and European Politics: Contemporary Feminism and Public Policy*. Brighton: Harvester.

Luckmann, T. (1967). *The Invisible Religion: The Problem of Religion in Modern Society*. New York: Macmillan.

—— (1979). 'The Structural Conditions of Religious Consciousness in Modern Societies'. *Japanese Journal of Religious Studies* 6: 121–37.

—— (1991). *Die unsichtbare Religion*. Frankfurt: Suhrkamp.

Luhmann, N. (1977). *Funktion der Religion*. Frankfurt: Suhrkamp.

Lundmark, C. (1990). 'The Perfect Politician: From a Liberal to a Feminist Perspective on Democracy'. *Statsvetenskaplig Tidskrift* 93: 235–45.

Luskin, R. C. (1987). 'Measuring Political Sophistication'. *American Journal of Politics* 76: 856–99.

Lybeck, J. (1985). 'Is the Lipset–Rokkan Hypothesis Testable?' *Scandinavian Political Studies* 8: 105–13.

Lyotard, J. F. (1984). *The Postmodern Condition*. Minneapolis: University of Minnesota Press.

Maag, G. (1990). *Gesellschaftliche Werte: Strukturen, Stabilität, Funktion*. Opladen: Westdeutscher Verlag.

MacCorquodale, K., and Meehl, P. (1948). 'On the Distinction between Hypothetical Constructs and Intervening Variables'. *Psychological Review* 55: 95–107.

MacIntyre, A. (1981). *After Virtue*. London: Duckworth.

Maffesoli, M. (1988). *Le Temps des tribus*. Paris: Klincksieck.

Mann, M. (1978). *Consciousness and Action Among the Western Working Class*. London: Macmillan.

Mannheim, K. (1952). 'The Problems of Generations'. In *Essays on the Sociology of Knowledge*, ed. P. Kecskemeti. London: Routledge and Kegan Paul.

—— (1960). *Ideology and Utopia*. London: Routledge and Kegan Paul.

Maquire, M. (1983). 'Is There Still Persistence? Electoral Change in Western Europe, 1948–79'. In *West European Party Systems*, ed. H. Daalder and P. Mair. London: Sage.

Marsh, A. (1977). *Protest and Political Consciousness*. Beverly Hills, Calif.: Sage.

Marshall, G. (1988). 'Some Remarks on the Study of Working-Class Consciousness'. In *Social Stratification and Economic Change*, ed. D. Rose. London: Hutchinson.

—— Newby, H., Rose, D., and Vogler, C. (1988). *Social Class in Modern Britain*. London: Hutchinson.

Martin, B. (1981). *A Sociology of Contemporary Cultural Change*. Oxford: Basil Blackwell.

Martin, D. (1978). *A General Theory of Secularization*. Oxford: Basil Blackwell.

Marx, G. T. (1967). 'Religion: Opiate or Inspiration of Civil Rights Militancy among Negroes?' *American Sociological Review* 32: 64–72.

Maslow, A. (1954). *Motivation and Personality*. New York: Harper and Row.

Mason, W., House, J. S., and Martin, S. S. (1980). 'Political Alienation in America'. In *Sociological Methodology*, ed. N. B. Tuma. San Francisco: Jossey Bass.

McAdam, D. (1986). 'Recruitment to High-Risk Activism: The Case of Freedom Summer'. *American Journal of Sociology* 92: 64–90.

McCarthy, J. D., and Zald, M. (1977. 'Resource Mobilization and Social Movements: A Partial Theory'. *American Journal of Sociology* 82: 1212–39.

McCracken, D. J. (1949). 'The Concept of Value as an A Priori Concept'. *Proceedings of the Tenth International Congress of Philosophy*. Amsterdam.

McGuire, W. J. (1985). 'Attitudes and Attitude Change'. In *Handbook of Social Psychology*, ii, *Special Fields and Applications*, ed. G. Lindzey and E. Aronson. New York: Random House.

McKinnon, M. H. (1989a). 'Calvinism and the Infallible Assurance of Grace: The Weber Thesis Reconsidered'. *British Journal of Sociology* 39: 143–77.

—— (1989b). 'Weber's Exploration of Calvinism: The Undiscovered Provenance of Capitalism'. *British Journal of Sociology* 39: 178–210.

McLaughlin, B. (1965). 'Values in Behavioral Science'. *Journal of Religion and Health* 4: 258–79.

Meadows, D. H., et al. (1972). *The Limits to Growth: A Report for the Club of Rome Project on the Predicament of Mankind*. New York: Universe.

Melucci, A. (1980). 'The New Social Movements: A Theoretical Approach'. *Social Science Information* 19: 199–226.

—— (1985). 'The Symbolic Challenge of Contemporary Movements'. *Social Research* 52: 789–816.

Meyrowitz, J. (1985). *No Sense of Place: The Impact of Electronic Media on Social Behaviour*. Oxford: Oxford University Press.

Michelat, G., and Simon, M. (1977a). *Classe, religion et comportement politique*. Paris: Presses de la Fondation Nationale des Sciences Politiques.

—— —— (1977b). 'Religion, Class, and Politics'. *Comparative Politics* 10: 159–90.

Middendorp, C. P. (1978). *Progressiveness and Conservatism: The Fundamental Dimensions of Ideological Controversy and their Relationship to Social Class*. New York: Mouton.

—— (1991). *Ideology in Dutch Politics: The Democratic System Reconsidered 1970–1985*. Assen: Van Gorcum.

Milbrath, L. W. (1968). 'The Nature of Political Beliefs and the Relationship of the Individual to the Government'. *American Behavioral Scientist* 12: 28–36.

—— (1981). 'Political Participation'. In *The Handbook of Political Behavior*, iv, ed. S. L. Long. New York: Plenum.

Miller, A. H. (1974). 'Political Issues and Trust in Government'. *American Political Science Review* 68: 951–72.

—— and Listhaug, O. (1990). 'Political Parties and Confidence in Government: A Comparison of Norway, Sweden, and the United States'. *British Journal of Political Science* 20: 357–86.

Mills, C. W. (1959). *The Sociological Imagination*. New York: Oxford University Press.

Morley, D. (1986). *Family Television: Cultural Power and Domestic Leisure.* London: Comedia.

Morris, R. T. (1956). 'A Typology of Norms'. *American Sociological Review* 21: 610–13.

Mort, F. (1989). 'The Politics of Consumption'. In *New Times*, ed. S. Hall and M. Jacques. London: Lawrence and Wishart.

Moscovici, S. (1981). 'On Social Representation'. In *Social Cognition: Perspectives on Everyday Understanding*, ed. J. Forgas. London: Academic Press.

——— (1984). 'The Phenomenon of Social Representations'. In *Social Representations*, ed. R. Farr and S. Moscovici. Cambridge: Cambridge University Press.

Mughan, A. (1985). 'Belgium'. In *Electoral Change in Western Democracies: Patterns and Sources of Electoral Volatility*, ed. I. Crewe and D. Denver. London: Croom Helm.

Muller, E. N. (1970). 'The Representation of Citizens by Political Authorities: Consequences for Regime Support'. *American Political Science Review* 64: 1149–66.

Müller-Rommel, F. (1982). 'Ecological Parties in Western Europe'. *West European Politics* 5: 68–74.

——— (1985*a*). 'New Social Movements and Smaller Parties: A Comparative Perspective'. *West European Politics* 8: 41–54.

——— (1985*b*). 'The Greens in Western Europe: Similar but Different'. *International Political Science Review* 6: 483–99.

——— (ed.) (1989). *New Politics in Western Europe: The Rise and Success of Green Parties and Alternative Lists.* Boulder, Colo.: Westview.

——— (1990). 'New Political Movements and New Politics Parties in Western Europe'. In *Challenging the Political Order: New Social and Political Movements in Western Democracies*, ed. R. J. Dalton and M. Küchler. Oxford: Polity Press.

Myers, F. (1973). 'Dilemmas in the British Peace Movement since World War II'. *Journal of Peace Research* 10: 81–90.

Næss, A. (1973). 'The Shallow and the Deep, Long-Range Ecology Movements: A Summary'. *Inquiry* 16: 95–110.

Nava, M. (1991). 'Consumerism Reconsidered: Buying and Power'. *Cultural Studies* 5: 25–34.

Neubauer, D. (1969). 'Some Conditions of Democracy'. In *Empirical Democratic Theory*, ed. C. Cnudde and D. Neubauer. Chicago: Markman.

Nie, N., Verba, S., and Petrocik, J. (1976). *The Changing American Voter.* Cambridge, Mass.: Harvard University Press.

Niemi, R. G. (1974). *The Politics of Future Citizens.* San Francisco: Jossey-Bass.

——— Craig, S. C., and Mattei, F. (1991). 'Measuring Internal Efficacy in the

1988 National Election Study'. *American Political Science Review* 85: 1407–13.

Nye, F. I. (1967). 'Values, Family, and a Changing Society'. *Journal of Marriage and the Family* 27: 241–8.

Oakeshott, M. (1962). *Rationalism in Politics*. London: Methuen.

—— (1975). *On Human Conduct*. Oxford: Clarendon Press.

O'Connor, J. (1973). *The Fiscal Crisis of the State*. New York: St Martin's Press.

OECD (1985). *National Accounts*. Paris: OECD.

—— (1986). *Economic Outlook: Historical Statistics 1960–1984*. Paris: OECD.

—— (1991). *Economic Outlook: Historical Statistics 1960–1989*. Paris: OECD.

—— (1992). *Economic Outlook: Historical Statistics 1960–1990*. Paris: OECD.

Offe, C. (1985a). *Disorganized Capitalism*. Cambridge: Polity Press.

—— (1985b). 'New Social Movements: Challenging the Boundaries of Institutional Politics'. *Social Research* 52: 817–68.

—— (1987). 'Challenging the Boundaries of Institutional Politics: Social Movements since the 1960s'. In *Changing Boundaries of the Political*, ed. C. S. Maier. Cambridge: Cambridge University Press.

Oficina de Estadistica y Sociologia de la Iglesia (OESI) (1989). *Estadistica de la Iglesia Catolica 1989*. Madrid: Editorial de la Conferencia Episcopal Española.

Olsen, J. P., and Sætren, H. (1980). *Aksjoner og demokrati*. Oslo: Universitetsforlaget.

Olson, M., Jr. (1963). 'Rapid Growth as a Destabilizing Force'. *Journal of Economic History* 23: 529–53.

Onis, F. de (1934). *Antologia de la Poesia Espanola e Hispanoamericana, 1882–1923*. Madrid: Las Americas Publishing Co.

O'Riordan, T. (1981) (2nd edn.). *Environmentalism*. London: Pion.

Oudhof, J. (1988). 'Kerkelijke gezindten in 1988'. *Sociaal-Cultureel Berichten* 11: 1–20. The Hague: CBS.

—— and Beets, G. C. (1982). 'Kerkelijke gezindten in Nederland, 1971–81'. *Sociaal-Cultureel Kwartaalbericht* 4: 9–25.

Pahl, R., and Wallace, C. (1988). 'Neither Angels in Marble nor Rebels in Red: Privatization and Working-Class Consciousness'. In *Social Stratification and Economic Change*, ed. D. Rose. London: Hutchinson.

Pappi, F. U. (1984). 'The West German Party System'. *West European Politics* 7: 7–26.

—— (1990). 'Neue soziale Bewegungen und Wahlverhalten in der Bundesrepublik'. In *Wahlen und Wähler: Analysen aus Anlass der Bundestagswahl 1987*, ed. M. Kaase and H.-D. Klingemann. Opladen: Westdeutscher Verlag.

Paris, R. (1989). 'Der kurze Atem der Provokation'. *Kölner Zeitschrift für Soziologie und Sozialpsychologie* 41: 33–52.

Parisi, A., and Pasquino, G. (1979). 'Changes in Italian Electoral Behaviour: The Relationships Between Parties and Voters'. *West European Politics* 2: 6–30.

Parkin, F. (1968). *Middle Class Radicalism*. New York: Praeger.

—— (1972). *Class Inequality and the Political Order*. London: Paladin.

Parsons, T. (1935). 'The Place of Ultimate Values in Sociological Theory'. *International Journal of Ethics* 45: 282–316.

—— (1942). 'Some Sociological Aspects of the Fascist Movement'. *Social Forces* 21: 138–47.

—— (1968). 'On the Concept of Value Commitments'. *Sociological Inquiry* 38: 135–60.

Pateman, C. (1983). 'Feminism and Democracy'. In *Democratic Theory and Practice*, ed. D. Graeme. Cambridge: Cambridge University Press.

—— (1988). *The Sexual Contract*. Cambridge: Polity Press.

Pedersen, M. (1979). 'The Dynamics of European Party Systems: Changing Patterns of Electoral Volatility'. *European Journal of Political Research* 7: 1–26.

Pekonen, K. (1989). 'Symbols and Politics as Culture in the Modern Situation'. *In Contemporary Political Culture: Politics in a Postmodern Age*, ed. J. R. Gibbins. London: Sage.

Pepper, S. C. (1958). *The Sources of Value*. Berkeley: University of California Press.

Petersson, O., and Valen, H. (1979). 'Political Cleavages in Sweden and Norway'. *Scandinavian Political Studies* 2: 313–31.

Pierce, R., and Converse, P. E. (1990). 'Attitudinal Sources of Protest Behavior in France: Differences between Before and After·Measurement'. *Public Opinion Quarterly* 54: 295–316.

Pin, E. (1956). *Pratiques religieuses et classes sociales dans une paroisse urbaine Saint-Pothin à Lyon*. Paris: Pes.

Pitts, J. R. (1976*a*). 'The Hippie Movement as a Socialization Agency'. In *Explorations in General Theory in Social Science*, ed. J. J. Loubster, R. C. Baum, A. Effrat, and V. M. Lidz. New York: Free Press.

—— (1976*b*). 'The Millenarium Movement Organization as a Socialization Agency'. In *Explorations in General Theory in Social Science*, ed. J. J. Loubster, R. C. Baum, A. Effrat, and V. M. Lidz. New York: Free Press.

Poguntke, T. (1987*a*). 'Grün-alternative Parteien: Eine Neue Farbe in Westlichen Parteiensystemen'. *Zeitschrift für Parlamentsfragen* 3: 368–82.

—— (1987*b*). 'New Politics and Party Systems: The Emergence of a New Type of Party?' *West European Politics* 10: 76–88.

—— (1988). 'New Politics Parties in Western Democratic Countries'. Paper presented at the 14th IPSA World Congress, Washington, DC.

Polsky, A. J. (1991). *The Rise of the Therapeutic State*. Princeton: Princeton University Press.

Popper, K. R. (1963). *Conjectures and Refutations: The Growth of Scientific Knowledge*. London: Routledge.

Porrit, J. (1986). *Seeing Green*. Oxford: Basil Blackwell.

—— and Winner, D. (1988). *The Coming of the Greens*. London: Fontana.

Postman, N. (1985). *Amusing Ourselves to Death: Public Discourse in the Age of Show Business*. New York: Viking Penguin.

Poulantzas, N. (1979). *Classes in Contemporary Capitalism*. London: Verso.

Powell, G. B. (1986). 'American Voting Turnout in Comparative Perspective'. *American Political Science Review* 80: 17–44.

Prewitt, K. (1968). 'Political Efficacy'. In *International Encyclopedia of the Social Sciences*, xii, ed. D. L. Sills. Glencoe, Ill.: Free Press.

Pye, L. W. (ed.) (1963). *Communications and Political Development*. Princeton: Princeton University Press.

Reimer, B. (1988). 'No Values—New Values? Youth and Postmaterialism'. *Scandinavian Political Studies* 11: 347–59.

—— (1989). 'Postmodern Structures of Feeling: Values and Life-styles in the Postmodern Age'. In *Contemporary Political Culture: Politics in a Postmodern Age*, ed. J. R. Gibbins. London: Sage.

—— (1994). *The Most Common of Practices: On Mass Media Use in Late Modernity*. Stockholm: Almqvist and Wiksell.

Rescher, N. (1969). *Introduction to Value Theory*. Englewood Cliffs, NJ: Prentice-Hall.

Robinson, J. A. (1963). *Honest to God*. London: SCM.

Rohrschneider, R. (1988). 'Citizen's Attitudes towards Environmental Issues: Selfish or Selfless?' *Comparative Political Studies* 21: 347–67.

—— (1990). 'The Roots of Public Opinion towards New Social Movements: An Empirical Test of Competing Explanations'. *American Journal of Political Science* 34: 1–30.

Rokeach, M. (1973). *The Nature of Human Values*. New York: Free Press.

—— (1976) (1st edn. 1968). *Beliefs, Attitudes, and Values: A Theory of Organisation and Change*. San Fransisco: Jossey-Bass.

Rokkan, S. (1970). *Citizens, Elections, Parties*. Oslo: Universitetsforlaget.

Rorty, R. (1979). *Philosophy and the Mirror of Nature*. Princeton: Princeton University Press.

—— (1990). *Contingency, Irony, and Solidarity*. Cambridge: Cambridge University Press.

Rose, A. M. (1956). 'Sociology and the Study of Values'. *British Journal of Sociology* 7: 1–17.

Rose, D. (1988). *Social Stratification and Economic Change*. London: Hutchinson.

—— Vogler, C., Marshall, G., and Newby, H. (eds.) (1984). 'Economic

Restructuring: The British Experience'. *Annals of the American Academy of Political and Social Science* 475: 137 –57.

Rose, R. (ed.) (1974). *Electoral Behaviour: A Comparative Handbook*. New York: Free Press.

———— and McAllister, I. (1986). *Voters Begin to Choose: From Closed-Class to Open Elections in Britain*. London: Sage.

———— and Urwin, D. (1969). 'Social Cohesion, Political Parties, and Strains in Regimes'. *Comparative Political Studies* 2: 7–67.

———— ———— (1970). 'Persistence and Change in Western Party Systems since 1945'. *Political Studies* 18: 287–319.

Rosenau, P. M. (1992). *Post-Modernism and the Social Sciences*. Princeton: Princeton University Press.

Ross, G. (1978). 'Marxism and the New Middle Classes: French Critiques'. *Theory and Society* 5: 163–90.

Rothschild-Whitt, J. (1979). 'The Collectivist Organization: An Alternative to Rational Bureaucratic Models'. *American Sociological Review* 44: 509–27.

Russett, B. M., Hayward R. A., Jr, Deutsch, K. W., and Lasswell, H. D. (1964). *World Handbook of Political and Social Indicators*. New Haven: Yale University Press.

Rustow, D. (1968). 'Modernization and Comparative Politics: Prospects in Research and Theory'. *Comparative Politics* 1: 37 –51.

Särlvik, B., and Crewe, I. (1983). *Decade of Dealignment: The Conservative Victory of 1979 and Electoral Trends in the 1970s*. Cambridge: Cambridge University Press.

Saunders, P. (1979). *Urban Politics: A Sociological Perspective*. London: Hutchinson.

Scarbrough, E. (1984). *Political Ideology and Voting*. Oxford: Clarendon Press.

Scharpf, F. W. (1987). *Crises and Choice in European Social Democracy*. Ithaca, NY: Cornell University Press.

Schimank, U. (1985). 'Funktionale Differenzierung und reflexiver Subjektivismus: Zum Entsprechungsverhältnis von Gesellschafts und Identitätsform'. *Soziale Welt* 36: 447–65.

Schluchter, W. (1981). 'Die Zukunft der Religionen'. *Kölner Zeitschrift für Soziologie und Sozialpsychologie* 33: 605–22.

Scholl-Schaaf, M. (1975). *Werthaltung und Wertsystem: Ein Plädoyer für die Verwendung des Wertconcepts in der Sozialpsychology*. Bonn: Bouvier.

Schumpeter, J. A. (1942). *Capitalism, Socialism, and Democracy*. New York: Harper and Row.

Schweisguth, E. (1983). 'Les Salariés moyens sont-ils des petits-bourgeois?' *Revue Française de Sociologie* 24: 679–704.

———— (1986). 'Les Avatars de la dimension droite–gauche'. In *La Drôle de défaite de la gauche*, ed. E. Dupoirier and G. Grunberg. Paris: Presses Universitaires de France.

—— (1988). 'La Dimension droite–gauche en France'. Paper presented at the 14th World Congress of the International Political Science Association, Washington, DC.

Scott, W. A. (1965). *Values and Organizations*. Chicago: Rand McNally.

Shamir, M. (1984). 'Are Western Party Systems "Frozen"?' *Comparative Political Studies* 17: 35–79.

Siegert, J., and Ulrich, D. (1986). *Wenn das Spielbein dem Standbein ein Bein Stellt . . . zum Verhältnis von Grüner Partei und Bewegung*. Kassel: Weber, Zucht.

Siisiäinen, M. (1985). 'Interests, Voluntary Associations, and the Stability of the Political System'. *Acta Sociologica* 28: 293–316.

Silverstone, R. (1991). 'From Audiences to Consumers: The Household and the Consumption of Communication and Information Technologies'. *European Journal of Communication* 6: 135–54.

Smart, M. (1989) (5th edn.). 'Party Representation in West European Parliaments since 1946: A Research Note'. In *Politics in Western Europe: A Comparative Analysis*, ed. G. Smith. Aldershot, Surrey: Gower.

Smelser, N. (1962). *The Theory of Collective Action*. New York: Free Press.

Sniderman, P. M., Brody, R. A., and Tetlock, P. E. (1991). *Reasoning and Choice: Explorations in Political Psychology*. Cambridge: Cambridge University Press.

Snow, D. A. (1980). 'Social Networks and Social Movements: A Microstructural Approach to Differential Recruitment'. *American Sociological Review* 45: 787–801.

Somervell, D. (ed.) (1946). *A Study of History by Arnold Toynbee*. Oxford: Oxford University Press.

Spretnak, C., and Capra, F. (1985). *Green Politics: The Global Promise*. London: Paladin.

Stark, R., and Bainbridge, W. S. (1985). *The Future of Religion: Secularization, Revival and Cult Formation*. Berkeley: University of California Press.

Statens Offentliga Utredningar (SOU) (1990). *Demokrati och Makt i Sverige*, no. 44. Stockholm: SOU.

Statistics Sweden (1992). *About Women and Men in Sweden and the European Communities: Facts on Equal Opportunities 1992*. Jönköping: SOU.

Stephens, J. D. (1981). 'The Changing Swedish Electorate: Class Voting, Contextual Effects, and Voter Volatility'. *Comparative Political Studies* 14: 163–204.

Studlar, D. T. and Welch, S. (1981). 'Mass Attitudes on Political Issues in Britain'. *Comparative Political Studies* 14: 327–55.

Styrkarsdottir, A. (1986). 'From Social Movement to Political Party: The New

Women's Movement in Iceland'. In *The New Women's Movement*, ed. D. Dahlerup. London: Sage.

Summers, R., and Heston, A. (1991). 'The Penn World Table (Mark 5): An Expanded Set of International Comparisons, 1950–1988'. *Quarterly Journal of Economics* 106: 327–68.

Svensson, P., and Togeby, L. (1991). *Højrebølge?* Århus: Politica.

Swanson, G. E. (1960). *The Birth of the Gods: The Origin of Primitive Beliefs*. Ann Arbor: University of Michigan Press.

Taylor, C. (1985). *Philosophical Papers*, i, *Human Agency and Language*. Cambridge: Cambridge University Press.

—— (1989). *Sources of the Self: The Making of the Modern Identity*. Cambridge, Mass.: Harvard University Press.

Taylor, C. L., and Hudson, M. C. (1972) (2nd edn.). *World Handbook of Political and Social Indicators*. New Haven: Yale University Press.

—— and Jodice, D. A. (1983) (3rd edn.). *World Handbook of Political and Social Indicators*. New Haven: Yale University Press.

Thomas, W. I., and Znaniecki, F. (1918). *The Polish Peasant in Europe and America*, i. Boston: Badger.

Thomassen, J. J. A. (1989). 'Economic Crisis, Dissatisfaction, and Protest'. In M. K. Jennings, J. W. van Deth, *et al.*, *Continuities in Political Action: A Longitudinal Study of Political Orientations in Three Western Democracies*. Berlin: de Gruyter.

Thompson, K. H. (1971). 'A Cross-National Analysis of Intergenerational Social Mobility and Political Orientations'. *Comparative Political Studies* 4: 3–20.

Thurstone, L. L. (1928). 'Attitudes Can Be Measured'. *American Journal of Sociology* 33: 529–54.

Tilly, C. (1978). *From Mobilization to Revolution*. Reading, Mass.: Addison-Wesley.

—— and Rule, J. (1965). *Measuring Political Upheaval*. Princeton: Princeton University Press.

—— and Schweitzer, R. A. (1982). 'How London and its Conflicts Changed Shape 1758–1834'. *Historical Methods* 15: 67–77.

Tilly, L. L., and Tilly, C. (eds.) (1981). *Class Conflict and Collective Action*. New York: Sage.

Togeby, L. (1985). 'Starka, aktiva och arga kvinnor'. *Kvinnovetenskaplig Tidskrift*. 6: 3–16.

—— (1989). 'Besøgs-og telefoninterview: To sammenligninger'. In *To folketingsvalg*, ed. J. Elklit, and O. Tonsgaard. Århus: Politica.

Topf, R. (1989). 'Political Change and Political Culture in Britain 1959–87.' In *Contemporary Political Culture: Politics in a Postmodern Age*, ed. J. R. Gibbins. London: Sage.

—— (1993). 'Science, Public Policy, and the Authoritativeness of the

Governmental Process'. In *The Politics of Expert Advice: Creating, Using, and Manipulating Scientific Knowledge for Public Policy*, ed. A. Barker and B. Peters. Edinburgh: Edinburgh University Press.

Touraine, A. (1974). *The Post-Industrial Society: Tomorrow's Social History: Classes, Conflicts, and Culture*. London: Wildwood House.

Toynbee, A. (1939). *A Study of History*, i–iv. Oxford: Oxford University Press.

Turner, B. (1989). 'From Postindustrial Society to Postmodern Politics'. In *Contemporary Political Culture: Politics in a Postmodern Age*, ed. J. R. Gibbins. London: Sage.

Turner, G. (1990). *British Cultural Studies: An Introduction*. Boston: Unwin Hyman.

Valen, H. (1981). *Valg og politikk: Et samfunn i endring*. Oslo: NKS-forlaget.

—— and Aardal, B. O. (1983). *Et valg i perspektiv: En studie av Stortingsvalget 1981*. Oslo and Kongsvinger: Statistisk Sentralbyrå.

Van Deth, J. W. (1980). 'Politics, Protest, and Participation: Problems of Measurement Equivalence in Eight Western Countries'. Paper presented at the annual meeting of the European Consortium for Political Research, Florence.

—— (1983*a*). 'Ranking the Ratings: The Case of Materialist and Post-materialist Value Orientations'. *Political Methodology* 9: 407–31.

—— (1983*b*). 'The Persistence of Materialist and Post-Materialist Value Orientations'. *European Journal of Political Research* 11: 63–79.

—— (1984). *Politieke Waarden*. Amsterdam: CT-Press.

—— (1986). 'A Note on Measuring Political Participation in Comparative Research'. *Quality and Quantity* 120: 261–72.

—— (1992). 'On the Relation of Value Change and Political Involvement in Western Europe'. In *Staat und Demokratie in Europa*, xviii, *Wissenschaftlicher Kongress der DVPW*, ed. B. Kohler-Koch. Opladen: Leske Budrich.

Veen, H.-J. (1989). 'The Greens as a Milieu Party'. In *Greens in West Germany*, ed. E. Kolinsky. Providence, RI: Berg.

Verba, S., Nie, N. H., and Kim, J.-O. (1978). *Participation and Political Equality*. Cambridge: Cambridge University Press.

Von Beyme, K. (1985). *Political Parties in Western Democracies*. Aldershot, Surrey: Gower.

Voyé, L., and Dobbelaere, K. (1992). 'D'une religion instituée à une religiosité recomposée'. In *Belges, heureux et satisfaits: Les Valeurs des belges dans les années 90*, ed. L. Voyé *et al.* Brussels: De Boeck Université.

Warner, W. L., Meeker, M., and Eells, K. (1949). *Social Class in America: A Manual of Procedure for Measurement of Social Status*. Chicago: Science Research Associates.

Weale, A. (1992). *The New Politics of Pollution*. Manchester: Manchester University Press.

Webber, C., and Wildavsky, A. (1986). *A History of Taxation and Expenditure in the Western World*. New York: Simon and Schuster.

Weber, M. (1958). *The Protestant Ethic and the Spirit of Capitalism*, trans. T. Parsons. New York: Charles Scribner's.

—— (1975) (7th edn.). *Gesammelte Aufsätze zur Religionssoziologie*, i. Tübingen: Mohr.

Welch, S., and Clark, C. (1975). 'Determinants of Change in Political Efficacy: A Test of Two Hypotheses'. *Journal of Political and Military Sociology* 3: 207–17.

Westle, B. (1994) (2nd edn.). 'Politische partizipation'. In *Die EG-Staaten im Vergleich. Strukturen, Prozesse, Politikinhalte*, ed. O. Gabriel and F. Brettschneider. Opladen: Westdeutscher Verlag.

White, R. K. (1951). *Value Analysis: The Nature and Use of the Method*. Glen Gardner, NJ.: Libertarian Press.

Whyte, J. (1974). 'Ireland: Politics Without Social Bases'. In *Electoral Behaviour: A Comparative Handbook*, ed. R. Rose. New York: Free Press.

Willi, V. J. (1966). *Grundlagen einer empirischen Soziologie der Werte und Wertsysteme*. Zürich: Orell.

Williams, R. (1961). *The Long Revolution*. London: Chatto and Windus.

Williams, R. M., Jr. (1968). 'The Concept of Values'. In *International Encyclopedia of the Social Sciences*, xii, ed. D. L. Sills. Glencoe, Ill.: Free Press.

Wilson, B. R. (1976). *Contemporary Transformations of Religion*. Oxford: Oxford University Press.

—— (1985). 'Secularization: The Inherited Model'. In *The Sacred in a Secular Age*, ed. P. Hammond. Berkeley: University of California Press.

Wilson, G. (1979). *Manual for the Wilson–Patterson Attitude Inventory*. Windsor: NFER.

Woodruff, A. D., and Divesta, F. J. (1948). 'The Relationship between Values, Concepts, and Attitudes'. *Educational and Psychological Measurement* 8: 645–59.

Wright, E. O. (1985). *Classes*. London: Verso.

Wright, J. D. (1976). *The Dissent of the Governed: Alienation and Democracy in America*. New York: Academic Press.

—— (1981). 'Political Disaffection'. In *The Handbook of Political Behaviour*, iv, ed. S. L. Long. New York: Plenum Press.

Wright, Q. (1955). *The Study of International Relations*. New York: Appleton.

Young, M. (1958). *The Rise of Meritocracy 1870–2033: An Essay on Education and Equality*. Harmondsworth, Middx: Penguin.

Zald, M., and McCarthy, J. (eds.) (1979). *The Dynamics of Social Movements*. Cambridge, Mass.: Winthrop.

Zapf, W., and Flora, P. (1971). 'Some Problems of Time Series Analysis in Research on Modernization'. *Social Science Information* 10: 53–102.

Ziehe, T. (1986). 'Inför avmystifieringen av världen: Ungdom och kulturell modernisering'. In *Postmoderna tider*, ed. M. Löfgren and A. Molander. Stockholm: Nordstedts.

Zinn, H. (1990) (1st edn. 1980). *A People's History of the United States*. New York: Harper Perennial.

AUTHOR INDEX

Author Index

SUBJECT INDEX